Data Structures with C++
Using STL

clock to produce the seed. In some simulation programs, you might want to repeat the same sequence of chance events. For instance, a flight simulator uses the same sequence of random numbers to produce events that compare the effectiveness of two pilots responding to in-flight situations. Each pilot reacts to the same sequence of events. For this application, use the same value to seed the random sequence.

The member functions in the class produce integer and real random numbers. The function frandom() returns a random real number in the range $0.0 \leq x < 1.0$. For integers, the programmer can use two versions of the function random(). The first version does not have an argument and returns a 32-bit random integer in the range $0 \leq m < 2^{31} - 1$. The second version takes an argument n and returns a random integer in the range $0 \leq m < n$. The following is the randomNumber API:

CLASS randomNumber   **Constructors**   **"d_random.h"**

randomNumber(int seed = 0);
   Sets the seed for the random-number generator.
   Postconditions: With the default value 0, the system clock initializes the seed;
                     otherwise, the user provides the seed for the generator.

CLASS randomNumber   **Operations**   **"d_random.h"**

double **frandom**();   *float random #*
   Return a real number $x, 0.0 <= x < 1.0$.

int **random**();   *largest int on computer*
   Return a 32-bit random integer $m, 0 <= m < 2^{31} - 1$.

int **random**(int n);
   Return a random integer $m, 0 <= m < n$.

Example 1-1

1. We use the constructor to declare two random-number generators. The system clock seeds rndA, while the user-defined value 100 seeds rndB.

   ```
   randomNumber rndA, rndB(100);
   ```

2. The loop generates five integer random numbers in the range 0 to 40 and five real random numbers in the range 0 to 1.

   ```
   int item, i;
   double x;

   for (i = 0; i < 5; i++)
   {
       item = rndA.random(40);      // 0 ≤ item < 40
       x = rndB.frandom();          // 0.0 <= x < 1.0
       cout << item << "   " << x;
   }
   ```

```
Possible Output:

17   0.00224779
32   0.503245
15   0.135261
2    0.161128
35   0.79557
```

3. (a) The toss of a die has six possible outcomes in the range 1 to 6. We use random-number object rndA and the function random(6) to represent the six possible outcomes in the range 0 to 5. Adding +1 to each outcome places the result in the range 1 to 6, which corresponds to a die toss.

```
dieValue = rndA.random(6) + 1; // 1 <= dieValue <= 6
```

(b) When tossing a coin, there is a 50-50 chance it will land as "heads." The function frandom() simulates the tossing of a coin. If the result is less than 0.5, set the Boolean variable tossHead to *true*. Otherwise, the simulated coin lands as a "tails."

```
bool tossHead = rndB.frandom() < 0.5;
```

Application: The Game of Craps

The game of CRAPS is a feature of casino gambling. The game has a simple set of rules that pits a player against the house. The game begins by having the player toss two dice. Depending on the total, we can have an immediate winner. Otherwise, the game continues.

Initial Toss: If the total is a 2, 3, or 12, the house wins.
If the total is a 7 or an 11, the player wins.
If the total is a 4, 5, 6, 8, 9, or 10, the game continues.

The total from the initial toss becomes the target value. The player continues tossing the two dice until the total matches the target or the total is 7. If the total is 7, the house wins; otherwise, the player wins. Throughout this process, the house has the advantage, because the total 7 occurs from any of pairs (1,6), (2,5), (3,4), (4,3), (5,2), or (6,1). A 7 is the most likely total when throwing two dice.

PROGRAM 1-2   GAME OF CRAPS

The program simulates playing the game of craps. Perform the dice-toss simulation by declaring a randomNumber object, *die*, that uses automatic seeding. The value of the expression

$$(1 + die.random(6)) + (1 + die.random(6))$$

is a random integer in the range from 2 through 12, because each term in the expression is a random integer in the range from 1 to 6. The algorithm for the main program makes an initial toss and determines possible winners. Otherwise, a loop carries out repeated tosses until a match or a 7 occurs.

```cpp
// File: prg1_2.cpp
// the program simulates playing the game of Craps.
// if die is a randomNumber object, simulate tossing
// the dice with the expression

// (1 + die.random(6)) + (1+ die.random(6))

// make an initial toss and determine if the player
// or house wins. otherwise, execute a loop that
// continues until a toss matches the initial toss
// or totals 7

#include <stream>

#include "d_random.h"        // randomNumber class

using namespace std;

int main()
{
    randomNumber die;
    int initToss, nextToss;

    // make the initial toss of 2 dice
    initToss = (1 + die.random(6)) + (1 + die.random(6));

    // check for immediate win. house wins with 2, 3, or 12
    // player wins with 7 or 11
    if (initToss == 2 || initToss == 3 || initToss == 12)
      cout << "Initial toss is " << initToss << " House wins" << endl;
    else if (initToss == 7 || initToss == 11)
       cout << "Initial toss is " << initToss << " Player wins" << endl;
    else
    // initial toss becomes the target; continue tossing until the
    // target occurs (player wins) or craps = 7 occurs (house wins)
    {
       cout << "Target is " << initToss << "  Play on" << endl;
       do
       {
          nextToss = (1 + die.random(6)) + (1 + die.random(6));
          cout << "Next toss " << nextToss << endl;
       }  while (nextToss != 7 && nextToss != initToss);
       if (nextToss == 7)
          cout << "    Craps - House wins" << endl;
       else
          cout << "    Match - Player wins" << endl;
    }

    return 0;
}
```

```
Run 1:
Initial toss is 12  House wins

Run 2:
Initial toss is 7  Player wins

Run 3:
Target is 6  Play on
Next toss 5
Next toss 2
Next toss 11
Next toss 6
    Match - Player wins

Run 4:
Target is 6  Play on
Next toss 9
Next toss 9
Next toss 4
Next toss 8
Next toss 11
Next toss 11
Next toss 7
    Craps - House wins
```

1-8   STRINGS

A string is a sequence of characters that programs use to identify names, words, and sentences. C++ provides programmers with two different string-data structures. The first, called a _C-style string_, has its origins in the C programming language and consists of an array of characters terminated by the NULL character (ASCII value 0). The second structure is a class that defines a string as an object and provides operations to access individual characters and collections of characters within the string. The standard C++ library provides the _string class_, which a programmer accesses using the directive

```
#include <string>
```

In this section, we begin with a brief discussion of the C-style string type, because it defines variables and literals that are used in the declaration of string objects. The main focus of the section is on the string class and its operations. Our study can only scratch the surface. Modern C++ compilers provide a string class that contains a very extensive and highly flexible set of operations for string handling. We introduce a partial string API, so that you can gain some familiarity with the string type and see how it is used. The help system with your C++ compiler will provide more complete information.

The C++ programming environment includes C-style strings in the declaration of many classes. You have already experienced this fact in the stream open() function that requires a C-style string to identify the file.

```
ifstream fin;                    // input stream
fin.open(<C-style string>);   // the C-style string is the filename type
```

A *string literal*, which is a sequence of characters enclosed in double quotes, is a C-style string. The following declaration creates a character array and assigns a string literal to the array:

```
char str[] = "A String";
```

The string is stored in memory as a nine-element character array.

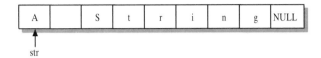

Because the string is stored in an array, its name identifies the address of the first character, and the location of NULL identifies the end of the string. For instance, str[0] is A and str[8] is the NULL character. The length of a C-style string is the number of characters preceding the NULL character. The length of string *str* is eight.

Example 1-2

A character array is not a C-style string until it contains a NULL character that indicates the end of the string:

```
char arr[10];
```

By placing a NULL character in the array block, we create a C-style string:

```
arr[0] = 'C';
arr[1] = '+';
arr[2] = '+';
arr[3] = 0;       // arr is now the string "C++"
```

This book uses C-style strings in the context of string literals. The tutorial on the book's Web site contains a discussion of C-style strings and the free function library, <cstring>, which provides an extensive series of string operations.

C-style strings

The string Class

A string object is a sequence of characters with an associated length. Like an array, a string has an index operator to access and update individual characters. Other operations handle the entire sequence of characters, enabling a programmer to copy one string to another (=), join strings together (concatenation, +, +=) and use the relational operators to compare strings (< >, <=, etc.). In <string>, C++ provides the string I/O operators << and >>, as well as the free function getline() that inputs lines of text. Unlike a C-style string, a string object has the member function length(), which returns the number of characters in the string. The following example illustrates these operations and highlights the distinction between the operator >> and getline().

Example 1-3

---

1. Declare string objects by using string literals (C-style strings), and apply to them the length, index, and concatenation operations.

```
// initialize state and city using C-style strings. cityState
// is an empty string
string state = "California", city = "Oakland", cityState;
cout << state.length();          // output 10

cityState = city + ", " + state; // "Oakland, California"
```

2. The programmer may compare string objects using the familiar relational operators:

```
string s1 = "John", s2 = "Johnson", s3 = "John";


s1 < s2 is true   s1 > "Rene" is false
s1 == s3 is true   s1 != s2 is true
```

3. The input operator >> reads whitespace-separated strings. The getline() function allows for general string input. It is more powerful than the simple ">>" operator, because it lets the programmer specify the input of all characters up to a delimiter. By removing the delimiter from the stream, successive calls to getline() can extract fields of information separated by the delimiter.

```
// input characters from istr and assign them to string str. stop
// when encountering the character delim and do not place it in
// the string. if delim is omitted, it defaults to '\n' (newline)
// and the function inputs an entire line of text. the function
// returns istream& so the programmer can test the state of the
// stream after the input
istream& getline(istream& istr, string& str, char delim = '\n');
```

As an example, for the string object s, assume the input is the following line of text:

```
New York
```

The input statement

```
cin >> s;
```

gives *s* the value "New". However, the statement

```
getline(cin, s);
```

results in the value *s* = "New York".

An operating-system password file might use a ':' delimiter to separate the user name and password:

```
jdoe:v^&aq#@95<*        (entry for John Doe)
```

A series of two getline() statements extracts the information:

```
string userName, userPwd;    // declare string objects
ifstream fin;                // declare a stream
    ...
getline(fin, userName,':');  // read user name jdoe
getline(fin, userPwd,'\n');  // read password  v^&aq#@95<*
```

Additional String Functions and Operations

The *string* class provides string-handling functions that enable a programmer to search for characters within a string, extract consecutive sequences of characters called substrings, and modify a string by adding or removing characters. We describe some of the key functions.

The functions find_first_of() and find_last_of() perform simple pattern matching that looks for a single character *c* in the string. The function find_first_of() looks for the first occurrence of the character *c* in the string, and the function find_last_of() looks for the last occurrence of *c*. The index of the match is the return value. If no match occurs, the functions return −1.

> *int find_first_of(char c, int start = 0):*
> Look for the first occurrence of *c* in the string, beginning at index start. Return the index of the match if it occurs; otherwise, return −1. By default, *start* is 0, and the function searches the entire string.

> *int find_last_of(char c):*
> Look for the last occurrence of *c* in the string. Return the index of the match if it occurs; otherwise, return −1. The search seeks a match in the tail of the string, so no starting index is provided.

Example 1-4

```
string str = "Mississippi";
int index;
```

```
// 's' occurs at indices 2, 3, 5, 6
index = str.find_first_of('s',0);      // index is 2
index = str.find_first_of('s',4);      // index is 5
index = str.find_first_of('s',7);      // index is -1
// last occurrence of 's' is at index = 6
index = str.find_last_of('s');

// the while loop outputs the index of each 'i'.
while ((index = str.find_first_of('i',index))!= -1)
{
    cout << "index " << index << " ";
    index++; // restart search at next index
}
```

Output: index 1 index 4 index 7 index 10

The function substr() extracts from the string a consecutive sequence of characters called a *substring*. The operation assumes a starting index and a count for the number of characters.

string substr(int start = 0, int count = −1):
> Copy count characters from the string beginning at index start, and return the characters as a substring. If the tail of the string has fewer than *count* characters or *count* is −1, the copy stops at end-of-string. If we call substr() without any arguments, then *start* and *count* take their default values, and the function copies the tail of the string. If the function call includes only the index *start*, then substr() returns the tail of the string starting from the index.

The find() function locates a specific pattern in the string. The function takes a string *s* and an index start as arguments and looks for match of *s* as a substring.

int find(const string& s, int start = 0):
> The search takes string *s* and index *start* and looks for a match of *s* as a substring. Return the index of the match if it occurs; otherwise, return −1. By default, *start* is 0, and the function searches the entire string.

Example 1-5

```
string fullname = "Mark Tompkin", firstname, lastname;
int index;

index = str.find_last_of(' ');    // index is 4
// firstname = "Mark"  lastname = "Tompkin"
firstname = fullname.substring(0,index);
lastname = fullname.substring(index+1);
```

```
index = fullname.find("kin");        // match "kin" at index = 9
index = fullname.find("omp",0);      // match "omp" at index = 6
index = fullname.find("omp",7);      // index is -1 (no match)
```

String concatenation $(+, +=)$ adds characters onto the end of a string. The insert() function extends this capability by allowing the addition of a string at an arbitrary index. To delete characters from a string, the erase() function deletes characters, beginning at a specified index.

void insert(int start, const string& s):
  Place the substring *s* into the string beginning at index start. The insertion expands the size of the original string.

void erase(int start = 0, int count = −1):
  Delete *count* characters from the string, beginning at index *start*. If fewer than *count* characters exist or *count* is −1, delete up to end-of-string. By default, *start* is 0, and the function removes characters from the beginning of the string. Also by default, the function removes the tail of the string. Note that calling erase() with no arguments truncates the string to the empty string, with length 0.

Example 1-6

```
string str = "endfile";
string s = "string object type";
str += " mark";
str.insert(3, "-of-");   // str is "end-of-file mark"
s.erase(7,7);            // s is "string type"
// erase 4 characters beginning at index 3
s.erase(3,4);
cout << s;               // Output: "strtype"
```

The member function c_str() returns the address of an equivalent C-style string. It provides conversion from a string object to a C-style string.

*char *c_str():*
  Return the address of a C-style string equivalent to the string object. The return type, char *, refers to the address of the first character of the C-style string. Chapter 5 discusses the notation char *.

Example 1-7

```
string fileName = "input.dat");

// open requires the file name as a C-style string
fin.open(fileName.c_str());
```

A program dealing with files might have to analyze file names. Such algorithms provide a good application of string handling. A file can be specified by a *pathname* that contains a collection of names distinguished by the separator \. The sequence of names prior to the last \ is called the *path*. The last name is the *filename* and can have an *extension*.

Pathname	\class\programs\testfile.cpp
Path	\class\programs
Filename	testfile.cpp
Extension	cpp

PROGRAM 1-3   FILE NAMES USING THE STRING CLASS

For our filename analysis, we read a full pathname from the keyboard and output the path and the filename. If the filename has the extension "cpp," we create an executable filename that replaces the extension with "exe." The following is an outline the structure of the program, along with an explanation of how it uses the string functions:

1. Input the pathname, and use the function find_last_of() to search for the last occurrence of \ in the string. This character defines the end of the path and the beginning of the filename.

2. The path is the substring of all characters prior to the final \. The filename is all characters after the final \. Use the index of the last \ and substr() to extract both the path and the filename.

3. The extension is the string following the last dot in the filename. Call find_last_of() to search for the index of the last dot. If there is a dot, use substr() to see if the remaining characters match "cpp." If so, copy the filename, erase the current extension, and append the new extension, "exe." Output the resulting executable filename.

```
// File prg1_3.cpp
// the program prompts the user for the pathname of a file.
// it uses string class operations to identify and output
// the pathname and filename. if the filename has the
// extension "cpp", create and output the name
// of an executable file whose extension "exe" replaces
// the extension "cpp"

#include <iostream>
#include <string>

using namespace std;

int main()
{
    string pathname, path, filename, executableFile;
    // index of '\' and '.'
    int backslashIndex, dotIndex;
```

```
cout << "Enter the path name: ";
cin >> pathname;

// identify index of last '\'. note: because
// escape codes such as '\n' begin with \,
// C++ represents \ by '\\'
backslashIndex = pathname.find_last_of('\\');

// pathname is characters prior to the last '\'
path = pathname.substr(0,backslashIndex);

cout << "Path:        " << path << endl;

// tail of pathname is the filename
filename = pathname.substr(backslashIndex+1,-1);
cout << "Filename:   " << filename << endl;

// see if the filename has the extension '.cpp'.
// first find the index of the last '.'. if there
// is no '.', dotIndex is -1
dotIndex = filename.find_last_of('.');
// test if there is a '.' and the remaining characters are "cpp"
if (dotIndex != -1 && filename.substr(dotIndex+1) == "cpp")
{
    // setup string executable by erasing "cpp" and appending "exe"
    executableFile = filename;
    executableFile.erase(dotIndex+1,3);
    executableFile += "exe";
    cout << "Executable: " << executableFile << endl;
}

return 0;
}
```

```
Run 1:

Enter the path name: \class\programs\testfile
Path:        \class\programs
Filename:   testfile


Run 2:

Enter the path name: programs\strings\filedemo.cpp
Path:        programs\strings
Filename:   filedemo.cpp
Executable: filedemo.exe
```

```
Run 3:

Enter the path name: \program.cpp
Path:
Filename:    program.cpp
Executable: program.exe
```

CHAPTER SUMMARY

- A data structure is a systematic way of organizing and accessing data. This book discusses programmer-defined data structures that object-oriented programming describes with classes. These structures bundle data with operations that manipulate the data. A container is a data structure that stores large collections of data. It has operations to access items, insert items, and remove items from the collection.

- The array is a very useful data structure, but it has limitations. An array has a fixed size and does not grow automatically to meet the needs of an application. The vector container solves this problem. Like an array, however, a vector is not an efficient storage structure for insertion and deletion at an intermediate position in the sequence. The operations involve the overhead of shifting blocks of elements. The list container provides very fast insertion at any point in a sequence of data elements. Arrays, vectors, and lists store elements by position. To access an element efficiently, we must know its position in the list. Otherwise, we have to revert to an item-by-item search of the list to locate the element. We also consider alternative types of containers that store elements by value rather than position. A map is such a container.

- To understand the design of a data structure, we use an abstract model that specifies the type of data stored and the operations that support the data. The model is called an abstract data type (ADT). The term "abstract" implies that we give an implementation-independent view of the data structure. We are interested in what the structure does, and not in how it does it. Before the data structure can be used in an application, we must provide an implementation. In the design and coding of the implementation, we address the runtime efficiency of the operations. Viewing a data structure as an ADT allows a programmer to focus on an idealized model of the data and its operations. A main feature of an ADT is a simple and clear description of the input to an operation, the action of the operation, and its return type. Part of the description of an operation should include a listing of the preconditions that must apply in order for the operation execute successfully. Operations often alter the value of data. The description also includes postconditions that indicate changes to the object's data caused by the operation.

- An ADT is realized by a C++ class. The public-member functions of the class correspond to the operations of the ADT. The private section of a class contains the data and operations that the public-member functions use in their implementation. The splitting of a class into public and private parts is known as *informa-*

tion hiding. A class encapsulates information by bundling the data items and operations within an object. This book illustrates the class declaration by using the *time24* class, which maintains time in 24-hour format.

- The implementation of C++ class-member functions is no different from the implementation of free functions, except that each function name must include the class scope operator ::, which designates class membership. The constructor is a special function with no return type. The constructor initializes the data members of the class by using its initialization list. The book illustrates the class implementation process by using the *time24* class.

- A class should be placed in a header file that the main program accesses through the C++ *include* directive. In this way, a class can be "plugged" into any program that requires it. The book illustrates this process by developing an application that uses the *time24* class.

- A member function can be implemented inside the class declaration by using in-line code. Replace the semicolon (;) in the function prototype by the function body. The compiler inserts the statements in the function body in place of the function call and thus avoids the function call and return mechanism. The process provides efficiency at the expense of increased code size. Use inline code for functions with only a few statements. The book illustrates inline code by developing the rectangle class.

- After the declaration and implementation of a class, the programmer might choose to create an application programming interface (API) description of the class. This allows other programmers to use the public interface of the class without having to view the technical details of the class declaration or implementation. The book illustrates the concept by providing an API for the randomNumber class that generates uniformly distributed pseudo random integer and real numbers.

- Many applications use strings of characters, and C++ provides two approaches to string handling. The C-style string is a character array that designates the end of the string by using the NULL character. This method of string handling is used by the C programming language and older C++ programs. A modern program uses the *string* class, which provides a large public interface containing many useful operations. Among these are I/O operations and functions that provide pattern-matching capabilities.

CLASSES AND LIBRARIES IN THE CHAPTER

Name	Header File
randomNumber	d_random.h
rectangle	d_rect.h
string	<string>
time24	d_time24.h

REVIEW EXERCISES

1. **(a)** Distinguish between the terms *object* and *class*.
   (b) Using the rectangle class, illustrate the differences between the two terms.
2. **(a)** Give an ADT for the *object* type triangle, which stores real numbers b, c, and *theta* that represent the lengths of two sides of a triangle and the included angle. The operation thirdSide() returns the length of the third side of the triangle formed by b, c, and angle *theta*.

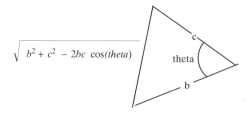

$$\sqrt{b^2 + c^2 - 2bc \ cos(theta)}$$

   (b) Assume that the default value for the data member b is 3.0 for c is 4.0 and for theta is 90. Give the C++ class declaration for triangle.
3. Identify syntax errors in the C++ class declarations. There might be several in each example.

   (a)
   ```
   class demoCL
   {
       public
           demoCL(initValue  int);
       private
           int t;
   }
   ```

   (b)
   ```
   class demoCL
   {
       private:
           int p, q;
           void demoCL(int n, m)
   };
   ```

4. The ADT circle specifies a measurement tool that identifies the radius, area, and circumference of a circle figure. Its objects store the radius as a real number and have the following operations:

   getRadius():
   > Return the radius of the circle.

   setRadius:
   > Set the radius to the value of the input argument, r.
   > Precondition: The new radius, r, must be positive
   > Postcondition: The new radius has the value r.

   area:
   > Compute and return the area with the formula $\pi * radius^2$.

   circumference:
   > Compute and return the circumference with the formula $2*\pi*radius$.

   (a) Give the class declaration.
   (b) Implement the constructor as an external function. Use a constructor initialization list.
   (c) Implement the function setRadius() as an external function.
   (d) Implement the circle class using inline code. Use the following constant declaration for PI:

   ```
   const double PI = 3.141592653589793;
   ```

5. Why should you pass an object of programmer-defined type by constant reference when the object cannot be modified?

6. A free function readDouble() prompts for the input of two *double* values, *value1* and *value2*, and then reads their values. The function has a string argument, *prompt*, and the two *double* values as reference arguments.
  (a) Give the function prototype.
  (b) Give the function implementation.
  (c) Declare two *double* values *x* and *y*, and show how to call readDouble() with the prompt "Enter two real numbers:."

7. What is a private-member function? From what code blocks can such a function be called? For what purpose is a private-member function used?

8. Declare a *time24* object *t* that has an initial time of 8:30 PM. Use member functions to update the time by three hours and five minutes and to output the result.

9. What is the range of possible values for each random-number expression?

```
randomNumber rnd;
double x;
int n;
```

  (a) *x* = rnd.frandom()*5 + 2;
  (b) *n* = rnd.random(50) + 8;
  (c) *n* = rnd.random(50) + rnd.random(25);

10. Statistics shows that one fifth of the automobiles in a state fail to meet smog emission standards. Use the randomNumber object *rnd* and the operation frandom() in a conditional expression to indicate whether a randomly selected car meets the standards.

11. (a) Consider the string object declarations

```
string s1, s2;
```

  and the input statements

```
cin >> s1;
getline(cin,s2,'\n');
```

  What is the value of *s1* and *s2* for the input line "George flies!"?
  (b) What is the value of *s1[3]* and *s1[5]*? Of *s2[0]* and *s2[6]*?

12. What is the output of the following program?

```cpp
#include <iostream>
#include <string>

using namespace std;

int main()
{
    string str = "baseball park", s;
    int index;

    index = str.find_first_of('e');
    cout << index << endl;

    index = str.find("ball");
    cout << index << endl;
```

```
str.erase(0,4);
str.insert(0,"foot");
cout << str << endl;

s = str.substr(4);
cout << s << endl;

str.erase(9);
cout << str << endl;

str += "stadium";
cout << str << endl;

return 0;
}
```

Answers to Review Exercises

1. **(a)** A <u>class</u> is a template that describes the encapsulation of data and operations on the data. An <u>object</u> is a specific instance of a class.
   (b) The rectangle class declaration is the class. The *rectangle* object rect is an instance of *rectangle*.

   ```
   rectangle rect(3,5);      // a 3 x 5 rectangle
   ```

2. **(a)** A triangle object stores the length of two sides *b* and *c* of a *triangle* and the included angle. It has the operation thirdSide.

   thirdSide():
   > The member function computes the length of the third side using the formula $\sqrt{b^2 + c^2 - 2bc \cos(\theta)}$ and returns the value.

   (b)
   ```
   class triangle
   {
       public:
           triangle(double s = 3.0, double t = 4.0, double angle = 90);
           double thirdSide();
       private:
           double a, b, theta;
   };
   ```

3. **(a)**
   ```
   class demoCL
   {
       public:
           demoCL(int initValue);
       private:
           int t;
   };
   ```
   (b)
   ```
   class demoCL
   {
       public:
           demoCL(int n, int m);
       private:
           int p, q;
   };
   ```

4. (a) `class circle`

```
{
   public:
      circle(double r = 0.0);        // constructor. initialize radius
      double getRadius() const;      // return radius
      void setRadius(double r);      // set new radius  → does not return value
      double area() const;           // return area of circle
      double circumference() const;  // return circumference of circle
   private:
      double r;                      // radius
};
```

(b) `circle::circle(double r): radius(r)`   → means the same as radius = r;

```
{}
```

(c) `void circle::setRadius(double r)`   or : radius(r)

```
{
   radius = r;                        {}
}
```

(d) `const double PI = 3.141592653589793;`

```
class circle
{
   public:
      circle(double r = 0.0): radius(r)
      {}

      double getRadius() const
      { return radius; }

      void setRadius(double r)
      { radius = r; }

      double area() const
      { return PI * radius * radius; }

      double circumference() const
      { return 2.0 * PI * radius; }

   private:
      double radius;
};
```

5. Use *pass by constant reference* to avoid the copying of data members involved in *pass by value*. When a formal reference argument is declared, the address of the argument, rather than a copy of the argument, is passed. The address is used to access the actual argument. In effect, the formal argument is an alias for the actual argument.

6. A free function readDouble() prompts for the input of two *double* objects, *value1* and *value2*, and then reads their values. The function has a string argument *prompt* and the two *double* objects as reference arguments.

(a) `void readDouble(const string& prompt, double& value1, double& value2);`

(b) `void readDouble(const string& prompt, double& value1, double& value2)`
```
{
    cout << prompt;
    cin >> value1 >> value2;
}
```

(c) `double x, y;`

```
readDouble("Enter two real numbers: ", x, y);
```

7. A private-member function is a member function declared in the private section of the class. It can be called only by another class-member function. A private-member function is a utility function that is used to implement other class-member functions. The creation of such functions simplifies code structure and avoids code duplication.

8. `time24 t(20,30);`

   `t.addTime(185);`

   `t.writeTime();`

9. **(a)** $2 \le x < 7$ **(b)** n in range from 8 to 57   **(c)** n in range from 0 to 73

10. `if (rnd.fRandom() >= 0.2)`

    `cout << "car meets smog emission standards"`

11. **(a)** `s1 = "George"`, `s2 = "□files!"` (□ is a blank)
    (b) `s1[3] = 'r'`, `s1[5] = 'e'`, `s2[0] = '□'`, `s2[6] = '!'`

12. 3
    4
    football park
    ball park
    football
    football stadium

WRITTEN EXERCISES

13. A one-dimensional array is a language-defined data structure. It consists of a finite sequence of values or objects (elements) of the same data type. Access to elements in an array is provided by the index operator [], which takes a position value as an argument. The operator can be used to access (fetch) the value of an element in the array and to use the value in an expression. When used on the left-hand side of an assignment statement, the operator copies (stores) a new value into the position. For instance,

```
// value of arr[2] is fetched from the array and multiplied by 3
x = arr[2] *3;
arr[2] = 3;    // 3 is stored as the new value of arr[2]
```

Give an ADT representation of an array that describes two versions of the [] operator, corresponding to the fetch and store operations. Give examples using array index notation arr[i] rather than the formal function prototype for the [] operator.

14. The gradeRecord class maintains student records for the registrar. Its attributes include the string studentID, along with integers for the units (total number of units attempted) and gradepts (total grade points earned).

783-29-4716	100	345
studentID	units	gradepts

These data members can be used to compute the gpa of the student by using the formula

```
gpa = double(gradepts)/units;
```

The foregoing figure represents an object named studObj. The gpa, computed by the object, is 3.45. Describe the gradeRecord class as an ADT. The operations include gpa(), which computes and returns the GPA, and updateGradeInfo(), which takes new units and grade points as arguments and updates the grade record. The operation writeGradeInfo outputs the current status of the grade record in the following format:

Student: 783-29-4716   Units: 100   GradePts: 345   GPA: 3.45

15. Consider the class declaration

```
class demoClass
{
   public:
      // assign arguments as initial values for the data members
      demoClass(int a = 5, int b = 10);
      // function returns the maximum of itemA and itemB
      // int max() const;
   private:
      int itemA, itemB;
};
```

(a) Give the implementation of the constructor using an initialization list.

(b) Implement the member function max() as an external function.

(c) For each of the following object declarations, give the corresponding initial values for attributes itemA and itemB:

```
demoClass obj1(7,9);  // itemA = _____  itemB = _____
demoClass obj2(12);   // itemA = _____  itemB = _____
demoClass obj3;       // itemA = _____  itemB = _____
```

(d) What is the output from each statement, assuming the previous declarations?

```
cout << obj2.max();   // Output: _____
cout << obj3.max();   // Output: _____
```

16. Identify the syntax errors in the C++ class declarations. There could be several in each class.

(a)
```
className:class
   public
   {
      className(a, b):void
      setData(int a, b);
```

(b)
```
class className
   {  public@
         void className(int initValue)
         getValue() : int;
      private;
```

```
   }                                              int value;
private                              }
{
   int itemA, itemB
};
```

17. The *accumulator* class describes objects that maintain running totals. In the class, the constructor has a default argument of 0.0, and the addValue() member function adds a value to the total. If its argument is omitted, the default value of 1.0 is added. The following is the declaration for the accumulator class:

```
class accumulator
{
   public:
      accumulator(double value = 0.0);      // constructor
      double getTotal() const;              // return total
      void addValue(double value = 1.0);    // add value to total
   private:
      double total;
         // total accumulated by the object
};
```

(a) Give an implementation of the constructor that uses an initialization list.

(b) Implement the member functions addValue() and getTotal() as external functions.

(c) Trace the program, and determine the result of each output statement. Assume the accumulator class is declared and implemented in the header file "accum.h".

```
#include <iostream>

#include "accum.h"

using namespace std;

int main()
{
   accumulator obj;

   cout << obj.getTotal() << endl;    // output: _____
   obj.addValue(3);
   obj.addValue(obj.getTotal()+3);
   cout << obj.getTotal() << endl;    // output: _____

   // using the constructor, create an object and
   // assign it to obj
   obj = accumulator(8);
   obj.addValue();
   cout << obj.getTotal() << endl;    // output: _____

   return 0;
}
```

18. Distinguish between the public and private sections of a class. How do they support information hiding?

19. Use a random number to simulate each of the following situations:

   (a) The number of students in ECON 101 falls randomly in the range from 30 to 35. Use random() to specify the number of students in any selected semester.

   (b) Integers in the range from 0 to 51 represent cards in a deck. Use random() to return a card from a deck.

   (c) The weather bureau predicts a 10% chance that the baseball game will be canceled, a 25% chance it will be delayed, and a 65% chance of no interruption. Write C++ statements that use a *random-number* object and a series of nested *if* statements that indicate the outcome based on the value of the random object.

20. **(a)** Implement the function countHeads(), which simulates the tossing of *n* coins and returns the number of heads. In order for all calls to countHeads() to use the same random sequence, pass the randomNumber object to the function by reference:

```
int countHeads(int n, randomNumber& rnd);
```

   (b) The function empiricalHeadToss() returns the empirical probability of getting *m* heads when tossing n coins. Use countHeads() to simulate the action of tossing the coins. The function computes the empirical probability by tossing *n* coins NUMBER-TOSSES times and determining the number of tosses that total *m* heads.
   Implement the function empiricalHeadToss():

```
double empiricalHeadToss(int m, int n);
```

   Use the following declaration for NUMBERTOSSES:

```
const int NUMBERTOSSES = 5000000;
```

   Store the result in the integer variable mHeadCount. The return value is the ratio

```
double(mHeadCount)/ NUMBERTOSSES
```

21. The HiLow game is a one-person game that challenges a player to determine the value of a random number (target) between 1 and 1000 within the span of $n \leq 10$ guesses. The player inputs a number, and the program informs the player whether the target matches the number ("PLAYER WINS IN <*n*> GUESSES") , the target is less than the number ("LOWER"), or the target is greater than the number ("HIGHER"). After 10 unsuccessful guesses, the game terminates ("PLAYER LOSES—TARGET IS <target>").

   (a) Declare and implement with inline code the class playHiLow, which has the integer, *target*, and the randomNumber object, *rnd*, as data members. The constructor uses *rnd* to initialize the target to a value in the range from 1 to 1000. The member function makeGuess() takes an integer argument and returns an integer value. The argument represents a guess that the function compares with target. The return value is negative (-1) if the target is less than the guess, zero if the target and the guess are a match, and positive $(+1)$ if the target is greater than the guess. The function writeTarget() outputs the message

   Target = <target>

   (b) Write a code segment that declares a playHiLow object called player and uses a loop to control the playing of the game. For each iteration, input a guess by calling makeGuess(), and use the return value to indicate whether the player wins or the target is "HIGHER" or "LOWER." Terminate the loop after 10 iterations (guesses), output the fact that the player loses, and display the target.

22. Consider the string declaration

```
string strA("john"), strB("son"), strC;
```

For each statement, give the resulting string. Execute the statements consecutively.

    (a) `strC = strA + strB;`
    (b) `strA += strA + strB;`
    (c) `strC = strB + " of " + strA;`

23. Consider the string object declarations

```
string s1, s2;
```

and the input statements

```
getline(cin,s1,':');
getline(cin,s2,'\n');
```

(a) What are the values of *s1* and *s2* for the input line

```
Roberts, Larry:345678912
```

(b) What are the values of *s1*[2] and *s1*[5]? Of *s2*[3] and *s2*[7]?

24. Use the following declarations for each of the parts (a)-(h).

```
string s = "abc12xya52cba", t;
int index;
```

(a) What is the value of index = s.find_last_of ('c')?
(b) What is the value of index = s.find_first_of('a',3)?
(c) What is the value of index = s.find_first_of('y',8)?
(d) What is the value of s[6]?
(e) What is the value of *t* = s.substr(5,6)?
(f) What is the value of *t* after executing the instructions

```
t = s;
t.insert(5,"ABC");
```

(g) What is the value of index = s.find("a52",2)?
(h) What is the value of s after

```
s.erase(5,2);
```

25. (a) The function linkNames() takes string objects strA and strB and separator character ch as arguments and returns a new string of the form *<strA><ch><strB>*. For instance, if *strA* is "find", *strB* is "first", and *ch* is the underscore character(-), the return string is "find_first." Give the prototype for the function linkNames().
(b) Give the implementation for the function linkNames().
(c) Use the following declaration:

    string nameA ="Barney", nameB = "Betty";

Give the C++ statement that uses linkNames() to output "Barney&Betty."

    cout << _____ << endl;

26. The free function newString() takes string objects *strA* and *strB* as arguments. For its action, newString() compares the strings by using < and returns the concatenation of the arguments, with the lesser string coming first.
  (a) Give a function prototype for newString().
  (b) Give the implementation for newString().
  (c) The main program has the following string declarations, which should be used for parts **(i)** and **(ii)**.

```
string A = "String", B = "cat";
```

  (i) `cout << newString(A,B);`   `// Output: _____`
  (ii) `cout << newString(A,"C++");`   `// Output: _____`

27. (a) The free function strInsert() takes strings *strA* and *strB*, along with the integer pos, as arguments. The function inserts *strB* in strA beginning at position *pos*, provided that pos < strA.length(). Otherwise, *strB* is inserted at the end of *strA*. Implement the function by using only the string member functions substr() and +.

```
void strInsert(string& strA, const string& strB, int pos);
```

  (b) The free function strReplace() takes strings *strA*, *strB*, and *strC* as arguments. In strA, the function replaces all occurrences of *strB* with *strC*. Implement the function by using the string member functions find(), insert(), and erase().

```
void strReplace (string& strA, const string& strB,
                 const string& strC);
```

28. Trace the program by using the two given versions of the function func(). In each case, give the output provided by the "cout" statements.

```
int main()
{
    int a = 3, b = 8, c = 5, d = 3;

    func(a, b);
    cout << a << "   " << b << endl;  // Output: _____

    func(c, d);
    cout << c << "   " << d << endl;  // Output: _____


    return 0;
}
```

  (a) Use version #1 for func(). **(b)** Use version #2 for func().

```
void func(int x, int& y)          void func(int& x, int& y)
{                                 {
    if (x < y)                        if (x < y)
        x = 2 * y;                        x = 2 * y;
    else                              else
        y = 3 * x;                        y = 3 * x;
}                                 }
```

29. Declare the *time24* objects *time* and *oldTime*.

```
// time represents 8:00 AM, oldTime midnight
time24 time(8,0), oldTime;
```

Write a *while* loop that enters a series of five increasing times in the range from 8:01 AM to 11:59 PM. Indicate the number of hours and minutes between successive time intervals. Hint: Use the following statements to input a new time.

> oldTime = time;
> time.readTime();

30. Write a free function isLater() that takes two *time24* objects and determines whether the first time is later than the second.

```
bool isLater(const time24& t1, const time24& t2);
```

EXAMPLE: // time1 is 8:15 AM, time2 is 5:25 AM
          time24 time1(8,15), time2(5,25);

```
if (isLater(time1, time2))          // condition true
```

31. Create an API for the *time24* class.

PROGRAMMING EXERCISES

32. In the file "grade.h," give the C++ declaration and implementation of the gradeRecord class from Written Exercise 1-14.
    (a) Write a program that declares the gradeRecord object *tMartin* with initial values "716-29-4238" (studentID), 20 (units), and 50 (gradepts). Output the initial GPA. After completing the semester, the student represented by object *tMartin* adds 15 units and 40 grade points. Update the grade record, and output the new grade-record information.
    (b) Write a program that declares the following objects:

    > gradeRecord aDunn("455-27-9138", 14, 49), bLange("657-58-0331", 25, 50);

    Output the gpa for both *aDunn* and bLange. Assume *aDunn* completes 4 units with a grade of A (16 gradepoints). Update the corresponding grade record, and output the new grade-record information. Assume *bLange* takes 15 units in a semester. In a loop, determine the effect on the total GPA if the average grade for the 15 units is a C (two gradepts per unit), a B (three gradepts per unit), and an A (four gradepts per unit). Output the total GPA for each case.

33. Some schools have a grade-replacement policy: A student can retake a course, remove the old grade, and post the new grade in the record. Using the implementation of the gradeRecord class from Programming Exercise 1-32, create a new header file "xgrade.h" that adds the member function replaceGrade() to the gradeRecord class.

```
void replaceGrade(int oldUnits, int oldGradePts,
                  int newUnits, int newGradePts);
```

The function updates the grade record by first deleting the old units and grade points and then adding the new grade information.

Write a program that declares the gradeRecord object dHarris. After initially displaying the GPA, indicate the effect of replacing four units of D (one gradept per unit) with an A (four gradepts per unit) by displaying the new GPA. Show the effect of more grade re-placement by having *dHarris* substitute a B for an F in two four-unit classes.

```
gradeRecord dHaris("558-29-4424", 100, 180);
```

34. In the header file "accum.h," declare and implement the *accumulator* class from Written Exercise 1-17.
   (a) Enter and run the program from part (c) of the written exercise.
   (b) Declare two accumulator objects *negTotal* and *posTotal*. Scan the array

```
double arr[8] = {4, −8, 6, 9, −2, 10, −14, 5};
```

   and determine separate totals for the negative and positive array elements. Output each of the totals.

35. Place the *circle* class in Review Exercise 1-4 in the file "circle.h." Write a program that prompts the user to enter a radius. Using this value, declare a *circle* object circ and a *rectangle* object rect that circumscribes the circle. Output the area in the shaded region.

36. (a) Extend the *rectangle* class in "d_rect.h" by adding the member function diagonal(), which returns the length of the diagonal. Implement the function, and use the file "xrect.h" to store the new rectangle class. Note that the length of the diagonal is given by sqrt($length^2 + width^2$) and that the sqrt() function is part of the math library in <cmath>.
   (b) A designer builds custom windows that include both stained and clear glass in various patterns. The cost for stained glass is $.75 per square inch and the cost for clear glass is $.40 per square inch. One pattern begins with a square frame whose sides are of length s. The midpoints of each side are joined to form a square that contains clear glass. The remainder of the frame contains stained glass. Write a program that enters the length of a side *s* for the inner square (clear glass). Declare the rectangle object innerSq, and use its diagonal value to declare the rectangle object frame. Compute and output the total cost of the window.

   (c) Write a program that uses the new class and the circle class implemented in Review Exercise 1-4. It is assumed that the circle class is in the header file "circle.h." The program computes a series of values for a combination of circle and rectangle objects. Begin by reading a radius r that is used to declare the circle object innerCircle. With this radius, declare a square, called innerSquare, that circumscribes the circle. A third object, outerCircle, circumscribes the square. Output the ratio of the perimeter of the outer circle to that of the inner square. Also, output the ratio of the area of the inner square to that of the inner circle. Run the program several times, and determine whether there is a pattern.

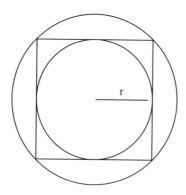

37. Random integers are uniformly distributed within a range of values. Write a program that uses simulation to see whether the units digits of the random numbers are uniformly distributed. Begin by declaring count as a 10-element array of integers. Using a loop, generate one million random integers in the range from 0 to 99,999. For each value, extract the units digit (value % 10), and increment the corresponding value in the array. Output the array values as a ratio to one million.

38. Use the function empiricalHeadToss() from Written Exercise 1-20(b). Prompt for n, the number of coins and m, the number of heads. Call empiricalHeadToss(), and output the result. Include runs with $n = 5, m = 3$ and $n = 5, m = 1$. The mathematical probabilities for these results are 0.3125 and 0.15625, respectively. How close does your simulation come to the mathematical results?

39. Use the specification of the HiLow game from Written Exercise 1-21. Write a program that includes the code segment developed for part (b) of the exercise.

40. Write a program that declares the following string objects:

```
string algs = "Algorithms ",
dataStruc = " Data Structures ",
programs = " Programs",
title;
```

By using the function linkNames() defined in Written Exercise 1-25, the program should assign to title the string value

Algorithms + Data Structures = Programs

and output it.

41. Declare an array containing the following words:

Arizona walk government C++ beach

For each word, output the first and the last letter, and count how many vowels are in the word.

42. Implement part (c) of Written Exercise 1-26 as a main program.

43. This exercise uses the functions strInsert() and strReplace(), developed in Written Exercise 1-27. Input a line of text into a string line by using getline(). Prompt for a replacement string rep. Replace all occurrences of "<pat>" in line by rep, and insert the string

"+++" in the middle of line at index line.length()/2. Output the modified string. Test your program with the following data:

line: Alfred the snake h<pat>ed because he m<pat>ed his M<pat>y.
rep: iss

The output should be

Alfred the snake hissed b+++ecause he missed his Missy.

44. Input a series of lowercase words until the end of file, converting each one to pig latin: If the word begins with a consonant, move the first character of the word to the last position and append "ay" to the end of word. If the word begins with a vowel, simply append "ay" to the end of the word. For example,

Input: this is simple
Output: histay isay implesay

45. Write a program that declares a *time24* object clock that is initially set to 9:00 AM. In a loop, enter a sequence of *minutes* values. Use each to increment time, and output the new value. Terminate the loop when *clock* exceeds 5:00 PM, and output the final time. Use the free function isLater(), developed in Written Exercise 1-30. ——→ *takes two time24 objects + determines whether the first time is later than the second.*

PROGRAMMING PROJECTS

46. Declare a class *geometry* that contains two (2) data items, *measure1* and *measure2*, of type double. The constructor has two formal arguments that correspond to the data members. The second argument has the default value 0.0, which allows a *geometry* object to be declared with a single runtime argument. When *measure2* is 0.0, the figure represented is a circle; otherwise, it is a rectangle.

```
// represent a circle of radius 1 and a rectangle with
// dimensions 3 X 5
geometry circ(1), rect(3,5);
```

The function border() returns the perimeter of the object. The functions area() and diagonal() return the area and diagonal of the object, respectively. Implement the *geometry* class in the file "geometry.h," and develop the following application.

Input the radius of a circle, and declare a geometry object that represents it. Use this radius to declare a square that circumscribes the circle. Declare a circle that circumscribes the square. Output the area and perimeter of each figure.

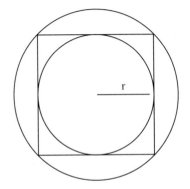

47. Allocate an array of 50 string objects. Read the lines from a file "formlet.txt," placing each line in an array element. Each line might contain the special symbols # and &. For example,

> Dear #:
>
> Your lucky gift is available at &. By going to & and identifying your name, the attendant will give you
> your prize. Thank you, #, for your interest in our contest.
>
> Sincerely,
> The String Man

Create a file "replace.txt" that contains lines in the format

> poundstr#ampstring

Each string *poundstr* substitutes for all occurrences of # in your document, and *ampstring* substitutes for all occurrences of &. For each line in "replace.txt," traverse the array of strings, perform the substitutions, and output the form letter. Separate all the form letters by a form-feed character, which you can output with the statement

```
cout << '\f' << endl;
```

CHAPTER 2

Object Design Techniques

OBJECTIVES

- To understand the phases of the software life cycle.
- To understand the difference between the traditional structured approach to program design and the modern object-oriented approach.
- To understand that it is important to design the public interface of a class carefully before beginning a class implementation.
- To understand that it is important to develop algorithms for implementing class-member functions carefully before beginning a class implementation.
- To understand that testing is a critical component of the software-development cycle. Without proper testing, an application could fail as a commercial product.
- To understand that program maintenance is as important as the creation of the original product, because failure to update an application causes it to become obsolete rapidly.
- To study the calendar class as a simple example of the software life cycle.
- To learn fundamental methods of handling program runtime errors: The calling code should handle the error, not the member or free function that encounters the error.
- To understand the basics of using C++ exceptions and to understand why exceptions are the superior mechanism for handling errors.
- To understand that object composition is a fundamental object design technique and that it facilitates software reuse.
- To understand the use of the constructor initialization list in providing initial values for objects included by composition.
- To understand that operator overloading is an object design technique that makes using a class easier and more flexible.
- To understand how a binary or a unary operator can be represented as an operator function and how operator functions form the basis for overloading most operators.
- To understand that most binary operators are overloaded either as free functions or as special free functions called *friend functions*, which are not class members.
- To understand how to overload the stream operators $<<$ and $>>$ as friends of a class, to allow class objects to be used in streams just like primitive variables.
- To understand that some operators cannot be overloaded as a *friend function* or that it is more convenient to declare the function as a class member.
- To understand that a function overloaded as a class member has one argument fewer than the corresponding operator function declaration.

OUTLINE

In Chapter 1, we developed an object view of a data structure as a class. We introduced the design process for a data structure that begins with an ADT and its realization as the public members of a class. The public members form the programmer interface for the data structure. Chapter 1 also discussed class implementation, including a design feature that uses private-member functions to streamline the writing of function code. The chapter concluded with a definition of an API, which is a documentation scheme that allows a programmer to use a data structure in an application without knowledge of the ADT design and the class declaration.

In this chapter, we extend the topics from Chapter 1 and view data structures in the broader context of a software system that solves a problem. We begin in Section 2-1 by describing the software-development life cycle, which is a systematic way of designing software for a problem posed by a client. The development cycle identifies progressive stages in the building of a software system that include analysis, design, and implementation. It also highlights the importance of testing to verify that the application design components meet the specifications of the client and that the code runs correctly.

In the designing of a class, some member functions have preconditions that must be satisfied in order for the operation to execute successfully. Handling the violation of preconditions and other errors during function execution is an important aspect of program design. Section 2-2 discusses three fundamental ways to handle errors and concludes that the best alternative is to use the C++ exception mechanism. When a function detects an error, it throws an exception, which is normally an object of a special class that handles the exception. The throw bypasses the normal function return mechanism and follows the chain of previous function calls until it locates an exception handler. The handler normally outputs an error message and either takes corrective action or terminates the program.

In Chapter 1, we described classes whose data members were primitive C++ data types. In object design, a data member of a class is often an object of some other class. This concept, called object composition, promotes code reuse and greatly simplifies the implementation of a class. Object composition is discussed in Section 2-3.

An important feature of object design in C++ is the addition of overloaded operators to a class, which is the topic of Section 2-4. Operator overloading redefines an operator to accept operands of the class type. For instance, you have used the string class in Chapter 1 and have taken advantage of its concatenation operator, +. This operator allows the concatenation of two string objects, using the familiar notation

```
str = str1 + str2;
```

The string class redefines the + operator to form the concatenation of its two operands. Designing a class to take advantage of familiar operator notation makes the class easier to use and extends its flexibility.

SOFTWARE DESIGN   2-1

A computer program begins with a problem that somebody (the *client*) wants solved. The process of building the program starts with an analysis of the problem and proceeds through a series of stages to produce a product that the client hopes is reliable and easy to maintain. The process has an analogy to building a house, where the client first engages an architect to design the structure and then a contractor to build it. In the early days of computing, software systems evolved without using standards for software design. As features were needed, programmers added code and functionality to the system with little attention to their integration into the system. Eventually, the systems deteriorated and became so difficult to update that programmers had to develop new software to replace them. In an attempt to address this problem, the computer industry developed principles of software engineering to control the design and implementation of a software system. Researchers organized the principles into a development model, called the *software-development life cycle*. Although the techniques vary, the model includes the following stages and agents:

Request:	A client perceives a need for a software system to solve a problem. A computer consultant undertakes a feasibility study for the project.
Analysis:	A systems analyst develops the requirements of the system and creates a *functional specification* that includes a list of needs and special requirements.
Design:	A software engineer translates the functional specification into an abstract model of the system. The engineer identifies the components of the system and develops algorithms that will be used for implementation.
Implementation:	Programmers use the design specification and language features to code the different components of the system.

Testing: The agents involved in the design and implementation of the program check that they are both solving the correct problem and solving it correctly. Testing procedures seek to identify logical and runtime errors and verify that the system meets the specifications of the client.

Maintenance: The development cycle is an ongoing process. It must periodically update the software system to stay current and to respond to the changing needs of the client.

An analysis of the software-development life cycle is the focus of a course in software engineering. The study would look at a sophisticated software system like one needed to deal with a proposal from the Department of Motor Vehicles:

Problem: The Department of Motor Vehicles proposes to provide motorists with an interactive Web-based system to schedule appointments for license renewal and auto registration.

The software development for this problem involves extensive analysis to understand the client's needs. The design includes a Web interface and the choice of data structures to store and access appointment data. Implementation involves the transfer of Web documents between a network server and the client, and so forth. Discussing the development cycle for such a problem lies beyond the scope of this book. We choose a much simpler problem that prints a calendar for a specified month and year. The problem allows us to illustrate in some detail the different features in the development cycle. The problem has the primary components of a more significant application.

Problem: The user enters the month and year, and the program displays a calendar. For instance, entering month 4 and year 2002 results in the calendar

```
                  April 2002
     Sun   Mon   Tue   Wed   Thu   Fri   Sat
            1     2     3     4     5     6
      7     8     9    10    11    12    13
     14    15    16    17    18    19    20
     21    22    23    24    25    26    27
     28    29    30
```

Request and Problem Analysis

In the initial phases of the software cycle, computer professionals meet with the client to discuss the needs and requirements for a software system. The client might perceive that a new system would improve the efficiency and organization of the company, would attract new customers, or would add quality controls in the manufacturing of a product. The analysis should involve a feasibility study to see whether building a software system is cost effective. After completion of the study, the analysis phase should determine the system requirements. This is the responsibility of a *systems analyst*, who acts as the intermediary between the client and the software engineers who will build the program. The result of the analysis phase of the cycle is a *functional specification* of the software system that includes a list of needs and special requirements.

There are many different ways to write functional specifications for a problem. At a minimum, the specifications must include clear statements about the inputs and outputs of the program, along with a detailing of the assumptions and processing requirements.

Calendar Analysis. In our calendar problem, the client wants a program that prompts the user to enter a month (in the range from 1 to 12) and a year (1900 or later). The output displays a calendar with the name of the month and the year in a label and the dates listed in a table below the days "Sun," "Mon," ..., "Sat." We assume that January 1, 1900, is a Monday and use this fact as the base reference in the creation of a calendar. The client wants the flexibility to take our program and produce a yearlong calendar by calling the monthly calendar display for each month in the year.

Program Design

The design phase of the software-development life cycle translates the functional specifications from the analysis phase into an abstract model of the problem. A traditional design method uses a top-down approach that assumes the existence of a top administrator who understands the problem and delegates tasks to managers. The model views a system as a layered set of subprograms. Execution begins in the main program, and information flows through the system via a series of function calls and return values.

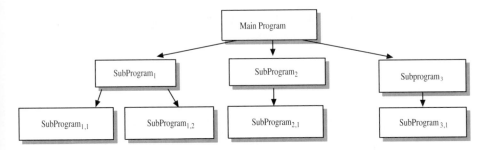

When the problem becomes too large, however, this approach can fail, because its complexity overwhelms the ability of a single person to manage the hierarchy of subprograms. Also, simple design changes in subprograms near the top of the hierarchy can require expensive and time-consuming changes in the subprograms at lower levels in the chart.

Object-oriented programming uses a different design model. It views the problem as a set of objects that interact to carry out tasks. The software system represents each object by a class consisting of data and of operations that manage that

data. Object-oriented programming employs a bottom-up approach that first identifies the objects and their operations and then builds scenarios that describe how the
objects should interact.

Model building in the design phase of the problem has similarities to the actions of an architect in creating blueprints for a house. The first set of blueprints addresses the client's needs and desires by laying out the rooms and creating hallways
for efficient flow of traffic. In software development, a second aspect of the design
phase is responsible for identifying the objects that are the building blocks of the
program and for determining how these objects should collaborate and interact to
solve the problem. In the process, this aspect creates the declarations of the classes,
including their attributes and public-member functions. It also describes how the
classes are related to each other and designs the algorithms that allow the classes to
interact efficiently. Just as the architect creates a second set of blueprints to specify
how the contractor should build the house, the design phase must also create struc-
tural blueprints that programmers can use to implement the individual components
and relate them in the overall system.

Designing the Calendar Class

Our design begins by viewing a calendar month as an object. We begin by creating a
calendar class whose public-member functions meet the specifications given by the
client. The class data store the month and year. A user will input the month and
year, so the constructor uses these values to initialize the data. The operation dis-
playCalendar() outputs the calendar. The client wants the flexibility to output a
yearly calendar by displaying the individual calendars for each month in the year. To
provide this capability, we add the functions getMonth() and getYear() to access the
data and the functions setMonth() and setYear() to update the data. The constructor and the set functions have preconditions that ensure the month and the year are
within their correct ranges.

CLASS calendar	Declaration	"d_cal.h"

```
class calendar
{
   public:
      calendar(int m = 1, int y = 1900);
      // initialize the month and year for display.
      // precondition: month is in the range 1 to 12 and year
      // is 1900 or later

   void displayCalendar() const;
      // display the calendar with a header and a table of dates

   int getMonth() const;
      // return the current month for the calendar

   int getYear() const;
      // return the current year for the calendar
```

```
    void setMonth(int m);
       // update the month for the calendar
       // precondition: m must be in the range 1 to 12

    void setYear(int y);
       // update the year for the calendar
       // precondition: y must be >= 1900

    private:
       . . .
};
```

Designing the displayCalendar() Algorithm. The member function display-Calendar() outputs both the calendar label and the grid of dates and names for the days in the week. These are distinct tasks. For instance, to display the label, we need to convert the integer value for the month to a string that gives the name of the month. Displaying the dates under the correct names for the days in the week requires knowing the day corresponding to the first day of the month, the number of days in the month, and so forth. To isolate the tasks, our implementation design creates two private-member functions, displayTitle() and displayDates(). Chapter 1 discusses the role of private-member functions in a class implementation.

The key element in the design of the calendar problem is the algorithm for displayDates(). Let us explore some of the issues. In the process, we will discover some object design techniques that we will discuss in detail in subsequent sections. We use the building of the grid for the April 1999 calendar as a specific example. The first day of the month is Thursday. Subsequent dates cycle through the days from Thursday to Saturday and then back to Sunday of the next week, stopping at date 30, which is the number of days in the month. To implement the algorithm, we require two pieces of information.

Requirement 1:   We require the day of the week on which the first of the month falls.

This information is important, because we must skip space in the first week in order to position the first of the month below the label "Thu" (Figure 2-1).

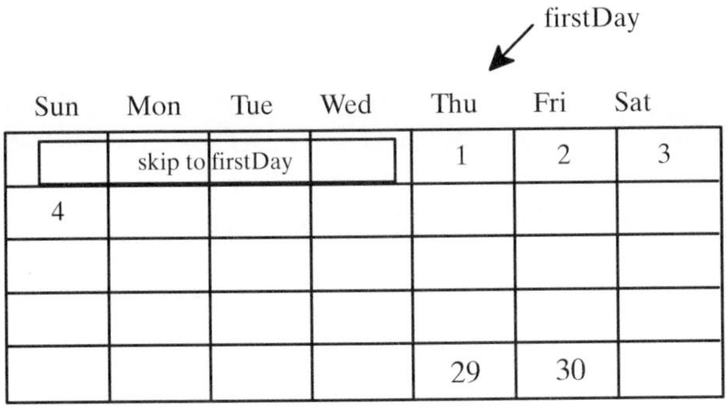

Figure 2-1
Identifying Thursday as the first day of April

Requirement 2:   We require the number of days in the calendar month.

Once displayCalendar() begins placing dates in the calendar grid, it must know when to stop. We must have access to the number of days in the month, including special attention to February in case of a leap year.

Finding the Day for the First of the Month. To find the day on which the first of the month falls, we use a brute-force calculation. Assume that the integer value 0 represents Sunday, 1 represents Monday, and so forth. We use the fact that January 1, 1900, fell on a Monday. This is the starting point for the calculation. For each subsequent year, we identify the day for January 1 by adding either 365 days or 366 days, depending on whether the previous year was a leap year. The day corresponds to the remainder after division by 7. For instance, year 1900 is not a leap year, so we add 365 days to 1 (Monday). The result, 366 % 7 = 2, indicates that January 1, 1901, was a Tuesday. By continuing the process, we identify that January 1, 1999, was a Friday (value 5). With this information, we can compute the first day of April by adding the number of days from January 1 to April 1. In 1999, that is 90 days: 31 days in January, 28 days in February, and 31 days in March. By adding 90 to 5 (Friday) and dividing by 7, we find that the result is 4 (Thursday).

The algorithm assumes that we can determine whether a year is a leap year, because the calculation adds 366 days in this case. If the calendar displays a month from March to December in a leap year, we use 29 days for February to find the day on which the first falls. We could design a function to determine a leap year, a second function to determine the number of days from January 1 to the first of the month, and a third function to return the number of days in the month. As frequently happens, designers identify operations that are already available in an existing class. Many compilers provide a date class that facilitates date computations. The software supplement provides a class date having member functions that determine leap years, evaluate the number of days in the month, properly increment dates that fall into the next year, and so forth. As part of our design, we give an API for the date class that lists the relevant operations for the calendar problem.

CLASS date	**Constructor**	**"d_date.h"**

date(int mm = 1, int dd = 1, int yy = 1900);
     Initializes the date with default January 1, 1900.

CLASS date	**Operations**	**"d_date.h"**

int **daysInMonth**();
     Returns the number of days for the month. If the year is a leap year, month 2 (February) returns 29.

int **getMonth**();
     Returns the month for the current date.

int **getYear**();
> Returns the year for the current date.

bool **isLeapYear**();
> Returns *true* if the year is a leap year; otherwise, returns *false*.

int **numberOfDays**();
> Returns the number of days into the year from January.

void **setMonth**(int mm);
> Updates the month in the current date.

void **setYear**(int yy);
> Updates the year in the current date.

To use the facilities of the date class, we define a date object *d* as a private member of the calendar class and use the object to store the month and year for the calendar display. This design technique is called *object composition*; in it, an object of class type is a data member. We develop this concept in Section 2-3. By using object composition, we have a data member that not only stores information, but also provides its own member functions for implementation of class operations. For instance, we can use the function calls

```
d.isLeapYear(), d.numberOfDays(), d.daysInMonth()
```

to implement displayDates(). When initializing *d*, we provide the constructor with an argument list consisting of the input values for month and year and a day argument of 1.

We summarize the implementation design for the calendar class by giving the declaration of the private members.

CLASS calendar   **Declaration**   **"d_cal.h"**

```
class calendar
{
    public:
        . . .
    private:
        date d;
            // date object representing the 1st day in the
            // specified month and year

        int firstDay() const;
            // return day of the week (0-6) holding first day of month
```

```
void displayTitle() const;
   // output month and year followed by names for days
   // of the week

void displayDates() const;
   // output the dates under the correct days of the week
```

Program Implementation

The implementation phase of the software development cycle uses the syntax and features of a programming language like C++ to convert the design into a program. Typically, a design includes a series of classes and functions to direct the interaction among the objects. We start by implementing the classes independently and verifying the actions of their member functions. The next stage implements program units that coordinate object interaction and concludes with the coding of the main program that manages the overall execution of the software system. In the development cycle, implementation should ideally follow design. The programmer should be able to use the design specifications much as a contractor builds a home from an architect's blueprint. In reality, there is a dynamic interaction between design and implementation. Often, errors and deficiencies in design are understood only during the implementation phase of a program. When this occurs, we will need to modify and update the initial design.

Implementing the Calendar Class

We illustrate the implementation phase of the development cycle with two examples from the calendar class. The member function setMonth() takes an integer argument and updates the month that is stored within the date object *d*. The implementation allows us to illustrate two important object-technology principles. The function has a precondition that requires the argument to be in the range from 1 to 12, so we need to test the precondition and take appropriate action if it is violated. We develop various techniques to handle this situation in Section 2-2. We focus on exception handling, which enables the program to identify the error and take remedial action. If the month is invalid, the function throws the dateError exception containing an error-message string. The implementation of setMonth() also allows us to illustrate the power of object composition, as we call the date member function setMonth() to perform the action of the corresponding calendar function.

setMonth():
```
// update the current month
void calendar::setMonth(int mm)
{
   // verify that mm is a valid month
   if (mm < 1 || mm > 12)
     throw dateError("calendar setMonth():", mm, "invalid month");
```

```
        // set d to new month
        d.setMonth(mm);
    }
```

A second example is the private-member function displayDates(). With the
date object *d* and the function firstDay(), we have the tools needed to write the
dates under the correct day of the week. The number of days in the month is determined by using the daysInMonth() function from the date class. The integer variable *days* advances through the days of the week, starting with 0, which represents
Sunday. Before writing the first date, we must skip space to the first day of the
month. Assign to the integer variable *first* the result of calling firstDay() and output
spaces until *day* has value *first*. Once we start filling the calendar, we move to a new
week after displaying the date for *day* = 6 (Saturday). Conclude by skipping any unused days of the last week. These two actions are implemented by outputting a newline character.

displayDates():

```
// output dates of the calendar under the correct days of week
void calendar::displayDates() const
{
    // set number of days in the month
    int monthLength = d.daysInMonth();
    int dayValue = 1;
    int day = 0, first = firstDay();

    // skip spaces up to the first day of the month
    while (day < first)
    {
        cout << setw(7) << " ";
        day++;
    }

    // output the dates 1 .. monthLength
    while (dayValue <= monthLength)
    {
        cout << setw(7) << dayValue;
        dayValue++;
        // is next day Sunday of a new week?
        if (day == 6)
            cout << endl;
        day = (day+1)%7;
    }

    // skip unused days in the last week
    if (day != 0)
        cout << endl;
}
```

Program Testing and Debugging

The analysis, design, and implementation phases of the software-development cycle reflect a logical progression in the building of a software system. Only in an ideal world are the phases sequential. Typically, the design phase identifies weaknesses in the analysis and requires reworking of the problem specifications. In the implementation phase, programmers often discover that the design did not adequately account for critical data and operations and did not provide control modules that allow proper interaction among objects. Analysis, design, and implementation are interactive processes that bring about modifications and corrections to the specifications and the code. Effective interaction among the phases depends on frequent and systematic testing. We not only need to test the classes and functions that are the individual units of the software system; we also must perform integrative testing. This type of testing ensures that the units fit together to create a program that runs correctly and efficiently and meets the specifications of the client. Automobile makers have long understood this dynamic. Subcontractors for the body style, engine, and transmission work together to ensure that their individual components fit together to produce an attractive, but functional, safe, and efficient, car. Each component and its integration into the final product are subject to constant testing and retesting as modifications are made.

The goal of the software-development cycle is to produce a program that meets the specifications set out by the client. At each stage in the process, we can do testing to see whether this goal is being advanced. The testing process, called *program verification*, checks on whether the original analysis creates functional specifications that meet the needs and desires of the client. In subsequent stages, verification determines that the design specifications create an abstract model consistent with the functional specifications and that the programmers correctly code the classes and functions in the design. In the process, verification identifies test data that will check how the individual components and the system as a whole will operate.

The development cycle for software starts with a set of specifications. These specifications could be wrong, on account of inadequate understanding of the problem or of indecision and changing goals on the part of the client. Throughout the development, we must use *program validation testing* that involves the client and the software developers to ensure that we are solving the correct problem. Program verification determines that we are solving the problem correctly, while program validation determines that we are solving the correct problem.

There is a variety of testing strategies that enble developers to verify the correctness of a program. The strategies fall into two categories, _blackbox_ tests and _whitebox_ tests. Blackbox tests focus on the input and output behavior of the program, without concern for the internal structure of its classes and functions. A programmer performs blackbox testing by choosing input data for which the output is known. The test checks whether the function takes the inputs and produces the correct result. Whitebox testing focuses on the internal structure of the program. The test requires data that will exercise each line of code in each function. Special attention is paid to selection statements and loops within the code. To help with whitebox testing, many compilers provide a software tool, called a _profiler_, that lists how often each statement in the program executes. For given test data, a profiler can identify statements that fail to execute and thus give the programmer clues for new inputs that should be added to the test bank. *Unit testing* combines the two testing techniques and focuses on the design and implementation of the classes and functions that control the interaction among the objects. Use blackbox testing to verify functionality of a component and whitebox testing to test the internal structure of the component.

An individual unit can have errors from a variety of sources. In writing function code, a programmer might use incorrect punctuation or fail to declare an object properly. The compiler identifies these *syntax errors* and supplies messages that can suggest solutions. We can identify other errors when attempting to execute the code. We discover *runtime errors*, which can occur when a programmer fails to account for preconditions or when code execution results in data overflow or memory-allocation errors. *Logical errors* are the most difficult to detect. The code executes and produces incorrect results. The source is often faulty algorithm design or incorrect coding of the algorithm.

To find runtime and logical errors, we need a systematic way to create a set of test inputs that is likely to detect the problems. For the test data to be effective, we must know the output expected when the code runs correctly. We can determine that output by using pencil and paper, a calculator, or some method other than the algorithm used by the code. In the case of the calendar problem, we can use a wall calendar to discover the correct result. Besides data that should produce a correct result, the test inputs should also include data that are likely to cause an error.

Creating test data requires design much like the design of the classes and the control modules. Typically, program specifications require that a user provide input data within ranges of values in order for the program to execute correctly. The test bank should include several examples of data within these ranges and then examples that deliberately fall outside the ranges. The latter data typically violate some precondition and should cause an error. Lying between the ranges of good and bad input are *boundary values*. These input values are one step away from changing program behavior. These values often require special handling by the code. For instance, the function max() returns the largest element in an array. Boundary values would include arrays with zero elements and one element or an array whose values are all the same. Testing should always include input of boundary values.

Calendar Testing. The calendar problem requires that the user enter a month in the range from 1 to 12 and a year later than 1899. A ready choice of input data is the current month and year, which are easy to verify by looking at a wall calendar. Other inputs should look at a month or year that is not in range. For example, month 13 and year 1899 test how the program handles errors. Creating a calendar requires attention to leap years. Test inputs that involve leap-year calculations are good boundary values. For instance, display the calendar for February 2004 (a leap year) and then the calendar for March 2004. These values test whether the program identifies a leap year and accounts for 29 days in February when creating the March calendar. Other boundary data should look at calendars for the year 2000, which is a leap year, and for 2100, which is one of those "every four years" that is not a leap year. By now, you probably have penciled in January 1900 as another good test value.

The client sets out in the problem specification a desire to create a yearlong calendar by using the monthly calendar for each month in the year. In the exercises, we have you write this program. It tests the effectiveness of our design of the calendar class.

Good developers should never shortchange testing. In the long run, testing is one of the most cost-effective activities in the development cycle. Clients won't tolerate hard-to-use, bug-ridden software, and word of such a product quickly spreads to other potential customers.

PROGRAM 2-1   TESTING THE CALENDAR CLASS
_____

The upcoming program tests the calendar class by prompting for a month and year and displaying the calendar. Runs include the valid months February 2003, February 2004, and March 2004. Entering the month August 1899 and month 13 of 1938 tests the program's response to errors.

The program places the calls to the calendar-class functions setYear() and setMonth() in a *try* block (try {...}), because the month or year may be in error. If either call generates an error, the *catch* block (catch {...}) that follows catches the error, outputs the error message in the exception object, and terminates the program by using exit() from <cstdlib>. If no error occurs, a call to displayCalendar() outputs the calendar for the specified month and year.

```cpp
// File: prg2_1.cpp
// the program tests the calendar class by prompting for a month
// and year and displaying the calendar. runs include invalid
// input that test the program's response to errors.

#include <iostream>
#include <cstdlib>       // for exit()

#include "d_cal.h"       // use calendar class

using namespace std;

int main()
{
    // month and year entered by the user
    int month, year;
    // default month January, 1900
    calendar cal;

    cout << "Enter the month and year: ";
    cin >> month >> year;
    cout << endl;

    // either setYear() or setMonth() can cause an error.
    // place the calls in a try block
```

```
try
{
   // set the year and month
   cal.setYear(year);
   cal.setMonth(month);
}

// catch the dateError exception if setYear()
// or setMonth() throws it
catch(const dateError& de)
{

   // output the error string and return
   cerr << de.what() << endl;
   exit(1);
}

// display the calendar
cal.displayCalendar();

return 0;
}
```

```
Run 1:

Enter the month and year: 2 2003

                 February 2003

   Sun   Mon   Tue   Wed   Thu   Fri   Sat
                                       1
    2     3     4     5     6     7     8
    9    10    11    12    13    14    15
   16    17    18    19    20    21    22
   23    24    25    26    27    28

Run 2:

Enter the month and year: 2 2004

                 February 2004
   Sun   Mon   Tue   Wed   Thu   Fri   Sat
    1     2     3     4     5     6     7
    8     9    10    11    12    13    14
   15    16    17    18    19    20    21
   22    23    24    25    26    27    28
   29
```

```
Run 3:

Enter the month and year: 3 2004
                        March 2004
     Sun    Mon    Tue    Wed    Thu    Fri    Sat
             1      2      3      4      5      6
      7      8      9     10     11     12     13
     14     15     16     17     18     19     20
     21     22     23     24     25     26     27
     28     29     30     31

Run 4:

Enter the month and year: 8 1899

calendar setYear(): 1899 is prior to 1900

Run 5:

Enter the month and year: 13 1938

calendar setMonth(): 13 invalid month
```

Program Maintenance

In an ideal situation, the analysis, design, and implementation phases of the soft-ware-development cycle produce an error-free application that meets all of the client's needs. This situation seldom occurs, and program maintenance must begin as soon as the client installs the system. Under the scrutiny of heavy usage, the client identifies bugs or features that must be changed or added. Over time, a client adds new hardware and finds new applications for the software. Modern software systems must be regularly upgraded, or eventually they will become obsolete and unusable. Software upgrades are part of the program-maintenance process.

2-2   HANDLING RUNTIME ERRORS

In the *time24* class, the function duration() has a precondition requiring the argument to be no earlier than the current time. When implementing any function, a programmer must be aware that the code will execute in a runtime environment that includes not only the computer system, but also a user. Good program design attempts to anticipate errors and to create code that can maintain the integrity of the program and the system as a whole. When such an error is identified, the code should often take some form of remedial action. In this section, we discuss different types of actions, including C++ exceptions, which are the most flexible and effective way of enabling the program to take corrective steps. The function duration() provides a common example.

Terminate Program

A simple error-handling strategy treats the error as fatal and immediately terminates the program. The function duration() executes correctly only if the time argument is at or after the current time. The upcoming code is an implementation of the function that treats the error as fatal. The function exit() from <cstdlib> terminates the program. The argument, 1, indicates that the termination is due to an error in the application.

Implementing duration() by terminating the program in case of error:

```
time24 time24::duration(const time24& t)
{
    // convert current time and time t to minutes
    int currTime = hour * 60 + minute;
    int tTime = t.hour * 60 + t.minute;

    // if t is earlier than the current time, throw an exception
    if (tTime < currTime)
    {
        cerr << "time24 duration(): argument is an earlier time";
        exit(1);
    }
    else
        return time24(0, tTime-currTime);
}
```

This approach is drastic and gives the application no chance to take corrective action. If the program is running in batch mode, there is no user interaction, and the displaying of an error message to cerr has no effect. If the program is running in a GUI (Graphical User Interface) environment, messages to cerr are not handled conveniently.

Set a Flag

In designing an error-handling strategy, you want the block of code that calls a function to be responsible for dealing with an error. After all, the calling block ideally knows the state of its objects before calling the function, and so it can take corrective action when it discovers that the operation does not execute correctly. If the application is running in console mode (cin/cout/cerr used for I/O), it can output a message to cerr; otherwise, the application can bring up a dialog that indicates the error. A simple way for the function to alert the calling statement is to provide a return value or a reference argument indicating that an error has occurred. This strategy assumes that the calling statement will check the value and either take corrective action or terminate the program. For instance, the duration() function can be redefined to have a reference argument of type *bool*. The value is *true* when the operation succeeds and *false* otherwise.

Implementing duration() with an error flag:

```
time24 time24::duration(const time24& t, bool& success)
{
    // convert current time and time t to minutes
    int currTime = hour * 60 + minute;
    int tTime = t.hour * 60 + t.minute;
    // time returned. default value of 0:00 is the return
    // time if an error occurs
    time24 returnTime;

    // assume that no error will occur
    success = true;

    // if t is earlier than the current time, assign false to success
    if (tTime < currTime)
      success = false;
    else
        // successful. assign duration to returnTime
        returnTime = time24(0, tTime-currTime);

    return returnTime;
}
```

The programmer can check whether duration() executes successfully by including an if statement immediately after the function call:

```
bool success;
time24 currTime, nextTime, interval;
    ...
interval = currTime.duration(nextTime, success);
if (success == false)  // check success and deal with an error
{
    <take appropriate action>
}
```

A problem with this approach is that the programmer might choose to ignore the return value and let the program continue in an incorrect state.

C++ Exceptions

The most flexible form of error reporting uses C++ exceptions. This strategy is generally the superior technique in object design. An *exception* is an object that contains information that is transmitted without using the normal function return process. The point at which an error occurs is the result of a chain of function calls. For instance, in Figure 2-2, the main program executes the member function f() for object objA. In f(), object objB is declared, and a subsequent call is made to function g(). The error occurs in the execution of g(). The programmer might want the calling statement in objA or the original calling statement in the main program to

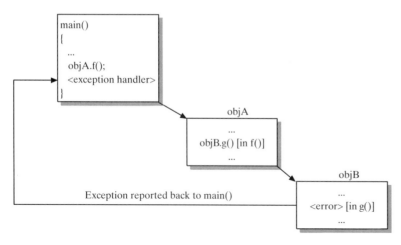

Figure 2-2
C++ exception

be notified of the error and take remedial action. To permit this option, the function g() *throws* an exception at the point of the error. The exception moves in reverse order through the chain of function calls until it finds a block of code
designed to *catch* the exception. This block of code is called the *exception handler*;
it is responsible for displaying an error message and for either taking corrective
action or terminating the program. In Figure 2-2, the exception handler is in the
main program.

The C++ syntax for throwing an exception is

put in appropriate object

```
throw object;
```

where object is the exception.

The file "d_except.h" of the software supplement provides classes whose objects are exceptions. This book develops the tools for the implementation of these
exception classes in Chapter 13, during the discussion of C++ inheritance. For now,
we will simply use these classes to generate and handle exceptions. Each class has a
constructor that takes a string argument and stores it in a data member. The string
contains a message describing the error. The member function what() returns the
stored string. Use the function in the exception handler to output an error message.

The *time24* class member function duration() throws an exception of type
rangeError when its argument represents an earlier time. The rangeError class is
one of the classes declared in "d_except.h". The statement

```
throw rangeError("time24 duration(): argument is an earlier time");
```

creates a rangeError exception object that includes a message indicating that the
member function duration() identified the argument error. The throw operation
throws the object back to the calling statement.

Implementing duration() by throwing an exception:

```
time24 time24::duration(const time24& t)
{
    // convert current time and time t to minutes
    int currTime = hour * 60 + minute;
    int tTime = t.hour * 60 + t.minute;

    // if t is earlier than the current time, throw an exception
    if (tTime < currTime)
        throw rangeError(
            "time24 duration(): argument is an earlier time");
    else
        return time24(0, tTime-currTime);
}
```

The previous discussion shows how to generate an exception with a throw statement. We now have to determine how a calling statement can be put on alert for a possible exception, catch it when one is thrown, and take appropriate action. The actions of the calling block and the function that throws an exception are part of an exception-handling process that follows a very specific sequence of steps. A program block places one or more statements that could generate an exception in a *try block* that consists of the keyword *try* followed by the statements enclosed in braces:

```
try
{
    statement;
        ...
    statement;
}
```

The try block must be followed immediately by one or more exception handlers that catch any exceptions generated when the try block executes. Implement an exception handler as a *catch block* with the syntax

```
// catch an exception that is thrown elsewhere
catch (<declaration of exception argument>)
{
    <remedial action in response to the exception>
}
```

The catch block takes an exception object as an argument. The programmer supplies a response to the exception within the catch block.

Example 2-1

The statements of the example prompt for the current time and for a time that must be later. A try block encloses a call to duration() and the output of its return value. If duration() throws a rangeError exception, control transfers out of the function and into the catch block that follows the try block. The catch block outputs the message in the rangeError object to the console and terminates the program. If the program runs in a graphical environment, the catch block will likely bring up a dialog that identifies the error. If no error occurs, the statement following the catch block executes.

```
time24 currentTime, nextTime, interval;

cout << "Enter the current time and a later time: ";
cin >> currentTime >> nextTime;

try
{
    interval = currentTime.duration(nextTime);
    cout << "The interval between the two times is "
        << interval << endl;
}

catch (const rangeError& re)
{
    // output the message in re and exit the program
    cerr << re.what() << endl;
    exit(1);
}
    ... continue the program ...
```

Example of input with no error. The function duration() executes successfully, and the return value becomes part of the subsequent cout statement.

```
Enter the current time and a later time: 6:15 15:35
The interval between the two times is 9:20
```

Example of input with an error. The function duration() halts execution when it identifies that the argument is an earlier time and throws a rangeError exception. Execution in the try block immediately terminates, and program control passes to the catch block, which calls what() to output the error message.

```
Enter the current time and a later time: 5:45 2:15
time24 duration(): argument is an earlier time
```

The statements within a try block can have the capacity to generate one of multiple possible exceptions. To handle this likelihood, a programmer can include two or more catch blocks. If no exception occurs in the try block, all of the catch blocks are ignored, and execution continues after the last catch block. For instance,

```
try
{
    <statement A>
    . . .
    <statement B>
}
```

```
catch (<exception>)                   // exception from statement A
{ . . .}

catch (<exception>)                   // exception from statement B
{ . . .}

// execution continues normally if no exception occurs in try block
 . . .
```

If an exception occurs, and the system cannot locate a corresponding catch block in the execution sequence, the exception is marked as *uncaught*, and the system executes a function that terminates the program. In the Windows environment, a dialog window appears, and UNIX creates a core dump. In either case, the programmer can use a debugger to detect the reason for the error. In this book, when a serious error occurs in an application, we will not use try and catch blocks and will allow the exception to terminate the program. For instance, calls to the time24 function duration() will not be enclosed in a try block. This book uses try and catch blocks selectively in situations where error recovery is possible. Examples of these situations occur in Program 2-2 of Section 2-3 and in Chapter 7 during the development of algorithms for expression evaluation.

2-3   OBJECT COMPOSITION

In a class, data members can include a variety of data types. In some cases, the members are variables having such primitive C++ language types as numbers, characters, and arrays. In other cases, the data involve programmer-defined class types. For instance, the Department of Motor Vehicles uses an appointment class to maintain information on the scheduling of license renewals and car registration for motorists. The class has data members for the motorist's name, the date, and the time of the appointment. The data types for the members are string, date, and time24, respectively.

The appointment class is an example of object composition. The term *object composition* refers to a condition that exists when a class contains one or more data members that are objects of class type. A class that is included by composition is called the *supplier class*. The class that includes an object by composition is the *client class*. For instance, the appointment class is the client class, and string, date, and time24 are the supplier classes.

```
class appointment
{
    . . .
  private:
    string motoristName;      // string supplier class
    date apptDate;            // date supplier class
    time24 apptTime;          // time24 supplier class
};
```

Object composition is an implementation feature of a class. When including a data member by composition, a programmer not only stores data, but also gains access to all of the member functions in the supplier class. The programmer can use the supplier-provided operations to implement a client-member function rather than repeating code to carry out the task. Using existing operations promotes *code reuse*. Composition is one of the most powerful tools in object-oriented programming.

We illustrate the concept of object composition by using the timeCard class, which has a constructor and two simple operations. The example allows us to see how the client-class constructor initializes the supplier objects and how a programmer employs code reuse to implement the class.

The timeCard Class

A timeCard object allows a company to pay a worker for a day's labor. The worker uses the time card to punch in at the beginning of the day and punch out upon quitting. The company immediately pays the worker based on the hourly rate and the length of time on the job. The data members in the timeCard class include the string object workerID and a real number specifying the hourly pay rate. The data also include two time24 objects named punchInTime and punchOutTime and a *bool* variable hasPunched that indicates whether the employee has punched out. In the language of object composition, time24 and string are supplier classes, and timeCard is the client class.

timeCard Data Members:

```
string workerID;                      // string composition
time24 punchInTime, punchOutTime;     // time24 composition
double payrate;
bool hasPunched;
```

598-81-2936	15.00	8:30	16:30
workerID	payrate	punchInTime	punchOutTime

The Constructor with Composition. In the declaration of a client object, the runtime system calls the client constructor to initialize the data members. In its execution, the constructor calls, in turn, the constructor for each of the supplier-class objects. For instance, in the declaration of a timeCard object, the system calls the string constructor for the workerID object and the *time24* constructor for the time objects punchInTime and punchOutTime. When declaring an object, the client-class constructor can provide arguments for a supplier-class object, or it can allow the system to call the default constructor for a supplier-class object. The choice is critical to the design of the client-class constructor. If the programmer chooses to pass arguments to a supplier-class constructor, the arguments must be included in the argument list for the client constructor. Let us see how this fact applies in the timeCard class.

When declaring a timeCard object, we initialize the workerID, the pay rate, the punchInTime for the day's work, and hasPunched. The arguments for the time-Card constructor include a string for the ID, a real number for the rate, and integers that specify the hour and minute that work begins. No arguments are required for punchOutTime; the timeCard constructor calls the *time24* default constructor for this data member. Initially, punchOutTime has the default value 0:00 (midnight). The constructor sets hasPunched to false.

Constructor Prototype:

```
// include separate arguments for the data members hour and
// minute in the time24 object punchInTime
timeCard(const string& ssno, double rate, int punchInHour,
         int punchInMinute);
```

Other timeCard Member Functions. Besides a constructor, the timeCard class has the member function punchOut() that takes a time24 argument and uses it to update the data member punchOutTime. A second member function, called writeSalaryInfo(), computes the day's wages and displays a log that includes the worker's ID, the starting and the ending time for the work, and the salary (based on time worked and hourly pay rate). The format of the function output is shown next. Any part of the output description enclosed in angle brackets (<...>) denotes an expression that will be filled with specific output.

Worker:	ID
Start time:	<punchInTime> End time: <punchOutTime>
Total time:	<time worked in hours and fraction of an hour> hours
Salary:	At $<pay rate> per hour, the day's earnings are
	$<payrate * hours worked>

Before displaying the salary information, the function writeSalaryInfo() tests the precondition that the worker has previously punched out on the time card (hasPunched == true). The function throws the rangeError exception if hasPunched is false.

The following is the declaration of the timeCard class.

CLASS timeCard   **Declaration**   **"d_tcard.h"**

```
class timeCard
{
   public:
      timeCard(const string& ssno, double rate, int punchInHour,
               int punchInMinute);

      void punchOut(const time24& t);
         // assign t to punchOutTime and set hasPunched to true,
```

```
        void writeSalaryInfo();
          // output a log that includes the beginning and ending times for
          // the day's work, the amount of time worked, the pay rate
          // and the earnings.
          // precondition:  throw a rangeError exception if worker has not
          // punched out (hasPunched == false)

     private:
         string workerID;
         time24 punchInTime, punchOutTime;        // supplier-class objects
         double payrate;
         bool hasPunched;
};
```

Example 2-2

The worker "598-81-2936" punches in at 8:30 and punches out at 16:30 (4:30 PM). The day's salary, based on an hourly rate of $15.00, is $120.00.

```
// the constructor arguments include the ssno, rate, and the hour
// and minute the work begins
timeCard worker("598-81-2936", 15.00, 8, 30);


worker.punchOut(time24(16,30));
worker.writeSalaryInfo();
```

```
Output:
Worker:      598-81-2936
Start time:  8:30 End time: 16:30
Total time: 8.00 hours
At $15.00 per hour, the days earnings are $120.00
```

Implementing the timeCard Class

The implementation of the timeCard class makes extensive use of time24 member functions. Let us begin with the constructor that has arguments to initialize the data members' workerID, payrate, punchInTime, and hasPunched. In the initialization list, include four data members with arguments enclosed in parentheses. In the case of punchInTime, the arguments are the integers punchInHour and punchInMinute.

Constructor:

```
// use initialization list to initialize data members. the value
// for hasPunched is the Boolean literal false
timeCard::timeCard(const string& ssno, double rate, int punchInHour,
                   int punchInMinute):
       workerID(ssno), payrate(rate), hasPunched(false),
       punchInTime(punchInHour, punchInMinute)
   {}
```

In its execution, the timeCard constructor calls the constructors for the supplier-class objects workerID, punchInTime, and punchOutTime. With a supplier-class object in the initialization list, the supplier constructor is called with the specified arguments. In our example, we call the string constructor for workerID with argument *ssno* and the *time24* constructor for punchInTime with arguments punchIn-Hour and punchInMinute. The initialization list does not include the *time24* object punchOutTime. For this object, the default *time24* constructor initializes punchOut-Time to 0:00 (midnight).

☞
Note

C++ allows a programmer to set initial values for data members within the constructor body without using an initialization list. In this case, the client-class constructor first calls the default constructors for each supplier-class object and then uses an assignment statement in the body of the constructor to assign initial values. For instance, the following is an alternative implementation for the timeCard constructor:

```
// initialize data members in the function body
timeCard(const string& ssn, double rate, int punchInHour,
         int punchInMinute)
{
    workerID = ssn;            ⟶ strng
    payrate = rate;           ⟶ double
    hasPunched = false;       ⟶ bool
    punchInTime = time24(punchInHour, punchInMinute);    ⟶ class
}
```

This technique works only because the string and time24 classes have default constructors. In general, use an initialization list to implement a client-class constructor instead.

The function punchOut() has a time24 argument that indicates when the worker finishes the day. Update the data member punchOutTime and set hasPunched to true.

punchOut():
```
void timeCard::punchOut(const time24& t)
{
    punchOutTime = t;
    hasPunched = true;
}
```

☞
Note

The function writeSalaryInfo() outputs real-number data, such as the day's earnings. It is often necessary to control the number of decimal places in a display of a real number. For instance, we should output a day's pay as $128.93, and not as $128.931756. For this purpose, the header file "d_util.h" of the software supplement implements the manipulator setreal(). Recall that a stream manipulator is an operation that changes stream characteristics. Examples include the familiar endl and setw manipulators. The manipulator setreal() takes integer arguments *w* and *p*, where *w* gives the number of output positions to use and *p* the number of decimal places. The argument *w* applies only to the next item in the stream. By using □ to represent a space, the following examples illustrate setreal().

```
cout << setreal(10,3) << 23.476;    // Output: □ □ □ □ 23.476

cout << setreal(8,2) << 3.567;      // Output: □ □ □ □ 3.57
                                    // (with rounding)

cout << setreal(1,5) << 163.567;    // Output: 163.56700
cout << setreal(1,1) << 163.567;    // Output: 163.6
```

The time24 operations play a fundamental role in implementing the write-SalaryInfo() member function. Its implementation uses the time24 operation write-Time() to output the times the worker punches in and punches out. It also uses the operation duration() to determine the total work time as a *time24* object. To compute the salary, we call getHour() and getMinute() to determine the amount of time worked as a fractional number of hours. By multiplying by the hourly rate, we have the day's earnings. Note the use of setreal() to control the number of decimal places in the display of the real-number data.

writeSalaryInfo():

```
void timeCard::writeSalaryInfo()
{
    // throw an exception if the worker did not punch out
    if (hasPunched == false)
        throw rangeError("timeCard: writeSalaryInfo() called before "
                          "punching out");

    // total time worked
    time24 timeWorked = punchInTime.duration(punchOutTime);
    // hours and fraction of an hour worked
    double hoursWorked = timeWorked.getHour() +
                         timeWorked.getMinute()/60.0;

    // format the output
    cout << "Worker: " << workerID << endl;
    cout << "Start time: ";
    punchInTime.writeTime();
    cout << " End time: ";
    punchOutTime.writeTime();
    cout << endl;
    cout << "Total time: " << setreal(1,2) << hoursWorked
         << " hours" << endl;
    cout << "At $" << setreal(1,2) << payrate
         << " per hour, the days earnings are $"
         << setreal(1,2) << payrate*hoursWorked << endl;
}
```

PROGRAM 2-2   HANDLING TIME CARDS

Assume a plant hires temporary workers at various times during the day. Each employee works until the plant closes at time CHECKOUT, which is 17:00 (5:00 PM), and receives a salary determined by the posted value PAYRATE. When a worker arrives, the supervisor notes the time of arrival, obtains the social security number, and creates a time card. When the plant closes, workers punch out and receive their wages for the day. It is possible that a worker forgets to punch out. In this situation, the supervisor punches out for the employee.

Let's look at a program that simulates this activity by prompting for the hour and minute of arrival at work and the social security number. These data, along with the constants PAYRATE and CHECKOUT, allow the declaration of a timeCard object called *employee*. Assume that three out of every four workers personally punch out. Simulate this situation by generating a random real number and punching out the employee if its value is > .25. A call to writeSalaryInfo() will output the salary data for the day's work. Because there is a probability of .25 that the employee did not punch out, its call can alternatively generate the rangeError exception. Place the call to writeSalaryInfo() in a try block and immediately follow the try block with a catch block that outputs the error string, has the supervisor punch out for the employee, and outputs the salary.

```cpp
// File: prg2_2.cpp
// the program simulates a temporary employees arriving
// at work and leaving when the plant closes at 5:00 PM.
// it prompts for the hour and minute of arrival at work
// and the social security number. it uses the timeCard
// class to determine the employee pay for the day. the
// program uses a random number to simulate that 3 out of
// every 4 employees punch out. in this situation,
// the program must handle a rangeError exception thrown by
// the timeCard class when an employee does not punch out.
// the catch block simulates the supervisor punching out for
// the employee

#include <iostream>

#include "d_tcard.h"    // use timeCard class
#include "d_random.h"   // randomNumber class

using namespace std;

int main()
{
    // posted pay rate
    const double PAYRATE = 12.50;
    // work ends at 5:00 PM
    const time24 CHECKOUT(17,0);
    // employee data input from the keyboard
    string id;
    int inHour, inMinute;
```

```
// simulate 1/4 of employees forgetting to punch out
randomNumber rnd;

cout << "Enter hour and minute of arrival at work: ";
cin >> inHour >> inMinute;
cout << "Enter social security number: ";
cin >> id;

// declare a timeCard object for the employee
timeCard employee(id, PAYRATE, inHour, inMinute);

// represents 3 out of 4 employees punching out
if (rnd.frandom() > .25)
    // punch out
    employee.punchOut(CHECKOUT);

// include writeSalary() call in a try block. it
// throws the rangeError exception if the employee
// has not punched out
try
{
    employee.writeSalaryInfo();
}

catch (const rangeError& re)
{
    // output the error string in the rangeError object re
    cerr << re.what() << endl;
    // supervisor punches out the employee. display salary info
    employee.punchOut(CHECKOUT);
    employee.writeSalaryInfo();
}

    return 0;
}
```

```
Run 1:

Enter hour and minute of arrival at work: 8 00
Enter social security number: 345-27-8156
Worker:        345-27-8156
Start time:    8:00 End time: 17:00
Total time:    9.0 hours
At $12.50 per hour, the days earnings are $112.50
```

```
Run 2:

Enter hour and minute of arrival at work: 9 15
Enter social security number: 766-25-6728
timeCard: writeSalaryInfo() called before punching out
Worker:         766-25-6728
Start time:     9:15 End time: 17:00
Total time:     7.75 hours
At $12.50 per hour, the days earnings are $96.88
```

2-4   OPERATOR OVERLOADING

Applications frequently need to compare variables or objects to determine whether they are equal or one is less than the other. For primitive number and character variables, the C++ language defines the operators == and < to carry out the comparisons. For programmer-defined objects, we need functions to enable the comparisons. For instance, a program can compare two *time24* objects by defining the free function equalTime() that returns the boolean value *true* if the objects are equal.

```
// compare two time24 objects
bool equalTime(const time24& a, const time24& b)

{  // a and b are equal if they have the same hour and minute values
   return a.getHour()== b.getHour() && a.getMinute() == b.getMinute();
}
```

Many applications involve comparing *time24* objects, so we might want to include a class-member function for this task. Comparison then becomes part of the programmer interface. For instance, let us add the member function equal() to the *time24* class. As a member function, the implementation has access to the attributes of the class.

```
class time24
{  public:
      . . .
      // compare obj and the current value of the time object
      bool equal(const time24& obj)
      {
         return hour == obj.hour && minute == obj.minute;
      }
      . . .
};
```

Example 2-3

---

1. Compare *time24* objects by using the free function equalTime():   → *compares a time24 instances*

```
time24 tA(3,30), tB(5,0);

tA.addTime(90);              // tA is now 5:00
if (equalTime(tA, tB))       // condition is true
    . . .
```

2. A loop outputs time from 9:30 to 13:00 in half-hour units. The loop test calls the member function equal() to determine when time *t* reaches stopTime.

```
time24 t(9,30), stopTime(13,30);

do
{
    t.writeTime();
    t.addTime(30);
}
while (!t.equal(stopTime));
Output: 9:30 10:00 10:30 11:00 11:30 12:00 12:30 13:00
```

The use of named operations like the free function equalTime() and the member function equal() represents two different ways of comparing *time24* objects for equality. C++ provides a third method, which allows a programmer to use the familiar binary == operator as though the *time24* objects were primitive variables. The concept, called *operator overloading*, allows the standard operator notation for objects of class type. For instance, we can use the expression tA == tB to compare two *time24* objects. Note how this technique would modify the code in Example 2-3:

```
// Example 2-3 (1)
   if (tA == tB)              // compare time24 objects for equality
    . . .

// Example 2-3 (2)
   do
   {
    . . .
   }
   while (!(t == stopTime));  // loop test checks for inequality
```

Without being formally aware of operator overloading, you have been using the concept with string objects. The string class defines overloaded versions of the operators < and == to compare strings, the + operator to combine (concatenate) strings, and the operators << and >> for input and output.

```
string str1 = "Johnson", str2 = "Smith", str3;
```

Comparison:
```
// comparison is true; in lexicographic order 'J' in Johnson
// comes before 'S' in Smith
str1 < str2

// str1 is equal to the string literal "Johnson"
str1 == "Johnson"        // strings are identical
```

Concatenation:
```
// create the string str3 = "Johnson and Johnson"
str3 = str1 + " and " + str1
```

Input and Output:
```
// input the string "load" from the keyboard
cin >> str3;

// change last letter to 'n' and output the result "loan"
str3[str3.length()-1] = 'n';
cout << str3;
```

In Chapter 1, we use descriptive names for the member functions in the time24 class. In many cases, the actions of these functions are analogous to arithmetic operations with numbers and can be defined with overloaded operators. For instance, addTime() has the effect of adding minutes to the current time, and duration() returns the difference between the current time and some later time. The operators += and − describe their action. The *time24* class performs I/O by using the member functions readTime() and writeTime(). We can overload the familiar C++ >> and << operators as an alternative way to handle I/O. Using operator overloading makes the use of a class more natural. We will soon discover many more advantages. Compare the code for an algorithm that inputs times for two successive classes in a student's schedule. Assuming that the instructor lectures for 50 minutes in the first course, we output the amount of time the student has until the next class:

Code Without Operator Overloading	Code With Operator Overloading
`time24 class1, class2, freeTime;`	`time24 class1, class2, freeTime;`

`// input times`
`class1.readTime();`
`class2.readTime();`
	`// input times`
	`cin >> class1 >> class2;`

`// add lecture time` `class1.addTime(50);`	`// add lecture time` `class1 += 50;`

`// compute and output free time`
`freeTime = class1.duration(class2);`
`freeTime.writeTime();`
	`// compute and output free time`
	`freeTime = class2 − class1;`
	`cout << freeTime;`

The concept of *operator overloading* is one of the most powerful and useful object design features in the C++ language. In this section, we introduce the syntax of operator overloading, including operator functions, friends, and member function overloading. To illustrate the concepts, we overload comparison operators, arithmetic operators, and I/O operators of the time24 class. In subsequent chapters, we extend operator overloading to the index operator, [], and the increment and decrement operators, ++ and −−.

Operator Functions

In programming, we write expressions involving the operators +, *, and < by using infix notation that places the operator between its two operands:

```
// op is the operator; lhs and rhs are the left and right operands
lhs op rhs
```

An infix expression corresponds to an *operator function* that contains the operands as arguments. The prototype of the operator function is

```
returnType operator op (type1 lhs, type2 rhs);
```
└→ + or == or − or & etc.

where the return type of the function is the type returned by the operator, and type1 and type2 are the types of the operands. For instance, assume that the string $s = $ "Hello" and $t = $ "World!." In this situation, both operands are strings, and the string expression $s + t$ returns a string that is the concatenation of s and t. The corresponding operator function for the operator + with arguments *lhs* and *rhs* and return type *string* is

```
string operator+ (const string& lhs, const string& rhs);
```

The runtime system executes the infix expression by calling the *operator* function. Figure 2-3 illustrates how the system passes the arguments (operands) and assigns the return value to string *u*.

The general form for an operator function includes the keyword *operator* followed by the operator symbol. The return type should be consistent with the initial language definition of the operator. For instance, a comparison operator should return a Boolean value. A binary-operator function has two arguments that represent

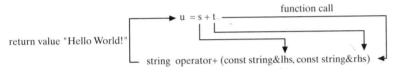

Figure 2-3
Execute u = s + t with a function call

the operands, at least one of which must be of *class* or *enum* type. The operator function form for a unary operator has a single operand of *class* or *enum* type. Assume *op* represents the C++ operator symbol. When declaring an operator function, replace *op* by the operator symbol.

> *Operator Function Prototype:*
>
> Binary operator with operands *lhs* and *rhs*. The infix notation is *lhs op rhs*.
> ```
> // one of typeLeft and typeRight must be a class or an enum
> returnType operator op (const typeLeft& lhs, const typeRight& rhs);
> ```
>
> Unary operator with operand *obj*. The infix notation is *op obj*.
> ```
> // type must be a class or an enum
> returnType operator op (const type &obj);
> ```

Operator Overloading with Free Functions

Operators can be overloaded as free functions or as class member functions. The concepts have important differences, so we deal with their syntax separately. Overload an operator as a free function by using the operator function format. In the introduction, we declared equalTime() as a free function to compare two time24 objects. The equivalent operator function == has the form

```
bool operator== (const time24& lhs, const time24& rhs);
```

The operator function is a free function, so its implementation must use the public-member functions in the time24 class to access the data:

> *operator == (Free Function)*
> ```
> bool operator == (const time24& lhs, const time24& rhs)
> {
>     return lhs.getHour() == rhs.getHour() &&
>            lhs.getMinute() == rhs.getMinute();
> }
> ```

Since private data can Not be directly accessed use a getfunctions

Example 2-4

An overloaded version of the subtraction operator returns the difference between successive times. If the lhs operand is later than the rhs operand, the operation throws a rangeError exception:

```
time24 operator- (const time24& lhs, const time24& rhs)
{
    // convert current time and time t to minutes
    int currTime = lhs.getHour() * 60 + lhs.getMinute();
    int tTime = rhs.getHour() * 60 + rhs.getMinute();

    // if rhs is earlier than current time, throw exception
    if (tTime < currTime)
```

```
        throw rangeError("time24 operator -: rhs < rhs");
    else
        return time24(0, tTime-currTime);
}
```

Operator Overloading with Friend Functions

Overloading an operator as a free function raises efficiency issues. Because the function is independent of the class, its implementation must use member functions to access the appropriate data members. The *time24* class provides access with getHour() and getMinute(), but their use requires the overhead of function calls. If a class does not provide the appropriate access functions, the operator cannot be overloaded as a free function. The C++ language recognizes these problems and allows a free function to be declared as a friend function in the class. A *friend function*, which we will simply call a *friend*, is a free function that has access to the private members of the class. We declare such a function in the class declaration by placing the keyword *friend* immediately before its prototype. Despite having access to the private data members, a friend is not a member function of the class.

```
// class declaration with an operator (#) overloaded as a friend
class className
{
    public:
      . . . .
        friend returnType operator# (const className& lhs, . . .);
    private:
        type dataValue;     // operator # may access dataValue
      . . . .
};
```

A friend function can be implemented by inline code or as an external function. In the latter case, the keyword friend is *not* included in the function header. Because a friend is not a member function, the external implementation does not include the class scope operator "className::."

```
// implementing the operator # as a friend function
returnType operator# (const className& lhs, . . .)
{
    < any statement may directly access dataValue >
      . . .
}
```

Using Friends to Overload *time24* Operators. With operator overloading, we can redesign the *time24* class to become easier to use. Several overloaded versions of the + operator enable a programmer to add two *time24* objects or a *time24* object, and integer minutes as either a left-or a right-hand operand. The overloaded binary operator − computes the time between two events and returns the value as a *time24* object. The original class does not allow for comparison of times. We address this problem by overloading the comparison operators == and <. The upcoming code is a partial declaration of the new *time24* class that includes these arithmetic and comparison operators. In the next section, we overload the stream I/O operators << and >>. These operators are equivalent to readTime() and writeTime() and allow a programmer to include *time24* objects in I/O statements as though they were primitive variables.

CLASS time24	Declaration	"d_time24.h"

```
class time24
{
  public:
     // constructor with starting time
     time24(int h = 0, int m = 0);


     // binary + operators: add minute and time24 objects
     friend time24 operator+ (const time24& lhs, const time24& rhs);
     friend time24 operator+ (const time24& lhs, int min);
     friend time24 operator+ (int min, const time24& rhs);

     // binary - operator: subtracts two time24 objects if rhs is not
     // earlier than lhs. if this precondition is not satisfied, throw
     // rangeError exception
     friend time24 operator- (const time24& lhs, const time24& rhs);

     // comparison operators
     friend bool operator== (const time24& lhs, const time24& rhs);
     friend bool operator< (const time24& lhs, const time24& rhs);
        . . .
  private:
     int hour, minute;        // data members
     void normalizeTime();     // put time units in range
};
```

The declaration of multiple versions of the + operator provides a programmer with the flexibility of using a variety of operands to increase the time of an object. The compiler selects the correct version of the operator by comparing the data types of the runtime arguments with the types of the formal arguments. For instance, consider the example of addition involving *time24* and *int* operands. Although each operation produces the same value for u (23:30 or 11:30 PM), the arguments for the corresponding operator functions have different operand types:

```
time24 s(22,0), t(1,30), u;    // s is 10:00 PM, t is 1:30 AM
int min = 90;

u = s + min;       // time24 + int
u = min + s;       // int + time24
u = s + t;         // time24 + time24
```

time24
  Declaration

time 24 (int h=0, int m=0)
// constructor

Implementing *time24* Friend Functions. Let's look at the implementation for two versions of the overloaded + operator. The *time24* constructor can be explicitly called to build an object for use in assignment statements, a return statement, or other expressions. Because the object is not associated with an identifier in a declaration, it is called an *anonymous object*. In the implementations, the constructor creates an anonymous *time24* object that becomes the return value.

> *time24 operator + (const time24& lhs, const time24& rhs);*
> ```
> // create an anonymous object with hour = lhs.hour + rhs.hour
> // and minute = lhs.minute + rhs.minute.
> time24 operator+ (const time24& lhs, const time24& rhs)
> {
>     return time24(lhs.hour+rhs.hour, lhs.minute+rhs.minute);
> }
> ```

> *time24 operator + (const time24& lhs, int min)*
> ```
> // create an anonymous object with hour = lhs.hour and
> // minute = lhs.minute + min.
> time24 operator+ (const time24& lhs, int min)
> {
>     return time24(lhs.hour, lhs.minute + min);
> }
> ```

To implement the overloaded comparison operator <, we convert the hour and minute values of each operand to minutes. The conversion creates minutes as a common unit of measure. The return uses the < operator for integers.

> *bool operator < (const time24& lhs, const time24& rhs);*
> ```
> // convert the hour and minute values for each operand to
> // minutes. compare lhs in minutes with rhs in minutes
> bool operator< (const time24& lhs, const time24& rhs)
> {
>     return (lhs.hour*60 + lhs.minute) < (rhs.hour*60 + rhs.minute);
> }
> ```

true or False

Overloading Stream I/O Operators

The C++ language defines overloaded versions of the >> and << operators for input and output of primitive integer, real, and character data. A programmer can use the same approach to handle the I/O of programmer-defined class objects. In this section, we add these operators to the *time24* class as a replacement for the member functions readTime() and writeTime(). We need some background before we can define the corresponding operator functions.

The file <iostream> has two classes, named *istream* and *ostream*, that provide stream input and stream output, respectively. The classes declare the stream operators >> and << for the primitive *char, int, short, long, float,* and *double* types. These are binary operators that contain a stream as the left operand and a variable or a literal as the right operand. You are familiar with these examples for integers:

```
int dataValue;
cout << dataValue;        // output to the standard cout stream
fin >> dataValue;         // input from the file stream fin
```

The operand on the left is a stream object, and the operand on the right is an integer variable. For output, the operator $<<$ takes the value of the variable on the right and inserts it into the stream without modifying its value. For input, the operator $>>$ extracts data from the stream and uses it to update the value of the variable. It is important to note that, like $+$ and $<$ the stream operators return a value. To understand this fact, we must look at more complex expressions that chain together a series of stream operators. Consider the $<<$ operator and the *cout* stream:

```
cout << "The value is " << dataValue;
```

The statement is equivalent to separate cout statements that include the string literal "The value is " in the first statement and the variable dataValue in the second statement:

```
cout << "The value is ";
cout << dataValue;
```

The compiler implements the single statement as

```
(cout << "The value is ") << dataValue;
```

The subexpression

```
cout << "The value is"
```

is evaluated first, and its return value is the stream object *cout*. The stream *cout* becomes the left-hand operand in the output of dataValue.

We use the design for input and output of primitive variables to describe how a class can overload the stream operators $<<$ and $>>$ as friend functions. The following is the operator function prototype for each operation:

(Output) $<<$:
```
friend ostream& operator<< (ostream& ostr, const className& obj);
```

(Input) $>>$:
```
istream& operator>> (istream& istr, className& obj);
```

In each case, the I/O stream object is the left-hand operand in an expression. Performing an operation on a stream changes its state, so we pass the stream by reference. The output operation uses only the value of the object, so we pass the object by constant reference. On the other hand, the input operation updates the object, so the object is passed by reference. We return the stream by reference so that we can use it in a statement that chains together a series of stream operators. The upcoming partial declaration lists the overloaded I/O functions for *time24* objects. Like the member functions readTime() and writeTime(), the operators handle time in the format *hh:mm*.

(handwritten: (cout << x) << y, stream, value, symbol, value, symbol, need to return the stream)

CLASS time24   **Declaration**   **"d_time24.h"**

```
class time24
{
   public:
      . . .

      friend istream& operator >> (istream& istr, time24& t);
         // input a time for object t

      friend ostream& operator<< (ostream& ostr, const time24& t);
         // output the time in t as hour:minute

   private:
      int hour, minute;          // data members
      void normalizeTime();      // put time units in range
};
```

(handwritten annotations: "need to return stream", "cout << t <<", "by reference", "this operation will change both", "will access private data member", "no change")

Implementing *time24* Stream Operators.   The implementation of an I/O operator function dictates what the operator does. If you so desire, output can produce the complete works of Shakespeare. More realistically, the operator should provide for readable input or output of the data members. For the *time24* class, the I/O operators replicate readTime() and writeTime(), respectively. With input, we read a time in the form *hh:mm*. We read the time as a triple, with the character : extracted as a separator. After the calling of normalizeTime(), the resulting values for *t.hour* and *t.minute* are in the ranges 0-23 and 0-59, respectively.

Implementation of >> for time24 class
```
      // overload stream operator >>. input has the form
      // hh:mm
      istream& operator>> (istream& istr, time24& t)
      {
         char separatorChar;

         istr >> t.hour >> separatorChar >> t.minute;
         // make sure hour and minute are in range
         t.normalizeTime();

         // return the stream
         return istr;
      }
```

(handwritten: → on the same op that is being overloaded)

The implementation of the output function displays the data members in the form hh:mm. Simply include the separator character : between the two data members.

Implementation of << for time24 class

```
// overload stream operator <<. output in the form
//    hh:mm
ostream& operator<< (ostream& ostr, const time24& t)
{
    // output hour and minute with : separator
    ostr << t.hour << ':' << t.minute;

    // return the output stream object
    return ostr;
}
```

In the file "d_time24.h", we enhance the implementation for the operator << to ensure that the value for minute is output with two digits, by adding a leading 0 if necessary. Consult the file for details. For instance,

```
time24 t(8,5);
cout << t;    // output: 8:05
```

Example 2-5

Input two *time24* values, and indicate how the times compare.

```
time24 s, t;

cin >> s >> t;              // both s and t use the cin stream object

if (s < t)
    cout << s << " is earlier than " << t;
else if (s == t)
    cout << "The times are equal";
else
    cout << s << " is later than " << t;
```

```
Input:    11:30    9:15
Output:   11:30 is later than ⟨9:15⟩

Input:    4:25   7:45
Output:   4:25 is earlier than 7:45

Input:    8:35 8:35
Output:   The times are equal
```

PROGRAM 2-3   SCHEDULING A NIGHT AT THE MOVIES

The following program handles a series of times involved with seeing a movie and returning on a bus. Prompt the user for the time the movie starts and the length of the movie. By using the + operator, determine the time when the movie ends. Assume a bus always arrives in front of the theater at 22:45 (10:45 PM). The program uses the − operator to compute the waiting time at the bus stop and outputs the time the movie ends and the waiting time.

```cpp
// File: prg2_3.cpp
// prompt the user for the time a movie starts and the
// length of the movie. use the time24 + operator to determine
// when the movie ends. a bus always arrives in front of
// the theater at 22:45. use the time24 − operator to compute
// the waiting time at the bus stop. output the time the movie
// ends and the waiting time

#include <iostream>

#include "d_time24.h"

using namespace std;

int main()
{
    time24 startMovie, movieLength, endMovie,
            busArrival(22,45), waitingTime;

    // prompt and input times for movie to start and its length
    cout << "Enter the time the movie starts and its length: ";
    cin >> startMovie >> movieLength;

    // compute time movie ends and waiting time for the bus
    endMovie = startMovie + movieLength;
    waitingTime = busArrival − endMovie;

    cout << "Movie ends at " << endMovie << endl;
    cout << "Waiting time for the bus is " << waitingTime << endl;

    return 0;
}
```

```
Run:

Enter the time the movie starts and its length: 20:15 1:50
Movie ends at 22:05
Waiting time for the bus is 0:40
```

Member Function Overloading

For most overloaded operators within a class, friend functions are appropriate. In some cases, however, using a member function is either necessary or more convenient. In Chapter 5, we introduce the assignment operator =, which must be overloaded as a member function. When a programmer has a choice, a simple principle applies: Use a member function to overload any binary operator whose action modifies the object itself. For instance, the operator += adds a value to the current object. Overload a unary operator as a member function. Overloading of unary operators will be discussed later in the book.

Member function overloading requires special understanding of the argument list. We illustrate these ideas with two versions of the overloaded += operator in the *time24* class. The prototypes for the functions are as follows:

```
// update time by adding a time24 object or an int
time24& operator+= (const time24& rhs);       // lhs += rhs
time24& operator+= (int min);                 // lhs += min
```

While += is a binary operator, you probably notice something strange about the functions: They seem to be missing an operand. This is not a mistake. Member function overloading has one less argument, since the object itself is an operand. In the case of the operator +=, the object is the left-hand side (*lhs*) operand. To see how C++ views the operation, consider the following two statements, with *time24* objects *objA* and *objB* and integer *m*:

```
objA += objB;
objA += m;
```

For each statement, the runtime system calls the += function in *objA*. In the first case, *objB* is passed as the argument. In the second case, the integer *m* is the argument.

```
objA.operator+= (objB);
objA.operator+= (m);
```

To understand the declaration of the += operator functions, you also need to see why they return a reference. C++ treats the result of the += operation as a new object that can be used in multiple-assignment statements. For instance, consider this chain of assignment statements that includes +=:

```
time24 r(3,15), s(6,30), t;

// first add r to s; then assign the result (s = s + r) to t
t = s += r;               // s = 9:45  t = 9:45
```

To allow the use of += in a multiple-assignment statement, the overloaded operator must return the new value. It is more efficient to return a reference than a copy of the object value. Assignment statements are evaluated from right to left. Each assignment operator returns a reference to the new value, so that it can be ac-

cessed by the next assignment on the left. For this and similar applications, C++ associates with each and every object the keyword *this* that represents the address of the object in memory. The expression *this* identifies the object itself. You will better understand the meaning of the keyword *this* and the expression *this* when we study pointers in Chapter 5. For now, you need only know that *this* is the current object and that any statement in a member function body can use *this* to identify the object. For instance,

```
<member function body>
{   (*this).dataValue = . . .;     // (*this).dataValue is dataValue

    return *this;                  // return the object itself
}
```

The *time24* += operator takes a *time24* argument and forms the sum of the current object (*this*) and the right hand side, *rhs*, by using the overloaded + operator. It then assigns the sum as the new value of the current object (*this*). To allow for multiple-assignment statements, the overloaded operator returns *this*, which is the current value of the object.

```
// implement += by using addition with operands *this and rhs
time24& time24::operator+= (const time24& rhs)
{
    // add *this and rhs using the overloaded + operator
    *this = *this + rhs;

    // return a reference to the current object
    return *this;
}
```

When the argument is an integer, the *time24* += operator forms the sum of the current object and the integer value. Again, *this* is the return value.

```
// implement += by using addition with operands *this and min
time24& time24::operator+= (int min)
{
    // add *this and min using overloaded + operator
    *this = *this + min;

    // return a reference to the current object
    return *this;
}
```

PROGRAM 2-4   LISTING AND ACCUMULATING APPOINTMENT TIMES

The upcoming program illustrates I/O for time24 objects, along with the overloaded operators + and +=. In a loop, the user enters the starting time for three appointments and the length of each appointment in minutes. Output displays the starting and ending time for each appointment. During the loop, the program uses the $+=$ operator to accumulate the total time required for the appointments.

```cpp
// File: prg2_4.cpp
// in a loop, the user enters the starting time for three
// appointments and the length of each appointment in minutes.
// using the time24 output and + operators, the program displays
// the starting and ending time for each appointment. during the
// loop, the program uses the time24 += operator to accumulate
// the total time required for the appointments

#include <iostream>

#include "d_time24.h"

using namespace std;

int main()
{
    time24 apptTime, totalApptTime;
    int apptLength;

    int i;

    for (i = 1; i <= 3; i++)
    {
        // input appointment time and length of appointment
        cout << "Enter start of appointment and length in minutes: ";
        cin >> apptTime >> apptLength;

        // output starting and stopping time for appointment
        cout << " Appointment " << i << ": Start: " << apptTime
             << " Stop: " << (apptTime + apptLength) << endl;
        totalApptTime += apptLength;
    }
    // output total time spent with appointments
    cout << "Total appointment time: " << totalApptTime << endl;
    return 0;
}
```

```
Run:

Enter start of appointment and length in minutes: 9:00 90
    Appointment 1: Start: 9:00 Stop: 10:30
Enter start of appointment and length in minutes: 11:30 120
    Appointment 2: Start: 11:30 Stop: 13:30
Enter start of appointment and length in minutes: 14:00 30
    Appointment 3: Start: 14:00 Stop: 14:30
Total appointment time: 4:00
```

[handwritten margin notes: Software-development Life Cycle — Request, Analysis, Design, Implementation, Testing, Maintenance]

CHAPTER SUMMARY

- The software-development life cycle consists of request, analysis, design, implementation, testing, and maintenance. Each component stage is important in the development of an application.

- In the request phase, computer professionals meet with the client to discuss the needs and requirements for a software system. This stage often involves a feasibility study to see whether building a software system is cost effective. After the completion of the study, the analysis phase should determine the system requirements. This stage is the responsibility of a systems analyst, who acts as the intermediary between the client and the software engineers who will build the program. The result of the analysis phase of the cycle is a functional specification of the software system that includes a list of needs and special requirements.

- The design phase of the software-development life cycle initially translates the functional specifications from the analysis phase into an abstract model of the problem. The design phase is responsible for identifying the objects that are the building blocks of the program and for determining how these objects should collaborate and interact to solve the problem. In the process, the design phase creates the declarations of the classes, including their attributes and public-member functions. It also describes how the classes are related to each other and designs the algorithms that allow the classes to interact effectively.

- The implementation phase of the software-development cycle uses a programming language to convert the design into a program. Typically, a design includes a series of classes and functions to direct the interactions among the objects. Implement the classes independently, and verify the action of their member functions. Then implement program units that coordinate object interaction, and conclude by coding the main program that manages the overall execution of the software system. Often, the implementation stage will discover errors or oversights in design.

- Analysis, design, and implementation are interactive processes that bring about modifications and corrections to the specifications and the code. Effective interaction among the phases depends on frequent and systematic testing. Test the classes and functions that are the individual units of the software system, and perform integrative testing to ensure that the units fit together to create a program that runs correctly and efficiently.

- Program maintenance must begin as soon as the client installs the system. Under the scrutiny of heavy usage, the client identifies bugs or features that must be changed or added. Over time, a client adds new hardware and finds new applications for the software. Modern software systems must be regularly upgraded, or they will eventually become obsolete and unusable.

- Handling errors during function execution is an important aspect of program design. There are three fundamental ways to handle errors. One method, although not preferred, is to output an error message and terminate the program. Another method is to return a Boolean flag from the function call that indicates whether an error occurred. This technique has the advantage of leaving the decision about how to handle the error to the calling code block. The last, and best, alternative is to use the C++ exception mechanism.

- C++ exceptions are handled by three keywords: *throw*, *try*, and *catch*. Place one or more function calls that could generate an exception and any code depending on those function calls in a *try* block. Follow the *try* block with a catch block that is the exception handler. When a function detects an error, it *throws* an exception object, which is normally an object of a special class that identifies the exception. The *throw* bypasses the normal function return mechanism and follows the chain of previous function calls until it locates a catch block that handles the exception. The *catch* block normally outputs an error message and either takes corrective action or terminates the program.

- Operator overloading is an important feature of object design in C++. Operator overloading redefines an operator to accept operands of the class type. For instance, the string class overloads the operator + to allow the concatenation of two string objects. Designing a class to take advantage of familiar operator notation makes the class easier to use and extends its flexibility.

- One way to overload an operator is to implement a free function that uses the operator function format. This method of overloading requires the use of class-member functions that give the function access to the private data of an object.

- A second method of overloading is to declare an operator function as a friend of a class. The function is not a class member, but has access to the private section of the class. This technique avoids calling class access functions. Overload most binary operators as friend functions.

- You must overload some operators as class member functions. The assignment operator = is a good example. In any case, it is customary to overload unary operators and binary operators that modify an object (+=) as member functions. An operator overloaded in this fashion has one operand fewer than the corresponding operator function does. In the case of a binary operator, the left operand is the object itself, and the right operand is the argument. A unary operator has no argument list.

CLASSES AND LIBRARIES IN THE CHAPTER

Name	Header File
calendar	d_cal.h
date	d_date.h
Exception classes	d_except.h
time24	d_time24.h
timeCard	d_tcard.h

REVIEW EXERCISES

1. Indicate to which component of the software-development life cycle each action belongs.
   (a) Run the program, and input boundary values.
   (b) Meet with the client, and determine the accounting needs of the business.
   (c) Users would like a new feature. Add it to the application.
   (d) Create a functional specification for a system that includes a list of needs.
   (e) Code the class-member functions and the functions that coordinate object activities.
   (f) Determine the public interface of classes and how classes interact.

2. Describe different ways that a function can handle errors.

3. Name the two classifications of testing.

4. (a) When should a function implementation throw an exception?
   (b) The function max() returns the maximum of an integer array of size n. The function throws a rangeError exception if n is 0. Implement max().
   (c) Write a code segment that calls max() and outputs the exception message if the array size is 0.

5. What is object composition? Give two examples.

6. A square is a special type of rectangle in which the length equals the width. The square class includes a rectangle object by composition:

```
class square
{
    public:
        square(double len);
            // constructor. sides of square have length len

        double getSide() const;
        void setSide(double len);
            // functions to retrieve and modify private data

        double perimeter() const;
        double area() const;
        double diagonal() const;
            // compute and return square measurements
    private:
        rectangle sq;
            // rectangle object represents a square
};
```

   (a) Implement the constructor for the square class by using an initialization list.
   (b) Complete the implementation for the member function setSide():

```
void square::setSide (double len)
    { _____; }
```

   (c) Give an implementation for the function area().
   (d) The diagonal of a square is sqrt(2 * $side^2$). Use this to implement the function diagonal().

7. The length class maintains length in feet and inches and features operator overloading:

```
class length
{
```

```
        public:           feet      inches
            length(int f = 0, int i = 0);
                // constructor initializes feet and inches
            _____

                // operator + adds two length objects; overload as friend
            _____

                // operator += adds i inches to current object. overload
                // as member function

            _____

                // operator << outputs the length in the format
                //    feet'  inches"

        private:
            int feet, inches;

            void normalize();
                // adjust feet and inches so that 0 <= inches < 12
      };
```

(a) Implement the constructor using inline code.

(b) Implement the private-member function normalize() using inline code.

(c) Give the declaration of the operator function + .

(d) Implement the overloaded operator + in (c).

(e) Give the declaration of the member function +=.

(f) Implement the overloaded operator += in (e) as an external function.

(g) Declare the overloaded operator <<, and implement it.

(h) Give the output for the following sequence of statements:

```
        length objA(3,20), objB(7), objC;

        objC = objA + objB;
        cout << objC;        // Output: _____
        objA += 18;
        cout << objA;        // Output: _____
```

Answers to Review Exercises

1. (a) Testing   (b) Request   (c) Maintenance

   (d) Analysis   (e) Implementation   (f) Design

2. (a) Output an error message, and terminate the program by calling exit(1).

   (b) Return a Boolean value that indicates whether an error occurred.

   (c) Throw an exception.

3. Blackbox and whitebox testing. Unit testing is a combination of the two.

4. (a) A function implementation should throw an exception if the call violates a precondition or if a fatal error, such as divide by 0, occurs during execution of the function.

(b)
```
int max(int arr[], int n)
{
    if (n == 0)
        throw rangeError("max(): the list is empty");

    int i, maxval = arr[0];

    for (i=1;i < n; i++)
        if (arr[i] > maxval)
            maxval = arr[i];

    return maxval;
}
```
(c)
```
try
{
    cout << "The maximum value in arr is " << max(arr, n)
        << endl;
}

catch(const rangeError& re)
{
    cerr << re.what() << endl;
}
        ...
```

5. With object composition, a class, called the client class, has data member(s) that are themselves classes. The types for the data members are called supplier classes. The calendar class of Section 2-1 and the timeCard class of Section 2-3 use object composition.

6. **(a)** Constructor: In the constructor initialization list, call the rectangle constructor for data member sq.

```
square::square(double len) : sq(len, len)
{}
```

(b)
```
void square::setSide(double len)
{ sq.setSides(len, len); }
```
(c)
```
double square::area() const
{ return sq.area(); }
```

(d)
```
double square:: diagonal() const
{ return sqrt(2)*getSide(); }
```

7. **(a)**
```
length(int f, int i): feet(f), inches(i)
{
    normalize();
}
```

(b)
```
void normalize()
{
    feet += inches/12;
    inches %= 12;
}
```
(c)
```
friend length operator+ (const length& lhs, const length& rhs);
```

(d) `length operator+ (const length& lhs, const length& rhs)`
```
    {
        return length(lhs.feet+rhs.feet, lhs.inches+rhs.inches);
    }
```
(e) `length& operator+= (int i);`
(f) `length& length::operator+= (int i)`
```
    {
        inches += i;
        normalize();

        return *this;
    }
```
(g) `// declaration of << in the class`
`friend ostream& operator<< (ostream& ostr, const length& obj);`
```
    // implementation of operator<<
    ostream& operator<< (ostream& ostr, const length& obj)
    {
        ostr << obj.feet << "' " << obj.inches << '"';

        return ostr;
    }
```
(h) `5' 3"`
`6' 2"`

WRITTEN EXERCISES

8. Design a class, displayYearCalendar, whose objects have the year as a data member. An object outputs a 12-month calendar for the specified year.
   (a) What member functions will you declare?
   (b) Is object composition necessary for the development of the class?
   (c) Give a class declaration.

9. The class hiLow describes objects that can play the "High-Low" game. The game starts with a random target in the range from 1 to 1000. The player is challenged to guess the number within n guesses, where typically $n <= 10$. The player is repeatedly asked to make a guess, which is then evaluated as being less than the target, greater than the target, or matching the target. The player wins when a match occurs within the allowed number of guesses.
   (a) Design the class so that an object can repeatedly play the game with a fixed number of allowed guesses.
   (b) What new design features would be required if the number of guesses can vary from game to game?
   (c) How would you modify the class design so that two players can alternately make guesses? The first player with a match wins.

10. The function
```
    removeDuplicates(int arr[], int& n);
```

modifies array *arr* with *n* elements by removing all duplicate values in the list. After duplicates have been removed, the function updates the reference argument *n* to reflect the number of distinct elements. Describe a set of inputs that would be appropriate for inclusion in a test bank that verifies the function.

11. (a) The function f() uses the function sqrt() from the mathematics library <cmath> to compute $\sqrt{x^3 - 1}$. The square root has no real value for a number less than 0, so f() throws a rangeError exception if $x < 1$. Implement f().

   (b) Write a code segment that inputs x and outputs f(x). If $x < 1$, catch the exception, output the exception string, and output f(1.0).

12. The box class provides measurement of a box that is defined by its length, width, and height. Store the base of the box as a rectangle object using object composition.

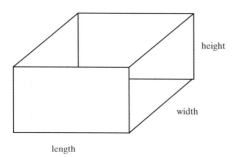

height

width

length

```
class box
{
    public:
        box (double l, double w, double h): _____, height(h)
        {}

        double volume()        // length * width * height
        { _____ }

        double getLength()
        { return _____ }
    private:
        rectangle base;
        double height;
};
```

   (a) Complete the initialization list for the constructor so that the rectangle object base gets initialized.

   (b) Give the return value for getLength().

   (c) Implement the member function volume().

13. Companies hire temporary workers at an hourly rate and pay them at the end of the day. A tempWorker object maintains information for a worker. It uses the composition of two time24 objects to indicate when the worker begins work and ends work. The third data member is the hourly pay rate.

```
class tempWorker
{
   public:
      tempWorker(const time24& start, const time24& end, double rate);
         // constructor has arguments to initialize both the time24
         // data and the rate per hour

      double pay() const;
         // return pay for the day

   private:
      time24 startWork, endWork;
      double ratePerHour;
};
```

(a) Implement the constructor by using an initialization list.

(b) Implement the function pay(). You may use overloaded operators in the time24 class.

(c) Declare the tempWorker object w, where the starting time is 8:30, the ending time is 16:00 (4:00 PM), and the hourly pay rate is $8.50 .

14. (a) Why should the stream operators $<<$ and $>>$ be overloaded as friends?

(b) Why does an implementation of a friend function as an external function not use the class scope operator "::"?

15. Suppose that className has the class declaration

```
class className
{
   public:
      . . .
      className operator- ();   // overloaded unary negation operator
   private:
      . . .
};
```

Assume a and b are objects of type className. The operation $b = -a$ is implemented as

(a) b = a.operator-(b)   **(b)** b = b.operator-()

(c) b = operator-(a)   **(d)** b = a.operator-()

16. In the implementation of the overloaded input operator $<<$ for the time24 class, what is the significance of providing a stream reference as the return value?

17. (a) Trace the following code segment, and fill in the missing statements using the overloaded time24 operators:

```
time24 getUp(6,45), breakfast(7,30), goToSchool;

// output the amount of time between your getting up and
// having breakfast
_____


// you go to school 40 minutes after breakfast. assign
// this time to the object goToSchool
_____
```

```
// you decide to increase getUp by 15 minutes
```

(b) A constructor for a class CL can serve as a *converter* from a type *T* to type CL. The constructor must take one argument of type *T*. Assume that *obj* is an object of type CL and *x* is a value of type *T*. The C++ compiler evaluates a statement of the form

```
obj = x;
```

by executing

```
obj = CL(x);
```

(i) Does the time24 class have a constructor that serves as a converter? Explain your answer.

(ii) What is the output?

```
time24 t;
t = 12;
cout << t << endl;
```

(c) Another type of converter takes an object of type CL and returns a value of type T. Declare such a converter as a member function of class CL using the following syntax:

```
operator T();
```

This unary operator takes the data in an object and returns a value of type T. There is no return type in the declaration, because it is understood that T is the return type. The programmer can apply the operator explicitly using the syntax T(obj), where obj is an object of type CL. If x is of type T, the compiler will apply the converter implicitly in statements like

```
x = obj;   // compiler evaluates this as x = T(obj)
```

(i) Give the declaration of a converter for the time24 class that returns the time in hours as a double value. For instance, if the time is 10:30, the converter returns 10.5.

(ii) Implement the converter.

(iii) What is the output?

```
time24 u(6,45);
double x, y;

x = double(u);
y = u;
cout << x << " " << y << " " << double(x) << endl;
```

18. Begin with the following declaration and inline implementation of the accumulator class.

```
class accumulator
{
   public:
      // constructor initializes total
      accumulator (int value = 0) : total(value)
      {}
```

```
        // access function
        int getTotal()
        { return total; }

        // update the data member total
        void addValue(int value)
        { total += value; }
    private:
        // total accumulated by the object
        int total;
};
```

(a) Add the overloaded operator += that has the same function as addValue(). Include both the prototype for the operator and its implementation as an external function.

(b) Add the negation operator, −, to the class. The operator changes the sign of the current value for total. Give the function prototype and the implementation as an external function.

(c) Add the + operator as a friend function. The operator takes two accumulator objects as arguments and returns a new accumulator object whose value is the sum of the data members. Include both the prototype for the operator and its implementation as an external function.

(d) Add an overloaded version of the output operator <<. Include both the prototype for the operator and its implementation as an external function.

(e) What is the output in the following code segment?

```
accumulator x(5), y(3), z(−9), w;

x += 3;
w = x + y;
z = −z;
cout << w << " " << z << endl;
```

19. The class modClass has a single integer data member, dataVal, in the range from 0 to 6. The constructor takes any positive integer v and assigns to dataVal the remainder after division by 7.

```
dataVal = v % 7;
```

The addition adds two objects by summing their data members and finding the remainder after division by 7. For instance,

```
// dataVal in a is 3, in b is 6, in c is 0
modClass a(10), b(6), c;
c = a + b;                    // dataVal in c is (3+6)% 7 = 2
c = a * b;                    // dataVal in c is (3*6)% 7 = 4
```

The following is the class declaration:

```
class modClass
{
    public:
        modClass(int v = 0);
```

```
         // throw a rangeError exception if v < 0
      friend modClass operator+ (const modClass& x, const modClass& y);
      friend modClass operator* (const modClass& x, const modClass& y);
      friend bool operator== (const modClass& x, const modClass& y);
      friend bool operator< (const modClass& x, const modClass& y);
      friend ostream& operator<< (ostream& ostr, const modClass& obj);
   private:
      int dataVal;
};
```

(a) Implement the class.

(b) The function inverse() takes a modClass object x != modClass(0) and returns the inverse of x. The inverse is defined as the object y such that x * y == modClass(1):

   modClass inverse(const modClass& x);

Implement the function inverse(). Hint: Use a while loop that multiplies x by modClass objects whose values are 1, 2, ... , 6. Terminate the loop when you find the object that produces the inverse. This becomes the return value.

PROGRAMMING EXERCISES

20. Write a program that prompts for the year and outputs a calendar for each month in the year. The program design should include a free function, displayYearCalendar(), that takes the year as an argument and uses a loop to display the calendar for each month.

```
// output a calendar for year
void displayYearCalendar(int year);
```

21. Take the square class from Review Exercise 2-6 and place the declaration and implementation in file "square.h." Place the declaration and implementation of the circle class from Review Exercise 1-4 in the file "circle.h." Write a program that declares objects innerSq, circ, and outerSq corresponding to the figure, which displays an inner square with length 4, a circumscribed circle, and a circumscribed outer square. Output the area of the "crossline" section of the circle and the perimeter of the shaded region. Hint: Use the function diagonal() in the square class to determine the radius of the circle.

22. Place the declaration and implementation of the class tempWorker from Written Exercise 2-13 in the header file "tworker.h". Write a program that inputs the rate per hour, the starting time, and the ending time for the job and outputs the worker's payment for the day. Use the data from part (c) of the exercise for your input.

23. Declare the following array of time24 objects:

```
time24 timeArr[8] = {time24(8,00), time24(9,30), time24(8,30),
                     time24(11,00), time24(13,00), time24(12,30),
                     time24(12,00), time24(16,00)};
```

Scan the array, and output the result of calling duration() for successive pairs. The program should catch any rangeError exception and output the error string. Note that for the first pair, 8:00 and 9:30, the output is 1:30. For the second pair, 9:30 and 8:30, catch the exception and output the message.

24. The time24 array cust is a list of times when five customers arrive at a restaurant for dinner. The restaurant serves an "early bird special" before 6:00 PM. Scan the array, and use the comparison operator < to determine whether a customer is eligible for the special. For each customer, output the time of arrival and the appropriate string "eligible for special" or "not eligible for special."

```
time24 cust[5] = {time24(17,15), time24(19,30), time24(17,45),
                  time24(18,10), time24(20,0)};
```

25. Written Exercise 2-18 develops the accumulator class that uses operator overloading. Place the declaration and implementation in the header file "accum_o.h". Write a program that uses the code segment from part (e).

26. The program tests the modClass developed in Written Exercise 2-19 by verifying the distributive law for modClass objects:

```
a*(b+c) = a*b + a*c
```

Define three objects, *a*, *b*, and *c*, which have initial values 10, 20, and 30, respectively. Your program should output the value of the expressions $a*(b + c)$ and $(a*b + a*c)$, respectively.

PROGRAMMING PROJECTS

27. The time24 class handles time with hours in the range 0 to 23 and minutes in the range 0 to 59. This exercise looks at the more familiar standard time and develops the time12 class that stores hours in the range 12, 1, 2, ..., 11 for both AM and PM. We could develop the new class "from scratch" by declaring the hour and minute data members and using them in the implementation of the member functions. A more efficient design uses composition and a time24 object to hold the time data. The time12 class has member functions that are similar to those of the time24 class, except that the constructor and I/O operations distinguish between AM and PM units. A private-member function, convert12To24(), converts time notation from standard to 24-hour time.

CLASS time12	Declaration	"time12.h"

```
// specifies clock time units
enum timeUnit {AM, PM};

// maintains clock time
class time12
{
   private:
      time24 t;
         // store time in 24-hour format
```

```
      time24 convert12To24(int h, int m, timeUnit tunit);
         // build t from standard time
   public:
      time12(int h=12, int m=0, timeUnit tunit = AM);
         // initialize time24 data member t
      void addTime(int m);
         // add m minutes to update current time

      void readTime();
      void writeTime();
         // I/O member functions use format HH:MM: AM (PM)
};
```

```
Example:
time12 t(8,15,AM);

t.writeTime();    // Output: 8:15 AM
t.readTime();     // Input: 12:00 PM
t.addTime(180);   // add 3 hours to t
t.writeTime();    // Output: 3:00 PM
```

(a) Implement the class, and place it in the file "time12.h." Figure 2-4 depicts the algorithm that should be used to implement the private-member function convert12To24().

(b) In Frankfurt, Germany, time is six hours ahead of the U.S. Eastern time zone. Write a program that uses the time12 class to output the time in Frankfurt that corresponds to midnight on New Year's Eve in New York City.

(c) Write a program that inputs the time at which an auto mechanic begins a job. The mechanic asks the customer to pick up the car in five hours and 20 minutes. Output the time that the car will be available to the customer.

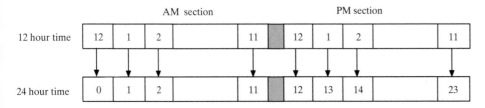

Figure 2-4
Conversion between clock time and 24-hour time

28. A complex number is of the form x + iy, where $i^2 = -1$. Complex numbers have vast applications in mathematics, physics, and engineering. Complex numbers have an arithmetic governed by a series of rules including the following:

Let $u = a + ib, \quad v = c + id$

$\quad$ Magnitude$(u) = \sqrt{a^2 + b^2}$

$\quad$ Complex number corresponding to real number f is $u = f + i0$

Real Part of $u = a$

Imaginary Part of $u = b$

$u + v = (a + c) + i(b + d)$

$u - v = (a - c) + i(b - d)$

$u*v = (ac - bd) + i(ad + bc)$

$u/v = \dfrac{ac + bd}{c^2 + d^2} + i\,\dfrac{bc - ad}{c^2 + d^2}$

$u == v$ if $(a == c)$ and $(b == d)$

(a) In the header file "complexx.h," implement the class complex whose declaration is

```
class complex
{
  public:
     complex(double x = 0.0, double y = 0.0);
        // constructor

     double magnitude() const;  // return magnitude
     double realPart() const;   // return real part
     double imagPart() const;   // return imaginary part
        // access member functions

     friend complex operator+ (const complex& lhs,
                                 const complex& rhs);
        // complex addition
     friend complex operator- (const complex& lhs,
                                 const complex& rhs);
        // complex subtraction

     friend complex operator* (const complex& lhs,
                                 const complex& rhs);
        // complex multiplication

     friend complex operator/ (const complex& lhs,
                                 const complex& rhs);
        // complex division

     friend bool operator== (const complex& lhs,
                                 const complex& rhs);
        // equality of complex numbers

     complex operator- () const;
        // negation of a complex number

     friend ostream& operator<< (ostream& ostr,
                                 const complex& x);
        // output in format (real,imag)
     friend istream& operator>> (istream& ostr,
                                 complex& x);
```

```
        // input complex number in format (real,imag)
   private:
      double real;      // real part
      double imag;      // complex part
};
```

(b) To test your work, run the following program:

```
#include <iostream>

#include "complexx.h"

using namespace std;

int main()
{
   // complex number i = 0 +1i
   complex i(0,1), z1, z2;

   // input values
   cout << "Enter two complex numbers: ";
   cin >> z1 >> z2;

   cout << "Test the binary arithmetic operators:" << endl;
   cout << " z1 + z2 = " << (z1 + z2) << endl;
   cout << " z1 - z2 = " << (z1 - z2) << endl;
   cout << " z1 * z2 = " << z1 * z2 << endl;
   cout << " z1 / z2 = " << z1 / z2 << endl;

   // test relational equality
   if (z1 == z2)
      cout << z1 << " = " << z2 << endl;
   else
      cout << z1 << " != " << z2 << endl;

   // verify that i*i = -1 and that -i*i = 1
   cout << "i*i = " << i * i << endl;
   cout << "-i*i = " << -i * i << endl;

   return 0;
}
```

Run:

Enter two complex numbers: (3,5) (8,6)
Test the binary arithmetic operators:
z1 + z2 = (11,11)
z1 - z2 = (-5,-1)
z1 * z2 = (-6,58)

z1 / z2 = (0.54,0.22)
(3,5) != (8,6)
i*i = (-1,0)
-i*i = (1,0)

(c)   Write a function, f(z), that evaluates the complex polynomial function

$$f(z) = z^3 - 3z^2 + 4z - 2$$

Evaluate the polynomial for the following values of z:

z = 2+3i, -1+i, 1+i, 1-i, 1+0i

Note that the last three values are roots of f(z).

CHAPTER 3

Introduction to Algorithms

OBJECTIVES

- To understand the simple sorting technique known as the selection sort and its implementation as a C++ function. We demonstrate the algorithm for integer data.
- To understand the sequential-search algorithm for locating a data value in an unordered array. We demonstrate the algorithm for integer data.
- To understand the binary search for locating a value in a sorted array and to discover that the algorithm is, in general, much faster than a sequential search when used on the same array.
- To gain an intuitive understanding of running-time analysis, using Big-O notation.
- To see that the running time of an algorithm tends to fall into one of the common orders of magnitude, ranging from $O(1)$ to $O(2^n)$.
- To apply Big-O analysis to the sequential search and see that its running time is $O(n)$.
- To see intuitively that the binary search has running time $O(\log_2 n)$.
- To understand that many algorithms, such as the selection sort and the binary search, work the same way for any data type. Using C++ template function notation makes these algorithms generic.
- To understand function template syntax and how the runtime expansion of a template function takes place.
- To see the template versions of the selection sort, the sequential search, and the binary search.
- To understand that some algorithms are recursive by nature and that it may be natural to implement such an algorithm with a recursive function.
- To understand that the implementation of recursion involves implementing a series of function calls until reaching a stopping condition. A series of function returns computes the result.
- To see the elegant recursive algorithms for solving the Tower of Hanoi and finding the greatest common divisor of two numbers.
- To realize that not all problems should be solved recursively. Often, iteration is much more efficient. The computation of the Fibonacci numbers illustrates this point.

OUTLINE

The primary aim of this book is a study of data structure based on a systematic development of the corresponding container classes. The study also includes criteria for selecting the appropriate data structure in the design of application software. To accomplish this task, we must discuss algorithms whose design is integral to the efficient implementation of the data structures and their use in programs. In this chapter, we introduce several classical searching and sorting algorithms, including the selection sort, sequential search, and binary search. The selection sort is an algorithm that illustrates many of the common features of sorting algorithms. In subsequent chapters, we develop a range of other, more efficient sorting techniques, including quicksort and the heap sort.

Searching a list to locate a target value is a basic problem in computing. For instance, the registrar uses the Social Security Number as a target to look up a student record in a database. Overnight-mail providers make use of an airbill number to track the status of a package. The simplest form of searching is the sequential search, which compares the target with every element in a list until it obtains a match or reaches the end of the list. For some applications, we maintain a list in sorted order. For these lists, a special search technique, called the binary search, may be used. The search exploits the structure of an ordered list to produce very fast access times.

This chapter introduces the concept of algorithm efficiency. In Section 3-3, we describe factors that determine efficiency and introduce Big-O notation as a measure of efficiency. A book on algorithms makes a formal study of algorithm efficiency, including the underlying mathematical justification for the different measures. Our approach is more intuitive. Nevertheless, the resulting Big-O measure for an algorithm gives you a tool to compare and contrast different algorithms. We use the measure throughout the book. In Section 3-4, we discuss the efficiency of the sequential and binary searches by developing simple Big-O estimates of their performance. A test program provides timing data that clearly reveal the greater efficiency of the binary search.

We use functions to implement algorithms. Up to this point, all of our function prototypes use specific data types for the arguments in the argument list. This approach severely limits the ability of a function to implement a general algorithm. For instance, finding the largest element in a list is a general algorithm that scans the elements and uses the $<$ operator to compare values. The algorithm applies to integers, strings, and time24 objects, because they all define the $<$ relationship. Unfortunately, the need to specify the data type forces us to create three versions of the max() function, one for an int list, one for a string list, and one for a time24 list. C++ recognizes that requiring a programmer to write essentially identical source code for multiple versions of a function is tedious and limits the use of abstraction. To address the problem, the language provides a template mechanism that allows a programmer to write a single version of a function with general type arguments. The compiler evaluates each call to max() and creates a version of the function corresponding to the specific data type. The task of creating multiple versions of the same function falls to the compiler, and not to the programmer. In Section 3-5, we present template functions and develop template-based (generic) versions of the selection sort and the binary search.

Recursion is an important problem-solving tool in computer science and mathematics. Programming languages use recursive definitions to describe language syntax. Searching and sorting algorithms and functions that traverse the elements of a list or tree use recursion. The use of recursion occurs frequently in operation research models, in game theory, in the study of graphs, and in the development of exhaustive search techniques. The chapter introduces recursion as an algorithm technique whose implementation involves the function calling itself. We describe how the technique works by presenting several examples, including the Tower of Hanoi puzzle. Recursive algorithms often have iterative solutions that are far more efficient. We discuss situations in which recursion should and should not be used. Recursion is a limited, but important, application in data structures. We revisit the topic in Chapters 10 and 15, when we introduce recursive tree structures and develop a variety of advanced algorithms.

SELECTION SORT   3-1

Sorting algorithms begin with a sequence of items in a list and use some rearrangement strategy to order successive elements. The algorithm implements the strategy. We begin with a very simple example of sorting, called the _selection sort_, that proceeds through the list position by position, starting at the beginning of the list. At each position, the algorithm selects the correct element and copies its value into the position.

There is a kind of natural progression to our development of a sorting algorithm. All of us have experience sorting items in our everyday lives. For instance, when a bank returns our monthly checks, we arrange them by check number. Teachers and student graders sorts exams and assignments by name before returning the papers to the class. Depending on the items, we have experience with different sort strategies without formally understanding them as algorithms. Relating a sort to our experiences is an important starting point. The problem with our experiences, however, is that we order items almost subconsciously. By using a sample list and carrying out the sort step by step, we make explicit the process and thus set out a design for the algorithm. The final step is the declaration of the sort function, including its argument list. The implementation of the function is a generalization of the example.

Let us illustrate these ideas in the development of the function selectionSort(). We begin by recalling our early days in school, when the teacher lined up the children in the order of their height. Follow the teacher as she starts with the line Tom, Debbie, Mike, and Ron.

Step #1: First Position

Step 1. She identifies Ron as the smallest child in the line and asks him to exchange positions with Tom, the first child in the line. The effect is to place the smallest child at the front of the line

Step 2. The line consisting of Debbie, Mike, and Tom remains unordered. The teacher repeats the selection process, identifies that Tom is the smallest child in the group of remaining children, and asks him to exchange positions with Debbie.

Step 3. With Ron and Tom in position, only the last two children in line must be ordered. The teacher identifies Debbie as the next-smallest child and asks her to exchange places with Mike.

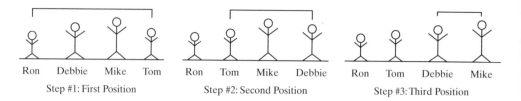

Step #1: First Position   Step #2: Second Position   Step #3: Third Position

After step 3, the four children are in order. Mike, the tallest child, is correctly positioned as part of the exchange with Debbie.

Selection-Sort Algorithm

We develop the selection-sort algorithm for an array of n elements. The resulting list is in ascending order, with

```
arr[0] <= arr[1] <= arr[2] <= . . . <= arr[n-2] <= arr[n-1]
```

The algorithm starts at position 0 and determines the index of the smallest element in the list. Once it has been selected, we exchange the element with the contents of arr[0]. This step places the smallest element in arr[0] and leaves the rest of the list in unsorted order. The process moves to position 1, and the selection determines the location of the smallest element in the sublist arr[1] ... arr[n − 1]. After that exchange has been completed, elements in the first two positions are ordered, and the process repeats for positions 2 through n − 2. No selection occurs at position n − 1, because arr[n − 1] is the largest element. The selection sort algorithm involves n − 1 iterations, which we refer to as *passes*, because each involves a traversal of elements in a sublist to locate the index of the smallest element.

We illustrate the algorithm with a sample array *arr* consisting of the n = 5 integer values 50, 20, 40, 75, and 35. Figure 3-1 displays the state of the list after each of the four passes. The passes start at 0, because the first pass stores the smallest element in arr[0].

Pass 0: Scan the entire list from arr[0] to arr[4], and identify 20, at index 1, as the smallest element. Exchange 20 with arr[0] = 50, the first element in the list. After the completion of pass 0, the first element is correctly positioned, and the remaining sublist from arr[1] to arr[4] is unordered.

Pass 1: Scan the sublist 50, 40, 75, and 35. Exchange the smallest element, 35, at index 4, with arr[1] = 50. The front of the list (20, 35) is ordered, and the sublist from arr[2] to arr[4] remains unordered.

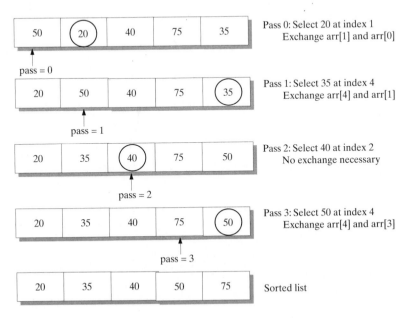

Pass 0: Select 20 at index 1
Exchange arr[1] and arr[0]

pass = 0

Pass 1: Select 35 at index 4
Exchange arr[4] and arr[1]

pass = 1

Pass 2: Select 40 at index 2
No exchange necessary

pass = 2

Pass 3: Select 50 at index 4
Exchange arr[4] and arr[3]

pass = 3

Sorted list

Figure 3-1
Ordering an integer array with the selection sort

Pass 2: Locate the smallest element in the sublist 40, 75, and 50. No exchange
           is necessary, because 40 is already the smallest element in the sublist.
           The sublist from arr[3] to arr[4] remains unordered.

Pass 3: Two elements remain to be sorted. Scan the sublist 75, 50, and ex-
           change the smaller element with arr[3]. The exchange places 50 at
           index 4 in arr[3]. Only the one element sublist arr[4] remains, and it
           must contain the largest element.

The function selectionSort() implements the algorithm for an integer list. Its
prototype includes the array *arr* and its size *n* as arguments.

selectionSort(): (Integer array)
     void selectionSort(int arr[], int n);

The coding of the algorithm consists of nested for loops. The outer loop establishes the $n - 1$ passes over the list. The control variable, called *pass*, ranges from 0
to $n - 2$. For each iteration, an inner loop scans the unordered sublist arr[pass] to
arr[$n - 1$] and identifies the index of the smallest element. If the index, called
smallIndex, is not equal to pass, we exchange arr[pass] and arr[smallIndex}. This assigns arr[smallIndex] to its correct position in the sorted order.

```
void selectionSort(int arr[], int n)
{
    int smallIndex; // index of smallest element in the sublist
    int pass, j;
    int temp;

    // pass has the range 0 to n-2
    for (pass = 0; pass < n-1; pass++)
    {

        // scan the sublist starting at index pass
        smallIndex = pass;

        // j traverses the sublist arr[pass+1] to arr[n-1]
        for (j = pass+1; j < n; j++)

        // if smaller element found, assign smallIndex to that position
        if (arr[j] < arr[smallIndex])
            smallIndex = j;

        // if smallIndex and pass are not the same location,
        // exchange the smallest item in the sublist with arr[pass]
        if (smallIndex != pass)
        {
            temp = arr[pass];
```

```
            arr[pass] = arr[smallIndex];
            arr[smallIndex] = temp;
      }
   }
}
```

You can find the declaration and implementation of selectionSort() in the header file "d_sort.h".

Example 3-1

The selection sort orders an array of 15 random integers in the range from 0 to 99.

```
// declare an integer array and a random number generator
int arr[15];
int i;
randomNumber rnd;

// initialize and output the unsorted array
cout << "Original array" << endl;

// fill the array with random integers in the range 0 to 99
for (i = 0; i < 15; i++)
{
   arr[i] = rnd.random(100);
   cout << arr[i] << "   ";
}
cout << endl << endl;

// call selectionSort() to order the array and then output it
selectionSort(arr,15);

cout << "Sorted array" << endl;
for (i=0;i < 15; ++)
   cout << arr[i] << "   ";
cout << endl;
```

```
Output:

Original array
66   20   33   55   53   57   69   11   67   70   81   39   83   13   29

Sorted array
11   13   20   29   33   39   53   55   57   66   67   69   70   81   83
```

3-2   SIMPLE SEARCH ALGORITHMS

An array is a sequence of elements with an index that identifies elements in the list. Search algorithms start with a target value and employ some strategy to visit the elements looking for a match. If the target is found, the corresponding index of the matching element becomes the return value. Otherwise, the return value indicates that the target is not found. A search frequently wants to cover the entire array, but we design the algorithms to allow for searches in a sublist of the array. A sublist is a sequence of elements whose range of indices begin at index *first* and continue up to, but not including, index *last*. We denote a sublist by its index range [first, last). In Figure 3-2, array arr contains nine elements. The shaded elements are the sublist [2,6). The array itself is the sublist [0,9). In each case, note that arr[last] is not an element in the sublist.

Sequential Search

The simplest search algorithm for an array is the sequential search. The algorithm begins with a target value and indices that define the sublist range. It scans the elements in the sublist item by item, looking for the first occurrence of a match with the target. If successful, the algorithm returns the index of the match. The search is not successful if the scan reaches the index *last* before matching the target. In this case, index *last* is the return value.

The function seqSearch() implements the sequential-search algorithm. For arguments, the function has an array, the two indices *first* and *last* that specify the index range, and the target value. The return value is an index of type *int*. To prohibit the modification of array elements, the prototype precedes the array formal argument with the reserved word *const*.

seqSearch() (assuming an integer array):
```
int seqSearch(const int arr[], int first, int last, int target);
```

To illustrate the action of seqSearch(), consider the integer array
```
int arr[8] = {6, 4, 2, 9, 5, 3, 10, 7};
```

The figure describes the algorithm with a target of 3 and a target of 9.

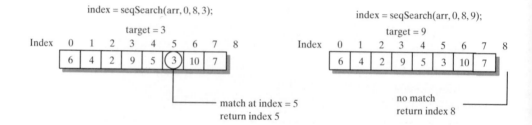

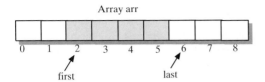

Array arr

first   last

Figure 3-2
Sublists in an array

The implementation of seqSearch() uses a while loop with control variable *i* to scan the array elements in the range [first, last). Iterations continue so long as the index is in range and no match is found. The scan terminates when arr[*i*] == target (success) or index *i* = last (failure). In either case, the index *i* is the return value.

```
int seqSearch(const int arr[], int first, int last, int target)
{
    int i = first;

    // scan indices in the range first <= i < last; test for a match
    // or index out of range.
    while(i != last && arr[i] != target)
        i++;

    return i;      // i is index of match or i = last if no match
}
```

You can find the declaration and implementation of seqSearch() in the file "d_search.h."

Example 3-2

```
int list[7] = {5, 3, 100, 89, 5, 6, 5}, index;
```

1. Search the entire array list, looking for the first occurrence of 100, and output the return value.

```
index = seqSearch(list,0,7,100);
cout << index;                      // output: 2 (search succeeds)
```

2. Search the sublist arr[0] ... arr[2] with index range [0,3), looking for the first occurrence of 100, and output the return value.

```
index = seqSearch(list,0,3,100);
cout << index;                      // output: 2 (search succeeds)
```

3. Search the sublist arr[3] ... arr[4] with index range [3,5), looking for the first occurrence of 100, and output the return value.

```
index = seqSearch(list,3,5,100);
cout << index;                      // output: 5 (search fails)
```

4. We use the fact that seqSearch() can search a subrange to find all occurrences of the element 5 in the list. After identifying the location (*index*) of the first 5, continue the search in the subrange [*index* + 1, 7). Continue the process until the search fails (*index* = 7).

```
// search for 5 in the range [0,7)
index = seqSearch(list,0,7,5);
cout << "5 occurs at indices ";
while (index != 7)
{
    cout << index << "   ";
    // search the range [index+1,7)
    index = seqSearch(list, index+1,7,5);
}
```

```
Output:
5 occurs at indices 0   4   6
```

Binary Search

The sequential search is a general search algorithm that applies to any array. It methodically scans the elements, one after another, until it succeeds or it exhausts the range. A more efficient search strategy can be employed when the array is ordered. You use this strategy when looking up a phone number in a telephone book. Suppose you want to find "Swanson." A phone book maintains names in alphabetical order, so you look for Swanson somewhere near the back of the book. If you jump to an approximate location and land in the P's, you know to look further back in the book. A second selection may land you in the U's, which is too far, and so a third choice is made somewhere between the first two locations—and so forth. This approach is clearly superior to a sequential search, which would laboriously scan the A's, then the B's, and successive letters in the alphabet. Our problem is to turn the rather haphazard phone lookup strategy into an algorithm that will work for any ordered array. The solution is the *binary-search algorithm*. Given a target value, the algorithm begins the search by selecting the midpoint in the list. If the value at the midpoint matches the target, the search is done. Otherwise, because the list is ordered, the search should continue in the first half of the list (lower sublist) or in the second half of the list (upper sublist). If the target is less than the current midpoint value, look in the lower sublist by selecting its midpoint; otherwise, look in the upper sublist by selecting its midpoint. The process can continue by looking at midpoints of ever smaller and smaller sublists. Eventually, we either find the target value or reduce the size of the sublist to 0 and conclude that the target is not in the list.

To get a more formal understanding of the binary-search algorithm, we need to specify the meanings of *midpoint* and *sublists* in terms of array indices. Assume *arr* is an array with n items and that the search looks for the item called *target*. The indices for the full list are in the index range first $= 0 \leq i < n =$ last, or $[0, n)$. Start the search process by computing the index *mid* as the midpoint in the list and assigning the value *arr[mid]* to midValue.

```
mid = (first + last)/2;      // midpoint
midValue = arr[mid];         // midpoint value is arr[mid]
```

Comparison of midValue with target can lead to three possible outcomes, which trigger three separate actions:

Case 1. A match occurs. The search is complete, and *mid* is the index that locates target.

```
if (midValue == target)      // found match
    return mid;
```

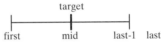

first   mid   last-1   last

Case 1: target = midvalue
Search is done

Case 2. The value in target is less than that in midValue, and the search must continue in the lower sublist. The index range for this sublist range is [first, mid). Reposition the index *last* to the end of the sublist (last = mid).

```
// search the lower sublist
if (target < midValue)
    <reposition last to mid>
    <search sublist arr[first]...arr[mid-1]
```

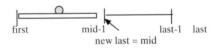

first   mid-1   last-1   last
new last = mid

Case 2: target < midvalue
Search lower sublist

Case 3. The value in target is greater than that in midValue, and the search must continue in the upper sublist. The indices range for this sublist is [mid+1, last), because the sublist begins immediately to the right of mid. Reposition the index *first* to the front of the sublist (first = mid + 1).

```
// search upper sublist
if (target > midValue)
    <reposition first to mid+1>
    <search sublist arr[mid+1]...arr[last-1]>
```

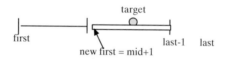

Case 3: target > midvalue
Search upper sublist

The process terminates when a match is found or the sublist is empty. An empty sublist occurs when *first* and *last* cross each other (first >= last).

Example 3-3

The example gives a few snapshots of the binary-search algorithm as it looks for a target in the nine-element integer array *arr*.

	0	1	2	3	4	5	6	7	8	9
arr	-7	3	5	8	12	16	23	33	55	Null

The first case finds target = 23 and returns the index 6. The second case looks for target = 4 and returns 9, because the item is not in the array.

1. Search for target = 23

STEP 1. Indices first = 0, last = 9, mid = (0 + 9)/2 = 4.

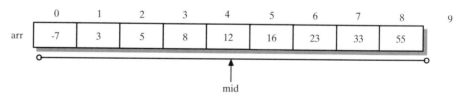

target = 23 > midValue = 12, so step 2 searches the upper sublist with first = 5 and last = 9.

STEP 2. Indices first = 5, last = 9, mid = (5 + 9)/2 = 7.

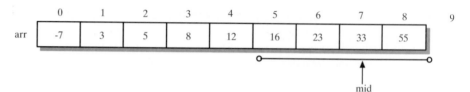

target = 23 < midValue = 33, so step 3 searches the lower sublist with first = 5 and last = 7.

STEP 3. Indices first = 5, last = 7, mid = (5 + 7)/2 = 6.

0	1	2	3	4	5	6	7	8	9
-7	3	5	8	12	16	23	33	55	

arr

mid

target = midValue = 23, so a match is found at index mid = 6.

2. Search for target = 4.

STEP 1. Indices first = 0, last = 9, mid = (0 + 9)/2 = 4.

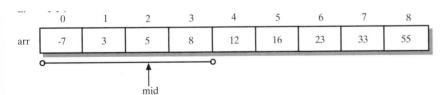

arr

mid

target = 4 < midValue = 12, so step 2 searches the lower sublist with first = 0 and last = 4.

STEP 2. Indices first = 0, last = 4, mid = (0 + 4)/2 = 2.

0	1	2	3	4	5	6	7	8
-7	3	5	8	12	16	23	33	55

arr

mid

target = 4 < midValue = 5, so step 3 searches the lower sublist with first = 0 and last = 2.

STEP 3. Indices first = 0, last = 2, mid = (0 + 2)/2 = 1.

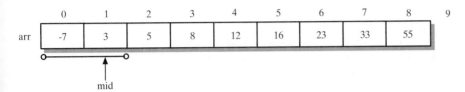

arr

mid

target = 4 > midValue = 3, so, step 4 should search the upper sublist with first = 2 and last = 2, but first ≥ last, so the target is not in the list, and we return index last = 9.

The function binSearch() implements the binary-search algorithm. For an integer list, the function has four arguments: an identification of the array, the starting index (first), the index upper bound (last) for the list, and the target. The function returns the array index that identifies the first occurrence of a match, or the value *last* when the target is not found.

binSearch():
```
int binSearch(const int arr[], int first, int last, int target);
```

The implementation of the function uses an *iterative* (looping) process on progressively smaller sublists [first, last). Iteration continues so long as the sublist is not empty (first < last) and no match occurs. After determining the middle index of the range and the corresponding array value, multiple selection statements compare the value with the target and treat the three possible outcomes.

```
int binSearch(const int arr[], int first, int last, int target)
{
    int mid;                    // index of the midpoint
    int midValue;               // object that is assigned arr[mid]
    int origLast = last;        // save original value of last

    while (first < last)        // test for nonempty sublist
    {
        mid = (first+last)/2;
        midValue = arr[mid];
        if (target == midValue)
            return mid;         // have a match
        // determine which sublist to search
        else if (target < midValue)
            last = mid;         // search lower sublist. reset last
        else
            first = mid+1;      // search upper sublist. reset first
    }
    return origLast;            // target not found
}
```

You can find the declaration and implementation of binSearch() in file "d_search.h".

Example 3-4
_____

Consider the declarations

```
int arr[10] = {-7, 12, 5, -1, 7, 2, 3, 55, 8, 33};
// int objects for the target value and the return index
int target, index;
```

We first sort the 10-element integer array by using selectionSort() and then call bin-Search() to locate a user-supplied target value. The output gives the return index from the search and a message indicating whether the item is found.

```
// sort the array prior to using binary search
selectionSort(arr,10);

cout <<"Enter an integer target: ";
cin >> target;

// call binSearch() to look for target
index = binSearch(arr,0,10,target);
if (index != 10)
    cout << target << " is in the list at index "
         << index << endl;
else
    cout << target << " is not in the list" << endl;
```

```
Input 1:

Enter an integer target: 33
33 is in the list at index 9

Input 2:

Enter an integer target: 6
6 is not in the list
```

ANALYSIS OF ALGORITHMS   3-3

A programmer judges the code that executes an algorithm by its correctness, its ease of use, and its efficiency—in simple terms, does it work, is it friendly, is it fast. The design and testing of the code are the key factors that contribute to its correctness and ease of use. The question of efficiency is more difficult to pin down, because the algorithm can be judged by different performance criteria. In this section, we describe system criteria, memory utilization criteria, and the internal complexity of the algorithm as three different ways to judge performance. The first two criteria depend on external resources and are more properly covered in a course on operating systems. We focus on complexity criteria that depend on the design of the algorithm. We are particularly interested in algorithms that apply to container objects for which the underlying storage structure might hold a large collection of data. For these algorithms, we develop measures of efficiency that depend on n, the number of data items in the container.

System/Memory Performance Criteria

An algorithm ultimately runs on a computer system with a specific instruction set and peripheral devices. If the algorithm is designed to target a particular machine, a programmer can code the function to take full advantage of the system resources. The resulting function will outperform a different implementation that assumes a generic machine. We say that the first algorithm has greater *system efficiency*. This is a relative measure that applies to two or more algorithms that carry out the same task. By running the algorithms on the same machine with the same data sets, we can determine the relative times by using a system-timing mechanism. The ranking of the times becomes the measure of system efficiency for each of the algorithms. For instance, to refresh a window, one algorithm might more effectively use the cache and operations of the video card and thus be more efficient on the particular system.

Algorithms use memory to store and process data. When comparing two algorithms, we might note that one requires a large temporary storage that limits the size of the initial data set or forces the system to use time-consuming disk swapping. The second algorithm might be less system efficient, but require less memory for its execution. On a system with limited memory, the first algorithm might not execute at all or might be very inefficient, while the second algorithm runs adequately within the memory constraints. *Space efficiency* is a measure of the relative amount of internal memory used by an algorithm. Depending on the memory resources of the system, the space efficiency of an algorithm dictates what kind of computer is capable of running the function and its impact on overall system efficiency. The issue of space efficiency is becoming less important on modern computers, because of the rapid increase in the size of available memory.

Algorithm Performance Criteria: Running-Time Analysis

For the study of data structures, we want performance criteria for algorithms that are based on their efficiency in accessing large collections of data. Traditionally, computer scientists use criteria that measure the amount of computation involved in executing the algorithm. The criteria often include the number of comparison tests and the number of assignment statements used by the algorithm. These types of measures are independent of any particular computer system and depend solely on the design and implementation of the algorithm. The criteria describe the *computational complexity* of an algorithm. When applied to a data structure, computational complexity measures the computational efficiency of the algorithm relative to n, the number of data items. The computational complexity of an algorithm indicates how fast it performs, so the term *running time* is often used instead, and we will adopt that term in this book.

To analyze the running time of a data structures algorithm, we need to identifying the key operations of the algorithm and determine how frequently they execute relative to the size of the data set. As a by-product of the analysis, we define a function $T(n)$ that counts the frequency of the key operations in terms of n. In the next section, we will use $T(n)$ to create a *Big-O*($O(n)$) measure of the algorithm. Let us see how we can carry out this analysis for a variety of algorithms that include the finding of the minimum element in an array, the selection sort, and the sequential search.

Running Time: min() Function. Locating the minimum element in an array is a simple algorithm whose primary operation involves comparing data items. For an array with n elements, the algorithm takes the first element as the implied minimum and performs $n - 1$ comparisons with the other elements in the array. The function $T()$ is a count of the number of comparisons:

$$T(n) = n - 1$$

Running Time: Selection Sort. Trying to find a function $T()$ that measures the running time of the selection sort is more involved, because the algorithm requires a series of passes, with comparisons performed on each pass. If arr is an array with n elements, the selection sort executes $n - 1$ passes. Each pass locates the minimum value in the unsorted sublist $[pass, n)$. The following is a description of the algorithm with a count of the number of comparisons on each pass. After each pass, the sorted elements are designated with an x.

Pass 0:   Within the range 0 to $n - 1$, find the index of the smallest element in the list. If smallIndex $\neq$ 0, exchange arr[smallIndex] with arr[0]. The number of comparisons $= n - 1$.

Pass 1:   Within the range 1 to $n - 1$, find the index of the smallest element in the list. If smallIndex $\neq$ 1, exchange arr[smallIndex] with arr[1]. The number of comparisons $= n - 2$.

Pass 2:   Within the range 2 to $n - 1$, find the index of the smallest element in the list. If smallIndex $\neq$ 2, exchange arr[smallIndex] with arr[2]. The number of comparisons $= n - 3$.

Pass $n - 2$:   Within the range $n - 2$ to $n - 1$, find the index of the smallest element in the list. If smallIndex $\neq n - 2$, exchange arr[smallIndex] with arr[$n - 2$]. The number of comparisons is 1.

	0	1	2	3	4		n-2	n-1	
Pass n-2 arr	x	x	x	x	x	...	x	x	1 comparison

The total number of comparisons in the selection sort is the sum of the comparisons for passes from 0 to $n - 2$. We record this sum as the value for the function $T(n)$:

$$T(n) = (n - 1) + (n - 2) + \cdots + 3 + 2 + 1$$

From mathematics, we recognize $T(n)$ as the arithmetic series of the terms from 1 to $n - 1$, which can be evaluated in terms of n:

$$T(n) = \left(\frac{n(n - 1)}{2} \right) = \left(\frac{n^2}{2} - \frac{n}{2} \right)$$

Running Time: Sequential Search: The analysis of the sequential search requires some statistical reasoning. Assume that the search looks for a match within a sublist containing n elements. If the target happens to be the first element in the sublist, the search requires one comparison. At the other extreme, the target might be the last element of the sublist or might not be present in the sublist. In this case, the algorithm requires n comparisons. In general, we cannot predetermine the exact number of comparisons, because a match can occur anywhere in the list or not at all. However, we can use statistical reasoning to determine an expected (average) number of comparisons if the search were repeated for a large number of targets. Some matches will occur quickly near the front of the sublist, but others will require an exhaustive scan through the entire sublist, so the expected number of comparisons is $n/2$. We use this average number of comparisons as the value for function $T(n)$:

$$T(n) = n/2 \qquad // \text{ expected number of comparisons}$$

Running Time: Best—Worst—Average Case. The efficiency of some algorithms depends on the initial ordering of the data. This gives rise to the notion of "best case," "worst case," and "average case" performance of the algorithm. For instance, the sequential search exhibits all three cases. The best case occurs when the target is the first element of the sublist. In this situation, the search requires only one comparison, and thus

$$T(n) = 1$$

The average case assumes that the sublist contains a random set of data values. We looked at the average case in the previous discussion. The running time for this case is the expected number of comparisons under the assumption that the search is repeated for a large number of targets:

$$T(n) = n/2$$

The worst case occurs when the algorithm either locates the target as the last element of the sublist or finds no match. In this case,

$$T(n) = n$$

The notion of best, average, and worst case can apply even to an algorithm in which the value $T(n)$ is the same for each case. Consider the selection sort. The algorithm always requires $n(n - 1)/2$ comparisons for the $n - 1$ passes. However, the initial ordering of the data can affect the algorithm in terms of the number of exchanges. For a list that has already been ordered, each successive pass does not require an exchange, because the smallest element in the tail sublist is already in the correct position. This is the best-case condition and represents the most efficient running of the algorithm. For a list that is sorted in descending order, each pass requires an exchange. This is the worst-case condition for the sorting algorithm. The average case has data randomly distributed in the list, and the algorithm requires number of exchanges between the numbers required for the best and worst cases. The value of $T(n)$ is the most important measure of running time. Nevertheless, the analysis of an algorithm should take into account special ordering of the data and distinguish a *best-case*, *worst-case*, and *average-case* performance for the algorithm.

Example 3-5

1. We have seen that the problem of finding the minimum value in an unordered array requires n $-$ 1 comparisons. There is no distinct best, average, or worst case. All three cases have running time

$$T(n) = n - 1$$

2. The analysis of the minimum-value problem is quite different if we know the list is ordered. For a list in ascending order, the minimum value occupies the first position (arr[0]). For a list in descending order, the minimum value is at the rear (arr[$n - 1$]). The running time for finding the minimum value involves a single data access independent of the number of elements in the array. The function $T()$ for the best, average, and worst cases is the constant function 1:

$$T(n) = 1$$

Big-O Notation

In analyzing the running time of an algorithm, we identify the activity that most affects overall performance. For instance, performing comparisons is the primary activity in searching and sorting algorithms, as well as in locating the minimum value in an array. As a measure of running time, a function $T(n)$ evaluates the number of times the algorithm performs the primary activity. In the previous section, we determined a value of $T(n)$ for the minimum-value problem for sorted and unsorted arrays, the selection sort, and the sequential search.

Algorithm	Function $T(n)$
Minimum value in the array (random list)	$T(n) = n - 1$
Minimum value in the array (ordered list)	$T(n) = 1$
Sequential search	$T(n) = n/2$
Selection sort	$T(n) = n^2/2 - n/2$

$T(n)$ is a function that depends on the size of the list. Its impact as a measure of the algorithm performance takes on more meaning as n becomes larger. To get an approximate measure of $T(n)$ for larger and larger n, we identify the term that has the greatest impact on its value—the term that "dominates" the expression. For instance, to find the minimum value in an unordered array, $T(n) = n - 1$:

$$n = 100: \qquad T(100) = 100 - 1 \;\; = 99$$
$$n = 500: \qquad T(500) = 500 - 1 \;\; = 499$$
$$n = 2000: \quad\;\; T(2000) = 2000 - 1 = 1999$$

As the example illustrates, n is clearly the dominant term. To get an approximate measure of $T(n)$, we define an expression that involves the dominant term. The expression is called the "Big-O" measure for the algorithm. In the case of the minimum value, the expression is $O(n)$, which is read as "Big-O" of n. For the selection sort, the number of comparisons is $T(n) = n^2/2 - n/2$. Again, let us look at a few values of n:

$n = 100: \qquad T(100) = 100^2/2 - 100/2 = 10000/2 - 100/2 = 5000 - 50 = 4,950$

$n = 1,000: \quad\; T(1000) = 1000^2/2 - 1000/2$
$$= 1000000/2 - 1000/2 = 500,000 - 500 = 499,500$$

$n = 10,000:\; T(10000) = 10000^2/2 - 10000/2 = 100000000/2 - 10000/2$
$$= 50,000,000 - 5000 = 49,995,000$$

The dominant term is $n^2/2$. After discarding the constant coefficient, we say that the Big-O measure for the selection sort is $O(n^2)$ and that the selection sort has running time $O(n^2)$.

Example 3-6

---

1. The function $T(n) = n/2$ computes the expected number of comparisons required by the sequential search to locate the target. The dominant term is n, and $O(n)$ is the measure of efficiency for the algorithm.

2. Finding the minimum value in an ordered array requires only one comparison. $T(n)$ has the constant value 1, independent of n and $O(1)$ is the measure of efficiency of the algorithm.

3. Assume that analysis of an algorithm results in the following values for $T(n)$:

    (a) $T(n) = 6n^3 + 2n^2 - 7n + 8$

    The dominant term is $6n^3$. After discarding $2n^2 - 7n + 8$ and the coefficient 6, we say that the algorithm has running time $O(n^3)$.

    (b) $T(n) = \sqrt{n + 1} + n + 5$

    The term n is dominant, and the running time of the algorithm is $O(n)$.

    (c) $T(n) = n^{\frac{3}{2}} + n + 5$

    The term $n^{\frac{3}{2}}$ is dominant, and the running time of the algorithm is $O(n^{\frac{3}{2}})$.

Our notion here of Big-O is entirely intuitive. A course in the theory of algorithms develops a mathematical definition of Big-O notation, along with other measures that refine the notion of running time for an algorithm.

An algorithm could have different running times for the best, worst, and average cases, so we compute a specific Big-O estimate for each case. The best case for an algorithm is often not important, because the circumstances are exceptional and thus not a useful criterion when choosing an algorithm. The worst case can be important, despite its exceptionality. Its efficiency could be so poor that an application could not tolerate the performance. In some cases, a designer might prefer an algorithm with better worst-case behavior even though the average performance is not as good.

Common Orders of Magnitude

In the previous section, we identified algorithms whose Big-O estimates are $O(n)$, $O(n^2)$, and $O(1)$. You might be apprehensive, thinking that algorithms can exhibit hundreds of these Big-O measures of running time. In reality, a small set of measures defines the running time of most algorithms. The following are categories for the different measures, along with sample algorithms.

Constant Time. An algorithm has efficiency $O(1)$ when its running time is independent of the number of data items. The algorithm runs in *constant time*. For instance, the algorithm for finding the minimum value in an ordered array has efficiency $O(1)$. No matter what the size of the array, just access the value of the first element. Another example involves assigning an element at the rear of an array list, provided that you maintain an index that identifies this location. The storing of the element involves a simple assignment statement and thus has efficiency $O(1)$.

Direct Insert at Rear

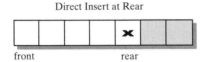

front   rear

Linear. An algorithm has efficiency $O(n)$ when its running time is proportional to the size of the list. Such an algorithm is said to be *linear*. When the number of elements doubles, the number of operations doubles. For instance, finding the minimum value in an n-element unordered list is $O(n)$. The output of elements in an n-element array is also an example of a linear algorithm.

Quadratic and Cubic. Algorithms whose running time is $O(n^2)$ are *quadratic*. Most simple sorting algorithms, such as the selection sort, are $O(n^2)$. Quadratic algorithms are practical only for relatively small values of n. Whenever n doubles, the running time of the algorithm increases by a factor of 4. An algorithm exhibits *cubic* time if its running time is $O(n^3)$. The efficiency of such algorithms is generally poor, because doubling the size of n causes the running time of the algorithm to increase eightfold. Matrix multiplication involves computing n^3 products and thus is an $O(n^3)$ algorithm.

Logarithmic. Recall that the logarithm of n, base 10, is the exponent for which $10^{exp} = n$. For instance, $\log_{10}(10) = \log_{10}(10^1) = 1$, and $\log_{10}(100) = \log_{10}(10^2) = 2$. Normally, the logarithm is a real number. For instance, $\log_{10}(125) = 2.0969....$ The logarithm of n, base 2, is more commonly used when analyzing computer algorithms. Just use 2 as the base instead of 10. In this case, $\log_2(2) = 1$, $\log_2(32) = \log_2(2^5) = 5$, $\log_2(75) = 6.2288...$, and so forth. When compared with the functions n and n^2, the function $\log_2 n$ grows very slowly, as depicted in Figure 3-3.

Some algorithms have running times $O(\log_2 n)$ and $O(n \log_2 n)$. They are termed *logarithmic*. These running times occur when the algorithm repeatedly subdivides the data into sublists whose size are 1/2, 1/4, 1/8,..., of the original list size. The binary search has average and worst case running time of $O(\log_2 n)$. For instance, when $n = 1024$, $\log_2 n = 10$, and when $n = 1,000,000$, $\log_2 n = 19.9315...$ This type of algorithm running time is good indeed! The famous quicksort has running time $O(n \log_2 n)$, which is far better than the $O(n^2)$ running time of the selection sort. For instance, if $n = 1000$, $n^2 = 1,000,000$, and $n \log_2 n = 9965.78...$ In choosing a sort algorithm for an array with 1000 elements, we can determine that the quicksort is approximately 100 times more efficient than the selection sort.

Exponential. Some algorithms deal with problems that involve searching through a large number of potential solutions before finding a answer. Such algorithms often have running time $O(a^n)$, $a > 1$. This is termed *exponential running time*. In Section 3-7, we will see that the recursive solution to the problem of generating Fibonacci numbers has an exponential running time. Exponential algorithms are useful only for very small values of n.

The *traveling-salesperson problem* provides an excellent example of exponential running time. The problem statement is as follows:

A salesperson is planning a trip that will visit n cities. A road connects each city to some of the other cities. To minimize travel time, the salesperson wants to determine a shortest route that starts at the salesperson's home city, visits each of the cities exactly once, and concludes at the home city.

All known solutions involve checking the length of a very large number of possible routes. All these algorithms have running time at least $O(2^n)$. Running them with $n = 1000$ on a present-day computer is unthinkable.

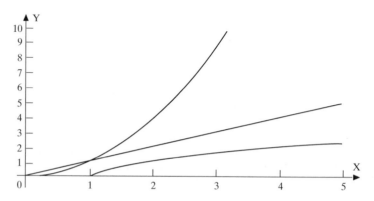

Figure 3-3
Growth of various functions

TABLE 3-1   VARIOUS ORDERS OF MAGNITUDE

n	$\log_2 n$	$n \log_2 n$	n^2	n^3	2^n
2	1	2	4	8	4
4	2	8	16	64	16
8	3	24	64	512	256
16	4	64	256	4096	65,536
32	5	160	1024	32,768	4,294,967,296
128	7	896	16,384	2,097,152	3.4×10^{38}
1024	10	10,240	1,048,576	1,073,741,824	1.8×10^{308}
65,536	16	1,048,576	4,294,967,296	2.8×10^{14}	Forget it!

Memorize! order

Table 3-1 gives the linear, quadratic, cubic, exponential, and logarithmic orders of magnitude for selected values of n. Clearly, you should avoid cubic and exponential algorithms unless n is small.

ANALYZING THE SEARCH ALGORITHMS   3-4

In this section, we run a simulation that allows us to compare experimentally the efficiencies of the sequential and binary-search algorithms. We provide you a timer class to evaluate total time required to perform 50,000 searches on an array of 100,000 integers. The simulation gives empirical data that allow us to verify the relative running time of the two search algorithms.

Before developing the simulation, let us analyze the running time of the binary search and obtain a Big-O measure of efficiency.

Binary-Search Running Time

The binary search is an algorithm that applies to ordered lists. Because the algorithm discards one half of the elements on each iteration, its running time is significantly better than that of the sequential search. The best-case outcome occurs when we find the match at the midpoint of the list. This requires only one iteration and a single equality comparison. The running time is $O(1)$. The running time for the worst case is $O(\log_2 n)$, which occurs when the item is not in the list. Some intuitive analysis explains this fact. When an iteration fails to find a match, the length of the sublist is reduced by a factor of 2. The sizes of the sublists are successively

$$\frac{n}{1} \frac{n}{2} \frac{n}{4} \frac{n}{8} \ldots 1 \quad \text{or} \quad \frac{n}{2^0} \frac{n}{2^1} \frac{n}{2^2} \frac{n}{2^3} \cdots \frac{n}{2^m} = 1$$

The worst case occurs when the iterative process shrinks the size of the sublist down to a length of 1 without finding a match. The splitting of sublists requires m iterations. If $n = 1024$, then $m = 10$, because $2^{10} = 1024$. In general, m is $\log_2 n$ truncated to an integer value, which, using C++ notation, is int($\log_2 n$). For instance, assume that $n = 87$. The following calculations show that $m = $ int($\log_2 87$) = 6:

$$n = 87, \quad \frac{1}{2} n = 43, \quad \frac{1}{2^2} n = 21, \quad \frac{1}{2^3} n = 10, \quad \frac{1}{2^5} n = 5, \quad \frac{1}{2^5} n = 2, \quad \frac{1}{2^6} n = 1$$

The initial iteration compares the target with the midpoint of the list. The algorithm follows this iteration by a series of $int(\log_2 n)$ iterations. Because each iteration requires two comparison operations ($==$ and $>$), the total number of comparisons is $2(\ 1\ +\ int(\log_2 n)\ )$. As a result, the worst-case condition for the binary search has Big-O measure $O(\log_2 n)$. It can be shown that the average-case running time is also $O(\log_2 n)$.

Example 3-7

This example computes the running time for both the sequential-search and binary-search algorithms, assuming the array contains 100,000 elements.

1. With the sequential search, the best case requires one comparison, and the worst case requires 100,000 comparisons. For the average case, the expected number of comparisons is 50,000.
2. If the array is sorted, the best case for the binary search requires one comparison. The maximum number of comparisons is $2(\ 1\ +\ int(\log_2 100{,}000)\ ) = 2(1 + 16) = 34$.

Comparing Search Algorithms

For large ordered arrays, the binary search is evidently more efficient than the sequential search. After all, the binary search eliminates one half of the data items on each iteration, whereas the sequential search methodically moves through the list element by element. The analysis in Example 3-7 provides expected results for the sequential search and worst-case results for the binary search when the array has 100,000 elements.

We can verify these results empirically by designing a program that executes a large number of searches on a common data set. The program must compare the computation time required by the two search algorithms. For a test, use a random-number generator to initialize two identical 100,000 element integer arrays, list1 and list2, with random numbers in the range from 0 to 999,999. The binary search requires a sorted array, so the selection sort orders list2. To compare the two search algorithms, create a third array, called targetList, which consists of 50,000 random numbers in the range from 0 to 999,999. Evaluate the efficiency of the searches empirically by executing two loops that take each element in targetList as a target value. The first loop uses the sequential search with list1, and the second loop uses the binary search with list2.

For timing algorithm execution, we provide a timer class that has operations start() and stop() that capture the time on the system clock at the start of a code sequence and then again at the completion of the sequence. The function time() returns the length of time in seconds required to execute the code sequence. The following is the API for the timer class:

CLASS timer	**Constructor**	**"d_timer.h"**

timer();
   Initializes the timer.

Postconditions:　Set the starting and ending event times to 0. This creates an
event whose time is 0.0.

| **CLASS timer** | **Operations** | **"d_timer.h"** |

void **start**();
　　Start timing an event.
　　Postcondition:　Record the current time as the starting time.

void **stop**();
　　Stop timing an event.
　　Postcondition: Record the current time as the ending time.

double **time**() const;
　　Return the time the event took in seconds by computing the difference be-
　　tween the ending and starting times.

To time the execution of a code sequence, create a timer object. Enclose the
sequence in calls to the functions start() and stop(), respectively. The member function time() returns the execution time of the sequence in seconds.

```
timer t;                        // declare a timer
double timeRequired;

t.start();                      // call start() before execution
t.stop();                       // call stop() when sequence finishes
timeRequired = t.time();        // return the execution time
```

PROGRAM 3-1　　SEARCH-ALGORITHM EFFICIENCY

The upcoming program declares integer arrays list1 and list2 of size ARRAY_SIZE =
100,000. The same random integers in the range from 0 to 999,999 initialize both list1 and
list2. Assign the array targetList, having TARGET_SIZE = 50,000 elements, another random
sequence from the same range. As a condition for the binary search, apply the selection sort
to list2, and use timer object *t* to compute the time required. Use the elements in array targetList as target values for the sequential search and for the binary search. Compute the execution time of each algorithm by using object t. By displaying the execution time for each
search, we demonstrate the relative efficiency of the algorithms.

```
// File: prg3_1.cpp
// the program compares the efficiency of the sequential
// and binary search by timing algorithm execution using the
// timer class. two integer arrays list1 and list2
// of size ARRAY_SIZE are initialized with the same random
// integers in the range 0 to 999,999. initialize the array
// targetList having TARGET_SIZE elements to contain other
```

```
// random numbers in the same range. time the selection sort
// as it sorts list2 and output the result. using the
// elements in array targetList as target values for the
// sequential and binary searches, time each algorithm and
// output the results

#include <iostream>

#include "d_search.h"     // sequential and binary searches
#include "d_sort.h"       // selection sort

#include "d_random.h"     // random number generation
#include "d_timer.h"      // time events

using namespace std;

int main()
{   const int ARRAY_SIZE = 100000, TARGET_SIZE = 50000;

    // arrays for the search
    int list1[ARRAY_SIZE], list2[ARRAY_SIZE], targetList[TARGET_SIZE];
    int i;

    // t used for timing the search algorithms
    timer t;
    // random number object
    randomNumber rnd;

    // initialize the arrays with random numbers in the
    // range 0 to 999,999
    for (i = 0; i < ARRAY_SIZE; i++)
     list1[i] = list2[i] = rnd.random(1000000);

    // initialize targetList with random numbers in the
    // same range 0 to 999,999
    for (i=0;i < TARGET_SIZE; i++)
       targetList[i] = rnd.random(1000000);

    // sort list2
    cout << "Timing the Selection Sort" << endl;
    t.start();       // start timer
    selectionSort(list2,ARRAY_SIZE);
    t.stop();        // stop timer
    cout << "Selection Sort takes " << t.time()
         << " seconds." << endl;

    cout << endl << "Timing the Sequential Search" << endl;
    t.start();       // start timer
    // perform sequential search with elements from list2
    for (i = 0; i < TARGET_SIZE; ++)
       seqSearch(list1,0,ARRAY_SIZE,targetList[i]);
```

```
    t.stop();       // stop timer
    cout << "Sequential Search takes " << t.time()
         << " seconds." << endl;

    cout << endl << "Timing the Binary Search" << endl;
    t.start();       // start timer
    // perform binary search with elements from list2
    for (i = 0; i < TARGET_SIZE; i++)
        binSearch(list2,0,ARRAY_SIZE,targetList[i]);
    t.stop();        // stop timer
    cout << "Binary Search takes " << t.time()
         << " seconds." << endl;

    return 0;
}
```

```
Run:

Timing the Selection Sort
Selection Sort takes 126.912 seconds.

Timing the Sequential Search
Sequential Search takes 132.889 seconds.

Timing the Binary Search
Binary Search takes 0.08 seconds.
```

Evaluating the Search Comparison Simulation. Note how much faster the binary search performs, once the program sorts the array. The sort took 126.912 seconds, so the time needed by the binary search is 126.992 seconds, as compared with 132.889 seconds for the sequential search. Even with time to sort the list, it is advantageous in this situation to use the binary search. The results are even more dramatic if the program uses an $O(n \log_2 n)$ sorting algorithm.

Example 3-7 shows that the expected number of comparisons for the sequential and binary searches of an ordered array with 100,000 elements are 50,000 and 34, respectively. The ratio of these values is 50,000/34 = 1470.6. The ratio of our empirical timing results is 132.889/0.08 = 1661.1, which is quite close to the theoretical result.

MAKING ALGORITHMS GENERIC   3-5

In Section 3-1, we introduced the selection sort to order items in an integer list. The fact that integers are used is not essential to the structure of the algorithm, because it relies only on a definition of the operator < to compare items and the ability to exchange their position in the list. With essentially the same set of instructions, we could have implemented the selection sort to order arrays of real numbers, strings, and so forth. Unfortunately, with our current understanding of C++, we could not use the integer version of selectionSort() for lists with different types. We would have to declare and implement separate versions of the function to accommodate the different types, even though the same algorithm would apply. One version of the function would sort integers, another version real numbers, yet another version strings, and so forth. To illustrate how redundant this task would be, consider the listing of the int and string versions of the selection sort functions. Note that the algorithms are identical; only the types of the objects are different.

Integer Version of the Selection Sort

```
void selectionSort(int arr[], int n)
{
    . . .
    int temp;        // int temp used for the exchange

    for (pass = 0; pass < n-1; pass++)
    {
        . . .
        if (arr[j] < arr[smallIndex])      // compare integers
            . . .
    }
}
```

String Version of the Selection Sort

```
void selectionSort(string arr[], int n)
{
    . . .
    string temp;     // string temp used for the exchange
    for (pass = 0; pass < n - 1; pass++)
    {
        . . .
        if (arr[j] < arr[smallIndex])         // compare strings
            . . .
    }
}
```

The C++ language recognizes the problem of expecting a programmer to create multiple versions of the same function. In response, the language allows a programmer to write one version of the function, called a *template function*, using a generic type, and then leaves the task of creating separate versions to the compiler. To understand this feature, we need to develop syntax to declare, implement, and use template functions.

Template Syntax

The prototype and implementation of a template function begins with a *template argument list*. Its syntax includes the keyword *template*, followed by a nonempty list of formal types enclosed in angle brackets. In the argument list, each type is preceded by the keyword *typename*, and types are separated by commas.

```
// argument list with a single template type
template <typename T>

// argument list with multiple template types
template <typename T, typename U, typename V, ...>
```

Although it is not required, C++ programmers typically use the letter *T* to represent the type in the template argument list. When a program uses a template function, the compiler will associate with *T* an actual C++ type, such as int or char, or with a programmer-defined class type and will create a version of the function with *T* replaced by the specific C++ type. Most applications of templates have an argument list with a single type *T*. In later chapters, we will introduce the use of multiple-template types.

Except for the initial template argument list, the declaration and implementation of a template function follow the standard rules of function coding. A programmer can use the template type for function arguments, for the return type, and for the declaration of local objects within the body. At the same time, there are two important restrictions. First, at least one argument in the function argument list must have template type *T*. Second, C++ statements within the function body can use objects of type *T* but only with operations that are valid for the actual type corresponding to *T*. For instance, a program could not use a template function that includes the $<$ operator for rectangles, because the class does not define the operation. Of course, a program could include an overloaded version of the operator and then use rectangle objects. Operator overloading is a powerful feature in C++ that extends the flexibility and usefulness of template functions.

```
template <typename T>
returnType funcName (T arg, . . . .)
{
    // C++ statements may use type T but only with
    // operations that are valid for T
}
```

We are familiar with the code for the integer version of selectionSort(). A template version of the function would handle different array data types. Begin with a template argument list having a single type *T* representing the data type of the array. The function prototype and body replaces the specific int type with the generic type *T*.

```
template <typename T>
void selectionSort(T arr[], int n)
{
    int smallIndex; // index of smallest element in the sublist
    int pass, j;
    T temp;

    // pass has the range 0 to n-2
    for (pass = 0; pass < n-1; pass++)
    {
```

```
        // scan the sublist starting at index pass
        smallIndex = pass;

        // j traverses the sublist a[pass+1] to a[n-1]
        for (j = pass+1; j < n; j++)
        // update if smaller element found
        if (arr[j] < arr[smallIndex])
            smallIndex = j;

        // if smallIndex and pass are not the same location,
        // exchange the smallest item in the sublist with arr[pass]
        if (smallIndex != pass)
        {
            temp = arr[pass];
            arr[pass] = arr[smallIndex];
            arr[smallIndex] = temp;
        }
    }
}
```

Example 3-8

---

1. The template function max() returns the larger of two data items. In its implementation, the function uses type *T* for the return value and the arguments.

```
template <typename T>
T max (const T& a, const T& b)
{   return a < b ? b : a;   }          // return larger of a and b
```

2. The template function writeArray() outputs the elements in array arr, whose size is *n*. The function implementation resides in the header file "d_util.h".

```
// function to output an n element array of type T
template <typename T>
void writeArray(const T arr[], int n)
{
    int i;

    for(i=0;i < n;i++)
        cout << arr[i] << "   ";
    cout << endl;
}
```

Runtime Template Expansion

When a compiler recognizes that a statement calls a template function, it identifies the type of the calling arguments and creates an instance of the function code with the specific type. For instance, the upcoming statements call selectionSort() for integer, double, and string arrays. The compiler recognizes that the array type for the first call is int and thus creates the instance of selectionSort() corresponding to the integer version of the function. To handle the second and third calls, the compiler creates versions of the sort function using types double and string. The resulting compiled code has multiple versions of the sort function. In the upcoming code, we list the resulting ordered arrays, using the template function writeArray(). The compiler creates three versions of writeArray(), corresponding to the data types int, double, and string.

```
intList[8] = {2, 9, 14, 7, 3, 1, 8, 12};
double realList[5] = {2.9, 7.3, 23.5, 30.8, 5.6};
string words[6] = {"john","rebecca","sara","jack","bob","joe"};

// sort the arrays having element of different types
selectionSort(intList, 8);      // use int version
selectionSort(realList, 5);     // use double version
selectionSort(words, 6);        // use string version

// output the ordered arrays
writeArray(intList, 8);
writeArray(realList, 5);
writeArray(words, 6);
```

```
Output:

1  2  3  7  8  9  12  14
2.9  5.6  7.3  23.5  30.8
bob  jack  joe  john  rebecca  sara
```

Example 3-9

A program can use the function max() of Example 3-8, with any data type that defines the < operator. For instance, data types int, string, and time24 support the operator:

```
// runtime arguments have type int; compiler uses T = int
cout << max(4,5);                 // output: 5

// with string arguments, compiler uses T = string
string s = "template", t = "function";
cout << max(s,t);                 // output: template

// with time24 arguments, compiler uses T = time24
time24 tA(9,30), tB(7,15);
cout << max(tA,tB);               // output: 9:30
```

The template function max() could not be used with rectangle objects, because the class does not provide the < operator. The statement a < b is not valid for rectangle objects:

```
Rectangle r(4,5), s(9,2), t;
t = max(r,s);                     // invalid! < is not defined
```

Suppose the programmer first overloads the < operator for rectangles by using some criteri-on, such as comparing the area of the objects. A call to max() is then valid:

```
// t = r, since r.area() = 20 and s.area() = 18
t = max(r,s);
```

When the compiler processes a call to a template function, it must be able to deter-mine the type *T* in an unambiguous fashion. If it determines that *T* can be of two or more possible types, the compiler outputs an error message. For instance, suppose *f*() is the tem-plate function

```
template <typename T>
T f(T x, T y)
{
    return x + y;
}
```

and that we have the following variable declarations:

```
int x = 3, y = 5;
long z = 124567, w = 127468;
```

The statement

```
cout << f(x,y) << "  " << f(z,w) << endl;
```

will compile, because it is clear to the compiler that the first call to f() uses *T* = int and the second call uses *T* = long. However, the statement

```
cout << f(x, z) << endl;
```

will generate an error message, because the compiler cannot unambiguously determine whether *T* is of type long or of type int. Our compiler produces the following message:

```
error C2782: 'T f(T,T)' : template parameter 'T' is ambiguous
            could be 'long'
            or 'int'
```

Template-Based Searching Functions

The sequential search is a general searching algorithm that uses the == operator to identify a match. We provided an integer version of seqSearch() in Section 3-2. Using the template mechanics of adding a template argument list and replacing type int by the generic type *T* for the array and the target, we can produce a template ver-sion of the function. A program can call the template version for any array whose type supports the == operator.

```
template <typename T>
int seqSearch( const T arr[], int first, int last, const T& target)
{
    int i = first;
```

```
// scan indices in the range first < i < last; test for a match
// or index out of range.
while(i != last && arr[i] != target)
    i++;

return i;      // i is index of match or i = last if no match
}
```

The binary search applies to any type that defines the comparison operators == and <. The following is an implementation of a template version of binSearch():

```
template <typename T>
int binSearch( const T arr[], int first, int last, const T& target)
{
    int mid;                   // index of the midpoint
    T midvalue;                // object that is assigned arr[mid]
    int origLast = last;       // save original value of last

    while (first < last)       // test for nonempty sublist
    {
        mid = (first+last)/2;
        midvalue = arr[mid];
        if (target == midvalue)
            return mid;        // have a match
        // determine which sublist to search
        else if (target < midvalue)
            last = mid;        // search lower sublist. reset last
        else
            first = mid+1;     // search upper sublist. reset first
    }

    return origLast;           // target not found
}
```

You can find the template versions for both seqSearch() and binSearch() in the file "d_search.h".

Example 3-10

This example uses template versions of the sequential search and the binary search to find string objects in a list, because the string class provides a definition for the == and < operators. Before executing the binary search, order the array by calling selectionSort(). Assume stateList is a list of names for the 50 U.S. states.

```
string stateList [50];
string stateTarget = "West Virginia";
int index;

// value of index depends on the location of 'West Virginia'
index = seqSearch(stateList, 0, 50, stateTarget);
```

```
// order the array of states
selectionSort(stateList, 50);

// value of index is 49
index = binSearch(stateList,0,50, stateTarget);
```

3-6   THE CONCEPT OF RECURSION

To this point in the chapter, we have explored algorithms whose design uses repetitive processes. For instance, the selection sort uses iterative steps for both the passes and the location of the smallest element in the unsorted sublist at the tail of the array. The sequential search repeatedly scans the elements in an array, looking for a match with the target value. For each of these algorithms, we implement the corresponding functions by means of loops to carry out the repetition. In the next two sections, we introduce a new repetition strategy called _recursion_. Understanding this strategy requires a new way of viewing an algorithm. You will also discover how to create recursive functions whose implementation hides the repetition. We begin our study by exploring a variety of iterative processes that have alternative recursive definitions.

Consider the problem of evaluating the power x^n, where x is a real number and n is a nonnegative integer. An iterative view of the problem involves repeated multiplication by the term x:

```
xⁿ = x * x * . . . * x      // multiply x a total of n times
```

A programmer can take this iterative process and implement the function power() by using a loop that fills in the missing terms represented by the ellipses (...):

Iterative power():
```
double power (double x, int n)
{
    double product = 1;
    int i;

    for (i = 1; i <= n; i++)
       product *= x;

    return product;
}
```

We can view the problem in a different way. Consider the evaluation of 2^9. From your experience with computers, you may know that $2^8 = 256$. The solution for 2^9 is simply the next larger multiple of 2, whose value is 256×2:

$$2^9 = 2^8 * 2 = 256 * 2 = 512$$

If you know only that $2^5 = 32$, then the solution requires a little more work. Successive steps double the previous result until you stop at exponent 9:

$$2^6 = 2^5 * 2 = 64$$
$$2^7 = 2^6 * 2 = 128$$
$$2^8 = 2^7 * 2 = 256$$
$$2^9 = 2^8 * 2 = 512$$

After determining a starting point, each step uses a known power of 2 and doubles it to compute the next result. Using this process gives us a new definition for the power function, x^n. Because we want the definition to apply to all exponents $n \geq 0$, we choose $x^0 = 1$ as the starting point. We compute all successive powers of x by multiplying the previous value by x. The following is a definition of x^n for any $n \geq 0$. The form, called a recursive definition, distinguishes between the exponent $n = 0$ (starting point) and $n \geq 1$, which assumes that we already know the value x^{n-1}.

$$x^n = \begin{cases} 1.0, & n == 0 \\ x^{n-1}*x, & n \geq 1 \end{cases}$$

The term *recursion* applies when the algorithm solves a problem by partitioning it into subproblems that are solved by using the same algorithm. The problem of computing x^n for $n \geq 1$ first involves computing x^{n-1}. In the partitioning process, we determine the value of x^{n-1} by first computing x^{n-2}, and so forth.

In executing a recursive algorithm, the partitioning process cannot go on indefinitely. The process must terminate at one or more simple problems that can be directly solved. We refer to the simple problems as *stopping conditions*, because they can be solved without any further partitioning. When the partitioning process arrives at a stopping condition, a final solution of the problem can be obtained by revisiting the recursive steps in reverse order, using the result from the previous step. We use a recursive function to implement a recursive algorithm. The design of a recursive function consists of the following elements:

1. One or more *stopping conditions* that can be directly evaluated for certain arguments.
2. One or more *recursive steps*, in which a current value of the function can be computed by repeated calling of the function with arguments that will eventually arrive at a stopping condition.

The recursive definition of the power function has a single stopping condition, $n = 0$. In this case, the value of x^0 is 1. The recursive step is the definition of x^n for $n \geq 1$:

$$x^n = x^{n-1} * x, \, n \geq 1$$

The expression on the right-hand side uses an exponent decremented by 1. Repeated execution of the recursive step will eventually arrive at exponent 0, which is the stopping condition. To see the interaction between the recursive step and the stopping condition, consider the problem of evaluating 3^4. The calculation requires four recursive steps before arriving at the stopping condition:

Step 1: $3^4 = 3^3 * 3$
Step 2: $3^3 = 3^2 * 3$
Step 3: $3^2 = 3^1 * 3$
Step 4: $3^1 = 3^0 * 3$

The evaluation of 3^0 is the stopping condition with result 1. We obtain the solution to 3^4 by revisiting the steps in reverse order. At each step, the product $3 * 3^{(n-1)}$ is evaluated and the result made available at the next step.

Step 4: $3^1 = 3^0 * 3 = 1 * 3 = 3$
Step 3: $3^2 = 3^1 * 3 = 3 * 3 = 9$
Step 2: $3^3 = 3^2 * 3 = 9 * 3 = 27$
Step 1: $3^4 = 3^3 * 3 = 27 * 3 = 81$

Implementing Recursive Functions

The design of a recursive function must carefully distinguish between the stopping conditions and the recursive step. A programmer can implement the distinction with an if/else statement. The if portion () handles the stopping conditions, and the else portion handles the recursive step. In the case of the power function, the if portion evaluates the single stopping condition $n == 0$ and returns a result of 1.0. The else portion first calls power() with exponent $n-1$, to compute x^{n-1}, and then returns the result of the expression $x * x^{n-1}$.

Recursive power():
```
double power(double x, int n)        // n is a nonnegative integer
{
   if (n == 0)
       return 1.0;                   // stopping condition
   else
       return x * power(x,n - 1);    // recursive step
}
```

Example 3-11

---

1. The function $S(n)$ computes the sum of the first n positive integers:

$$S(n) = \sum_{1}^{n} i = 1 + 2 + \cdots + n$$

A recursive definition of the function evaluates $S(n)$ by first computing the sum of the first $n-1$ terms and then adding n. For instance, $S(4) = 1 + 2 + 3 + 4 = 10$. The sum of the first five terms is

$$S(5) = S(4) + 5 = 10 + 5 = 15$$

The stopping condition occurs at $S(1)$, which has one term that is the sum:

$$S(n) = \begin{cases} 1, & n = 1 \\ S(n-1) + n, & n > 1 \end{cases}$$

The function sumToN() is the C++ implementation of the mathematical function $S(n)$. The algorithm uses a simple if/else to distinguish the stopping condition and recursive step:

```
int sumToN(int n)
{
    if (n == 1)
        return 1;
    else
        return sumToN(n - 1) + n;
}
```

2. In a recursive function, the recursive step must ultimately give rise to a stopping condition, so that the process does not endlessly make recursive function calls. Consider the following recursive definition for $f()$:

$$f(n) = \begin{cases} 0, & n=0 \\ f(n/4 + 1) + n, & n \geq 1 \end{cases}$$

While the function looks harmless, it has problems. Watch what happens when we start with $f(5)$:

```
f(5) = f(5/4 + 1) + 5;
    // to evaluate f(5), make a recursive call to f(5/4 + 1) = f(2)
f(2) = f(2/4 + 1) + 2;
    // to evaluate f(2), make a recursive call to f(2/4 + 1) = f(1)
f(1) = f(1/4 + 1) + 1;
    // to evaluate f(1), make a recursive call to f(1/4 + 1) = f(1)
. . .
```

The function never reaches the stopping condition at $n = 0$, but rather executes an infinite series of recursive calls to $f(1)$.

How Recursion Works

A recursive algorithm is an alternative form of an iterative process. What makes recursive algorithms difficult to understand is the fact that the function implementation uses only a simple if/else statement that hides the underlying repetitive process. In this section, we introduce a recursive definition for factorials and trace the series of steps executed by the recursive function factorial().

The factorial of a nonnegative integer n has an iterative definition specifying the result as the product of all positive integers less than or equal to n. The mathematical notation $n!$ denotes factorial(n):

```
n! = n * (n–1) * (n–2) * ...* 2 * 1
```

For instance,

$$\text{factorial}(4) = 4! = 4*3*2*1 = 24$$
$$\text{factorial}(6) = 6! = 6*5*4*3*2*1 = 720$$
$$\text{factorial}(2) = 2! = 2*1 = 2$$
$$\text{factorial}(0) = 0! = 1 \qquad\qquad \text{// special definition}$$

Like the power function, there is a recursive definition for factorial(n). The value $n!$ is n times the product of the first $n - 1$ terms, which is $(n - 1)!$. For instance, with 4!, the first term is 4, and the remaining terms $(3 * 2 * 1)$ are 3!. A similar result is true for 6!, which is the product of 6 and 5!. The factorial is defined such that $n = 0$ has the value 1. This becomes the stopping condition in the recursive definition of factorial(n).

$$\text{factorial}(n) = \begin{cases} 1 & n = 0 \\ n * \text{factorial}(n - 1), & n \geq 1 \end{cases}$$

As a C++ function, factorial() takes an integer as an argument and uses an if/else statement to evaluate both the stopping condition and recursive step:

Recursive factorial():

```
int factorial(int n)                    // n is a non-negative integer
{
    if (n == 0)
        return 1;                       // stopping condition
    else
        return n * factorial(n - 1);    // recursive step
}
```

Executing the function factorial() sets in motion a whole series of function calls and calculations. To understand this underlying activity, we trace the execution of factorial(4). Think of factorial(n) as a machine (n-Fact) that computes $n!$ by carrying out the multiplication $n * (n-1)!$. In order to operate, it must be networked with a series of other n-Fact machines that pass information back and forth. The 0-Fact machine is the exception: It can work independently and produce the result 1 without assistance from another machine. The following is a description of the networking and interaction of machines, starting with 4-Fact, that computes 4! (Figure 3-4):

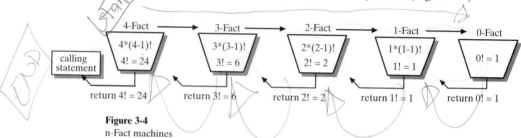

Figure 3-4
n-Fact machines

4-Fact starts up the 3-Fact machine and waits for it to return the value 3! before computing 4*3!

3-Fact starts up the 2-Fact machine and waits for it to return the value 2! before computing 3*2!

2-Fact starts up the 1-Fact machine and waits for it to return the value 1! before computing 2*1!

1-Fact starts up the 0-Fact machine and waits for it to return the value 0! before computing 1*0!

Once 0-Fact is activated, it immediately computes 0! = 1 and returns the value to the 1-Fact machine, which is then capable of completing the operation 1 * 0! = 1. The 2-Fact machine uses the return value of 1 from 1-Fact to complete the operation 2 * 1! = 2. In turn, 3-Fact uses the result 2 from 2-Fact to evaluate 3 * 2! = 3 * 2 = 6. Obtaining 6 as the return value from 3-Fact enables 4-Fact to compute the final result 4 * 3! = 24 and return this value to the calling statement.

The factorial machine is a useful tool for viewing the operation of a recursive function at the abstract level. In the actual implementation of recursion by a C++ function, the program pushes the function arguments and the return address of the function onto the runtime stack. The pushing and popping of this stack directs the execution of the function. Section 7-2 discusses this process.

Example 3-12

A loop inputs four integers and outputs their factorial value:

```
int i, n;

cout << "Enter 4 positive integers: ";
for (i = 0; i < 4; i++)
{
    cin >> n;
    cout << n << "! = " << factorial(n) << endl;
}
```

```
Run:

Enter 4 positive integers: 0 7 1 10
0! = 1
7! = 5040
1! = 1
10! = 3628800
```

Our experience with the execution of factorial(*n*) should alert you to the runtime demands and potential inefficiency of recursive functions. They often provide an elegant solution of a problem, but they may not be the method of choice, particularly if an equivalent iterative solution is available. This is the case with factorial(). An iterative form of the function simply performs the multiplications and is more efficient:

```
int factorial(int n)
{
    int fact = 1;

    while (n > 0)
    {
        fact = fact * n;
        n--;
    }

    return fact;
}
```

Section 3-7 discusses criteria a programmer can use to choose between a recursive and an iterative solution to a problem.

Application: Multibase Output

Output statements in most programming languages display numbers in decimal by default. It is sometimes useful to display numbers in other bases. For instance, the number $n = 70$ has the following representations in bases 2, 3, 5, and 8:

$$70 = 1000110_2 \qquad // \ 70 = 1(2^6) + 0(2^5) + 0(2^4) + 0(2^3) + 1(2^2) + 1(2^1) + 0$$
$$70 = 2121_3 \qquad\quad // \ 70 = 2(3^3) + 1(3^2) + 2(3^1) + 1$$
$$70 = 240_5 \qquad\quad\ // \ 70 = 2(5^2) + 4(5^1) + 0$$
$$70 = 106_8 \qquad\quad\ // \ 70 = 1(8^2) + 0(8^1) + 6$$

An integer n can be output in different bases by using repeated division. The process generates the digits for the number from right to left by using the % and / operators. The remainder is the next digit, and the quotient identifies the remaining digits. For instance, $n = 85$ is 125 base 8. The process identifies digits for the base-8 number in the order 5, 2, and 1:

```
85 % 8 = 5      // remaining digits: 85/8 = 10
10 % 8 = 2      // remaining digits: 10/8 = 1
 1 % 8 = 1      // remaining digits: 1/8  = 0 STOP!
```

For output, the digits appear in the opposite order of their discovery. The recursive function displayInBase() implements the algorithm by using repeated division. The recursive step first looks at the quotient (remaining digits) by calling displayIn-Base() with n/base as the argument and then outputs the remainder (next digit). The stopping condition occurs when the function passes the quotient 0 as the argument. This becomes the stopping condition. In this case, there are no remaining digits, and the algorithm can begin to output the digits in reverse order. Figure 3-5 illustrates the series of recursive steps used by displayInBase() to output $n = 85_{10}$ in base 8 (octal). Note that, because the recursive step first calls the function and then outputs the digit, the output begins with the leftmost digit and proceeds to the next digit on the right as the recursive calls are revisited in reverse order.

The function displayInBase() implements the algorithm for $2 \leq base \leq 10$:

```
// output n with base b
void displayInBase(int n, int base)
{
    // if n != 0, have another significant digit to display
    if (n > 0)
    {
        // output the digits in n/base
        displayInBase(n/base, base);

        // output the remainder
        cout << n % base;
    }
}
```

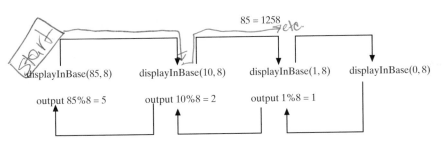

Figure 3-5
Function calls for displayInBase(85,8)

PROGRAM 3-2   DISPLAYING INTEGERS IN MULTIBASES

The upcoming program prompts the user to enter a nonnegative decimal number and a corresponding base in the range $2 \leq base \leq 10$. It calls the recursive function displayInBase() to output the number in the desired base.

```cpp
// File: prg3_2.cpp
// the program prompts the user to enter a non-negative
// decimal number and a corresponding base in the range
// 2 <= base <= 10, it calls the recursive function
// displayInBase() that outputs the number in the
// desired base

#include <iostream>
#include <string>

using namespace std;

// output n with base 2 <= b <= 10
void displayInBase(int n, int b);

int main()
{
    int number, base;

    // prompt for number and base
    cout << "Input number and base: ";
    cin >> number >> base;

    if (base >= 2 && base <= 10)
    {
        // output statement with function call
        cout << " " << number << " (base 10) = ";
        displayInBase(number,base);
        cout << " (base " << base << ")" << endl;
    }
    else
        cout << "The base must be in the range 2 << base << 10"
             << endl;
    return 0;
}
/* the function displayInBase() is implemented in the
   program discussion */
```

```
Run 1:

Input number and base:  85 8
     85 (base 10) = 125 (base 8)

Run 2:

Input number and base:  25 2
     25 (base 10) = 11001 (base 2)

Run 3:
```

```
Input number and base:  9 4
    9 (base 10) = 21 (base 4)
Run 4:

Input number and base:  1555 3
    1555 (base 10) = 2010121 (base 3)
```

PROBLEM SOLVING WITH RECURSION   3-7

Our introductory study of recursion has involved algorithms with alternative iterative solutions that are simple to code and more efficient to execute. The examples are a good illustration of the design and implementation of recursive functions. They do not, however, let you appreciate the true importance of recursion as an algorithm design strategy. One of the most powerful features of recursion is its ability to allow a programmer to solve problems that would be difficult to design and implement as an iterative process. In this section, we illustrate this feature with the famous *Tower of Hanoi* puzzle, which has an elegant solution as a recursive problem. We also use recursive design in creating a function that computes the greatest common divisor of two integers. We include a fairly detailed mathematical justification for the gcd() implementation.

Tower of Hanoi

Puzzle fans have long been fascinated with the *Tower of Hanoi* problem, which involves a stack of *n* graduated disks and a set of three needles called A, B, and C. The initial setup places the *n* disks on needle A. The task for the player is to move the disks one at a time from needle to needle until the process rebuilds the original stack, but on needle C. The challenge is the fact that at no time can a larger disk be placed on top of a smaller disk.

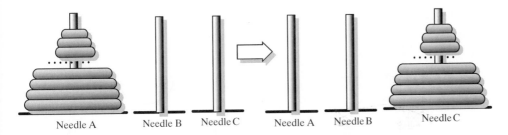

| Needle A | Needle B | Needle C | Needle A | Needle B | Needle C |

Legend has it that the puzzle originated with priests in the Temple of Brahma who were given a brass platform with three diamond needles and 64 golden disks. The mission of the priests was to solve the problem so as to quicken the end of the world. If the legend is true, then we can be assured that the priests are still busy at work, because the solution requires $2^{64} - 1$ moves. At one move per second, the task requires over 500 billion years.

At first glance, you might think that solving the Tower of Hanoi puzzle would be a daunting problem in terms both of time and of strategy. Somewhat surprisingly, however, the Tower of Hanoi has a relatively simple recursive solution. We illustrate the algorithm by looking at the simple three-disk Hanoi puzzle. Watch the steps as we move disks from needle A to C by way of the intermediate needle B. For discussion purposes, we break up the moves into separate stages encompassing several steps. These stages will be used later to develop the recursive function hanoi().

The first stage uses three moves to shift the top two disks from needle A to needle B:

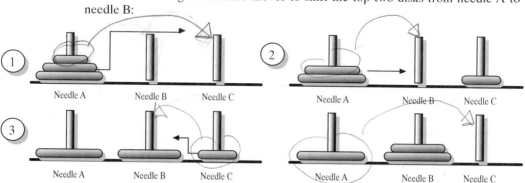

After completing the first stage, only the largest disk remains at needle A. In stage two, a simple move shifts this disk from needle A to needle C:

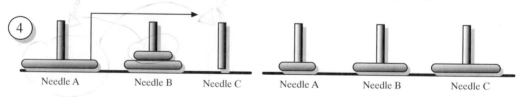

A third stage takes three steps to move the two disks from needle B to needle C:

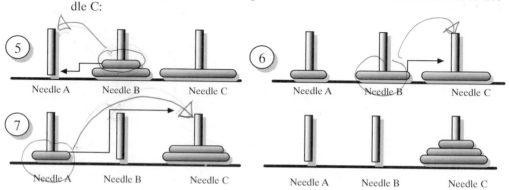

To understand the recursive nature of the process, note that stage 1 and stage 3 both describe separate Tower of Hanoi problems with 2 disks. In the first stage, two disks move from needle A to needle B, with needle C serving as temporary storage. In the third stage, two disks move from needle B to needle C, with needle A serving as temporary storage. The fact that the Tower of Hanoi algorithm involves a smaller version of the algorithm makes it recursive.

   The recursive function hanoi().   The recursive process translates into the function called hanoi(). The arguments include n, the number of disks, and three string arguments that denote the name of the starting needle (initNeedle), the destination needle (endNeedle), and the intermediate needle (tempNeedle) that temporarily holds disks during the moves. The following is the function prototype:

```
// move n disks from initNeedle to endNeedle using tempNeedle for
// temporary storage
void hanoi(int n, const string& initNeedle, const string& endNeedle,
           const string& tempNeedle);
```

Stage 1 and stage 3 correspond to recursive steps. The first stage involves $n - 1$ disks that are moved from needle initNeedle (needle A) to tempNeedle (needle B) by using endNeedle (needle C) for temporary storage:

```
// recursive call for stage 1
hanoi(n-1, initNeedle, tempNeedle, endNeedle);
```

Stage 3 moves $n - 1$ disks from tempNeedle to endNeedle by using initNeedle for temporary storage:

```
// recursive call for stage 3
hanoi(n-1, tempNeedle, endNeedle, initNeedle);
```

After the completion of stage 1, the big disk is left on initNeedle and the other $n - 1$ smaller disks are on tempNeedle. The big disk can be moved directly to endNeedle. An output statement describes this move:

```
cout << "Move " << initNeedle << " to " << endNeedle << endl;
```

The recursive steps continue to move shorter and shorter stacks of disks from one needle to another until the stack size is one disk. This is the stopping condition, and the solution is simply to move the one disk to the correct needle. The upcoming code is the code for the hanoi() function. Note that there are two separate calls to hanoi(), corresponding to the stages 1 and 3. In each case, there is a different order of needles in the argument list.

```
// move n disks from initNeedle to endNeedle, using tempNeedle
// for intermediate storage of the disks
void hanoi(int n, const string& initNeedle,
           const string& endNeedle, const string& tempNeedle)
{
```

(handwritten margin notes:)
initNeedle — needle where the piece to be moved starts @

tempNeedle — Nothing happens @ this needle.

endNeedle — needle where the piece to be moved ends up.

```
// stopping condition: move one disk
if (n == 1)
 cout << "move " << initNeedle << " to "
      << endNeedle << endl;
else
{
   // move takes n—1 disks from initNeedle to
   // tempNeedle using endNeedle for temporary storage
   hanoi(n—1,initNeedle,tempNeedle,endNeedle);

   // move largest disk to endNeedle
   cout << "move " << initNeedle << " to "
        << endNeedle << endl;

   // move takes n—1 disks from tempNeedle to
   // endNeedle using initNeedle for temporary storage
   hanoi(n—1,tempNeedle,endNeedle,initNeedle);
}
}
```

PROGRAM 3-3   SOLVING THE TOWER OF HANOI PUZZLE

Let's look at a program that prompts for the number of disks and uses the hanoi() function to solve the Tower of Hanoi puzzle. The run gives a listing of the moves for the case where $n =$ 3. Compare the results with the seven moves in the example.

```
// File: prg3_3.cpp
// prompt for the number of disks and call the function
// hanoi() to solve the Tower of Hanoi puzzle

#include <iostream>
#include <string>

using namespace std;

// move n disks from initNeedle to endNeedle, using tempNeedle
// for intermediate storage of the disks.
void hanoi(int n, const string& initNeedle,
           const string& endNeedle, const string& tempNeedle);

int main()
{
    // number of disks and the needle names
    int n;
    string beginneedle  = "A",
           middleneedle = "B",
           endneedle    = "C";

    // prompt for n and solve the puzzle for n disks
    cout << "Enter the number of disks: ";
```

```
    cin >> n;
    cout << "The solution for n = " << n << endl;
    hanoi(n, beginneedle, endneedle, middleneedle);

    return 0;
}
/* implementation of hanoi() given in the algorithm discussion */
```

```
Run:

Enter the number of disks: 3
The solution for n = 3
move A to C
move A to B
move C to B
move A to C
move B to A
move B to C
move A to C
```

Number Theory: The Greatest Common Divisor

Number theory is a branch of mathematics that studies the properties of integers. Many of its results find important applications in computer science. Finding the *greatest common divisor* of two nonnegative integers a and b that are not both 0 is an example of a very useful number-theory algorithm. The greatest common divisor, denoted by $\gcd(a, b)$ is the largest integer that divides (evenly into) both a and b. For instance,

$$\gcd(10, 4) = 2 \qquad \gcd(4, 12) = 4 \qquad \gcd(54, 30) = 6$$
$$\gcd(630, 132) = 6 \qquad \gcd(67, 0) = 67 \qquad \gcd(45, 16) = 1$$

The Greek mathematician Euclid provided an elegant recursive algorithm for computing $\gcd(a, b)$, The algorithm, appropriately called the *Euclidean Algorithm*, computes $\gcd(a, b)$ by using repeated application of the % operator until the result is 0. The following recursive step and stopping condition implement $\gcd(a, b)$:

$$\gcd(a,b) = \begin{cases} a, & b = 0 \\ \gcd(b, a\%b), & \text{otherwise} \end{cases}$$

To see how the algorithm works, consider the following examples:

Let $a = 54, b = 30$ $\gcd(54, 30) = 24$ // $a = 54\ b = 30$ $\lceil a\% \ b = \lceil 54\% \ 30 \rceil = 24.$
                         $\gcd(30, 24) = 6$ // $a = 30\ b = 24$ $a \% b = 30 \% 24 = 6$
                         $\gcd(24, 6) = 0$ // $a = 24\ b = 6$ $a \% b = 24 \% 6 = 0$
                         $\gcd(6, 0) = 6$ // stopping condition: $b == 0$

b   Answer

Let $a = 45, b = 16$ $\gcd(45, 16) =$ // $a = 45$ $b = 16$ $a \% b = 45 \% 16 = 13$

$\gcd(16, 13) =$ // $a = 16$ $b = 13$ $a \% b = 16 \% 13 = 3$

$\gcd(13, 3) =$ // $a = 13$ $b = 3$ $a \% b = 13 \% 3 = 1$

$\gcd(3, 1) =$ // $a = 3$ $b = 1$ $a \% b = 3 \% 1 = 0$

$\gcd(1, 0) = 1$ // stopping condition: $b == 0$

In the next section, we give the mathematical justification for the algorithm. For now, let us assume the recursive definition is correct . We can implement the function gcd() by using an if/else statement to distinguish the stopping condition and the recursive step:

Greatest Common Divisor gcd():

```
// compute the greatest common divisor of the nonnegative
// integers a and b where both a and b cannot be 0
int gcd(int a, int b)
{
   if (b == 0)
      return a;            // a divides a and 0
   else
      return gcd(b, a%b);  // recursive step
}
```

Mathematical Justification of the Euclidean Algorithm: We give a proof of the Euclidean algorithm in two stages that treat the recursive step and the stopping condition separately. The first stage establishes the identify $\gcd(a, b) = \gcd(b, a\%b)$; the second stage establishes that the algorithm finally reaches the stopping condition ($b == 0$), with the result $\gcd(a, 0) = a$.

Stage 1:   Verify: $\gcd(a, b) = \gcd(b, a\%b)$.

Assume that c divides into both a and b, so that there are integers h_1 and h_2 such that

$$a = h_1 c \quad \text{and} \quad b = h_2 c$$

If r is the remainder $a\%b$ and q is the quotient a/b, we can record the result of the integer division problem as

$$r = a - qb, 0 \leq r \leq b - 1 \qquad b \overline{\smash{\begin{array}{r} q \\ a \\ qb \\ \hline a - qb = r \end{array}}}$$

Substituting for the values a and b, the equation becomes

$$r = a - qb = h_1 c - q h_2 c = c(h_1 - q h_2)$$

Thus, c also divides $r = a\%b$. We have shown that any number that divides a and b also divides b and $a\%b$, respectively. Assume now that d divides b and $a\%b$, so that

$$b = h_3 d \quad \text{and} \quad a\%b = h_4 d$$

Then

$$a = qb + r = qh_3 d + h_4 d = d(qh_3 + h_4)$$

As a result, any number that divides into b and $a\%b$ also divides into a and b. Because the pairs (a, b) and $(b, a\%b)$ have the same set of divisors, they must have the same greatest common divisor, so $\gcd(a, b) = \gcd(b, a\%b)$.

Stage 2:   The Euclidean algorithm applies to nonnegative integers that are not both 0. If $b = 0$, however, $\gcd(a, 0) = a$, because a is the largest integer that divides into a and 0. This is the stopping condition. The problem in stage 2 reduces to showing that the recursive step will lead to this condition for any valid combination of a and b.

For values of a and b, we can assume that $b \le a$ (because if $b > a$, $a\%b = a$), and so the recursive step yields

$$\gcd(a, b) = \gcd(b, a\%b) = \gcd(b, a)$$

If $b = a$, the stopping condition occurs in one step, since $a \% a = 0$:

$$\gcd(a, b) = \gcd(a, a) = \gcd(a, 0) = a$$

If $b < a$, each application of the recursive step involves computing $a\%b$, whose result is in the range from 0 to $b - 1$. The arguments $(b, a\%b)$ keep getting smaller, so that eventually $a\%b$ must reach 0, which is the stopping condition.

Application of gcd—Rational Numbers

The _rational numbers_ are the set of quotients p/q, where p and q are integers and $q! = 0$. The integer values p and q are the numerator and denominator, respectively. The following are examples of rational numbers:

$$2/3 \quad 6/7 \quad 8/2 \quad 10/1 \quad 0/5$$

A rational number is a ratio between the numerator and denominator and hence represents one member of a collection of equivalent numbers. For instance,

$$2/3 = 10/15 = 50/75 \quad \text{(equivalent rational numbers)}$$

Within the collection of equivalent rational numbers, one member has a reduced form in which the numerator and denominator have no common divisor. For instance, in the collection {2/3, 10/15, 50/75}, 2/3 is the member in reduced form. To create the reduced form for any rational number p/q, divide the numerator and denominator by their greatest common divisor $gcd(p, q)$. We say that p/q is reduced to lowest terms. For instance,

$$10/15 = 2/3$$
$$(gcd(10, 15) = 5 \quad (10/5 = 2, 15/5 = 3)$$

$$24/21 = 8/7$$
$$(gcd(24, 21) = 3 \quad (24/3 = 8; 21/3 = 7)$$

$$5/9 = 5/9$$
$$(gcd(5, 9) = 1 \quad (5/1 = 5; 9/1 = 9)$$

You have experience with integers and rational numbers (fractions) from your early schooling. Remember the teacher"s refrain to 'reduce the fraction to lowest terms and give your answer as a mixed number if the fraction is greater than one." We will take this refrain to heart and write a program does just this for any fraction (rational number). A mixed number consists of a whole part and a fractional part that is less than 1. For instance, the rational number 324/88 has the mixed-number representation

$$3\ 60/88$$

which, in reduced form, is

$$3\ 15/22$$

PROGRAM 34   DISPLAYING MIXED NUMBERS
_____

The upcoming program asks the user to input a rational number in the form p/q and displays it as a mixed number. The input is two integer values separated by a /.

1. Compute the whole part of the number as follows:

       wholePart = numerator / denominator;

2. The fractional part of the number is the rational number

       (numerator % denominator) / denominator

3. To output the fractional part in reduced form, divide its two components by

       gcd(numerator % denominator, denominator)

The program handles the special cases where the fractional part or the whole number part is 0 by omitting output in these situations.

```
// File: prg3_4.cpp
// the program prompts the user to input a rational
// number in the form p/q and displays it as a mixed number.
#include <iostream>
```

```
using namespace std;

// compute the greatest common divisor of the nonnegative
// integers a and b where both a and b cannot be 0
int gcd(int a, int b);

int main()
{
    int numerator, denominator, wholePart, remainder, divisor;
    char slash;

    cout << "Enter a rational number (numerator/denominator): ";
    cin >> numerator >> slash >> denominator;

    // compute the quotient (whole part) and the remainder
    wholePart = numerator / denominator;
    remainder = numerator % denominator;

    if (remainder == 0)
        // the rational number is an integer
        cout << wholePart << endl;
    else
    {
        // number in mixed form is "wholePart remainder/divisor"
        // output wholePart if it is not 0
        if (wholePart != 0)
            cout << wholePart << ' ';

        // compute the greatest common divisor of the remainder
        // and the denominator
        divisor = gcd(remainder, denominator);
        // output the fractional part in lowest terms by dividing
        // the remainder and denominator by their gcd
        cout << remainder/divisor << '/' << denominator/divisor
             << endl;
    }

    return 0;
}
/* the implementation of gcd() is given in the program discussion */
```

```
Run 1:

Enter a rational number (numerator/denominator): 6/8
3/4

Run 2:

Enter a rational number (numerator/denominator): 535/1
535
```

```
Run 3:

Enter a rational number (numerator/denominator): 535/2
267 1/2

Run 4:

Enter a rational number (numerator/denominator): 324/88
3 15/22
```

Evaluating Recursion

The value of using a recursive function depends upon the problem. Sometimes recursion is not appropriate, because a far more efficient iterative version exists. For some problems, like the Tower of Hanoi, a recursive solution is elegant and easier to code than the corresponding iterative solution. In this section, we use the Fibonacci numbers to compare and contrast iterative and recursive functions. Our discussion will outline some of the advantages and disadvantages of recursion.

Fibonacci numbers are the sequence of integers
```
0, 1, 1, 2, 3, 5, 8, 13, 21, 34, ...
```

The first two terms are 0 and 1 by definition. They start a sequence that uses a calculation for all subsequent terms. Starting at $n = 2$, the next term is the sum of the two previous terms. Hence $1 = 1 + 0$ ($n = 2$), $2 = 1 + 1$ ($n = 3$), $3 = 2 + 1$ ($n = 4$), and so forth. The Fibonacci sequence has a recursive definition for $n \geq 0$. Define the first two terms explicitly as 0 and 1 (stopping conditions). From that point on, each term is the sum of the previous two terms (recursive step).

$$\text{fib}(n) = \begin{cases} 0, & n = 0 \\ 1, & n = 1 \\ \text{fib}(n-1) + \text{fib}(n-2), & n \geq 2 \end{cases}$$

The recursive function fib() takes a single argument, n, and returns Fibonacci number n:

```
int fib(int n)
{
   if (n <= 1)                        // stopping conditions
      return n;
   else
      return fib(n–1) + fib(n–2);    // recursive step
}
```

The implementation of fib() is a simple and straightforward translation of the recursive definition for terms in the Fibonacci sequence. The execution of the function is far from straightforward. Consider the function calls required to compute fib(5). Figure 3-6 is a hierarchy tree of nodes representing calls to fib() for $n = 5, 4, 3, 2, 1$, and 0. For the recursive step, a node spawns two other nodes corresponding to the

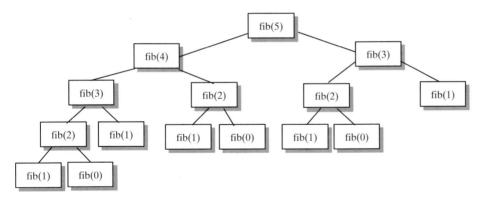

Figure 3-6
Tree of recursive calls for fib(5)

statement fib($n - 1$) + fib($n - 2$). Nodes at the bottom of the tree identify stopping conditions.

Note that the function makes multiple calls to itself with the same argument. The evaluation computes fib(3) two times and fib(1) five times. The 15 nodes on the tree represent the number of recursive calls required to compute fib(5) = 5. The total number of recursive calls to evaluate the nth Fibonacci number is directly related to the value fib(n). Assuming the number of calls is given by the function num-Call(), it can be shown that

```
numCall(n) = 2 * fib(n+1) - 1
```

For instance,

```
numCall(5)  = 2 * fib(6)  - 1 = 2 * 8 - 1 = 15
numCall(35) = 2 * fib(36) - 1 = 2 * 14930352 - 1 = 29,860,703
```

Since the Fibonacci numbers get large very quickly, it is clear that their recursive computation is not efficient. In fact, the recursive computation has an exponential running time.

It can be shown that

Note

$$\text{fib}(n) = \frac{1}{\sqrt{5}}\left[\left(\frac{1 + \sqrt{5}}{2}\right)^n - \left(\frac{1 - \sqrt{5}}{2}\right)^n\right]$$

for all $n \geq 0$. The second term in the parentheses is approximately $(-0.618034)^n$, so, as n gets large, the term gets smaller and smaller. It follows that fib(n) is approximately

$$\frac{1}{\sqrt{5}}\left(\frac{1 + \sqrt{5}}{2}\right)^n$$

The number of function calls necessary for the evaluation of fib(n) is 2 * fib($n + 1$) $-$ 1, which is approximately

$$\frac{2}{\sqrt{5}} \left(\frac{1 + \sqrt{5}}{2} \right)^{n+1} - 1$$

The value increases exponentially, so the recursive computation of the Fibonacci numbers has an exponential running time.

The example illustrates a cruel irony of recursion. Often, it simplifies both the algorithm design and coding, only to fail for lack of runtime efficiency.

Fibonacci Numbers using Iteration. An iterative version of the function fib() uses a simple loop and two integer variables, oneback and twoback, that maintain a record of the last two Fibonacci numbers. Each iteration of the loop updates these variables. The iterative version has the name fibiter():

```
int fibiter(int n)
{
    // integers to store previous two Fibonacci value
    int oneback = 1, twoback = 0, current;
    int i;

    // return is immediate for first two numbers
    if (n <= 1)
        return n;
    else
        // compute successive terms beginning at 3
        for (i = 2; i <= n; i++)
        {
            current = oneback + twoback;
            twoback = oneback;    // update for next calculation
            oneback = current;
        }

    return current;
}
```

For Fibonacci number $n \geq 2$, the iterative form requires $n - 1$ additions and one function call, so the running time is O(n). For $n = 35$, the iterative form requires 34 additions, while the recursive function requires 29,860,703 function calls.

PROGRAM 3-5   EVALUATING RECURSION (FIBONACCI EXAMPLE)

The upcoming program evaluates fib(45) by using the iterative and recursive versions of the function. The nonrecursive version executes in a fraction of a second, and so the program uses a timer object only to display the computation time of the recursive version.

```cpp
// File: prg3_5.cpp
// the program evaluates Fibonacci number 45 using
// an iterative and a recursive algorithm. the iterative
// algorithm executes in a fraction of a second. the program
// uses a timer object to output the computation time
// of the very inefficient recursive algorithm (exponential
// running time)

#include   <iostream>

#include "d_timer.h"

using namespace std;

// prototypes for the recursive and iterative versions
int fib(int n);
int fibiter(int n);

int main()
{
    timer t;         // time recursive version
    int fib_45;

    // evaluate fib() using iteration and recursion
    cout << "Value of fib(45) by iteration is ";
    cout << fibiter(45) << endl;

    cout << "Value of fib(45) by recursion is ";
    // start/stop timer object for recursive process
    t.start();
    fib_45 = fib(45);
    t.stop();

    cout << fib_45 << endl;
    cout << "    Time required by recursive version is " << t.time()
         << " sec" << endl;

    return 0;
}
/* implementation of fibiter() and fib() given in the program discussion */
```

```
Run:

Value of fib(45) by iteration is 1134903170
Value of fib(45) by recursion is 1134903170
    Time required by recursive version is 72.584 sec
```

Criteria for Using Recursion: The example of Fibonacci numbers should alert you to potential problems with recursion. With the overhead of function calls, a simple recursive function could significantly deteriorate runtime performance. In the case of the Fibonacci numbers, the O(n) iterative solution is preferred over the recursive version.

Having provided the foregoing warnings, we can still state that recursion remains an important design and programming tool. Many algorithms naturally lend themselves to a recursive implementation that distinguishes the stopping conditions and recursive steps. The Tower of Hanoi is a good example. In Chapter 15, we use recursion to solve a maze and the 8-Queens problem. These are elegant algorithms that demonstrate how recursion can solve some difficult problems. Equivalent iterative algorithms would be more difficult to devise. In the same chapter, we use recursion to implement the divide-and-conquer strategy for the famous quicksort, an extremely efficient algorithm for sorting an array.

While recursion is not an object-oriented concept, it has some of the good characteristics of object design. It allows the programmer to manage the key components in the algorithm while hiding some of the complex implementation details. There is no simple rule describing when to use recursion. Use it when it enhances the algorithm design and provides a function implementation that runs with reasonable space and time efficiency.

CHAPTER SUMMARY

- The design of algorithms is integral to the efficient implementation of data structures.

- The selection sort is an algorithm that illustrates many of the common features of sorting algorithms. The algorithm uses comparisons and exchanges to order a list.

- The simplest form of searching is the sequential search, which compares the target with every element in a list until matching the target or reaching the end of the list. If the list is in sorted order, the binary-search algorithm is more efficient. This search exploits the structure of an ordered list to produce very fast search times.

- Big-O notation measures the efficiency of an algorithm by estimating the number of certain operations that the algorithm must perform. For searching and sorting algorithms, the operation is data comparison. Big-O measure is very useful when selecting among competing algorithms.

- The running time of the sequential search is O(n) for the worst and the average cases. However, the worst and average case for the binary search is O($\log_2 n$). Timing data obtained from a program provides experimental evidence to support the greater efficiency of the binary search.

- Algorithms, such as for the selection sort and binary search, work the same way with integer data as they do with time24 data. To address this situation, C++ provides a template mechanism that allows a programmer to write a single version of a function with general type arguments. If a main program wants to call the function several times with different runtime arguments, the compiler looks at the types of the runtime arguments and creates different versions of the function that matches the types.

- An algorithm is recursive if it calls itself for smaller problems of its own type. Eventually, these problems must lead to one or more stopping conditions. The solution at a stopping condition leads to the solution of previous problems. In the implementation of recursion by a C++ function, the function calls itself.

- The alternative to recursion is iteration, in which the solution to a problem results from looping rather than recursive function calls. Iteration is often more efficient than recursion.

- Some algorithms are elegantly described using recursion. The Tower of Hanoi puzzle is an example of a complex problem that can be clearly defined and solved by using recursion.

- Use recursion with care and only if it makes the solution to a problem easier to understand and not too inefficient. The computation of the Fibonacci numbers is an excellent example wherein the recursive solution is simple, but extremely inefficient.

CLASSES AND LIBRARIES IN THE CHAPTER

Name	Header File
binSearch()(integer)	d_search.h
binSearch()(template)	d_search.h
randomNumber	d_random.h
selectionSort()(integer)	d_sort.h
selectionSort()(template)	d_sort.h
seqSearch()(integer)	d_search.h
seqSearch()(template)	d_search.h
timer	d_timer.h
writeArray()(template)	d_util.h

REVIEW EXERCISES

1. Show the order of elements in the array after each pass of the selection-sort algorithm applied to the array

```
int arr[6] = {5, 1, 8, 2, 7, 9};
```

2. Use the sequential search to locate an integer value *target* in the array *list* and give the return value.

```
int list[5] = {15, 5, 3, 17, 12}, retValue;
```

   (a) retValue = seqSearch(list, 0, 5, 3);   // retValue = _____
   (b) retValue = seqSearch(list, 2, 4, 17);   // retValue = _____

(c) `retValue = seqSearch(list, 0, 2, 3);`   `// retValue = _____`

3. An iteration of the binary search occurs each time the algorithm compares the target with the middle value of the current sublist. For the upcoming data and target value, compute the number of iterations required by the binary search:

Target = 50

Vector	3	6	8	10	15	18	22	25	35	43	50	55

Number of iterations: _____

4. Perform a Big-O analysis for each function. In each case, give the result as O(g), where g is some function of n.

    (a) $n - 18$ **(b)** $n^3 + 6n + 5$ **(c)** $\sqrt{n} + 9$ **(d)** $\dfrac{n^2 + 7}{n + 1}$

5. Indicate the running time of each algorithm or code segment.
    (a) Selection sort.
       (i) O(n^2)   **(ii)** O(n)   **(iii)** O($n \log_2 n$)   **(iv)** O(2^n)
    (b) Finding the minimum of an n element array (unordered).
       (i) O(n^2)   **(ii)** O(n)   **(iii)** O($n \log_2 n$)   **(iv)** O(n^3)
    (c) Finding the maximum of an n element ordered array.
       (i) O(n^2)   **(ii)** O(n)   **(iii)** O(1)   **(iv)** O($\log_2 n$)

    (d)
```
for(i=1; i < n; i++)
    for(j=1; j < n; j++)
        sum += i+j;
```

       (i) O(n^2)   **(ii)** O(n)   **(iii)** O(1)   **(iv)** O(n^3)

    (e)
```
for(i=1; i < n; i++)
    for(j=1; j < i*i; j++))
        count++;
```

       (i) O(n^2)   **(ii)** O(n)   **(iii)** O(1)   **(iv)** O(n^3)

    Note that $1^2 + 2^2 + 3^3 + \cdots + n^2 = \dfrac{n(n + 1)(2n + 1)}{6}$

6. **(a)** Use the sequential search to find a target value in a list of 10,000 items.
       (i) What is the fewest number of comparisons the search will require?
       (ii) What is the maximum number of comparisons the search will require?
       (iii) What is the expected number of comparisons for the search?
    (b) Use the binary search to find a target value in a list of 10,000 items.
       (i) What is the fewest number of comparisons the search will require?
       (ii) What is the maximum number of comparisons the search will require?

7. Use the following code, which contains a template function:

```
#include <iostream>
#include <string>

using namespace std;
```

```
template <typename T>
void dp(const T& a, const T& b);

int main()
{ string s = "Time", t = "Marches";
  dp(4,5);
  dp(s,t);

  return 0;
}

template <typename T>
void dp(const T& a, const T& b)
{ cout << a + b << endl; }
```

(a) What is the output from dp(4, 5)?_____
(b) What is the output from dp(s, t)?_____

8. Trace the following function:

```
template <typenameT>
T func(const T list[], int n)
{ T m1 = list[0], m2 = list[0];
  int i;

  for(i = 1;i < n; i++)
  {
     if (list[i] < m1)
        m1 = list[i];
     if (list[i] < m2)
        m2 = list[i];
  }
  return m1 - m2;
}
```

What is the output of the following code?

```
int intArr[] = {7, 5, 2, 3, 8, 9};
time24 timeArr[] = {time24(5,15), time24(15,45), time24(12,0)};

cout << func(intArr,6) << endl;      // output: _____
cout << func(timeArr,3) << endl;     // output: _____
```

9. What sequence does the upcoming function produce when executing func() with arguments
1, 2, 3, ...?

```
long func(int n)
{
   if (n == 1 || n == 2)
      return 1;
   else
      return 2*func(n-2) + func(n-1);
}
```

(a) 1, 1, 2, 3, 5, 8, ... **(b)** 2, 4, 6, 8, 16, 32, ...
(c) 1, 1, 3, 5, 11, 21, ... **(d)** 1, 1, 5, 13, 41, 121, ...

10. What is an equivalent iterative version of the upcoming function?

```
int func(int n)
{
    if (n > 1)
        return func(n−1) + n;
    else
        return 1;
}
```

11. Pass the string argument str = "Hello" to the recursive function f().

```
void f(const string& s, int i)
{
    if (i < s.length())
    {
        cout << s[i];
        f(s,i+1);
    }
}
```

(a) What is the output from the function call f(str, 0)? _____
(b) What is the output from the function call f(str, 3)? _____
(c) What is the output for the calls to f() in parts (a) and (b) if f(s, i + 1) comes before cout << $s[i]$?

Answers to Review Exercises

1. Pass 0: 1 5 8 2 7 9
   Pass 1: 1 2 8 5 7 9
   Pass 2: 1 2 5 8 7 9
   Pass 3: 1 2 5 7 8 9
   Pass 4: 1 2 5 7 8 9

2. **(a)** `retValue = 2`   **(b)** `retValue = 3`   **(c)** `retValue = 3`
3. Number of iterations: 4.
4. **(a)** $O(n)$ **(b)** $O(n^3)$ **(c)** $O(\sqrt{n})$ **(d)** $O(n)$

   For (d), divide $n + 1$ into $n^2 + 7$:

$$\frac{n^2 + 7}{n + 1} = n - 1 + \frac{8}{n + 1}$$

5. **(a) (i)** $O(n^2)$ **(b) (ii)** $O(n)$ **(c) (iii)** $O(1)$ **(d) (i)** $O(n^2)$ **(e) (iv)** $O(n^3)$
6. **(a) (i)** 1   **(ii)** 10,000   **(iii)** 5000
   (b) (i) 1   **(ii)** $2*(1 + \lfloor \log_2 n \rfloor) = 2(1 + 13) = 28$
7. **(a)** 9   **(b)** TimeMarches
8. 7
   10:30

9. (c) 1, 1, 3, 5, 11, 21, 43, 85,...

10.
```
// form the sum of the integers 1, 2, 3, .., n
int f(int n)
{
    int sum = 0, i;

    for f(i = 1; i <= n; i++)
        sum += i;

    return sum;
}
```

11. (a) Hello   **(b)** lo   **(c)** Output for (a): olleH. Output for (b): ol.

WRITTEN EXERCISES

12. Assume an array has values {19, 13, 7, 12, 16}. Show the order of elements in the array after each pass of the selection-sort algorithm.

13. Indicate how to modify the selection-sort algorithm so it sorts the list in descending order.

14. Use the sequential search to locate an integer value *target* in the array *list* and give the return value.

```
int list[10] = {1, 5, 8, 2, 5, 18, 23, 55, 4, 9}, retValue;
```

(a) retValue = seqSearch(list, 0, 10, 5);   // retValue = _____
(b) retValue = seqSearch(list, 2, 10, 5);   // retValue = _____
(c) retValue = seqSearch(list, 1, 10, 5);   // retValue = _____
(d) retValue = seqSearch(list, 4, 10, 5);   // retValue = _____
(e) retValue = seqSearch(list, 6, 10, 5);   // retValue = _____
(f) retValue = seqSearch(list, 7, 9, 4);   // retValue = _____

15. The template function find_last_of() is a variation of the sequential search. The arguments include an array, the range [first, last) for the search, and a target value. The function searches for the final occurrence of the target in the array and returns its index if found; otherwise, it returns last.

(a) Give a prototype for the template function find_last_of().

(b) Implement the function.

16. Recall that pass i of the selection sort, $0 \le i < n$, finds the smallest of the elements in the sublist {arr[i], arr[i + 1], ..., arr[$n-1$]} and exchanges it with arr[i]. A variation of this algorithm, called the *double-ended selection sort*, locates both the smallest and largest of the elements in each sublist and positions them at the beginning and the end of the sublist, respectively. Pass 0 locates the smallest and largest elements in {arr[0], arr[1], ..., arr[n − 1]} and places them at indices 0 and n − 1, respectively. Pass 1 locates the smallest and largest elements in {arr[1], ..., arr[n − 2]} and locates them at indices 1 and n − 2, respectively. Continue in this way until the leftmost index becomes equal to or greater than the rightmost index. The sort makes $n/2$ passes.

(a) Assume an array has values {13, 5, 2, 25, 47, 17, 8, 21}. Show the order of elements in the array after each pass of the double-ended selection sort.

(b) Write the function deSelSort() that implements the double-ended selection sort algorithm.

```
template <typename T>
void deSelSort(T arr[], int n);
```

(c) Intuitively, what do you think is the worst-case running time for deSelSort()? Explain your answer.

17. This exercise develops the bubble-sort algorithm. During multiple passes through the array, a flag notes whether any local activity occurs. On a pass, compare adjacent elements, and exchange their values when the first element is greater than the second element. Set a Boolean flag *true* if an exchange occurs. At the end of the pass, the largest element has "bubbled up" to the top of the array. Subsequent passes order the array from back to front. The sort requires at most $n - 1$ passes, with the process terminating if the flag notes that no swapping occurs during a pass. The upcoming figure illustrates two passes of the bubble sort for array arr = {35, 10, 40, 15}. The boxed elements are in their correct location.

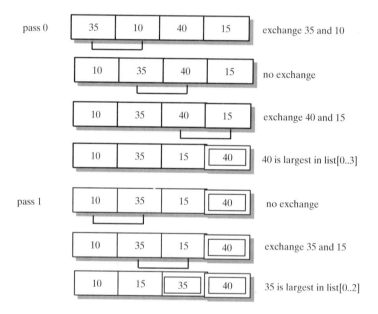

Implement the template bubble-sort function:

```
template <typename T>
void bubbleSort(T arr[], int n);
```

18. **(a)** Trace the following code segment, and give the resulting output:

```
int arr[8] = {2, 6, 2, 9, 8, 8, 2, 7};
int k = 0, i, index, target;

for (i = 0; i < 8; i++)
{
```

```
        target = arr[i];
        if ((index = seqSearch(arr, 0, i, target)) == i)
          if ((index = seqSearch(arr, i+1, 8, target)) == 8)
            k++;
  }
  cout << k;  // Output: _____
```

(b) If the code is applied for an arbitrary array arr, what does it compute?

19. Consider the integer array

```
  int arr[8] = {1, 2, 5, 8, 9, 10, 15, 25};
```

List the sequence of steps to execute the binary-search algorithm. For each step, give the values of first, last, and mid for the appropriate sublist. Then give the return value from the function.
(a) binSearch(arr, 0, 8, 2);
(b) binSearch(arr, 0, 8, 16);

20. Each iteration of the binary search compares the target with the value at the midpoint of [first, last). Indicate the number of iterations required by the binary-search algorithm to locate each target in the entire list. The array is

```
  int arr[9] = {9, 16, 21, 32, 40, 57, 60, 75, 80};
```

(a) target = 75   **(b)** target = 21   **(c)** target = 9

21. The following are Big-O estimates for the running times of three sorting algorithms:

Algorithm 1: $O(n^2)$ Algorithm 2: $O(n \log_2 n)$ Algorithm 3: $O(2^n)$

Rank the algorithms in order of preference.

22. Perform a Big-O analysis for each function. In each case, give the result as $O(g)$, where g is some function of n.

(a) $n + 5$ **(b)** $n^2 + 6n + 7$ **(c)** $6\sqrt[3]{n} + \sqrt{n} + 7$ **(d)** $\dfrac{n^3 + n^2}{n + 1}$

23. (a) For what value of $n > 1$ does 2^n become larger than n^3?
(b) Show that $2^n + n^3$ is $O(2^n)$.

(c) Give a Big-O estimate for $\dfrac{n^2 + 5}{n + 3} + \log_2 n$.

24. Maintain a list of n integers in an array.
(a) What is the running time of printing the last element in the array?
(b) What is the running time of printing the entire array?

25. Both functions in this problem contain a loop as their primary component. Use Big-O notation to express the worst-case running time for each function in terms of n.
(a) `bool g(const int a[], int n, int k)`

```
  {
      int i;
      for(i=0; i < n; i++)
        if (a[i] == k)
            return true;
      return false;
  }
```

(b)
```
void h(int a[], const int b[], int n)
{
    int i;
    for (i=0; i < n; i++)
        for (j=0; j < n; j++)
            a[i] += b[j];
}
```

26. Search a list with n elements for the maximum value.
    (a) What list ordering will always result in running time O(1)?
    (b) What is the running time of the computation for an unordered list?

27. **(a)** Use the sequential search to find a target value in a list of 50,000 items.
    (i) What is the fewest number of comparisons the search will require?
    (ii) What is the maximum number of comparisons the search will require?
    (iii) What is the expected number of comparisons for the search?
    (b) Use the binary search to find a target value in a list of 50,000 items.
    (i) What is the fewest number of iterations the search will require?
    (ii) What is the maximum number of iterations the search will require?

28. Use the template function f() for parts (a) and (b). In each case, give the resulting value of m and the contents of array bList.

```
template <typename T>
void f(const T aList[], int n, T bList[], int& m, const T& target)
{
    int i, j = 0;

    for (i=0;i < n; i++)
        if (aList[i] != target)
        {
            bList[j] = aList[i];
            j++;
        }
    m = j;
}
```

(a)
```
int intListA[5] = {1, 9, 3, 9, 5}, intListB[5];

int m;
f(intListA, 5, intListB, m, 9);
```

(b)
```
string strListA[7] = {"cat", "rat", "bird", "dog", "rat", "fish",
                      "rat"}, strListB[7];
int m;

f(strListA, 7, strListB, m, string("rat"));
```

29. The upcoming function takes an array arr of n integer values and creates a second array, cumArr. Element i in cumArr is the cumulative sum of the elements in the range from arr[0] to arr[i].

```
void makeCumArray(int arr[], int n, int cumArr[])
{
    int i;
```

```
      cumArr[0] = arr[0];

      for (i=1; i < n; i++)
          cumArr[i] = cumArr[i-1] + arr[i];
  }
```

   (a) Write a template version of makeCumArray().

   (b) For an array with elements of type T, what operation(s) must T support in order for the array to be an argument for makeCumArray()?

   (c) List the elements in the cumulative array for each of the upcoming:

      (i)   `int intArray[5] = {6, 2, -3, 9, -8},` `cumIntArray[5];`

      (ii) `time24 timeArray[4] = {time24(4,30),` `time24(13,15),`

                                     `time24(1,45), time24(16,0)},`

             `cumTimeArray[4];`

      (iii) `string strArray[3] = {"the", "string", "man"}, cumStrArray[3];`

30. Give the first six terms in the numerical sequence generated by the recursive function f().

```
  int f(int n)
  {
      if (n == 0)
          return 1;
      else if(n == 1)
          return 2;
      else
          return 2*f(n - 2) + f(n - 1);
  }
```

31. Explain the problem that occurs when executing the recursive function f():

```
  int f(int n)
  {
      if (n == 1)
          return 1;
      else
          return f(n + 1) + n ;
  }
```

32. Use the recursive function rs() for parts (a)–(c):

```
  void rs(const string& s, int n)
  {
      cout << s[n-1];
      if (n > 0)
          rs(s, n-1);
  }
```

   (a) What is the output from the function call rs("animal", 6)?

   (b) What is the output from the function call rs("level", 5)?

33. Trace the following recursive function and give the output for the specified function calls:

```
  void f(int n)
  {
      if (n >= 0 && n <= 9)
```

```
    {
        cout << n << "   ";
        f(n-1);
    }
    else
        cout << endl;
}
```

(a) f(4)   **(b)** f(7)   **(c)** f(0)

34. Assume that the output statement and the recursive call in Written Exercise 3-33 are reversed:

```
f(n-1);
cout << n << "   ";
```

What is the output for the following function calls?

(a) f(4)   **(b)** f(7)   **(c)** f(0)

35. Assume that the recursive call in Written Exercise 3-33 is f(n + 1) in stead of f(n - 1):

```
cout << n << "   ";
f(n+1);
```

What is the output for the following function calls?

(a) f(4)   **(b)** f(7)   **(c)** f(0)

36. Trace the recursive function h(), and give the output for the specified function calls:

```
void h(char ch, int n)
{
    if (n <= 0)
        cout << endl;
    else
    {
        h(ch-1, n-1);
        cout << ch;
    }
}
```

What is the output for each of the following function calls?

(a) h('f',4)   **(b)** h('d',3)   **(c)** h('x',1)

37. Assume that the output statement "cout << ch" in function h() of Written Exercise 3-36 occurs before the if statement. What is the output for the function call h('f',4);

38. Trace the recursive function f(), and give the output for the specified function calls:

```
int f(int n)
{
    if (n < 1)
        return 0;
    else
        return f(n/2) + 1;
}
```

What is the output for each of the following function calls?

(a) f(15)   **(b)** f(8)   **(c)** f(3)

39. Implement the recursive function isPal(), which determines whether a string *str* is a simple palindrome. A simple palindrome is a string consisting entirely of the characters *a-z* that reads the same forward and backward. For instance, the upcoming are palindromes:

dad   level   mom   madamimadam

Use the following declaration of isPal():

```
bool isPal(const string& str, int startIndex, int endIndex);
```

It returns true when the substring of str in the index range [startIndex, endIndex) is a palindrome. The conditions are

Stopping Condition:
Result is true when startIndex >= endIndex − 1.
Result is false when str[startIndex] != str[endIndex − 1].

Recursive Step:
Determine whether the substring of str in the index range [startIndex + 1, endIndex − 1) is a palindrome.

40. Program 3−2 uses the recursive function displayInBase() to output a base-10 integer in a number base between 2 and 9. Implement a modified version of the function, called dec2bin(), that outputs a base-10 number as a fixed-length binary number. Assume that the length is sufficient to output all the significant digits of the number.

```
// output integer n as a fixed length base 2 (binary) number
void dec2bin(int n, int length);
```

For instance, dec2bin(11, 5) is 01011, and dec2bin(49, 8) is 00110001.

41. The upcoming is a recursive definition for f(a, b), where a and b are integer values:

$$f(a,b) = \begin{cases} a - b & a == 0 \text{ or } b == 0 \\ f(a - 1, b) + f(a, b - 1) & \text{otherwise} \end{cases}$$

(a) Write a recursive function that implements f().
(b) Display the 'calling tree' that lists the function calls that are required to execute f(3, 2). Use Figure 3-6 as an example.

PROGRAMMING EXERCISES

42. Use the function find_last_of() from Written Exercise 3-15 in a program that declares the upcoming arrays:

```
int intArr[10] = {2, 5, 3, 5, 4, 7, 5, 1, 8, 9};
char charArr[] = "mathematics";
string strArr[5] = {"june", "joe", "glenn", "joe", "glenn"};
```

Using find_last_of(), output the index for the last occurrence of 5 in intArr, of "a" in charArr, and of "glenn" in strArr.

43. Write a program that generates an array of 10 random integers in the range from 0 to 999. Output the array using the template function writeArray(), and then call the function bubbleSort() developed in Written Exercise 3-17 to sort the list. Output the sorted list.

44. Use the algorithm in Written Exercise 3-18 to implement the template function numUnique():

```
// returns the number of elements that occur only once in the array
template <typename T>
int numUnique(T arr[], int n);
```

Write a program that declares arrays of integer, string, and time24 type. Use these arrays as arguments for numUnique(), and output the return value.

45. Assume a file contains whitespace separated words, some of which may be the C++ keywords "if," "break," "switch," "case," "class," "template," "bool," and "catch." After prompting for the file name, the program should input the file word by word and count the number of occurrences of each keyword. To recognize a keyword, use the binary search.

46. Write a program that uses the recursive function isPal() from Written Exercise 3-39 to determine whether a string containing no blanks or punctuation marks is a palindrome. Input five strings, and use isPal() to determine whether each is a palindrome. Include the following strings:

> amanaplanacanalpanama
> gohangasalamiimalasagnahog
> abcdecba

47. Write a program that uses the recursive function dec2bin() from Written Exercise 3-40. The program should read a number n and a length len and call dec2bin() to output n with len binary digits. Include a loop so that you can repeat the process five times. In the runs, use the following inputs:

> 11   597   820   613   465   7

48. The following formula evaluates the sum of the first n integers:

$$1 + 2 + 3 + \cdots + n = n(n + 1)/2$$

Write a program that gives separate output for the values $n*(n + 1)/2$ and sumToN(n), which is the recursive function in Example 3-11 that sums the first n integers. Output for $n = 1$ to $n = 10$.

49. Implement the recursive function sumDigits(), which sums the digits of a nonnegative integer n:

$$\text{sumDigits}(n) = \begin{cases} n & \text{if } n/10 == 0 \\ \text{sumdigits}(n/10) + n\%10 & \text{if } n/10 \mathrel{!}=0 \end{cases}$$

Include sumDigits() in a program that enters an integer and outputs the sum of its digits. Run the program three times with input 23, 1234, and 90513.

50. For a random list of integers, the maximum number of comparisons required to find a target value by using the binary search is $2(1 + \text{int}(\log_2 n))$. This result can be tested experimentally. Modify the function binSearch() to return the number of comparisons the algorithm executes in a successful search and the negative of the number of comparisons required for an unsuccessful search. We provide the code for binSearch():

```
template <typename T>
int binSearch(const T arr[], int first, int last,
const T& target)
{
    int mid;
    T midvalue;             // object that is assigned arr[mid]
    int count = 0;

    while (first < last)   //test for nonempty sublist
    {
        mid = (first + last)/2;
        midvalue = arr[mid];
        if (target == midvalue)
        {
            count++;           // count == before return
            return count;   // have a match
        }
        // determine which sublist to search
        else if (target < midvalue)
            last = mid;        // search lower sublist. reset last
        else
            first = mid+1;  // search upper sublist. reset first
        count += 2;        // count == and <
    }
    return -count;         // target not found
}
```

Write a program that declares an integer array arr of ARRSIZE integers and two integer objects sumBinSearchSuccess and sumBinSearchFail.

```
const int ARRSIZE = 50000,
          RANDOMVALUES = 100000,
          RANDOMLIMIT = 200000;
int arr[ARRSIZE];
int sumBinSearchSuccess = 0, sumBinSearchFail = 0;
int success = 0;
```

After initializing arr with ARRSIZE random integers in the range from 0 to RANDOM-LIMIT − 1, apply the selection sort to arr. In a loop that executes RANDOMVALUES times, generate a random target in the range from 0 to RANDOMLIMIT − 1, and search for it in list using the modified binary search. If the search is successful, increment the integer counter success, and increment sumBinSearchSuccess by the number of comparisons returned from binSearch(); otherwise, increment sumBinSearchFail by the negative of the number of comparisons returned by binSearch(). At the conclusion of the loop, output the following:

```
cout << "Empirical average case: "
     << sumBinSearchSuccess/double(success) << endl;
```

```
cout << "Empirical worst case: "
    << sumBinSearchFail/double(RANDOMVALUES-success)
    << "  Theoretical bound for worst case: "
    << 2.0*(1.0 + int(log(double(ARRSIZE ))/log(2.0))) < endl;
```

Note: Include <cmath> to access the function log().

How do your empirical results for the worst case compare with the theoretical bound? The analysis of the average case for a successful search is difficult. The average number of comparisons performed in a successful search should be less than the number performed in an unsuccessful search. Do your empirical results verify this reasoning? Based on your empirical results, by how many iterations do the average and worst cases differ?

51. Make Example 3-1 into a program. Use the function deSelSort() from Written Exercise 3-16 instead of selectionSort() to order the array.

PROGRAMMING PROJECT

52. This project uses the bubble sort, which is developed in Written Exercise 3-17. In parts (a) and (b), model your answers after the running-time analysis for the selection sort.

(a) What is the best-case condition for the bubble sort? Give the Big-O measure of running time.

(b) What is the worst-case condition? Give the Big-O measure of running time. How many interchanges are performed in this case?

(c) The average-case analysis for the bubble sort is difficult. What do think the running time is?

(d) Write a program that compares the efficiency of the bubble and selection sorts. Model your program after Program 3-1, which compares the efficiency of the sequential and binary searches. Declare two arrays:

```
int arr1[50000], arr2[50000];
```

Fill each array with the same set of random numbers in the range from 0 to 999999, and time the execution of the algorithms. Fill each array with the sequence 1, 2, 3, ... , 50,000, and time the algorithms. Then fill the arrays with the sequence 50,000, 49,999, ... , 2, 1, and time the algorithms. Do your results correspond the Big-O running time?

◆

CHAPTER 4

The Vector Container

OBJECTIVES

- To understand that the Standard Template Library organizes its classes into three categories: sequence containers, adapters, and associative containers.
- To understand that the vector container provides index access to data and grows at the rear to meet the needs of an application. Although insertion and deletion at the rear are efficient, such operations inside a vector are not efficient.
- To understand that access to items in a list container does not use an index. Rather, we must move from element to element until the desired data value has been located. However, insertion and deletion are O(1) operations at any list location.
- To understand that a stack is an adapter implementing LIFO access.
- To understand that a queue is an adapter implementing FIFO access.
- To understand that a priority queue is an adapter for which deletion returns the largest (or smallest) value.
- To understand that the set container has a series of operations that allow a programmer to determine whether an item is a member of the set and to insert and delete items very efficiently.
- To understand that a map is a storage structure allowing a programmer to use a key as an index to the data. The key does not have to be an integer.
- To understand how to construct a class with generic data, called a *template class*.
- To learn the C++ mechanics necessary to declare and implement a template class.
- To master the fundamental public interface for the STL vector class as supplied by an API.
- To study programs that use the vector class.
- To understand the design and the running-time analysis for the insertion-sort algorithm.

OUTLINE

The previous chapters have introduced software design principles and the basic concepts of algorithm analysis. We are now in a position to draw on these topics to begin the study of containers, which form the basis for our treatment of data structures. A container is a class that stores a collection of data. It has operations that allow a programmer to insert, erase, and update elements in the collection. In this book, we use containers from the Standard Template Library (STL). The library includes most of the classic data structures that programmers use in writing sophisticated computer applications. In Section 4-1, we provide an overview of the STL containers. You can use this section as a road map for our development of data structures in the remainder of the book.

In Chapter 3, we introduced template functions that provide a mechanism for writing generic algorithms. The C++ template mechanism allows a programmer to abstract the data type on which the algorithm operates from the algorithm itself. The same template mechanism allows us to declare generic classes. The objects for a generic class store data of different types and have operations that access the data without reference to the specific type. For instance, the class may have objects that store int, string, and time24 data. In Section 4-2, we develop the syntax for declaring template classes and implementing their member functions. This section is significant, because all of the STL container classes are template classes.

The simplest STL container is the vector, which generalizes and improves upon the C++ array. Unlike an array, a vector has dynamic sizing that allows the container to grow and contract to meet the runtime demands of the application. Vectors have a particular significance in this book. We use them to implement the stack container class, as well as other more advanced data structures. Section 4-3 develops the structure of a vector and provides the vector class API. Section 4-4 provides two applications of vectors, including the insertion sort, which is a quadratic sorting algorithm ($O(n^2)$) that does not perform data swapping.

4-1   OVERVIEW OF STL CONTAINER CLASSES

The Standard Template Library consists of 10 container classes. The library categorizes the containers according to the ordering of the elements and the different types of operations that access the data. The three categories for STL container classes are sequence containers, adapter containers, and associative containers. A *sequence container* stores data by position in linear order: first element, second element, and so forth:

Sequence Container

Position 0   Position 1   Position 2   Position 3   Position 4

An *associative container* stores elements by key, such as name, social security number, or part number. A program accesses an element in an associative container by its key, which may bear no relationship to the location of the element in the container. An *adapter* contains another container as its underlying storage structure.

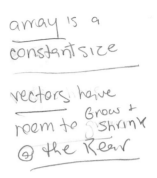

The programmer interface for an adapter, however, provides only a restricted set of operations from the underlying storage structure.

Sequence Containers	Adapter Containers	Associative Containers
vector	stack FILO	set, multiset
deque	queue FIFO	map, multimap
list	priority_queue	

The Vector Container A vector is a generalized array that stores a collection of elements of the same data type. Like an array, a vector allows access to its elements by using an index in the range from 0 to $n - 1$, where n is the size of the vector. Unlike an array, however, a vector has operations that allow the collection to grow and contract dynamically at the rear of the sequence, to meet the runtime needs of an application.

v[0]	v[1]	v[2]	...	v[n-1]	room to grow
0	1	2		n-1	

The ability to grow or shrink dynamically at the rear of the sequence is a key feature of the vector container. Insertion or deletion in the interior of the sequence is not an efficient vector operation. Programmers use a vector as the data structure of choice when an application needs a dynamic sequence and the ability to directly access any element by its position. We introduce the vector container in this Chapter. In Chapter 5, we develop the syntax and operations for dynamic memory management, which are the tools needed to implement a vector class.

The List Container. A list is a data structure that stores elements by position. Each item in the list has both a value and a memory address (*pointer*) that identifies the next item in the sequence. In order to access a specific data value in the list, you must start at the first position (*front*) and follow the pointers from element to element until you locate the data value. Hence, a list is not a direct-access structure.

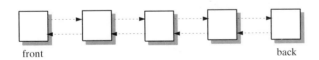

front   back

The power of a list container is its ability to add and remove items efficiently at any position in the sequence. You can think of a list as a chain consisting of a series of connected links. The algorithm to add an element follows the model of inserting a new link in a chain. In Figure 4-1, we add the value 15 immediately after element 12 in an integer list. The operation involves updating 12 to point at the new element and completing the connection by having 15 point to 6.

Figure 4-1
Inserting into the list container

Because the insert process requires only two updates, it occurs in constant O(1) running time independently of the number of other items in the list. A list container is ideal for applications that require sequential access to data while also needing frequent insertion and deletion of elements. We introduce the list class in Chapter 6 and use linked lists from Chapter 9 for its implementation.

The Stack and Queue Containers. Both a stack and a queue are storage structures that restrict how elements enter and leave a sequence. A stack allows access at only one end of the sequence, called the *top*. A rack to hold serving trays in a cafeteria is a good model of a stack. The adding of an object to the sequence is referred to as *pushing* the object onto the stack. The new item is on the top of the stack, and all other items currently on the stack are "pushed lower" to make room. The operation of removing an item from a stack is called *popping* the stack. In Figure 4-2 (a), objects A, B, and C are pushed onto the stack in that order. A series of pop operations (Figure 4-2 (b)) begins to clear the stack by removing the top element.

Note that items come off a stack in the reverse order of original insertion into the stack. We refer to this as *last-in and first-out* (*LIFO*) ordering. We introduce stacks in Chapter 7 and use them to illustrate the runtime handling of recursive function calls and in the development of algorithms used by a compiler to evaluate arithmetic expressions.

A *queue* is a container that allows access only at the front and rear of the sequence. Items enter at the rear and exit from the front. This is the model for a waiting line at a grocery store or bank. Figure 4-3 provides a view of a queue after adding elements A, B, C, and D, in that order. An insertion adds E to the end of the list, and a deletion removes the first element A from the list.

Items leave the queue in the same order as their arrival; hence, the container provides a *first-in first-out* (*FIFO*) order. We introduce the queue container in

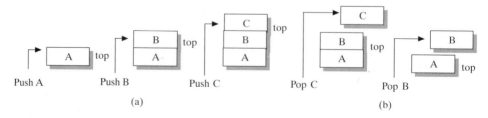

(a)   (b)

Figure 4-2
Push and pop operations on a stack

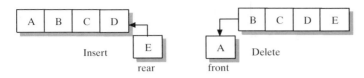

Figure 4-3
Insert and delete operations on a queue

Chapter 8 and illustrate its use with the radix-sort algorithm and an event-driven simulation.

The Priority Queue Container. A *priority queue* is a storage structure that has restricted-access operations similar to those of a stack or queue. Elements can enter the priority queue in any order. Once in the container, a delete operation removes the largest (or smallest) value. You can visualize a priority queue as a filtering system that takes in elements and then releases them in priority order. We introduce the priority queue in Chapter 8, but delay its implementation until Chapter 14, when we cover heaps.

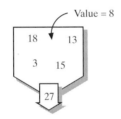

The Set Container. A *set* is a collection of unique values, called keys or set members. The set associative container has a series of operations that allow a programmer to determine whether an item is a member of the set and to insert and delete items very efficiently. The mathematical description of a set is a good abstract model of a set container. We introduce sets in Chapter 14 and illustrate applications that use the familiar set operations union (∪) and intersection (∩). A *multiset* is similar to a set, but the same value can be in the set more than once; in other words, the multiset container allows duplicates. This book provides a brief introduction to multisets and a program that illustrates their application.

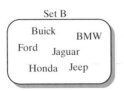

The Map Container. A map is a storage structure that implements a key–value relationship. It allows a programmer to use a key for access to the corresponding value. For instance, the key could be a part number, such as "A29-468,"

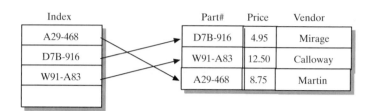

Figure 4-4
The map container

that corresponds to a part with price $8.75 and manufacturer Martin. Maps do not
store data by position; but allow the use of a key as an index. Programmers can use
the key to access an element in a map as though it is a vector or array (Figure 4-4).
We discuss the associative map container in Chapter 11, which provides a general
treatment of associative containers. A *multimap* is similar to a map, but the container allows duplicates.

4-2   TEMPLATE CLASSES

Chapter 3 introduced the template mechanism for creating generic functions. The
syntax enables a programmer to call a function with any data type that supports the
function implementation. For instance, the template-based selection sort can order
any array whose data type implements the < operator. The template mechanism applies to container classes. STL uses this fact in the declaration of each of its container classes. They can store int, string, time24 objects, and others. By having template
containers, STL allows a programmer to use a single data structure in a variety of
applications. In this section, we develop a simple template class, called *store*, that has
a single data member called value and operations to initialize, access, and update the
data member. You can think of store as a primitive container class. After all, it does
hold one element. While the store class does not have profound applications, it provides us an opportunity to define the template syntax used in the declaration and
implementation of generic classes.

Constructing a Template Class

A template version of a class has a template argument list followed by the class declaration. The data members can use the template type as an object type, and the
member functions can use the template type for their arguments and return types.
The following is the general structure for a template-based class:

```
template <typename T>
class templateClass
{
    public:
        templateClass (const T& item);
            // constructor with argument of type T
```

```
        T f();
            // member function returns a value of type T

        void g(const T& item);
            // member function has an argument of type T
        ...
    private:
        T dataValue;
        ...
};
```

The template argument list is the first item in the declaration. The actual class declaration follows the usual format with public and private sections. All of the data members and functions can reference template type *T*. Typically, the function arguments in a template class are passed by constant reference. For programmer-defined types, this avoids the copying required by call-by-value argument passing and still applies to the C++ primitive types.

The store Class. In the store class, the constructor has an argument of type *T* that initializes its data member called *value*. To access and update the data, the class has operations getValue() and setValue(). An overloaded version of the << operator displays the data member *value*. To declare a store object, the output operator must be defined for type *T*.

CLASS store	Declaration	"d_store.h"

```
template <typename T>
class store
{
    public:
        store(const T& item = T());
            // initialize value with item or the default object of type T

        T getValue() const;
            // retrieve and return data member value

        void setValue(const T& item);
            // update the data member value to item

        friend ostream& operator<< (ostream& ostr, const store<T>& obj);
            // display output in the from "Value = " value
    private:
        T value;// data stored by the object
};
```

In the declaration, note the syntax for the arguments in both the constructor and overloaded << operator. The constructor uses "*T*()" as a default value to initialize the store object when the program does not explicitly provide the value. The notation *T*() represents the object of type *T* that is created by calling the default constructor for *T*. For instance, if *T* represents the time24 type, *T*() is the time24 object 0:00 (midnight). For primitive types, C++ defines int() as 0, double() and float() as 0.0, and char() as the NULL character. The second argument in the overloaded << operator has an object of store class type. With template classes, all references to the class as a type must include the class name and the template type *T* enclosed in angle brackets. For this reason, we use store<*T*> as the object type for *obj*.

Implementing the Store Class. Programmers can implement member functions in a template class as in-line code or as external functions outside of the class body. In-line code has the usual format that places the function body inside of the class body. For instance,

setValue() (using in-line code)
```
// assign the argument as the new data member value
void setValue(const T& item)
{ value = item; }
```

An external function that implements a template class-member function is itself a template function. Its declaration must include a template argument list. In order to associate the function with the class, the function header attaches the class scope operator expression "store<*T*>::" to the function name. Recall that a template-free function must have an argument of type *T*. Because the type *T* is part of the class scope operator expression, a member function is not subject to that requirement.

We implement the store class constructor, the access function getValue(), and the overloaded operator << as external functions. Note that the template syntax applies primarily to the template header and the function header and does not significantly affect the code in the function body.

Constructor: store()
The constructor has a single argument that initializes the data member, *value*. The constructor still has the class name *store*, while the class scope operator references the template class with store<*T*>.

```
// use an initialization list to assign value
template <typename T>
store<T>::store(const T& item): value(item)
{}
```

Access Function: getValue()
The function getValue() retrieves the stored value of type *T* and returns it:

```
// return the current value
template <typename T>
T store<T>::getValue() const
{ return value; }
```

Overloaded Operator $<<$

The current value is output along with the label "Value = ." Since the operator is a friend and not a member function, the class scope operator store<*T*>:: is not used.

```
template <typename T>
ostream& operator<< (ostream& ostr, const store<T>& obj)
{
    ostr << "Value = " << obj.value;
    return ostr;
}
```

Declaring Template-Class Objects

To declare an object whose type is a template class, the compiler needs to create a specific instance of the class for a specified type. To do this, place the type in brackets immediately after the class name:

```
templateClass<type> object(argument list);
```

The declaration creates an instance of the class with the type used for the data members and operations. For instance, the following declarations create store objects with different data types:

```
store<int> intStore(5);          // data value has type int

store<char> charStore('.');      // object stores char '.' (period)

store<double> realStore;         // initially data value is 0.0

store<string> strStore("Template");  // class instance for a string
```

PROGRAM 4-1   STORING DIFFERENT TYPES

The following program uses the store class to create objects associated with different types. The objects intStore, realStore, and strStore store data of type int, double, and string, respectively. We call the overloaded << operator to output the value in each object. The program illustrates the member functions getValue() and setValue() by first returning the value "Template" from object strStore. After appending " Class," the new string updates the data value in strStore.

```
// File: prg4_1.cpp
// the program uses the store class to create objects associated
// with int, double, and string types. using the overloaded <<
// operator, it outputs the value in each object. the program
// illustrates the member functions getValue() and setValue()
// for the store object with string data
#include <iostream>
#include <string>
```

```cpp
#include "d_store.h"          // use store class

using namespace std;

int main()
{
    // declare three different types of store objects
    store<int> intStore(5);
    store<double> realStore(2.718);
    store<string> strStore("Template");

    cout << "The values stored by the objects are:" << endl;
    cout << intStore << endl;
    cout << realStore << endl;
    cout << strStore << endl;
    cout << endl;

    cout << "The concatenation of 'Template' in strStore and "
         << "'Class' is:" << endl;
    // access current value strStore and concatenate " Class"
    // update the value in strStore with the new string
    strStore.setValue( strStore.getValue() + " Class" );
    cout << strStore << endl;

    return 0;
}
```

```
Run:

The values stored by the objects are:
Value = 5
Value = 2.718
Value = Template

The concatenation of 'Template' in strStore and 'Class' is:
Value = Template Class
```

4-3   THE VECTOR CLASS

An array is a fixed-size collection of values of the same data type. It is a language-defined sequence container that stores the n (size) elements in a contiguous block of memory. The storage mechanism allows a programmer to use an index in the range from 0 to $n - 1$ to reference the value of each element in the sequence (Figure 4-5).

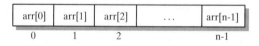

Figure 4-5
Array arr of size n with index in the range from 0 to $n - 1$

The use of an index allows a programmer to select any item in the array without referencing any of the other items. This feature characterizes an array as a *direct-access container*. A string object is also a direct-access container. The word "LIMEAR" is stored as a sequence of six characters. The letter "M" in the word is incorrect. Changing the third letter to "N" corrects the spelling:

```
string str = "LIMEAR";        // declare string object
str[2] = 'N';
cout << str:                  // Output: LINEAR (corrected spelling)
```

You first discovered the array concept in an introductory programming course. At this point, arrays are probably your only experience with containers, so let us look at them critically, to evaluate their effectiveness as a storage structure. In the process, we will discover that arrays have severe limitations that make them inappropriate or inconvenient to use in many applications. An understanding of these limitations becomes the motivation for the design of the vector container, which we introduce in the next section.

Evaluating an Array as a Container.   The size of an array is fixed at the time of its declaration and cannot be changed to meet the runtime demands of the application. For instance, assume that a statistics program reads its data from a file referenced by the input *istream fin*. For storage, the program declares an array of 100 elements of type double. We can use a loop to enter the data and store it in array statArr. The loop terminates on "end of file."

```
// read data into statArr
double statArr[100];
int i = 0;
        ...
// read data until end of file
while (fin >> statArr[i])
   i++;
```

The program fails if the file contains more than 100 values. To safeguard itself, the program could declare an array size of 1000 or larger. This new size might waste space or still not be large enough to handle the input. Being a fixed-size storage structure, an array cannot dynamically adjust its size to meet the demands of the application. This is a serious problem that precludes the use of arrays in many programs.

Other limitations of arrays create programmer inconvenience. Functions that have an array argument must also have a separate size argument, because the array itself does not provide this information. The calling statement must have explicit access to the size of the array and pass the size as a second argument. Recall the function writeArray() from "d_util.h" that outputs the elements in an array:

```
// size must be included as a second argument
template <typename T>
void writeArray(const T arr[], int size)
{
    int i;

    for(i = 0; i < size; i++)
        cout << arr[i] << " ";
    cout << endl;
}
```

Some applications need to create a copy of an array in temporary storage, so that the copy can be sorted or updated without destroying the original array. Unfortunately, C++ arrays do not allow the assignment of one array to another, and the programmer must create the copy with a loop that uses the array size as an upper bound.

```
T arr[100], tempArr[100];


// invalid statement
tempArr = arr;

// perform assignment by a loop that copies the elements from
// one array to the other using an index in the range 0 to arraySize-1
for(i=0; i < arraySize; i++)
    temparr[i] = arr[i];
```

Our evaluation of an array is not intended to be a negative criticism, but rather a positive assessment of the container as a storage structure. For applications that require a fixed-length sequence whose elements can be directly accessed by position, an array is a very useful data structure. When an application needs a storage structure that can dynamically grow and contract, we need a different container type. That was the problem faced by the designers of STL. Seeing the strengths and weaknesses inherent in an array, programmers saw the need to have a storage structure that maintains the positive features of an array, particularly its use of an index for direct access to its elements. At the same time, the new structure should allow for dynamic resizing, have a way to store the size internally, and allow for assignment of one object to another. With these design specifications, programmers created the vector container, whose objects are "super" arrays or "programmer-friendly" arrays. In turn, an evaluation of the vector type will reveal limitations of this structure and the need for additional container types. Exploring the pros and cons of each container is the dynamic force that has created the modern study of data structures and is the motivation behind the classification and choice of different containers in the

Standard Template Library. In the end, we have access to a range of data structures and the opportunity to choose the one that is most appropriate for an application.

In the next section, we introduce the vector container. Before we look at the vector, let us explain our approach, which will apply to all new containers. We begin with a basic description of the data structure that emphasizes how it stores elements. With this information, we discuss features that make the container appropriate for certain types of applications. We develop the operations for the container, using examples and pictures, and then conclude with the container API. We are not in the business of designing a formal ADT for the data structure and a declaration of its class. These tasks have been performed by the STL developers. For each container, we are looking at a finished product. Our description and the use of examples gives you a feel for the structure. The API provides documentation that gives you the prototypes for the constructors and the member functions, along with comments that give the action and the pre- and postconditions for each operation. The API allows you to use the data structure in applications without having to deal with the formal declaration of the class.

Introducing the Vector Container

The vector is a template-based class that stores elements of the same data type. Like an array, a vector object allows direct access to the elements via an index operator. Unlike an array, however, a vector retains information on its size and provides an associated size() function that gives the programmer access to the number of elements in the vector. The following is a view of a vector v with length v.size(). The indices for the vector elements are in the range from 0 to v.size() $- 1$.

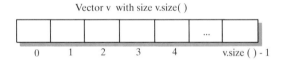

Vector v with size v.size( )

| | 0 | 1 | 2 | 3 | 4 | ... | v.size ( ) - 1 |

A vector object allows the use of the index operator on either side of an assignment statement. For instance, assume that v is a vector of integers. The following statements update or access an element by using the index operator:

```
v[5] = 15;        // assign integer 15 to the vector at index 5

// access element at index 5, double it, and assign to value
value = v[5]*2;
```

When used on the left-hand side of the assignment statement, $v[5]$ is the address of the sixth element in the vector, and the assignment copies the integer 15 to that address. On the right-hand side, the expression $v[5]*2$ accesses the value of the sixth item in the vector.

Because the size() function returns the length of a vector, algorithms that use a vector argument do not require a second size argument. For instance, the output function writeVector() requires only a constant reference vector argument:

Vector Output Function writeVector()

```
// number of elements in list is v.size()
template <typename T>
void writeVector(const vector<T>& v)
{
    // capture the size of the vector in n
    int i, n = v.size();

    for(i = 0; i < n; i++)
        cout << v[i] << " ";
    cout << endl;
}
```

an integer

For your convenience, the function is in the library file "d_util.h."

Declaring Vector Objects. Because vector is a class, the declaration and initialization of an object involves using a constructor. The class provides great flexibility by including three different constructors. The first version includes two arguments consisting of the size and an initial value of type *T*. The second argument has the default value *T*(). The action of the constructor is to allocate a vector with the specified size and assign the initial value to each of the elements. The upcoming statements declare vector objects with only a size argument. The initial value becomes the default value *T*(). For the integer vector, the initial value is 0, which is the default value for the int type. The elements in the vector of strings have the initial value "" (empty string).

```
// vector of size 5 containing the integer value 0
vector<int> intVector(5);
// vector of size 10; each element contains the empty string
vector<string> strVector(10);
```

Declaring a vector by using only the size argument parallels the declaration of an array. The following arrays correspond to the vectors intVector and strVector:

```
int intArray[5];         // array of 5 integers
string strArray[10];     // array of 10 strings.
```

The fact that the constructor allows an initial value as a second argument provides added flexibility in a declaration. In the following statements, we declare a vector of 80 characters, with each element initially set to blank. The time24 vector openTime is a list of 7 elements with an initial value of 9:00:

```
vector<char> line(80, ' ');
vector<time24> openTime(7, time24(9,0));
```

9	2	7	3	12
0	1	2	3	4

Figure 4-6
Declaring a vector with initial
values copied from an array

A second version of the vector constructor initializes its values from an array. Unlike with an array, you cannot use an initialization list enclosed in braces when declaring a vector. This task must be performed by first declaring an array and then passing the range of array addresses to the constructor as arguments. For instance, the following declaration creates a five-element vector with initial values copied from array intArray (Figure 4-6):

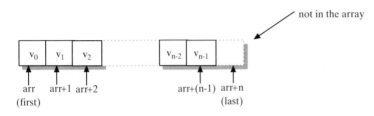

```
int intArray[5] = {9,2,7,3,12};      // array with initial values
vector<int> intVector(intArray, intArray+5);
```
> initial values
> # of elements

To understand the syntax for this version of the constructor, you need to draw on your understanding of array addresses. Assume we declare the array *arr* of type *T* and initialize it as follows:

```
T arr[n] = {v₀, v₁, v₂, ..., vₙ₋₁};
```

The array name, *arr*, is the address of arr[0], the first element of the array; arr + 1 is the address of arr[1]; arr + 2 is the address of the element arr[2]; and so forth. The last element in the array has address arr + (*n* − 1), and arr + *n* is the address just past the end of the array (Figure 4-7).

Mathematics defines a half-open interval [*a*, *b*) as the set of values between *a* and *b* including value a, but not b. We use this notation to define the *address range* for array arr as [arr, arr + *n*). In the declaration of vector intVector, the arguments are the addresses in the address range for the array intArray.

The compiler has knowledge of the number of bytes required to store an element of any data type. As a result, C++ has a unary operator *sizeof* that takes either a type or an object or variable as its operand. The operator returns the number of bytes of memory required to store data of the specified type or the number of bytes required for the specific object or variable. For an array argument, sizeof returns the number of bytes of memory used by the array. For this reason, if *T* is the type of the elements in array arr, then the number of elements in arr is

Note

not in the array

v₀	v₁	v₂		vₙ₋₂	vₙ₋₁

arr   arr+1 arr+2   arr+(n-1) arr+n
(first)   (last)

Figure 4-7
Addresses of arr [i] in array where $0 \le i < n$

sizeof(arr)/sizeof(T). Determining the number of array elements using this approach guarantees that we can add additional array elements and recompile the program without having to change the vector declaration. In our previous example, we can declare the vector intVector as follows:

```
int intArray[] = {9,2,7,3,12};        // allocate array
int arrSize = sizeof(intArray)/sizeof(int);
vector<int> intVector(intArray, intArray+arrSize );
```

Suppose we modify intArray to have seven elements.

```
int intArray[] = {9,2,7,3,12,18,25};
```

The vector declaration does not require any change, and the resulting sequence has seven elements.

Note: From this point on in the book, we will not include a size in the declaration of an initialized array. We will use the sizeof operator to determine the number of array elements.

The vector class has a third constructor, the default constructor. No argument is included in the declaration, and the resulting vector is empty, with size = 0. An empty vector is of no value if we cannot add new elements. We will introduce such an operation in the next section.

```
// empty vectors designed to hold real numbers and strings
vector<double> dblVector;
vector<string> v;
```

Adding and Removing Vector Elements.   After the declaration of an array, its size is fixed, and you cannot add or remove any elements from the sequence. You can change the value of elements but you cannot physically alter the size of the array. The vector class, on the other hand, has operations that allow a programmer to modify the rear of the sequence by using the member functions push_back() and pop_back(). These operations lie at the heart of the vector class. The function push_back() takes an element of type T and adds it at the rear of the vector. The vector size automatically increases by 1. The operation "grows" the vector. For instance, v. push_back(10) adds the element 10 on the back of the integer vector v and increases its size to five (Figure 4-8).

Figure 4-8
Using push_back() to add an integer to vector v

We refer to the last element in a vector as the back of the vector. Its value is $v[\text{v.size}() - 1]$. The vector class provides the function back() as an alternative way of accessing and updating this element. For nonconstant vectors, the function can be used on either side of an assignment statement. For constant vectors, back() provides read-only access to the value of the last element in the list. The following declarations use an array to create a vector of characters with the five vowels as initial values:

```
char vowel[] = {'a', 'e', 'i', 'o', 'u'};
int vowelSize = sizeof(vowel)/sizeof(char);
vector<char> v(vowel, vowel+vowelSize);          → initial values
                                                  → # of elements
cout << v.back();       // output: 'u'
v.push_back('w');       // add 'w' onto end of vector
v.back() = 'y';         // changes back from 'w' to 'y'
```

Just as elements can be added to the back of a vector, they can also be removed from the back. The function pop_back() deletes the last element in the vector at index size() − 1 and reduces the vector size by 1. The operation has the precondition that the vector not be empty. Programmers can test this condition by calling the function empty(), which returns a Boolean value true when size() == 0. Figure 4-9 displays a two-element vector v of real numbers. A second call to pop_back() will create an empty vector.

```
cout << v. back();      // Output: 6.8
v.pop_back();           // remove element 6.8 (See figure 4.9)
v.pop_back();           // remove element 4.6
v.empty()               // returns true
```

v.size ( ) = 2

4.6	6.8
0	1

Before

v.size ( ) = 1

4.6
0

After v.pop _back()

Figure 4-9
Removing an element from the back of a vector

Example 4-1

---

1. An application can start with an empty vector and use push_back() to build the list dynamically. In the evaluation of an array as a sequence container, we described a statistics program that reads data from an input stream and stores the values in a list. The size of the list depends on the size of the file. A vector becomes an ideal storage structure for the data.

```
vector<double> statList;            // declared as an empty vector
double dataElt;

      ...
// read data until end of file
for (;;)
{
```

```
      fin >> dataElt
      if (!fin)
         break;

      // store the dataElt at the back of the vector
      statList.push_back(dataElt);
   }
```

2. The pairing of the functions back() and pop_back() enables a program to access and then delete the element at the end of a vector. The upcoming statements declare a vector with initial integer values. A loop displays the values in the vector in reverse order, by repeatedly removing the back element until the vector is empty.

```
int arr[] = {3,5,8,1,3,8};
int arrSize = sizeof(arr)/sizeof(int);
vector<int> v(arr, arr+arrSize);

while (!v.empty())
{
   cout << v.back() << " ";
   v.pop_back();
}
cout << endl;   // output: 8 3 1 8 5 3
```

Resizing a Vector.   The function resize() uses an argument *n* to change the size of the vector. The function allows a second argument that specifies the fill value. By default, the fill value is *T*(). If the new size is greater than the current size, the vector grows by adding *n* − size() new elements. All of the existing elements remain fixed, and the new elements are assigned the fill value. If the new size is less than the current size, the resize() operation contracts the vector by "chopping off" elements at the tail of the vector. The first *n* elements remain fixed, and the vector discards the other size() − *n* elements. In the following example, a vector object initially has 5 elements. By resizing, it doubles to 10 elements and then contracts to 4 elements. Figure 4-10 displays the initial vector and its contents after the two resize() operations. A third resize() operation rebuilds the vector to 10 elements with a fill value 1.

```
int arr[] = {7, 4, 9, 3, 1};
int arrSize = sizeof(arr)/sizeof(int);

vector<int> v(arr,arr+arrSize);
v.resize(2*arrSize);      // vector size is doubled; fill value is 0
v.resize(4);              // vector is contracted. data is lost
v.resize(10,1);           // vector grows to size 10 with fill 1
```

The Vector API

The previous section has described the key operations in the vector class and has provided examples. The vector API documents the class.

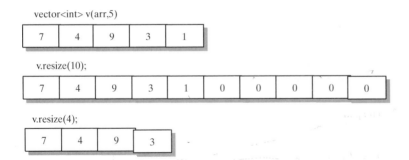

Figure 4-10
Resizing a vector

CLASS vector	Constructors	<vector>

vector();
 Create an empty vector. This is the default constructor.

vector(int *n*, const *T*& value = *T*());
 Create a vector with *n* elements, each having a specified value. If the value
 argument is omitted, the elements are filled with the default value for type *T*.
 Type *T* must have a default constructor, and the default value of type *T* is
 specified by the notation *T*().

vector(*T* *first, *T* *last);
 Initialize the vector using the address range [first, last). The notation *first* and
 last is an example of pointer notation that we cover in Chapter 5.

CLASS vector	Operations	<vector>

T& **back**();
 Return the value of the item at the rear of the vector.
 Precondition: The vector must contain at least one element.

const *T*& **back**() const;
 Constant version of back().   why a?.

bool **empty**() const;
 Return *true* if the vector is empty and *false* otherwise.

T& **operator[]** (int *i*);
 Allow the vector element at index *i* to be retrieved or modified. The notation
 in the prototype is explained in Chapter 5.
 Postcondition: If the operator appears on the left side of an assignment
              statement, the expression on the right side modifies the
              element referenced by the index.

const *T&* **operator[]** (int *i*) const;
　　Constant version of the index operator.

void **push_back**(const *T&* value);
　　Add a value at the rear of the vector.
　　Postcondition:　The vector has a new element at the rear, and its size
　　　　　　　　　　increases by 1.

void **pop_back**();
　　Remove the item at the rear of the vector.
　　Precondition:　　The vector is not empty.
　　Postcondition:　The vector has a new element at the rear or is empty. Its size
　　　　　　　　　　decreases by 1.

void **resize**((int *n*, const *T&* fill = *T*()));
　　Modify the size of the vector. If the size is increased, new elements with value
　　fill are added to the tail of the vector. If the size is decreased, the original
　　values at the front are retained.
　　Postcondition:　The vector has size *n*.

int **size**() const;
　　Return the number of elements in the vector.

☞
Note

When an object is constant, the programmer can call only a member function
that the class declares with the const specifier. The member function back() and
the index operator [] have separate implementations declared const, so these
functions are available for a constant object. For instance, consider the function
writeVectorEnds():

```
template <typename T>
void writeVectorEnds(const vector<T>& v)
{
    if (v.size() > 0)
        cout << v[0] << " " << v.back() << endl;
}
```

Without the const versions of the index operator and back(), this function will
not compile.

4-4　VECTOR APPLICATIONS

This section includes two algorithms that demonstrate use of the vector class. The
function join() concatenates one vector onto the end of another by using
push_back(). In Chapter 3, we introduced the selection-sort algorithm, which orders

an array in ascending order. The algorithm makes $n - 1$ passes over the data, selecting the smallest element in the unordered sublist at the tail of the array. An exchange repositions this smallest element at the location of the current pass. We here introduce a new sorting algorithm, called the *insertion sort*, and apply it to vectors. The algorithm makes only comparisons and does not perform exchanges.

Joining Vectors

The concatenation of one string onto the end of another is the model for the joining of two vectors. The function join() takes two vectors vA and vB as arguments. A loop scans the elements of vB and copies them onto the end of vA by using push_back() (Figure 4-11). Vector vA is a reference argument, because the operation grows the vector by adding the elements from vB. The argument vB is a constant reference argument, because copying elements to vA does not modify vB.

join():

```
template <typename T>
void join (vector<T> &vA, const vector<T>& vB)
{
    // capture the size of vB in sizeB
    int i, sizeB = vB.size();

    // use index i to access the elements of vB and push_back()
    // to add the elements to the rear of vA
    for (i = 0; i < sizeB; i++)
        vA.push_back(vB[i]);
}
```

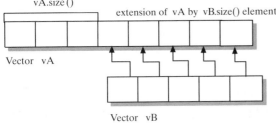

vA.size()

extension of vA by vB.size() elements

Vector vA

Vector vB

Figure 4-11
Join of vector vB onto the end of vector vA

The Insertion Sort

Teachers often have the chore of putting exams in alphabetical order before returning the papers. By looking in on the process, we discover the insertion-sort algorithm. Initially, the papers are in random order. Assuming that the first name is correctly positioned, the sort begins with the name on the second paper. If it is out of order, move it forward to the front of the pile. The third paper might be in order ($name_3 > name_2$). If not, slide it forward in front of the second paper and make another comparison. If it is still out of order, move it forward in front of the first paper.

Repeat this process for the fourth, fifth, and subsequent papers. For each new paper, we know that the papers in the front of the pile (previously processed papers) are in order. By successive comparison of the name on the new paper with each preceding paper, we find the place to insert the new paper. Let's look at the insertion-sort algorithm for a list of five names: Monroe, Chin, Flores, Stein, and Dare.

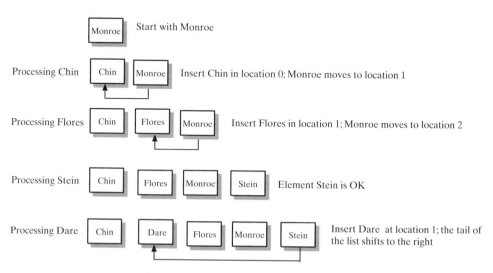

The insertionSort() Function: The function insertionSort() takes a vector v by reference and implements the insertion-sort algorithm. The ordering assumes that the first element is in its correct position, so the function requires $n - 1$ passes in the range from 1 to v.size() $- 1$ to order the remaining elements. For a general pass i, the elements in the range from 0 to $i - 1$ are already sorted. The task is to locate $v[i]$ in the proper position within the sublist from 0 to i by scanning the previously sorted sublist. Copy $v[i]$ to a temporary object called target. Scan down the list, comparing the target with items $v[i - 1], v[i - 2]$, and so forth. The process stops at the first element $v[j]$ that is less than or equal to the target or at the beginning of the list ($j = 0$). The latter condition is true when $v[i]$ is smaller than any previously sorted element and thus will occupy the first position in the newly sorted sublist. During the scan, move each element that is greater than the target one position to the right ($v[j] = v[j - 1]$). As soon as the correct location is determined, copy target (original $v[i]$) to that location. Unlike the selection sort, the insertion sort slides data to the right and does not perform exchanges.

insertionSort():

```
// sort a vector of type T using insertion sort
template <typename T>
void insertionSort(vector<T>& v)
{
    int i, j, n = v.size();
    T target;
```

```
// place v[i] into the sublist
//    v[0] ... v[i—1], 1 <= i < n,
// so it is in the correct position
for (i = 1; i < n; i++)
{   // index j scans down list from v[i] looking for
    // correct position to locate target. assigns it to
    // v[j]
    j = i;
    target = v[i];
    // locate insertion point by scanning downward as long
    // as target < v[j—1] and we have not encountered the
    // beginning of the list
    while (j > 0 && target < v[j-1])
    {
        // shift elements up list to make room for insertion
        v[j] = v[j-1];
        j--;
    }
    // the location is found; insert target
    v[j] = target;

}

}
```

You can find the function insertionSort(), along with a vector version of the template-based selectionSort(), in the header file "d_sort.h."

Running Time. Assuming that $n = $ v.size(), the insertion sort requires $n - 1$ passes. For a general pass i, the insertion occurs in the sublist $v[0]$ to $v[i - 1]$ and requires on the average $i/2$ comparisons. The average total number of comparisons is

$$T(n) = 1/2 + 2/2 + 3/2 + \cdots + (n - 2)/2 + (n - 1)/2 = n(n - 1)/4$$

From the dominant term in $T(n)$, the average-case running time of the algorithm is $O(n^2)$, which measures the number of comparisons. The best case occurs when the original list is already sorted. In pass i, the insertion occurs at $v[i]$ after only one comparison. The total number of comparisons is $n - 1$, with running time $O(n)$. The worst case occurs when the list is in descending order. For each pass i, we must scan the entire sorted sublist from $i - 1$ down to 0 and insert $v[i]$ at the front of the list in $v[0]$. The scan requires i comparisons. The total number of comparisons is $n(n - 1)/2$ with running time $O(n^2)$.

In general, the insertion sort exhibits the best performance among the quadratic sorting algorithms. Programming Project Exercise 33 deals with this issue. The quadratic algorithms are efficient for a list having a small number of elements, say $n \leq 15$. Recall that the insertion sort is linear ($O(n)$) when the list is already sorted. The insertion sort is still linear when the list is "almost sorted." This condition occurs when many of its elements are already in their correct places. Some more advanced sorting algorithms exploit this fact by partially sorting a vector and "finishing up" with insertion sort.

PROGRAM 4-2 JOINING SORTED SUBLISTS

Let's look at a program that uses join() and insertionSort() to create an ordered vector. The program begins by creating 12 random integers in the range from 100 to 999. Add each number to vector vSmall, vMedium, or vLarge, depending on its value (Figure 4-12). The insertion sort orders each of the vectors separately. A call to join() appends the elements from vMedium onto the end of vSmall. A second call to join() appends the elements from vLarge onto the end of vSmall, which already contained all of the elements from vSmall and vMedium. The final list in vSmall is sorted. The function writeVector() from "d_util.h" displays the initial set of elements in each vector and the final sorted list.

Figure 4-12
Distribution of values for Program 4-2

```
// File: prg4_2.cpp
// the program generates 12 random integers in the range
// 100 to 999. add each number value to vector vSmall if
// value < 400, to vector vMedium if 400 <= value < 700
// and to vLarge if 700 <= value < 1000. apply the insertion
// sort to order each vector. use join() so that vSmall is
// the concatenation of the three vectors. The final list
// in vSmall is created as a sorted list. display the initial
// set of elements in each vector and the final sorted list
// by calling writeVector()

#include <iostream>
#include <vector>

#include "d_random.h"      // for randomNumber
#include "d_sort.h"        // for insertionSort()
#include "d_util.h"        // for writeVector()

using namespace std;

// attach vB onto the end of vA
template <typename T>
void join (vector<T> &vA, const vector<T>& vB);

int main()
{
   // declare 3 integer vectors
   vector<int> vSmall, vMedium, vLarge;
   // use a random number generator
   randomNumber rnd;

   int i, value;
```

```
      for (i = 0; i < 12; i++)
      {
         value = rnd.random(900) + 100;

         if (value < 400)
            vSmall.push_back(value);
         else if (value < 700 )
            vMedium.push_back(value);
         else
            vLarge.push_back(value);
      }

      // sort the vector of integers in the range
      // 100 <= n < 400 and output
      insertionSort(vSmall);
      cout << "Small:   ";
      writeVector(vSmall);

      // sort the vector of integers in the range
      // 400 <= n < 700 and output
      insertionSort(vMedium);
      cout << "Medium: ";
      writeVector(vMedium);

      // sort the vector of integers in the range
      // 700 <= n < 1000 and output
      insertionSort(vLarge);
      cout << "Large:   ";
      writeVector(vLarge);

      // join vMedium onto the end of vSmall
      join(vSmall, vMedium);
      // join vLarge onto the end of the modified vSmall
      join(vSmall, vLarge);

      // output the new vector
      cout << "Sorted: ";
      writeVector(vSmall);

      return 0;
   }

/* implementation for join() provided in the preceding discussion */
```

```
Run:

Small:   176 213 269 287 357
Medium: 482 535 551 649 687
Large:   843 901
Sorted: 176 213 269 287 357 482 535 551 649 687 843 901
```

CHAPTER SUMMARY

- The Standard Template Library (STL) provides 10 container classes for solving a wide range of problems. The containers fall into three classifications: sequence containers, adapters, and associative containers.

- The vector sequence container provides direct access through an index and grows dynamically at the rear as needed. It is an alternative to the use of an array. Insertion and deletion at the rear of the sequence is very efficient, but these operations inside a vector are not efficient.

- The list sequence container stores elements by position. In order to access a specific data value in the list, you must start at the first position (front) and move from element to element until you locate the data value. The power of a list container is its ability to add and remove items at any position in the sequence efficiently.

- Both a stack and a queue are adapter containers that restrict how elements enter and leave a sequence. A stack allows access at only one end of the sequence, called the *top*. A queue is a container that allows access only at the front and rear of the sequence. Items enter at the rear and exit from the front. Like a stack or queue, the priority queue adapter container restricts access operations. Elements can enter the priority queue in any order. Once in the container, only the largest element can be accessed.

- A set is a collection of unique values, called *keys* or *set members*. The set container has a series of operations that allow a programmer to determine whether an item is a member of the set and to insert and delete items very efficiently.

- A map is a storage structure that allows a programmer to use a key as an index to the data. Maps do not store data by position; instead they implement key-access to data, which allows a programmer to use the key as an index similar to an array or vector.

- The template mechanism can also be applied to container classes. Template classes enable us to create and use very flexible generic containers. Section 4-2 introduces template classes by developing a simple template class, *store*, that has a single data member named value and member functions to initialize, access, and update the data value. The class also overloads the output operator <<. The remainder of the book will be devoted to the development of template container classes.

- The array data structure defines a block of consecutive data values of the same type and is an example of a sequence container. Because an array allows the use of an index to select any item in the list without referencing any of the other items, it is known as a direct-access container. Some sequence containers, such as the list container, do not allow direct access.

- The vector sequence container extends the functionality of arrays. Arrays have inherent problems, such as fixed size, lack of a built-in size attribute, and lack of an ability to assign one array object to another directly. The vector container solves these problems and provides a simple-to-use public interface, described by an API in Section 4-3.

- Vectors are easy to use in applications in place of C++ arrays. Section 4-4 implements the function join(), which appends one vector onto the end of another, and also develops insertion sort. This $O(n^2)$ algorithm sorts a vector in ascending order without using data exchanges. This algorithm is the best of the quadratic ($O(n^2)$) algorithms and is effective for small vectors.

CLASSES AND LIBRARIES IN THE CHAPTER

Name	Header File
insertionSort()	d_sort.h
randomNumber	d_random.h
store	d_store.h
vector	<vector>

REVIEW EXERCISES

1. **(a)** What is a sequence container? Name three types of sequence containers.
   (b) How does a sequence container differ from an associative container?

2. The class storeMax maintains an integer value. In parts (a) to (e), modify storeMax so it is a template class storing a generic data type.

```
class storeMax
{ public:
      storeMax(int item = 0): value(item)
      {}

      int getValue() const
      { return value; }

      void updateValue(int item)
      { if (item > value)
         value = item;
      }
  private:
      int value;
};
```

   (a) The declaration of storeMax as a template class is
   - **(i)** template <typename *T*>
       class storeMax<*T*>
   - **(ii)** class <template *T*>
       class storeMax
   - **(iii)** template <typename *T*>
       class storeMax
   - **(iv)** template <*T*>
       classstoreMax
   (b) The declaration of the value data member is
   - **(i)** int<T> value
   - **(ii)** template<typename T> value
   - **(iii)** template value<T>
   - **(iv)** T value

(c) The prototype for the constructor is
    (i)   storeMax<T>(const T& item = 0);   **(ii)** storeMax(const int& item<T>)
    (iii) storeMax(const T& item = T());   **(iv)** storeMax<T> (int item)

(d) The prototype for the function getValue() is
    (i)   int getValue();   **(ii)** T getValue();
    (iii) T& getValue();   **(iv)** void getValue(T& value);

(e) Give the implementation of updateValue(), assuming inline code is not used.

3. Fill in information at the indicated points in the following code:

```
int arr[] = {3, 5, 2, 7, 9};
int arrSize = sizeof(arr)/sizeof(int);
vector<int> v, w(arr, arr+arrSize);
    // (a) v = _____  w = _____

v.push_back(8);
v.push_back(10);                 // (b) v = _____

w.pop_back();
w.pop_back();                    // (c) w = _____

cout << v.back();                // (d) output: _____
cout << w.size();                // (e) output: _____

w.push_back(18);
w.resize(7);                     // (f) w = _____
```

4. Trace the following function:

```
template <typename T>
void func(vector<T> & v)
{
   if(v.size() >= 2)
   {
      v[v.size()-2] = v.back();
      v.pop_back();
   }
}
```

What is the output of the following code?

```
string str[] = {"AA", "AB", "AC", "AD", "AE"};
int strSize = sizeof(str)/sizeof(string);
vector<string> v(str, str+strSize);
int i;

func(v);
for (i=0;i < v.size();i++)
   cout << v[i] << " ";         // output: _____
```

5. Show the vector after each pass of the insertion sort:

```
int arr[] = {5, 1, 3, 2, 9, 6};
int arrSize = sizeof(arr)/sizeof(int);
vector<int> v(arr, arr+arrSize);
insertionSort (v);
```

Answers to Review Exercises

1. **(a)** A sequence container stores data by position in linear order: first element, second element, and so forth. Three types of sequence containers are the array, vector, and list.
   (b) A sequence container accesses a value by its position within the linear collection. An associative container implements fast insertion, access, and removal of elements by key, such as social security number. The key could bear no relationship to the location of the element in the container.

2. **(a)** (iii)   **(b)** (iv)   **(c)** (iii)   **(d)** (ii)

```
template <typename T>
void storeMax<T>::updateValue(const T& item)
{
    if (item > value)
    value = item;

}
```

3. **(a)** v is empty $w = \{3, 5, 2, 7, 9\}$ **(b)** $v = \{8, 10\}$ **(c)** $w = \{3, 5, 2\}$
   (d) 10   **(e)** 3   **(f)** $w = \{3, 5, 2, 18, 0, 0, 0\}$

4. output: AA   AB   AC   AE

5. Pass 0:$\{1, 5, 3, 2, 9, 6\}$
   Pass 1: $\{1, 3, 5, 2, 9, 6\}$
   Pass 2: $(1, 2, 3, 5, 9, 6\}$
   Pass 3: $\{1, 2, 3, 5, 9, 6\}$
   Pass 4: $\{1, 2, 3, 5, 6, 9\}$

WRITTEN EXERCISES

6. For each part, select the container type that best relates to the descriptive phrase.

   (a) If a larger number is considered more important, the container deletion operation returns the largest number.
      (i) queue   **(ii)** priority queue   **(iii)** stack   **(iv)** vector
   (b) Go directly to a data value stored in a consecutive sequence of data values .
      (i) queue   **(ii)** stack   **(iii)** list   **(iv)** vector
   (c) Input a word from a file, and determine if it is in a collection of correctly spelled words.
      (i) stack   **(ii)** set   **(iii)** list   **(iv)** vector
   (d) The next value out is the last one in.
      (i) queue   **(ii)** stack   **(iii)** list   **(iv)** vector
   (e) To get to a value three fourth of the way through the list, move through the preceding data values.
      (i) queue   **(ii)** array   **(iii)** list   **(iv)** vector
   (f) The first data value in is the first data value out.
      (i) queue   **(ii)** set   **(iii)** list   **(iv)** vector
   (g) Input a word, look it up in the container, and output its definition.
      (i) queue   **(ii)** set   **(iii)** map   **(iv)** vector

7. What is the main difference between a vector object and an array object? between a vector and a list object?

A vector
can only insert
& delete at front &
back

8. What is the problem with using a vector container if the application needs to perform multiple insertions and deletions at random positions in a sequence?

9. The upcoming code is the template-based accumulator class, which maintains a total value for the object. The constructor, which initializes total, can use the default constructor for the object type *T* as a default value. The data member is updated by addValue() and accessed by getTotal().

```
template <typename T>
class accumulator
{
   public:
      accumulator(const T& value = T());      // constructor
      T getTotal() const;                     // return total
      void addValue(const T& value);          // add (+) value to total
   private:
      // total accumulated by the object
      T total;
};
```

(a) Implement the class. Do not use inline code.
(b) Declare an accumulator object with the specified type and value:
   (i)   int with initial value 25.
   (ii) double with initial default value.
   (iii) string with initial value "Walker."
(c) Write a series of statements for the accumulator object strAcc storing data of type string. The statements create and output the string "template-based container." Recall that the operator + for strings performs string concatenation.

```
_____      // declare strAcc with value "template"
_____      // update strAcc to "template-based'
_____      // update strAcc with " container"
_____      // access and output final string
```

10.(a) Declare a vector object v that stores 30 elements of type double.
   (b) Declare a vector object *v* that stores the elements in the array

```
char vowel[] = {'a', 'e', 'i', 'o', 'u'};
int vowelSize = sizeof(vowel)/sizeof(char);
```

   (c) Declare a vector object *v* that stores 25 real numbers with initial values 1.0.

11. What are the initial times for elements in vector *t*?

```
vector<time24> t(10);
```

12. Implement a vector version of the sequential-search algorithm:

```
int seqSearch(const vector<T>& v, int first, int last, const T& target);
```

13. The template-based function pop_front() erases the first element in a vector and returns its value. It throws the underflowError exception if *v* is empty.

```
T pop_front(vector<T>& v);
```

Implement the function. (Hint: Shift all of the elements from position 1 to the back (vsize − 1) to the left one position, and erase the element at the back of the vector.)

14. Give the value of v.size() after executing each of the following statements:

```
vector<int> v(25);
v.push_back(-4);
v.resize(40);
m = v.back();
v.pop_back();
```

15. Given the declarations

```
int arr[] = {4, 6, 2, 9, 3, 8, 7, 1};
int arrSize = sizeof(arr)/sizeof(int);
vector<int> v(arr,arr+arrSize);
```

what is the list of elements in v after the execution of the statement v.resize(5)?

16. Trace the following code, and give the output:

```
int arr[] = {4, -6, 22, 7, 13, 8};
int arrSize = sizeof(arr)/sizeof(int);
vector<int> v(arr,arr+arrSize);

while (!v.empty())
{   cout << v.back() << " ";
    v.pop_back();
}
```

17. Implement two versions of the reverseVector() function, which reverses the order of elements in a vector.

(a) `template <typename T>`
    `void reverseVector(vector<T>& v);`

Strategy: Let n = v.size(). Exchange successive pairs of elements in the following sequence of indices i, j:

$$i = 0/j = n - 1, \quad i = 1/j = n - 2, \quad i = 2/j = n - 3, \ldots, \text{while } i \geq j$$

(b) `template <typename T>`
    `vector<T> reverseVector(const vector<T>& v);`

Strategy: Copy the elements of v in reverse to the back of a new vector, and return the new vector.

18. The function removeDup() takes a vector object as an argument and removes all duplicate elements.

```
template <typename T>
void removeDup(vector<T>& v);
```

For instance, if T = int:
    Initial vector v: 1 7 2 7 9 1 2 8 9
    Revised vector v: 1 7 2 9 8

Hint   Scan the vector v with an index i. Declare a second index j that specifies the location in v for assignment of the next nonduplicate entry. Because the first element in v is not a duplicate, initialize j = 1. The index j is incremented only after it is determined that $v[i]$ is not located within the values $v[0], v[1], ...,v[j-1]$. Resize v before returning from the function.

19. The function removeDup() in Written Exercise 4-18 can be implemented by using the function seqSearch() in Written Exercise 4-12. Follow the hint for Written Exercise 4-18 by declaring index j. To determine whether $v[i]$ is a duplicate value, call the sequential search with index first $= 0$ and index last $= j$.

20. The exchange sort is another basic sort algorithm that repeatedly scans a vector and swaps elements until the list is placed in ascending order. The algorithm exchanges a pair of elements when a smaller element is out of order. We illustrate the three-pass process for the four-element list 8, 3, 6, 2:

Pass 0:   Consider the full list 8, 3, 6, 2 . The entry at index 0 is compared with each other entry in the vector at index 1, 2, and 3. For each comparison, if the larger element is at index 0, the two entries are exchanged. After all the comparisons, the smallest element is stored at index 0.

Pass 0: Compare v[0] with v[1], v[2], v[3]

Initial List				Action	Resulting List			
8	3	6	2	Exchange	3	8	6	2
3	8	6	2	NoExchange	3	8	6	2
3	8	6	2	Exchange	2	8	6	3

Pass 1:   Consider the sublist 8, 6, 3. With the smallest element already located at index 0, only entries in the vector from index 1 to the end are considered. The entry at index 1 is compared with the other entries at index 2 and 3. For each comparison, if the larger element is at index 1, the two entries are exchanged. After all the comparisons, the smallest element in the new list is stored at index 1.

Pass 1: Compare v[1] with v[2], v[3]

Initial List				Action	Resulting List			
2	8	6	3	Exchange	2	6	8	3
2	6	8	3	Exchange	2	3	8	6

Pass 2:   Consider the sublist 8, 6. With the two smallest elements already located at index 0 and 1, only entries in the list from index 2 to the end are considered. The entry at index 2 is compared with the only other element in the vector, at index 3. After the comparison, the smallest element in the new list is stored at index 2. The resulting vector is ordered.

Pass 2: Compare v[2] with v[3]

Initial List				Action	Resulting List			
2	3	8	6	Exchange	2	3	6	8

(a) Implement the exchange sort for vector objects by using nested for loops. The outer loop has iterations for pass $= 0$ to pass $= $ v.size() $- 2$. The inner loop compares $v[\text{pass}]$ with each of the elements at

$$v[\text{pass} + 1], \quad v[\text{pass} + 2], \ldots, \quad v[v.\text{size}() - 1].$$

(b) Distinguish the best and worst cases for the exchange sort. Do a Big-O analysis for the number of comparisons in each case.

(c) Do an average-case analysis for the number of comparisons in the exchange sort.

21. (a) Implement the binary search for a vector object.

```
template <typename T>
int binSearch(const vector<T>& v, int first, int last,
              const T& target);
```

(b) Implement the binary search recursively. The function prototype remains the same.

22. Implement a recursive version of the insertion sort for a vector, using the upcoming function description as a guide.

If first $=$ last, then simply return. If first $<$ last, call insertionSort() with arguments v, first, and last-1. Then insert v[last-1] so that the range [first, last) is in order.

```
// use insertion sort to order the range [first, last)
template <typename T>
void insertionSort(vector<T>& v, int first, int last);
```

23. The Shell sort, named after its inventor Donald Shell, provides a simple and efficient sorting algorithm. The sort begins by subdividing an n-element vector into k sublists, which have members

```
arr[0],   arr[k+0],   arr[2k+0], ...
arr[1],   arr[k+1],   arr[2k+1], ...
          . . .
arr[k-1], arr[k+(k-1)], arr[2k+(k-1)], ...
```

A sublist starts with a first element arr[i] in the range from arr[0] to arr[$k-1$] and includes every successive kth element. For instance, with $k = 4$, the following vector splits into four sublists:

7 5 8 6 2 4 9 1 3 0

Sublist$_0$: 7 2 3
Sublist$_1$: 5 4 0
Sublist$_2$: 8 9
Sublist$_3$: 6 1

Sort each sublist using the insertion-sort algorithm. In our example, we obtain the sublists

Sublist$_0$: 2 3 7
Sublist$_1$: 0 4 5
Sublist$_2$: 8 9
Sublist$_3$: 1 6

and the partially sorted vector

2 0 8 1 3 4 9 6 7 5

Repeat the process with successively smaller values of k, and continue through $k = 1$. When $k = 1$, the algorithm corresponds to the ordinary insertion sort that assures the vector is in order. The values of k the algorithm uses are called the *increment sequence*. It can be shown that a very effective increment sequence is to choose as the starting value of k the largest number from the sequence 1, 4, 13, 40, 121, 364, 1093, 4193, 16577, ... that is less than or equal to $n/9$. After each iteration, replace k with $k/3$ so that the increments move backward in the sequence from the starting value of k through $k = 1$. The data swapping occurs in noncontiguous segments of the vector, which moves an element a greater distance toward its final location than a swap of adjacent entries in the ordinary insertion sort. It can be shown that the Shell sort does less than $O(n^{3/2})$ comparisons for this increment sequence.

Implement the Shell sort algorithm in the template function shellSort().

```
template <typename T>
void shellSort(vector<T>& v);
```

You may use the following code to find the starting value for k.

```
for(k=1;k <= n/9;k = 3*k+1);
```

PROGRAMMING EXERCISES

24. Write a program that declares a vector of real numbers, and inputs values until a 0 is entered. Add the values to the vector by using push_back(), and compute both the average and the maximum value of the numbers. Output the average and the maximum. Use the upcoming statements that initialize max to have the value $-\infty$. The first real number entered will become the new maximum.

```
double zero = 0.0;
// start max at -infinity
double max = -1.0/zero;
```

25. Write a program that initializes a vector with array values.

```
int arr[] = {1, 6, 2, 9, 12, 15, 33, 28};
int arrSize = sizeof(arr)/sizeof(int);
```

Compute the average value, and then output each value along with its deviation $(+/-)$ from the average.

26. Use the accumulator class from Written Exercise 4-9, and place your implementation in the file "accum_t.h." Write a program that uses the instructions specified in part (c) of the exercise.

27. Use the accumulator class from Written Exercise 4-9, and place your implementation in the file "accum_t.h." Write one program that does the following:

(a) Inputs six integer values and outputs the average. For input, use the values {4, 6, 1, 6, 9, 10}.

(b) Declares a vector of 10 accumulator objects:

```
vector<accumulator<int> > count(10);
```

Generate a million random integers in the range from 0 to 9. For each value, increment count[value]. Output the value of each element in the vector count.

28. Use the function seqSearch() in Written Exercise 4-12. Write a program that inputs a number n and then declares a vector v of n elements. Fill the vector with random integers in the range from 0 to 9, and output the vector using the function writeVector(). Output the number of occurrences of the element at the rear of the list.

29. Write one program that determines the nonduplicate values in a list by using three different approaches. Declare a vector v and then input a number n. Insert n random integers in the range from 0 to 9 at the back of the vector, and output the vector using writeVector().

   (a) Use nested for loops. The outer loop scans index range from 0 to $n - 1$. For each $v[i]$!= -1, an inner loop scans the indices $i + 1, i + 2, ..., n - 1$ and replaces each occurrence of $v[i]$ by -1. Output the values that are not -1.
   (b) Use the function removeDup() in Written Exercise 4-18. Output the values from the revised vector.
   (c) Use the function removeDup() from Written Exercise 4-19, and rename the function removeDup2(). Output the values in the revised vector.

30. **(a)** Written Exercise 4-17(a) defines the function reverseVector(). In a program, declare a vector v by using the integer array arr.

```
int arr[] = {9, 12, 6, 24, 16, 8, 3, 19, 11, 4};
int arrSize = sizeof(arr)/sizeof(int);
```

   Use reverseVector() to reverse the order of the elements. Output the elements in the modified vector.
   (b) Using part (a) as a guide, develop a program that calls the version of reverseVector() from Written Exercise 4-17(b).

31. Write a program that inputs a number n and then inputs n integers into the integer vector v. Use the insertion sort to order the list. The *median* is the value $v[n/2]$. Output the median value. For your runs, use the following data:

```
Run 1:   {9,16,3,8,2,12,6}
Run 2:   {15,34,18,6,55,78}
```

32. Do Programming Exercise 4-31 by using the exchange sort from Written Exercise 4-20.

PROGRAMMING PROJECT

33. Develop a program that compares the execution times of the selection, insertion, bubble, exchange, and Shell sorts. Written Exercise 3-17 discusses the bubble sort, and Written Exercises 4-20 and 4-23 present the exchange and Shell sorts, respectively. Create integer vectors with 10,000 entries, and generate timing data for the following cases:

```
1,2,3, . . ., 9999,10,000(ascending order)
10,000,9999, . . . ,3,2,1(descending order)
vector of 10,000 random integers in the range from 0 to 999,999
```

   Implement your program by developing the function timeSort():

```
enum sortType {Selection, Insertion, Bubble, Exchange, Shell};
enum testType {Rand, Ascending, Descending};

// create a vector with vecSize entries whose values are determined
```

```
// by the argument tst. apply the sort stype and output the time
// in seconds required by the sort
void timeSort(sortType stype, testType tst, int vecSize);
```

Hint: Use switch statements and the timer class presented in Section 3-4 to implement timeSort().

Do your empirical data support the running-time analysis for the various sorts? Which of the quadratic sorts appears to be the best, in general? Is the Shell sort much better than the $O(n^2)$ sorts?

◆

CHAPTER 5

Pointers and Dynamic Memory

OBJECTIVES

- To understand the declaration and use of the pointer primitive type for array access.
- To understand the basics of pointer arithmetic.
- To learn the use of the operator $->$ for accessing a member function through a pointer.
- To learn why a program might need dynamic memory and how to create and delete it.
- To understand that any class allocating dynamic memory must implement a destructor, a copy constructor, and an overloaded assignment operator.
- To become familiar with the application of the keyword *this.*
- To understand the basics of the vector class implementation by looking at the implementation of a small subset of the vector class named miniVector.
- To understand how to implement the overloaded index operator.
- To note the limitations of the C++ multidimensional array and to learn how to overcome these limitations by developing a matrix container.

OUTLINE

Up to this point in the book, we have declared variables, arrays, and objects without consideration of their location in computer memory. In this chapter, we declare a new type of variable, called a *pointer*, which allows a program to identify data through its memory address. We begin the chapter by showing you how to declare a pointer variable and then assign it an address associated with one or more items in memory. You are familiar with the fact that an array name is the address of the first item in the sequence. Given that a pointer is an address, an array name can initialize a pointer. This allows us to use pointer techniques for accessing arrays.

A compiler is responsible for converting source code into machine instructions. With declaration statements, a compiler designates the amount of space that will be required to store the data. When a user directs the operating system to execute a program, the system copies the instructions into memory and allocates a fixed block of space for the data. Once the program begins to execute, it can request additional memory from a system-provided resource, called a *heap*. C++ uses pointers and the operations *new* and *delete* to allow a program to allocate and then deallocate memory from the heap. The program can dynamically use (borrow) and then return this memory to meet the runtime needs of the application. The availability of dynamic memory allows container objects, such as a vector, to grow and contract as elements are added or removed from the container. The use of pointers to manage dynamic memory is their most important function in data structures.

An object that uses dynamic memory must have pointer data members that can maintain the address of the data on the heap. The corresponding class must provide constructors that not only initialize the nonpointer data members of the object, but also allocate memory from the heap and assign its address to the pointer member. When the object is destroyed, another member function, called a *destructor*, must return the previously allocated memory to the heap. In Sections 5-3 and 5-4, we show you how to design member functions for a class that uses dynamic memory so that the objects work correctly and do not waste available system memory resources.

With dynamic structures, we can design and allocate arrays whose sizes are set by the runtime requirements of the application. These are called *dynamic arrays*. The dynamic array is the basis for the implementation of the vector class, introduced in Chapter 4. In Section 5-5, we develop a template-based class, miniVector, that includes a dynamic array as the underlying storage structure. The programmer interface for the miniVector class is a simplified subset of the STL vector class interface. We use the same prototypes for the member functions, so you will not have to use a separate API. We never intend for you to use miniVector objects in applications. Rather, the class provides you with an overview of the vector class implementation.

A matrix is a two-dimensional array of elements. C++ includes two-dimensional arrays as part of the language definition. The structure has a limited number of applications, because a programmer must declare the two-dimensional arrays as a fixed-length array of one-dimensional arrays. We noted a similar problem with fixed-size arrays and used the problem to motivate the need for the vector container. In Section 5-6, we develop the matrix class, which uses vectors to generalize the C++ two-dimensional array. A matrix object has resizing capability and an overloaded version of the index operator, [], which allows a programmer to use a pair of indices to access any element in the matrix.

Pointers have great historical significance in the C programming language and have been adopted and enhanced by C++. They are part of most professionally written C++ programs. Understanding pointers requires studying them in a variety of applications. The material in this chapter is fundamental to your subsequent study of data structures and advanced C++ programming.

C++ POINTERS   5-1

To understand the concept of a pointer, we must look at the internal storage of data in memory. Memory consists of a sequence of eight-bit groups called *bytes*. Each location in the sequence has an associated address, and the contents at that address define a byte.

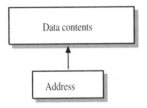

Figure 5-1 provides a physical view of memory as a sequence of bytes. As a vertical display, the memory locations resemble numbered lines on a sheet of paper. The horizontal view displays memory as contiguous series of bytes along a row.

A byte is a physical unit of data storage. As programmers, we are interested in numeric, character, or object data whose representation might require multiple bytes of storage. The number of bytes to store a data item depends on its type. For instance, an integer typically requires four bytes of memory while a real number requires eight bytes. In the case where a data item occupies more than one byte, we associate with the item the address of its first byte. For example, the integer 50 has address 5000 and occupies bytes 5000 through 5003, and the character *S* uses a single byte and has address 5004.

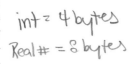

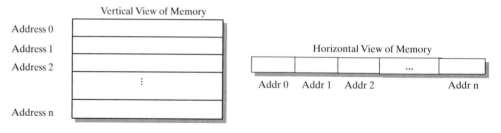

Figure 5-1
Vertical and horizontal view of memory

To make addresses more meaningful, C++ provides _pointer variables_. A pointer variable (simply called a _pointer_) holds the address of an object of a specified type. We can declare integer pointers, character pointers, time24 pointers, and so forth. Each is called a pointer because its value "points at" a data item of some type. Pointer variables have values that are memory addresses, such as 5000 or 5004. The address provides access to the data at the address. For instance, if we know that an integer pointer has value 5000, we can access the four-byte block beginning at the address and identify the integer 50. Similarly, a character pointer with value 5004 provides access to the data value _S_. To understand a pointer we must determine how to declare it as a variable. To use the pointer in the program we must have a way to give it a value (address) so that it actually points at something and then have operations to access the associated data (contents).

Declaring Pointer Variables

Declaring a pointer is much like declaring any other variable: Begin with the type, followed by the variable name, but add an * immediately before the name:

```
type *ptr;
```

The pointer _ptr_ is a variable whose value is the address of a data item of the designated type. For instance, the following are declarations of pointers to integer data and character data, respectively:

```
int *intPtr;
char *charPtr;
```

Assigning Values to Pointers

A simple declaration of a pointer does not give the variable a value, and thus it does not initially reference any object in memory. A program must assign a specific memory address to the pointer before using it. We will discover a variety of ways to make the assignment. For starters, C++ supplies the _"address-of" operator_ &, which retrieves the memory address of a variable or object declared within the program. To

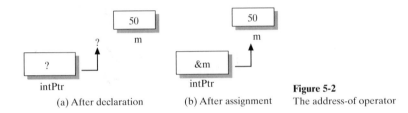

(a) After declaration   (b) After assignment

Figure 5-2
The address-of operator

access the address, attach the operator to the front of a variable or object name. By assigning the address to the pointer of the appropriate type, we give the pointer a value and create an association between the pointer and the data item. For instance, assume that a declaration creates the integer *m* with initial value 50 and an integer pointer *intPtr*. Note that a single statement can declare both type of variables:

```
int m = 50, *intPtr;
```

Then &m is the address of the integer in memory, and the assignment statement

```
intPtr = &m;
```

sets intPtr to point at an actual data item. Figure 5-2 illustrates the status of the two variables from the declaration statement and the resulting status after the assignment of &m to intPtr.

Example 5-1

Figure 5-3 assumes that integer *t* has initial memory address 8050 and rectangle *r* has initial memory address 8068. Through use of the & operator, the declarations illustrate how we can create a pointer and give it an initial value within the statement itself.

Declare pointer *p*, and initialize it to reference integer *t*, which has value 100:

```
int t = 100, *p = &t;
```

Declare pointer rectPtr and initialize it to reference the four-by-five rectangle *r*:

```
rectangle r(4,5), *rectPtr = &r;
```

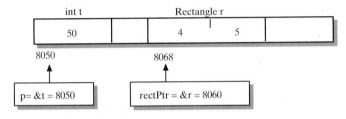

Figure 5-3
Creating a pointer and initializing it within the statement itself

Accessing Data with Pointers

Once a pointer has a value, a program can use the pointer to access the data item that it references. The syntax requires attaching the * operator immediately before the pointer name. When it is used in this way, *ptr is the contents of the data item the pointer references. For instance,

```
double x = 2.98, *dPtr = &x;
cout << *dPtr;      // Output: 2.98
*dPtr = -3.6;       // assigns -3.6 to the real number referenced by dPtr
```

The operator * is called the _dereference operator;_ it combines with the pointer to allow access to the contents referenced by the pointer.

Now that we can declare pointers and use them in statements with the & and * operators, we consider a series of examples, along with pictures that give a view of memory before and after each statement.

Example 5-2

Assume there is a declaration that creates two integer variables x and y, along with two integer pointers px and py. In the declaration, px is set to point at x, and py is set to point at y:

```
int x = 50, y = 100, *px = &x, *py = &y;
```

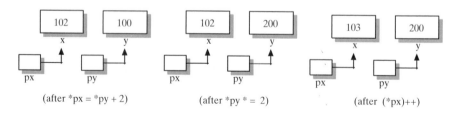

1. Expressions combine the pointers and the dereference operator * to update the values of x and y:

```
*px = *py + 2;      // assign to x the value y + 2 = 102
*py *= 2;           // double the value of y to 200
(*px)++;            // increment x from 102 to 103
```

(after *px = *py + 2)   (after *py * = 2)   (after (*px)++)

2. Pointers are variables, and thus an assignment statement could copy the value of one pointer into another pointer. The variable on the left-hand side gets a new value (address) and references the same data item as the pointer on the right-hand side:

```
py = px;    // py points to the same object referenced by px
```

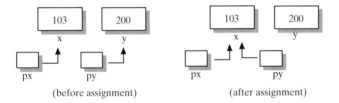

(before assignment)   (after assignment)

After the assignment, *px* and *py* reference the same value: *x*. The integer *y* still has the value: 200.

```
cout << *px << " " << *py;       // output: 103 103
cout << x << " " << y;           // output: 103 200
```

Arrays and Pointers

An array is a sequence of data items of the same type occupying consecutive memory locations. In its declaration, the array name is the starting address of the list:

```
int arr[7];
```

When processing the declaration of *arr*, the compiler allocates space for seven integer objects and assigns to *arr* the starting address of the memory block. The array name *arr* becomes a pointer constant whose value is the address of *arr*[0] (Figure 5-4).

From the declaration, the compiler also associates with the pointer the type, and thus the size, of the data item it references. In this case, the compiler identifies that the data item is a four-byte integer. As a result, the pointer *arr* can be part of an arithmetic expression of the form *arr* + *i*, where *i* is an integer. The value of the expression is the address of the *i*th element in *arr*:

```
arr+1 is the address of arr[1]
arr+2 is the address of arr[2]
. . .
arr+7 is the address immediately past the end of the array
```

By using the dereference operator with the pointer expression, we have

```
*arr = arr[0];
*(arr+1) = arr[1];
. . .
*(arr+6) = arr[6];
```

Figure 5-4
The array name arr is a constant integer pointer containing the address of arr[0].

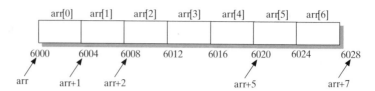

Figure 5-5
Using pointer arithmetic to compute the value of a pointer expression

☞

Note

An expression of the form *arr* + *i* involves pointer arithmetic. The compiler evaluates the address by taking the value of *i*, the size of an integer, and the value of *arr* (the starting address of the array):

$$\text{Address}(arr + i) = arr + i * 4.$$

For instance, if *arr* is address 6000 in memory, then *arr* + 2 is the physical address 6008 and *arr* + 5 is physical address 6020. The address immediately following the array is 6028 (*arr* + 7). See Figure 5-5 .

Because an array name is an address, it can be used to assign a value to a pointer variable. For instance, the statements shown next declare the integer pointer *p* and then assign it the address *arr*. The initialization could be done in the declaration.

```
int *p;       // Equivalent action: int *p = arr
p = arr;
```

The pointer *p* references the first element in *arr*, and **p* = *arr*[0]. C++ syntax allows a pointer variable to use both pointer arithmetic and the index operator []. For instance,

```
p[1] = *(p + 1) = arr[1]
```

The increment (++) and decrement (−−) operators apply to a pointer, and the programmer can use them to perform operations on array values. The statement *p*++ moves *p* forward one array location and the statement p−− moves *p* back one array location. Similar expressions using *arr* are not valid, because *arr* is a pointer constant and thus cannot be updated.

Example 5-3
___

Consider the following seven-element array of double values and pointer *p*:

```
double arr[] = {1.2, 4.5, 6.7, 2.3, 7.8, 3.5, 8.9}, *p = arr;
// let the compiler determine the size of arr
int arrSize = sizeof(arr)/sizeof(double);
```

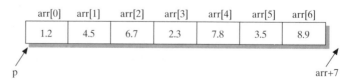

1. The loop uses the pointer *p* and the ++ operator to scan the array and doubles each of its values. The loop terminates when *p* has the address just beyond the end of the list (*arr* + 7):

```
while (p != arr+arrSize)
{
    *p += 2.0;
    p++;
}
```

2. After initializing the pointer to a location past the end of the array, the loop outputs the elements of the array in reverse order. The decrement operator, −−, moves the pointer down through the list until it reaches the first element at address *arr*:

```
p = arr + arrSize;          // initialize p past end of array
while (p != arr)
{
    p--;                    // set p to previous array element
    cout << *p << " ";      // output element pointed to by p
}
```

```
Run:
8.9  3.5  7.8  2.3  6.7  4.5  1.2
```

3. To initialize the pointer *p* to some intermediate array element *arr*[*i*], use the reference *arr* + *i* or the & operator:

```
p = arr+i = &arr[i];     // p points at arr[i]
```

The fact that *arr* and *arr* + *i* are addresses is the rationale behind the constructor that initializes a vector object from an existing array. This form of the constructor uses the address range [*arr*, *arr* + *N*) as arguments, where *N* is the size of the array. The first argument is the location of *arr*[0], and the second argument is the address of the location immediately past the end of the array. For instance,

```
double arr[] = {1.2, 4.5, 6.7, 2.3, 7.8, 3.5, 8.9};
int arrSize = sizeof(arr)/sizeof(double);

vector v(arr, arr+arrSize);
```

Pointers and Class Types

In all of our previous examples, the pointers reference data items having primitive number and character types. The examples illustrate basic pointer concepts, but we need to introduce pointers that reference objects. We will learn new notation that allows us to use the pointer to call the member functions for the associated data object. We develop the ideas by using a rectangle object and a rectangle pointer.

The upcoming declaration creates a two-by-five rectangle called _box_ and the pointer variable rectPtr. By using the operator &, we assign to rectPtr the address of box.

```
rectangle box(2,5), *rectPtr;        // a 2 by 5 rectangle and a pointer

rectPtr = &box;                      // set rectPtr to point at box
```

The dereference operator, *, allows a pointer to access the data item it references. In this case, *rectPtr is the rectangle box. We can combine the * operator and the . (dot) operator to execute member functions:

```
// (*rectPtr).area() is box.area()
cout << (*rectPtr).area();      // area of the box is 10

(*rectPtr).setSides(7,10);      // update dimensions of *rectPtr (box)
```

The use of parentheses with *rectPtr is necessary, because the * operator has a lower precedence than the dot operator and so would execute after the dot operator. Without the parentheses, the compiler interprets the expression *rectPtr.area() as *(rectPtr.area()), which is a syntax error, because rectPtr.area() is not a pointer, but a value of type double.

C++ recognizes that the need to enclose *rectPtr in parentheses is somewhat clumsy and provides the operator −> as a shortcut. Type the operator by entering the characters − and > adjacent to each other. Its use has the general form

```
ptr-> f()
```

where *ptr* is a pointer to an object and *f()* is a member function. The syntax ptr−> f() is shorthand for (*ptr). f(). For instance, we can use the pointer rectPtr with −> to call rectangle member functions:

```
// rectPtr is address of 4 x 5 rectangle box
cout << rectPtr-> area();       // output the area 10
rectPtr->setSides(7,10);        // *rectPtr (box) to 7x10 rectangle
```

The −> operator, which is referred to as the *dereference and select operator,* is used only with pointers to objects. The operator is a shortcut; it accesses an object member by using the pointer name and member name as operands, rather than the dereferenced object (*ptr) in parentheses and the dot operator.

Example 5-4

The following declaration creates the time24 object *t* with initial value 12:00 (noon) and a time24 pointer, tPtr, set to point at *t*:

```
time24 t(12,0), *tPtr = &t;
```

1. The pointer and the −> operator provide a shortcut to call getHour():

```
cout << tPtr-> getHour();       // output: 12
```

2. With expressions involving overloaded time24 operators, use the deference operator, *, for an operand:

```
*tPtr += 75;            // *tPtr is object t
cout << *tPtr;          // Output:  13:15
```

DYNAMIC MEMORY   5-2

In Chapter 4, we introduced the vector container as an extension of arrays. One of its key features is the ability to grow and contract in response to the storage demands of an application. In order to understand how a vector implements this feature, we need to introduce the concept of a heap. Our discussion starts with the compilation process. When a source-code statement declares a variable or object, the compiler creates information that specifies the amount of memory the variable or object will occupy. For instance, the information from the declaration of a time24 object *t* specifies that the object will need eight bytes for its two integer data members, hours and minutes:

```
time24 t(9,45);
```

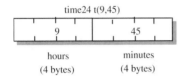

The compilation process creates an executable file in which the memory requirements for each variable and object are defined. We say that all of the program variables and objects are *statically allocated*, because the compiler determines their size. During runtime, a program could need additional memory. The amount of memory could not be anticipated by the programmer and included in source-code declaration statements, so the compiler makes no provisions to allocate space. Recognizing this problem, the runtime system makes available to the program an additional memory resource, called the *heap*. You can think of the heap as a bank of memory, much like a financial bank that maintains a reserve of money. A program can borrow (allocate) memory from the heap when additional storage space is required and then pay it back (deallocate) when it is no longer needed. We refer to memory from the heap as *dynamic memory*, because the program uses runtime instructions to allocate and deallocate the resource.

In this section, we show you how to use pointers and the operations *new* and *delete* to access dynamic memory. In Section 5-4, we use these operations to implement the miniVector class, which uses a dynamic array as the underlying storage structure for the elements. In subsequent chapters, we will see how the other STL container classes use dynamic memory to provide their objects with almost unlimited storage capacity.

The Memory Allocation Operator new

A program informs the system that it requires heap memory through the use of the operator *new* in conjunction with a pointer variable. To understand the syntax and action of the operator, assume *T* is a primitive type and ptr is a pointer to type *T*. The operator requests memory space from the heap for a variable of type *T*. If the memory is available, the system reserves the appropriate number of bytes and returns the starting address of the memory. If memory is not available, the system returns the value 0, which is called the *NULL pointer*. The file <iostream> defines the constant NULL. Use an assignment statement to give ptr the value of the return address:

```
// allocate unitialized memory for variable of type T
ptr = new T;
```

If the object of type *T* is to have an initial value on the heap, include the value in parentheses after the type name:

```
// allocate memory for type T and initialize the value to initValue
ptr = new T(initValue);
```

Example 5-5

The upcoming statements allocate C++ variables on the heap. In the figure, we assume the system heap begins at address 5000.

1. Before allocating memory from the heap, a program must declare a pointer to hold the address of the memory. To allocate an integer, first declare the integer pointer intPtr:

```
int *intPtr;
```

```
// assign to intPtr the address of an uninitialized integer
// on the heap
ptrInt = new int;
```

The operation *new* returns the address 5000 from the heap and assigns the value to the pointer. Thus, intPtr = 5000. The runtime system maintains a heap allocation table which indicates that the four bytes starting at address 5000 are in use.

2. If the operation *new* includes an initial value, the operation allocates memory on the heap, assigns it the initial value, and returns the address:

```
double *dblPtr;
```

```
// request space for a double with initial value 5.3
// pointer dblPtr is assigned the address 5004
dblPtr = new double(5.3);
```

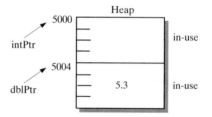

If the heap does not have sufficient memory to allocate the requested variable or object, the *new* operation returns the value NULL. In this book, we throw a memoryAllocation exception when the operations fails:

```
if (dblPtr == NULL)
{
    throw memoryAllocation("Memory allocation error";
}
```

The *new* operator can also dynamically allocate objects. A programmer must, however, take into account the constructor, which is called whenever the program allocates an object of type className. When dynamically allocating a single object, the operator *new* allows constructor arguments immediately following the type name. If no arguments are present, the operation calls the default constructor.

```
ptr = new className;              // calls the default constructor
ptr = new className(arguments);   // pass arguments to constructor
```

For instance, the operator new assigns to pointers *p* and *q* the address of time24 objects on the heap. The initial value of **p* is 00:00 (default constructor), and the initial value of **q* is 8:15 (constructor arguments 8, 15). Figure 5-6 gives a view of the memory allocated on the heap.

```
time24 *p, *q;

p = new time24;            // *p is 00:00 (midnight)
q = new time24(8, 15);     // *q is 8:15 AM
```

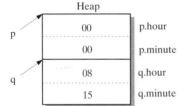

Figure 5-6
Dynamically allocated time24 objects

Dynamic Array Allocation

The power of dynamic memory allocation is most evident with arrays whose size requirements are often not known until runtime. C++ extends the syntax of the *new* operator to use the index symbol [] with the array size as an argument. The operator requests memory from the heap for *n* objects of type *T*, which is a dynamic array of size *n*.

```
T *ptr;

ptr = new T[n];    // ptr is the address of an array of n elements
```

When *T* is a primitive type, the elements in the dynamic array are uninitialized. However, when *T* is a class, the system calls the default constructor to build each array element. For instance,

```
int *pList;

// allocate array pList with 25 uninitialized integers
pList = new int[25];

rectangle *rList;
// allocate array rList with 10 rectangles initialized by the
// default constructor as 0 x 0 rectangles
rList = new rectangle[10];
```

☞
Note

When an array is dynamically allocated, the pointer that holds the return address can be used just like an ordinary array name. For instance, if pList is the pointer, pList[0] is the first element of the dynamic array, pList[1] is the second element, and so forth.

Example 5-6

1. The operator new attempts to allocate space for an array of 1000 doubles. If memory is not available, the program throws an exception. The elements of the array dArr do not have initial values.

```
double *dArr;

dArr = new double [1000];
if (dArr == NULL)
{
    throw memoryAllocation("Memory allocation error!";
}
```

2. Let timeList be a time24 pointer. The upcoming statements use the operator new to allocate an array of 10 time24 objects that are initially assigned the default value 0:00 (midnight). A loop uses the pointer , the −> operator, and the time24 member function setHour() to assign to array elements the times 1:00 am through 10:00 am.

```
time24 *timeList;
int i;

// an array of 10 time24 objects initially set to 0:00
timeList = new time24[10];
// assign array elements the times 1:00 AM through 10:00 AM
for (i=0;i < 10;i++)
    timeList[i]-> setHour(i+1);
```

The Memory Deallocation Operator delete

In an application, the program is responsible for providing efficient memory management. Understanding that the heap is a finite resource, the program should prudently request (allocate) memory from the heap and then return (deallocate) the memory when it is not needed. C++ provides the *delete* operator to return un-used memory to the heap. The operator deallocates memory that was previously allocated by the *new* operator. The syntax is very simple and relies on the fact that the system retains information about the address and the size of memory allocat-ed by each call to the operator *new*. When freeing the dynamic memory allocated to a single object, the *delete* operator takes a pointer operand that was previously assigned a value by the operator *new* and deallocates the corresponding memory.

```
ptr = new T;       // allocate dynamic storage
delete ptr;        // deallocate same dynamic storage
```

When deallocating a dynamic array, use a slightly different form of *delete*: Place square brackets, [], between *delete* and the pointer variable's name. The sys-tem deallocates all of the memory originally assigned to the dynamic array.

```
arr = new T[ARRSIZE];    // allocated space for ARRSIZE objects
delete [] arr;           // deallocate dynamic array storage
```

For instance, assume that *t* is a dynamic 20-element array of time24 objects:

```
// allocate a dynamic array with 20 time24 objects.
time24 *t = new time24[20];
```

Deallocate the dynamic array using the operator *delete*:

```
delete [] t;    // deallocate the array memory from the heap
```

Example 5-7

Be careful to distinguish between allocating a single object with an initial value and allocating an array with a specified size:

```
// allocate a single integer variable with initial value 100
int *p = new int(100);

// allocate a dynamic array of 100 unitialized integers.
int *q = new int[100];
```

The corresponding `delete` operations deallocate the single integer variable and the array of 100 integers, respectively:

```
delete p;        // deallocate memory for single integer
delete [] q;     // deallocate memory for 100 integer elements
```

5-3   CLASSES USING DYNAMIC MEMORY

In the previous section, we distinguished between memory that is statically allocated to store the variables and objects from the program's declaration statements, and dynamic memory that the program dynamically allocates from the heap. While a program executes, the runtime system is constantly allocating and deallocating memory to service function calls, create and later destroy local variables, and so forth. We refer to this runtime activity as *memory management*. For statically allocated data items, such as function arguments, the compiler provides instructions to the runtime system for their memory management. With dynamically allocated data items, however, the programmer must include instructions that direct the memory management. For instance, the programmer must include a *new* operation to allocate an array dynamically. When the array is no longer needed, the programmer must include a *delete* statement to direct the runtime system to deallocate the memory. To see the importance of maintaining good memory management, consider a GUI (graphical user interface) application that allows a user to open and close windows. Each *open* operation uses *new* to acquire memory for the window surface and components. Suppose the *close* operation does not include a *delete* statement. Its execution would shut down the window, but would not free the corresponding memory on the heap. We refer to this situation as a *memory leak*, because the operation loses a memory resource. If windows are repeatedly opened and closed, all of the available heap space would eventually be designated as "in use," and the application could no longer create a new window.

Classes often use dynamic memory to store data. We associate the term *dynamic class* to designate these types of classes. The programmer is responsible for the management of dynamic memory in the design and implementation of the classes. To handle memory management, a dynamic class typically includes constructors that allocate the dynamic memory for an instance of the class and a destructor that deallocates the memory when the object is destroyed. If the class allows for the assignment of one object to another, its implementation must include an overloaded version of the assignment operator, =, that copies the corresponding dynamic data values from the object on the right-hand side to the object on the left-hand side of the operator. To illustrate the design and implementation of the constructors, destructor, and overloaded assignment operator, we use a simple template-based class, called dynamicClass, that has a static data member and a dynamic data member. While the class serves only for demonstration, it illustrates the essential action of class operations to handle dynamically allocated data members. You will be able to use the principles to understand the design and implementation of container classes that use larger blocks of dynamic memory to store the elements.

The Class dynamicClass

The data members in dynamicClass consist of the statically allocated object member1 of type T and a pointer, *member2, that references a data item of type T. Actually, both of the data members are statically allocated when a program creates a dynamicClass object. What is not allocated is the data item pointed to by member2.

This requires the action of the constructor, which contains two arguments, *m1* and *m2*, of type *T*:

```
dynamicClass(const T& m1, const T& m2);
```

The constructor uses argument *m1* to initialize the data value member1. Action for member2 requires allocating memory for data of type *T* and giving it an initial value *m2*. The upcoming code is an implementation of the constructor. The initialization list uses argument *m1* to initialize member1. The function body has a statement with the operator *new* to allocate the dynamic memory for member2 and assigns the associated data item on the heap the value *m2*. Because dynamicClass is a demonstration class, we include an output statement that indicates the action of the constructor. We use the same strategy for the other memory management operations. A series of programs will use dynamicClass objects to illustrate the operations. The output for these programs will portray the action of the operations.

dynamicClass Constructor:

```
// constructor with arguments to initialize the data members.
// use constructor initialization list to give member1 the
// value m1
template < typename T>
dynamicClass<T>::dynamicClass(const T& m1, const T& m2):
    member1(m1)
{
    // allocate dynamic memory. initialize it with value m2
    member2 = new T(m2);
    cout << "Constructor: " << member1 << '/'
        << *member2 << endl;
}
```

Example 5-8

The next statement declares a dynamicClass< int> object obj. The accompanying figure illustrates the allocation of memory on the heap.

```
dynamicClass<int> obj(1,100), *ptrDynamicObj;
```

  1. The object obj has arguments 1 and 100 that initialize the data members. The constructor assigns to obj.member2 the address of the dynamically allocated integer on the heap. The pointer and the dereference operator, *, identify the integer data item on the heap.

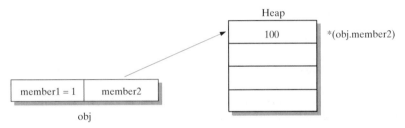

2. We can allocate a dynamicClass object dynamically using the operator *new*. The following declaration defines a dynamicClass< int> pointer ptrDynamicObj and allocates a corresponding object with arguments 2 and 200:

```
ptrDynamicObj = new dynamicClass<int> (2,200);
```

The action of the operator *new* includes a call to the dynamicClass constructor, which itself makes a call to *new* in order to allocate the dynamic integer for member2. The initial call to *new* allocates space for the data members member1 and member2. Initially member1 is 2, and the pointer member2 is uninitialized. The call to new in the constructor allocates additional space for an integer that has an initial value of 200. The return address from this operation becomes the value for member2.

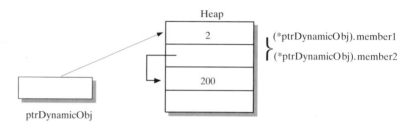

In the figures for part 1 and part 2, we include the heap to emphasize the action of new in allocating memory. To illustrate other dynamicClass objects, we employ a simpler and more functional view of the objects (Figure 5-7).

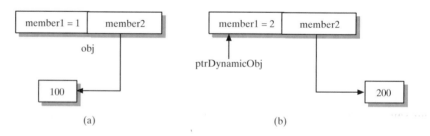

Figure 5-7
dynamicClass objects featuring the two data members and the dynamic data on the heap

The Destructor

During execution of a program, the runtime system allocates variables and objects in response to declaration statements in the main program and in response to function calls that set up arguments and local data within the function body. When the function completes execution, the runtime system destroys any temporary data used by the function. Before executing the return statement in the main program, the runtime system destroys any data declared in the program. When a class has objects that allocate dynamic memory, the action of the runtime system destroys the objects, but not any associated dynamic memory. Consider the function destroyDemo(), which creates a dynamicClass object obj having integer data and then simply returns. The function illustrates the need for a member function in dynamicClass that "undoes" the action of the constructor.

```
void destroyDemo(int m1, int m2)
{
    dynamicClass<int>  obj(m1,m2);
}
```

Before executing the return from destroyDemo(), the system destroys obj, but does not deallocate the dynamic memory associated with the object. Figure 5-8 illustrates this situation.

For effective memory management, we need to deallocate the dynamic data within the object as part of the process of destroying the object. Otherwise, the memory resides on the heap, while the pointer that references the memory is no longer available. This memory on the heap is inaccessible for the remainder of the program, and the situation creates a memory leak. To prevent this problem, the programmer needs to provide the runtime system with an operation that reverses the action of the constructor that originally allocated the dynamic data. The C++ language provides a member function, called the *destructor*, which the runtime system calls when an object is destroyed. For any class, the prototype of the destructor uses the class name and the character ~. For example, the prototype for the destructor in class className is

```
~className();          // no return type
```

For dynamicClass, the destructor has the declaration

```
~dynamicClass();
```

The character "~" represents "complement," so ~dynamicClass is the complement of a constructor. A destructor never has an argument or a return type. For our sample class, the destructor is responsible for deallocating the dynamic data for member2.

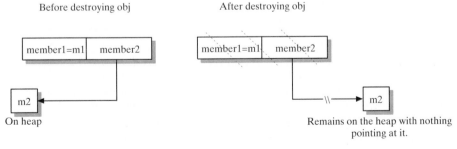

Before destroying obj   After destroying obj

Figure 5-8
Need for a destructor

dynamicClass Destructor:

```
// destructor. deallocates the dynamic memory allocated
// by the constructor
template <typename T>
dynamicClass<T>::~dynamicClass()
{
    cout << "Destructor: " << member1 << '/'
        << *member2 << endl;
    delete member2;
}
```

When a program terminates, the runtime system calls the destructor for all objects declared in the main program. For local objects created within a block, the program calls the destructor when the program exits the block.

Now that we have introduced the constructor and destructor for dynamicClass, we give a partial declaration of the class that includes the data members and these two member functions.

CLASS dynamicClass	Declaration	"d_dynam.h"

```
template <typename T>
class dynamicClass
{
  public:
    // constructor
    dynamicClass(const T& m1, const T& m2);
        // initializes member1 and dynamic object associated
        // with member2

    // destructor
    ~dynamicClass();

  private:
    T member1;
    T *member2;
};
```

PROGRAM 5-1   THE DESTRUCTOR

Let's look at a program that illustrates the destructor by using three dynamicClass objects with integer data. The main program statically allocates the object obj1 and dynamically allocates an object pointed to by ptrObj2 . The program includes a call to the function destroyDemo(), which declares an object obj. We include annotations that mark the different calls to the constructor and destructor. In the run, you can identify the order of operations.

```
// File: prg5_1.cpp
// dynamicClass objects are declared in the main program
// and in the function destroyDemo(). output indicates when
// the system calls the constructor and destructor for each
```

```
// object

#include <iostream>

#include "d_dynam.h"

using namespace std;

void destroyDemo(int m1, int m2);

int main()
{
    // create object Obj_1 with member1=1, *member2=100
    dynamicClass<int> obj1(1,100);          ◄──────────── Constructor for obj1(1,100)

    // declare a pointer to an object
    dynamicClass< int>   *ptrObj2;

    // allocate dynamic object pointed to by ptrObj2 with
    // member1 = 2 and *member2 = 200
    ptrObj2 = new dynamicClass<int>   ◄─────── Constructor for * ptrObj2(2,200)

    // call function destroyObject() with arguments 3/300
    destroyDemo(3,300);

    // explicitly delete object pointed to by ptrObj2
    delete ptrObj2;                    ◄─────── Destructor for *ptrObj2

    cout << "Ready to exit program." << endl;


    return 0;                          ◄─────── Destructor for obj1
}

void destroyDemo(int m1, int m2)
{
    dynamicClass< int>   obj(m1,m2);   ◄─────── Constructor for obj3(3,300)
}                                      ◄─────── Destructor for obj3
```

```
Run:
Constructor: 1/100
Constructor: 2/200
Constructor: 3/300
Destructor: 3/300
Destructor: 2/200
Ready to exit program.
Destructor: 1/100
```

5-4   ASSIGNMENT AND INITIALIZATION

Assignment and initialization are basic operations that apply to C++ variables and to objects. Initialization is part of a declaration statement in which the value of an existing data item initializes a new variable or object. Assignment involves copying the value of an existing data item on the right-hand side into an existing variable or object on the left-hand side. The initialization and assignment operations both have the effect of producing a data item that is the copy of an existing item. For objects that allocate dynamic data, the class must provide special member functions, called the copy constructor and the overloaded assignment operator, that enable the run-time system to execute the operations. Before we look at these member functions, let us see what happens with objects for classes that do not have dynamic data. For these classes, the compiler provides default versions of the copy constructor and overloaded assignment operators that perform a byte-by-byte copy of the data from an existing item. For instance, consider the time24 objects x, y, and z. The declaration of y uses the existing time24 object x for its initial value (Figure 5-9). The assignment of x to z copies the values for x.hour and x.minute to the corresponding data members of z (Figure 5-9 (b)).

```
// create time24 objects x and y. the data in x initializes
// the data in y. z has the default time 0:000
time24 x(15,30), y = x, z;


z = x;      // time 3:30 PM overwrites time 0:00 in z
```

With classes that allocate dynamic memory, the default versions for initialization and assignment do not manage memory properly and potentially produce runtime errors. As we continue the development of dynamicClass, we illustrate the problems with the default operations and design new ones that correctly manage memory.

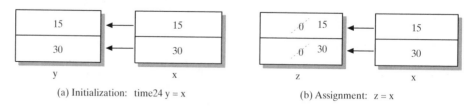

(a) Initialization: time24 y = x   (b) Assignment: z = x

Figure 5-9
Using the default copy constructor and overloaded assignment operator, =, for time24 objects

Assignment Issues

Assume that a declaration statement creates two dynamicClass objects, objA and objB. The constructor allocates separate dynamic data items pointed to by objA.member2 and objB.member2, respectively (Figure 5-10).

```
dynamicClass< int>  objA(1,2), objB(3,4);
```

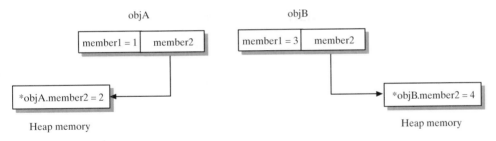

Figure 5-10
Declaration of dynamicClass objects objA and objB

If dynamicClass uses the default assignment operation, the statement objB = objA causes the byte-by-byte copying of the data in objA to objB:

```
// copies statically allocated data from objA to objB
member1 of objB = member1 of objA
// copies the pointer from objA to objB
member2 of objB = member2 of objA
```

The problem occurs with the default copy of the pointer objA.member2 into pointer objB.member2. Both pointer variables reference the same location in memory. The action leaves the dynamic memory that originally belongs to objB on the heap and thus results in a memory leak (Figure 5-11).

A runtime error can occur if objA is destroyed and the program continues to access objB. The action of destroying objA calls the destructor of the object, which deallocates the data pointed to by objA.member2. These are the same data referenced by objB.member2. An instruction involving objB that attempts to access the deallocated data will likely cause a fatal application error.

The default assignment action copies the pointer member2 in objA to the pointer member2 in objB. We really want to leave the pointer *values* the same, but copy the *contents* pointed to by member2 of objA to the *contents* pointed to by member2 of objB. We use this design strategy in the next section, when we develop the algorithm for a programmer-defined version of the overloaded assignment operator (Figure 5-12).

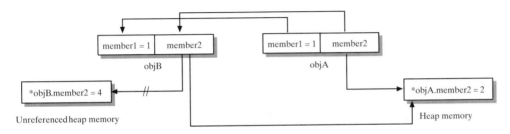

Figure 5-11
Action of using the default assignment operator for the statement objB = objA

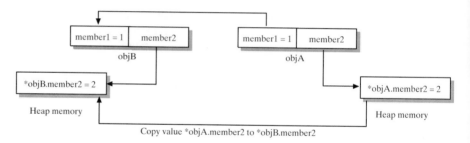

Figure 5-12
Design of the overloaded assignment operator, =, in dynamicClass

Overloading the Assignment Operator

C++ allows for overloading the assignment operator, =, as a member function. The prototype for the operator function in dynamicClass is

```
dynamicClass<T>& operator= (const dynamicClass<T>& rhs);
```

The argument *rhs* represents the right-hand side operand. For instance,

```
objB = objA;      // implemented as objB.operator= (objA)
```

For each assignment statement involving dynamicClass objects, the runtime system executes the overloaded operator = instead of using the default version of the operator. The overloaded operator assigns the data value member1 for object rhs to the data value member1 of the current object. The assignment also copies the contents pointed to by member2 in rhs to the contents pointed to by member2 in the current object. The pointers are unchanged, because they must continue to reference different dynamic data. For demonstration purposes, we include an output statement that indicates the action of the operation.

dynamicClass Assignment Operator:
```
// overloaded assignment operator. returns a reference to
// current object
template <typename T>
dynamicClass<T>& dynamicClass<T> ::operator=
                (const dynamicClass<T>& rhs)
{
  // copy static data member from rhs to the current object
  member1 = rhs.member1;
  // contents of dynamic memory must be same as that of rhs
  *member2 = *rhs.member2;
  cout << "Assignment Operator: "<< member1 << '/'
       << *member2 < <  endl;

  return *this;
}
```

The implementation uses the reserved word *this*, which we introduced in Chapter 2. The identifier returns a reference to the current object. When combined with the dereference operator, *this is the object itself. Because the operator = returns a reference to the current object, we can chain together two or more assignment statements. For instance,

```
objC = objB = objA;// assign the result of (objB = objA) to objC
```

The Pointer this

Now that you have an understanding of pointers, we can clarify the meaning of the reserved word *this*. The identifier is a pointer to the current object, and *this is the object itself. A programmer can use the identifier *this* only inside of a class member function. For instance, within object objA of type dynamicClass,

```
*this is the object objA;
this-> member1 is member1, the data value in objA
this-> member2 is member2, the pointer in objA
```

For the assignment operator, the return value is a reference argument. The expression *return *this* returns a reference to the current object.

Initialization Issues

Object initialization is an operation that creates a new object that is a copy of another object. In addition to its use in a declaration, initialization also occurs during the passing of an object as a value argument in a function and during the returning of an object as the value of a function. For instance, assume function f() has a value argument, obj, of type dynamicClass< int> . The function returns the argument as its value:

```
dynamicClass<int> f(dynamicClass<int> obj)     // value argument
{
    return obj;
}
```

In a function call that uses object objA as the actual argument, the pass-by-value action copies objA into obj:

```
dynamicClass<int>   objA(3,5), objB(0,0);

objB = f(objA);
```

When returning from f(), the system makes a copy of obj, calls the destructor for the object obj, and returns the copy as the value of the function.

While both initialization and assignment involve the copying of data from one object to another, the operations are different. Initialization involves creating a new object that is a copy of the existing one. With assignment, both objects already exist from prior declarations, and the action focuses on the copy. The runtime system performs initialization by calling a member function, referred to as the *copy constructor*. The name is descriptive of its action. The function is a constructor that initializes the object by copying values from an existing object.

For dynamicClass, we can combine features of the simple constructor and the overloaded assignment operator to design the copy constructor for the class. Recall that the simple constructor allocates a dynamic data item referenced by member2. This action is required in the copy constructor. The simple constructor uses arguments *m1* and *m2* of type *T* to initialize the data values member1 and *member2. With the copy constructor, we perform the initialization by copying the data values from an existing object. Let us look at the design of the copy constructor in the following example:

```
dynamicClass<int> objA(3,5), objB = objA;
```

The simple constructor creates objA by assigning 3 to objA.member1 and then allocates a dynamic integer pointed to by objA.member2 with initial value 5. The copy constructor creates objB in a three-step process. First, copy the value of objA.member1 to objB.member1. This takes care of the data member that does not reference dynamic memory. Second, allocate a dynamic integer pointed to by objB.member2. This step is also part of the simple constructor, but is not required with assignment, where the dynamic data item already exists. Third, complete the initialization by copying the value of the dynamic data item in objA to its counterpart in objB. Figure 5-13 illustrates the three steps in the copy constructor algorithm.

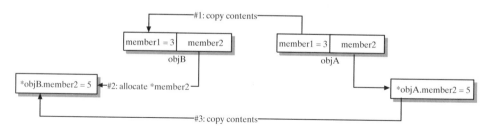

Figure 5-13
Copy Constructor algorithm for the declaration of dynamicClass objA(3,5),objB 5 objA

Creating a Copy Constructor

In order to handle properly classes that allocate dynamic memory, C++ provides the copy constructor to allocate dynamic memory for the new object and initialize its data members. The copy constructor is a constructor, so the member function uses the class name as the function name. An object of the same class type is the single argument, and the function has no return values. The prototype for the copy constructor in dynamicClass is

```
dynamicClass(const dynamicClass<T>& obj);     // copy constructor
```

The dynamicClass copy constructor copies the data in member1 from obj to the current object. For the dynamic data, the copy constructor allocates memory pointed to by member2 and initializes it to the value *obj.member2:

dynamicClass Copy Constructor:
```
// copy constructor. initialize new object to have the
// same data as obj. use constructor initialization
// list to give member1 the value obj.member1
template < typename T>
dynamicClass< T> ::dynamicClass(const dynamicClass<T>& obj):
    member1(obj.member1)
{
    // allocate dynamic memory and initialize it with
    // value *obj.member2.
    member2 = new T(*obj.member2);
    cout <<  "Copy Constructor:  " <<  member1
        <<  '/' <<  *member2 <<  endl;
}
```

The runtime system calls the copy constructor to perform initialization and create a new object. If the class does not provide an explicit version of the copy constructor, the runtime system calls a default version that simply copies data members from the existing object to the new object. With a dynamic class, the default version is likely to produce an error.

Note

The programmer must pass the argument for the copy constructor by reference. The consequence of failing to do so would be catastrophic if the compiler did not recognize the error. Assume that you declare the copy constructor with a call-by-value argument. Note what happens.

```
dynamicClass(dynamicClass<T>  obj);
```

The system calls the copy constructor whenever a function argument is specified as call by value. In the copy constructor, assume that a call passes object objA to the argument obj by value.

objA ⟶

dynamicClass(dynamicClass<T>obj)

Because we pass objA to obj by value, the copy constructor must be called to handle the copying of objA to obj. This call, in turn, needs the copy constructor, and we have an infinite chain of copy-constructor calls. Fortunately, the compiler catches this potential trouble and indicates that the argument must be passed by reference. In addition, the reference argument obj should be declared constant; we certainly do not want to modify the object we are copying.

We conclude this section by giving a partial declaration for dynamicClass that gives the interface for the constructor, copy constructor, and overloaded assignment operator. Program 5.2 features the use of these operations.

CLASS dynamicClass	Declaration	"d_dynam.h"

```
template <typename T>
class dynamicClass
   {
   public:
      dynamicClass(const T& m1, const T& m2);
         // initializes member1 with m1 and the dynamic data item pointed
         // to by member2 with m2

      dynamicClass(const dynamicClass<T>& obj);
         // creates new object with values copied from obj

      dynamicClass< T> & operator= (const dynamicClass<T>& rhs);
         // copies values from rhs to the current object
};
```

PROGRAM 5-2   USING DYNAMICCLASS

The next program illustrates the action of the dynamicClass member functions by using integer data. Extensive comments facilitate understanding of the program.

```
// File: prg5_2.cpp
// the program arranges for the dynamicClass constructor,
// destructor, copy constructor, and overloaded assignment
// operator to be called in a variety of circumstances.
// output from the function calls traces their order of
// execution

#include <iostream>
#include "d_dynam.h"
using namespace std;

template <typename T>
dynamicClass<int> demo(dynamicClass<T> one,
                       dynamicClass<T>& two, const T& m)

int main()
{
   /* objA(3,5) calls the constructor (member1=3, *member2=5)

      objB = objA calls copy constructor to initialize object objB
      from object objA. (member1=3, *member2=5)

      object objC calls the constructor (member1=0, *member2=0)
   */
   dynamicClass<int>  objA(3,5), objB = objA, objC(0,0);
```

```
    /* call the function demo(). the copy constructor creates
       the value argument one (member1=3, *member2=5) by copying
       object objA. argument two is passed by reference, so the copy
       constructor is not called. upon return, a copy is made
       of the local object obj. this copy is assigned to object objC
    */
    objC = demo(objA,objB,5);

    // all remaining objects are destroyed upon program exit.
    return 0;
}

template <typename T>
dynamicClass<int> demo(dynamicClass<T> one, dynamicClass<T>& two,
                       const T& m)
{
    // calls the constructor (member1 = m, *member2 = m)
    dynamicClass<T> obj(m,m);

    // a copy of obj is made and returned as the
    // value of the function
    return obj;

    // the temporary object one is destroyed upon
    // return from demo()
}
```

```
Run:
Constructor: 3/5
Copy Constructor:  3/5
Constructor: 0/0
Copy Constructor:  3/5
Constructor: 5/5
Copy Constructor:  5/5
Destructor: 5/5
Destructor: 3/5
Assignment Operator: 5/5
Destructor: 5/5
Destructor: 5/5
Destructor: 3/5
Destructor: 3/5
```

THE MINIVECTOR CLASS 5-5

In Chapter 4, we introduced the vector API, which provides a description of the container and a listing of the operations that manage the data. There was no effort to declare and implement the underlying vector class. Professional programmers often use this approach. They become familiar with a container class from its API and understand how to use its operations from the member-function prototypes. The professionals access the code for the container class from a library and then begin declaring and using its objects in applications. When a library such as STL is used, programmers have an implicit trust in the code, based on the expertise of its authors, the quality of testing, and years of use.

A design feature of this book is to illustrate how professionals use data structures. At the same time, we must be students of data structures, which involves understanding how to design and implement them. We could carry out this study by looking at the actual STL code. This is neither practical nor instructive in a data structures course. The STL classes are complex, because their aim is to be efficient and to provide as much generality as possible. You need to see a simple and straightforward implementation of container classes. We provide this implementation by creating template-based minicontainer classes that have the look and feel of the corresponding STL classes. Our minicontainer classes have a restricted set of member functions with the same interface as the STL classes. The main difference is in their implementation. We implement member functions in such a way that you can understand the overall design of the algorithm and its translation to C++ code. We do not expect you to use our minicontainer classes in applications, because you have access to the STL versions of the containers. We present the minicontainer classes only to illustrate implementation features of the containers.

In this section, we develop the miniVector class, which is a simplified version of the STL vector class. Like the other containers, the miniVector is a *dynamic class*, because it contains dynamically allocated memory. In this section, we introduce the private data members for a miniVector that includes a dynamic array to store the elements and accompanying size information. Because the class uses dynamic memory, Sections 5-3 and 5-4 tell us that the miniVector class must have a destructor, a copy constructor, and an overloaded assignment operator.

You are familiar with the update functions push_back() and pop_back() from the vector class. We discuss the design and implementation of these member functions. A vector is a generalized array that allows access to elements with the index operator. In the miniVector class, we create an overloaded version of the [] operator, so a miniVector object also acts like an array. We use exceptions to handle the violation of preconditions or for any errors that occur during execution.

Design of the miniVector Class

At the heart of a miniVector object is a dynamically allocated array that reserves space to store the elements. The amount of available space is called the *capacity* of the object. The actual number of elements in the miniVector object is called its *size*. You can think of the capacity as being the number of available lots in a housing subdivision. The size is the actual number of houses that are built on the lots. Hence, the size is always less than or equal to the capacity. A vector can grow into unused capacity without allocating more dynamic memory. When a vector continues to execute push_back() operations and exhausts all of its capacity, the vector allocates additional capacity and copies existing elements into the space. When pop_back() operations execute, the vector size decreases, but the capacity does not. In this way, the vector can grow again without having to allocate additional memory.

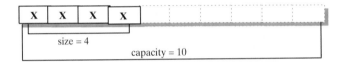

To implement this dynamic storage strategy, the miniVector class has a pointer, called vArr, that specifies the dynamically allocated array, along with integers vSize and vCapacity that maintain the size of the vector and the available space in the array, respectively.

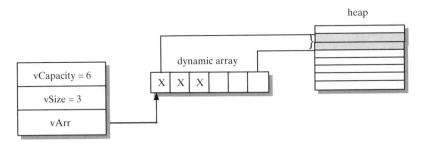

The miniVector constructor has a size argument with a default value of 0. The constructor dynamically allocates space for the designated size and then fills each location with T(), which is the default value for type T. In the resulting object, the size and capacity are equal. Using the housing-subdivision analogy, the constructor uses the size argument to allocate lots and then builds houses on each of the lots. A program could add new elements to the list by using push_back() and remove the element at the end of the list with pop_back(). The function push_back() allocates additional space when the current space is full (capacity $==$ size). The function back() provides access to the element at the rear of the vector. A program can access the elements in a miniVector object directly by using an index in the range from 0 to vSize $-$ 1. The class provides this facility by overloading the index operator [].

The upcoming code is a declaration of the miniVector class that includes the data members, the constructor, and the member functions that provide a basic programmer interface. The declaration also includes the required memory management operations provided by the destructor, copy constructor, and overloaded assignment operator. Except for the memory management functions, you are familiar with the other operations from the STL vector API.

CLASS miniVector	Declaration	"d_vector.h"

```
template <typename T>
class miniVector
{
   public:
      miniVector(int size = 0);
         // constructor.
         // Postconditions: allocates array with size number of elements
```

```
    // and capacity. elements are initialized to T(), the default
    // value for type T

miniVector(const miniVector<T> & obj);
    // copy constructor
    // Postcondition: creates current vector as a copy of obj

~miniVector();
    // destructor
    // Postcondition: the dynamic array is destroyed

miniVector& operator= (const miniVector<T> & rhs);
    // assignment operator.
    // Postcondition: current vector holds the same data
    // as rhs

T& back();
    // return the element at the rear of the vector.
    // Precondition: the vector is not empty. if vector
    // is empty, throws the underflowError exception

const T& back() const;
    // const version used when miniVector object is a constant

T& operator[] (int i);
    // provides general access to elements using an index.
    // Precondition: 0 <= i < vSize. if index is out
    // of range, throw indexRangeError exception

const T& operator[] (int i) const;
    // const version used when miniVector object is a constant

void push_back(const T& item);
    // insert item at the back of the vector.
    // Postcondition: the vector size is increased by 1

void pop_back();
    // remove element at the back of the vector.
    // Precondition: vector is not empty. if the vector is
    // empty, throws the underflowError exception

int size() const;
    // return current list size

bool empty() const;
    // return true if vector is empty and false otherwise

int capacity() const;
    // return the current capacity of the vector
```

```
private:
    int vCapacity;    // amount of available space
    int vSize;        // number of elements in the list
    T *vArr;          // the dynamic array

    void reserve(int n, bool copy);
        // called by public functions only if n > vCapacity. expands
        // the vector capacity to n elements, copies the existing
        // elements to the new space if copy == true, and deletes
        // the old dynamic array. throws the memoryAllocationError
        // exception if memory allocation fails
};
```

Example 5-9

The example illustrates the use of the constructor, the index operator, and the functions size(), capacity(), and push_back() for miniVector objects.

```
miniVector<int>  vInt;       // an integer vector with 0 elements
// a 1-element vector of strings with initial value ""
miniVector<string> vStr(1);
int i;

// output: 0  1
cout <<  vInt.size() << " " << vStr.size() <<  endl;

// elements are: 0 1 2 3 4
// capacity grows to 8
for (i = 0; i < 5; i++)
    vInt.push_back(i); see implementation of push-back()

// output: 5  8
cout << vInt.size() << " " << vInt.capacity() <<  endl;

// add a string to vStr; capacity grows to accommodate the new element
vStr[0] = "mini";
vStr.push_back("vector");
// output: 2  2
cout << vStr.size() <<  " " << vStr.capacity() << endl;
```

Reserving More Capacity

The private-member function reserve() allocates capacity for the vector. Memory management functions including the constructors, the assignment operator, and push_back() call the function when the vector requires a capacity of *n* elements and vCapacity $< n$. The function increases the capacity by allocating a dynamic array and copies the current vector elements into the front of the new space if the Boolean argument copy is true. Memory allocation fails if the call to *new* returns a NULL value. In this situation, reserve() throws the memoryAllocationError exception. Before returning, the function deletes the old array from the heap. Figure 5-14 gives a view of the size and capacity of an object before and after calling reserve().

reserve():

```
// set the capacity to n elements
template < typename T>
void miniVector<T>::reserve(int n, bool copy)
{
    T *newArr;
    int i;

    // allocate a new dynamic array with n elements
    newArr = new T[n];
    if (newArr == NULL)
        throw memoryAllocationError(
            "miniVector reserve(): memory allocation failure");

    // if copy is true, copy elements from the old list to the new list
    if (copy)
        for(i = 0; i < vSize; i++)
            newArr[i] = vArr[i];

    // if vArr is NULL, the vector was originally empty
    // and there is no memory to delete: otherwise delete
    // original array.
    if (vArr != NULL)
        delete [] vArr;
    // update vCapacity and vArr
    vCapacity = n;
    vArr = newArr;
}
```

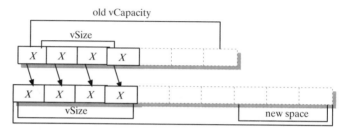

new vCapacity

Figure 5-14
Using reserve() to expand vCapacity

The miniVector Constructor, Destructor, and Assignment

The constructor initially sets the vector size and capacity to 0 and assigns the NULL pointer to vArr. If the miniVector is empty (size = 0), the constructor just returns. If size is greater than 0, the constructor calls reserve() with arguments *n* = size and copy = false. This call allocates the dynamic array, vArr, that has *size* elements. The Boolean argument for reserve() is false, because there is no existing dynamic array. After assigning size to vSize, the constructor copies the default value T() into each array element.

miniVector() constructor:

```
// constructor. initialize vSize and vCapacity.
// allocate a dynamic array of vSize integers
// and initialize the array with T()
template <typename T>
miniVector<T>::miniVector(int size):
   vSize(0), vCapacity(0), vArr(NULL)
{
   int i;

   // if size is 0, vSize/vCapacity are 0 and vArr is NULL.
   // just return
   if (size == 0)
      return;

   // set capacity to size. since we are building the vector,
   // copy is false
   reserve(size, false);
   // assign size to vSize
   vSize = size;

   // copy T() into each vector element
   for (i=0;i < vSize;i++)
      vArr[i] = T();
}
```

The Destructor.   If the vector is not empty, the destructor deletes the dynamic array vArr.

~miniVector():

```
// destructor. deallocate the dynamic array
template <typename T>
miniVector<T>::~miniVector()
{
   if (vArr != NULL)
      // deallocate memory for the array
      delete [] vArr;
}
```

The Assignment Operator. The miniVector class must provide its own version of the overloaded assignment operator for proper management of dynamic memory. The assignment operator copies the elements in the dynamic array rhs.vArr into the dynamic array vArr. If the capacity of the current object is sufficient (vCapacity $\geq$ rhs.vSize), it is not necessary to allocate new dynamic memory (Figure 5-15(a)). If the capacity of the dynamic array vArr for the current object is too small (vCapacity < rhs.vSize), then the assignment operator must first allocate new memory by calling reserve() with arguments n = rhs.vSize and copy = false (Figure 5-15(b)). The Boolean argument for reserve() is false, because there is no reason to copy existing elements to the new memory. After assigning the new size as rhs.vSize, the assignment operator copies the data from the array rhs.vArr to the array vArr. and uses *this to return a reference to the current object.

miniVector Assignment Operator:

```
// replace existing object (left-hand operand) by
// rhs (right-hand operand)
template <typename T>
miniVector<T> & miniVector<T>::operator= (const miniVector<T> & rhs)
{
    int i;

    // check vCapacity to see if a new array must be allocated
    if (vCapacity < rhs.vSize)
        // make capacity of current object the size of rhs. don't
        // do a copy, since we will replace the old values
        reserve(rhs.vSize, false);

    // assign current object to have same size as rhs
    vSize = rhs.vSize;

    // copy items from the rhs.vArr to vArr array
    for (i = 0; i < vSize; i++)
        vArr[i] = rhs.vArr[i];

    return *this;
}
```

We do not include an implementation of the copy constructor; the algorithm is similar to that for the overloaded assignment operator. The copy constructor must always call reserve() with arguments obj.vSize and copy = false, because the current object does not have an existing dynamic array to store the elements. The function uses obj.vSize to initialize the data members vSize and vCapacity in the current objects and concludes by copying the elements from obj.vArr to vArr.

Adding and Removing Elements from a miniVector Object

A miniVector object uses push_back() to add an element after the current last element. The operation is not complicated as long as the vector has enough capacity to add a new item. If this is the case, push_back() merely adds the item at index vSize and increments the size. If the array does not have enough capacity (vSize == vCa-

pacity), then the function must first add additional space by calling reserve() and require it to copy existing elements. The only problem is determining how much new
capacity to allocate. This is a matter of a design strategy. Having the capacity grow
by 1 would be inefficient, because then each call to push_back() would immediately
fill the available space. To handle a large number of insertions, the system would be
bogged down with repeated calls to reserve(), which must allocate new space and
copy the existing elements. A better design grows the capacity in anticipation of
adding more elements. The strategy the miniVector class uses is to double the capacity whenever an allocation must be done. In this way, the capacity of a miniVector object grows from 1 to 2, 2 to 4, 4 to 8, and so forth.

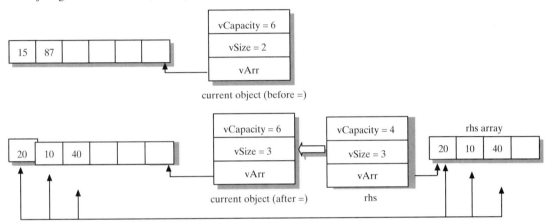

(a) Assignment without calling reserve()

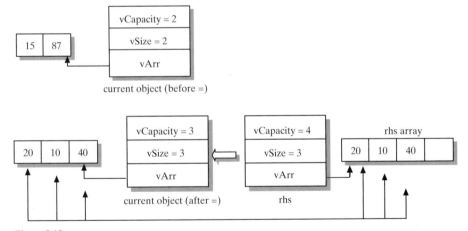

Figure 5-15
Assignment of miniVector objects

push_back():
```
// ensure that list has sufficient capacity,
// add the new item to the list, and increment vSize
```

```
template <typenameT>
void miniVector<T>::push_back(const T& item)
{
   // if space is full, allocate more capacity
   if (vSize == vCapacity)
   {
      if (vCapacity == 0)
         // if capacity is 0, set capacity to 1.
         // set copy to false because there are
         // no existing elements
         reserve(1,false);
      else
         // double the capacity
         reserve(2 * vCapacity, true);
   }

   // add item to the list, update vSize
   vArr[vSize] = item;
   vSize++;
}
```

Example 5-10

The example illustrates the distinction between the capacity and size of a miniVector object. Initially, v*A* is an integer vector with five elements (v*A*.vCapacity = v*A*.vSize = 5) and v*B* is empty (vB.vCapacity = vB.vSize = 0). A loop inserts the integers 1 through 8 into each vector by using push_back(), and another loop removes three elements from v*A*. Shaded boxes show the size and capacity at various stages, using the format vSize/vCapacity.

```
// two miniVector objects with initial size/capacity for vA is 5/5
// and for vB is 0/0
miniVector<int> vA(5,), vB;

// insert 8 items in each vector. the table gives size/capacity
// after each iteration
for (i=1; i <= 8; i++)
{
   vA.push_back(i);
   vB.push_back(i);
}
/* i       vA      vB              i       vA      vB
   1       6/10    1/1             2       7/10    2/2
   3       8/10    3/4             4       9/10    4/4
   5       10/10   5/8             6       11/20   6/8
   7       12/20   7/8             8       13/20   8/8
*/

// delete 2 items from vA. the size/capacity after pop 1
// is 12/20 and after pop 2 is 11/20/
vA.pop_back();
va.pop_back()
```

A miniVector object uses pop_back() to remove an element. The operation, which occurs only at the end of the sequence, assumes the vector is not empty. If this condition fails, the function throws an underflowError exception. The function reduces the size of the list by one element without changing the capacity. The space remains the same; only the number of items filling the space changes. In the housing-subdivision model, the function bulldozes the last house and leaves a vacant lot, which becomes available for the next insertion (push_back()) of an element.

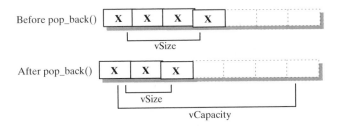

In the upcoming implementation, the function pop_back() checks vSize and throws an exception when the value is 0. Otherwise, it decrements vSize.

pop_back():
```
// if not empty, just decrement the size
template <typename T>
void miniVector<T>::pop_back()
{
   if (vSize == 0)
      throw underflowError(
         "miniVector pop_back(): vector is empty");

   vSize--;
}
```

The function pop_back() removes the back of the list without returning its value. To gain access to the value at the rear of the vector, use back(). The operation first tests that the list is not empty; then it either throws an underflowError exception or returns the value of the array element at index vSize − 1.

back():
```
// check vSize and throw an underflowError exception if the
// value is 0; otherwise return the element vArr[vSize-1]
template <typename T>
T& miniVector<T>::back()
{
   if (vSize == 0)
      throw underflowError(
         "miniVector back(): vector empty");
   return vArr[vSize-1];
}
```

The complexity of pop_back() is O(1), because all it does is decrement vSize. The operation push_back() is more involved. A reallocation must be done when the vector's capacity is full. If the capacity is *n* at the time, then the function copies the existing vector elements into another dynamic array with capacity 2*n*. The running time of push_back() in this case is O(*n*). A new allocation of space would not occur for the next *n* calls to the function push_back(), and so these *n* operations have running time O(1). When the total effort is averaged (amortized) over the number of insertions, the average running time is constant. Complexity theory designates such operations as having *amortized running time* O(1).

Overloading the Index Operator

C++ defines the *index operator, []*, to access elements in an array. A programmer uses the operator in an expression of the form arr[*i*] to reference the element at address arr + *i*. When the index operator occurs on the left-hand side of an assignment statement, the compiler must know the address of the element in which to store the value from the right-hand side. In this situation, arr[*i*] must evaluate to the address. Otherwise, the compiler simply accesses the value at the index.

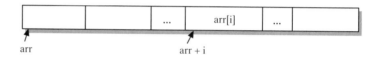

```
arr[i] = 30;         // arr[i] is the address into which 30 is copied
t = arr[i] + 4;      // add 4 to the value of the element at arr[i]
```

A programmer can overload the binary operator [] only as a member function. In the miniVector class, the function uses the index argument, *i*, to access the element at index *i* in the dynamic array vArr. The function prototype for the overloaded index operator returns a reference of type *T* (*T&*). You can think of *T&* as being the address of the element at location *i* in the array:

```
T& operator[] (int i);
```

When a miniVector object uses the index operator, the compiler is responsible for using the return reference properly. If *v*[*i*] occurs on the left side of an assignment statement, the reference identifies the address of element vArr + *i*. This address receives the new data. If *v*[*i*] occurs in an expression on the right side of an assignment statement, the compiler uses the value of the element at address vArr + *i*. The index operator performs bounds checking. An attempt to access an element with an index out of the range from 0 to vSize − 1 creates an indexRangeError exception whose arguments include an error message, the value of the invalid index, and the size of the vector. Index checking is a feature of miniVector class that is not provided by the STL vector class. In Chapter 13, we illustrate how a programmer might use inheritance to extend the STL vector class to a new class that includes index-range check-ing. The new class, as well as the miniVector class, are referred to as a *safevector* class.

Operator []:

```
// provides general access to array elements
template <typename T>
T& miniVector<T>::operator[] (int i)
{
   if (i < 0 || i > = vSize)
      throw indexRangeError(
         "miniVector: index range error", i, vSize);

   return vArr[i];
}
```

PROGRAM 5-3   HANDLING MINIVECTOR EXCEPTIONS

The upcoming program illustrates exception handling for the miniVector class. After declar-ing an empty vector *v*, a try block calls the function pop_back(), which throws an underflow-Error exception, because the vector is empty. The corresponding catch block handles the exception by calling what() to output the error message. The same catch block uses push_back() to add 99 to the empty vector. We include this statement in the catch block to il-lustrate that the exception handler can perform tasks other than simply displaying the error message. A second try block outputs the value at *v*[0] and attempts to output *v*[1]. The second index operation creates an indexRangeError exception. The corresponding catch block out-puts information specifying the invalid index and the current vector size.

```
// File: prg5_3.cpp
// the program illustrates the use of exceptions with the miniVector
// class. during execution, the underflowError and indexRangeError
// exceptions each occur once

#include <iostream>

#include "d_vector.h"

using namespace std;

int main()
{

   miniVector<int> v;

   // try block tests for empty vector; catch block catches
   // underflowError exception from pop_back()
   try
   {
      v.pop_back();
   }
```

```
catch (const underflowError& e)
{
    cout << e.what() << endl;
    // store element in v[0]
    v.push_back(99);
}

cout << "The size of v = " <<  v.size() <<  endl;

// try block enables index bound checking ; catch block catches
// indexRangeError exception from operator[]
try
{
    cout << "v[0] = " << v[0] << endl;
    cout << "v[1] = " << v[1] << endl;
}
catch (const indexRangeError& e)
{
    cout << e.what() << endl;
}

return 0;
}
```

```
Run:
miniVector pop_back(): vector is empty
The size of v = 1
v[0] = 99
miniVector: index range error  index 1  size = 1
```

5-6   THE MATRIX CLASS

An array is a list of elements of the same type that can be referenced by a single index. As such, an array is referred to as *one dimensional.* The C++ languages supports multidimensional arrays, which are collections of elements that can be referenced by two or more indices. In this section, we discuss two-dimensional arrays that correspond to a row–column table of entries of a specified data type. These arrays are commonly called *matrices* and have important engineering and scientific applications.

A programmer references a matrix element by using a pair of indices that specify the row and column location in the table. For instance, assume that *mat* is a matrix of integer values with three rows and four columns (Figure 5-16). The element mat[0][3] is −2, and mat[1][2] is 4.

In general, if mat is a matrix with numRow rows and numCol columns, then mat[i][j] is the entry in row i and column j, where $0 \leq i <$ numRow and $0 \leq j <$ numCol. The C++ declaration for the matrix in Figure 5-16 is

```
int mat[3][4] = { {8,1,7,-2}, {0,-3,4,6}, {10,-14,1,0} };
```

Figure 5-16
Three-by-four matrix of integers

C++ treats a matrix as an array of one-dimensional arrays. For instance, mat[0] is the one-dimensional integer array $\{8, 1, 7, -2\}$, mat[1] is the array $\{0, -3, 4, 6\}$, and mat[2] is the array $\{10, -14, 1, 0\}$. C++ stores a matrix in memory by rows. The first row (mat[0]) is immediately followed by the second row (mat[1]), and so forth. As a result, the array elements cannot be accessed correctly unless the compiler knows the number of elements in each row, which is precisely the number of columns. This requires that a function accepting a matrix argument must specify the number of elements in each column. This limits the generality for such functions. For instance, assume that a programmer wishes to create a function matSum() that returns the sum of the elements in a matrix. A general prototype like

```
int matSum(int mat[][], int numRows, int numCols);
```

is invalid, because it does not explicitly specify the number of columns in the matrix argument. A correct prototype must include a constant value for the column index. For instance,

```
int matSum(int mat[][4], int numRows, int numCols);
```

The limitation is obvious. A programmer could call this version of matSum() only for a 1×4 matrix, a 2×4 matrix, and so forth. Any attempt to call matSum() with a matrix that does not have exactly four columns generates a compilation error. In addition to the requirement of specifying the number of columns in the function arguments, matrices suffer from the same problems we noted for one-dimensional arrays. A matrix has fixed size that cannot be changed dynamically to accommodate the storage needs of an application. The size is not internally maintained by the matrix, and so a programmer must pass the number of rows and the number of columns to any function that has a matrix argument.

Confronted with these limitations imposed by C++ one-dimensional arrays, the standard template library (STL) provides the vector class to extend arrays and allow dynamic storage and resizing operations. In this section, we do the same thing for C++ two-dimensional arrays. The result is the template-based *matrix* container.

Describing the Matrix Container

In the design of the template-based matrix class, we store elements in a vector of vectors. The private data member mat holds the entries in the matrix:

```
vector<vector<T> > mat;     // private member stores matrix elements
```

The outer vector corresponds to the rows of the matrix. The elements in the inner vector of type T correspond to the column entries for each vector row. Thus, mat[0]

is the vector of column entries corresponding to row 0, mat[1] is the entries in row 1, and so forth.

Note

> When a declaration nests one template type inside another, the programmer must make sure that two > symbols do not occur in succession. The compiler will confuse the token >> with the stream input operator. For instance, in our declaration of mat, note that there is a blank between the first > and the succeeding one.

The constructor for the class has integer arguments for the number of rows and the number of columns in the matrix, along with an initial value for the entries. By default, the matrix has one row and one column, with entries set to the default value for type *T*. For instance, the following declaration of intMat creates a three-by-four integer matrix, all of whose entries are 0. The two-by-five time24 matrix has 10 elements initially set to 8:30.

```
matrix<int>   intMat(3,4);
matrix<time24>  timeMat(2,5,time24(8,30));
```

A program can adjust the dimensions of a matrix object at runtime by using resize(). It takes a row and a column size as arguments and uses the vector class resize() function to modify the matrix so that it has the new dimensions. Depending on the dimensions, resize() saves the original values in the new matrix. Any new elements the function creates have the default value for type *T*. For instance, the upcoming resize operation converts intMat into a two-by-seven matrix. The resizing eliminates row 2 and fills the extra three columns in rows 0 and 1 with 0.

```
intMat.resize(2,7);              // convert intMat to a 2 by 7 matrix
```

In order for a matrix object to use the familiar [*row*][*col*] index notation, the class overloads the index operator []. This allows a matrix object to appear on each side of an assignment statement.

```
intMat[i][j] = 7;         // assign 7 to matrix at indices i and j
n = intMat[i][j] * 2;     // access the value of element intMat[i][j]
```

The public-member functions rows() and cols() return the number of rows and columns in the vector, respectively.

The upcoming code is the declaration of the matrix class. After illustrating its use in a program, we implement the constructor and the overloaded index operator.

CLASS matrix   **Declaration**   **"d_matrix.h"**

```
template <typename T>
class matrix
{
   public:
      matrix(int numRows = 1, int numCols = 1, const T& initVal = T());
```

```
        // constructor.
        // Postcondition: create array having numRows x numCols elements
        // all of whose elements have value initVal

    vector<T> & operator[] (int i);
        // index operator.
        // Precondition: 0 <= i < nRows. a violation of this
        // precondition throws the indexRangeError exception.
        // Postcondition: if the operator is used on the left-hand
        // side of an assignment statement, an element of row i
        // is changed

    const vector<T>& operator[](int i) const;
        // version for constant objects

    int rows() const;
        // return number of rows
    int cols() const;
        // return number of columns

    void resize(int numRows, int numCols);
        // modify the matrix size.
        // Postcondition: the matrix has size numRows x numCols.
        // any new elements are filled with the default value of type T

  private:
    int nRows, nCols;
        // number of rows and columns

    vector<vector<T> > mat;
        // matrix is implemented as nRows vectors (rows),
        // each having nCols elements (columns)
};
```

troduction of two-dimensional arrays, we noted the difficulty in declaring In the introduction of two-dimensional arrays, we noted the difficulty in declaring the matSum() function for an array. The prototype requires a specific number of columns as part of the array argument. With the matrix class, we can declare a template-based version of matSum() that applies to any type supporting the operator $+=$. The member functions rows() and cols() return the number of rows and columns, so only the matrix object needs to be passed as an argument. The function returns the sum as an object of type *T*.

matSum():
```
    // return the sum of the entries in mat
    template <typename T>
    T matSum(const matrix<T>& mat)
    {
        // declare sum and initialize it to the default value for T
```

```
    T sum = T();
    int i, j;

    // scan the rows and columns, adding each element to
    // the running sum
    for (i = 0; i < mat.rows(); i++)
       for (j = 0; j < mat.cols(); j++)
          sum += mat[i][j];

    // return the sum as object of type T
    return sum;


}
```

PROGRAM 5-4   SUMMING A MATRIX

The next program declares an integer matrix intMat and a time24 matrix timeMat and reads
the data for the elements from the file "mat.dat". The first line of input is the number of rows
and the number of columns for intMat. The function resize() uses these values to set the dimensions of the matrix. Subsequent input provides the row and column values for the matrix.
The data for timeMat follow the same format. The program calls matSum() to compute the
sum of the values in each matrix and then outputs the return value.

```
// File: prg5_4.cpp
// the program initializes an integer and a time24 matrix object by
// reading their data from a file. by calling the function matSum(),
// the program outputs the sum of the values in each matrix

#include <iostream>
#include <fstream>
#include <cstdlib>

#include "d_matrix.h"
#include "d_time24.h"

using namespace std;

// return the sum of the entries in mat
template <typename T>
T matSum(const matrix<T> & mat);

int main()
{
   matrix<int>   intMat;
   matrix<time24>   timeMat;

   int numRows, numCols;
   int i,j;
   ifstream fin("mat.dat");
```

```
      if (!fin)
      {
         cerr << "Cannot open 'mat.dat'" << endl;
         exit(1);
      }

      fin >> numRows >> numCols;
      intMat.resize(numRows, numCols);
      for (i = 0; i < numRows; i++)
         for (j = 0; j < numCols; j++)
            fin >> intMat[i][j];
      cout << "Sum of integer matrix is " << matSum(intMat) << endl;

      fin >> numRows >> numCols;
      timeMat.resize(numRows, numCols);
      for (i = 0; i < numRows; i++)
         for (j = 0; j < numCols; j++)
            fin >> timeMat[i][j];
      cout << "Sum of time24 matrix is " << matSum(timeMat) <<  endl;
      return 0;
}
/* the function matSum() is implemented in the program discussion */
```

```
File "mat.dat"
3   4
8      1   7  -2
0     -3   4   6
10  -14   1   0
2   5
1:00    2:30   0:30   0:45   2:00
3:00    0:15   0:45   1:45   3:15


Run:
Sum of integer matrix is 18
Sum of time24 matrix is 15:45
```

Implementing Matrix Functions

The constructor for the matrix class takes arguments numRows and numCols and an initial value for the entries. The arguments numRows and numCols set values for the private data members nRows and nCols. The interesting part of the constructor implementation is the use of the initialization list to create mat, the internal vector of vectors that stores the matrix elements. The list includes the expression

```
      mat(numRows, vector<T> (numCols, initVal))
```

The compiler interprets the expression by calling the vector constructor for mat with numRows as the size and vector< T> (numCols, initVal) as the initial value for each element in mat. The elements in mat are the rows of the matrix. The process of assigning an initial value to each row creates a second call to the inner vector constructor with arguments numCols and initVal. The initial value for each row element thus becomes a vector of elements with value initVal that constitute the column entries for the row.

matrix constructor:
```
template <typename T>
matrix<T>::matrix(int numRows, int numCols, const T& initVal):
    nRows(numRows), nCols(numCols),
    mat(numRows, vector<T> (numCols,initVal))
{}
```

Overloaded matrix index operator. The C++ compiler interprets the expression intMat[i][j] as (intMat[i])[j], where intMat[i] is the vector of column elements for row i. Because intMat[i] is a vector, the index [j] is evaluated by the overloaded index operator in the vector class. This access gives us the value at row i, column j of the matrix. The role of the index operator in the matrix class is to evaluate [i] and return mat[i], where mat is the private data member that stores the matrix elements. Index bounds checking assures that i is a valid matrix row index.

matrix index operator (nonconstant version):
```
// provides general access to matrix elements
template <typename T>
vector<T>& matrix<T>::operator[] (int i)
{
    if (i <0 || i > = nRows)
        throw indexRangeError(
            "matrix: invalid row index", i, nRows);
    return mat[i];
}
```

Note

For a reference mat[*i*][*j*], the matrix class index operator detects only whether *i* is an improper row index. The vector class uses *j* to access the element in the column. Unfortunately, the vector class performs no index bounds checking. Using an improper column index will cause the program either to terminate with a fatal error or just to produce incorrect results. In Chapter 13, we discuss the use of inheritance in adding index bounds checking to a vector object.

CHAPTER SUMMARY

- A pointer contains the address of data in memory. By applying the dereference operator, *, the programmer can access the data pointed at. Operators such as +, ++, and += apply to pointers. With such operators, pointers can be used for algorithms involving array traversal, but their primary application is in the allocation and maintenance of dynamic memory.

- Using dynamic memory, we can allocate arrays whose sizes are set by the runtime requirements of the application. A program can use the operator *new* to request memory from the heap at runtime for single objects and arrays. When the memory is no longer needed, release it by using the operator *delete*.

- When a class uses dynamic memory to store data, it must define a destructor that deallocates the memory when an object is destroyed. This avoids memory leaks.

- By default, C++ performs assignment and initialization by performing a byte-by-byte copy of data members. When a class uses dynamic memory, this action copies the *pointers to the dynamic data*, not the *data itself*. This results in two objects pointing at the same dynamic memory. The action produces a memory leak, and subsequent references to the dynamic memory will likely result in a fatal error. The programmer handles these problems by adding an overloaded assignment operator and a copy constructor to the class.

- It is important for a student of data structures to understand the basics of vector implementation. The vector class is too complicated to study directly. The implementation of the miniVector class illustrates the key points. It allocates dynamic memory, and so it has a destructor, a copy constructor, and overloaded assignment operator. Because it implements push_back(), it must control vector capacity in order to minimize dynamic-memory reallocation. It allows access to elements by using an index, and so the class implements an overloaded index operator. In addition, it does index bounds checking and thus implements a safe array.

- A two-dimensional array has many uses in engineering and scientific applications. C++ two-dimensional arrays have the same problems as one-dimensional arrays, including their fixed size and their lack of an attached size attribute. In addition, if such an array is a function argument, it is necessary to specify the number of columns as a constant. These problems can be avoided by the creation of a matrix class that uses a vector of vectors for its implementation. By applying the vector resize() function, the programmer can change the number of rows and columns of a matrix object. Overloading the index operator enables the expression mat[i][j] to refer to the data in row i, column j of object mat.

CLASSES AND LIBRARIES IN THE CHAPTER

Name	Header File
dynamicClass	d_dynam.h
matrix	d_matrix.h
miniVector	d_vector.h
time24	d_time24.h

REVIEW EXERCISES

1. What are the final values of *x* and *y*?

```
int x = 3, y = 15, *px = &x, *py = &y;

*px = 8;
px = py;
*px += 6;
```

2. What are the final values in the array *arr*?

```
int arr[] = {45, 24, 16, 3, 2, 8};
int *parr = arr;

*parr = 3;
parr += 4;
*parr = 5;
parr = parr-3;
*parr = 15;
parr[4] *= 2;
```

Final values in the array arr = {_____, _____, _____, _____, _____, _____}

3. What is the result of the following declaration?

```
int *a = new int(35);
```

(a) *a* is an array of 35 integers.
(b) *a* is an integer with initial value 35.
(c) *a* is an integer with initial value 35.
(d) *a* is an array of 35 integers with initial value 35.

4. Assume the declaration

```
int   *p;
```

Give a declaration that creates a dynamic integer array *p* with 25 elements. Perform error checking.

5. Assume that className is a class with a member function f() and *p* is a pointer to a dynamic className object:

```
className *p;
p = new className;
```

Write two expressions that execute f().

_____ _____

6. Allocate **p* as follows:

```
miniVector< int>   *p;
p = new miniVector<int> ;
```

Show how to insert the values 3 and 5 at the rear of the vector.

7. What is a memory leak? How are memory leaks avoided when you develop a C++ class?

8. (a) Assume the class CL has data member *value*. Are the following expressions equivalent?

```
this-> value
(*this).value
```

(b) In general, distinguish between the meanings of *this* and **this*.

9. In class *demo*, which of the following is a valid implementation of operator += ?

```
class demo
{ public:
       friend demo operator+ (const demo & lhs, const demo & rhs)
       {  return demo(lhs.v + rhs.v); }

       demo & operator+= (const demo & rhs)
       { _____
       }
   private:
       int v;
};
```

(a) `demo& demo::operator+= (const demo& rhs)`

```
{
    *this = this.v + rhs.v;
    return *this;
}
```

(b) `demo& demo::operator+= (const demo& rhs)`

```
{
    this.v += rhs.v;
    return this;
}
```

(c) `demo& demo::operator+= (const demo& rhs)`

```
{
    this = this + rhs;
    return *this;
}
```

(d) `demo& demo::operator+= (const demo& rhs)`

```
{
    *this = *this + rhs;
    return *this;
}
```

10. Explain the difference between initialization and assignment. Suppose that CL is a class whose constructor requires two integer arguments. Illustrate your answer by using CL objects.

11. Explain the need for a class copy constructor and for a class overloaded assignment operator.

12. (a) Declare a matrix object *mat* containing integer data and having 5 rows and 7 columns. The initial value 0 should fill the entries of mat.

(b) Give a statement that will resize mat so it has 10 rows and 5 columns.

(c) Implement a function writeMatrix(), which outputs the elements of a matrix object, one row per line.

```
// output mat, one row per line
template <typename T>
void writeMatrix(const matrix<T> & mat);
```

Answers to Review Exercises

1. $x = 8, y = 21$

2. Final values in the array arr = $\{3, 15, 16, 3, 5, 16\}$

3. (b)

4.
```
p = new int [25];
if (p == NULL)
{
   cerr << "Memory allocation failure" << endl;
   exit(1);
}
```

5. p-> f();
   or
   (*p).f();

6. p-> push_back(3);
     p-> push_back(5);

7. A memory leak occurs when all pointer references to a block of memory on the heap are lost. The memory consumes space that cannot be used. Memory leaks are avoided by implementing a destructor, copy constructor, and overloaded assignment operator in a class that uses dynamic memory.

8. **(a)** The two expressions are equivalent.

     (b) The reserved word *this* can be used only in the implementation of a member function and is a pointer to the currently executing object. The expression **this* is the object itself.

9. **(d)**

10. Initialization creates a new object by copying an existing object. Initialization occurs through the use of = in a declaration, in pass by value, and when returning an object as the value of a function. Here is an example using the CL class:

```
CL one(2,3), two = one;    // initialize two to have value one
```

Assignment replaces the value of an existing object by the value of another object. For instance,

```
CL one(3,5), two(6,8);

two = one;
```

11. By default, C++ performs initialization and assignment by doing a byte-by-byte copy. If a class has one or more members that refer to dynamic memory, this action copies the pointers and not the data pointed to. As a result, the two objects involved in the operation

both point at the same dynamic memory. If the destructor for one object is called, the remaining object's dynamic data is invalid. Any attempt to reference it will likely result in a
fatal application error. The copy constructor and overloaded assignment operator have
another object as an argument. Each function ensures that the current object has its own
dynamic memory and that the contents of the dynamic memory are identical to that of
the other object.

12. (a) `matrix<int> mat(5,7);`
   (b) `mat.resize(10,5);`
   (c)
```
// output mat, one row per line
template <typename T>
void writeMatrix(const matrix< T> & mat)
{
    int i, j;

    for (i=0; i <  mat.rows(); i++)
    {
        for (j=0; j <  mat.cols(); j++)
            cout < <  mat[i][j] < <  "   ";
        cout < <  endl;
    }
}
```

WRITTEN EXERCISES

13. Assume that p is a pointer to an integer that is stored in four bytes:

```
int *p;
```

A memory view includes four integer values with pointer p set at location 5000:

| 7000 | 4500 | 1000 | 2500 |

5000

p

   (a) What is the value of $*p + 3$?
   (b) What is the value of $*(p + 2)$?
   (c) What is the value of $p + 1$?

14. (a) Declare p as a pointer to a character.
   (b) Declare p as a pointer to a time24 object.
   (c) Declare p as a pointer to a vector of integer values.

15. Assume the declaration

```
int m = 35, *intPtr;
double x, *dblPtr;
```

   (a) Assign intPtr a value so that it points to m.
   (b) Assign dblPtr a value so that it points to x, and then use the pointer to assign x
       the value 5.3.

16. Use the declaration

```
string str("soccer"), *p;
```

    (a) Assign p to point at str.
    (b) Give a C++ statement that outputs str and its length by using p.

17. Repeat the following declaration for each part, (a)–(d). Fill in the value for $*p$ and $*q$.

```
int a = 15, b = 25, *p = &a, *q = &b;
```

    (a) $*p = *q + 2$ $*p =$ _____
    (b) $*q += 10$ $*q =$ _____
    (c) $(*q)++$ $*q =$ _____
    (d) $q = p$ $*p =$ _____ $*q =$ _____

18. Identify the errors that occurs in the following statements:

    (a) `const int STARTVAL = 100;`
            `int *ptr = &STARTVAL;`
    (b) `int arr[20];`
            `arr++;`
    (c) `int *p = {1,4,9};`
    (d) `int *p;`
            `p = new int[3]{4, 9, 1};`

19. The upcoming declaration includes integer and pointer variables. For parts (b)–(e), repeat the declaration and use the results from part (a).

```
int x = 6, y = 5, *px, *py;
```

    (a) Write two assignment statements that set px and py to point at integers x and y, respectively.
    (b) Write an output statement using px that prints the contents of x.
    (c) Write a statement using py that assigns 20 as the contents of y.
    (d) What is the resulting value of $*py + *px$?
    (e) After executing $*py = *px$, are $&x$ and py equal?

20. The following statement declares both an array and a pointer:

```
int arr[] = {9, 2, -3, 5, -1}, *px;
```

    (a) Give a statement that sets px to point at array arr.
    (b) Give a cout statement using px that outputs the value 9 from the array.
    (c) Give a cout statement using px that outputs the value -3 from the array.
    (d) Give a statement that sets px to point at element arr[1]. After executing this statement,
           (i) what is the value of $*(px + 2)$?
           (ii) what is the value of $*px + 2$?

21. Trace the following function:

```
template <typename T>
T *f(T *arr, int n)
{
    T *cum = new T[n];
    T *p = cum, *end = cum + n;

    *p = *arr;
```

```
        p++;
        arr++;

        while (p < end)
        {
            *p = *(p-1) + *arr;

            arr++;
            p++;
        }

        return cum;
    }
```

(a) `int arr[] = {3, 5, 7, -9, 6}, *p;`
    `p = f(arr, sizeof(arr)/sizeof(int));`

What are the contents of the dynamic array p after $f()$ has been called?

(b) `string str[] = {"C", "+", "+", " Programs"}, *p;`
    `p = f(str, sizeof(str)/sizeof(string));`

What are the contents of p after $f()$ has been called?

22. What does p point to after the execution of each of the following declarations?
    (a) `int *p = new int(20);`
    (b) `int *p = new int[25];`
    (c) Give the *delete* statements that would deallocate the dynamic memory for parts (a) and (b).

23. Use the following declaration for parts (a)–(d):

    ```
    rectangle *r;
    ```

    (a) Dynamically allocate a six-by-eight rectangle.
    (b) Use the dereference operator, *, and the dot operator to output the perimeter of the rectangle.
    (c) Use the -> operator to output the area of the rectangle.
    (d) Using setSides(), double the length and width of the rectangle.

24. The function createArray() has the task of creating a dynamic array of real numbers whose elements have an initial value initValue. Both size and initValue are passed as arguments, and a pointer to the array is the return value. Implement the function.

    ```
    double *createArray(int size, double initValue);
    ```

25. Use the following declaration for parts (a)–(c):

    ```
    miniVector<int>  *pVec;
    int i;
    ```

    (a) Dynamically allocate an empty vector pointed to by pVec.
    (b) Using push_back(), assign to the vector the values 10, 20, 30, and 40.
    (c) Using the dereference operator, *, and the index operator, [], write a loop that outputs the elements of the vector in reverse.

26. Use the insertion sort algorithm to implement the function sortMiniVector(), which takes a miniVector object and rearranges the elements in descending order:

```
template <typename T>
void sortMiniVector(miniVector<T> & v);
```

27. Consider the class called className.
   (a) Explain why you cannot declare a copy constructor as

```
className (const className obj);
```

   (b) Explain why you would not want to use the following declaration for an overloaded assignment operator:

```
void operator = (const className& rhs);
```

28. What is the meaning of the keyword *this*? Explain why it is valid only in the implementation of a member function.

29. The class dynamicClass uses its constructor, copy constructor, assignment operator, and destructor for memory management.
   (a) Consider the following declaration and statement:

```
dynamicClass<int>  one(5,7), two = one, three;

three = two;    // statement *
```

   (i)   Which operation is called to create object *one*? Describe the action.
   (ii) Which operation is called to create *two*? Describe the action.
   (iii) Which operation does the system use to implement statement *? Describe the action.

   (b) Function *f()* and the calling statement use dynamicClass objects:

```
dynamicClass<int> obj1(9,30), obj2(5,6);

template <typenameT>
dynamicClass<T> f(dynamicClass<T> x, const T& value)
{
    dynamicClass<T> obj = x, y(value,value);

    obj = y;

    return y;
}
```

Describe all of the class operations that are used by the system to execute the statement

```
obj2 = f(obj1, 8);
```

30. Function *f()* is a member of class demoCL. Four different implementations of *f()* include the *this* pointer. Use the different implementations to answer questions (a) to (c). Use the declaration for demoCL for each question.

```
class demoCL
{
   public:
      demoCL (int d);      // d initializes the data member
```

```
        demoCL f();            // return a demoCL object
    private:
        int data;
};
```

```
Implementation 1:              Implementation 2:
    demoCL demoCL::f()             demoCL demoCL::f()
    {                             {
        demoCL tmp = this;           this-> data *= 2;
        tmp.data *=2;                return *this;
        return tmp;               }
    }
```

```
Implementation 3:              Implementation 4:
    demoCL demoCL::f()             demoCL demoCL::f()
    {                             {
        demoCL tmp = *this;          demoCL tmp = *this;
        tmp.data *= 2;               tmp.data *= 2;
        return tmp;                  return *tmp;
    }                             }
```

(a) Identify the implementations for *f*() that contain syntax errors. Describe the errors.

(b) Identify the implementation for *f*() that takes the data value of the current object and creates a new object whose data value is twice that of the original. The function returns the new object.

(c) Identify the implementation for *f*() that doubles the data value of the current object and returns the current object.

31. Consider the class dynamicInt, which has a single dynamic data member:

```
class dynamicInt
{
    public:
        dynamicInt(int m = 0);
            // constructor

        ...
            // destructor

        dynamicInt(const dynamicInt& obj);
            // copy constructor

        ...
            // assignment operator

        int getData()const;
            // return value of dynamic member

        friend ostream& operator<< (ostream& ostr,
                                    const dynamicInt& obj);
            // output stream operator << as a friend function
```

```
    private:
        int *ptr;
            // dynamic data member
};
```

(a) Declare the destructor for dynamicInt.

(b) Declare the overloaded assignment operator.

(c) Implement the copy constructor. Throw the memoryAllocationError exception if no dynamic memory is available.

(d) Implement the overloaded operator << as a friend of the class.

(e) The function *f*() takes a dynamicInt object as an argument and has a dynamicInt object as its return value. The function is called in the main program.

```
dynamicInt f(dynamicInt obj)
{
    dynamicInt localObj(5 + obj.getData());

    return localObj;
}

int main()
{
    dynamicInt  obj1(10), obj2;

    obj2 = f(obj1);    // call the function
    cout << obj2.getData() << endl;

    return 0;
}
```

(i)   Indicate the number of times that the copy constructor is used.

(ii) Indicate all of the times that the destructor is called.

(iii) What is the output value from obj2.getData()?

32. Use the class dynamicInt from Written Exercise 5-31 and the operator *new* to allocate objects pointed to by *p* dynamically:

```
dynamicInt *p;
```

(a) Allocate a single dynamicInt object with an initial data value of 30.

(b) Allocate an array with five dynamicInt elements. What is the data value for each object in the array?

(c) Give the *delete* statements that deallocate the dynamic memory used in questions (a) and (b).

33. Give the implementation of the class dynamicInt of Written Exercise 5-31 as the template class dynamicType. Do not use inline code.

```
template <typename T>
class dynamicType
{
    public:
        dynamicType(const T& value);
        dynamicType(const dynamicType<T> & obj);
            // constructor and copy constructor
```

```
  ~dynamicType();
    // destructor

  dynamicType<T> & operator= (const dynamicType<T>& rhs);
    // assignment operator


  T getData() const;
    // data access

  friend ostream& operator<< (ostream& ostr,
                              const dynamicType<T>& obj);
    // stream output
private:
  T *ptr;
};
```

34. This exercise uses the class dynamicInt from Written Exercise 5-31 and the class dynamicType from Written Exercise 5-33. Declare the object

```
dynamicType<dynamicInt>  d(dynamicInt(5));
```

What is the output from the following statements?

```
cout << d << endl;
cout << d.getData().getData() << endl;
cout << d.getData() << endl;
```

35. Using the matrix class, implement as friends the overloaded arithmetic operators that add and subtract matrices. Each matrix must have the same dimension.

```
friend matrix<T>  operator+ (const matrix<T> & left,
                             const matrix<T> & right);
  // Precondition:left.rows() == right.rows()]
  //                     and
  //            left.cols() == right.cols()

  // result[i][j] = left[i][j] + right[i][j],
  // 0 <= i < left.rows() and 0 <= j < left.cols()

friend matrix<T> operator- (const matrix<T> & left,
                            const matrix<T> & right);
  // the same precondition applies as that for operator+.
  // result[i][j] = left[i][j] - right[i][j],
  // 0 < = i < left.rows() and 0 < = j < left.cols()
```

PROGRAMMING EXERCISES

36. Write a program that prompts for the number of rooms in a house. Use the input, n, to declare an array of rectangles dynamically. In a loop, input the dimensions for the n rooms, and then output the total area of the house. Scan the array to identify the room with the largest perimeter, and output its dimensions.

37. Implement the class dynamicInt of Written Exercise 5-31, and place it in the header file "dynint.h." Test the class with the following program, which includes function *f*():

```
#include <iostream>

#include "dynint.h"

using namespace std;

dynamicInt f(dynamicInt obj);

int main()
{
   dynamicInt a(3), b;

   b = f(a);
   cout << b << endl;

   return 0;
}

dynamicInt f(dynamicInt obj)
{
   obj = dynamicInt(7);

   return obj;
}
```

38. Use the function createArray() from Written Exercise 5-24 to allocate an array *arr* of size 5 and having initial values 1.0:

```
double *arr;
```

The program should include the following features: output the elements in arr; scan the array arr and modify the values to create the sequence 1.0, 2.0, 3.0, 4.0, 5.0; output the new values. You can output the array using the function writeArray() from "d_util.h."

39. Write a program that stores in miniVector *v* a list of 15 random integers in the range from 0 to 99. Output the vector. Use the function sortMiniVector() from Written Exercise 5-26 to order the elements in the vector and then output their values.

40. Place your implementation of the class dynamicType in Written Exercise 5-33 in the header file "dynt.h." Test your class by entering and running the following program:

```
#include < iostream>
#include < vector>

#include "dynt.h"

using namespace std;

template <typename T>
dynamicType<T> sum(const vector< dynamicType<T> >& v);
```

```
int main()
{
    dynamicType<int> arr[5] = {
        dynamicType<int> (3), dynamicType<int> (5),
        dynamicType<int> (8), dynamicType<int> (7),
        dynamicType<int> (2) };
    vector<dynamicType<int> > v(arr, arr+5);

    cout << sum(v) << endl;

    return 0;
}

template <typename T>
dynamicType<T> sum(const vector< dynamicType<T> > & v)
{
    T sum = T();
    int i;

    for (i=0;i < v.size(); i++)
        sum += v[i].getData();

    return dynamicType<T> (sum);
}
```

41. Written Exercise 5-36 discusses the implementation of overloaded operators + and − for the matrix class. Place your modified class in the header file "mat.h". Use the class to develop a program that declares the following two matrices and inputs their values. The program should compute and output the sum and difference of the two matrices.

$$matrix\ A = \begin{bmatrix} 1 & 2 & 3 \\ 4 & 5 & 6 \\ 7 & 8 & 9 \end{bmatrix}, \quad matrix\ B = \begin{bmatrix} 0 & 0 & 0 \\ 1 & 1 & 1 \\ 2 & 2 & 2 \end{bmatrix}$$

PROGRAMMING PROJECT

42. Consider these new member functions for the miniVector class:

```
void insert(int i, const T& item);
    // insert item at index i in the vector.
    // Precondition vector is not empty and 0 <= i <= vSize.
    // Postcondition the vector size increases by 1

void erase(int i);
    // erase the item at index i in the vector.
    // Preconditions vector is not empty and 0 <= i < vSize.
    // Postcondition the vector size decreases by 1
```

(a) Implement insert(). Note that the implementation of insert() allows $i = $ vSize. The operation in this situation is equivalent to push_back(item). A reallocation is necessary if vSize $==$ vCapacity.

   Recall that push_back() has amortized running time $O(1)$. In general, what is the amortized running time of insert()?

(b) Implement erase(). Note that for miniVector v, v.erase(v.size()-1) is equivalent to v.pop_back().

   Recall that pop_back() has running time $O(1)$. In general, what is the running time of erase()?

(c) Use the *new* operation to implement the following algorithm:

```
// v is in increasing order
// v[0] <= v[1] <= v[2] <= ... <= v[v.size()-1]
// insert item into v so that v remains in increasing
// order
template <typename T>
void insertOrder(miniVector<T>& v, const T& item);


// v is in increasing order. erase duplicate values
// from v. for example, if T = int, transform the
// vector
//    v = {1, 1, 2, 3, 3, 3, 7, 7, 8, 9, 9, 10}
// to
//    v = {1, 2, 3, 7, 8, 9, 10}
template <typename T>
void removeDuplicates(miniVector<T>& v);
```

(d) Place the implementation for the modified class in the file "minivec.h." Write a program that generates 15 random integers in the range from 0 to 19. Place each value into the miniVector object randInt, using insertOrder(). Output the values in randInt. Call removeDuplicates(), and output the modified vector.

◆

CHAPTER 6

The List Container and Iterators

OBJECTIVES

- To understand that a list is a sequence of values stored by position, but that no index operator is available for direct access to list elements.
- To understand that, unlike a vector, element insertion and removal has O(1) running time for any point in the list.
- To become familiar with the STL list class API and how to use its operations in an application.
- To understand that an iterator is a generalized pointer to container elements.
- To understand that all STL container classes have nested iterator classes that facilitate access to elements in the container.
- To understand that an iterator must have a starting value pointing to the first list element and that this value is supplied by the container begin() member function.
- To understand that any list traversal must have an ending point. It is supplied by the container member function end(), which returns an iterator pointing just past the end of the list.
- To understand the difference between constant and nonconstant iterators.
- To study the use of the iterator concept for implementing the sequential search of a list object.
- To understand that container operations to insert and erase objects inside a list require an iterator argument.
- To apply the general insert() and erase() operations for creating ordered lists and removing duplicates from a list.
- To view a case study that makes extensive use of list operations.

OUTLINE

In Chapter 4, we began a study of containers with the vector class, which is a sequence container modeled after an array. As a storage structure, a vector can grow to meet the needs of an application by efficiently inserting and removing items at the rear of the list. Programmers use a vector as the data structure of choice when an application needs a dynamic list with direct access to the elements. A vector has serious limitations, however, when the application frequently needs to insert and delete elements at intermediate positions in the list. For instance, the application may want to maintain an ordered list. With a vector, these operations require shifting of large blocks of data to open new positions or close unused gaps in the list. A different sequence container, called a *list*, provides a better alternative. The list container is specifically designed to store elements sequentially and still allow for very efficient adding and removing of items at any position. Section 6-1 begins a discussion of the list class with operations that allow for access and modification of items at either end of the list. We document the STL versions of these operations with an API.

While a list is a sequence container that store elements by position, the structure does not provide an index for direct access to an element at a specific position. To access the elements, list objects use iterators. Section 6-2 introduces the notion of a container iterator, one of the most important concepts in data structures. The iterator concept allows the development of algorithms that will work with any container type (vector, list, set, map, and so forth). While all containers have iterators, list iterators are the easiest to understand. They provide a foundation that can be applied and extended to all other containers.

With an iterator, we can define general insert and erase operations for a list object. In Section 6-3, we define these list operations and use them to solve some problems, including the removal of duplicate items from a list and the creation of an ordered list. An API documents the STL prototype and description of the operations. We conclude the section with a case study on graduation lists. The case study makes extensive use of list objects and iterators.

This chapter presents lists as an ADT. In Chapter 9, we introduce singly and doubly linked lists. Once you understand linked lists, you will have the tools to see how a list class is implemented. We use a doubly linked list to implement the miniList class. Like the miniVector class, the miniList class uses the STL list container function prototypes as its interface, but provides a simpler and more accessible implementation.

6-1   THE LIST CONTAINER

A vector is a sequence container that uses an array for the underlying storage of its elements. As a result, data occupy contiguous memory locations, and an index is able to access the data directly. The storage mechanism also allows data updates to the list, but only at one end, because there is additional space at the end of the memory block.

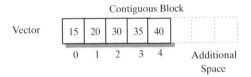

In Chapter 4, we evaluated the array container and noted several limitations that made it inappropriate for certain applications. Based on the evaluation, we introduced the vector container, whose design specifically addresses the array limitations. An evaluation of the vector class will likewise reveal problems and create design specifications for a new container class called a list.

While the vector functions push_back() and pop_back() allow for efficient modification of elements at the end of the sequence, there are no comparable operations to modify the front of the sequence. Overall, a vector is not an efficient storage structure for general insertion and deletion of items at an arbitrary position in the sequence. Because the data items must reside in a contiguous block of memory, an insertion requires shifting a block of elements to the right to make room for the new item. Similarly, a deletion requires shifting a block of elements to the left to fill the gap created by the removed item. Figure 6-1 illustrates the action required to add the element 25 to an ordered vector and the action required to remove the element 20 from the sequence.

The general insert and erase operations in a vector have running time O(n). If these operations are a significant part of an application, their execution imposes on the program extra overhead to maintain the storage structure. For applications that require a sequential container with efficient insert and erase operations, STL has a different data structure, called a *list container.*

A list container is a data structure that maintains elements by position. Unlike a vector, however, there is no external indexing mechanism to access an element directly at its position. Rather, each element in a list contains links that identify both the next and the preceding item in the sequence. The items are laid out in a row,

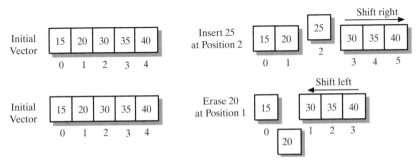

Figure 6-1
Shifting blocks of elements to insert or delete a vector item

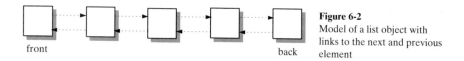

Figure 6-2
Model of a list object with
links to the next and previous
element

starting at the first element, called *front*, and proceeding in successive order to the last element, called *back*. Figure 6-2 provides a model for a list that illustrates the links with arrows that identify adjacent elements.

The process of locating an element uses a sequential scan that begins at the front of the list and moves forward from item to item until the element is identified. A similar scan could begin at the back of the list and proceed toward the front of the list until a match occurs.

You are familiar with lists from your everyday experiences. For instance, a restaurant maintains a reservation list for its dining customers. Items are added by customer name and include the number in the party and the time of reservation. When a customer arrives, the reservation name is removed (crossed out) from the list. Figure 6-3(a) illustrates a portion of the reservation list at Pasta Delectica Restaurant. Another example is that before going to a grocery store, you often create a shopping list on a sheet of paper, with the items appearing in a column down the page (Figure 6-3(b)). A third example illustrates a telephone company sending signals to rural customers by draping lines on a series of poles (Figure 6-3(c)).

Figure 6-3
Sample lists: a reservation list, a grocery list, and phone lines

The List ADT

We begin a study of the template-based list class with an overview of its operations. The list API documents the member function prototype and pre- and postconditions. The class provides three constructors to declare a list object. The format is identical to those used by the vector class. The default constructor creates an empty list; the other two versions allocate a list object with initial values. One version takes a size *n* and an value of type *T* as arguments and creates a list with *n* elements all set to the specified value. A second version initializes the list object with distinct values. The programmer first declares an array with the values and then passes the address range of the array as arguments. Figure 6-4 illustrates the lists created by different list constructors. From now on, in drawings of list objects, we will omit the arrows that represent the links between the elements.

```
// create an empty list that stores integer values
list<int> intList;

// allocate a list with 8 elements and value 0.0 (Figure 6-4 (a))
list<double> realList(8);

// list 6 time24 objects initially set at 8:30 (Figure 6-4 (b))
list<time24> timeList(6, time24(8,30));

// use the array address range to initialize a list with three strings
// Figure 6-4 (c))
string strArr[3] = {"array", "vector", "list"};
list<string> strList(strArr, strArr+3);
```

(a) list<double> realList(8)

| 0.0 | 0.0 | 0.0 | 0.0 | 0.0 | 0.0 | 0.0 | 0.0 |

(b) list<time24> timeList(6, 8:30)

| 8:30 | 8:30 | 8:30 | 8:30 | 8:30 | 8:30 |

(c) list<string> strList(strArr,strArr+3)

| array | vector | list |

Figure 6-4
Creating a list object having initial values

All STL containers share a common set of member functions. A copy constructor, destructor, and overloaded assignment operator provide runtime memory management tools. The operations allow a programmer to use an existing object to initialize a new container object or assign one a new value. Each container object also has a size() and an empty() function, which provide information on the current number of elements in the list. For instance, with the list class, we can do the following:

```
// copy constructor creates containerList as a clone of strList
list<string> containerList = strList;
cout << newList.size();                // output: 3
```

The list class has a set of operations that allow a programmer to add or remove elements at the both ends of the sequence, as well as operations for general insertion and deletion of items at intermediate positions. The general insert and erase operations require an understanding of iterators, which are introduced in the Section 6-2. The functions push_front() and pop_front() modify the first element in the list. To access or update the value of the first element, the class has the member function front(). Like a vector, a list object uses functions push_back(), pop_back(), and back() to deal with the back of the list.

To illustrate these access and update functions, assume intList is an empty list of integers. The push functions build the list by adding a new element. You should observe that successive calls to push_front() add elements in reverse order; successive calls to push_back() add the elements in the normal order.

```
intList.push_front(5);
intList.push_front(20);
intList.push_back(10);
intList.push_back(25);
```

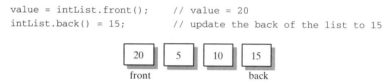

A program can use front() and back() to access the elements at the ends of the list. The operations can be used on the left side of an assignment statement to update the value.

```
value = intList.front();    // value = 20
intList.back() = 15;        // update the back of the list to 15
```

The pop operations remove an element from the list. For a list with two elements, the operations update *front* and *back* to point at the same element.

```
intList.pop_front();
```

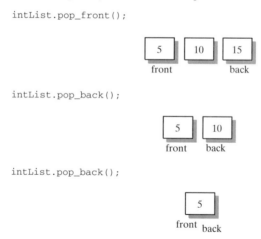

```
intList.pop_back();
```

```
intList.pop_back();
```

The List API

The upcoming API is a partial listing of the STL list operations, which include the constructors, size functions, and the access and update functions for the ends of a list. With the introduction of a list iterator in the next section, we will extend the

API. Use the system header file <list> to include the corresponding STL class. We do not include prototypes for the destructor, copy constructor, and overloaded assignment operator, because you are familiar with the format from the miniVector class. Note that many of the member functions have the same name and operation as corresponding functions in the vector class. This is a deliberate design feature of STL, which attempts to provide a programmer with a common interface for all container classes.

CLASS list ·	Constructors	<list>

list();
> Create an empty list. This is the default constructor.

list(int *n, const T& value* = *T*());
> Create a list with *n* elements, each having a specified value. If the value argument is omitted, the elements are filled with the default value for type *T*. Type *T* must have a default constructor, and the default value of type *T* is specified by the notation *T*().

list((*T *first, T *last)*;
> Initialize the list, using the address range [*first, last*).

CLASS list	Operations	<list>

T& **back**();
> Return the value of the item at the back of the list.
> Precondition: The list must contain at least one element.

bool **empty**() *const*;
> Return true if the list is empty, false otherwise.

T& **front**();
> Return the value of the item at the front of the list.
> Precondition: The list must contain at least one element.

void **push_back**(const *T& value*);
> Add a value at the back of the list.
> Postcondition: The list has a new element at the back, and its size increases by 1.

void **pop_back**();
> Remove the item at the back of the list.
> Precondition: The list is not empty.
> Postcondition: The list has a new element at the back or is empty.

void **push_front**(const *T& value*);
> Add a value at the front of the list.
> Postcondition: The list has a new element at the front, and its size
>   increases by 1.

void **pop_front**();
> Remove the element at the front of the list.
> Precondition: The list is not empty.
> Postcondition: The list has a new element at the front or is empty.

int **size**() *const*;
> Return the number of elements in the list.

Application: A List Palindrome

A palindrome is a sequence of values that reads the same forward and backward. For instance, the characters in the string "level" are a palindrome, as are the digits in the integer 2002. The function isPalindrome() takes a list object as an argument and returns a value of true if the sequence of elements is a palindrome. The algorithm begins by making a copy of the list, using the assignment operator. Working on the copy, the process begins by comparing the elements on opposite ends of the list, using front() and back(). If they match, the elements are deleted, and the comparison on the list that now has two fewer elements is repeated. If the comparison fails, the function is exited immediately with the value false. Otherwise, the process is continued until the size of the list is less than 2. This occurs when the list is a palindrome, and the return value of true notes this fact.

```
template <typename T>
bool isPalindrome(const list<T>& alist)
{
   list<T> copyList;
   copyList = alist;     // create a copy of the original list
   // check values at ends of list as long as list size > 1
   while (copyList.size() > 1)
   {
      // compare values on opposite ends; if not equal, return false
      if (copyList.front() != copyList.back())
         return false;
      // delete the objects
      copyList.pop_front();
      copyList.pop_back();
   }
   // if still have not returned, list is a palindrome
   return true;
}
```

PROGRAM 6-1   PALINDROME STRINGS

The program uses the list function isPalindrome() to determine whether a string is a palindrome. We use the more common notion of string palindrome to refer to any sequence of letters that reads the same forward and backward. Hence, the string "Madam I'm Adam" is a palindrome, once the blanks are removed. The program begins by prompting the user to enter a string, which could include blank letters and punctuation marks. The function getline() reads the string. A loop scans the individual characters in the string and copies all letters in lowercase to the list charList by using push_back(). This removes the blanks and punctuation marks. After isPalindrome() is called with charList as the argument, a message indicates whether the original string is a palindrome.

Three runs include test strings that are palindromes with blanks, punctuation, and both lowercase and uppercase letters, along with a string that is not a palindrome:

```cpp
// File: prg6_1.cpp
// the program prompts the user to enter a string which
// may include blank letters. it scans the individual characters in
// the string and copies all nonblank letters to the list charList.
// a call to the function isPalindrome() with charList as the argument
// determines whether the original string is or is not a palindrome

#include <iostream>
#include <string>
#include <list>
#include <ctype.h>           // for isalpha() and tolower()

using namespace std;

// check whether the values in a list read the same forward and
// backward. if so, return true; otherwise return false.
template <typename T>
bool isPalindrome(const list<T>& alist);

int main()
{
   string str;
   list<char> charList;      // empty list of characters
   int i;
   char ch;

   // prompt the user to enter a string that may include blanks
   cout << "Enter the string: ";
   getline(cin, str, '\n');;

   // copy all of the nonblank letters as lowercase characters
   // to the list charList
   for (i = 0; i < str.length(); i++)
   {
      ch = str[i];
      if (isalpha(ch))
         charList.push_back(tolower(ch));
   }

   // call isPalindrome() and use the return value to designate
   // whether the string is or is not a palindrome
```

```
    if (isPalindrome(charList))
        cout << "'" << str << "' is a palindrome" << endl;
    else
        cout << "'" << str << "' is not a palindrome" << endl;

    return 0;
}
/* implementation of isPalindrome() given in the program discussion */
```

```
Run 1:
Enter the string: A man, a plan, a canal, Panama
'A man, a plan, a canal, Panama' is a palindrome

Run 2:
Enter the string: Go hang a salami, I'm a lasagna hog
'Go hang a salami, I'm a lasagna hog' is a palindrome

Run 3:
Enter the string: palindrome
'palindrome' is not a palindrome
```

6-2   ITERATORS

A vector can access each element in the sequence by using an index. A list has no such tool. Except for the front and the back, we have no way to identify the elements. However, the items in a list contain pointers that identify both the next and the previous elements in the sequence. These pointers are designed to scan the list in both directions, from the front or from the back. Up to this point, we have seen no way to utilize the pointer attributes of an element and thus cannot scan the list to find an element and access its value. The concept of an list iterator addresses this issue.

The Iterator Concept

A *list iterator* is an object that accesses the elements in a list in their positional order. You can think of an iterator as a "locator" that slides back and forth across the range of elements in the list. At any position in the list, the iterator can access the value of the corresponding element. By using the links to the next and previous element, the iterator can move to the right and to the left, one position at a time. An iterator object is a generalized pointer that uses pointer notation for its interface. The dereference operator, *, accesses the value of the element referenced by the iterator. The increment operator, ++ (or decrement operator, −−) resets the iterator to point at the next (previous) element in the list. The operators == and != compare two iterator objects that are pointing at elements in the list. The two iterators are equal if they point at the same element in the list and are not equal if they point at different elements. You are familiar with pointer notation from

Chapter 5, so we describe the corresponding iterator operations by using a modified API format.

CLASS list::iterator	Operations	<list>

*:   Accesses the value of the item currently pointed to by the iterator. For example,

       *iter;

++:   Moves the iterator to the next item in the list. For example,

       iter++;

−−:   Moves the iterator to the previous item in the list. For example,

       iter−−;

==:   Takes two iterators as operands and returns true when they both point at the same item in the list. For example,

       iter1 == iter2

!=:   Returns true when the two iterators do not point at the same item in the list. For example,

       iter1 != iter2

Example 6-1

The list<int> object contains the following five consecutive integers in the sequence. Assume iterA and iterB are iterators that point to elements 22 and 70, respectively:

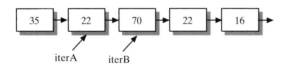

1. The expression *iterA is 22, which is the value of the element pointed to by iterA.
2. Currently, iterA != iterB, because the two iterators point at distinct elements. By using the ++ operator, iterA moves to the next element in the list. The resulting iterators are equal, because they point at the same element.

```
iterA++           // iterator moves to next position (element 70)
iterA == iterB    // true: two iterators point to same element
```

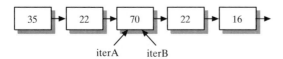

A similar result would occur if iterB were to move to the previous location (element 22), by means of using the operator $--$.

(c) Just as with C++ pointers, we distinguish between an iterator and the value of the element to which it points. Assume iterA and iterB point at elements 22 and 70, respectively. Clearly, the iterators are not equal. If iterB moves to the next element, then *iterA and *iterB are both 22, yet the iterators are still not equal.

```
iterB++            // iterator moves to next position (element 22)
*iterA == *iterB   // true: values referenced by iterators are equal
iterA != iterB     // true: iterator objects are distinct
```

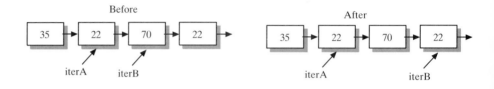

Declaring and Using Iterators. Example 6-1 illustrates how you can manipulate iterators as though they are pointers, without having to understand their underlying implementation in the list class. To use iterators in a program, however, we must learn how to declare them and then position them at an element in a specific list.

The list class includes *iterator* as a nested class within its declaration. As a result, the declaration of an iterator object must include the class name "iterator" along with the scope operator expression "list<T>::". The scope operator identifies the iterator as belonging to the list class. All STL container classes have a nested iterator class. Declaring the iterator class inside the container identifies it with the container. The iterator uses knowledge of the container structure to access an element with the * operator and to scan the elements by using the ++ and $--$ operators. The list iterator uses the fact that a list stores elements by position to scan the sequence.

```
// list iterator declaration
list<T>::iterator iter;
```

For instance, the following are declarations of iterators that reference an integer list and a string list:

```
list<int>::iterator listIter;
list<string>::iterator iter;
```

Like a C++ pointer, an iterator object is ineffective until it is has an initial value. The program must associate the iterator with a specific position in a specific list. To initialize a list iterator, the list class provides two member functions, called begin() and end(). The begin() function returns an iterator value that points to the beginning of the list. The end() function returns an iterator value that points just past the back of the list. It is appropriate that a list object provide these two member functions, because only the object knows which element occupies the front of the list and which element is at the back of the list. Note that end() is the iterator position *past* the end of the list and is not the last element (back) of the list.

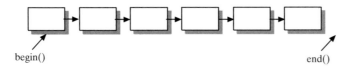

begin()   end()

For instance, the following statements declare the integer list intList and then initialize listIter to the front of the list:

```
list<int> intList;              // declare list
listIter = intList.begin();     // initialize listIter to front of list
```

To set an iterator at the last element in the list, use end() to give it a value past the end of the list, and then reposition the iterator to the last element with the −− operator:

```
listIter = intList.end();       // location past the end of the list
listIter--;                     // move to last element
cout << *listIter;              // output the last list element
// Note: *listIter and intList.back() are the same
```

> List iterators move through the list in a circular fashion. When an iterator is at end(), the operation ++ moves the iterator to the first list element, at location begin(). Similarly, when an iterator is at begin(), the operation −− moves the iterator to end().

Note

Example 6-2
_____

The function find_last_of () takes a list and a value of type *T* as arguments. The function returns the iterator that locates the last occurrence of that value in the list. If the value is not found, the function returns the iterator end().

```
template <typename T>
list<T>::iterator find_last_of(list<T>& alist, const T& value)
{
    // declare iterator and set it just beyond the end of the list
    list<T>::iterator iter = alist.end();

    // scan in reverse order until a match occurs or until the iterator
    // exhausts the list; at the front of the list, iter--moves
    // the iterator to position a list.end()
    do
        iter--;         // move iterator to previous position
    while (iter != alist.begin() && !(*iter == value));
    return (iter;       // returns iterator at match or alist.end()
}
```

The next set of statements apply the function find_last_of() to intList by searching for the last occurrence of 3 and then the last occurrence of 7. When the function locates 3, the code outputs that value and its successor in the list. The value 7 does not occur in the list.

```
int arr[] = {1,3,3,4,5};
int arrSize = sizeof(arr)/sizeof(int);
list<int> intList(arr, arr+arrSize);
list<int>::iterator iter;

iter = find_last_of(intList, 3);
if (iter != intList.end())
{
    cout << "iter << "  ";
    iter++;
    cout << *iter << endl;
}

iter = find_last_of(intList, 7);
if (iter != intList.end())
    cout << "7 is in the list" << endl;
else
    cout << "7 is not in the list" << endl;
```

```
Output:

3   4
7 is not in the list
```

Constant Iterators

C++ uses the *const* attribute to specify that an object cannot be modified. Typically, a programmer passes an object by constant reference in an argument list when the function will only access, and not modify, the value of the object. The const attribute carries over to list iterators. The STL list class has a second iterator, called a *constant iterator*, that functions much like a simple (nonconstant) iterator, but with one notable exception: The programmer cannot apply the dereference operator, *, to a constant iterator on the left side of an assignment statement. In the next section, we will observe that a constant iterator cannot be used with list insert() and erase() functions, because both of these operations modify the list.

In the list class, constant iterators have the object type name *const_iterator*. Like a nonconstant iterator, a constant iterator includes the scope operator expression *list<T>::* in its declaration.

```
list<T>::const_iterator iter;
```

A constant iterator has the operations ++ and −− to move forward and backward in the list. The * operator allows a constant iterator to access the value of an element in the list, but not to update the value. Iterator and const_iterator objects have different types, so the list class provides separate versions of begin() and end() to assign to a constant iterator the extreme locations in the list. The rule for deciding between a constant iterator and a nonconstant iterator is very simple:

> RULE: Use a constant iterator to access and scan a constant list. Use a
>   nonconstant iterator to access and scan a nonconstant list.

In practice, you will come across constant lists primarily as function arguments. Whenever you have such a list, remember to use the const_iterator object type for the iterator. To illustrate the use of constant iterators, consider the function writeList(), which outputs the elements in a list and follows each element by *separator*, a string that has a default value consisting of two blanks. The function passes the list by constant reference, and a constant iterator scans the elements. The * operator simply accesses the value of each element.

writeList():
```
// display the list. follow the output of each list element
// by separator. default value of separator = "  "
template <typename T>
void writeList(const list<T>& alist, const string& separator = "  ")
{
   list<T>::const_iterator iter;

   for (iter = alist.begin(); iter != alist.end(); iter++)
      cout << *iter << separator;
   cout << endl;
}
```

If you pass the string "\n" as the separator, output occurs with one item per line. The implementation of writeList() is in the library file "d_util.h."

In the previous section, we gave a partial listing of the STL list operations. We extend the API to include a description of the functions begin() and end(), which return both iterator and const_iterator values.

CLASS list	Operations (continued)	<list>

iterator **begin**();
> Returns an iterator that references the first position (front) of the list. If the list is empty, the iterator value end() is returned.

const_iterator **begin**();
> Returns a const_iterator that points to the first position (front) of a constant list. If the list is empty, the const_iterator value end() is returned.

iterator **end**();
> Returns an iterator that signifies a location immediately out of the range of actual elements. A program must not dereference the value of end() with the * operator.

const_iterator **end**();
> Returns a const_iterator that signifies a location immediately out of the range of actual elements in a constant list. A program must not dereference the value of end() with the * operator.

The Sequential Search of a List

In Chapter 3, we discussed the sequential-search algorithm, which scans a sublist of an array or vector looking for a target value. In "d_search.h," we implemented a template version of the function seqSearch() for a vector container. The function takes the vector object, the index range [*first, last*), and the target value as arguments. The return value is the index of a match, or *last* if a match does not occur. In this section, we extend the sequential-search algorithm to lists and create another version of the function seqSearch(). This function takes an iterator range [*first, last*) and a target value of type *T* as arguments. The return value is a list<*T*>:: iterator that points at the first element in the range matching the target, or is the iterator value *last* if no match occurs. While the functions perform the same task, their prototypes differ significantly.

```
// vector version of the sequential search
template <typename T>
int seqSearch(const vector<T>& v, int first, int last, const T& target);

// list version of the sequential search
template <typename T>
list<T>::iterator find(list<T>::iterator first,
                       list<T>::iterator last, const T& target)
```

Note that the list version does not need the list object as a separate argument, because the iterators first and last reference locations in the list. With the dereference operator, *, an iterator can access a list element. In the vector version, an index in the range must be combined with the associated vector object in order to access an element.

seqSearch():
```
// perform the sequential search for target in the list
// iterator range [first, last). return an iterator pointing
// at the target in the list or last if target is not found
template <typename T>
list<T>::iterator seqSearch (list<T>::iterator first,
                        list<T>::iterator last, const T& target)
{
```

```
        // start at location first
        list<T>::iterator iter = first;

        // compare list elements with target until either
        // we arrive at last or locate target
        while(iter != last && (*iter != target))
            iter++;

        // iter either points at target or is last
        return iter;
    }
```

You might wonder why the function passes the iterators by reference and not by constant reference. If the argument list specifies the range by using constant iterators, the return type must be const_iterator. Typically, a programmer calls seqSearch() to locate an element and then subsequently uses the return iterator and the operator * to update the value. Update operations are not valid for a constant iterator. The implementation for seqSearch() is in the file "d_search.h."

☞

Note

Recall that iterator is a nested class declared in a list. It is possible that the C++ compiler will not determine the template type T for the iterator arguments of seqSearch() without assistance. When calling the function, place the actual template type in angle brackets after its name to inform the compiler about the type. For instance, suppose you want to search an integer list intList from beginning to end for the value 5 and assign the result to *iter*. Use the function call

   iter = seqSearch<int> (intList.begin(), intList.end(), 5);

In general, whenever the compiler is not able to determine the template type for a function call, using this construct will instruct the compiler to use the specified type.

Example 6-3
_____

Declare the following list and list iterators:

```
        int arr[] = {2, 5, 2, 15, 10, 3, 5, 5};
        int arrSize = sizeof(arr)/sizeof(int);
        list<int> intList(arr, arr + arrSize);
        list<int>::iterator result;
```

1. Search for 15 in the entire list, and, if it is found, replace it by 55:

```
        result = seqSearch<int> (intList.begin(), intList.end(), 15);

        // search is successful if result is not intList.end()
        if (result != intList.end())
            *result = 55;
```

2. Output the modified list:

```
writeList(intList);
```

Output: 2 5 2 55 10 3 5 5

3. The function numUnique() determines the number of unique (nonduplicate) elements in a list. Each iterator value iter defines the two sublists [aList.begin(), iter) and [iterNext, aList.end()), where iterNext is the position immediately after iter. The value *iter is unique if the sequential search verifies that it is not present in either sublist.

```
template <typename T>
int numUnique(list<T>& aList)
{
    list<T>::iterator iter, iterNext;
    int uniqueCount = 0;

    // scan the list element by element using iter
    iter = aList.begin();
    while (iter != aList.end())
    {
        // is target (*iter) in range [aList.begin(),iter)?
        if (seqSearch<T>(aList.begin(), iter, *iter) == iter)
        {
            // target is not in the lower sublist. is it
            // in the sublist [iterNext,aList.end())?
            // set iterNext to position past iter
            iterNext = iter;
            iterNext++;
            if (seqSearch<T>(iterNext, aList.end(),
                            *iter) == aList.end())
                // target is unique. increment uniqueCount
                uniqueCount++;
        }
        iter++;
    }

    return uniqueCount;
}
```

Call numUnique() for list intList, and output the number of unique elements:

```
cout << numUnique(intList);     // Output: 5
```

Application: Word Frequencies

To illustrate the use of a list, we design an application that reads a document from a file and outputs the distinct words and their frequencies in alphabetical order. The application uses the class wordFreq, which stores a word and the number of times the word has occurred (the word frequency). The class has a constructor that initializes the word and sets its frequency to 1. For each subsequent occurrence of the word, use the member function increment() to increase the frequency by 1. A list stores wordFreq objects, and the application uses seqSearch() to determine whether the next word in the file is already in the list or must be added to the list. In the former case, a call to increment() updates the frequency. In the latter case, the word is embedded in a wordFreq object and added to the list using push_back(). In order to use seqSearch(), the class overloads the operator $==$ by comparing two words. The operator $<<$ outputs a wordFreq object in the format "word (frequency)".

The STL list class includes a sort() member function. In order to use this member function, the wordFreq class must define the operator $<$, which enables the sorting of elements in ascending order.

```
// prototype for the STL list function
void sort();
```

The sort() function for a list object has running time $O(n \log_2 n)$. For instance, if *wf* is an object of type list<wordFreq>, the statement

```
wf.sort();
```

places the list in alphabetical order.

CLASS wordFreq　　　　　　**Declaration**　　　　　　**"d_wfreq.h"**

```
// maintains a word and its frequency of occurrence
class wordFreq
{
   public:
      // initialize word and set freq to 1
      wordFreq(const string& str): word(str), freq(1)
      {}

      // add 1 to the frequency
      void increment()
      { freq++; }

      // equality operator compares the word for the objects
      friend bool operator== (const wordFreq& lhs, const wordFreq& rhs)
      { return lhs.word == rhs.word; }

      // less than operator compares the word for the objects
      friend bool operator< (const wordFreq& lhs, const wordFreq& rhs)
      { return lhs.word < rhs.word; }

      // output an object in the format word (freq)
      friend ostream& operator<< (ostream& ostr, const wordFreq& w)
      {
         ostr << w.word << " (" << w.freq << ')';
         return ostr;
      }
```

```
private:
    string word;
    // number of times word found
    int freq;
};
```

PROGRAM 6-2   WORD FREQUENCIES

The program prompts for the name of a file containing words. After the opening of the file
and error checking, a loop inputs words until the end-of-file marker is reached and stores the
frequency information in the list *wf* of wordFreq objects. Insert a word into the list with frequency 1 if a call to seqSearch() determines that the word is not already in the list. If the
word is already in the list, use the iterator value returned by seqSearch() to execute the member function increment(), which increases the word frequency by 1. After handling all the
words in the file, use the list class member function sort() to place the words in alphabetical
order. Using writeList() with separator = "\n," output each word and its frequency on a separate line.

```cpp
// File: prg6_2.cpp
// the program uses the class wordFreq, which stores a word
// and the number of times it has occurred in a document. declare
// a list, wf, of wordFreq objects. prompt the user for the name
// of a file containing words, and read the file word by word. if
// a word is in the list, increase its frequency by 1; otherwise,
// insert the word into the list with frequency 1. sort the final
// list, and output each word and the number of times it occurs
// in the file.

#include <iostream>
#include <fstream>
#include <cstdlib>          // for exit()
#include <list>
#include <string>

#include "d_search.h"       // for list seqSearch()
#include "d_wfreq.h"        // for wordFreq
#include "d_util.h"         // for writeList()

using namespace std;

int main()
{
    ifstream fin;
    // words read from file and inserted into wf
    list<wordFreq> wf;
    // use for seqSearch() and displaying the list
    list<wordFreq>::iterator iter;
    //prompt for the name of the file
    string fileName, word;
```

```
   cout << "Enter name of the file containing the words: ";
   cin >> fileName;

   // error checking
   fin.open(fileName.c_str());
   if (!fin)
   {
      cerr << "Cannot open " << fileName << endl;
      exit(1);
   }
   // read a word until end-of-file
   while (fin >> word)
   {
      // declare a wordFreq object with frequency 1
      wordFreq obj(word);

      // search for word in the list wf
      iter = seqSearch<wordFreq> (wf.begin(), wf.end(), obj);

      // did we locate the word?
      if (iter != wf.end())
         // yes. increment the word frequency
         (*iter).increment();
      else
         // word is new. insert obj into the list
         wf.push_back(obj);
   }

   // list member function sort() orders the list
   wf.sort();

   // output each object on a separate line
   cout << endl;
   writeList(wf, "\n");

   return 0;
}
```

```
File "wf.dat"

peter piper picked a peck of pickled peppers
a peck of pickled peppers peter piper picked
if peter piper picked a peck of pickled peppers
where is the peck that peter piper picked
Run:

Enter the name of the file containing the words: wf.dat

a (3)
if (1)
```

```
is (1)
of (3)
peck (4)
peppers (3)
peter (4)
picked (4)
pickled (3)
piper (4)
that (1)
the (1)
where (1)
```

6-3   GENERAL LIST INSERT AND ERASE OPERATIONS

The desire to have a sequence container that allows for efficient insertion and deletion of elements is the motivation behind the design of the list container. The list class
provides insert() and erase() functions, which add or remove an element at an iterator
position, respectively. Before we describe the prototype for the functions, let us use
the operations in a series of examples. Note carefully how an insert or erase operation
affects iterator values after a new element is added or removed from the list.

Consider an integer list with the iterator *iter* pointing at the second element.
Figure 6-5 gives a before-and-after view of the list for an insert operation that adds
the element 4 at the iterator position. Initially, *iter = 7. The insertion places the
new element in the list immediately before element 7 and returns an iterator pointing at the new element (*newIter = 4). The original iterator continues to point at
the same element 7.

```
int arr[5] = {2, 7, 3, 9, 5};
int arrSize = sizeof(arr)/sizeof(int);
list<int> intList(arr, arr + arrSize);
list<int>::iterator iter, newElt;

iter = intList.begin();
iter++;                              // move to 2nd list element
newIter = intList.insert(iter, 4);   // insert before iter
cout << *newIter << "  " << *iter;   // output: 4   7
```

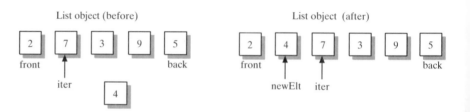

Figure 6-5
Insert the element 4 into a list. The iterator iter continues to point at the element 7, and
newIter points to the new element, 4.

The erase() operation removes the element from the list at the current iterator position. The operation destroys the element, so the iterator becomes invalid. Figure 6-6 gives a before-and-after view illustrating removal of the element 7 from the integer list. The object iter must be reinitialized before its next use in an algorithm.

```
iter = intList.begin();
iter++;
intList.erase(iter);
```

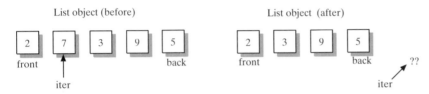

Figure 6-6
Removal of the element 7 from a list

A second version of the erase function takes an iterator range [*first, last*) and removes all elements within the range. When the range specifies the entire list, the erase() function has the effect of clearing the list:

```
// clear the list
erase(alist.begin(), alist.end());
```

We complete the API documentation for the list class by including the prototypes, actions, and pre- and postconditions for the member functions insert() and erase() operations.

CLASS list   **Operations (continued)**   **<list>**

void **erase**(*iterator pos*);
    Erase the element pointed to by *pos*.
    Precondition: The list is not empty.
    Postcondition: The list has one fewer element.

void **erase**(*iterator first, iterator last*);
    Erase all list elements within the iterator range [*first, last*).
    Precondition: The list is not empty.
    Postcondition: The size of the list decreases by the number of elements in the
                range.

iterator **insert** (*iterator pos, const T& value*);
    Insert *value* before *pos*, and return an iterator pointing to the position of the
    new value in the list. The operation does not affect any existing iterators.
    Postcondition: The list has a new element.

The programmer can use the operator ++ with the iterator argument in the erase() function. Two actions occur: The current value of the iterator becomes the argument to erase(), and then the iterator moves to the next element in the list. The effect is significant. Rather than having the erase() function invalidate the iterator, the increment operator sets the iterator at the next item in the list, immediately following the element that was removed.

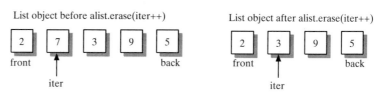

Example 6-4

1. The function doubleData() takes a list and modifies it to repeat every element. For instance, the integer list 2, 3, 7, 5 becomes 2, 2, 3, 3, 7, 7, 5, 5.

```
template <typename T>
void doubleData(list<T>& aList)
{
    list<T>::iterator p = aList.begin();

    while (p != aList.end())
    {
        // insert current list value before the current position
        p = aList.insert(p,*p);
        p++;      // move forward to the next value
    }
}
```

2. The function eraseSmallValues() takes a list and a target value as arguments and removes from the list all elements whose value is less than the target. The use of the increment operator, ++, in the erase() function is critical to the implementation.

```
template <typename T>
void eraseSmallValues(list<T>& aList, const T& target)
{
    // declare iterator and set to start of the list
    list<T>::iterator iter = aList.begin();

    // scan the entire list
    while (iter != aList.end())
        // compare current value with target and remove if necessary.
        // increment the iterator in either case
        if (*iter < target)
            aList.erase(iter++);
        else
            iter++;
}
```

3. Use the function erase(), whose argument is a range, to erase an entire list.

```
int arr[] = {2, 6, 12, 35, 99, 55};
int arrSize = sizeof(arr)/sizeof(int);
list<int> intList(arr, arr+arrSize);
    . . .
// erase all the elements in the list
intList.erase(intList.begin(), intList.end()):
cout << intList.size(); // output: 0
```

Ordered Lists

In many applications, we wish to maintain an ordered list of data, with the values in ascending or descending order. An algorithm to create such a list must scan the list to identify the correct location for the new data value and then insert it. The following discussion illustrates the process of creating a list in ascending order.

To enter data value *item*, we first scan the list and position a list iterator *curr* at the first element whose data value is greater than or equal to *item*. The insert() function can then add the new value immediately in front of *curr*. The upcoming examples illustrate the algorithm. Assume intList initially contains the integers 60, 65, 74, and 82.

Position the iterator *curr* at the front of the list by using begin().

```
curr = intList.begin();
```

Insert the element 50 in the list: The first item in the list has value 60, which is greater than or equal to 50, so the scan immediately terminates with *curr = 60. The insertion places the value 50 at the front of the list:

```
intList.insert(curr, 50);
```

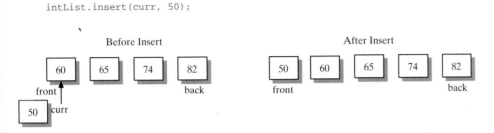

Insert the element 70 in the list: In the scan, *curr* stops at value 74, which is the first item in the list that is greater than or equal to 70. Insert 70 at position *curr*:

```
intList.insert(curr, 70);
```

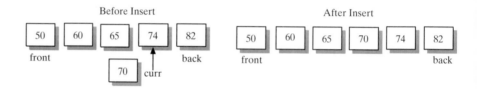

Insert the element 90 in the list: We scan the entire list and cannot find an element greater than or equal to 90 (*curr* == intList.end()). The new value is greater than all other values in the list and hence will occupy the rear of the list. An insert at *curr* = intList.end() adds the element at the rear of the list. This is equivalent to the list operation push_back().

```
intList.insert(curr, 90);
```

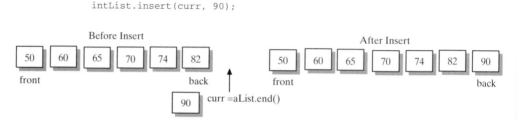

The function insertOrder() takes the list and the new item as arguments and implements the algorithm. By using the function to build the list, you create an ordered sequence of elements. You can locate insertOrder() in the file "d_listl.h."

insertOrder():
```
// insert item into the ordered list
template <typename T>
void insertOrder(list<T>& orderedList, const T& item)
{
    // curr starts at first list element, stop marks end
    list<T>::iterator curr = orderedList.begin(),
                      stop = orderedList.end();
    // find the insertion point
    while ((curr != stop) && (*curr < item))
        curr++;

    // do the insertion using insert()
    orderedList.insert(curr, item);
}
```

The efficiency of the insertOrder() algorithm depends on the value of the new item. If the list has *n* elements, the worst-case performance occurs when the insert occurs at the end of the list. This case requires *n* comparisons and has running time O(*n*). On average, we expect to search half the list to find an insertion point. As a result, the average running time is O(*n*). Of course, the best case is O(1).

Removing Duplicates

An algorithm to remove duplicates in a list provides an interesting application of list iterators. The process involves scanning the list with the iterator *curr*. Begin by setting *curr* to point at the front of the list, and record its data value. This provides a target at which to start looking for duplicates in the remainder of the list. Position a second iterator, *p*, at the element immediately to the right of *curr*, and scan the tail of the list, using iterator *p* to erase all elements whose data value matches the target. Then move the iterator *curr* forward one position, and continue the process until reaching the end of the list. Figure 6-7 illustrates the algorithm, assuming that iterator *curr* identifies the element with target value 5. Iterator *p* points at element 7, which is immediately to the right of *curr*. After deleting all occurrences of the value 5, iterator *curr* moves to the next element in the list, which has a value of 7.

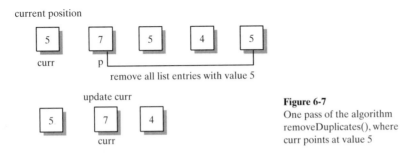

remove all list entries with value 5

Figure 6-7
One pass of the algorithm removeDuplicates(), where curr points at value 5

The function removeDuplicates() takes a list by reference. The algorithm modifies the list to have only unique values stored in the same order as in the original list. You can locate the implementation of removeDuplicates()in the file "d_listl.h".

removeDuplicates:
```
template <typename T>
void removeDuplicates(list<T>& aList)
{   // current data value
    T currValue;
    // the two list iterators we use
    list<T>::iterator curr, p;

    // start at the front of the list
    curr = aList.begin();

    // cycle through the list
    while(curr != aList.end())
    {
        // record the current list data value
        currValue = *curr;
```

```
                    // set p one element to the right of curr
                    p = curr;
                    p++;

                    // move forward until end of list, removing
                    // all occurrences of currValue
                    while(p != aList.end())
                      if (*p == currValue)
                          // erase current element and advance p to next
                          aList.erase(p++);
                      else
                          p++;      // move to the next list element
                    // duplicates of currValue removed. move to the next
                    // data value and repeat the process
                    curr++;
                }
        }
```

PROGRAM 6-3 ORDERED LIST WITHOUT DUPLICATES

This program illustrates the functions insertOrder() and removeDuplicates(). The unordered integer array *arr* contains duplicate values. By scanning the array and calling insertOrder(), we create the ordered list intList. Before and after removing duplicates, the program outputs the list by using the function writeList().

```
// File: prg6_3.cpp
// the program declares an unordered integer array,
// arr, containing duplicate values. it builds the
// ordered list, intList, by inserting each element
// of arr into the list using insertOrder(). calling
// removeDuplicates() transforms intList into a list
// of unique values. the program uses writeSeqList()
// to output the list before and after removing
// duplicates.

#include <iostream>
#include <list>

#include "d_list1.h"     // for insertOrder() and removeDuplicates()
#include "d_util.h"      // for writeList()

using namespace std;

int main()
{
    // declare an unordered array with duplicate values
    int arr[] = {7, 2, 2, 9, 3, 5, 3, 9, 7, 2}, i;
    int arrSize = sizeof(arr)/sizeof(int);
    list<int> intList;
```

```
    // build the ordered list using elements from the array
    for (i = 0; i < arrSize; i++)
        insertOrder(intList, arr[i]);

    // output the ordered list with duplicates
    cout << ""Ordered list with duplicates: ";
    writeList(intList);

    // remove duplicate values
    removeDuplicates(intList);

    // output the ordered list that has no duplicates
    cout << "Ordered list without duplicates: ";
    writeList(intList);

    return 0;
}
```

```
Run:

Ordered list with duplicates: 2  2  2  3  3  5  7  7  9  9
Ordered list without duplicates: 2  3  5  7  9
```

> With an ordered list, such as the one created in Program 6-3, the removal of   ☞
> duplicates can be done more efficiently. See Written Exercise 6-21.   Note

Splicing Two Lists

The function splice() is the list equivalent of insert() for strings. The operation inserts a list, called sourceList, at a specified iterator position in a second list, called destList. For instance, if destList = {7, 3, 4, 5} and sourceList = {15, 16}, a splice at value 3 (position 1) in destList inserts the two elements from sourceList immediately before the element 3. The resulting list is {7, 15, 16, 3, 4, 5 }. In the prototype for the function, we pass the source list by constant reference, because its contents should not be modified. In the function implementation, access to the source list must be through a const_iterator.

The implementation defines the constant iterator sourceIter, which scans the elements in sourceList and inserts each one at position *pos* in destList. Figure 6-8 illustrates the action of splice() for the sample data.

splice():
```
    template <typename T>
    void splice(list<T>& dest, list<T>::iterator pos,
                const list<T>& source)
    {
        list<T>::const_iterator sourceIter;
```

```
sourceIter = source.begin();

    // insert each element of source before the
    // position pos
    while (sourceIter!= source.end())
    {
        dest.insert(pos, *sourceIter);
        sourceIter++;
    }
}
```

The file "d_listl.h" contains the implementation of the function splice().

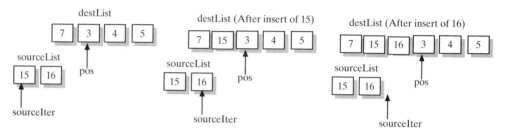

Figure 6-8
splice() Inserts a Two-Element Source List into the Destination List at Position pos.

6-4   CASE STUDY: GRADUATION LISTS

This case study follows the activities of the registrar and the dean of a university in organizing the distribution of diplomas to students during the end-of-year commencement ceremonies. The registrar gathers the names of eligible graduates and then turns the list over to the dean, who is responsible for the ceremonies.

Problem Analysis

For each eligible graduate, the registrar creates a student record that includes the student's name and the type of degree (BA or BS). The records are stored in a file and transmitted to the dean at the end of the semester. For a period of time before graduation, the dean creates records that include the names of those students who do not plan on attending the ceremonies. To handle all of the data, the dean wants to create a program that will read student records from the registrar file and student records from the file of nonattendees and create a list of names in alphabetical order, with all BS degree graduates coming first and BA degree graduates coming last.

Program Design

In order to maintain information on each eligible graduate, we create the graduate class, which contains strings for the name and degree. The class has a default constructor. The member function getDegree() returns the degree type for the graduate. The rest of the class consists of a series of overloaded operators. The input operator, $>>$, reads a student record from a stream and creates a graduate object. The operator assumes that the input files use a tab separator to distinguish the name from the degree. The output operator, $<<$, displays the student and degree information to a stream. For the purpose of creating an ordered list and later scanning the lists to erase elements, we include overloaded versions of the operators $==$ and $<$. These operators compare graduate objects by name. The following is the declaration of the graduate class.

CLASS graduate　　　　　　**Declaration**　　　　　　　**"d_grad.h"**

```
class graduate
{
    public:
        graduate();
        // default constructor

        string getDegree() const;
            // return the degree type of the graduate

        friend bool operator== (const graduate& lhs, const graduate& rhs);
            // two objects are equal if they have the same name

        friend bool operator< (const graduate& lhs, const graduate& rhs);
            // compare two objects by the alphabetic ordering of their name

        friend istream& operator>> (istream& istr, graduate& grad);
            // input name and degree from a file. each line contains
            // the name and degree separated by a tab character
        friend ostream& operator<< (ostream& ostr,
                                    const graduate& grad);
            // output the name and degree for the graduate
    private:
        string name;
        string degree;
};
```

For data gathering in the dean's office, we specify three lists that contain the BA graduates, the BS graduates, and the complete list of graduates stored in the order they will receive their diplomas.

```
list<graduate> gradBA_list, gradBS_list, diplomalist;
```

From the registrar file "gradlist.dat," we read student records one at a time and store the corresponding graduate object in the appropriate list by calling insertOrder(). We identify the correct list by calling getDegree() for the graduate object. The resulting lists store students by name in alphabetic order. From the nonattendee file, "noattend.dat," we read each student record. In order to remove the graduate from the appropriate degree list, we define the function removeGraduate(), which takes a list and the target graduate as arguments and deletes the object from the list:

```
void removeGraduate(list<graduate>& gradList, const graduate& grad)
```

Once this task is completed, we are in a position to create the diploma list that contains the BS degree graduates and then the BA degree graduates. By assigning gradBS_list to diplomalist, we copy the BS graduates to the diploma list. A call to splice() appends the gradBA_list onto the tail of diplomalist.

Program Implementation

The implementation of removeGraduate() uses the algorithm seqSearch() for lists. If seqSearch() locates the graduate, the member function erase() removes the object.

removeGraduate():
```
    void removeGraduate(list<graduate>& gradList, const graduate& grad)
    {
      // search for grad in the list
      list<graduate>::iterator iter =
         seqSearch<graduate> (gradList.begin(), gradList.end(), grad);
         // if found, call erase() to remove the element
      if (iter != gradList.end())
         gradList.erase(iter);
    }
```

PROGRAM 6-4   GRADUATION LIST

This program is an implementation of the graduation-list problem design. We divide the algorithm for the main program into separate activities.

1. After declaring the list objects and input streams, gradIn and noAttIn, for the registrar and noattendee records, respectively, the program begins by opening registrar file "gradlist.dat" and uses the overloaded input operator, >>, to read the student records into a graduate object. Depending on the degree type of the graduate, the object is stored in either gradBS_list or gradBA_list by using insertOrder().

2. The list of students not attending the ceremonies is stored in the file "noattend.dat". After opening the file, the program reads the student records. A call to removeGraduate() deletes the object from the appropriate degree list. The algorithm determines which list to access by calling getDegree() to identify the degree type of the graduate.

3. Two additional operations create the final diploma list. First, assign gradBS_list to diplomalist, and then call splice() with destination location diplomalist.end() to copy the gradBA_list graduates onto the tail of diplomalist.

4. The program concludes by using the overloaded output operator, <<, in the graduate class and the list display function writeList() to output the name and degree
for each student in the order he or she will receive a diploma.

The run includes a sample listing of names and degrees for both the registrar file
"gradlist.h" and the nonattendee file "noattend.dat."

```cpp
// File: prg6_4.cpp
// the class graduate stores the name of a degree candidate
// and the type of degree (BA or BS). the file "gradlist.dat"
// contains a list of degree candidates. the program reads
// the file and inserts each graduate into one of two lists
// of graduate objects, gradBS_list or gradBA_list. it uses
// insertOrder() so each list is in order by graduate name.
// the program next reads the file "noattend.dat" containing
// a list of graduates who will not attend the graduation
// ceremonies. using the function removeGraduate(), it erases
// each graduate in this file from either the list gradBS_list
// or gradBA_list, depending on the degree. using the function
// splice(), it joins the two lists together in the list
// diplomalist. the BS candidates are first, followed by the BA
// candidates. displaying this list gives the order in which
// the degree recipients will march in the graduation ceremony

#include <iostream>
#include <fstream>
#include <cstdlib>
#include <string>
#include <list<

#include "d_util.h"    // for writeList()
#include "d_grad.h"    // contains the graduate class
#include "d_listl.h"   // for insertOrder() and splice()
#include "d_search.h"  // for list seqSearch()

// remove the object grad from the appropriate list
void removeGraduate(list<graduate>& gradList, const graduate& grad);

int main()
{
    // object read as an entry from the files
    graduate grad;

    // list holds graduates in two sections "BS" and "BA"
    list<graduate> gradBA_list, gradBS_list, diplomalist;

    // streams to input registrar's list and dean's list
    ifstream gradIn, noAttIn;
```

```
// open registrar's list file
gradIn.open("gradlist.dat");
if (!gradIn)
{
   cerr << "Cannot open file 'gradlist.dat'" << endl;
   exit(1);
}

// read registrar's list to end-of-file and add to list
while(true)
{
   gradIn >> grad;
   if (!gradIn)
      break;
   if(grad.getDegree() == "BS")
      insertOrder(gradBS_list, grad);
   else
      insertOrder(gradBA_list, grad);
}

gradIn.close();

// open file of those not attending graduation
noAttIn.open("noattend.dat");
if (!noAttIn)
{
   cerr << "Cannot open file 'noattend.dat'" << endl;
   exit(1);
}

// read list of those not attending to end-of-file and
// remove each graduate from the list
while(true)
{
   noAttIn >> grad;
   if (!noAttIn)
      break;
   if (grad.getDegree() == "BS")
      removeGraduate(gradBS_list,grad);
   else
      removeGraduate(gradBA_list, grad);
}

diplomalist = gradBS_list;
splice<graduate>(diplomalist, diplomalist.end(), gradBA_list);

// output list of graduates at ceremony by sections. use
// a newline separator between names
cout << "Students at Graduation" << endl << endl;
writeList(diplomalist, "\n");
```

```
      return 0;
}

/* implementation of removeGraduate() presented in the application discussion
*/
```

```
<File "gradlist.dat">

Peterson, Bradley BA
Frazer, Thomas BA
Harnes, Bailey BA
Kilmer, William BA
Barnes, Nancy BS
Miller, Sara BS
Neeson, Rebecca BS
Bailey, Julie BS
Nelson, Harold BS
O'Dell, Jack BA
Johnson, Shannon BS

<File "noattend.dat">
Frazer, Thomas BA
Johnson, Shannon BS
Barnes, Nancy BS

Run:

Students at Graduation

Bailey, Julie      BS
Miller, Sara       BS
Neeson, Rebecca    BS
Nelson, Harold     BS
Harnes, Bailey     BA
Kilmer, William    BA
O'Dell, Jack       BA
Peterson, Bradley  BA
```

CHAPTER SUMMARY

- A list is a sequence of elements stored by position. Index access is not available, so to access the value of an element, we must pass through its preceding elements. However, all insert and erase operations have running time O(1), even those performed inside the list. In contrast, the corresponding vector operations inside the sequence have running time O(n). The list class has the familiar operations push_back() and pop_back(). However, the list adds the corresponding operations push_front() and pop_front() for the front of the list. As is the case with every container class, lists provide the size() and empty() access operations.

- A list iterator is a generalized pointer that moves through a list element by element, either in the forward or backward direction. At any point, the * operator accesses the value of a list item.

- The list class has two iterator types, iterator and const_iterator. A const_iterator must be used with a constant list object. Each type is a nested class of list and must be accessed by using the scope operator :: (e.g., list<int>::iterator). The * operator cannot be combined with a const_iterator on the left-hand side of an assignment statement.

- Give an iterator an initial value that points to the first element by using the list member function begin(). The member function end() returns an iterator pointing just past the last element of the list.

- The sequential search of a list object is readily implemented by using an iterator range [*first*, *last*). Its implementation returns an iterator that points at the target value or has value *last* if the target is not in the list.

- The list class member functions insert() and erase() use an iterator argument to modify a list. The function insert(*pos value*) places *value* in the list before the data referenced by the iterator *pos*. The function erase(*pos*) removes the data item referenced by *pos* from the list.

- As an application of iterators and the member function insert(), the function insertOrder() places an item in a list so that the list retains ascending order. Using iterators and the erase() member function, the algorithm removeDuplicates() modifies a list so that it contains only unique values. The function splice() uses the insert() member function to place all the values in one list into another at a specified iterator position.

- The case study dealing with graduation lists provides a significant example of list operations. It uses the functions seqSearch(), insertOrder(), splice(), and writeList(), which were developed throughout the chapter.

CLASSES AND LIBRARIES IN THE CHAPTER

Name	Implementation File
graduate	d_grad.h
insertOrder(), removeDuplicates(), splice()	d_listl.h
list	<list>
seqSearch()	d_search.h
wordFreq	d_wfreq.h
writeList()	d_util.h

REVIEW EXERCISES

1. Let *alist* be a list of integer values.
   (a) Display the list created by the following sequence of operations:

```
alist.push_back(40);
alist.push_front(10);
```

```
alist.push_front(15);
alist.push_back(30);
```

(b) What is the sum of the expression alist.back() + alist.front()?

2. **(a)** Declare a five-element list object *alist* with initial integer value 2.
   (b) Display the list after executing the following loop:

```
for (int i = 1; i <= 4; i++)
{
    alist.push_front(alist.back() + alist.front());
    alist.pop_back();
}
```

3. What is an iterator?

4. An iterator is implemented as a(n) _____ class.

5. **(a)** Declare a list object *alist* whose elements are initialized from the array

```
int arr[7] = {5, 2, 3, 8, 9, 25, 35};
int arrSize = sizeof(arr)/sizeof(int);
```

   (b) Declare a list iterator *iter*.
   (c) Give a statement that initializes iter so that it points at the first element of alist.
   (d) Assume the result of part (c). Give the value of *iter after the statement

```
iter++;
```

   (e) Give the value of *iter after the statements

```
iter = alist.end();
iter++;
```

   (f) Give the value of *iter after the statements

```
iter = alist.end();
iter--;
iter--;
```

6. After the execution of the following statements, what is the resulting sequential list?

```
list<char> aList;
list<char>::iterator i;

aList.push_front('t');
aList.push_front('a');
i = aList.begin();
i++;
aList.insert(i,'m');
aList.insert(i,'x');
```

7. Assume that the five-element list charList contains the characters in the string "train."
   What is the sequence of list values after executing the following instructions?

```
list<char> charList;
list<char>::iterator iter;

iter = charList.begin();
iter++;
```

```
charList.erase(iter++);
charList.erase(iter);
charList.push_back('t');
```

8. Implement the function maxElement(), which returns an iterator pointing at the maximum value in a list:

```
template <typename T>
list<T>::iterator maxElement(list<T>& alist);
```

9. What is the key difference between an iterator object and a const_iterator object?

10. Assume that intList is an empty list of integer values and *iter* is an iterator for the same type of list.

   (a) Display the list created by the following sequence of statements:

```
intList.push_front(0);
iter = intList.begin();
for (int i = 1; i <= 4; i++)
{
    intList.push_front(i);
    insert(iter, i);
}
```

   (b) What is the list if the insert() statement in (a) is replaced by insert(iter, *iter)?
   (c) What is the list if push_back replaces push_front in (a)?

11. What is the action of the function func() on a list of elements?

```
void func(list<T>& alist);
{
    list<T>::iterator iter = alist.begin();

    while(iter != alist.end());
    {
        alist.push_front(*iter);
        erase(iter++);
    }
}
```

Answers to Review Exercises

1. **(a)** alist: 15 10 40 30   **(b)** 45
2. **(a)** list<int> alist(5, 2);   **(b)** 10 8 6 4 2
3. An iterator is a generalized pointer that is used to sequence through a container. At a minimum, an iterator has the * (dereference), ++, ==, and != operators and is initialized by the container member function begin(). The container member function end() is used to detect the end of the container data.
4. An iterator is implemented as a nested class.
5. **(a)** list<int> alist(arr, arr+arrSize)   **(b)** list<int>::iterator iter
   (c) iter = alist.begin()   **(d)** 2
   (e) 5   **(f)** 25

6. aList: a m x t

7. charList: t i n t

8.
```
template <typename T>
list<T>::iterator maxElement(list<T>& alist)
{
    list<T>::iterator iter, maxvalIter;

    if (alist.empty())
        return alist.end();

    // assume maximum is at the first list element
    maxvalIter = iter = alist.begin();
    // start scan at 2nd list element
    iter++;
    // move through list, updating maxvalIter as necessary
    while (iter != alist.end())
    {
        if (*iter > *maxvalIter)
            maxvalIter = iter;
        iter++;
    }

    return maxvalIter;
}
```

9. A programmer must use a const_iterator whenever it traverses a constant list object. A const_iterator cannot use the dereference operator, *, on the left-hand side of an assignment statement.

10. **(a)** intList: 4 3 2 1 1 2 3 4 0
   (b) intList: 4 3 2 1 0 0 0 0 0
   (c) intList: 1 2 3 4 0 1 2 3 4

11. Reverses the order of the elements in alist.

WRITTEN EXERCISES

12. Describe a sequential list.

13. Consider the C++ array

```
int arr[] = {-15, 5, 35, -19, -12, 17, -4};
int arrSize = sizeof(arr)/sizeof(int);
```

   (a) Declare the list object intList that holds the integers from the array *arr*.
   (b) Declare the iterator *iter* for an integer list.
   (c) Initialize the iterator iter to the beginning of the list intList.
   (d) Assume iter is set to the start of the list.

```
iter++;
iter++;                          // what value does iter point at?
```

```
cout << *iter;              // what is the output?
iter = intList.end();
iter--;
iter--;                     // what value does iter point at?
cout << *iter;              // what is the output?
iter = intList.end();
iter++;                     // what value does iter point at?
cout << *iter;              // what is the output?
```

    (e) Use the iterator to write a code segment that scans the list elements and replaces each negative value by the corresponding positive number.

14. Use list<char> objects chList and revList and their member functions:

```
list<char> chList, revList;
char ch;
```

    (a) Give the status of chList after each of the following instructions:

```
chList.push_front('t');  _____
chList.push_front('a');  _____
chList.push_back('j');   _____
chList.pop_front();      _____
```

    (b) Write a code segment with a while loop that deletes the characters from chList and stores them in revList, but in reverse order. Use the member functions pop_front(), push_front(), and empty().

15. Declare tList, amList, and pmList as three list objects holding time24 objects as elements. Write a code segment that uses a list iterator *iter* to scan tList and insert the current object at the rear of amList if the time falls in the AM period and at the rear of pmList if the time falls in the PM period.

16. Assume the following declarations:

```
list<string> strList;
list<string>::iterator strIter;
```

    Also assume that the list has the following contents:

        vector list begin insert

    What are the contents of the list after each statement sequence?

    (a) `strIter = strList.begin();`
       `strList.insert(strIter,"template");`

    (b) `strIter = strList.end();`
       `strList.insert(strIter,"switch");`

    (c) Assume that *strIter is "begin."
       `strIter++;`
       `strList.erase(strIter);`

17. Assume that strList is a list object that stores a sequence of strings and that strIter is an iterator for the object. Write a code segment that scans the elements in the list and outputs only those strings whose length is greater than four elements.

18. Use list<char> objects chList and newList and their member functions:

```
list<char> chList, newList;
```

Trace the following code:

```
while (chList.size() != 0)
{ newList.push_front(chList.front());
  newList.push_back(chList.front());
  chList.pop_front();
}
```

(a) Assume that chList has the three characters in the string "C++. What is the resulting sequence of characters in newList?

(b) What is the sequence if chList has the characters in the string "walk"?

19. Trace the following code, and display the resulting elements in the list:

```
int arr[] = {1,2,3,4};
int arrSize = sizeof(arr)/sizeof(int);
list<int> intList(arr, arr+arrSize);
list<int>::iterator iter = intList.begin();
int i;

for (i=1; i <= arrSize; i++)
    intList.insert(iter++, i);
```

20. Trace function inList, which inserts new items into a list:

```
template <typename T>
void inList(list<T>& aList, const T& item)
{
    list<T>::iterator iter;

    iter = aList.begin();

    while (iter != aList.end())
    {
        if (item == *iter)
            return;
        iter++;
    }
    aList.push_back(item);
}
```

(a) Assume that the list<int> object intL is originally empty. What are the elements in the resulting list after making six calls to function inList() with data values 5 2 4 5 7 2?

(b) Assume that the list<char> object charL is originally empty. Make 11 calls to the function with characters from the string "mississippi". What are the resulting elements in the list charL?

21. Implement the function rmOrderedDuplicates(), which removes duplicate values from an ordered list:

```
template <typename T>
void rmOrderedDuplicates(list<T>& aList);
```

For instance, assume that the integer list intList contains the values {2 2 7 8 8 8 15 20 20}. After rmOrderedDuplicates() has been called, the list has values {2 7 8 15 20}. Hint:

Modify removeDuplicates from Section 6-3 so that the second iterator stops under one of two conditions: when it locates the end of the list or when it finds a data value unequal to the one referenced by the first iterator.

22. (a) Implement a function reverseOutput() that outputs the items in a list object in reverse order. Use an iterator that moves backward in the list.

```
template <typename T>
void reverseOutput(const list<T>& aList);
```

(b) Implement a recursive function r_reverseOutput() that outputs the elements in the iterator range [*first,last*) in reverse order.

```
template <typename T>
void r_reverseOutput(list<T>::iterator first,
                     list<T>::iterator last);
```

23. Implement, according to the instructions in parts (a) and (b), the function count(), which takes *item* as argument and returns the number of times *item* occurs in a list.

```
template <typename T>
int count(const list<T>& aList, const T& item);
```

(a) Implement the function by scanning the list and maintaining a count of the number of occurrences of *item*.

(b) Implement the function by making repeated calls to seqSearch() until the return iterator is aList.end().

24. Write a function afterNoon() that takes a list<time24> argument timeList and a time24 object *t*, representing a time at or later than noon (12:00). The function outputs all times from noon through *t*.

```
void afterNoon(const list<time24>& timeList, const time24& t);
```

For instance, if timeList = 9:45, 8:15, 11:15, 12:25, 12:00, 14:38, 15:30, 16:45, 17:00 and *t* = 15:30, the output should be 12:25 12:00 14:38 15:30.

25. Write a function

```
template <typename T>
void split(const list<T>& aList, list<T>& list1, list<T>& list2);
```

that takes a list *aList* and creates two new lists, list1 and list2. The object list1 contains the first, third, fifth, and successive odd-numbered elements; list2 contains the even-numbered elements.

PROGRAMMING EXERCISES

26. Declare the following two integer lists:

```
int a[] = {5, 8, 4, 1, 7}, b[] = {12, 3, 15, 6, 23, 1, 2};
int sizeA = sizeof(a)/sizeof(int), sizeB = sizeof(b)/sizeof(int);

list<int> list1(a, a+sizeA), list2(b, b+sizeB);
```

Use the function splice() from the library "d_listl.h" to copy list2 onto the end of list1. Use writeList() to output list1.

27. Implement the function maxLoc(), which returns an iterator pointing at the largest element in a list.

```
// return an iterator pointing to the largest element
// in the list
template <typename T>
list<T>::iterator maxLoc(list<T>& aList);
```

Write a program that tests maxLoc(), using the following declarations:

```
string strArr[] = {"insert", "erase", "template", "list"};
int strSize = sizeof(strArr)/sizeof(string);
list<string> strList(strArr, strArr+strSize);
```

The program should repeatedly call maxLoc(), output the largest value, and then delete the value, until the list is empty.

28. Implement the function maxIter(), which takes an iterator range and returns the location of the largest value within the range.

```
// return an iterator pointing to the largest element
// in the range [first,last)
template <typename T>
list<T>::iterator maxIter(list<T>::iterator first,
                          list<T>::iterator last);
```

You will use maxIter() in a list version of the selection sort:

```
// use selection sort to order aList
template <typename T>
void selectionSort(list<T>& aList);
```

In a loop that executes aList.size() times, use the iterator passIter to scan the list elements, starting at aList.begin(). In each iteration, use maxIter() to find the maximum value in the range [*passIter, aList.end*()). Push the maximum value onto the front of aList, and then delete the value.

   In a program, generate 10 random integers in the range from 0 to 24, and store the values in a list named intList. Call selectionSort() to order the numbers, and then output them with writeList(). Hint: In your calls to maxIter(), use the syntax

```
... = maxIter<T> (...);
```

29. In a program, use the function count() developed in Written Exercise 6-23(a), which counts the number of times a value occurs a list. Generate 20 random numbers in the range from 0 to 4. For each number, output its value and insert it into an integer list by using push_back(). In a loop, call the function count(), and display the number of occurrences of each value (0 to 4) in the list.

30. Repeat Programming Exercise 6-29, but with the following exception: Use the function count() from Written Exercise 6-23(b) to maintain the count.

31. In a program, write a function loadOddEven() that takes an integer list and an integer vector as arguments. The function scans the vector and loads each odd integer at the front of the list and each even integer element at the rear of the list.

```
void loadOddEven(list<int>& aList, const vector<int>& v);
```

Output the elements from the resulting list. For instance, the six-element vector 6 2 9 8 3 1 translates to the list 1 3 9 6 2 8.

32. Two lists, $L = \{L_0, L_1, ..., L_i\}$ and $M = \{M_0, M_1, ..., M_j\}$, can be merged pairwise to produce the list $\{L_0, M_0, L_1, M_1, ..., L_i, M_i, ... M_j\}$, $j \geq i$. Write a program using the list class that prompts for the values of i and j and generates a list L with i numbers ($1 \leq i \leq 5$) and a list M with j numbers ($1 \leq j \leq 10$). The entries in list L are random numbers in the range from 0 to 99, and the entries in M are random numbers in the range from 100 to 199. The program should output the initial lists L and M, merge them into a new list N, and output the resulting list.

33. Write a program that enters five integers into a list by using the following algorithm:

For each input N, insert N at the front of the list. Scan the remainder of the list, deleting all nodes that are less than N.

Run the program three times, using the following input:

1,2,3,4,5
5,4,3,2,1
3,5,1,2,4

Output the resulting list.

34. The program in this exercise illustrates the circular behavior of a list. First, declare the list

```
string str[] = { "Joe", "Glenn", "Dave", "Bret",
                 "Bryce", "Heather"};
int strSize = sizeof(str)/sizeof(string);
list<string> strList(str, str+strSize);
```

Start at "Dave", and output the list elements in reverse order. The output should be

Dave Glenn Joe Heather Bryce Bret

35. Declare the list

```
list<char> charList;
```

Use the random-number generator to create 35 random characters in the range from a to z, and insert them into the list in order. Use the function rmOrderedDuplicates() from Written Exercise 6-21 to remove all duplicate characters. Output the size of charList and the characters by using writeList().

36. Use the list class for this exercise. The data consists of objects of the type intEntry:

```
class intEntry
{
   public:
      intEntry(int v, int c = 1);
         // initialize the integer value and its count

      int getValue() const;
         // return value

      int getCount() const;
         // return count

      void increment();
```

```
                // increment count

    friend bool operator< (const intEntry& lhs,const intEntry& rhs);
    friend bool operator== (const intEntry& lhs,const intEntry& rhs);
        // compare lhs and rhs using value
    friend ostream& operator<< (ostream& ostr, const intEntry& obj);
        // output obj in format "value value ... value" (count times)

private:
    int value;
        // integer value
    int count;
        // number of occurrences of value
};
```

Implement the class using inline code, and place it in the header file "intentry.h." In the main program, input 10 integers, and create an ordered list of intEntry nodes. Do this by modifying the function insertOrder() of Section 6-3 to update an entry when a duplicate is found. Output the resulting list.

PROGRAMMING PROJECT

37. A positive integer n ($n > 1$) can be written uniquely as a product of prime numbers. This is called the *prime factorization* of the number. For instance,

$$12 = 2*2*3; \quad 18 = 2*3*3; \quad 11 = 11$$

The function loadPrimes() uses the intEntry class of Programming Exercise 6-36 to create a list that identifies the different primes and the number of occurrences of the primes in the factorization of a number. For instance, with 18, the prime 2 occurs 1 time and the prime 3 occurs 2 times.

```
void loadPrimes(list<intEntry>& primes, int n)
{   int i = 2;
    int nc = 0;

    do
    {
        if (n % i == 0)
        { nc++;
            n = n/i;
        }
        else
        {
            if (nc > 0)
                primes.push_back(intEntry(i, nc));

            nc = 0;
            i++;
        }
    }
```

```
    while (n > 1 || nc != 0);
}
```

Write a program that enters two integers *m* and *n* and uses the function loadPrimes() to create a list of the primes. Add comments to loadPrimes() that explain how it works. Scan the list, and output the prime factorization of each number. For instance, assume *m* = 60 and *n* = 18.

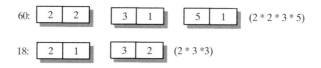

Create a new list that consists of all the primes that are common to the *m* and *n* lists. As you identify each such prime, take the minimum count in the two nodes, and use that as the count in the node for the new list. For instance, 2 is a prime factor of 60, and 2 is a prime factor of 18:

$$60 = 2*2*3*5 \qquad // \ 2 \ \text{has count} \ 2$$
$$18 = 2*3*3 \qquad\quad // \ 2 \ \text{has count} \ 1$$

In the new list, 2 is a value with count 1 (minimum of 1 and 2). The product of the primes is the greatest common divisor of *m* and *n*, gcd(*m*, *n*). Output the list, and compute gcd(*m*, *n*).

new list

CHAPTER 7

Stacks

OBJECTIVES

- To understand that the stack ADT defines LIFO access.
- To understand how to use the stack API for solving problems whose solutions require a stack.
- To understand that the implementation of recursion uses a stack of activation records.
- To view the implementation of the miniStack class that uses a vector.
- To understand how STL implements the stack API. (OPTIONAL)
- To understand postfix (RPN) notation and how to evaluate postfix expressions by using a stack.
- To study in detail the use of a stack to convert an infix expression into a postfix expression.

OUTLINE

In the previous chapters, we introduced the vector and the list containers, which are the basic sequence storage structures. Each class provides an extensive interface that allows a programmer to scan and access all of the data items. A list also provides operations to insert or remove an element at any position in the sequence. In this chapter, we introduce a new storage structure called a *stack*, which is a very different type of container. Unlike the general interface of a vector or a list, a stack is a container that supports only a restricted set of access and update operations.

A stack stores elements sequentially, but allows the insertion and removal of items at only one end of the sequence. A pack of paper in the paper tray of a laser printer is a good model of a stack. The tray can hold a large number of sheets; however, the printer feeds only the sheet on the top. If you want to run a letterhead sheet through the printer, you must put the sheet on the top of the pile. In Section 7-1, we introduce the stack ADT, with operations that provide limited access to the data.

As you will see in this chapter, the stack storage structure is ideal for some applications. Much of this chapter discusses these types of applications. Section 7-1 employs a stack to output integer values in number bases other than base 10. It also describes an algorithm that uses multiple stacks to maintain an order of elements. Section 7-2 illustrates how the runtime system uses a stack to handle a function call and return. You will learn how recursion works by observing each phase of the recursive function calls for *n* factorial (*n*!).

The miniStack class, presented in Section 7-3, shows how to implement a stack easily from a vector by using object composition. The section concludes with optional material showing how STL constructs its stack class from a vector, a list, or a container called a *deque*.

Compilers use algorithms for the evaluation of arithmetic expressions. Section 7-4 presents a simple and elegant algorithm that evaluates an expression in postfix (RPN) format. In this format, an operator appears after its two operands. The class postfixEval implements the expression evaluation algorithm, which uses a stack to store operands.

You are probably more familiar with arithmetic expressions in *infix* format, which puts an operator between its two operands. Evaluating an infix expression is far more interesting and challenging than evaluating an RPN expression. The algorithm must account for the order of precedence and the associativity of operators, as well as for subexpressions enclosed in parentheses. In the case study in Section 7-5, we provide the object design and implementation of the infix expression evaluation algorithm.

7-1   THE STACK ADT

A *stack* is a sequence of items that are accessible at only one end of the sequence. Think of a stack as a collection of items that are piled one on top of the other, with access limited to the topmost item. Figure 7-1 provides a model of a stack as a collection of food trays you might find in a school cafeteria.

A stack has operations that add and remove items from the top of the stack. A *push()* operation adds an item to the topmost location on the stack. Once it is on the stack, we can see and access only the new item. All items that were formerly on the

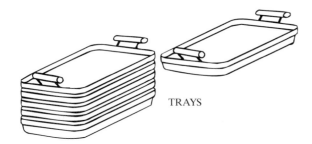

TRAYS

Figure 7-1
Model of a stack as a pile of
food trays

stack are pushed down out of sight. A *pop()* operation removes an element from the stack. Consider the problem of putting vegetables onto a skewer prior to placing the skewer on a barbecue. In Figure 7-2, the cook pushes the vegetables onto the tip of the skewer (1) in the order onion, green pepper, mushroom, and a second onion. Before putting the skewer onto the grill, a guest indicates that he cannot eat mushrooms and needs to have them removed. To satisfy the request, the cook removes (pops) first the onion from the end of the skewer (2) and then the mushroom (3). The onion can then be pushed back onto the skewer (4).

Figure 7-3 illustrates a sequence of push() and pop() operations for character values. Because a pop operation removes the item last added to the stack, we say that a stack has *LIFO* (last-in/first-out) ordering.

The push and pop operations change the stack. In some situations, it is necessary to access the topmost element of the stack without removing it. For this purpose, the ADT provides the operation *top()*. Only this operation provides access to an element in the stack, because only the topmost element is visible. There is no access to elements below the topmost element in the stack.

The abstract concept of a stack allows for an arbitrarily large sequence of data. Hence, the push() operation has no precondition. The same is not true for top() or pop(); because the topmost item cannot be accessed or removed successfully unless

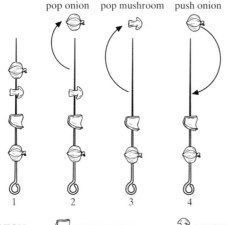

pop onion   pop mushroom   push onion

1   2   3   4

🧅 ONION   🫑 GREEN PEPPER   🍄 MUSHROOM

Figure 7-2
A vegetable stack

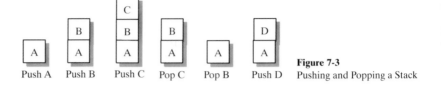

Figure 7-3

Push A   Push B   Push C   Pop C   Pop B   Push D   Pushing and Popping a Stack

the stack has at least one element (not empty). The operation *empty()* indicates whether the stack has elements, and the operation *size()* returns the number of elements on the stack.

In order to use the stack ADT in applications, STL provides a stack class. The following is the API for the class, including a constructor that declares an empty stack.

| **CLASS stack** | **Constructor** | **<stack>** |

stack();
    Create an empty stack.

| **CLASS stack** | **Operations** | **<stack>** |

bool **empty**() *const*;
    Check whether the stack is empty. Return true if it is empty, false otherwise.

void **pop**();
    Remove the item from the top of the stack.
    Precondition: The stack is not empty.
    Postcondition: Either the stack is empty or the stack has a new topmost
                         item from a previous push.

void **push**(*const T & item*);
    Insert the argument *item* at the top of the stack.
    Postcondition: The stack has a new item at the top.

int **size**() *const*;
    Return the number of items on the stack.

T& **top**();
    Return a reference to the value of the item at the top of the stack.
    Precondition: The stack is not empty.

const T& **top**() *const*;
    Constant version of top().

Example 7-1 illustrates the declaration of a stack object and the use of its member functions. The stack API provides us with sufficient information to interpret the meaning of the statements.

Example 7-1

1. Declare a stack object *s*, containing integer data. Push the values 1, 2, 3, 4, 5 onto the
   stack; after they are all on, repeatedly pop the stack until it is empty. On each iteration, we first call top() to access the topmost value before it comes off the stack with
   a pop(). The stack is a LIFO structure, so output of the data occurs in the reverse
   order of their storage on the stack.

```cpp
#include <stack>
    ...
stack<int> s;  // Creates an empty Stack
int i;

for (i=1; i <= 5; i++)
    s.push(i);

cout << "Stack size = " << s.size() << endl;
cout << "Popping the stack" << endl;
while (!s.empty())
{
    cout << s.top() << " ";
    s.pop();
}
cout << endl;
```

```
Output:   Stack size = 5
          Popping the stack
          5 4 3 2 1
```

2. The fact that top() returns a reference to the item at the top of the stack allows the
   programmer to modify its value. For instance, the following statements push 2, 3,
   and 99 onto the stack and then change the top from 99 to 5:

```cpp
stack<int> s;

s.push(2);
s.push(3);
s.push(99);
cout << s.top() << endl;

// change top to 5
s.top() = 5;
while (!s.empty())
{
    cout << s.top() << " ";
    s.pop();
}
```

```
Output:     99
            5 3 2
```

Note

Finite Stack: The stack ADT assumes that a stack can grow without bounds. Theoretically, a cafeteria could stack food trays to the sky and beyond; but can a cook place an indefinite number of vegetables onto a skewer? In reality, a dispenser holds only a finite number of food trays, and the length of the skewer allows only a limited number of vegetables. Some applications assume a bounded (finite) stack. In this case, the push operation has a precondition that prevents the addition of a new item when the stack is full. For such applications, we need a new ADT with a maxStackSize attribute. The maximum size of the stack can be set by using the constructor or the setMaxSize() function. The getMaxSize() operation allows an application to determine the current limit of the size of the stack. The Boolean function full() indicates whether the stack is full. Written Exercise 7-20 discusses the implementation of a bounded stack.

Multibase Output

Output statements in most programming languages display integer values in decimal (base 10) as the default format. For some applications, particularly systems programming, you may want to output a number in binary (base 2), octal (base 8), or hexadecimal (base 16). To provide this ability, we design a function multibaseOutput(), which takes an integer value and a base in the range from 2 to 16 as arguments and returns a string with the digits in the specified base. The implementation uses a stack to convert numbers to other bases. For instance, the number $n = 75$ would have the following representations in bases 2, 8, and 16:

```
75 = 1001011₂     // 75 = 1(⁶) + 0(2⁵) + 0(2⁴) + 1(2³) + 0(2²) + 1(2¹) + 1
75 = 113₈         // 75 = 1(8²) + 1(8¹) + 3
75 = 4B₁₆         // 75 = 4(16²) + B
```

A hexadecimal (hex) number consists of digits chosen from $0, 1, \ldots, 9, A, B, C, D, E, F$, where the letters represent the values 10–15.

An algorithm to convert a nonnegative integer N to a designated base B uses repeated division by the base. At each step, the remainder $N\%B$ identifies the next digit, and the quotient N/B becomes the next value to divide. The process terminates when the quotient is 0. For instance, we identify the digits for 75 base-8 in three steps:

$$
\begin{array}{lll}
\textbf{Step 1:} & \textbf{Step 2:} & \textbf{Step 3:} \\
9 & 1 & 0 \\
8\overline{)75} & 8\overline{)9} & 8\overline{)1} \\
72 & 8 & 0 \\
\overline{3} & \overline{1} & \overline{1}
\end{array}
$$

$$
\begin{array}{ll}
8\overline{)75} & R = 3 \\
8\overline{)9} & R = 1 \\
8\overline{)1} & R = 1
\end{array}
\qquad 1 \quad 1 \quad 3
$$

The division process identifies the digits for the final output, but in reverse order. By using a stack, with its LIFO ordering, we store the successive digits as characters. After the stack is emptied, the number is stored in the string numStr, with its digits in the correct order. To convert each, remainder to the corresponding digit character, we declare the string digitChar and use the remainder as an index:

```
string digitChar = "0123456789ABCDE";
```

For instance, if the remainder is 7, digitChar[7] = 7. The conversion to a hexadecimal number could have a remainder 13. The corresponding hex digit is digitChar[13]= D.

Figure 7-4 illustrates the conversion of $n = 431$ to base 16 (hex). The figure describes the growth of the stack while creating the three hex digits for n. Clearing the stack with a sequence of pop() operations produces the string 1AF. The successive remainders upon division by 16 are 15 (hex F), 10 (hex A), and 1 (hex 1).

The function multibase() takes a positive integer *num* and an integer base *b* in the range $0 <= b <= 15$. The return value is a string representing the value of *num* to the specified base *b*.

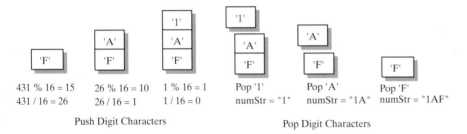

Figure 7-4
Using a stack to create a multibase numbers

multibaseOutput() :

```
string multibaseOutput(int num, int b)
{
    // digitChar[digit] is the character that represents
    // the digit, 0 <= digit <= 15
    string digitChar = "0123456789ABCDEF", numStr = "";

    // stack holds the base-b digits of num
    stack<char> stk;
    // extract base b digits right to left and push on stack s
    do
    {
        // push right-most digit on the stack
        stk.push(digitChar[num % b]);
        num /= b;                  // remove right-most digit from num
    } while (num != 0);            // continue until all digits found
```

```
      while (!stk.empty())         // flush the stack
      {
         numStr += stk.top();      // add digit on top of stack to numStr
         stk.pop();                // pop the stack
      }

      return numStr;
}
```

PROGRAM 7-1   MULTIBASE OUTPUT

Each iteration of the loop in this program prompts the user to enter a nonnegative decimal number and a corresponding base. Using multibaseOutput(), the program displays the number in the specified base. The loop terminates when the user enters the number 0 and base 0.

```
// File: prg7_1.cpp
// the user enters a nonnegative decimal number and a base in the
// range 2 <= base <= 16. a call to the function multibaseOutput()
// displays number in the specified base. the program terminates
// when the user enters a number of 0 and a base 0

#include <iostream>
#include <stack>
#include <string>

using namespace std;

// output integer num in base b
string multibaseOutput(int num, int b);

int main()
{
   int num, b; // decimal number and base

   // prompt for a number >= 0 and base 2 <= B <= 16
   cout << "Enter a non-negative decimal number and base "
        << "(2 <= B <= 16)" << endl << "or 0 0 to terminate: ";
   cin >> num >> b;

   // continue until the user enters a base of 0
   while (b != 0)
   {
      cout << " " << num << " base " << b << " is "
           << multibaseOutput(num, b) << endl;

      cout << "Enter a non-negative decimal number and base "
           << "(2 <= B <= 16)" <<  endl << "or 0 0 to terminate: ";
```

```
      cin >> num >> b;
   }

   return 0;
}

string multibaseOutput(int num, int b)
{
   // digitChar[digit] is the character that represents
   // the digit, 0 <= digit <= 15
   string digitChar = "0123456789ABCDEF", numStr = "";

   // stack holds the base-b digits of num
   stack<char> stk;

   // extract base b digits right to left and push on stack s
   do
   {
      // push right-most digit on the stack
      stk.push(digitChar[num % b]);
      num /= b;              // remove right-most digit from num
   } while (num != 0);       // continue until all digits found

   while (!stk.empty())      // flush the stack
   {
      numStr += stk.top();   // add digit on top of stack
      stk.pop();             // pop the stack
   }

   return numStr;
}
```

(handwritten annotation: to main( ))

```
Run:

Enter a nonnegative decimal number and base (2 <= B <= 16)
or 0 0 to terminate: 27 2
    27 base 2 is 11011
Enter a nonnegative decimal number and base (2 <= B <= 16)
or 0 0 to terminate: 300 16
    300 base 16 is 12C
Enter a nonnegative decimal number and base (2 <= B <= 16)
or 0 0 to terminate: 75 8
    75 base 8 is 113
Enter a nonnegative decimal number and base (2 <= B <= 16)
or 0 0 to terminate: 0 0
```

Uncoupling Stack Elements

In a large city, groups of shippers load freight cars at their respective warehouses. Engines take the cars to a railroad switching yard,where they are coupled together to form a single train. While traveling cross-country, the train stops at different locations and drops off individual cars. Figure 7-5 illustrates how a switching yard might use a side track to uncouple car C from a five-car chain. Consider the train to be a stack with car E at its top. The two cars at the front of the train (D, E) are uncoupled and pulled to the side track in the order E, D. Think of the side track as another stack, with E followed by D pushed onto this stack. At the end of these operations, C is on the top of the original stack of cars, and D is on top of the side track. This action permits C to be uncoupled and pulled clear. After removing C, the cars from the side track can reconnect with car A, and the train can proceed. This amounts to popping the stack on the side track and pushing each car onto the original stack.

Motivated by this example, we develop an algorithm, uncouple(), that uses a second stack to search for and remove the first occurrence of an element *target* from an existing stack. Repeatedly remove the element at the top of the stack and push it onto the second stack until locating *target*. Pop *target* from the original stack, and restore the initial ordering of the sequence by popping each element from the second stack and pushing it at back onto the original stack. If the uncouple operation occurs, the function returns true; otherwise, it returns false.

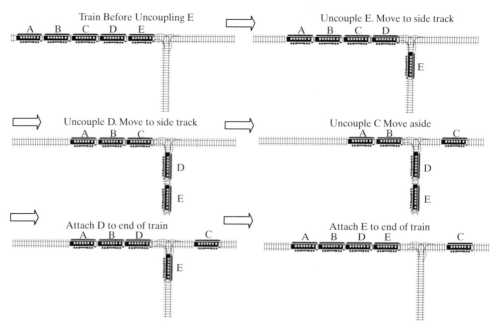

Figure 7-5
Uncoupling a freight car

```
// remove the first occurrence of target (if any) from stack s.
// return true if target was removed and false otherwise
template <typename T>
bool uncouple(stack<T>& s, const T& target)
{

    stack<T> tmpStk;
    // assume the target is on the stack
    bool foundTarget = true;

    // pop elements from the stack s and push
    // them onto tmpStk until we locate target
    // or the stack becomes empty
    while (!s.empty() && s.top() != target)
    {
        tmpStk.push(s.top());
        s.pop();
    }

    // the while loop locates item if s is not empty
    if (!s.empty())
        s.pop();
    else
        // the target is not on the stack
        foundTarget = false;

    // restore the items from tmpStk by popping
    // it and pushing each element onto s
    while (!tmpStk.empty())
    {
        s.push(tmpStk.top());
        tmpStk.pop();
    }

    return foundTarget;
}
```

Note

The pop() Return Type: The reader may wonder why pop() returns void, instead of type *T*. That is, why is it necessary to use top() and then pop() to access and remove the element at the top of the stack, rather than combining the two in a single member function that returns type *T*? There is a good reason for this design. If pop() returns the element on the top of the stack, it would have to return it by value rather than by reference. Returning it by reference is not feasible, because the element is no longer on the stack and must be saved somewhere before returning a reference to it. If the choice is to use dynamic memory, a memory leak will result unless the dynamic memory is eventually deleted. Returning it by value is inefficient, because it involves a call to the copy constructor for type *T*. Having pop() return a value will lead either to potential memory problems or to inefficiency, so it is more sensible for it to return no value at all and to require the calling block to use top() to inspect the value on the top of the stack.

PROGRAM 7-2 UNCOUPLE LIST ELEMENTS

This program illustrates the function uncouple(). Begin with the stack intStack, whose initial values come from an array. After the generic function writeArray() is called to display the elements in their stack order, make two calls to uncouple() to remove the elements 14 and 11, respectively, from the stack. A loop pops and displays each item from the modified stack.

```cpp
// File: prg7_2.cpp
// program initializes an integer stack with values from an array.
// push the numbers on the stack from the array back to the front.
// top of the stack is the first array element. output contents of
// the stack using writeArray() to display array elements. call the
// function uncouple() to remove elements 14 and 17 from the
// stack, and then pop stack until empty, outputting each stack
// element

#include <iostream>
#include <stack>

#include "d_util.h"     // for writeArray()

using namespace std;

// remove the first occurrence of target (if any) from stack s.
// return true if target was removed and false otherwise
template <typename T>
bool uncouple(stack<T>& s, const T& target);

int main()
{
   int arr[] = { 19, 14, 37, 43, 11, 12}, i;
   int arrSize = sizeof(arr)/sizeof(int);
   stack<int> intStack;

   cout << "Creating a stack with values (top to bottom):   ";
   writeArray(arr, arrSize);
   cout << endl;
   // push items in arr onto intStack in order
   // arr[arrSize-1] ... arr[0], so arr[0] is on the
   // top of the stack
   for (i= arrSize-1;i >= 0;i--)
      intStack.push(arr[i]);
```

```
// attempt to remove 14 and 17 from intStack
if (uncouple(intStack, 14))
    cout << "Uncoupled 14" << endl;
else
    cout << "14 is not on the stack" << endl;

if (uncouple(intStack, 17))
    cout << "Uncoupled 17" << endl;
else
    cout << "17 is not on the stack" << endl;

cout << "Final stack (top to bottom):    ";
while (!intStack.empty())
{
    cout << intStack.top() << " ";
    intStack.pop();
}
cout << endl;

return 0;
}

/* implementation of uncouple() given in the program discussion */
```

```
Run:

Creating stack with values (top to bottom): 19 14 37 43 11 12

Uncoupled 14
17 is not on the stack
Final stack (top to bottom): 19 37 43 11 12
*/
```

RECURSIVE CODE AND THE RUNTIME STACK   7-2

A function is a sequence of instructions that are executed in response to a function call. The execution process begins by having the calling statement set up an *activation record*, which includes the list of runtime arguments, space for local variables and objects in the function, and a return address. The address is the location of the next instruction to execute after the function returns to the calling statement.

Runtime arguments	Space for local variables and objects	Return Address <next instruction>

Activation Record

At the point of a function call, the runtime system pushes the activation record onto a system-supplied stack called the *runtime stack*. Control then transfers to the statements in the function, where the data in the record are available for use in the function body. Upon exiting from the function, the runtime system extracts the return address from the activation record and then pops the record from the stack.

A recursive function makes repeated calls to itself by using a modified argument list for each call. The process pushes a chain of activation records onto the stack until the function identifies a stopping condition. The subsequent popping of the records gives the recursive solution. The factorial function, fact(), illustrates the use of activation records and the runtime stack. Assume the main program makes a call to fact(4). After executing the function, program control returns to location RetLoc1, where an assignment statement places the value 24 (4!) in factValue.

```
int main()
{
    int factValue;
    . . .
                                              RetLoc1
    factValue = fact(4);
    cout << "Value fact(4) = " <<factValue <<endl;

    return 0;
}
```

The recursive calls in the function body return to location RetLoc2, which computes the product $n * (n - 1)!$.

```
int fact(intn)
{
    if (n== 0)
        return 1;
    else
        return  n * fact(n-1);
}
                                              RetLoc2
```

The activation record for the fact() function has three fields. The runtime argument is the integer argument n. Because the function fact() has no local variables, the compiler does not allocate local variable storage in the activation record. The final field is the return address. In the example, the argument n has values 4, 3, 2, 1, and 0. The record that the call fact(4) creates in the main program has return address RetLoc1. All other records have return address RetLoc2. For convenience, we omit the empty local variable field from the activation record figures.

Argument int n	Return Address RetLoc1 orRetLoc2

Activation Record

The call of fact(4) in the main program initiates a sequence of five function calls. Figure 7-6 displays the stack of activation records for each function call. The call from the main program always occupies the bottom of the stack.

The stopping condition occurs in fact(0) and begins a sequence of return actions. Each step pops the activation record on the top of the stack and passes

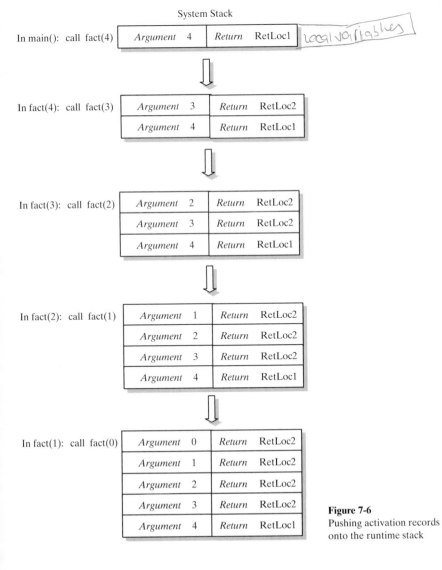

Figure 7-6
Pushing activation records
onto the runtime stack

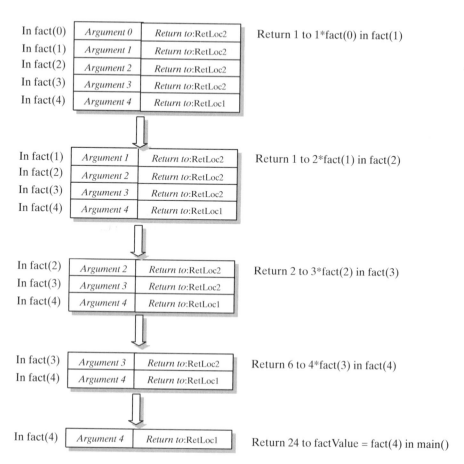

In fact(0) — Argument 0 — Return to:RetLoc2 — Return 1 to 1*fact(0) in fact(1)
In fact(1) — Argument 1 — Return to:RetLoc2
In fact(2) — Argument 2 — Return to:RetLoc2
In fact(3) — Argument 3 — Return to:RetLoc2
In fact(4) — Argument 4 — Return to:RetLoc1

In fact(1) — Argument 1 — Return to:RetLoc2 — Return 1 to 2*fact(1) in fact(2)
In fact(2) — Argument 2 — Return to:RetLoc2
In fact(3) — Argument 3 — Return to:RetLoc2
In fact(4) — Argument 4 — Return to:RetLoc1

In fact(2) — Argument 2 — Return to:RetLoc2 — Return 2 to 3*fact(2) in fact(3)
In fact(3) — Argument 3 — Return to:RetLoc2
In fact(4) — Argument 4 — Return to:RetLoc1

In fact(3) — Argument 3 — Return to:RetLoc2 — Return 6 to 4*fact(3) in fact(4)
In fact(4) — Argument 4 — Return to:RetLoc1

In fact(4) — Argument 4 — Return to:RetLoc1 — Return 24 to factValue = fact(4) in main()

Figure 7-7
Popping activation records from the runtime stack

program control to the return location. Figure 7-7 illustrates the operations that describe the clearing of activation records from the runtime stack.

The completion of all the return processes leaves the stack empty and assigns the value fact(4) = 24 to factValue in the main program.

7-3   STACK IMPLEMENTATION

In keeping with our strategy of providing the reader with some understanding of how STL implements container classes, we develop the class miniStack. This class actually implements all of the STL stack operations. The stack stores data sequentially and allows for access at only one end of the sequence. A vector is a sequence container that implements very efficient access and modification at the back of the sequence. We choose the vector as the underlying storage structure and associate the concept of "back" in the vector with "top" in the stack. Think of the elements of the stack as lying horizontally in a sequence. Initially, the stack is empty and the size of the vector is 0. Pushing an item onto the stack corresponds to adding an element at the back of the vector with push_back() and increasing its size by 1. Popping an item from the stack corresponds to using pop_back() to remove the last element (back) of the vector and decreasing its size by 1. For instance, the next figure shows a stack of characters. After three push operations, C is on the top of the stack.

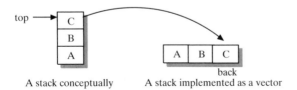

A stack conceptually   A stack implemented as a vector

We use object composition and declare a vector object as a private data member. The vector operations implement the stack class. For instance, implement the stack operation top() by applying the vector operation back() to the vector. The implementation becomes almost trivial.

The upcoming code is the declaration of the miniStack class. You will notice the lack of the member functions begin() and end(). Stacks do not have iterators. This makes sense, because the programmer uses an iterator for general access and updates at any location in a container.

CLASS miniStack	**Declaration**	**"d_stack.h"**

```
class miniStack
{
   public:
      miniStack();
         // constructor. create an empty stack

      void push(const T& item);
         // push (insert) item onto the stack.
         // Postcondition: the stack has a new topmost element and
         // the stack size increases by 1

      void pop();
         // remove the item from the top of the stack.
         // Precondition: the stack is not empty.
         // if the stack is empty, the function throws
         // the underflowError exception

      T& top();
         // return a reference to the element on the top
         // of the stack.
         // Precondition: the stack is not empty.
         // if the stack is empty, the function throws
```

His version of the STL stack class

```
            // the underflowError exception

        const T& top() const;
            // constant version of top()

        bool empty() const;
            // determine whether the stack is empty

        int size() const;
            // return the number of elements in the stack

    private:
        vector<T> stackVector;
            // a vector object maintains the stack items and size
};
```

return StackVector.empty() (handwritten annotation)

Example 7-2

You can use the miniStack class to solve any of the problems in this chapter. This example illustrates the declaration and use of miniStack objects.

1. Declare a miniStack object stk, and use it to reverse the first and last name of "John Doe." While on the stack, "John" is changed to "Jack" by using the fact that the operation top() returns a reference. The resulting string, fullname, becomes "Doe, Jack."

```
string firstname = "John", lastname = "Doe", fullname;
miniStack<string> stk;

// push first and last name on stack in that order
stk.push(firstname);
stk.push(lastname);

// set fullname to lastname(top of stack) and pop element
fullname = stk.top();
stk.pop();

// change the first name (top of stack) to "Jack"; then
// concatenate ", " and firstname (top of stack)
stk.top() = "Jack";
fullname += ", " + stk.top();
stk.pop();
```

2. If the preconditions for pop() and top() are not satisfied, the operations throw the exception underflowError:

```
miniStack<int> s;

try
{
    ...
```

```
      n = s.top();
      s.pop();
      ...
  }

  catch (const underflowError& e)
  {
      cout << e.what() << endl;
  }
```

---

miniStack Class Implementation

The miniStack class uses the vector data member stackVector by composition to hold the elements. The client class is miniStack, and vector is the supplier class. Implement the empty(), size(), and push() operations by using corresponding vector functions. For instance, the stack size() function returns stackVector.size(). For the operation push(), insert an item at the top of the stack by placing it at the back of stackVector by using push_back().

push():

```
// push item on the stack by inserting it at rear of vector
template <typename T>
void miniStack<T>::push(const T& item)
{
    stackVector.push_back(item);
}
```

The operations pop() and top() require additional logic to handle error checking for the "stack empty" condition. If the condition is true, the functions throw the exception underflowError. The interested reader will find the source for the exception class in the header file "d_except.h." For the top() operation, identify the top of the stack by using the vector operation back(). This operation returns a reference to the rear of the vector.

top():

```
// the top of the stack is at the rear of the vector
template <typename T>
T& miniStack<T>::top()
{
    // check for an empty stack
    if (empty())
        throw underflowError("miniStack top(): stack empty");

    // return the element at the rear of the vector
    return stackVector.back();
}
```

The pop() operation removes the element by using the vector function pop_back().

pop():
```
// pop the stack by removing the item at rear of vector
template <typename T>
void miniStack<T>::pop()
{
    // check for an empty stack
    if (empty())
        throw underflowError("miniStack pop(): stack empty");

    // pop the stack
    stackVector.pop_back();
}
```

The running time of the miniStack operations depend on the running time of push_back() and pop_back() for the vector class. The running time of pop_back() is O(1), so the running time of miniStack pop() is O(1). The operation push_back() has constant amortized running time (Section 5-4). As a result, the miniStack push() operation has this same running time.

Implementation of the STL Stack Class (Optional)

The STL stack class provides a programmer with more flexibility than does our miniStack, because the STL stack class allows *several* underlying storage structures. Besides the vector implementation, a programmer can choose the list or deque implementation. A deque is a sequence container that resembles a double-ended vector. In addition to allowing access to elements with an index, a deque allows the sequence to efficiently grow dynamically at both the front and the back. The structure provides the functions front(), push_front(), and pop_front(), along with operations back(), push_back(), and pop_back() for the back of the sequence.

STL allows the programmer to choose the underlying storage container by declaring the stack class with two template arguments. The first argument, *T*, represents the type of the elements on the stack. The name of the second argument is Container, and it represents the type of storage structure specified by the programmer. STL implements the stack class by using the operations size(), push_back(), and so forth that are available in the vector, list, and deque classes. By default, the deque container is chosen; that is why we needed to specify only the object type when declaring an STL stack object.

```
template <typename T, typename Container = deque<T> >
class stack
{
    public:
        ...
        void push(const T& x)
        { c.push_back(x); }
```

```
    int size()
    { return c.size(); }
      ...
  private:
    Container c;
};
```

An *adapter class* is a container that uses the interface provided by one class to implement the interface required by another. The STL stack container is an adapter class, because it uses either a vector, deque, or list to implement the behavior of a stack. From this point of view, miniStack is an adapter class, because it implements a stack by using a vector.

Example 7-3

This example illustrates how a programmer can specify the underlying storage structure when declaring a stack. The first case declares a stack of integers, using a list container to hold its elements. The second template argument is the container list<int>. The second case is a stack of strings, using an underlying vector.

```
stack<int, list<int> > intStack;

stack<string, vector<string> > strStack;
```

deque
is a double ended
queue

Choosing the Stack Container: Each of the underlying storage structures for a stack has different performance criteria. Hence, a programmer should choose the container most suited to the application. In general, a vector is the most efficient for relatively small stacks. A vector loses efficiency when it must frequently be resized to accommodate the size of the stack. In this case, the deque container is a better choice; the deque manages memory more efficiently than a vector. A list container is specifically designed to allow for general insertion and deletion at any position. Because a stack does not use this feature, there is little reason for using a list to store the stack's elements.

Note

POSTFIX EXPRESSIONS 7-4

Electronic calculators illustrate one of the primary applications of a stack. The user enters a mathematical expression by pressing a sequence of numbers (operands) and operators. After the = key has been pressed, the calculator computes and displays the result. The calculator assumes that the user enters the expression in a specific expression format. For instance, an integer expression such as

$$8 + (4*12 + 5\%2)/3$$

contains *operands* $(8, 4, 12, 5, 2, 3)$, *binary operators* $(+, *, /, \%)$, and *parentheses* that create subexpressions. The operators are termed binary because each requires two operands. We say the expression is in *infix* format, because each binary operator appears between its operands, and each unary operator precedes its operand. Infix is the most common format for writing expressions and is the expression format of choice for most programming languages and calculators.

Some calculators allow the alternative *postfix* format, where an operator comes after its operands. The format is also called *RPN*, or *Reverse Polish Notation*. The term "Polish" refers to the fact that the notation was developed by the Polish mathematician Jan Lukasiewicz. The infix expression "*a* + *b*" has the equivalent postfix form "*a b* +." With postfix format, one enters an operator in the expression as soon as its two operands are available. To understand how this applies, consider the translation of the following infix expressions to postfix:

1. **Infix:** *a* + *b* * *c*   **Postfix:** *a b c* * +
   Because * has higher precedence than +, the evaluation of *b**c must come first. The operator + has operands *a* and *b**c. The evaluation of + occurs only after the computation of the value of the subexpression *b c* *.

2. **Infix:** (*a* + *b*) * *c*   **Postfix:** *a b* + *c* *
   The parentheses create the subexpression *a b* + as the left operand for the operator *. The + applies to the operands *a* and *b*, and the operator * forms the product of the left operand *ab*+ and the right operand *c*.

3. **Infix:** (*a**b + *c*)/*d* + *e*   **Postfix:** *a b* * *c* + *d* / *e* +
   The subexpression is *a b* * *c* +. Division (/) is the next operator and occurs immediately after the operand *d*. The result after division is the left operand for the + operator, which immediately follows its right operand, *e*.

We can summarize the conversion from infix to postfix with two simple rules:

Rule 1: Scan the infix expression from left to right. Immediately record an operand as soon as you identify it in the expression.

Rule 2: Record an operator as soon as you identify its operands.

Example 7-4

Let us test your understanding of conversion from infix to postfix format. The upcoming expressions are a series of four infix expressions. We provide four equivalent postfix expressions, but in random order. Test your ability to make the conversion, and then check the result. Note that parentheses are not necessary with postfix format.

InfixExpressions:

1. a*b − c/d   2. a*b*c*d*e*f
3. a+(b*c + d)/e   4. (b*b − 4*a*c)/(2*a)

PostfixExpressions:

(a) ab*c*d*e*f*   **(b)** bb * 4a * c * − 2a*/
(c) ab*cd/−   **(d)** abc * d + e/ +

Answers: 1(c), 2(a), 3(d), 4(b)

Postfix Evaluation

The algorithm for evaluating a postfix expression scans each term of the expression from left to right and uses a single stack to hold the operands. If a term is an operand, push it onto the stack. If the term is a binary operator, we can evaluate its result, because its two operands already reside on the stack, in the top two positions. To carry out the evaluation of the operator, pop the stack twice to retrieve the operands, evaluate the expression, and then push the result back onto the stack. After the terms in the expression have been processed, there will be a single value on the top of the stack, which is the result. Consider the expression "4 3 5 * + ." Its evaluation requires five steps:

Steps 1–3:   Read operands 4, 3, 5, and push each value onto the stack.

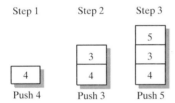

Step 1   Step 2   Step 3

Push 4   Push 3   Push 5

Step 4:   Read operator *, and evaluate the expression by popping the two operands 5 and 3 from the stack and computing 3 * 5. The value 5 was last pushed onto the stack, so it comes off first and is the right operand for the operator. The operand 3 becomes the left operand. Push the result, 15, back onto the stack, and make it available as an operand for a subsequent operator.

Step 4

Step 5:   Read operator +, and evaluate the expression by popping the two operands 15 and 4 from the stack and computing 4 + 15. Push the result, 19, back onto the stack.

Step 5

Stack after
evaluating +

After the postfix expression has been scanned, the result is the value of the one element that resides on the stack. In our case, the result is 19.

Detecting Errors: Errors can occur during the evaluation of a postfix expression. At each step in the algorithm, the state of the stack allows us to identify whether an error occurs and the cause of the error. For instance, the expression

$$3\ 8+*\ 9$$

has too many successive operators. Put another way, the binary operator * is missing a second operand. We identify this error when we input * and note that the stack has only one element 11 (3 8 +). We cannot evaluate the * operation, because it requires that there be two operands on the stack. We can conclude that * has too few operands.

After pushing   After evaluating +
operands 3 and 8

Another error occurs when an expression contains too many operands. We identify this error only after processing the entire expression. At the conclusion of the process, the stack contains more than one element. It should contain only the result. For instance, consider the postfix expression

$$9\ 8+7$$

The following figure traces the steps of the algorithm:

After pushing   After evaluating +   After pushing 7
operands 9 and 8

The final stack should contain only the result. Upon noting that the stack size is 2, we can conclude that the expression has too many operands.

The postfixEval Class

In keeping with the principles of object technology, we design a class, postfixEval, that takes a postfix expression contained in a string and evaluates it. We assume that the operands are single-digit nonnegative integers. This simplifies the process of distinguishing between an operator and an operand. The class handles the standard binary integer operators +, -, *, /, and %. In addition, the class evaluates expressions containing the binary exponentiation operator, ^. That operator takes two operands a and b, and computes

$$a \wedge b = a^b$$

The postfixEval class contains a default constructor and the operation set-PostfixExp(), which takes a string argument containing the postfix expression. The access member function getPostfixExp()) enables a programmer to retrieve the current expression. The key member function, evaluate(), attempts to compute the value of the postfix expression. If successful, it returns the value of the expression. If the expression contains an error, the function throws the expressionError exception, which is defined in "d_except.h." In this case, the calling block can catch the exception and output the message contained in the expressionError object.

Designing the Function evaluate(). The public-member function evaluate() scans each character in the string postfixExpression. The characters in the string include operands, operators, and whitespace characters, such as blanks and tabs. The postfix expression algorithm in evalute() uses the stack operandStack to store the operands during evaluation. To implement the algorithm, the class provides three utility functions:

isOperator():
    Determines whether a character is one of the valid operators $(+, -, *, /, \%, \wedge)$.

getOperands():
    Pops the left and right operands from the stack. The function checks that the stack is not empty before each pop operation. An empty stack indicates that there are too many operators, and the function throws an expression-Error exception.

compute():
    Evaluates an operation and pushes the result onto the stack. For the divide (/) and remainder (%) operators, compute() checks the right-hand operand (divisor) to see if it is 0. In this case, the function throws an expressionError exception with the message "Divide by 0." For the exponential operator $(\wedge)$, compute() checks for $(0, 0)$ and throws an expressionError exception, since there is no definition for 0^0.

The function evaluate() carries out the algorithm by looking at each non-whitespace character in the string. A call to isOperator() determines whether the character is an operator. If so, evaluate() calls getOperands() to retrieve the two operands and then calls the function compute() to evaluate the operation and push the result onto the stack.

CLASS postfixEval	Declaration	"d_rpn.h"

```
class postfixEval
{
   public:
```

```
        postfixEval();
          // default constructor. postfix expression is NULL string

        string getPostfixExp() const;
          // return the postfix expression

        void setPostfixExp(const string& postfixExp);
          // change the postfix expression

        int evaluate();
          // evaluate the postfix expression and return
          // its value. the function throws expressionError
          // if an error occurs during evaluation

    private:

        string postfixExpression;
          // the postfix expression to evaluate
        stack<int> operandStack;
          // stack of operands

        void getOperands(int& left, int& right);
          // pop left and right operands from stack.
          // Precondition: the stack must have at least two entries.
          // if the stack is empty prior to a pop() operation, the
          // function throws the exception expressionError

        int compute(int left, int right, char op) const;
          // compute "left op right". if right is 0 and op
          // is '/' or '%', the function throws expressionError

        bool isOperator(char ch) const;
          // is ch one of '+','-','*','/','%','^'
};
```

Example 7-5

This example illustrates how you can use a postfixEval object, exp, to evaluate a postfix expression. Input the expression into the string rpnExp, and assign the string to exp by using the member function setPostfixExp(). Enclose the call to evaluate() in a try block in case an error occurs. A catch block follows the try block and uses the what() member function of expressionError to display the error. The runs include the infix format for the expressions that do not contain an error.

```
        // object used to evaluate postfix expressions
        postfixEval exp;
        // postfix expression input
```

```
string rpnExp;
cout << "Enter the postfix expression: ";
getline(cin, rpnExp);

// assign the expression to exp
exp.setPostfixExp(rpnExp);

// call evaluate() in a try block in case an error occurs
try
{
   cout << "The value of the expression = "
        << exp.evaluate() << endl << endl;
}

// catch block outputs the error using what()
catch (const expressionError& ee)
{
   cout << ee.what() << endl << endl;
}
```

```
Output:

    Run 1: (2 + 5)*3 - 8/3

    Enter the postfix expression: 2 5 + 3 * 8 3 / —
    The value of the expression = 19

    Run 2: 2³ + 1

    Enter the postfix expression: 2 3 ^ 1 +
    The value of the expression = 9

    Run 3: 2^{2^3}/4

    Enter the postfix expression: 2 2 3 ^ ^ 4 /
    The value of the expression = 64

    Run 4:

    Enter the postfix expression: 1 9 * /
    postfixEval: Too many operators

    Run 5:

    Enter the postfix expression: 2 3 5 +
    postfixEval: Too many operands
```

Implementing evaluate(). To understand the implementation of evaluate(), we must first look at the private-member (utility) functions. When the current character in the scan is an operator (isOperator() returns true), the function getOperands() pops the top two values off the stack and assigns them to output arguments *left* and *right*. During the operation, the stack might be empty, and then values cannot be found for both arguments *left* and *right*. The function getOperands() checks for this condition before attempting to pop a value and throws an expressionError exception that indicates the expression has too many operators. The following is the code for getOperands():

getOperands():

```
void postfixEval::getOperands(int& left, int& right)
{
    // can we pop the right operand?
    if (operandStack.empty())
        throw expressionError("postfixEval:   Too many operators");

    // pop right operand
    right = operandStack.top();
    operandStack.pop();

    // can we pop the left operand?
    if (operandStack.empty())
        throw expressionError("postfixEval:   Too many operators");

    // pop left operand
    left = operandStack.top();
    operandStack.pop();
}
```

The function compute() has operands called left and right and the operator symbol *op*. A switch statement provides the case selection for the operators $(+, -, *, \%, /, \wedge)$, performs the operation corresponding to the selection value *op*, and pushes the result onto the stack. The function handles an attempt to divide by 0 (*right* $== 0$) or to evaluate 0^0 by throwing an expressionError exception.

compute():

```
int postfixEval::compute(int left, int right, char op) const
{
    int value;

    // evaluate "left op right"
    switch(op)
    {
        case '+':   value = left + right;
                    break;
```

```
        case '-':    value = left - right;
                     break;

        case '*':    value = left * right;
                     break;

        case '%':    if (right == 0)
                         throw
                             expressionError("postfixEval: divide by 0");
                     value = left % right;
                     break;

        case '/':    if (right == 0)
                         throw
                             expressionError("postfixEval: divide by 0");
                     value = left / right;
                     break;

        case '^':    // make sure we are not computing 0^0
                     if (left == 0 && right == 0)
                         throw
                             expressionError("postfixEval: 0^0 undefined");

                     value = 1;
                     // general case. compute value = 1*left*...*left.
                     // if right == 0, skip the loop and left^0 is 1
                     while (right > 0)
                     {
                        value *= left;
                        right--;
                     }
                     break;
    }

    return value;
}
```

Rather than simply listing the code for evaluate(), we describe how it implements the algorithm. You can find a complete listing of the function in "d_rpn.h." The main loop in evaluate() scans each character of postfixExpression and terminates when all characters have been processed or when an error occurs.

```
// expValue contains the evaluated expression
int left, right, expValue;
char ch;
int i;

// process characters until the end of the string is reached
// or an error occurs
```

```
for (i=0; i < postfixExpression.length(); i++)
{
    // get the current character
    ch = postfixExpression[i];
    . . .
}
```

When the function isdigit() from the character classification library <ctype.h> determines that *ch* is a digit (isdigit(*ch*) is true if *ch* >= '0' && *ch* <= '9'), evaluate() pushes the corresponding integer value of the operand onto the stack.

```
// look for an operand, which is a single digit
// non-negative integer
if (isdigit(ch))
    // value of operand goes on the stack
    operandStack.push(ch - '0');
```

If the character *ch* is an operator, evaluate() calls getOperands() to obtain the left and right operands from the stack. The function compute() then executes the operator and pushes the resulting value onto the stack.

```
// look for an operator
else if (isOperator(ch))
{
    // pop the stack twice and get the
    // left and right operands
    getOperands(left, right);
    // evaluate "left op right" and push on stack
    operandStack.push(compute(left, right, ch));
}
```

If the character *ch* is neither an operand nor an operator, evaluate() uses the function isspace() from <ctype.h> to determine whether *ch* is a whitespace separator consisting of a blank, newline, or tab. If *ch* is not a whitespace character, the function throws an expressionError exception; otherwise, the loop continues with the next character in the string.

```
// any other character must be whitespace.
// whitespace includes blank, tab, and newline
else if (!isspace(ch))
    throw expressionError("postfixEval: Improper char");
```

Assuming the scan of the postfix expression terminates without an error, the value of a properly formed expression should be on the top of the stack. The function, evaluate(), extracts the value of the element before popping it from the stack. If the stack is then empty, the value is the final result and becomes the return value. If the stack still contains elements, evaluate() concludes that there are too many operands and throws an expressionError exception.

```
// the expression value is on the top of the stack.
// pop it off
expValue = operandStack.top();
operandStack.pop();

// if data remains on the stack, there are too
// many operands
if (!operandStack.empty())
    throw expressionError("postfixEval: Too many operands");
return expValue;
```

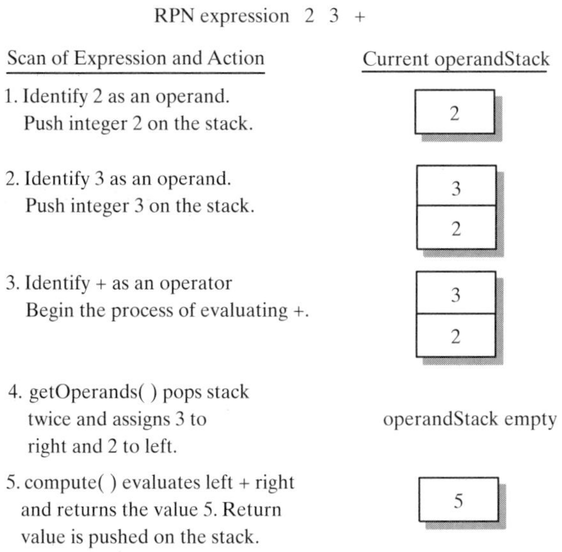

RPN expression 2 3 +

Scan of Expression and Action   Current operandStack

1. Identify 2 as an operand.
   Push integer 2 on the stack.

2

2. Identify 3 as an operand.
   Push integer 3 on the stack.

3
2

3. Identify + as an operator
   Begin the process of evaluating +.

3
2

4. getOperands( ) pops stack
   twice and assigns 3 to   operandStack empty
   right and 2 to left.

5. compute( ) evaluates left + right
   and returns the value 5. Return   5
   value is pushed on the stack.

Figure 7-8
Relationship among
evaluate(), getOperands(), and
compute()

Figure 7-8 illustrates the relationship between evaluate() and the private functions getOperands() and compute() for the simple postfix expression "2 3 + ."

CASE STUDY: INFIX EXPRESSION EVALUATION   7-5

Section 7-4 discussed the use of stacks for the evaluation of postfix expressions. The evaluate() algorithm in that section illustrates the scanning and processing of the expression. Postfix expressions are relative easy to evaluate, because they do not contain subexpressions and already account for precedence among operators. In addition, the implementation requires a stack that stores only operands. Unfortunately, postfix expressions have limited application. Most electronic calculators and programming languages assume that expressions are entered with infix notation rather than postfix notation. Evaluation of an infix expression is more difficult. The algorithm must have a strategy to handle subexpressions and must maintain the order of precedence and associativity for operators. For instance, in the expression

$$9 + (2 - 3) * 8$$

we evaluate the subexpression $(2 - 3)$ first and then use the result as the left operand for *. The operator * executes before the +, because it has higher precedence.

In this section, we develop an algorithm for evaluating infix expressions. We could use one of two approaches. One approach scans the infix expression and uses two stacks to produce the result directly. A second approach converts the infix expression to its equivalent postfix expression and then calls the postfix expression evaluator from Section 7-4 to compute the result. We use the latter approach, because it enables us to focus on strategies to handle operator precedence and subexpressions. You can get a fairly good understanding of the process from the upcoming discussion of the key concepts and steps required by the algorithm. We support the discussion with numerous examples and figures.

Infix Expression Attributes

Infix expressions consist of operands, operators, and pairs of parentheses that create subexpressions that are computed separately. There is an *order of precedence* and *associativity* among operators. The order of precedence dictates that you evaluate the operator with the highest precedence first. The concept of associativity refers to the order of execution for operators at the same precedence level. If more than one operator has the same precedence, the leftmost operator executes first in the case of left associativity (+, −, , /, %) and the rightmost operator executes first in the case of right associativity (^). A few examples will clarify the difference between left and right associativity. In the following expression, operators * and % have the same order of precedence. They are also left associative: They execute from left to right. Compute the successive products, and then evaluate the remainder:

$$7 * 2 * 4 \% 5 \quad \text{Evaluate:} \quad ((7 * 2) * 4) \% 5 = (14 * 4) \% 5 = 56 \% 5 = 1$$

The exponentiation operator, ^, is right associative. For instance, the following expression combines two successive ^ operations:

$$2 \wedge 3 \wedge 2 + 3 \quad \text{(Math form)} \quad 2^{3^2} + 3 = 2^9 + 3 = 512 + 3 = 515$$

Perform the second (rightmost) ^ operation ($3^2 = 9$), then execute the first (leftmost) ^ operation (2^9). The order of evaluation is then from right to left. In general, the additive operators (+, −) have the lowest precedence and are left-associative; next are the left-associative multiplicative operators (*, /, %). The right-associative exponentiation operator (^) has the highest precedence.

Example 7-6

---

    1. $8 + 2*3 = 14$ // * executes before +

    2. $(8 + 2) * 3 = 30$ // parentheses create a subexpression

    3. $8/9*5=0$ // operators are left associative. $8/9 = 0$ executes first

---

Rank of an Expression We restrict the infix-expression-evaluation algorithm to expressions that contain only binary operators. The algorithm to evaluate an infix expression uses the concept of *rank*, which assigns a value ($-1, 0,$ or 1) to each term in the expression:

Rank of an operand is 1.
Rank of the binary operators $+, -, *, /, \%, \wedge$ is -1.
Rank of left and right parentheses is 0.

With each term in the expression, we associate a *cumulative rank* that is the sum of the ranks of the individual terms, from the first symbol through the given term. Assuming that the cumulative rank starts at 0, its value must remain in the range from 0 to 1, because a valid infix expression ensures that each binary operator has two surrounding operands and that no successive operands exist without an infix operator. Furthermore, the cumulative rank for the entire expression should be +1, because there must be exactly one more operand than operator. For instance, in the simple expression

$$2 + 3$$

the successive rank values are

Scan 2:   Operand rank = +1   Cumulative rank = 1
Scan +:   Operator rank = −1   Cumulative rank = 1 + (−1) = 0
Scan 3:   Operand rank = +1   Cumulative rank = 1

Example 7-7

___

The following are invalid expressions that are identified by their cumulative rank:

Expression	Invalid Rank	Reason
1. 2 4 + 3	Rank at 4 is 2	Too many consecutive operands
2. 2 + * 3	Rank at * is –1	Too many consecutive operators
3. 2 + 3 −	Final rank is 0	Missing an operand

___

Infix-to-Postfix Conversion: Algorithm Design

The infix-to-postfix conversion algorithm takes an infix expression as an input string and returns the corresponding postfix expression as an output string. With postfix evaluation, the scan of an expression uses an operand stack to temporarily store operands and evaluates operators as they appear. The infix-to-postfix conversion does things in an opposite manner. During the scan of an expression, an operand is immediately written to the output string. As a result, the algorithm does not need to maintain an operand stack. Operators and left-parenthesis symbols, however, move to an operator stack for temporary storage. You must understand how the operator stack works to appreciate the algorithm, because it manages the order of precedence and associativity of operators and handles subexpressions. We motivate the use of the operator stack by looking at several examples which illustrate issues that must be addressed. By tracing the scan of the sample expression, you will then see how the stack is involved in the solution. In the process, we develop rules that describe the management of the stack.

Example 1: Expression $a + b * c$. This example illustrates how the stack temporally stores operators awaiting their right-hand-side operand. The resulting postfix expression is $abc*+$.

Read the operand a, and immediately write it to the postfix string. The next term is the operator +. The issue is what to do with it. For starters, we do not have a second operand in the postfix string, and so + cannot be output, because it can appear in the string only after we have its two operands. The solution is to park the operand on a stack and proceed with the scan (figure A). The operator will ultimately leave the stack after we discover its right operand. Read the operand b, and write it to the postfix string. We next find the operator *, which has higher precedence than + and hence must appear in the final postfix expression before +. Leave the lower precedence operator on the stack, and add the * to the stack (figure B). Read operand c, and write it to the postfix string. After completing the scan of the expression, clear the stack and write the operators to the output string. The result is the correct postfix expression: $a\ b\ c\ *\ +$ (figure C).

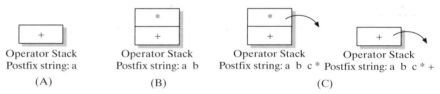

Operator Stack
Postfix string: a

(A)

Operator Stack
Postfix string: a b

(B)

Operator Stack
Postfix string: a b c *

Operator Stack
Postfix string: a b c * +

(C)

Example 2: Expression $a * b / c + d$. This example illustrates how to use the stack to handle operators that have the same or lower precedence. The resulting postfix expression is $ab*c/d+$.

Read the first three terms, writing the operands a and b to the postfix string and placing the operator * on the stack (figure A). The next item in the string is the operator /, which has the same precedence as *. Placing / immediately on the stack would bury the * and ultimately result in placing the / in the postfix string prior to the *. This violates the left associativity of the operators. We must extend the notion of stack handling. When scanning an operator, first remove all operators on the stack that have the same or higher precedence, and write them to the postfix string. Only then do we push the new operator on the stack (figure B). After handling the operand c, the scan reads the operator +. Before adding it to the stack, remove (pop) the *, which has higher precedence, and write it to the postfix string (figure C). Complete the scan with the operand d, and then remove the operator + from the stack (figure D).

Operator Stack
Postfix string : ab
(A)

Operator Stack
Postfix string : ab*
(B)

Operator Stack
Postfix string : ab*c/
(C)

Operator Stack
Postfix string : ab*c/d
(D)

Example 3:   Expression $a \wedge b \wedge c$. This example illustrates how to use precedence values to handle the exponential operator, $\wedge$, which is
right associative. The resulting postfix expression is $abc\wedge\wedge$ (a^{b^c}).

The $\wedge$ operator is right associative, which implies that we must evaluate the expression $b \wedge c$ first and use the result as the right operand of a ($a \wedge$ <operand>).
Handling the second $\wedge$ operator is the problem. After reading the symbols $a \wedge b$, the
operands a and b are in the postfix string and the operator $\wedge$ is on the stack (figure
A). We must next deal with the second $\wedge$ operator. In Example 2, we develop a rule
that indicates an input operator should not go onto the stack until we remove all operators of equal or greater precedence from the stack. If the input operator $\wedge$ has
the same precedence as the operator $\wedge$ on the stack, then first popping the operator
from the stack and writing it to the postfix string produces the expression $ab\wedge$. Placing the second $\wedge$ operator on the stack and proceeding with the scan results in a final
postfix expression $ab\wedge c\wedge$ $((a^b)^c)$. This violates the right associativity of the $\wedge$ operator. To create a solution, we develop a new strategy. When an operator is right associative, we assign it two different precedence values, called the *input precedence* and
the *stack precedence*. The stack precedence of an operator applies when it resides on
the stack. When we first read an operator, we compare its input precedence to the
stack precedence of the operator on the top of the stack. If the input precedence is
less than or equal to the stack precedence of the operator, pop the operator from
the stack and write it to the postfix string. Repeat the process for each subsequent
operator on the stack. If the input precedence is greater, push the operator on the
stack. In the case of $\wedge$, we give the operator input precedence 4 and stack precedence 3. When first scanning the second $\wedge$, we observe that it has input precedence
4, which is greater than the stack precedence of the $\wedge$ on the stack, and so the second
operator joins the $\wedge$ operator on the stack (figure B). The LIFO ordering assures us
that the second $\wedge$ operator will come off first, thus preserving right associativity (figure C). Table 7-1 gives a listing of the input precedence and stack precedence for
each operator. The following figure identifies the operators on the stack, along with
their stack precedence in square brackets ([]):

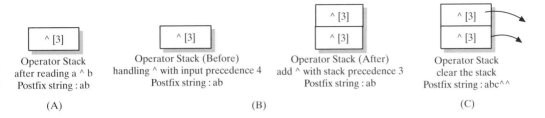

Operator Stack after reading a ^ b Postfix string : ab	Operator Stack (Before) handling ^ with input precedence 4 Postfix string : ab	Operator Stack (After) add ^ with stack precedence 3 Postfix string : ab	Operator Stack clear the stack Postfix string : abc^^
(A)	(B)		(C)

Example 4:   Expression $a * (b + c)$. This example illustrates how to handle left
and right parentheses that create a subexpression. The resulting
postfix expression is $abc+*$.

Dealing with a parenthesized subexpression causes problems that we can
solve by using existing concepts and strategies. When we read a left parenthesis, we
enter into a subexpression that we handle much like a regular infix expression. The
main difference is that the subexpression terminates on input of the corresponding

right parenthesis. We store the left parenthesis on the stack until we reach the end of the subexpression. Because the left parenthesis begins a new subexpression, all operators currently on the stack must remain there. We accomplish this by providing the left parenthesis with an input precedence that is greater than the stack precedence of any operators. Once on the stack, no operator in the subexpression may remove the left parenthesis until we identify the corresponding right parenthesis. We guarantee that the left parenthesis remains fixed by making its stack precedence -1, which is lower than the input precedence of any operator. Once we read the corresponding right parenthesis, we have a complete subexpression and can pop all operators on the stack down to the left parenthesis and write them to the postfix string. Complete the handling of the subexpression by removing the left parenthesis from the stack, and continue with the scan of the remaining expression. The figure illustrates how we would handle the subexpression $(b + c)$.

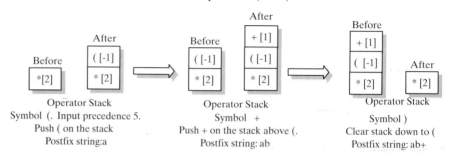

Table 7-1 gives input precedence, stack precedence, and rank used for the operators $+$, $-$, $*$, $/$, %, and $\wedge$, along with the parentheses. Except for the exponential operator, $\wedge$, the other binary operators are left associative and have their input and stack precedences equal.

TABLE 7.1   INPUT AND STACK PRECEDENCE WITH RANK

	Precedence		
Symbol	*Input Precedence*	*Stack Precedence*	*Rank*
+ −	1	1	−1
* / %	2	2	−1
^	4	3	−1
(	5	−1	0
)	0	0	0

Rules for Infix Expression Evaluation. In the upcoming examples, we describe a series of prescribed actions for handling the operands, operators, and parentheses in an infix expression. We summarize the actions as a series of rules:

RULE 1:   Check the cumulative rank after each symbol. The value must be in the range from 0 to 1. If the value becomes negative, the expression has too many operators. If the value is 2, the expression has too many operands. The final value for the cumulative rank must be 1.

RULE 2: If the input is an operand, immediately write it to the postfix string.

RULE 3: Upon input of an operator or a left parenthesis, compare the input precedence with the stack precedence of the topmost item on the stack. Pop the operator if the stack precedence is greater than or equal to the input precedence, and write the operator to the postfix string. Continue this process until the stack precedence is no longer greater than or equal to the input precedence. Then push the input symbol onto the stack.

RULE 4: If the input is a right parenthesis, the scan has reached the end of a subexpression. Pop all operators from the stack down to the corresponding left parenthesis and write them to the postfix string. Then pop the left-parenthesis symbol, and continue with the scan.

RULE 5: After reaching the end of the infix expression, pop all remaining operators from the stack, and write them to the postfix string.

Example 7-8

Consider the infix expression

$$3 * (4 - 2 \wedge 5) + 6$$

A series of figures traces the conversion of the expression to postfix. Each figure specifies the action of the algorithm and the resulting contents of the stack and the output (postfix) string. We give the stack precedence for each item on the stack within square brackets.

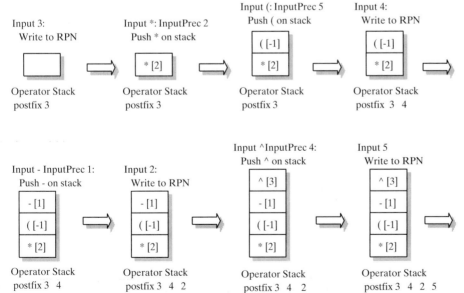

handwritten notes in right margin:
the decision to whether or not to pop or not is Based on the input Precedence vs. Stack Prec.

if iP > SP Push
if iP <= SP Pop
< = from stack write to postfix

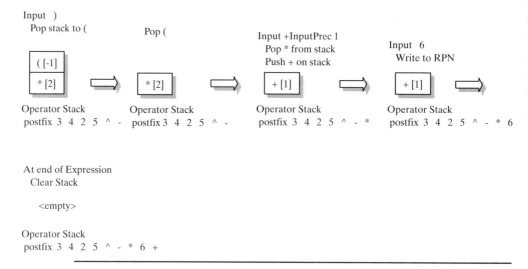

Input   )
Pop stack to (

Pop (

Input +InputPrec 1
Pop * from stack
Push + on stack

Input 6
Write to RPN

([-1]

* [2]

* [2]

+ [1]

+ [1]

Operator Stack
postfix 3 4 2 5 ^ -

Operator Stack
postfix 3 4 2 5 ^ -

Operator Stack
postfix 3 4 2 5 ^ - *

Operator Stack
postfix 3 4 2 5 ^ - * 6

At end of Expression
Clear Stack

<empty>

Operator Stack
postfix 3 4 2 5 ^ - * 6 +

Infix-to-Postfix Conversion: Object Design

The design of the infix-to-postfix expression algorithm uses two classes. The expressionSymbol class encapsulates each symbol (operator or parenthesis) along with the associated input and stack precedence values. In this way, we can use the associated expressionSymbol object to access precedence information. The expressionSymbol class has a default constructor and a constructor that takes the symbol as an argument. The nondefault constructor sets both the input precedence and the stack precedence of the operator.

The class has the member function getOp() to access the symbol and an overloaded >= operator that compares the stack precedence of the left operand with the input precedence of the right operand. We use this comparison operator to determine the symbols on the stack that we must pop before pushing the new symbol onto the stack. The following is the declaration of the expressionSymbol class.

CLASS expressionSymbol   Declaration   "d_expsym.h"

```
// a class that maintains the precedence of symbols
class expressionSymbol
{
   public:
      expressionSymbol();
         // default constructor
      expressionSymbol(char ch);
         // initializes the object for operator ch

      friend bool operator>= (const expressionSymbol& left,
                              const expressionSymbol& right);
         // return true if stackPrecedence of left is
         // >= inputPrecedence of right. determines whether
```

```
        // operator left on the stack should be output before
        // pushing operator right on the stack

     char getOp() const;
        // return operator
  private:
     char op;
        // operator
     int inputPrecedence;
        // input precedence of op
     int stackPrecedence;
        // stack precedence of op
};
```

The infix2Postfix class implements the algorithm by using a stack. The class stores the infix expression string, the postfix output expression created by the conversion, and a stack of expressionSymbol objects as private data members. The class provides a default constructor and a constructor that takes the infix expression as an argument. When using the default constructor, the programmer can call the member function setInfixExp() to initialize the infix expression string. The member function postfix() uses the conversion algorithm to build and return the equivalent postfix expression. You can use this string with the postfixEval class in order to evaluate the expression. We developed postfixEval in Section 7-4.

The following is the declaration of the infix2Postfix class.

| CLASS infix2Postfix | Declaration | "d_inftop.h" |

```
class infix2Postfix
{
   public:
      infix2Postfix();
         // default constructor. infix expression is NULL string
      infix2Postfix(const string& infixExp);
         // initialize the infix expression

      void setInfixExp(const string& infixExp);
         // change the infix expression

      string postfix();
         // return a string that contains the equivalent postfix
         // expression. the function throws expressionError if an
         // error occurs during conversion

   private:

      string infixExpression;
         // the infix expression to convert
```

```
        string postfixExpression;
          // built to contain the postfix equivalent of infixExpression
        stack<expressionSymbol> operatorStack;
          // stack of expressionSymbol objects

        void outputHigherOrEqual(const expressionSymbol& op);
          // the expressionSymbol object op holds the current
          // symbol. pop the stack and output as long as the symbol
          // on the top of the stack has a precedence {.}= that of
          // the current operator

        bool isOperator(char ch) const;
          // is ch one of '+','-','*','/','%','^'
};
```

Example 7-9

By using rank, the member function postfix() can identify errors in the expression while scanning the symbols. Whenever it encounters an error, it throws an appropriate expressionError exception. For this reason, we include the conversion code in a try block with the exception handler in a catch block.

```
        infix2Postfix exp("2 * (3 + 5) % 8");
        string postfixExp;

        try
        {
            postfixExp = exp.postfix();
            cout << "The postfix form is " << postfixExp << endl;
        }

        catch (const expressionError& e)
        {
            cout << e.what() << endl;
            exit(1);
        }
```

```
Output: The postfix form is 2 3 5 + * 8 %
```

---

infix2Postfix Class Implementation

The constructors and the function setInfixExp() simply initialize the string infixExpression. The function postfix() calls the private-member function outputHigherOrEqual() when it reads an operator or the symbol). The function pops those symbols from the stack whose stack precedence is greater than or equal to the input precedence of the new symbol. The function writes all of the symbols popped from the stack to the postfix string.

outputHigherOrEqual():

```
void infix2Postfix::outputHigherOrEqual(const expressionSymbol& op)
{
    expressionSymbol op2;

    while(!operatorStack.empty() &&
         (op2 = operatorStack.top()) >= op)
    {
        operatorStack.pop();
        postfixExpression += op2.getOp();
        postfixExpression += ' ';
    }
}
```

The function postfix() implements the infix-to-postfix conversion algorithm, which scans each character of the expression. The algorithm skips a whitespace character, while it immediately writes an operand to the postfix string. With an operator, the function outputHigherOrEqual() outputs higher or equal precedence operators before the input operator goes on the stack. If the input symbol is a right parenthesis, postfix() also calls outputHigherOrEqual() to output all the operators down to the left parenthesis. Upon input of an operator or an operand, postfix() updates the cumulative rank and throws an expressionError exception if it identifies an error. The input terminates at the end of the expression or if an error occurs. The function makes the following declarations:

```
expressionSymbol op;
// maintain rank for error checking
int rank = 0, i;
char ch;
```

The body of postfix() consists of a nested if/else statement that distinguishes the different types of characters in the infix expression. We describe the implementation of the function by indicating the action upon input of an operand, an operator or left parenthesis, a right parenthesis, or a whitespace character. We conclude by describing the action that occurs at the end of the expression:

Process an operand:

Increment the accumulated rank by 1, which should now equal 1. If the rank exceeds 1, the expression is invalid ("Operator expected"). Output the operand.

```
// ********  process an operand  ********
// an operand is a single digit non-negative integer
if (isdigit(ch))
{   // just add operand to output expression, followed by
    // a blank
    postfixExpression += ch;
    postfixExpression += ' ';
    // rank of operand is 1, accumulated rank must be 1
```

```
    rank++;
    if (rank > 1)
        throw
            expressionError("infix2Postfix: Operator expected");
}
```

Process an operator:

If the operator is not '(', decrease the accumulated rank by 1, which should now equal 0. If the rank is negative, the expression is invalid ("Operand expected"). By calling outputHigherOrEqual(), pop all operators from the stack that have stack precedence greater than or equal to the input precedence of the current operator. Push the new operator onto the stack.

```
// *********  process an operator or '(' **********
else if (isOperator(ch) || ch == '(')
{
    // rank of an operator is -1. rank of '(' is 0.
    // accumulated rank should be 0
    if (ch != '(')
        rank--;

    if (rank < 0)
        throw
            expressionError("infix2Postfix: Operand expected");
    else
    {
        // output the operators on the stack with higher
        // or equal precedence. push the current operator
        // on the stack
        op = expressionSymbol(ch);
        outputHigherOrEqual(op);
        operatorStack.push(op);
    }
}
```

Process a right parenthesis ')'

Using outputHigherOrEqual(), pop and output all operators on the stack that have stack precedence greater than or equal to the input precedence of ')' which is 0. Note that the stack precedence of '(' is −1, so the process stops when it encounters '('. The effect is to output all operators between the parentheses. If no '(' is found, the expression is invalid ("Missing '(' "). Pop the '(' from the stack.

```
// *********  process a right parenthesis **********
else if (ch == rParen)
{
```

```
        // build an expressionSymbol object holding ), which
        // has precedence lower than the stack precedence
        // of any operator except '('. pop the stack
        // and output operators from the subexpression until
        // '(' surfaces or the stack is empty. if the stack is
        // empty, a '(' is missing; otherwise, pop off '('.
        op = expressionSymbol(ch);
        outputHigherOrEqual(op);
        if(operatorStack.empty())
            throw expressionError("infix2Postfix:  Missing '('" );
        else
            operatorStack.pop(); // get rid of '('
    }
```

Handle whitespace:

```
    // ********* make sure ch is whitespace **********
    else if (!isspace(ch))
        throw expressionError("infix2Postfix: Invalid input");
```

At the end of the expression:

The rank must be 1. If the rank is less than 1, an operand is missing. Empty the stack, and output each operator. During this process, if a left parenthesis is found, the expression is invalid ("Missing ')' "). Conclude by returning postfixExpression.

```
    // finish processing
    if (rank != 1)
        throw expressionError("infix2Postfix: Operand expected");
    else
    {
        // flush the stack and complete expression evaluation.
        // if find left parenthesis, a right parenthesis is
        // missing.
        while (!operatorStack.empty())
        {
            op = operatorStack.top();
            operatorStack.pop();
            if (op.getOp() == lParen)
                throw expressionError("infix2Postfix: Missing ')' ");
            else
            {
                postfixExpression += op.getOp();
                postfixExpression += ' ';
            }
        }
    }

    return postfixExpression;
```

PROGRAM 7-3   EVALUATING AN INFIX EXPRESSION

The upcoming program illustrates the conversion of an infix expression to postfix and the
evaluation of the postfix expression. The program declares the infix2Postfix object iexp and
the postfixEval object pexp. Statements in a loop execute until the user enters an empty infix
expression from the keyboard. After assigning the expression to iexp by using setInfixExp(),
the function postfix() converts the expression to postfix form. If there is no error, the program displays the postfix form and uses the object pexp to evaluate the postfix expression. Its
value is that of the original infix expression. If an error occurs during the execution of post-
fix(), a catch block displays the error message of the expressionError object. The run illustrates the various errors that can occur in an infix expression.

```cpp
// File: prg7_3.cpp
// program inputs an infix expression until user enters an empty
// string. it uses class infix2Postfix to convert infix expression
// to postfix, handling errors by catching the corresponding
// expressionError exception. if no error, the postfix string is
// correctly formatted. use class postfixEval to evaluate postfix
// expression and output the result. this is the value of the
// original infix expression

#include <iostream>
#include <string>

#include "d_inftop.h" // infix2Postfix class
#include "d_rpn.h"    // postfixEval class

using namespace std;

int main()
{
    // use iexp for infix to postfix conversion
    infix2Postfix iexp;
    // infix expression input and postfix expression output
    string infixExp, postfixExp;
    // use pexp to evaluate postfix expressions
    postfixEval pexp;

    // input and evaluate infix expressions until the
    // user enters an empty string

    // get the first expression
    cout << "Enter an infix expression:    ";
    getline(cin, infixExp);

    while (infixExp != "")
    {
        // an exception may occur. enclose the conversion
        // to postfix and the output of the expression
```

infix to post fix class

Postfix Eval class

```
// value in a try block
try
{
    // convert to postfix
    iexp.setInfixExp(infixExp);
    postfixExp = iexp.postfix();
    // output the postfix expression
    cout << "The postfix form is " << postfixExp
        << endl;
    // use pexp to evaluate the postfix expression
    pexp.setPostfixExp(postfixExp);

    cout << "Value of the expression = "
        << pexp.evaluate() << endl << endl;
}

// catch an exception and output the error
catch (const expressionError& ee)
{
    cout << ee.what() << endl << endl;
}
// input another expression
cout << "Enter an infix expression: ";
getline(cin, infixExp);
}

return 0;
}
```

```
Run:
Enter an infix expression: 3 ^ 2 ^ (1+2)
The postfix form is 3 2 1 2 + ^ ^
Value of the expression = 6561

Enter an infix expression: 3 * (4 − 2 ^ 5) + 6
The postfix form is 3 4 2 5 ^ − * 6 +
Value of the expression = −78

Enter an infix expression: (7 + 8*7
infix2Postfix: Missing ')'

Enter an infix expression: (9 + 7) 4
infix2Postfix: Operator expected

Enter an infix expression: 2*4*8/
infix2Postfix: Operand expected

Enter an infix expression:
```

CHAPTER SUMMARY

- A stack is a structure whose insert (push) and erase (pop) operations occur at one end of a sequence, called the top of the stack. The last element in is the first element out of the stack, so a stack is a LIFO structure. The stack ADT defines the operations push() and pop(), which update the stack, and the operation top(), which returns a reference to the topmost element of the stack. The stack container has the standard operations size() and empty(). The standard library provides the class stack, and Section 7-1 presents its API. We illustrate the use of the stack API by presenting an application that outputs a number in any base $b, 2 <= b <= 16$. Another application shows the use of stack operations to remove the first occurrence of an item in a stack.

- When we introduced recursion in Chapter 3, we gave no indication of how programming languages implement recursion. In fact, its implementation is quite simple and uses a stack. The system maintains a stack of activation records that specify the function arguments, the local variables or objects, and the return address. The system pushes an activation record when calling a function and pops it when returning.

- There are a number of ways to implement a stack. One of the simplest is to include a vector object by using object composition. To implement push(), apply push_back() to the vector; to implement pop(), apply pop_back() to the vector. Implement top() by using the vector back() operation. For empty() and size(), execute the corresponding operations on the vector object. Section 7-3 applies this technique to develop the miniStack class. Unlike the standard library stack class, miniStack throws an underflowError exception if pop() or top() is applied to an empty stack. The section also discusses how STL implements a very general stack class by using two template arguments, the first of which specifies the sequence container to include by object composition. The available containers are vector, deque, and list.

- Postfix, or RPN, expression notation places the operator after its operands. Some calculators use this notation, and it has other applications. A postfix expression is easy to evaluate, using a single stack to hold operands. The rules are simple: Immediately push an operand onto the stack. For a binary operator, pop the stack twice to obtain its operands, perform the operation, and push the result onto the stack. At the end of a properly formed postfix expression, a single value remains on the stack. This is the value of the expression. It is possible to have too many operators (pop() needed, but the stack is empty) or too many operands (final stack has more than one entry). Section 7-4 carefully designs the postfixEval class to perform postfix expression evaluation and throws the expressionError exception if an error occurs.

- Infix notation is the most commonly used expression format. In this notation, a binary operator appears between its operands. Most programming languages and calculators use infix notation. The notation is more complex than postfix, because it requires the use of operator precedence and parentheses. In addition, some operators are left associative, and a few are right associative. Section 7-5 presents an algorithm for converting an infix expression into the equivalent postfix form. The algorithm uses a single stack that holds operators and the left-parenthesis symbols. Associated with each of these symbols is its input and stack precedence. Applying a set of rules defines the algorithm, and we carefully motivate each rule by an example. The class infix2Postfix applies the algorithm to convert an infix expression into postfix form. Using the concept of rank, the class performs error checking and throws the expressionError exception if an error occurs.

CLASSES IN THE CHAPTER

Name	Header File
infix2Postfix	d_inftop.h
miniStack	d_stack.h
postfixEval	d_rpn.h
stack	<stack>
vector	<vector>
writeArray()	d_util.h
expression Symbol	d_expsym.h

REVIEW EXERCISES

1. Circle all that apply. A stack is a structure that relies upon which of the following implementations?

   (a) first-in/last-out   **(b)** last-in/first-out   **(c)** first-come-first-serve
   (d) first-in/first-out   **(e)** last-in/last-out

2. What is the output from the following sequence of stack operations?

```
stack<int> s;
int x = 3, y = 5;

s.push(8);
s.push(x);
s.push(y);
x = s.top();
s.pop();
cout << x << endl;          // Output 1 _____
y = s.top();
cout << y << endl;          // Output 2 _____
s.pop();
s.push(25);
while (!s.empty())
{  y = s.top();
   s.pop();
   cout << y << "   ";      // Output 3 _____
}
```

3. **(a)** Describe the ordering in the integer vector v after function f() has been executed.

```
void f(vector<int>& v)
{  stack<int> s;
```

```
        int i;

        for (i = 0; i < v.size(); i++)
            s.push(v[i]);

        i = 0;
        while (!s.empty())
        {   v[i] = s.top();
            s.pop();
            i++;
        }
    }
```

(b) What is the ordering of the vector if the while loop is altered as follows?

```
        i = v.size()-1;
        while (!s.empty())
        {
            v[i] = s.top();
            s.pop();
            i--;
        }
```

4. Trace the upcoming program, and answer parts (a) and (b). Assume that function output-Stack() pops successive elements from the stack and displays them.

```
    #include <iostream>
    #include <stack>

    using namespace std;

    template <typename T>
    void f(stack<T>& s, stack<T>& t, int n);

    int main()
    {
        int arr[5] = {2, 1, 7, 4, 3}, i;
        stack<int> s, t; // declare two stack objects

        for (i = 0; i < 5; i++)
            s.push(arr[i]);

        f(s,t,4);
        outputStack(t);

        return 0;
    }

    template <typename T>
    void f(stack<T>& s, stack<T>& t, const T& item)
    {
        T svalue;
```

```
    while(!s.empty())
    {
        svalue = s.top();
        s.pop();
        if (svalue < item)
            t.push(svalue);
    }
}
```

   (a) What is displayed by outputStack()?
   (b) Assume that array *arr* has initial values {5, 30, 25, 10, 20} and f() is called with arguments f(s, t, 20). What is displayed by outputStack?

5. The miniStack and the standard library stack class use a sequence container for the implementation of the stack interface. As such, they are said to be _____ classes.

6. In a for loop, the first three elements of miniStack object s are popped and output on a separate line. Write a code segment to do this that uses the C++ constructs try and catch. The code must output an error message and terminate the program if a pop() operation occurs with an empty stack.

7. Implement a function bottom() that returns the element on the bottom of a nonempty stack:

```
// return true if the stack is not empty and assign the
// bottom of the stack to last. return false if the stack
// is empty. note that bottom() does not modify the stack
template <typename T>
bool bottom(const stack<T>& s, T& last);
```

8. Write the following infix expression in postfix form:

$$a*(b + c*d)/e$$

9. Write the following postfix expression in infix form:

$$8 a * bb * + cd+ /e+$$

10. Draw the sequence of stack configurations in the evaluation of the following postfix expression:

$$2\ 3\ 5\ *\ \%\ 6 +$$

11. Draw the sequence of stack configurations and the developing output string in the conversion of the following infix expression to postfix:

$$5 + (2 + 3) * 6$$

Answers to Review Exercises

1. (a), (b)
2. Output 1: 5   Output 2: 3   Output 3: 25 8
3. **(a)** $v = \{25,\ 18,\ 27,\ 15,\ 6,\ 9,\ 2,\ 5\}$
   (b) $v = \{5,\ 2,\ 9,\ 6,\ 15,\ 27,\ 18,\ 25\}$
4. 2 1 3
   5 10

5. adapter

6.
```
for (i=0; i < 3; i++)
{
    try
    {
      cout << s.top() << endl;
      s.pop();
    }

    catch (const underflowError& ue)
    {
      cout << ue.what() << endl;
      exit(1);
    }
}
```

7.
```
template <typename T>
    bool bottom(const stack<T>& s, T& last)
    {
        // record the size of s
        int size = s.size(), i;
        // make a copy of s. we cannot alter s
        stack<T> tmpStack = s;
        // assigned the return value
        bool retval;
        if (size == 0)
            // stack is empty. return false
            retval = false;
        else
        {
            // pop off all but the last element of tmpStack
            for (i=0;i < size-1;i++)
              tmpStack.pop();
            // assign last the remaining element, and indicate
            // we are successful
            last = tmpStack.top();
            retval = true;
        }

        return retval;
    }
```

8. $a\ b\ c\ d* + *e\ /$

9. $(8*a + b*b)/(c + d) + e$

10.

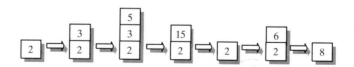

11.

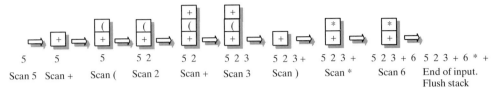

5	5	5	5 2	5 2	5 2 3	5 2 3 +	5 2 3 +	5 2 3 + 6	5 2 3 + 6 * +
Scan 5	Scan +	Scan (	Scan 2	Scan +	Scan 3	Scan)	Scan *	Scan 6	End of input. Flush stack

WRITTEN EXERCISES

12. Give two applications for stacks in a computer program.

13. What is the output from the following sequence of stack operations?

```
stack<int> intStack;
int x, y = 3;

intStack.push(8);
intStack.push(9);
intStack.push(y);
x = intStack.top();
intStack.pop();
intStack.push(18);
x = intStack.top();
intStack.pop();
intStack.push(22);
while (!intStack.empty())
{   y = intStack.top();
    intStack.pop();
    cout << y << " ";
}
cout << x << endl;
```

14. List the elements on the stack after each operation:

```
stack<int> intStack;
int i;

intStack.push(8);
intStack.push(5);
intStack.push(3);
intStack.push(intStack.top());
intStack.push(intStack.top() * 2);
i = intStack.top();
intStack.pop();
intStack.push(2*i);
```

15. Write a function

```
template <typename T>
void stackClear(stack<T>& s);
```

that clears a stack *s*. Why is it critical that *s* be passed by reference?

16. What is the action of the following code segment?

```
stack<T> s1, s2, tmp;
T x;
...
while (!s1.empty())
{
    x = s1.top();
    s1.pop();
    tmp.push(x);
}


// assume s2 is empty
while (!tmp.empty())
{
    x = tmp.top();
    tmp.pop();
    s1.push(x);
    s2.push(x);
}
```

17.(a) Write a function

```
template <typename T>
T second(const stack<T>& s);
```

that uses stack operations to return the second element on the stack. Note: If s.size() <2, throw the exception underflowError.

(b) Write a function

```
template <typename T>
void n2top(stack<T>& s, int n);
```

that moves the *n*th element (counting from the top, which is element 1) of the stack to the top, leaving the order of all other elements unchanged. For instance, the figure illustrates the action of *n*2top() for an integer stack and *n* = 4.

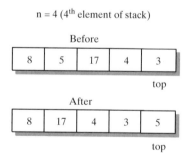

18. The function f() uses a second stack to modify the contents of an initial stack *s*:

```
template <typename T>
void f(stack<T>& s, const T& item)
{
```

```
stack<T> tmpStack;
T tmpVal;
bool have = true;

while (!s.empty() && s.top() != item)
{
   tmpVal = s.top();
   s.pop();
   tmpStack.push(tmpVal);
}

if (s.empty() == true)
   have = false;
else
   s.pop();

while (!tmpStack.empty())
{
   s.push(tmpStack.top());
   tmpStack.pop();
}

if (have)
   s.push(item);
}
```

Assume that *s* has the values

$$1 \; 5 \; 8 \; 10 \; 15 \; 22 \; 55$$

where 55 is on top of the stack. After executing

```
f(s, 5);
```

what is the output from the statements

```
while (!s.empty())
{
   cout << s.top() << " ";
   s.pop();
}
```

19. Trace the function f():

```
template <typename T>
void f(stack<T>& s)
{
   vector<T> v;
   int i;

   while (!s.empty())
   {
      v.push_back(s.top());
      s.pop();
   }
```

```
    for(i=0;i < v.size();i++)
        s.push(v[i]);
}
```

Assume that *s* has the values 3 4 9 12 15 8 3 5, where 5 is on the top of the stack. What is the output from the following statements?

```
f(s);
while (!s.empty())
{   cout << s.top() << " ";
    s.pop();
}
```

20. A classical implementation of a stack uses a static array to hold the elements. Consider the following bstack (bounded stack) class declaration.

```
// number of elements in the array that implements the stack.
// value is global, so it is accessible to any calling block
// and to all bstack objects, independent of their type
const int MAXSTACKSIZE = 50;

template <typename T>
class bstack
{
    public:
        bstack();
            // constructor. create an empty stack

        void push(const T& item);
            // push item onto the top of the stack.
            // Precondition: stack not full.
            // throws overflowError exception if stack is full.
            // Postcondition: the stack has a new topmost element
            // and the stack size increases by 1

        void pop();
            // remove the item from the top of the stack.
            // Precondition: the stack is not empty.
            // if the stack is empty, the function throws
            // the underflowError exception

        T& top();
            // return a reference to the element on the top
            // of the stack.
            // Precondition:. the stack is not empty.
            // if the stack is empty, the function throws
            // the underflowError exception
        const T& top() const;
            // constant version of top()

        bool empty() const;
            // determine whether the stack is empty
```

```
    int size() const;
        // return the number of elements in the stack

    bool full() const;
        // return true if stack has MAXSTACKSIZE elements

  private:
      // array holds the stack elements
      T stackList[MAXSTACKSIZE];
      // topIndex is the index of the stack's top
      int topIndex;
};
```

The constructor initializes top $= -1$, and the implementation of push() and pop()are outlined as follows:

push():
```
    topIndex++;
    stacklist[topIndex] = item;
```

pop():
```
    topIndex--;
```

Implement the bstack class.

21. Convert the following infix expressions to postfix:
  (a) $a + b*c$
  (b) $(a + b)/(d - e)$
  (c) $(b\textasciicircum 2 - 4*a* c)/(2*a)$

22. Write the following expressions in infix form:
  (a) $a\,b + c\,*$
  (b) $a\,b\,c + *$
  (c) $a\,b\,c\,de + + * * ef - *$

23. Draw the sequence of stack configurations in the evaluation of the following postfix expression:

$$4\ 5\ *\ 6\ 3\ +\ /\ 8\ +$$

24. Draw the sequence of stack configurations and the developing output string in the conversion of the following infix expression to postfix:

$$7*(5 + 2*3) - 2$$

PROGRAMMING EXERCISES

25. Prompt for an integer value n, and read n integers into a vector. Cycle through the vector from location 0 to location size() $-$ 1, and push each element onto a stack. Output the original vector using writeVector() from "d_util.h," and then output the stack by popping the elements. Of course, the second output lists the elements in reverse order.

26. Use the function second() from Written Exercise 7-17(a). Write a program that enters five integer values and pushes them onto a stack. The program should output the first and second element on the stack. Flush the stack, and output its elements.

27. Use the function n2top() from Written Exercise 7-17(b). Write a program that enters five integer values and pushes them onto a stack. The program should execute each of the following actions:
    a.   Move the second element to the top of the stack, leaving all elements beneath it unchanged. Output its value.
    b.   Move the last element of the stack to the top. Output its value.
    c.   Flush the stack, and output its elements.

28. A stack can be used to recognize certain types of patterns. Consider the pattern STRING1#STRING2, where neither string contains "#" and STRING2 must be the reverse of STRING1. For instance, the string 1&A#A&1 matches the pattern, but the string 1&A#1&A does not. Write a program that reads strings until the user enters an empty string. The program should then indicate whether each string matches the pattern.

29. Place your implementation of the array-based stack in Written Exercise 7-20 in the header file "bstack.h." Use the class to run Program 7-1.

30. Write a program that prompts for a file name and then reads the file to check for balanced curly braces, { }; parentheses, ( ); and square brackets, [ ]. Use a stack to store the most recent unmatched left symbol. The program should ignore any character that is not a parenthesis, curly brace, or square bracket. Note that proper nesting is required. For instance, [a(b]c) is invalid.

31. Use the following skeleton to form a program:

```
int main()
{
    string infixExp, rpnExp;
    ...
    return 0;
}
```

The program should input the string infixExp and an equivalent postfix expression rpnExp. Evaluate the postfix expression, and output the result. Convert the infix expression to postfix, evaluate the postfix equivalent, and output the result. Run the program three times, using the following strings for the first run:

infixExp: 8 + 2 ^ 3 ^ 2   rpnExp: 8 2 3 2 ^ ^ +

PROGRAMMING PROJECTS

32. A deque can be used to store two stacks. One stack updates its elements with push_front()/pop_front(), and the other stack uses push_back()/pop_back(). Of course, a count of the number of elements in each stack must be maintained.

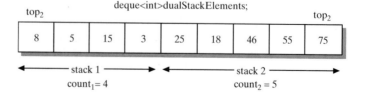

(a) In the header file "dualstk.h," implement the class dualStack whose declaration is given by

```
enum stackNumber {One, Two};
template <typename T>
class dualStack
{
   public:
      dualStack();
         // constructor. set counts to 0

      void push(const T& item, stackNumber n);
      void pop(stackNumber n);

      T& top(stackNumber n);
      const T& top(stackNumber n) const;

      bool empty(stackNumber n) const;
      int size(stackNumber n) const;

   private:
      deque<T> dualStackElements;
      int count1, count2;
};
```

(b) Write a program that reads a sequence of 20 integers, pushing all of the even integers onto one stack and all the odd integers onto the other. Output the contents of each stack by popping elements until it is empty.

33. Extend the class postfixEval by adding the unary minus, represented by the symbol @. For example, the expression @

$$"7 @ 9 +"$$

has value 2, because in RPN, the operator follows the operand(s). Place the class in the header file "xrpn.h". Test the class by placing Example 7-5 in a complete program. Your run must include the expressions

$$7 @ 9 +$$

and the postfix equivalent of the infix expression

$$@7 + (@4 + 9)*2$$

◆

CHAPTER 8

Queues and Priority Queues

OBJECTIVES

- To study the queue ADT and understand that a queue is a FIFO structure.
- To be able to use the STL queue API in applications.
- To understand the radix sort algorithm and note its running time relationship to other sorting algorithms.
- To study the implementation of the miniQueue class using the STL list class and to see how really simple it is.
- To see how STL implements the queue class by using either a list or a deque. (Optional)
- To experience a significant application of a queue by studying a program that simulates the operation of an automated car wash.
- To become familiar with the classical implementation of a bounded queue that treats an array as a circular structure.
- To understand the priority queue ADT and its applications.
- To become familiar with the STL priority_queue API and to note that its push() and pop() operations have running time $O(\log_2 n)$.
- To study an $O(n \log_2 n)$ sorting algorithm that uses a priority queue.
- To study the application of a priority queue to a problem in resource allocation for a secretarial pool.

OUTLINE

In Chapter 7, we developed the stack class, which allows elements to be accessed and updated at only one end of the sequence. In this chapter, we introduce a queue that is an analogous structure, but with operations at both ends of the sequence. A real-world example of a queue is the checkout line at a grocery store. Customers enter the checkout (waiting) line at the back, and the clerk serves them one by one from the front of the line (Figure 8-1).

Section 8-1 presents the queue ADT, which STL implements in the queue class. You will quickly discover the similarities between the queue and the stack interfaces. Most of the focus is on applications that illustrate the use of queues. A very interesting example is the sorting algorithm known as the radix sort. Rather than comparing elements within a sequence, the algorithm repeatedly uses a set of queues to partition the elements into progressively more ordered sublists.

As with other containers, we develop a miniQueue class that implements the queue ADT, using a sequential list. An optional section indicates how STL actually implements the queue class.

Simulation studies are a primary application for queues. A time-driven simulation is a study of a system over an interval of time. For instance, a bank might develop a simulation study that models the flow of customers in and out of the bank. The study could evaluate average customer waiting time, teller workload, and so forth. Section 8-4 provides a case study that simulates the arrival of customers and the flow of their cars through a drive-through car wash. The study evaluates the overall performance of the car wash.

The queue ADT assumes an unbounded sequence (waiting line). In some applications, a queue models a storage structure that has limited space. Section 8-5 discusses the implementation of a queue using an array of fixed size. In this situation, the queue can fill up. The implementation introduces a circular model of a queue.

In Section 8-6, we develop a variation of a queue, called a *priority queue*, that removes the item of highest priority from a container, rather than simply the first item in the sequence. The STL class priority_queue implements the ADT. The priority-queue container provides an efficient algorithm for sorting a vector. It also applies to situations where one activity should be performed before others. The section develops an application that models the control of work flow within a secretarial pool.

Figure 8-1
Grocery store checkout line as a model for a queue

8-1 THE QUEUE ADT

A *queue* is a sequential storage structure that permits access only at the two ends of the sequence. We refer to the ends of the sequence as the *front* and *back* (Figure 8-2). A queue inserts new elements at the back and removes elements from the front of the sequence.

Figure 8-2
A queue

The queue ADT provides essentially the same interface as does the stack. This is consistent with STL's philosophy to use a common interface for its classes. Hence, you will recognize the queue operations size(), push(), pop(), and empty() from the stack ADT. The operation push() adds an element at the back of the queue. The operation pop() removes the first element (front) of the queue. To access or modify the first element, the queue ADT provides the function front(). Figure 8-3 illustrates the push() and pop() operations.

You will note that a queue removes elements in the same order in which they were stored, and hence a queue provides *FIFO* (first-in/first-out), or *FCFS* (first-come/first-served), ordering. Applications use a queue to retrieve items in their order of occurrence. The abstract concept of a queue allows for an arbitrarily large sequence of data. Hence, the push() operation has no precondition. The same is not true for the functions pop() and front(), which assume that the queue has at least one element (i.e., the queue is not empty). The following is an API for a queue.

CLASS queue	**Constructor**	**<queue>**

queue();
    Create an empty queue.

CLASS queue	*Operations*	*<queue>*

bool **empty**() *const*;
    Check whether the queue is empty. Return true if it is empty, and false otherwise.

T& **front**();
    Return a reference to the value of the item at the front of the queue.
    Precondition: The queue is not empty.

const T& **front**() *const*;
    Constant version of front().

void **pop**();
    Remove the item from the front of the queue.
    Precondition: The queue is not empty.
    Postcondition: The element at the front of the queue is the element that was added immediately after the element just popped, or the queue is empty.

void **push**(*const T& item*);
>   Insert the argument *item* at the back of the queue.
>   Postcondition: The queue has a new item at the back.

int **size**() *const*;
>   Return the number of elements in the queue.

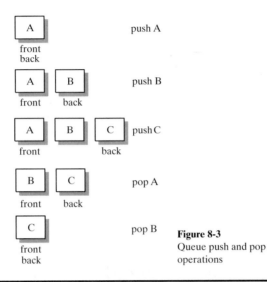

Figure 8-3
Queue push and pop
operations

Example 8-1

This example illustrates the operations in the queue ADT. From push(), the queue contains
the values 2, 3, and 99, from front to back. A loop outputs the elements in the queue by calling front() to access the value of the first element and then deletes the element with a pop().
The loop terminates when the queue is empty.

```
queue<int> q;

q.push(2);
q.push(3);
q.push(99);

while (!q.empty())
{
   cout << q.front() << "   ";
   q.pop();
}
```

Output: 2   3   99

Application: Scheduling Queue

Let us look at one of the main applications of a queue, namely a *process*, or *task*, *scheduler*. An executive secretary for a personnel director schedules a series of job interviews for applicants seeking an open position. The secretary uses a queue to store the starting times for the interviews. The figure illustrates a schedule of eight appointments beginning at 9:00 AM. The last appointment begins at 16:30 (4:30 PM). Because the office closes at 5:00 PM, the last appointment lasts at most for 30 minutes. Throughout the day, the director begins each interview by popping the queue and then calling front() to identify the time for the next interview. The information enables the director to determine the amount of time available for the interview.

Appointment Schedule

9:00	10:15	11:15	13:00	13:45	14:30	15:30	16:30

front   back

PROGRAM 8-1   JOB INTERVIEW SCHEDULING

The following program implements the interview scheduler. A prompt asks the executive secretary to input the time for the first interview, and then a loop continues to prompt for input of subsequent interview times. Input terminates when the secretary enters a time at or after 5:00 PM. A loop executes pop() operations until the queue is empty. Each iteration outputs the time that the appointment begins, along with the amount of time available for the director to carry out the interview. When the queue becomes empty, the time for the last interview is the difference between the office-closing time of 5:00 PM and the prior starting time for the last interview.

```cpp
// File: prg8_1.cpp
// the program outputs the interview schedule for a personnel director.
// the executive secretary constructs a queue of appointment times
// by reading the times from the keyboard. by cycling through the
// queue, the secretary outputs the time at which each appointment
// begins and the available time until the next scheduled
// appointment. the last interview ends at 5:00 PM

#include <iostream>
#include <iomanip>
#include <queue>

#include "d_time24.h"

using namespace std;

int main()
{
    time24 interviewTime;
    // queue to hold appointment time for job applicants
    queue<time24> apptQ;
```

```
   cout << "First interview of the day:   ";
   cin >> interviewTime;

   // construct the queue until input is 5:00 PM or later
   while (interviewTime < time24(17,0))
   {
      // push the interview time on the queue
      apptQ.push(interviewTime);

      // prompt for the next interview time
      cout << "Next interview: ";
      cin >> interviewTime;
   }

   // output the day's appointment schedule
   cout << endl << "Appointment    Available Interview Time" << endl;

   // pop the next applicant appointment time and determine available
   // time for interview by checking time for applicant at the front
   // of the queue
   while (!apptQ.empty())
   {
      interviewTime = apptQ.front();
      apptQ.pop();

      // output available time. if the queue is empty,
      // the interview ends at 5:00 PM
      cout << "  " << interviewTime << setw(17) << "  ";
      if (apptQ.empty())
         cout << (time24(17,0) - interviewTime) << endl;
      else
         cout << (apptQ.front() - interviewTime) << endl;
   }
   return 0;
}
```

```
Run:

First interview of the day: 9:00
Next interview: 10:15
Next interview: 11:15
Next interview: 13:00
Next interview: 13:45
Next interview: 14:30
Next interview: 15:30
Next interview: 16:30
Next interview: 17:00           // 17:00 (5:00 PM) terminates input
```

Appointment	Available Interview Time
9:00	1:15
10:15	1:00
11:15	1:45
13:00	0:45
13:45	0:45
14:30	1:00
15:30	1:00
16:30	0:30

8-2   THE RADIX SORT

In the early days of computing, data were stored on punched cards. To order the data, an operator ran the cards through a mechanical sorter. For integer data, the machine dropped each card into one of 10 bins that represented the digits 0–9. Each bin was a queue in which a card entered at the back and exited at the front. The mechanical sorter implemented the radix sort algorithm. To explain the process, we assume the cards contain two-digit numbers in the range 00–99. The numbers (cards) pass through the machine twice to separate the data, first by the ones digit and then by the tens digit. Each pass involves first distributing the cards into the bins and then collecting them back into a sequence.

Initial sequence: 91 6 85 15 92 35 30 22 39

Pass 0: Distribute the cards into bins according to the ones digit (10^0) .

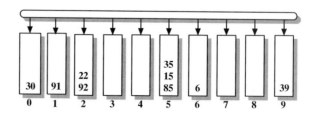

Hence, 30 falls into bin 0, 91 falls into bin 1, 92 and 22 fall into bin 2, and so forth. Collect the numbers from the bins in the order 0 to 9. This determines a sequence that is in order by the ones digit.

Sequence after pass 0:   30 91 92 22 85 15 35 6 39

Pass 1: Take the new sequence and distribute the cards into bins determined by the tens digit (10^1).

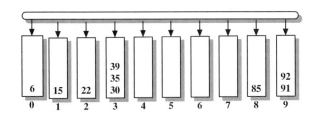

(margin handwritten notes: phase based on 10's digit. Remove in new order. Sorted! 1 digit)

Collect the cards from the bins in the order 0 to 9.

Sequence after pass 1:   6 15 22 30 35 39 85 91 92   (Sorted sequence)

A little intuitive analysis indicates why the process sorts the numbers after two passes. At the completion of pass 1, the sequence is ordered with elements distributed in groups with the zeros (range from 00 to 09), followed by the tens (range from 10 to 19), 20's, and so forth. Thus, any two numbers with different tens digits, such as 35 and 92, will be in the proper relative order, since the operator collects numbers from the 3 bin before numbers from the 9 bin. The analysis reduces to considering numbers with the same tens digit. Pass 0 deals with their ordering. To see this, consider the partially ordered sequence that results from pass 0. This sequence is divided into groups with all numbers ending in 0 located at the start of the sequence, followed by the group of numbers ending in 1, and so forth. In our example, for instance, the original sequence contains three numbers in the thirties, 30, 35, and 39. Pass 0 produces a partially ordered sequence in some manner like

Partially Ordered List After Pass 0

As these numbers move through the sorter on pass 1, they drop into the 3 bin in the order 30, 35, and 39. A similar situation occurs in the other bins. Pass 1 produces an ordered list of two-digit numbers .

Ordered List After Pass 1

6	15	22	30 35 39		85	91 92
0's	10's	20's	30's		80's	90's

Radix Sort Algorithm

We can extend the sorting process for two-digit numbers to d-digit numbers, $d >= 1$, by performing d passes. Recall that a base-10 number with d digits is a sum of products of its digits with powers of 10. Each digit x_i is in the range from 0 through 9.

$$value = x_{d-1}10^{d-1} + x_{d-2}10^{d-2} + \cdots + x_2 10^2 + x_1 10^1 + x_0 10^0$$

The first pass sorts by the ones digit (power 10^0), the second by the tens digit (power 10^1), the third by the hundreds digit (power 10^2), and so forth. The function radix-Sort() implements the algorithm. It requires as arguments an integer vector v and the maximum number of digits d of any integer in the vector:

```
// sort v using the radix sort. each integer has
// d digits
void radixSort(vector<int>& v, int d);
```

In the implementation, an array of 10 queues simulates the sorting bins 0 to 9.

```
queue<int> digitQueue[10];
```

The radixSort() function must execute d iterations, one for each digit. The ith iteration collects the numbers into digitQueue by using the digit corresponding to the power 10^i. For $i = 0$, collect the numbers into the queues according to the digit with power $10^0 = 1$. For $i=1$, collect the numbers into the queues according to the digit with power $10^1 = 10$, and so forth. Divide a number by the power, and take the remainder after division by 10 to obtain the required digit. For instance, suppose the number is 34,758 and *power* = 1000. Dividing by 1000 cuts off the low three digits, leaving a result of 34. Obtain the digit in the thousands position by finding the remainder after division by 10.

```
34758/1000 = 34,     34 % 10 = 4
```

The digit identifies the queue into which the algorithm should push the number:

```
digitQueue[(v[i] / power) % 10].push(v[i]);
```

The function distribute() implements the distribution of the numbers into the 10 queues. The arguments include the vector of elements, the queue containers, and the power that designates which digit defines the allocation of a number to a queue.

distribute():
```
// distribute vector elements into one of 10 queues
// using the digit corresponding to power
// power = 1     ==> 1's digit
// power = 10    ==> 10's digit
// power = 100   ==> 100's digit
// ...
void distribute(const vector<int>& v, queue<int> digitQueue[],
                int power)
{
    int i;

    // loop through the vector, inserting each element into
    // the queue (v[i] / power) % 10
    for (i = 0; i < v.size(); i++)
        digitQueue[(v[i] / power) % 10].push(v[i]);
}
```

After distribution of the numbers into the queues, the function collect() scans the array of queues in the order from 0 to 9 and moves all items from the queues back into the vector:

collect():

```
// gather elements from the queues and copy back to the vector
void collect(queue<int> digitQueue[], vector<int>& v)
{
    int i = 0, digit;
    // scan the vector of queues using indices 0, 1, 2, etc.
    for (digit = 0; digit < 10; digit++)
        // collect items until queue empty and copy items back
        // to the vector
        while (!digitQueue[digit].empty())
        {
            v[i] = digitQueue[digit].front();
            digitQueue[digit].pop();
            i++;
        }
}
```

The function radixSort() simply calls distribute(), followed by collect(), for power = 1, 10, 100, ..., 10^{d-1}.

radixSort():

```
// sort v using the radix sort. each integer has d digits
void radixSort(vector<int>& v, int d)
{
    int i;
    int power = 1;
    queue<int> digitQueue[10];

    for (i=0;i < d;i++)
    {
        distribute(v, digitQueue, power);
        collect(digitQueue, v);
        power *= 10;
    }
}
```

For convenience, we place the function radixSort() and its two support functions in the header file "d_sort.h."

PROGRAM 8-2   RADIX SORT

This program performs a radix sort for a vector intVector of five-digit integers. A loop assigns 50 random numbers in the range 0–99999 to intVector. The program calls displayVector() to display the sorted vector elements in six columns.

```cpp
// File: prg8_2.cpp
// the program initializes a 50-element vector with five-digit random
// integers in the range 0 to 99,999 and sorts the vector using the
// radix sort. it outputs the numbers in six columns using the
// function displayVector()

#include <iostream>
#include <iomanip>
#include <vector>

#include "d_random.h"
#include "d_sort.h"

using namespace std;

// output v, 6 elements per line
void displayVector(const vector<int>& v);

int main()
{
   // vector to hold the data that is sorted
   vector<int> intVector;
   randomNumber rnd;
   int i;

   // initialize vector with 50 random numbers in range 0 - 99999
   for (i = 0; i < 50; i++)
     intVector.push_back(rnd.random(100000));

   // apply the radix sort and output the sorted vector
   radixSort(intVector, 5);
   displayVector(intVector);

   return 0;
}

void displayVector(const vector<int>& v)
{
    int i;

    for (i=0; i < v.size(); i++)
    {
      // output each element in 12 spaces
      cout << setw(12) << v[i];
      if ((i+1) % 6 == 0)   // newline every 6 numbers
        cout << endl;
    }
    cout << endl;
}
```

```
Run:
     3930        6921        7801       10277       10680       12227
    12850       15897       16273       17178       18226       18702
    20133       20373       24554       26389       26988       27395
    30359       32636       35678       39582       41033       41385
    42447       47526       48484       53883       55710       59465
    59675       60133       64623       68462       70153       71142
    71296       75233       76463       82925       83973       85099
    86845       87009       89763       89832       91424       92877
    94422       95966
```

Efficiency of the Radix Sort   The radix sort orders a vector of size n that contains d-digit integers. Each pass inserts the n numbers into the 10 queues (bins) and then collects the numbers from the queues. The algorithm performs these $2*n$ queue operations d times. Section 8-3 discusses the fact that queue push() and pop() operations have running time O(1). It follows that the complexity of the radix sort for d-digit numbers is $O(2*d *n) = O(n)$. The radix sort is a linear algorithm and does not compare data items with each other. It appears to be superior to most *in-place sorting* algorithms, which reorder the data within the original sequence and do not use temporary storage. The in-place sorts have average-case running times of $O(n^2)$ or $O(n \log_2 n)$. The "superior" quality of the radix sort is deceiving, however, because one measure of the efficiency of an algorithm is the amount of memory it requires. The radix sort requires extra space proportional to the size of the vector that is being sorted. For very large data sets, the extra storage becomes a real liability.

The more general-purpose $O(n \log_2 n)$ algorithms, such as the quicksort, adapt to a broader variety of applications than does the radix sort. On a more technical note, the efficiency of the radix sort, as compared with that of an $O(n \log_2 n)$ sort, can depend on features of the computer hardware. For instance, some systems are more efficient with the division operation and with copying of large blocks of data. Another issue is the number of bins (queues) that are required. With integers, 10 queues are sufficient, but the algorithm would require almost 100 separate queues for arbitrary strings. The number of bins does affect the efficiency of the radix sort.

IMPLEMENTING THE MINIQUEUE CLASS   8-3

In Section 7-3, we develop the miniStack class, which illustrates how STL implements its stack class. We use a vector object by composition as the underlying storage structure. The member functions, such as size() and empty(), of a miniStack object actually reflect the status of the underlying vector. To access or modify the top of the stack or to add and remove an element at the top, the miniStack class uses the functions back(), push_back(), and pop_back() from the vector class.

We use the same approach with the miniQueue class. However, rather than using a vector to store the data, we use a list object, qlist. The reason is simple. A vector has operations that access the back of the sequence, but it does not efficiently remove an element at the front. The list class operation front() accesses the front of the sequence, and the function pop_front() efficiently removes it. These operations provide a simple implementation of the queue front() and pop() functions. The list class also has the function push_back(), which efficiently inserts an element at the back of the sequence. We will use this function to implement the queue push() operation. The list interface is ideal for the miniQueue class, because it has all of the operations that can efficiently implement the queue interface.

To understand how a list can represent a queue, think of the elements of the queue as organized horizontally in a waiting line. Initially, the queue is empty and the size of the list is 0. You may add items to the back of the list (push_back()), which increases the size by 1. You can also remove an item from the front of the list (pop_front()), which decreases the size by 1. At all times, we know the element at the front of the list (front()). We also know the size of the queue and whether it is empty, by extracting this information from the underlying list object.

Example 8-2

___

In this example, the miniQueue object miniQ holds integer values. A series of statements uses miniQueue operations. The following figure displays the resulting state of the queue and the underlying list, along with the list statement that implements the queue operation .

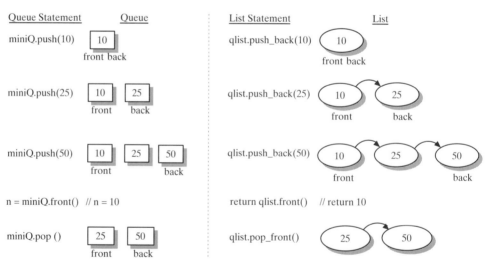

The upcoming code is a partial declaration of the miniQueue class that features the constructor and private section. You are familiar with the operations push(), pop(), front(), size(), and empty() from the API for the STL queue class.

___

CLASS miniQueue	Declaration	"d_queue.h"

```
template<typename T>
class miniQueue
{

   public:
     miniQueue();
        // constructor; create an empty queue


        . . .
        // member functions push(), pop(), front(), size(), empty()

   private:
     list<T> qlist;
        // a list object maintains the queue items and size
};
```

Implement the functions empty() and size() by returning the result from a call to the corresponding list functions. In the case of push(), insert an item at the back of the queue by placing it at the back of qlist, using push_back().

push():

```
// insert item into the queue by inserting it at
// the back of the list
template<typename T>
void miniQueue<T>::push(const T& item)
{
    qlist.push_back(item);
}
```

The operations pop() and front() require additional logic to test the "queue empty" condition. If the condition is true, the functions throw the underflowError exception specified in the header file "d_except.h." The implementation of front() uses the corresponding list function. Let us look at pop() to see how it performs exception handling:

pop():

```
// remove the element from the front of the queue
template<typename T>
void miniQueue<T>::pop()
{   // if queue is empty, throw underflowError
    if (qlist.size() == 0)
        throw underflowError("miniQueue pop(): empty queue");
    // erase the front
    qlist.pop_front();
}
```

Chapter 9 discusses the implementation of the list class that uses a doubly linked list. The list operations push_back() and pop_front() both have complexity O(1). It follows that the operations push() and pop() in the miniQueue class also have complexity O(1).

Implementation of the STL queue Class (Optional)

The STL queue class design is almost identical to that of the stack class (Section 7-3). A programmer can select the underlying storage container for the queue element. The choice can be any container that supports the operations size(), empty(), push_back(), front(), and pop_front(), because these are the operations that implement the queue's interface. A list is just such a container. On the other hand, a vector does not have the pop_front() operation and hence cannot be used as the underlying storage structure. Another container that effectively implements a queue is the deque. We have briefly discussed this data structure in Section 7-3 as one possible implementation structure for a stack. A deque is a direct-access container that supports O(1) insert and erase operations at both ends of the sequence. That is, the container implements efficient push_front()/pop_front() and push_back()/pop_back() operations. The term *deque* refers to the fact that it is a "double-ended queue." By default, STL uses the deque container to store queue elements.

Example 8-3

This example illustrates how a programmer can declare an STL queue object with either a list or a deque container to store the elements. The queue, qList, uses a list container, while the deque, qDeque, uses a deque container. In a loop, prompt the user for an integer value greater than or equal to 0. Terminate the loop upon input of 0. Add each even number to qList and each odd number to qDeque. On termination of the loop, display the values in each queue by clearing (popping) the elements.

```
queue<int,list<int> > qList;
queue<int,deque<int> > qDeque;
int value;

cout << "Enter an integer > 0 or 0 to quit: ";
cin >> value;

while (value != 0)
{

   if (value % 2 == 0)
     qList.push(value);
   else
     qDeque.push(value);

   cout << "Enter an integer > 0 or 0 to quit: ";
   cin >> value;
}
cout << endl << "Even numbers: ";
```

```
while (!qList.empty())
{   cout << qList.front() << "   ";
    qList.pop();
}
cout << endl << endl;

cout << "Odd numbers: ";
while (!qDeque.empty())
{
    cout << qDeque.front() << "   ";
    qDeque.pop();
}
cout << endl;
```

```
Run:

Enter an integer > 0 or 0 to quit: 3
Enter an integer > 0 or 0 to quit: 2
Enter an integer > 0 or 0 to quit: 8
Enter an integer > 0 or 0 to quit: 12
Enter an integer > 0 or 0 to quit: 35
Enter an integer > 0 or 0 to quit: 88
Enter an integer > 0 or 0 to quit: 5
Enter an integer > 0 or 0 to quit: 0

Even numbers: 2   8   12   88

Odd numbers: 3   35   5
```

The complexities of the STL queue class operations are O(1), because either a list or a deque has push_back() and pop_front() operations that are O(1).

Whether to Use a List or a Deque The list-class implementation adds each item to the list as an individual element. As pop() operations erase elements, the list class reclaims the memory and efficiently reuses it for subsequent insertions. By contrast, a deque allocates memory in blocks and performs insert and erase operations in a fashion similar to that for a vector. Generally, the deque implementation will be faster. However, the programmer should try the application both ways and determine which implementation performs the best.

Note

CASE STUDY: TIME-DRIVEN SIMULATION   8-4

A time-driven simulation is a study of a system over an interval of time. The purpose of the study is to evaluate how different values for key components affect the over-all efficiency of the system. In this application, customers bring their cars to a drive-through car wash. To simplify the statistics and allow us to focus on the simulation aspect, we assume that each car wash takes a fixed amount of time and that the like-lihood that a customer arrives at any minute during the simulation is a fixed proba-bility. For instance, if the probability is 25%, then there is a one in four chance that a customer arrives at any given minute. Put another way, one customer is likely to ar-rive every four minutes. During the simulation, of course, we will observe times when customers arrive on successive minutes and times when long gaps separate the ar-rivals. The assumptions for arrival and service times do not provide a realistic model for the car wash. In reality, the simulation should use more sophisticated probability measures such as the Poisson distribution of average arrival time. Our assumptions do not appreciably alter the overall design of the simulation, but they do simplify the implementation. The simulation seeks to identify the number of customers that ar-rive, the longest waiting time for a customer, the average time each customer must wait, and the percentage of time the automated equipment is utilized.

Let's speculate how different values might affect the efficiency of the system. Assume that, on average, one customer arrives every 4 minutes. In the simulation, there is a 25% probability that a customer arrives at any minute. If a car wash takes 10 minutes, the system will eventually produce long waiting lines, and the equipment will be busy almost 100% of the time. On the other hand, if the probability of arrival is 5% (an average of one customer every 20 minutes), and a car wash takes 3 min-utes, the system will be underutilized, and the equipment will be idle much of the time. Ideally, arrival times and the time to wash a car should be adjusted so that the system can run more efficiently, with reasonable waiting times for the customers and reasonable utilization of the equipment. The simulation can look at different combi-nations of data to produce greater efficiency.

To design the study, we need to identify objects that describe the customers and performance variables that gather information on the number of customers, the maximum waiting time for a customer, the total wait time for the customers, and the total time the equipment is operating. The simulation continuously updates the per-formance variables as it observes the flow of customers and the washing of cars. At the end of the run, we can provide a summary report of the overall performance of the system.

Simulation Design

In the design of the simulation, we rather impersonally denote a customer as a time24 object. Rather than associating the customer with a name like "Tom," we call the customer "9:15," to designate the time of arrival. We represent the waiting line with a queue of time24 objects.

Customer:
```
time24 carArrival;         // stores time of customer's arrival
queue<time24> waitQueue;   // queue for car arrival objects
```

The simulation runs over an interval of time subdivided into minutes. To main-tain a record of activities, we need a set of objects to identify key times and simula-tion parameters.

Simulation Data:

```
time24 totalWaitTime, maxWaitTime;      // total and max waiting times
time24 totalServiceTime;                // total time equipment used
time24 startTime, endTime;              // times for the simulation

randomNumber rnd;                       // use for arrivals
double probOfArrival;                   // probability customer arrives
int numberOfWashes = 0;                 // number of cars washed
int washTime;                           // fixed time for a wash
```

To execute the simulation, create a loop whose iterations look at the system each minute. The loop runs over the interval [startTime, endTime), with the time incremented in units of one minute. If startTime is 8:00 and endTime is 17:00 (5:00 P.M.), the simulation looks at a car wash over a typical day. Each iteration of the loop simulates the passing of one minute of the work day. Because the time24 class does not implement the ++ operator, the for loop uses the += operator to increment the control variable *t*:

```
for (t = startTime; t < endTime; t += 1)
{
    . . .
}
```

Simulation Implementation

Once the simulation design identifies the key data values and the basic loop design, efforts can focus on implementing the loop algorithm and producing final output. Each loop iteration represents the state of the car wash at any time *t*. An iteration is divided into phases. First, use a random number to determine whether a customer arrives:

```
rnd.frandom() <= probOfArrival
```

If the condition is true, store the current simulation time *t* in the object carArrival, and push it onto the queue. Then look at the activity of the car wash. The simulation uses two objects to monitor the state of the system. The boolean variable washAvailable indicates whether the car wash is currently operating. The time24 object finishWash is the time at which a current car in the wash will complete service. Initially, washAvailable is set to true. When a car enters the wash, set washAvailable to false. When the current simulation time *t* equals finishWash, set washAvailable back to true, because a car has just left the automated system.

```
if (!washAvailable && t == finishWash)
    washAvailable = true;
```

If the simulation recognizes that the car wash is not in use and a customer is waiting (waitQueue.empty() is false), remove the customer (time) at the front of the queue. Assign the value to the time24 object carArrival, because it specifies when the customer first arrived at the car wash. This information and the fact that a car wash takes a fixed amount of time allow the update of the key data for the simulation.

```
// find the waiting time of the next customer
waitTime = t - carArrival;
// update the maximum customer waiting time
if (maxWaitTime < waitTime)
   maxWaitTime = waitTime;
// add waiting time for customer to totalWaitTime.
totalWaitTime += waitTime;
// add time to wash car to totalServiceTime for the equipment
totalServiceTime  += washTime;
// determine the time the car will exit from the wash
finishWash = t + washTime;
// increment the number of customers served
numberOfWashes++;
// set washAvailable to false since equipment back in service
washAvailable = false;
```

When the simulation ends, the output summarizes the key elements of the system. This includes the number of customers served, the maximum customer waiting time, the average waiting time, the percentage of time the equipment is in use, and the number of customers left in the waiting queue.

Example 8-4

Assume that the simulation begins at 8:00 with the probOfArrival = 20% (an average of one customer every 5 minutes) and washTime = 4. The example illustrates how the system would manage hypothetical data during the first 13 minutes of the day. The value of rnd.frandom() is *x*.

Time	*Action*	*Queue*	*System*
8:00	Customer Arrives ($x <= 0.2$) Push 8: 00 on the queue Pop 8:00. Set finishWash to 8:04 maxWaitTime = 0 totalWaitTime = 0 totalServiceTime = 4	8:00 \<empty\>	idle busy
8:01	Customer Arrives (rnd $<= 0.2$) Push 8:01 on the queue	8:01	busy
8:02	No Arrival (rnd > 0.2)	8:01	busy
8:03	Customer Arrives (rnd < 0.2) Push 8:03 on the queue	8:01 8:03	busy
8:04	No arrival (rnd > 0.2) Car Leaves (finishWash $== 8:04$) Pop 8:01. Set finishWash to 8:08	8:01 8:03	busy

Time	Event	Queue	Wash
	maxWaitTime = 3 totalWaitTime = 3 totalServiceTime = 8	8:03	busy
8:05–8:07	No Arrival (rnd > 0.2)	8:03	busy
8:08	No Arrival (rnd > 0.2) Car Leaves (finishWash == 8:08) Pop 8:03. Set finishWash to 8:12	8:03	busy
	maxWaitTime = 5 totalWaitTime = 8 totalServiceTime = 12	<empty>	busy
8:09–8:11	No Arrival (rnd > 0.2)	<empty>	busy
8:12	No Arrival (rnd > 0.2) Car Leaves (finishWash == 8:12) Set washAvailable to true	<empty>	busy
8:13	Customer Arrives (rnd <= 0.2) Push 8:13 on the queue	8:13	idle
	Pop 8:13 Set finishWash = 8:17 maxWaitTime = 5 totalWaitTime = 8 totalServiceTime = 16	<empty>	busy

PROGRAM 8-3   TIME-DRIVEN SIMULATION

The upcoming program asks the user to enter the probability of arrival, the fixed length of time to wash a car, and the starting and ending times for the simulation.

Three runs illustrate the simulation running between the hours of 8:00 AM and 5:00 PM. Run 1 assumes that customers arrive on average every 10 minutes and that a wash takes 11 minutes. The results should indicate that the system backs up customers in the queue, causing a relatively long average waiting time. Run 2 looks at increased activity, where a customer arrives on the average every 5 minutes and takes 3 minutes for a wash. Customers should pass through the system with little wait. The equipment might be underutilized. Run 3 has customers arriving on the average every 4 minutes, with a wash taking 4 minutes to finish.

```
// File: prg8_3.cpp
// the program uses a queue to simulate the flow of customers
// in and out of an automated car wash. prompt the user for the
// fixed probability that a car will arrive at any minute of the
// day and the fixed number of minutes it takes for a
// car wash. also input the opening and closing times. the
// simulation steps from opening to closing time in increments
// of 1 minute. each iteration determines if a car arrives and,
// if so pushes the time of arrival in the queue of waiting
// customers. next, determine whether the car wash is busy. if
// it is avaiable, pop the longest waiting customer from the
// queue and update simulation parameters. when the simulation
// loop terminates, output the accumuated parameters, that
// include the total number of cars washed, the maximum waiting
```

```
// time for a customer, the average customer waiting time, the
// percentage of the day the car wash operates, and the number
// of customers remaining to serve when the car wash closes

#include <iostream>
#include <queue>

#include "d_time24.h"
#include "d_random.h"

using namespace std;

// returns the time t in minutes
int minutes(const time24& t);

int main()
{
   time24 carArrival;                  // stores time of customer's arrival
   queue<time24> waitQueue;            // queue for car arrival objects

   time24 waitTime, maxWaitTime;       // maxWaitTime initially 0: 00
   time24 totalWaitTime;               // total time customers wait
   time24 totalServiceTime;            // total time equipment is in use
   time24 startTime, endTime;          // times for the simulation
   time24 t, finishWash;               // used in simulation loop

   randomNumber rnd;                   // use for random number generation

   double probOfArrival;               // probability customer arrives
   int numberOfWashes = 0;             // number of cars washed in study
   int washTime;                       // fixed time for a wash in minutes

   bool washAvailable = true;          // indicates whether wash available

   // real number output is fixed format, with 1 decimal place
   cout.setf(ios::fixed, ios::floatfield);
   cout.precision(1);

   // series of inputs to customize the simulation run
   cout << "Enter probability of arrival and wash time: ";
   cin >> probOfArrival >> washTime;
   cout << "Enter time to start and end simulation: ";
   cin >> startTime >> endTime;
   cout << endl;

   // loop views and updates system each minute of the study
   for (t = startTime; t < endTime; t  += 1)
   { // if customer arrives; store arrival time in queue
      if(rnd.frandom() <= probOfArrival)
      {
```

```
         carArrival = t;
         waitQueue.push(carArrival);
     }


     // if car finishes wash, indicate wash is available
     if (washAvailable == false && t == finishWash)
         washAvailable = true;


     // if wash is available, get front car from queue
     if (washAvailable)
         if (!waitQueue.empty())
         {
             // pop next car from queue and update data for summary
             carArrival = waitQueue.front();
             waitQueue.pop();

             // find the waiting time of the next customer
             waitTime = t - carArrival;
             // update the maximum customer waiting time
             if (maxWaitTime  < waitTime)
                 maxWaitTime = waitTime;
             // add waiting time for customer to totalWaitTime.
             totalWaitTime  += waitTime;
             // add time to wash car to totalServiceTime for the equipment
             totalServiceTime  += washTime;
             // determine the time the car will exit from the wash
             finishWash = t  + washTime;
             // increment the number of customers served
             numberOfWashes++;
             // set washAvailable to false since equipment back in service
             washAvailable  = false;
         }
     }


     // output the summary data for the simulation including number of cars
     // washed, average customer waiting time and pct of time wash operates
     cout << "Total number of cars washed is " << numberOfWashes << endl;
     cout << "Maximum customer waiting time for a car wash is "
          << minutes(maxWaitTime) << " minutes" << endl;
     cout << "Average customer waiting time for a car wash is "
          << double(minutes(totalWaitTime))/numberOfWashes << "minutes"
          << endl;
     cout << "Percentage of time car wash operates is"
          << double(minutes(totalServiceTime))/minutes(endTime-startTime)*100.0
          << '%' << endl;
     cout << "Number of customers remaining at " << endTime
          << " is " << waitQueue.size() << endl;

     return 0;
}
```

```
int minutes(const time24& t)
{
    return t.getHour() * 60 + t.getMinute();
}
```

```
Run 1:

Enter probability of arrival and wash time: .1 11
Enter time to start and end simulation: 8:00 17:00

Total number of cars washed is 49
Maximum customer waiting time for a car wash is 100 minutes
Average customer waiting time for a car wash is 7.1 minutes
Percentage of time car wash operates is  99.8%
Number of customers remaining at 17:00 is 10

Run 2:

Enter probability of arrival and wash time: .2 3
Enter time to start and end simulation: 8:00 17:00

Total number of cars washed is 123
Maximum customer waiting time for a car wash is 9 minutes
Average customer waiting time for a car wash is 2.2 minutes
Percentage of time car wash operates is  68.3%
Number of customers remaining at 17:00 is 0

Run 3:

Enter probability of arrival and wash time: .25 4
Enter time to start and end simulation: 8:00 17:00

Total number of cars washed is 127
Maximum customer waiting time for a car wash is 29 minutes
Average customer waiting time for a car wash is 7.8 minutes
Percentage of time car wash operates is  94.1%
Number of customers remaining at 17:00 is 1
```

8-5   ARRAY-BASED QUEUE IMPLEMENTATION

Our approach to implementing the miniQueue class in Section 8-3 uses a state-of-the-art object-technology approach. The list container provides member functions that directly support the implementation of a queue. The list storage structure allows a queue to grow as necessary, and so there is no *queue full* condition. For some applications, however, the entries could need to reside in a memory area of fixed size. For instance, a hardware interface often inserts data from a peripheral device into a buffer that resides inside the interface itself. You are familiar with computer video cards that manage the screen. These cards have internal memory (RAM) that serves as the buffer. The amount of RAM, even though it is often four megabytes or more, nonetheless has a fixed size. The interface must organize all queue elements within the fixed-size buffer. For situations like this, a programmer might require a specialized queue that stores data in a fixed-size array. When the array fills up, the *queue full* condition is true (buffer overrun), and no more elements can be inserted into the queue.

In this section, we design a bounded-queue container class called *bqueue*. The implementation of the bounded-queue class introduces you to a classical computer algorithm. Keep in mind that a bounded queue is a modified queue container with only specialized applications. The bqueue class implements the queue ADT by using an array to hold the sequence of items and by declaring array indices that reference the front and back of the queue. The array has a fixed number of elements, specified by the constant MAXQSIZE. If the queue requires more or fewer than this maximum number of elements, change the declaration of MAXQSIZE and recompile the application.

The public interface for the queue class and for the bqueue class are almost identical. A notable difference is the presence of the member function full(), which indicates when the fixed-size array is full. When a program attempts to add an element to a full queue, push() throws an overflowError exception. You will note that we declare the constant MAXQSIZE outside of the class. The value is then global, and so it is accessible to any calling block and to all bqueue objects, independently of their type. The class defines the integer count, which maintains the size of the queue. This private member is updated by the push() and pop() operations.

CLASS bqueue	Declaration	"d_bqueue.h"

```
const int MAXQSIZE = 50;
template <typename T>
class bqueue
{
   public:
      bqueue();
         // constructor. create empty queue with MAXQSIZE slots

      void push(const T& item);
         // insert an element at the back of the queue.
         // Precondition: count < MAXQSIZE. throws an
         // overflowError exception if queue is full

      void pop();
         // remove an element from the front of the queue.
         // Precondition: the queue is not empty. throws exception
         // underflowError if the queue is empty
```

```
        T& front();
           // return the front of the queue.
           // Precondition: the queue is not empty. throws the
           // underflowError exception if the queue is empty
const T& front() const;
           // constant version

        int size() const;
           // return the queue size

        bool empty() const;
           // is the queue empty?

        bool full() const;
           // is the queue full?

private:
           // array holding the queue elements
           T queueArray[MAXQSIZE];
           // index of the front and back of the queue
           int qfront, qback;
           // number of elements in the queue, 0 <= count <= MAXQSIZE
           int count;
   };
```

Example 8-5

This example illustrates the declaration of a bqueue object and the use of full() to avoid attempting an insertion into a full queue. An exception occurs when we call push() from within a try block and attempt to add an element to a full queue.

```
        // declare an empty bounded queue
        bqueue<int> q;
        int i;

        // fill-up the queue
        for (i=1; i <= MAXQSIZE; i++)
           q.push(i);

        // output element at the front of q and the queue size
        cout << q.front() << "  " << q.size() << endl;

        if (!q.full())
           q.push(99);     // push() does not occur

        try
        {
           q.push(99);     // exception occurs
        }
```

```
catch (const overflowError& oe)
{
    cout << oe.what() << endl;
}
```

```
Output:
1  50
bqueue push(): queue full
```

Designing the Bounded Queue

The implementation of the bqueue class will involve a new model for managing the queue elements in the array. We illustrate the features of the model by using a queue with MAXQSIZE = 4 elements. Assume that the queue already contains three elements. The index *qfront* identifies the first element in the queue, and the index *qback* identifies the location at which the next insertion occurs:

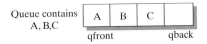

As we remove elements *A* and *B* from the queue, we could shift the remaining items forward in the array. This would be a happy situation for customers in a grocery checkout line, because the movement would get them closer to being served. This is not productive activity for a computer algorithm, however, because the movement takes processor time merely to maintain the array. Suppose the queue contains 1000 items. When we delete an entry from the front, 999 elements must move toward the front. A better solution leaves the remaining elements at their current location and moves qfront forward in the array:

A problem occurs if we attempt to add elements *D* and *E*. The first insertion places *D* at location qback, which is then positioned past the end of the array. There is no room for *E*, because an element cannot be added beyond the bounds of the fixed-length array. Nevertheless, the array does have room. Unfortunately this room is at the front of the array previously occupied by the deleted elements *A* and *B*:

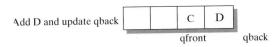

The situation leads us to a new way of viewing the queue. Think of the queue as a circular sequence. The circular path has a series of slots that elements enter in a

Figure 8-4
Circular-queue model

clockwise fashion. The exit point for an element is the slot designated by qfront, and the entry point for a new element is at the slot identified by qback. Let us retrace the activity in our four-element queue, assuming the circular storage model Figure 8-4.

In the circular model, element E can enter the queue at location qback. Note that qback is now the position that was formerly occupied by A and referenced by qfront. While the circular model is a good abstract view of how items enter and leave a queue, our implementation of the bqueue class must deal with the array, which stores elements sequentially. Treating the array as a circular sequence involves updating qfront and qback to cycle back to the front of the array as soon as they move past the end of the array (value = MAXQSIZE). Figure 8-5 illustrates how E would be added to the queue at the front of the array. Note that qback has a value that is less than that of qfront. This can be a little disconcerting, even counterintuitive, given our familiar linear view of a queue. Don't let this bother you; the circularity will be handled in the implementation of the class.

To have the indices qfront and qback cycle within the bounds of the array, we use the % operator, which computes the remainder after dividing by MAXQSIZE. On each insertion or deletion from the sequence, increment the appropriate index by 1, and assign it a new value modulo the array size. When the indices move past the end of the array, their values are reset to the start of the array:

Move qback forward: `qback = (qback + 1) % MAXQSIZE;`
Move qfront forward: `qfront = (qfront + 1) % MAXQSIZE;`

With our four-element array, if qfront has value 2, then the new value of qfront after popping an element from the queue is

$$qfront = (2 + 1)\%4, \text{ which has value } 3 \% 4 = 3$$

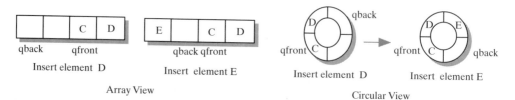

Insert element D   Insert element E   Insert element D   Insert element E

Array View   Circular View

Figure 8-5
Adding an element to a circular queue

If qback is at the end of the array (index 3) and we push a new element onto the queue, qback is updated to have the new value

$$\text{qback} = (3 + 1) \% 4, \text{which is the integer } 4 \% 4 = 0$$

Note that qback moves circularly around the array.

Implementing the Bounded Queue

We present the implementation of the bqueue functions push() and pop(). Because we view a queue as a circular sequence, the front(), pop(), and push() operations must use the locations qfront and qback when accessing or modifying the queue.

The push() operation adds an element to the back of the queue. If the queue is full (count == MAXQSIZE), the function throws the overflowError exception. Otherwise, add the element at location qback, increment count, and update qback to the next location in the circular queue.

push():
```
template<typename T>
void bqueue<T>::push(const T& item)
{
    // is the array filled up? if so, throw overflowError
    if (count == MAXQSIZE)
        throw overflowError("bqueue push(): queue full");

    // perform a circular queue insertion
    queueArray[qback] = item;
    qback = (qback + 1) % MAXQSIZE;
    // increment the queue size
    count++;
}
```

The pop() operation checks that the queue is not empty and then moves qfront forward circularly:

pop():
```
template<typename T>
void bqueue<T>::pop()
{
    // if queue is empty, throw underflowError
    if (count == 0)
        throw underflowError("bqueue pop(): empty queue");

    // perform a circular queue deletion
    qfront = (qfront + 1) % MAXQSIZE;

    // decrement the queue size
    count--;
}
```

Recall that the STL queue and the miniQueue operations push() and pop() have complexity O(1). In the bqueue class, these operations also have complexity O(1), because each function just accesses the array index qfront or qback.

8-6   PRIORITY QUEUES

A queue is a data structure that provides FIFO ordering of elements. A removal selects the first, or "oldest," element from the queue. Applications sometimes require a modified version of a queue in which elements exit from the sequence on the basis of a priority ranking instead of chronological order. This structure, called a *priority queue*, removes the element of highest priority from the sequence. The ranking of elements in a priority queue is determined by some external criterion. For instance, suppose a business provides a centralized secretarial pool to handle a variety of jobs for the staff. Company policy judges job requests by the president to be of highest priority (priority 3), followed by requests from managers (priority 2), from supervisors (priority 1), and finally from clerks (priority 0). A person's rank in the company becomes a criterion that measures the relative importance of a job. Instead of handling jobs on a first-come/first-served basis, the secretarial pool uses a priority queue to handle jobs in the order of their assigned importance. For instance, Figure 8-6 shows jobs 1–4 in the priority queue. The secretarial pool processes the jobs in the order #2, #1, #4, and #3.

The abstract model of a priority queue does not view the storage structure as a sequence container. The shape of the graphic in Figure 8-6 reflects this model. There is no assumption on how elements enter the priority queue, but only a criterion for their exit. Think of a priority queue as a collection of elements loosely tossed into a bucket. Removing an element involves reaching around in the bucket and pulling out the one with the highest priority.

Priority queues find applications in an operating system that maintains a waiting list for system tasks (processes) that is based on their urgency (priority). For instance, the operating system might give a "key pressed" event at the keyboard a high priority, because the character must be processed before the next key is pressed and data are lost. The system can postpone other tasks that are not as time critical. As another example, an operating system can insert print jobs into a priority queue on the basis of the number of pages required. In this situation, the higher priority jobs are those with the lower page count. It is reasonable to print the 2-, 7- and 10-page jobs before a 100-page job.

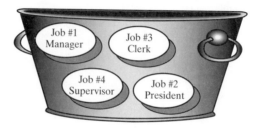

Figure 8-6

A priority queue for the secretarial pool

Priority-Queue ADT

The priority-queue ADT has essentially the same interface as the stack and queue containers. However, for the determination of priority, the data type T must implement the $<$ operator. The push() operation adds an element to the priority queue, and the pop() operation removes the element of highest priority. As with other containers, we can access the status of the priority queue with the size() and empty() functions. In particular, you should note how a priority queue references the next element that would be popped. Like a stack, the priority queue uses the operation top(). In contrast, a queue provides this access with the operation front(). The standard library implements the priority-queue ADT with the class priority_queue, whose API follows.

CLASS priority_queue	Constructor	<queue>

priority_queue();
    Create an empty priority queue. Type T must implement the operator $<$.

CLASS priority_queue	Operations	<queue>

bool **empty**() *const;*
    Check whether the priority queue is empty. Return true if it is empty, and false otherwise.

void **pop**();
    Remove the item of highest priority from the priority queue.
    Precondition: The priority queue is not empty.
    Postcondition: The priority queue has one fewer element.

void **push**(*const T& item*);
    Insert the argument *item* into the priority queue.
    Postcondition: The priority queue contains a new element.

int **size**() *const;*
    Return the number of items in the priority queue.

T& **top**();
    Return a reference to the element having the highest priority.
    Precondition: The priority queue is not empty.

const T& **top**() *const;*
    Constant version of top().

By default, the priority_queue class assumes that the element of highest priority is the one with the largest value; that is, if x and y are two elements in the priority queue and $x < y$, then y has higher priority than does x.

Example 8-6

This example illustrates how to declare a priority_queue object and use its member functions:

```
priority_queue<int> pq;
int n;

pq.push(20);
pq.push(10);
cout << pq.size() << "   "
     << pq.top();                      // output: 2   20
n = pq.pop();                          // n = 20 is removed
if (!pq.empty())
   pq.pop();
cout << pq.size();                     // output: o
```

☞

Note

Priority-Queue Ordering: When one is erasing an item from a priority queue, there could be several elements in the sequence with the same priority level. In this case, we could require that these items be treated like a queue. For instance, the secretarial pool could select jobs for workers at the same rank in the order in which they were submitted.

Job #1	Job #2	Job #3	Job #4
Clerk	Manager	Manager	Clerk

From the priority queue, select the manager jobs in the order Job #2 and Job # 3, and then the clerk jobs in the order Job #1 and Job #4. Programming Exercise 8-23 develops the queue model for a priority queue. The STL priority_queue class does not use this model. When deciding between two or more elements that have the same priority, the pop() operation makes no assumption about when the elements first entered the priority queue.

Implementing a Priority Queue Class: For the vector, stack, and queue, this book develops "mini" classes to illustrate implementation techniques. The efficient implementation of a priority queue requires a study of a data structure called a *heap*. A heap is a special version of a binary tree in which each parent node has a value that is $>=$ the value of its two children (maximum heap) or $<=$ the value of the children (minimum heap). This relationship is called the *heap property*. In Chapter 14, we use a maximum heap to implement a "mini" priority_queue class. With this structure, the largest element always occupies the root node. The pop() operation removes the root node. A heap has an operation, called adjustHeap(), that reorganizes the tree so that the new maximum element occupies the root and all other elements maintain the heap property. In its implementation, pop() calls the adjustHeap() operation. For instance, assume that a heap holds the elements of an integer priority queue. Figure 8-7, shows a maximum heap before and after the removal of the largest element.

From the illustration in Figure 8-7, you can gain some appreciation for the efficiency of using a heap to implement a priority queue. Elements in the heap are

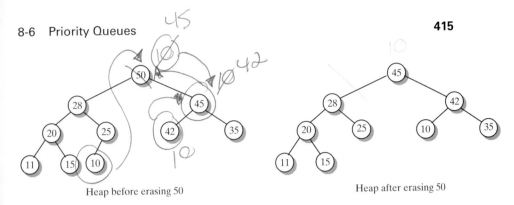

Heap before erasing 50   Heap after erasing 50

Figure 8-7
Heap before removing (popping) of the root and after a call to adjustheap()

densely packed near the root. Access to an element is along a relatively short path from the root. Adding an element (push) involves adding a node along the bottom of the tree. Deleting an element (pop) requires removing the root and then reposi-tioning the last element (node 10 in the figure) along a path on the other side of the tree. Both of these operations have running time $O(\log_2 n)$ (logarithmic complexity). The STL priority_queue class implements a priority queue by using a heap.

Sorting with a Priority Queue

A priority queue provides an efficient sorting algorithm. The algorithm first inserts the $n = $ v.size() elements of the vector into a priority queue and then empties the priority queue by using a loop. Because the priority queue releases the elements in descending order (highest priority to lowest priority), the sort copies the first ele-ment from the priority queue into $v[n - 1]$, the second into $v[n - 2]$, and so forth. Copy the last element coming from the priority queue into $v[0]$. The effect is to sort the vector v in ascending order. For example, the figure illustrates the sorting of the integer array 16, 27, 14, and 22.

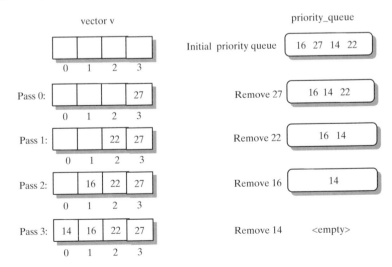

The function psort() implements the algorithm for a generic type T supporting the < operator:

```
// sort v using a priority queue
template<typename T>
void psort(vector<T>& v)
{
    priority_queue<T> pq;
    int i, n = v.size();

    // insert the vector elements in the priority queue
    for (i = 0; i < n; i++)
        pq.push(v[i]);

    // remove the elements from the priority queue and
    // copy them back into the vector. the largest element
    // goes in v[n-1], ..., the smallest in v[0].
    for (i = n-1; i >= 0; i--)
    {
        v[i] = pq.top();
        pq.pop();
    }
}
```

It is useful to investigate the complexity of psort(). The function inserts n elements into the heap, and each insertion has running time $O(\log_2 n)$, so the total insertion running time is $O(n \log_2 n)$. Similarly, the algorithm erases n elements with running time $O(n \log_2 n)$. It follows that the total algorithm has complexity $O(n \log_2 n)$. The famous heapsort algorithm, discussed in Chapter 14, is similar to psort(), but even more efficient.

Example 8-7

The statements initialize an integer vector v and use psort() to order the elements. At the initial stage and after the sort, the elements in the array are output by using the function writeVector() from "d_util.h."

```
// unordered integers
int arr[] = {16, 29, 14, 32, 18, 14, 87, 50, 64, 35};
int arrSize = sizeof(arr)/sizeof(int);
vector<int> v(arr, arr + arrSize);

cout << "Initial vector: ";
writeVector(v);

psort(v);

cout << "Sorted vector:  ";
writeVector(v);
```

```
Output:


Initial vector: 16   29   14   32   18   14   87   50   64   35
Sorted vector:   14   14   16   18   29   32   35   50   64   87
```

Company Support Services

At the beginning of this section, we motivated the use of priority queues by using a situation in which a common pool of secretaries supplies typing, photocopying, and other office services for a company's employees. To control the flow of work within the pool, the company ranks its employees, using the categories *president*, *manager*, *supervisor*, and *clerk*. The categories create priorities for tasks done by the pool. A job requested by a president has priority over a job requested by a supervisor, and so forth. To use the pool services, an employee must fill out a job request form that provides a job ID and includes the category status and an estimate of time required to finish the task. For this application, we simulate the activities within the secretarial pool.

We describe the categories as an enumeration type: → *newdate type*
                                                              "enumerated"

```
// employee priority level
enum staff {Clerk=0, Supervisor=1, Manager=2, President=3};
```

→ *variable*
staff title;

A job request form is an object of class type jobRequest. The class has three data members, called status, jobID, and jobTime, along with three corresponding access functions, getStatus(), getJobID, and getJobTime(). For the purpose of comparing two jobRequest objects, the class implements the overloaded < operator, which compares the status of two objects.

For input and output, the class overloads the operators >> and << The input of a job request assumes that the user specifies the status, the job ID, and the length of the job, in minutes, in the following format:

    status   jobID   jobTime

The overloaded version of << outputs a job request object in the same format. Consider the following statements, which input a 35-minute job request (ID = 1002) from a Manager and write the request to the screen:

```
jobRequest job;      // default values set to 0



    . . .
// input from ifstream 'fin': Manager  1002  35
fin >> job;

cout << job;         // output: Manager  1002  35
```

```
CLASS  jobRequest              Declaration              "d_job.h"
// class defining a job request
class jobRequest
{
   public:
       enum staff {Clerk=0, Supervisor=1, Manager=2, President=3};
          // employee priority level
       jobRequest();
          // default constructor. assign data members using stream
          // operator >>
       jobRequest(staff stat, int jid, int jtime);
       staff getStatus() const;
       int getJobID() const;
       int getJobTime() const;
       friend ostream& operator<< (ostream& ostr, const jobRequest& req);
       friend istream& operator>> (istream& istr, jobRequest& req);
          // I/O operations
       friend bool operator < (const jobRequest& a, const jobRequest& b);
          // compare job requests by status
   private:
       staff status;
       int jobID;
       int jobTime;
};
```

will default to these value if not assigned

The implementation of jobRequest is straightforward. You need to be aware of a syntax feature in the implementation of getStatus() outside the class declaration. The return type must be qualified with the scope operator jobRequest::staff, because the compiler processes the return type before it finds the scope operator identifying getStatus() as a jobRequest member function.

```
jobRequest::staff jobRequest::getStatus() const
{ return status; }
```

Consult the file "d_job.h" for the remaining implementation details.

PROGRAM 8-4   MANAGING A SECRETARIAL POOL

The application discussed next opens the file "job.dat," which contains a list of job requests. It inputs jobs by using the overloaded >> operator for jobRequest objects and inserts them into the priority queue jobPool. The application then removes the jobs from the queue in their order of priority and posts them by using the jobRequest << operator. The operator < for jobRequest objects implements this ranking of jobs. At its conclusion, the application outputs the total amount of time spent servicing each of the different types of employees. For this purpose, the program declares the integer vector jobServicesUse, all of whose entries are initially 0:

```
// time spent by the pool for each category of employee
vector<int> jobServicesUse(4,0); // initial time 0 for each category
```

As jobs are removed from the priority queue, the application adds the job time to the cumulative time for the corresponding type of employee by using getStatus() and getJobTime(). Note that int(job.getStatus()) = 0 (clerk), 1 (supervisor), 2 (manager), or 3 (president).

```
// accumulate job time for the category of employee
jobServicesUse[int(job.getStatus())]  += job.getJobTime();
```

After emptying the priority queue, the program concludes by displaying a summary of the services for each type of employee, using the function writeJobSummary():

```
// output total pool time allocated to each employee category
void writeJobSummary(const vector<int>& jobServicesUse)
{
   cout << "Total Pool Usage"  << endl;
   cout << "   Clerk        "  << setw(3)
        << jobServicesUse[0]   << endl;
   cout << "   Supervisor   "  << setw(3)
        << jobServicesUse[1]   << endl;
   cout << "   Manager      "  << setw(3)
        << jobServicesUse[2]   << endl;
   cout << "   President    "  << setw(3)
        << jobServicesUse[3]   << endl;
}
```

The following is a listing of the program:

```
// File: prg8_4.cpp
// the jobRequest class maintains information about the
// type of employee (Clerk, Supervisor, Manager, President),
// a job ID, and the number of minutes a job should take
// a company secretarial pool. the program inputs job data
// from the file "job.dat" inserts it into the priority queue
// jobPool. while popping elements from jobPool, the
// category of employee, job ID, and estimated job time
// are output. during the process, the vector jobServicesUse
// maintains the total service time for each category of
// employee. the function writeJobSummary() outputs the
// accumulated data

#include <iostream>
#include <fstream>
#include <iomanip>
#include <vector>
#include <queue>        // priority_queue class

#include "d_job.h"      // jobRequest class

using namespace std;

// output total pool time allocated to each employee category
void writeJobSummary(const vector<int>& jobServicesUse);

int main()
```

```
{
   // handle job requests
   priority_queue<jobRequest> jobPool;

   // job requests are read from fin
   ifstream fin;

   // time spent working for each category of employee
   vector<int> jobServicesUse(4,0); // initial time is 0

   jobRequest job;

   // open "job.dat" for input. exit program if open fails
   fin.open("job.dat");
   if (!fin)
   {
      cerr << "Cannot open file 'job.dat'" << endl;
      exit(1);
   }

   // read file. insert each job into priority queue jobPool.
   while (true)
   {
      fin  >> job;
      if  (!fin)
         break ;

      // insert job into the priority queue
      jobPool.push(job);
   }

   // delete jobs from priority queue and output information
   cout << "Category   Job ID    Job Time" << endl << endl;
   while (!jobPool.empty())
   {
      // remove a job from the priority queue and output it
      job = jobPool.top();
      jobPool.pop();
      cout << job;

      // accumulate job time for the category of employee
      jobServicesUse[int(job.getStatus())]  += job.getJobTime();
   }
   cout << endl;

   writeJobSummary(jobServicesUse);

   return 0;
}
/* implementation of writeJobSummary() given in the program discussion */
```

```
Input file "job.dat"

Supervisor 300 20
Clerk 301 30
Supervisor 302 40
President 303 25
Manager 304 10
Manager 305 40
President 306 50
Supervisor 307 70
Clerk 308 20
Clerk 309 20
Supervisor 310 60
Manager 311 30

Run:

Category       Job ID    Job Time

President       303         25
President       306         50
Manager         305         40
Manager         311         30
Manager         304         10
Supervisor      302         40
Supervisor      310         60
Supervisor      300         20
Supervisor      307         70
Clerk           301         30
Clerk           309         20
Clerk           308         20

Total Pool Usage
   Clerk          70
   Supervisor    190
   Manager        80
   President      75
```

CHAPTER SUMMARY

- A queue is a first-in-first-out (FIFO) data structure for which insertion operations (push()) occur at the back of the sequence and deletion operations (pop()) occur at the front. STL implements the queue ADT in the queue class, whose API we present in Section 8-1.

- The radix sort algorithm orders an integer vector by using 10 queues (bins). The sorting technique has running time O(n), but has only specialized applications.

The more general in-place $O(n \log_2 n)$ sorting algorithms are preferable in most cases.

- The miniQueue class provides a class with the same interface as the STL queue class. Its implementation uses a list object by composition. The implementation of each queue operation involves calling a corresponding member function for the embedded list object. The section concludes with an optional discussion of the STL queue class implementation. The programmer instantiates this class by specifying the sequence container to include by composition, as well as the type of the data. The acceptable containers are list and deque.

- Simulation applications often use queues. Section 8-4 presents a time-driven simulation for an automated car wash. The program enables the user to view the performance of the car wash as changes occur in the rate of customer arrival and the time it takes for a wash.

- For some specialized applications, it is necessary to implement a queue by using a fixed-size array. The class bqueue is describes a bounded-queue object that has a member function full() and a precondition for push(). The implementation of bqueue uses a fixed-size array with indices qfront and qback moving circularly through the array. The algorithm implements push() and pop() in $O(1)$ running time without wasting any space in the array.

- The priority queue ADT does not specify how push() stores a data value, but it requires that pop() must return the highest priority item in the container. The highest priority item is the largest (smallest) item. The standard library implements the priority queue ADT with the priority_queue class, whose API we present in Section 8-6. The class assumes that type T implements the < operator and, by default, it assumes that the highest priority item is the largest item in the container. The section uses a priority queue to implement a sorting algorithm and to develop an application that schedules jobs in a secretarial pool, where employees have priority ranging from president to clerk.

CLASSES AND LIBRARIES IN THE CHAPTER

Name	Header File
bqueue	d_bqueue.h
deque	<deque>
jobRequest	d_job.h
list	<list>
priority_queue	<queue>
queue	<queue>
radixSort	d_sort.h
randomNumber	d_random.h
time24	d_time24.h
vector	<vector>

REVIEW EXERCISES

1. What is the output from the following sequence of queue operations?

```
queue<int> s;
int x = 3, y = 5;

s.push(8);
s.push(x);
s.push(y);
x = s.front();
s.pop();
cout << x << endl;        // Output: 1 _____
y = s.front();
s.pop();
s.push(25);
while (!s.empty())
{ y = s.front();
s.pop();
cout << y << " ";      // Output: 2 _____
}
```

2. Trace the function f():

```
template<typename T>
void f(queue<T>& q)
{ vector<T> v;
  int n = q.size(), i;

  for(i=0;i < n/2;i++)
  { v.push_back(q.front());
    q.pop();
  }
  for (i=0;i < v.size();i++)
    q.push(v[i]);
}
```

Assume that *q* has the values 1 5 8 10 15 22 55, from front to back. What is the output from the following statements?

```
f(q);
while (!q.empty())
{
    cout << q.front() << "   ";
    q.pop();
}
```

3. What are the contents of the bins after Pass 1 of the radix sort for the following three-digit integers?

Data: 365 251 67 842 175 453 129 380 905 8 123 659 451 255 70l 123 49 598
535

bin 0	bin 1	bin 2	bin 3	bin 4	bin 5	bin 6	bin 7	bin 8	bin 9

4. What is the output from the following sequence of priority-queue operations?

```
priority_queue<int> pq;
int x = 8, y = 25;

pq.push(6);
pq.push(x);
pq.push(y);
x = pq.top();
pq.pop();
cout << x << endl;          // Output 1  _____
y = pq.top();
pq.pop();
pq.push(35);
while (!pq.empty())
{ y = pq.top();
  pq.pop();
  cout << y << "  ";        // Output 2  _____
}
```

5. Use a priority-queue object to reorder a vector of integers. What is the order of the vector

$$v = \{6, 12, 34, 15, 67, 45, 53, 3, 5\}$$

after the execution of function f()?

```
void f(vector<int>& v)
{  priority_queue<int> pq;
   int i;

   for (i = 0; i<v.size(); i++)
      pq.push(v[i]);

   i = 0;
   while (!pq.empty())
   { v[i] = pq.top();
     pq.pop();
     i++;
   }
}
```

6. Trace the following program, and answer parts (a) and (b):

```
#include <iostream>
#include <stack>
#include <queue>
```

```
using namespace std;

// function uses both a priority queue and stack object
template<typename T>
void f(priority_queue<T>& pq);

int main()
{   priority_queue<int> pq;
    int vals[] = {2,8,55,3,12,9}; // declare array of 6 integers

    for(int i=0;i < 6;i++)
        pq.push(vals[i]);
    f(pq);

    return 0;
}

template<typename T>
void f(priority_queue<T>& pq)
{   stack<T> s; // declare a local stack to store data
    T elt;

    while (!pq.empty())
    {   elt = pq.top();
        pq.pop();
        s.push(elt);
    }
    while (!s.empty())
        cout << s.pop() << "   ";
    cout << endl;
}
```

(a) What is the output?
(b) Assume that array vals has initial values {20, 50, 30, 20, 10, 40}. What is the resulting output?

Answers to Review Exercises

1. Output 1:   8   Output 2:   5 25
2. The function moves the first $n/2$ elements to the end of the queue.
Output: 10 15 22 55 1 5 8
3.

Bin 0	Bin 1	Bin 2	Bin 3	Bin 4	Bin 5	Bin 6	Bin 7	Bin 8	Bin 9
380	251	842	453	<empty>	365	<empty>	67	8	129
70	451		123		175			598	659
			123		905				49
					255				
					535				

4. Output 1:   25

Output 2:   35 6

5. The function sorts the vector ito descending order. After f() has been called, the vector v has contents

$$v = \{67, \ 53, \ 45, \ 34, \ 15, \ 12, \ 6, \ 5, \ 3\}$$

6. (a) 2 3 8 9 12 55   **(b)** 10 20 20 30 40 50

WRITTEN EXERCISES

7. A queue is a structure implementing which of the following properties (circle all that apply)?
   (a) first-in/last-out
   (b) last-in/first-out
   (c) first-come/first-serve
   (d) first-in/first-out
   (e) last-in/last-out

8. A queue is an applicable data structure for (circle all that apply)
   (a) expression evaluation
   (b) an operating-system job scheduler
   (c) simulation of waiting lines
   (d) printing a list in reverse order

9. What is the output from the following sequence of queue operations?

```
queue<int> q;
int x = 5, y = 3;

q.push(8);
q.push(9);
q.push(y);
x = q.front();
q.pop();
q.push(18);
x = q.front();
q.push(22);
while (!q.empty())
{
   y = q.front();
   q.pop();
   cout << y << "   ";
}
cout << x << endl;
```

10. List the elements in the queue after each of the following operations:

```
queue<int> intQueue;

intQueue.push(18);
intQueue.push(2);
intQueue.push(intQueue.front());
```

```
intQueue.push(intQueue.front());
intQueue.pop();
```

11. What is the action of function f()?

```
template<typename T>
void f(queue<T>& q)
{
    stack<T> s;
    T elt;

    while (!q.empty())
    {
        elt = q.front();
        q.pop();
        s.push(elt);
    }

    while (!s.empty())
    {
        elt = s.top();
        s.pop();
        q.push(elt);
    }
}
```

Why is it critical that *q* be a reference argument?

12. What is the action of the following code segment?

```
queue<int> q1, q2;
int x;
int n = 0, i;
    ...
// assume q2 is empty and n = 0
while (!q1.empty())
{
    x= q1.front();
    q1.pop();
    q2.push(x);
    n++;
}

for (i=0; i < n; i++)
{
    x = q2.front();
    q2.pop();
    q1.push(x);
    q2.push(x);
}
```

13. What is the action of function f()?

```
template<typename T>
T f(const queue<T>& q)
```

```
{
    queue<T> qtmp;
    int i, qsize = q.size();

    // assign q to qtmp
    qtmp = q;

    for(i=0;i < qsize-1;i++)
      qtmp.pop();

    return qtmp.front();
}
```

14. (a) What are the contents of each bin, 0–9, after Pass 0 of the radix sort? What is the order of the list after Pass 0?

   Data: 363 251 670 84 175 45 123 389 90 8 122 676 455 53 7 125 4 91 593 528

   (b) Show the contents of bins 0–9 after Pass 1 of the radix sort. What is the order of the list after Pass 1?
   (c) Show the contents of bins 0–9 after Pass 2 of the radix sort and the final sorted list.

15. Give the output of the following statements:

```
priority_queue<int> pq;
int arr[] = {10,  50,  30,  40,  60};
int i, x, y;

for(i=0;i < 5;i++)
  pq.push(arr[i]);

pq.push(25);
x = pq.top();
pq.pop();
pq.push(35);
y = pq.top();
pq.pop();
cout << x << "  " << y << endl;
while (!pq.empty())
{  cout << pq.top() << "  ";
   pq.pop();
}
cout << endl;
```

16. Give the output of the following statements:

```
priority_queue<int> intPQ; // empty priority queue

intPQ.push(5);
intPQ.push(27);
intPQ.push(25);
intPQ.pop();
intPQ.push(intPQ.top() * 2);
```

```
    intPQ.push(intPQ.top() * 5);
    while (!intPQ.empty())
    {   cout << intPQ.top() << "  ";
        intPQ.pop();
    }
    cout << endl;
```

17. Declare a stack, queue, and priority queue of integers, as follows:

```
    stack<int> s;
    queue<int> q;
    priority_queue<int> pq;
```

Assume that you input the integer sequence

5 8 12 15 1 3 18 25 18 35 2 55

and insert each value into each container in the order given. What is the output of the following statements?

```
    while (!s.empty())
    {
        cout << setw(5) << s.top() << setw(5)
             << q.front() << setw(5)
             << pq.top() << endl;
        s.pop(); q.pop(); pq.pop();
    }
```

18. Assume that a queue, intQueue, has the elements 5 1 3 9 8, from front to back.
    (a) Assume that you remove the elements from the queue and push them onto a stack. List the contents of the stack from top to bottom.
    (b) Assume that you remove the elements from the queue and push them onto a priority queue. Then remove the elements from the priority queue and push them onto a stack. List the contents of the stack from top to bottom.

19. Assume an array implementation of a queue with a maximum size of five elements. Initially, the queue has the elements 6, 2, 9, 5. Draw pictures of the array contents after each of the following queue operations with indices qfront and qback:

```
    q.push(8);
    q.pop();
    q.pop();
    q.push(25);
```

Be certain to indicate the positions of qfront and qback in your drawings.

20. Write a function

```
    template<typename T>
    void n2front(queue<T>& q, int n);
```

that moves the nth element (counting from the front, which is element 1) of the queue to the front, leaving the order of all other elements unchanged. The function throws the rangeError exception if $n < 1$ or $n > $ q.size(). The figure illustrates the action of n2front() for an integer queue and $n = 4$.

$n = 4$ (4th element of queue)

Before

8	5	17	3	7

front   back

After

3	8	5	17	7

front   back

21. Write a function

```
template<typename T>
void cut(queue<T>& q, int n, const T& item);
```

that inserts *item* into the queue as the *n*th element (counting from the front, which is ele-ment 1), leaving the order of all other elements unchanged. If *n* has value q.size() + 1, cut() inserts *item* at the back of the queue. The function throws the rangeError exception if $n < 1$ or $n > $ q.size() + 1. The figure illustrates the action of cut() for an integer queue, $n = 4$, and *item* = 9.

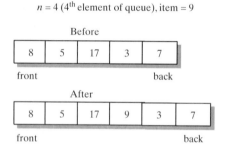

$n = 4$ (4th element of queue), item = 9

PROGRAMMING EXERCISES

22. Read a line of text in lowercase, placing each letter onto both a queue and stack. Verify whether the text is a palindrome.

23. Declare a vector *v* that has the following elements:

   1 3 5 7

   The program should copy the elements from *v* into a queue *q* and a stack *s*. Using stack and queue operations, double the size of the queue, with the tail having the initial values of the queue in reverse order. Flush the queue, and output its elements. Your output should be

   1 3 5 7 7 5 3 1

24. Use the function n2front() from Written Exercise 8-20. Write a program that enters eight integer values and pushes them onto a queue. Prompt for an integer *n*, and move the *n*th value in the queue to the front. Flush the queue, and output its elements.

25. Use the function cut() from Written Exercise 8-21. Write a program that enters eight integer values and pushes them onto a queue. Prompt for an integers *n* and *item*. Make *item* the *n*th value in the queue, flush the queue, and output its elements.

26. Declare a priority queue for integer objects. Using the random-number generator, load the priority queue with 15 values in the range from 0 to 4. Output the number of occurrences of 4, 3, 2, 1, 0. The number of occurrences should follow the number, using the format "*n*(*count*)." For instance, if the numbers are

→ pqint.cc

    2 3 0 1 2 4 4 2 1 2 4 1 2 3 2

the output should be

    4(3) 3(2) 2(6) 1(3) 0(1)

27. One way to implement a priority queue is to decide on the maximum priority possible, say MAXPRIORITY. Allocate an array *priority* of MAXPRIORITY + 1 queues. To insert an object of priority *p* into the priority queue, add it to the back of the queue *priority*[p]. Each queue contains only elements of equal priority, in the order of their insertion. When removing an element from the priority queue, find the nonempty queue of largest index, and pop the queue. Implement the class qpqueue in the header file "qpqueue.h", and use the class to run Program 8-4.

CLASS qpqueue	Declaration	"qpqueue.h"

```
const int MAXPRIORITY = 10;


template<typename T>
class qpqueue
{
   public:
      qpqueue ();

      void push(const T& item, int p);
         // insert item with priority p,
         // 0 <= p <= MAXPRIORITY
         // Postcondition:   the queue has one more element

      void pop();
         // find the non-empty queue with largest index and remove
         // its front element
         // Precondition:   the queue is not empty. the function
         // throws the underflowError exception if the queue is empty

      T& top();
         // find the non-empty queue with largest index and return
         // its front element
```

```
      // Precondition:   the queue is not empty. the function
      // throws the underflowError exception if the queue is empty

   const T& top() const;
      // constant version of top()

   bool empty() const;
      // is the queue empty?
   int size() const;
      // return the number of elements in the queue

 private:
   queue<T> priority[MAXPRIORITY +1];
      // priority[i] contains all elements with priority i
      // in the their order of insertion
   int pqsize;
      // number of elements in the priority queue
};
```

PROGRAMMING PROJECT

28. This exercise uses a vector object to implement a priority queue class vpriority_queue. Assume that the name of the vector object included by composition is pqVector. The following is an outline for the implementation of the class member functions:

(i) Use the size() operation in the vector class to implement the priority-queue functions size() and empty().

(ii) The push() operation inserts a new element at the back of the vector by using push_back(). The elements in the vector are not ordered in any way. Assign the boolean data member recomputeMaxIndex the value *true*, since the new value may be the largest in the priority queue. Part (iii) describes this variable.

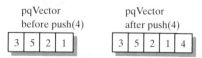

pqVector
before push(4)

| 3 | 5 | 2 | 1 |

pqVector
after push(4)

| 3 | 5 | 2 | 1 | 4 |

(iii) The functions top() and pop() must compute the largest of the pqVector.size() elements. Do this computation with the private-member function findMaxIndex (), which assigns to the data member maxIndex the index of the maximum element.

The functions top() and pop() both need the maximum value in the vec- lare a boolean data member recomputeMaxIndex, and initialize it to false. The functions top() and pop() use recomputeMaxIndex to avoid unnecessary calls to findMaxIndex().

(iv) The function top() returns the maximum value in pqVector. The function top() first checks to see whether the priority queue is empty. In that case, throw the exception underflowError. A second check looks at recomputeMaxIndex. If it is true, call findMaxIndex(), assign its return value to maxIndex, and set recomputeMaxIndex to false. In either case, top() returns the element pqVec- tor[maxIndex].

(v) If recomputeMaxIndex is true, the function pop() finds the maximum element
by calling findMaxIndex(). The function must remove the highest priority item
from the vector, which vacates a position. Sliding the tail of the sequence toward
the front of the vector is inefficient. Implement the removal process by locating
the last element in the vector (pqVector.back()) and copying its value into the
vacated position. Remove the last element by using pqVector.pop_back(), and
set the value of recomputeMaxIndex to true, indicating that a subsequent call to
top() or pop() requires a new maximum.

The figures show the sequence of values in pqVector as push() and pop() operations execute for the vpriority_queue object *pq*.

```
int arr[5] = {6, 2, 3, 5, 3};
vpriority_queue<int> pq;
int i;

for (i=0;i < 5; i++)
    pq.push(arr[i]);
```

pqVector

6	2	3	5	4

```
cout << pq.top() << " ";      // output: 6
pq.pop();
```

pqVector

4	2	3	5

```
cout << pq.top() << " ";      // output: 5
pq.pop();
```

pqVector

4	2	3

```
pq.push(10);
```

pqVector

4	2	3	10

```
pq.push(1);
```

pqVector

4	2	3	10	1

```
cout << pq.top() << " ";      // output: 10
pq.pop();
```

pqVector

4	2	3	1

```
cout << pq.top() << " ";      // output: 4
pq.pop();
```

pqVector

1	2	3

Implement the class vpriority_queue, whose class declaration follows. Place the class in the header file "vpqueue.h", and test the class by running Program 8-4.

CLASS vpriority_queue   **Declaration**   **"vpqueue.h"**

```
template<typename T>
class vpriority_queue
{
   public:
      vpriority_queue();
         // default constructor. create an empty priority queue

      void push(const T& item);
         // insert item into the priority queue.
         // Postcondition:   the priority queue has one more element

      void pop();
         // remove the highest priority (maximum) item from the
         // priority queue.
         // Precondition:   the priority queue is not empty. if it is
         // empty, the function throws the underflowError exception

      T& top();
         // return the highest priority (maximum) item in the
         // priority queue
         // Precondition:   the priority queue is not empty. if it is
         // empty, the function throws the underflowError exception

      const T& top() const;
         // constant version

      bool empty() const;
         // is the priority queue empty?

      int size() const;
         // return the size of the priority queue

   private:
      vector<T> pqVector;
         // vector that implements the priority queue
```

```
      int findMaxIndex() const;
          // find the index of the maximum value in pqVector
      int maxIndex;
          // index of the maximum value

      bool recomputeMaxIndex;
          // do we need to compute the index of the maximum element?
};
```

♦

CHAPTER 9

Linked Lists

OBJECTIVES

- To understand that a singly linked list is a sequence of values tied together by pointers, which serve as links in a chain.
- To understand that inserting or erasing in a singly linked list involves only pointer changes and that such operations have running time O(1).
- To understand that a pointer to the first node defines a singly linked list.
- To be able to build a singly linked list by inserting at the front of the list.
- To understand how to erase the front of a singly linked list.
- To become familiar with singly linked list algorithms that must insert or erase elements inside the list and to understand that such algorithms require the maintenance of a pointer to the current and the previous node.
- To understand that efficient insertion at the back of a singly linked list requires the maintenance of a pointer to the back of the list.
- To note that removal of the back of a singly linked list requires a scan of the list with running time O(n) and that a programmer rarely uses a singly linked list when an application requires this operation.
- To study the efficient implementation of the queue ADT that uses a singly linked list.
- To understand that a circular doubly linked list with a header node is a great improvement on the singly linked list, particularly when it comes to container-class implementation.
- To understand how to insert before any node of a doubly linked list, given only a pointer to the node.
- To understand how to erase any node of a doubly linked list, given only a pointer to the node.
- To understand that inserting at the front or back of a doubly linked list requires no special handling.
- To see how a doubly linked list elegantly and simply implements the miniList container, which is a subset of the STL list container.
- To see, for the first time, how to implement an iterator nested class.

OUTLINE

In Chapter 6, we introduced the list container, which is a data structure that allows sequential access to the elements. A list lays out the sequence in a row, starting at the first element (called *front*) and proceeding in successive order to the last element (called *back*). Each element in a list contains links that identify both the next and the preceding item in the sequence. Figure 9-1 provides a model for a list, illustrating the links with arrows that identify adjacent elements.

In the development of the list ADT, we focused on the fact that the container provides efficient operations to insert and delete an element at any position in the sequence. This was very important, because we needed to understand why a list is sometimes used in an application rather than a vector, which is another basic sequence container. We concluded that programmers select a list as the container of choice when an application wants to maintain elements by position and allow for frequent insertions and deletions.

In this chapter, we take up the task of implementing the list class. We could make our job very easy by choosing a vector as the underlying storage structure and declaring by composition a private data member listVector. There are some advantages to this approach. First of all, we understand vectors and would not have to learn a new structure. The front of the list is at index 0, and the back of the list is at index list Vector.size(). A list iterator can scan the list by using indices. Unfortunately, we must reject a vector as the underlying storage structure, for two important reasons. A vector does not permit efficient addition and removal of elements. We noted this fact in previous chapters. The problem with a vector is the fact that it stores its elements in consecutive memory locations. If a list object has elements 2, 7, 3, and 10 stored in listVector, the addition of value 5 as the third element in the sequence requires moving the tail of the vector (elements 3 and 10) to the right to accommodate the new data (Figure 9-2).

Removing an element requires a similar shift of vector elements to the left, in order to fill in the gap left by the deleted element. In general, a vector imple-

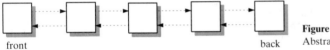

front   back

Figure 9-1
Abstract model of a list object

Insert 5 into list 2 7 3 10 at the 3rd position
Implementation shifts listVector [2] and listVector [3]

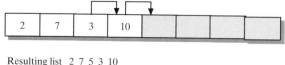

Resulting list 2 7 5 3 10
Implementation assigns 5 to listVector [2]

Figure 9-2

Implementing the insertion of element 5 into a list by the shifting of vector storage elements

mentation of the list insert() and erase() operations has running time O(*n*). For a large list, these operations would require excessive computing time merely to maintain the vector structure. This nullifies the whole rationale behind the design of the list container.

We need to design a new list storage structure that allows elements to be dispersed throughout memory and not necessarily packed into consecutive memory locations. To establish links between elements in the list, the structure of each element requires pointers that specify the location in memory of its adjacent list elements. Such an implementation structure is called a *linked list*.

In Sections 9-4 and 9-5, we develop the doubly linked list and use the structure in Section 9-7 to implement the miniList class, which is a simplified version of the STL list class. In a doubly linked list, each element, called a *node*, contains two pointers, which reference the next and previous element in the sequence. In the early sections of this chapter, we look at a simpler structure, called a *singly linked list*, in which each node has a single pointer that references only the next element in the list, and not its predecessor. Studying singly linked lists before doubly linked lists gives you a chance to understand the structure of a node and the ways in which nodes fit together to form a linked list. We will also explore the algorithms that insert and delete elements by updating the links between nodes. In the process, we will discover that a singly linked list is not a good implementation structure for the list class. Nevertheless, it is a good structure to represent a stack and a queue. In Section 9-3, we illustrate this fact by giving a linked-list implementation of the queue class. From an understanding of singly linked lists, the transition to doubly linked lists is relatively simple.

9-1   LINKED-LIST NODES

To gain some understanding of a singly linked list, you can think of each node as being an individual piece in a child's pop chain. A piece is a cylinder with a connector on one end and a hole in the back. To form a chain, insert the connector of one piece into the back of the next piece (Figure 9-3).

Individual Piece   Pop Chain

Figure 9-3

Physical model of a node and a singly linked list as pieces in a pop chain

Disconnect   Reconnect

Figure 9-4
Adding a piece at a position in the pop chain

   Inserting a new piece into the chain merely involves breaking a connection and reconnecting the chain at both ends of the new piece (Figure 9-4). Similarly, the removal of a piece from anywhere in the chain requires breaking its two connections, removing the piece, and then reconnecting the chain (Figure 9-5).

   The operations of adding and removing a piece in a pop chain involve only the connections at the single piece and do not affect the rest of the chain. The task has complexity $O(1)$, not $O(n)$, because the other pieces in the chain are not part of the process. This is the key feature we will carry over to our computer realization of a singly linked list.

Disconnect   Reconnect

Figure 9-5
Removing a piece from a pop chain

The node Class

The starting point for a computer representation of a linked list is a *node* that consists of a data value, called *nodeValue*, and a single pointer, called *next*, that points to the next node in the sequence. Using a piece in a pop chain as the model for a node, we model the pointer as the connector (Figure 9-6).

   The template-based node class defines the attributes of a node object and its constructors. In the public section, the class declares the data member *nodeValue* of type *T* and a pointer variable *next*. Allowing public data is something we have rarely done in the book and is an action that must never be taken lightly. Normally, the data in a class should be private, with access and updates controlled by public-member functions. However, the node class is used strictly for implementing a linked list. A node object is not intended for general-purpose use. When one is implementing a linked list, it is more efficient to access the data and pointer fields of a node directly, rather than requiring calls to member functions.

   The node class has two constructors. The default constructor has no arguments and allocates a node without an initial data value and with pointer value NULL. The second constructor includes the arguments for the data value and the pointer value. The pointer value is NULL by default. The following is a declaration of the node class, along with the implementation of the constructors, using inline code.

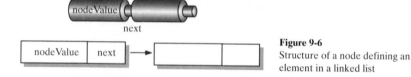

Figure 9-6
Structure of a node defining an element in a linked list

CLASS node	Declaration	"d_node.h"

```
// linked list node
template <typename T>
class node
{
   public:
      T nodeValue;      // data held by the node
      node<T> *next;   // next node in the list

      // default constructor with no initial value
      node() : next(NULL)
      {}

      // constructor. initialize nodeValue and next
      node(const T& item, node<T> *nextNode = NULL) :
         nodeValue(item), next(nextNode)
      {}
};
```

Note that the value of the data member *next* is a pointer to a node<*T*> object. The node class is a *self-referencing* structure, in which a pointer variable refers to an object of its own type.

A node is a single element in a linked list. In order that a list can grow and contract as values are added or removed, the nodes are dynamically allocated and deallocated. This implies that the node itself resides on the heap and requires a pointer to reference its address. The creation of a node involves first declaring a node<*T*> pointer and then using the operator *new* to allocate the node. For instance, the upcoming statements declare a pointer to an integer node and then allocate the node with initial value 10. The pointer value for the node is NULL, which we display with the following graphical symbol:

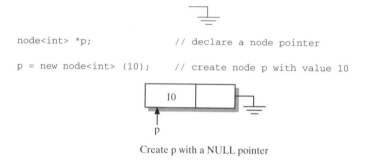

```
node<int> *p;              // declare a node pointer

p = new node<int> (10);    // create node p with value 10
```

Create p with a NULL pointer

We refer to the new node as "node p," although, more precisely, it is "the node pointed to by p." The actual node is *p. The shortcut description is more convenient, provided you understand that p is a node<T> pointer. To access the value and pointer fields of the node, use the pointer variable p and the operator $->$.

```
int n = p->nodeValue;      // n is 10 (See figure (a))

p->nodeValue = 5;          // update nodeValue to 5 (see figure (b))
```

```
┌──────────┬───┐              ┌──────────┬───┐
│    10    │   │──┐           │    5     │   │──┐
└──────────┴───┘  ─           └──────────┴───┘  ─
      ↑                              ↑
      p       (a)                    p       (b)
```

The expression $p->$nodeValue is a shortcut for (*p).nodeValue. The usefulness of the $->$ operator is particularly evident with nodes. You can use the notation $p->$nodeValue and $p->$ next to refer to the value and pointer fields of node p. The compiler reads these expressions as the nodeValue and pointer fields of the node pointed to by p.

Example 9-1

1. The node constructor gives the programmer flexibility in creating a node. If arguments for the operator *new* include the data value and the pointer to an existing node, the constructor creates the new node with a link to the existing node. If the pointer value is omitted, the new node is initially isolated from the list. The programmer must establish a link to a successor node by updating the pointer value *next*. In the example, p, q, r, and s are node<int> pointers.

   ```
   node<int> *p, *q, *r, *s;    // declare node pointers
   ```

   (a) The operator *new* allocates node p with value 5 and pointer value NULL. By including data value 8 and pointer value p, a second call to *new* allocates node q with a link to p.

   ```
   p = new node<int>(5);
   q = new node<int> (8, p);
   ```

   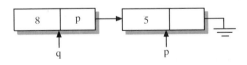

   (b) Node r is initially allocated as an isolated node with value 3. To attach node r to node q, update $r->$next.

   ```
   r = new node<int>(3);    // allocate r as isolated node
   r->next = q;             // link r to q
   ```

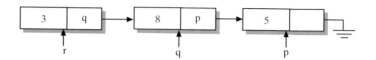

(c) Allocate node *s* (value 9), and insert it after node *q*. The operation requires updating the pointer values for both node *s* and node *q*.

```
s = new node<int>(9);
s->next = p;
q->next = s;
```

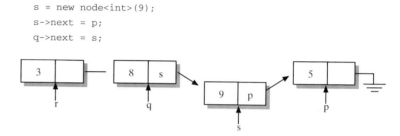

2. To move from one node to the next in a linked list, use the data member *next*. Assume that *p* points at a node with value 6. The pointer value *p*−>next is the successor node with value 9. (See part (a) of the next figure.) The assignment statement

```
p = p->next
```

updates p to point at the next node (value 9) in the list (see part (b) of the next figure.)

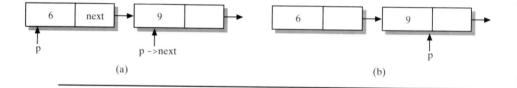

(a)   (b)

Adding and Removing Nodes

A fundamental problem in building a linked list is the insertion of a new node before the intermediate node *curr* in the list. The predecessor of *curr* has a link pointing to *curr*. Assume that the predecessor is node *prev*. The insertion process involves first allocating the new node and then updating pointers that attach it between *prev* and *curr*. Begin by declaring the node<*T*> pointer object newNode. A call to *new* with argument *item* allocates the new node and assigns *item* as its value. Initially, the pointer field for the node *prev* identifies *curr* as its successor, and newNode exists as an isolated node (Figure 9-7(a)). Connecting newNode to the list requires updating the values of newNode−>*next* and *prev*−>*next*. The pointer field for newNode must link to *curr*, and the pointer field for *prev* must link to newNode. The connections involve two steps (Figure 9-7(b)):

```
newNode->next = curr;     // step 1
prev->next = newNode;     // step 2
```

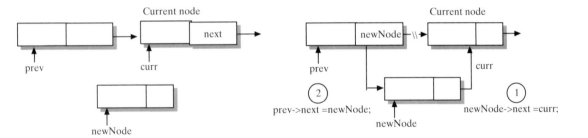

Figure 9-7
Inserting a new node before node curr in the list

The deletion algorithm for nodes in a list starts with a pointer that specifies a current position. Removing the current node requires the adjustment of the pointer in its predecessor. Assume that *curr* is the current node and *prev* is its predecessor. Set the pointer value for *prev* to reference the successor of *curr*. This has the effect of disconnecting *curr* from the list. Complete the algorithm by calling *delete*, which deallocates the memory for *curr* on the heap. The next set of statements implement the algorithm. Figure 9-8 describes the unlinking process.

```
node<T> *curr, *prev;

prev->next = curr->next;    // reconnect prev to the successor of curr
delete curr;                // delete the unlinked node
```

Current node

| | next |--//->| | | |->| | | |->

prev   curr   curr->next

prev->next = curr->next;

Figure 9-8
Unlinking a node

BUILDING LINKED LISTS   9-2

Section 9-1 focused on nodes, which are the building blocks for a linked list. After declaring the node class, we provided examples that illustrate how a programmer could allocate individual nodes and then link them together to create a chain. In this section, we step back and view the collection of nodes as a sequential storage structure. We begin by defining a singly linked list and then develop algorithms for displaying a linked list and for inserting and removing nodes at the ends of the list.

Defining a Singly Linked List

A singly linked list is a collection of nodes that has a pointer, which identifies the first node in the list. Traditionally, we call this pointer *front*. Each element except the last has a unique successor referenced by the pointer field *next*. The last element has pointer value NULL. For example, the chain of nodes shown in Figure 9-9 (a) is the linked-list representation of the integer list {7, 5, 3, 10}. An *empty list* occurs when *front* has the value NULL (Figure 9-9 (b)).

(a) Singly linked list with 4 integer valued nodes

```
// declaration of front
node<int> *front;
```

(b) Empty list

```
// template based declaration of front
node<T> *front = NULL;
```

Figure 9-9
Singly linked lists of nodes

The reason the pointer *front* is required is clear when you realize that a linked list is a sequential structure. The value of *front* locates the first node in the list. From there, you can use the pointer field *next* in the first node to reference the second node in the list. The next field in the second node references the third node, and so forth. The list ends when we arrive at a node whose pointer field is NULL. As we will see, *front* gives us access to the first node of the list, so the algorithms that insert and erase a node at the front of the list simply update the value of *front*.

We say that the pointer *front defines* the linked list. If you have *front*, you can access every element in the list. Without *front*, there is no entry point into the list, and all of the elements are inaccessible. We illustrate the importance of *front* in the implementation of the template function writeLinkedList(). The first argument is the pointer value *front*, which passes the list to the function. The second argument is the separator that the function outputs after each list value. Its default value is a string containing two blanks. You can access the function in the library file "d_nodel.h."

writeLinkedList():

```
// output a linked list with element followed by separator
template <typename T>
void writeLinkedList(node<T> *front, const string& separator = " ")
{
    // front points at first node. curr moves through the list
    node<T> *curr;
```

```
        curr = front;             // set curr to front of the list
        while (curr != NULL)      // continue until end of list
        {
              // output node value and move to the next node
              cout << curr->nodeValue << separator;
              curr = curr->next;
        }
    }
```

Inserting at the Front of a Linked List

Adding a node at the front of a linked list involves allocating the node and then attaching it to the current first node in the list. The process concludes by updating the value of *front* to point at the new node. When allocating the new node, we ask the constructor to create the link to the first node by passing *front* as the pointer argument for the operator *new*. For instance, the upcoming statements add the element *item* at the front of an integer list. Figure 9-10 (a) shows the addition of the node to an empty list. Figure 9-10 (b) displays the addition of the node to a list that initially has *front* pointing at a node with value 20.

```
        node<T> *front, *newNode;

        // allocate the new node so it points to front
        newNode = new node<T>(item, front);

        // front is now newNode
        front = newNode;
```

OR

front = new node <T>(item, front);

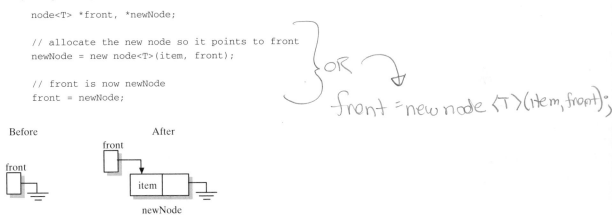

(a)

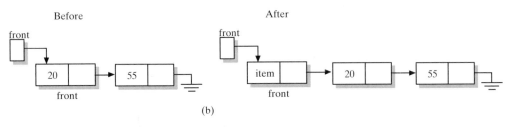

(b)

Figure 9-10
Adding a node with value item to the front of a list

Note that in the case of an empty list, the argument *front* for the constructor is the value NULL. The effect is to assign the pointer field for newNode the value NULL. With a nonempty list, the operation assigns the pointer field of newNode as the pointer to the current *front* node (node 20).

Example 9-2

This example builds the following linked list by repeatedly inserting at the front of the list:

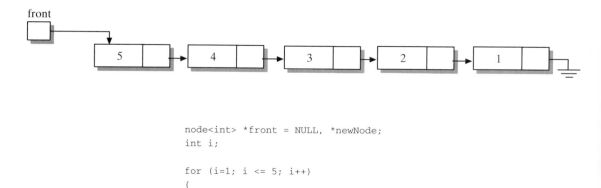

```
node<int> *front = NULL, *newNode;
int i;

for (i=1; i <= 5; i++)
{
   newNode = new node<int> (i, front);

   front = newNode;
}
```

Note

Allocating a node can be unsuccessful if the heap does not have sufficient memory. In this case, the application should throw an exception. A good strategy is to combine the allocation and testing into a function that returns the address of the node. The upcoming code defines the function getNode(), which takes the value and pointer field for a node and returns the address of the new node on the heap. The function throws a memoryAllocation exception if the heap does not have sufficient memory.

```
node<T>* getNode(const T& item, node<T> *nextNode = NULL)
{
   node<T> *newNode;

   // allocate the new node
   newNode = new node<T>(item, nextNode);
```

```
         // test for sufficient memory; if failure throw exception
         if (newNode == NULL)
            throw memoryAllocation("Node allocation error");

         // return the address of the new node on the heap
         return newNode;
    }
```

We will use getNode() as a private-member function in the implementation of the linkedQueue class in Section 9-3.

Erasing at the Front of a Linked List

The node at the front of a list can be erased only if the list is not empty. The operation merely updates *front* to point at the current second node in the list (*front−>next*). If the list has only one element, then front−>next is NULL. The algorithm begins by assigning *front* to a temporary pointer *p*. After *front* is updated to reference the second node in the list, the *delete* operator with argument *p* deallocates the memory initially assigned to the first node. Figure 9-11 illustrates the action for a list with one element and for a multinode list.

The following statements implement the algorithm:

```
node<T> *front, *p;

// can't erase the front of an empty list
if (front != NULL)
{
    // p set to original front pointer
    p = front;

    // move front to the next node
    front = front->next;

    delete p;
}
```

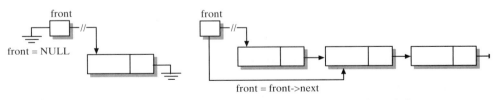

Deleting front of a 1-node list   Deleting front of a multi-node list

Figure 9-11
Deleting at the front of a linked list

Example 9-3

When a program no longer needs a linked list, the programmer should deallocate the memory occupied by its nodes. The following code clears the list by repeatedly deleting the *front* node until the list is empty (i.e., *front* = NULL):

```
node<T> *p;

// repeatedly remove the first node in the list
while(front != NULL)
{
    p = front;
    front = front->next;
    delete p;
}
```

Removing a Target Node

A programmer often wants to access or update nodes in a linked list via their value rather than their position in the list. We know how to remove the first node in a linked list. When an application calls for removal of a node with a specific value, the deletion could occur at some intermediate position in the list. The task involves a new approach. A scan of the list must first identify the location of the target node. This information is not sufficient to erase the node, because it is also necessary to know the location of the preceding node (Figure 9-8). The scan must use a pair of pointers that move in tandem down the list. One pointer references the current node in the scan, and the other the previous (predecessor) node. Figure 9-12 illustrates the relative location for the tandem pointers *curr* and *prev*. Once *curr* identifies the node that matches the target, the algorithm uses the pointer *prev* to unlink *curr*.

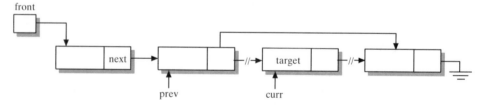

Figure 9-12
Positions of prev and curr for a deletion

To find the target node, initially set pointer *curr* to the front of the list. The pointer *prev* identifies the node just before *curr*. The first node in a linked list does not have a predecessor, so we assign *prev* the value NULL. Using *curr*, scan each successive node until you match the target or until *curr* reaches the end of the list (*curr* == NULL). During the scan of the list, the two pointers *curr* and *prev* move

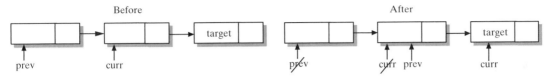

Figure 9-13
Update of pointers prev and curr in the scan of nodes in a linked list

as a tandem pair. The following statements move the pointers forward to the next node in the list (Figure 9-13):

```
prev = curr;          // update prev to next position (curr)
curr = curr->next;    // move curr to the next node
```

If the scan of the list identifies a match (*curr*−>node*Value* == *target*), *curr* points at the node that we must remove, and *prev* identifies the prior node. There are two possible situations, each of which requires different actions. The target node might be the first node in the list, or it might be at some intermediate position in the list. The value of *prev* distinguishes between the two cases.

Case 1:   Pointer *prev* is NULL, which implies that *curr* is *front*. The search identifies a match at the first node in the list. Delete the front of the list.

Case 2:   The match occurs at some intermediate node in the list. Both *curr* and *prev* have non-NULL values. Delete the current node by unlinking it from *prev* (*prev*−>*next* = *curr*−>*next*)

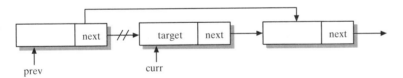

The function eraseValue() implements the algorithm that removes the first occurrence of a node having a specified value. The argument list includes the node<T> pointer front as a reference variable and the target value. Recall that a pointer is a variable. Its value just happens to be the address of another object in memory. The function could modify the pointer *front*, so it is a reference argument. Read the notation "node<T> * & *front*" as "*front* is a reference to a node<T> pointer."

eraseValue():
```
// if target is in the linked list, remove its first
// occurrence; otherwise, do not modify the list
template <typename T>
void eraseValue(node<T> * & front, const T& target)
{
    // curr moves through list, trailed by prev
  node<T> *curr = front, *prev = NULL;
```

```
                 // becomes true if we locate target
                 bool foundItem = false;

                 // scan until locate item or come to end of list
                 while (curr != NULL && !foundItem)
                 {
                    if (curr->nodeValue == target)        // have a match
                    {
                       if (prev == NULL)                  // remove the first node
                          front = front->next;
                       else
                          prev->next = curr->next;        // erase intermediate node

                       delete curr;

                       foundItem = true;
                    }
                    else
                    {
                       // advance curr and prev
                       prev = curr;
                       curr = curr->next;
                    }
                 }
              }
          }
```

Program 9-1   ERASING NODES IN DESCENDING ORDER

Let us look at a program that uses the linked-list algorithms from this section. A prompt asks
the user to enter the number of elements in the list. Building the list involves inserting at the
front random values in the range from 0 to 99. The function writeLinkedList() displays the sequence. The function getMax() scans the list and returns a pointer to the node with the maximum value. A loop calls getMax(), outputs the maximum value, and then deletes the
corresponding node by using eraseValue(). The loop terminates when the list is empty.

```
        // File: prg9_1.cpp
        // the program prompts the user for the size of an integer list and
        // inserts required number of random integers in the range 0 to 99
        // at the front of the list. after displaying the list using
        // writeLinkedList(), a loop repeatedly calls the function getMax()
        // that returns a pointer to the maximum value. after displaying
        // the maximum value, the loop calls function eraseValue() to erase
        // the maximum value from the list. output of the program is the
        // original list of integers in descending order

        #include <iostream>

        #include "d_node.h"
        #include "d_node1.h"
        #include "d_random.h"
```

```cpp
using namespace std;

// return a pointer to the maximum element in the linked list
template <typename T>
node<T> *getMax(node<T> *front);
// if target is in the linked list, remove its first
// occurrence; otherwise, do not modify the list
template <typename T>
void eraseValue(node<T> * & front, const T& target);

int main()
{
   node<int> *front = NULL, *p;
   randomNumber rnd;
   int listCount, i;

   cout << "Enter the size of the list:    ";
   cin >> listCount;

   for (i = 0; i < listCount; i++)
      front = new node<int> (rnd.random(100), front);
   cout << "Original List of Values:        ";
   writeLinkedList(front, "  ");
   cout << endl;

   cout << "Output in Descending Order:    ";
   while (front != NULL)
   {
      p = getMax(front);
      cout << p->nodeValue << "   ";
      eraseValue(front, p->nodeValue);
   }

   cout << endl;
   return 0;
}

template <typename T>
node<T> *getMax(node<T> *front)
{
   node<T> *curr = front, *maxPtr = front;

   while (curr != NULL)
   {
     if (maxPtr->nodeValue < curr->nodeValue)
         maxPtr = curr;
     curr = curr->next;
   }
   return maxPtr;
}

/* implementation of eraseValue() is in the program discussion */
```

```
Run:

Enter the size of the list: 9
Original List of Values:     62   44   55   40   39   81   30   91   95
Output in Descending Order: 95   91   81   62   55   44   40   39   30
```

9-3   HANDLING THE BACK OF THE LIST

A linked list is designed as an implementation structure for sequence containers. In evaluating this role, we need to assess the types of containers that can efficiently use a linked list as the underlying storage structure. In the previous section, we developed algorithms that add or remove an element at the front of the list. The corresponding functions simply update the *front* pointer and have running time O(1). A stack has operations that update only one end of the list. If we use a linked list to implement a stack and let the first element in the linked list represent the top of the stack (Figure 9-14), then implementing the push() and pop() functions would involve applying linked-list operations only at the front. We conclude that the stack class can be implemented efficiently by using a singly linked list.

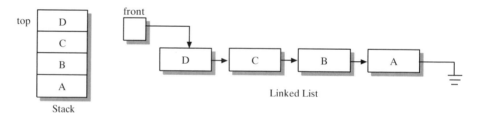

Figure 9-14
Implementing a stack by a linked list

A queue is a sequence container with operations at both ends of the list. If its implementation uses a singly linked list, and the first element represents the front of the queue, the pop() operation reduces to deleting the front of the list. The queue push() function adds an element at the end of the sequence. To implement this operation, we need access to the last node in the list. If the implementation design maintains only the *front* pointer, then locating the last node requires an O(*n*) scan (Figure 9-15).

```
node<T> *curr = front;

// back of the list is the node with pointer value NULL
while (curr->next != NULL)
    curr = curr->next;
```

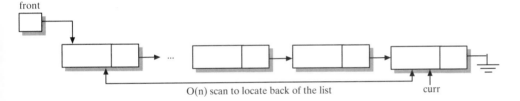

Figure 9-15
Scan list to set curr at the last element

Designing a New Linked-List Structure

In general, a singly linked list does not efficiently handle operations at the back of the list if we must rely on the pointer *front* to access the nodes. An alternative approach defines a second pointer, called *back*, that always points to the end of the list. Let us look at the insertion algorithm that adds a new node at pointer location *back*. To insert the value *item* in the list, allocate a new node whose pointer value is NULL and whose node value is *item*. The new node, called newNode, will become the back of the list. Make the connection by assigning to *back−>next* the pointer value newNode. Because there is a new element at the end of the list, complete the process by repositioning the pointer *back* at newNode (Figure 9-16).

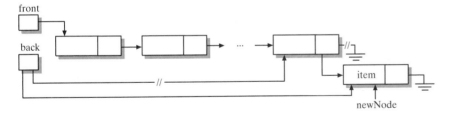

Figure 9-16
Inserting at the back of a nonempty list

When the list is empty (*front* == NULL and *back* == NULL), allocate a new node, and assign both *front* and *back* to point to it (Figure 9-17).

The following code implements the algorithm. An *if* statement must check whether the list is initially empty, because the insert in this situation requires that *front* be updated.

```
node<T> *front, *back, *newNode;

// allocate the new node with value item and pointer NULL
newNode = new node<T> (item);

if (front != NULL)
    // list not empty. link back to newNode
    back->next = newNode;
else
```

```
        // list empty. assign both front and back value newNode
        front = newNode;

    back = newNode;        // assign back to be newNode
```

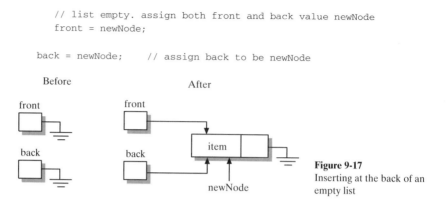

Figure 9-17
Inserting at the back of an
empty list

Note that insertion into the back of the list involves a fixed number of assignment statements and thus has running time O(1). If we use the two-pointer strategy as an implementation design, a singly linked list becomes an effective implementation structure for a queue. Both the push() and pop() operations are efficient. We illustrate this fact in the next section, where we develop a linked-list implementation for the queue class.

The use of two pointers to describe a singly linked list is not without problems. The algorithms to modify the front of the list become more complicated, because they can require a separate update for the pointer *back*. Consider, for instance, what happens when we add an element at the front of an empty list. The new node simultaneously becomes the front and the back of the list. In this case, the algorithm must update both *front* and *back* to point at the new node. Figure 9-18 illustrates the situation before and after the insertion.

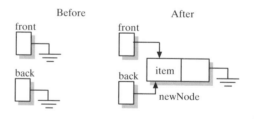

Figure 9-18
Adding a node with value item
to the front of an empty list

The code for the algorithm includes a separate *if* statement that tests whether the list is initially empty. If so, set *back* to point at newNode.

```
node<T> *front, *back, *newNode;

// allocate the new node so it points to front
newNode = new node<T>(item, front);

if (front == NULL)
    // the list is empty. after insertion at the front, the
    // list will have one element. back must point to the new node
```

```
    back = newNode;
// front is now newNode
front = newNode;
```

Erasing the node at the front of a list can affect the pointer *back* when the list has a single element. In this case, the deletion simultaneously removes the front and the back of the list. Besides updating *front*, the algorithm must also set *back* to NULL, because the resulting list is empty (Figure 9-19).

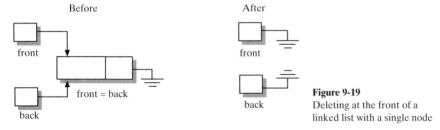

Figure 9-19
Deleting at the front of a
linked list with a single node

Like the *insert front* algorithm, code for the deletion includes an *if* statement that checks whether the list is empty (*front* == NULL) after unlinking the first node. The situation requires updating *back* to have the value NULL.

```
node<T> *front, *back, *p;

// can't erase the front of an empty list
if (front != NULL)
{
    // p set to original front pointer
    p = front;

    // move front to the next node
    front = front->next;
    // if front is now NULL, back must be NULL also
    if (front == NULL)
       back = NULL;

    delete p;
}
```

We hope that our brief discussion of singly linked list algorithms alerts you to some of the problems and workarounds that you must consider when using a list as an implementation structure. Stacks and queues are examples of sequence containers that can use a singly linked list. In the next section, we detail how a queue can use a linked list for its implementation.

IMPLEMENTING A LINKED QUEUE   9-4

A container ADT specifies an interface that is independent of its implementation. The ADT provides a set of operations that a programmer can use in an application. The implementation is a separate issue that allows a programmer to select from a variety of underlying storage structures. A programmer should evaluate the different storage structures based on issues of runtime efficiency. Let us look at the queue container. We can use a vector to implement a queue. The choice will work, but it is not efficient, because the implementation of pop() involves deleting the element at index 0 and shifting the remaining elements to the left one position. That operation has running time $O(n)$. In Chapter 8, we developed an implementation of the miniQueue class, using a list as the underlying storage structure. We chose a list object to store the data in order to take full advantage of the $O(1)$ running time for the push_back() and pop_front() operations that implement the queue push() and pop() operations.

In this section, we illustrate another implementation for the queue class that uses a singly linked list to store the elements. The class, called linkedQueue, declares a pointer *qfront* that locates the front of the linked list. The pointer value *qback* references the last element in the list. The pointer *qfront* gives us access to the front of the list for the implementation of pop() and front(). The pointer value *qback* allows the efficient implementation for push(). The integer *qsize* is the third data member in the class and maintains the number of elements in the queue. The operation size() returns this value. The linkedQueue class implementation of the queue ADT is as efficient as the miniQueue class implementation, with all operations having running time $O(1)$.

The linkedQueue Class

The public interface for the linkedQueue class is identical to the interface for the queue class, except for the copy constructor, destructor, and overloaded assignment operator required for dynamic memory management. Unlike the STL queue class, which does not provide exceptions, the linkedQueue operations pop() and front() throw an underflowError exception if the queue is empty. The class has three private-member functions that allocate a new node, copy another linkedQueue object, and clear the list in support of the dynamic memory management operations.

CLASS linkedQueue	Declaration	"d_lqueue.h"

```
// implements a linked queue
template <typename T>
class linkedQueue
{
   public:
      linkedQueue();
         // Constructor:   creates an empty queue.
         // Postcondition: qsize = 0, qfront = qback = NULL

      linkedQueue(const linkedQueue<T>& obj);
         // copy constructor. builds a copy of obj

      ~linkedQueue();
         // destructor. clear the linked list
```

```
linkedQueue<T>& operator= (const linkedQueue<T>& rhs);
    // assignment operator. copy rhs to the current object
void push(const T& item);
    // insert an element at the rear of the queue
    // Postcondition:   the queue has one more element

void pop();
    // remove an element from the front of the queue.
    // Precondition:   the queue is not empty. if the queue
    // is empty, throw an underflowError exception
    // Postcondition:   the queue has one fewer element

T& front();
    // return a reference to the front of the queue.
    // Precondition:   the queue is not empty. if the queue
    // is empty, throw an underflowError exception

const T& front() const;
    // constant version

int size() const;
    // return the current size of the queue

bool empty() const;
    // return true if queue empty; otherwise, return false
private:
    node<T> *qfront, *qback;
        // the linked list with qfront stores the elements.
        // qback points to the rear of the queue
    int qsize;
        // number of elements in the queue

    void copy(const linkedQueue<T>& q);
        // copy q so the current list is identical to q

    void clear();
        // clear the list. used by destructor and assignment operator
    node<T> *getNode(const T& item);
        // allocate a node with value item and pointer value NULL.
        // return a pointer to it. if memory allocation fails,
        // throw the memoryAllocationError exception
};
```

Implementing the linkedQueue Class

We begin the implementation by looking at the overloaded assignment operator. Most of the work is done by the private-member function copy(). We also provide an implementation of the constructor and the update functions push() and pop().

The Copy Utility. The function assumes that the current list is empty and performs a series of insertions at the back of the list, using qback. Each insertion is a copy of an element from *q*. The function concludes by setting the size of the current list (qsize) to the size of *q*.

copy():

```
template <typename T>
void linkedQueue<T>::copy(const linkedQueue<T>& q)
{
    // qback moves through the new list. p moves through the
    // list for q. repeat inserts after qback
    node<T> *newNode, *p = q.qfront;

    // initially, the list is empty
    qfront = qback = NULL;

    // nothing to do if p is NULL
    if (p != NULL)
    {
        // create the first node in the queue and assign
        // its address to qback
        qfront = qback = getNode(p->nodeValue);

        // move forward in the list we are copying
        p = p->next;

        // copy remaining items
        while(p != NULL)
        {
            // insert new node at the back
            newNode = getNode(p->nodeValue);
            qback->next = newNode;

            // qback is the new node
            qback = newNode;

            // move to the next node of the list we are copying
            p = p->next;
        }
    }

    // the size of the new list is the size of q
    qsize = q.qsize;
}
```

Implementing the Constructor. The constructor initializes the pointer variables to NULL and sets the size to 0. The effect is to create an empty linked list.

Constructor:
```
// create the empty list qfront = qback = NULL and qsize = 0
template <typename T>
linkedQueue<T>::linkedQueue(): qfront(NULL), qback(NULL), qsize(0)
{}
```

Implementing the Assignment Operator. The assignment operator calls clear() to delete the existing nodes and create an empty list. By calling copy() with argument rhs.qfront, it makes the current object identical to *rhs*.

operator=:
```
template <typename T>
linkedQueue<T>& linkedQueue<T>::operator= (const linkedQueue<T>& rhs)
{
   // delete the current list
   clear();

   // make the current object a copy of rhs
   copy(rhs);

   return *this;
}
```

Queue Update Operations. The function push() inserts an element at the back of the queue. If the list is not empty, the pointer *qback* identifies the position of the last element in the list. The push() operation simply links the new node to *qback*, updates *qback* to point at the new last element, and increments the size. If the list is empty, then the new element becomes simultaneously the front and back of the list. In this case, the operation must update both *qfront* and *qrear*.

push():
```
// insert item into the queue by inserting it at
// the back of the list
template <typename T>
void linkedQueue<T>::push(const T& item)
{
   // allocate space for the new node
   node<T> *newNode = getNode(item);

   // if the queue is empty, insert the new element at the front of
   // the list and update both qfront and qback
   if (qfront == NULL)
   {
      qfront = newNode;
      qback = newNode;
   }
   // in a nonempty list, insert new element at back, update qback
```

```
else
{
    qback->next = newNode;
    qback = newNode;
}

// increment the queue size
qsize++;
}
```

The pop() operation requires a nonempty queue. If the queue is empty, the algorithm throws an underflowError exception. The implementation of the operation deletes the first element in the list and updates both *qfront* and *qsize*. In order to maintain the pointer *qback*, the algorithm must check whether the new list is empty. In this case, the deletion removed both the front and the back of the queue, and the function must assign to *qrear* the value NULL.

pop():
```
// remove the item at the front of the queue by erasing
// the first element
template <typename T>
void linkedQueue<T>::pop()
{
    // save the location of the front of the queue
    node<T> *p = qfront;

    // if the queue is empty, throw underflowError
    if (qsize == 0)
        throw underflowError("queue pop(): empty queue");

    // move the front forward one node
    qfront= qfront->next;

    // if the queue is now empty, set qback to NULL
    if (qfront == NULL)
        qback = NULL;

    // delete the node
    delete p;

    // decrement the queue size
    qsize--;
}
```

Program 9-2   TESTING THE LINKEDQUEUE CLASS

With the implementation of the linkedQueue class, let us look at a simple program that uses many of its operations. The program begins by declaring an integer array *arr* and the linkedQueue object *q*. A loop uses push() to add each array element to the queue. After a display of the size of the queue, a second loop clears the queue by first displaying the value front(), which identifies the first element, and then erasing the element with pop(). With the resulting empty queue, a try/catch block responds to the exception thrown by a call to pop().

```cpp
// File: prg9_2.cpp
// the program tests the linkedQueue class by pushing
// the values in an array onto a queue. by using front()
// followed by pop(), the programs displays the contents
// of the queue as it empties it. when the queue is empty,
// a call to pop() causes the underflowError exception.
// after catching the exception and displaying an error
// message, the program terminates

#include <iostream>

#include "d_lqueue.h"
using namespace std;

int main()
{
    // declare an integer array and compute its size
    int arr[] = {6, 9, 2, 5}, i;
    int arrSize = sizeof(arr)/sizeof(int);

    // declare an empty queue of integer elements
    linkedQueue<int> q;

    // insert the array elements in q and output their value
    for (i = 0; i < arrSize; i++)
       q.push(arr[i]);

    // display the resulting size of the queue
    cout << "Queue size is " << q.size() << endl;

    // clear the queue
    while (!q.empty())
    {
       // display the element at the front and then
       // erase it from the queue
       cout << q.front() << " ";
       q.pop();
    }
    cout << endl;

    // handle the underflowError exception using a call to pop()
    try
    {
       q.pop();
    }
    catch (const underflowError& ue)
    {
```

```
        cout << ue.what() << endl;
    }

    return 0;
}
```

```
Run:
Queue size is 4
6  9  2  5
queue pop(): empty queue
```

9-5   DOUBLY LINKED LISTS

We began this chapter with the goal of implementing the list container. To this point, we have developed the concept of a singly linked list as a storage structure for a sequence of data items. In Section 9-3, we used a singly linked list to implement the linkedQueue class. We did not, however, attempt to use a singly linked list to implement the list class. This was not an oversight, as you will soon see.

Recall the abstract model for a list container (Figure 9-20). A list object has operations that access and update elements at the ends of the list at positions *front* and *back*. It also has a list iterator that allows for insertion and deletion of elements at intermediate locations in the list. The iterator scans the list in both directions by using the $++$ and $--$ operators.

Let us look at implementation design issues that would occur if we chose a singly linked list as the underlying storage structure for the list class. A singly linked list has algorithms that efficiently insert or erase at the front of the list. The problem with a singly linked list begins to surface when we consider the list operation pop_back(). From our discussion of insertion at the back of a singly linked list in Section 9-3, it follows in a similar fashion that the algorithm for pop_back() will have running time $O(n)$ (Figure 9-15). The problem is that we must scan the singly linked list to locate both the back and the predecessor to the back.

The implementation of the list class must also include list iterators. A list iterator is a generalized pointer, so it must have an underlying representation that corresponds to elements in the storage structure. If the structure is a singly linked list, the representation for an iterator must include a node pointer. In a singly linked list, a node pointer can scan the sequence only in the forward direction, starting at *front*. A list iterator must scan a list object in two directions. The issue of iterators carries over to the insert() and erase() functions in the list class. These operations add or remove an element at an iterator position. The implementation of these operations requires adding or removing a node at a pointer position in the linked list. For this reason, the iterator must maintain a pointer *prev* to the node immediately

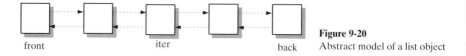

front   iter   back

Figure 9-20
Abstract model of a list object

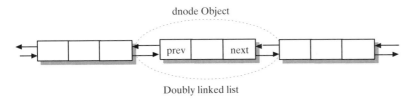

dnode Object

Doubly linked list

Figure 9-21
Doubly linked list with nodes having two pointer fields

before the current position. Recall that a singly linked list can link and unlink only the element after *prev*, because the operations require an update of the pointer field *next* in the previous node.

Our implementation design analysis points out the inefficiency of using a singly linked list to implement the list class. It does not imply that the implementation would be impossible, only inefficient. By slightly modifying the structure of a node, we can overcome many of the problems associated with singly linked lists. We begin by creating a new node, called a *dnode*, that has two pointer fields, which specify the addresses of both the previous node and the next node in the list. A sequence of dnode objects creates a list called a *doubly linked list*. Figure 9-21 gives a view of a dnode object with links to adjacent elements in a doubly linked list.

We begin our discussion by defining the dnode class, which specifies the structure of the objects that build a doubly linked list. In the next section, we modify the concept of a linked list by introducing the notion of a sentinel node. We also add circularity to the list, by having the last node point back to the front of the list. The resulting structure, called a *circular doubly linked list with a sentinel node*, will give us a very efficient and simple mechanism for implementing the list class and its associated iterator class.

dnode Objects

An element in a doubly linked list is a dnode object having a data member nodeValue that stores the value of the element and two pointer fields, *prev* and *next*, that identify the predecessor and successor of the node, respectively. The data members in the dnode class are public, because dnode objects are an implementation structure. Allowing direct access to the data members greatly simplifies the programmer's task of including dnode objects in a list. The class has two constructors. The default constructor creates a dnode object having value T(), the default value of type *T*. Of course, type *T* must have a default constructor. The second constructor provides an argument of type *T* to initialize nodeValue.

CLASS dnode	Declaration	"d_dnode.h"

```
template <typename T>
class dnode
{
   public:
```

```
       // the members of a dnode object are used for operations within a
       // doubly linked list; access is simplified by making them public
       T nodeValue;        // data value of the node
       dnode<T> *prev;     // previous node in the list
       dnode<T> *next;     // next node in the list

       dnode();
          // default constructor. creates object with value T(),
          // the default value of type T

       dnode(const T& value): nodeValue(value);
          // constructor with an argument to initialize nodeValue
   };
```

The fundamental reason for including two pointer values in a dnode object is to facilitate the addition or deletion of an element at the current position in a linked list. These operations require access to the pointer that references the previous element in the list. With a node object in a singly linked list, the operations used a second pointer, called *prev*. With a dnode object, pointer variable *prev* provides access to the previous element. The insert and erase algorithms for dnode objects are a little more complicated, because we must update two pointers, rather than a single pointer, as in the case of node objects.

Inserting a Node at a Position.   Assume that curr is a pointer to a dnode object in a doubly linked list. The insert algorithm allocates a new node and adds it to the list immediately before the node at a specified location. Assume that the insert occurs at pointer location *curr*. The pointer variable prev in node *curr* identifies prevNode (*curr* −>*prev*) as the predecessor. Figure 9-22 displays the steps required to allocate a new node with value item and update appropriate pointer fields in the new node, in node *curr*, and in node prevNode. Begin by allocating a new node (newNode), with the value set to item. The linking of newNode into the list requires setting its *prev* field to point to the predecessor of *p* and its next field to point to *p*.

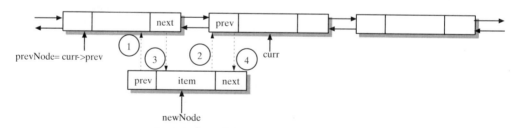

Figure 9-22
Inserting a node with value item before node curr in a doubly linked list

```
// declare the dnode pointer newNode and prevNode
dnode<T> *newNode, *prevNode;
```

```
// allocate a new node and assign prevNode to reference the
// predecessor of curr
newNode = new dnode<T>(item);
prevNode = curr->prev;

// update pointer fields in newNode
newNode->prev = prevNode; // statement 1
newNode->next = curr;     // statement 2
```

The algorithm concludes by having the predecessor of *curr* point forward to newNode and having *curr* point back to newNode.

```
// update curr and its predecessor to point to newNode
prevNode->next = newNode;    // statement 3
curr->prev = newNode;        // statement 4
```

Deleting a Node at a Position. A list with dnode objects allows for the deletion of an element at a specified pointer location. Assume that *curr* is the pointer location for a node. The delete operation requires access to both the predecessor and successor of the node. The pointer variables *prev* and *next* in node curr identify these adjacent nodes. The algorithm involves unlinking the node from the list by having the predecessor of *curr* and the successor of *curr* point to each other. Figure 9-23 indicates the two steps required by the operation. Assume that prevNode and succNode are pointers to the adjacent nodes. After updating the pointer fields for prevNode and succNode, the algorithm concludes by deallocating the memory for node *curr* by using the delete operator.

```
dnode<T> *prevNode = curr->prev, *succNode = curr->next;

// update the pointer variables in the adjacent nodes.
prevNode->next = succNode; // statement 1
succNode->prev = prevNode; // statement 2

// deallocate memory for node curr
delete curr;
```

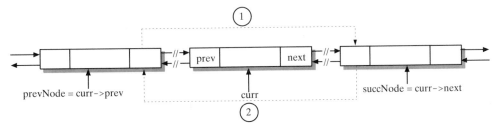

Figure 9-23
Deleting node curr in a doubly linked list

Circular Doubly Linked Lists

A doubly linked list is a sequence of dnode objects. Its structure differs from that of
a singly linked list in two significant ways. Rather than specifying a *front* pointer to
start the sequence and a NULL pointer to indicate the end of the sequence, a doubly linked list contains a *sentinel node* called *header*. The sentinel is a dnode object
containing the default value of type *T*. The linked-list structure never uses this
value. The data items in the doubly linked list begin with the node referenced by the
pointer variable *next* in header. The last node in the list has a *next* pointer that references *header*. In this way, the list is circular. Think of a doubly linked list as a
watch with a band consisting of flexible links. The header is the watch face, and the
actual nodes are the links in the band (Figure 9-24).

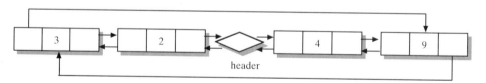

Figure 9-24
Watch model for doubly linked
list with a header node

Each node in a doubly linked list, including the header node, has a unique successor and a unique predecessor referenced by the pointer variables *next* and *prev*,
respectively. The role of the header is fundamental to a doubly linked list. With its
pointer field *next*, *header* references the first "real" node in the list. With its *prev*
pointer, *header* identifies the last real node in the list. Traversing a list can begin with
the header node and continue either forward or backward until the scan returns to
the header. Like the *front* pointer in a singly linked list, the header provides access
to all of the elements. Figure 9-25 illustrates a list of four integer nodes whose order
is 4 9 3 2, from front to back. If we follow the pointer variable *prev*, we visit the items
in the order 2 3 9 4. The figure denotes the header by using angle lines on the sides
of the node.

Figure 9-25
Doubly linked list with integer nodes having values 4 9 3 2

Declaring a Doubly Linked List. The header node defines a doubly linked
list. As a result, the declaration of the list begins with the declaration of the header
node. With the default constructor in the dnode class, we create an object with the
default value of type T() and with pointer fields that reference the node itself. The
default constructor is used primarily to allocate the header.

```
dnode<T> *header = new dnode<T>;
```

The result of the declaration is an "empty" list with a single header node and pointer values that point to the header itself:

```
header->next == header
```

```
header->prev == header
```

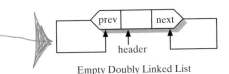

Empty Doubly Linked List

Conveniently, "itself" is the pointer *this,* which becomes the initial values for the
pointer variables *next* and *prev.*

Default Constructor:
```
dnode()
{
    next = this;
    prev = this;
}
```

Note the difference between the declaration of a singly linked list and that of
a doubly linked list. In the former case, the node<*T*> pointer *front* defines the list.
The declaration of the list begins by assigning to *front* the pointer value NULL. The
resulting singly linked list has no nodes. A doubly linked list always contains at least
one node, the header. The declaration allocating the header with the default constructor creates an empty doubly linked list. You test for an empty singly linked list
by comparing *front* with NULL. The comparison for a doubly linked list tests
whether *header—>next* or *header—>prev* is the header node (Figure 9-26).

```
Empty singly linked list:          front == NULL
Empty circular doubly linked list: header->next == header or
                                   header->prev == header
```

Example 9-4
_____

The function writeDLinkedList() scans the nodes in a doubly linked list and outputs
their values. A dnode pointer provides a loop control variable to scan through the range. For
greater flexibility, a programmer can pass a string to separate the output. By default, the separator is two blank spaces. The string "\n" outputs the node values on separate lines. The function writeDLinkedList() is included in the node library "d_nodel.h."

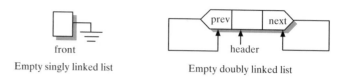

front   header

Empty singly linked list   Empty doubly linked list

Figure 9-26
Testing conditions for an empty singly linked list and an empty doubly linked list

writeDLinkedList():

```
// output a doubly linked list with each element followed by separator
template <typename T>
void writeDLinkedList(dnode<T> *header, const string& separator = " ")
{
    // header points at first dnode. p moves through the list
    dnode<T> *p = header->next ;

    while (p != header)     // continue until end of list
    {
        // output dnode value and move to the next dnode
        cout << p->nodeValue << separator;
        p = p->next;
    }
}
```

9-6   UPDATING A DOUBLY LINKED LIST

The ability to add and remove elements efficiently is the key motivation behind the design of doubly linked lists. In this section, we develop the algorithms for general insert and delete operations at any position in the list. The functions insert() and erase() implement all of the pointer updates to link and unlink a node. The presence of a header node allows a programmer to use these functions without modification when adding or removing nodes at the ends of the list. You do not want to lose sight of this fact. Unlike adding to or deleting from a singly linked list, which requires separate algorithms to add and delete elements at the front and back of the list, the same operations for a doubly linked list can be trivially derived by using only the general insert() and erase() functions. You can find an implementation of these functions in the node library "d_nodel.h."

The insert() Function

The insert operation adds a new element at a designated dnode pointer location in the list. The algorithm allocates a new node and adds it to the list immediately before the designated node. If the pointer location is the header, the insertion adds a new node at the rear of the list. The function insert() takes a dnode pointer *curr* and a new value as arguments. The return value is the address of the new node. The algorithm involves only updating four pointer values, so the algorithm has running time O(1). Use the accompanying figure to trace the update of the pointer values.

insert():

```
// insert a new node with value item immediately before node curr
template <typename T>
dnode<T> *insert(dnode<T> *curr, const T& item)
{
    // declare pointer variables for the new node and the previous node
    dnode<T> *newNode, *prevNode;

    // allocate new dnode with item as initial value
    newNode = new dnode<T>(item);

    // assign prevNode the pointer value of node before p
    prevNode = curr->prev;

    // update pointer fields in newNode
    newNode->prev = prevNode;
    newNode->next = curr;

    // update curr and prevNode to point at newNode
    prevNode->next = newNode;
    curr->prev = newNode;

    return newNode;
}
```

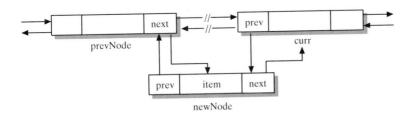

Example 9-5

Inserting an element into an empty list simultaneously creates both the first and the last node in the list. The header can reference this node by using *header−>next* (*first*) and *header−>prev* (*last*). The following figure illustrates an empty list before and after the insertion of a new node.

Before insert: empty list

After insert: list with one element

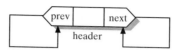

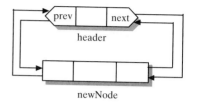

newNode

The erase() Function

The erase operation deletes an element at a specified dnode pointer location. The algorithm involves updating the pointer variables for the adjacent nodes and deallocating the memory for the deleted node. The function erase() takes a dnode pointer *curr* as an argument. If *curr* points back to itself (*curr−>next == curr*), *curr* is the header node of an empty list, and the function simply returns. The function assumes that the programmer will not attempt to delete the header of a nonempty list. The efficiency of the operation derives from the fact that node *curr* can identify both its predecessor and successor nodes. The update of the pointers requires only two statements, so erase() has running time O(1). Use the accompanying figure to trace the algorithm.

erase():

```
// erase dnode pointed to by curr
template <typename T>
void erase(dnode<T> *curr)
{
    // return if the list is empty
    if (curr->next == curr)
        return;

    // declare pointers for the predecessor and successor nodes
    dnode<T> *prevNode = curr->prev, *succNode = curr->next;

    // update pointer fields for predecessor and successor
    prevNode->next = succNode;
    succNode->prev = prevNode;

    // deallocate the memory used by the node
    delete curr;
}
```

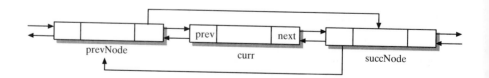

Modifying the Ends of a List. In a singly linked list, operations that add or delete nodes at the ends of the list require very distinct algorithms. Because a doubly linked list is a circular list with a header node, update operations at the ends of the list simply use insert() and erase(), with pointer arguments referenced by the header.

The pointer fields in the header reference the first node (*header−>next*) and the last node (*header−>prev*) in the list (Figure 9-27). The header itself defines the first position past the end of the list. This fact derives from the circular structure of the list. A scan begins at the first node and continues back around to the header. By using the familiar range notation [*first, last*) for iterators, we can say that the sequence of nodes in a doubly linked list has pointer values [*header−>next, header*).

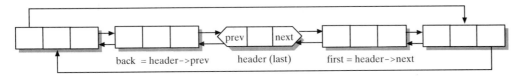

Figure 9-27
The header identifies the front and back nodes in a doubly linked list

Adding or removing a node at the front of a list involves calling insert() or erase() with the pointer argument *header−>next*. The insertion occurs immediately before the first node, with the pointer value *next* in the header referencing the new node (Figure 9-28). The function erase() removes the current first node in the list and updates the header to reference a new first node.

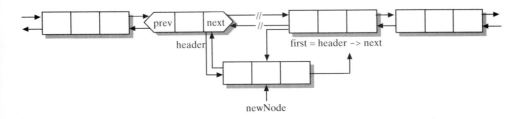

Figure 9-28
Insert node at the front of a list

With the realization that the header identifies the rear of the list, the algorithm to add a node at the rear involves calling insert() with the header as the pointer argument. The operation adds the node immediately before the header, hence at the back of the list (Figure 9-29). A call to the function erase() with pointer argument *header−>prev* deletes the last node in the list.

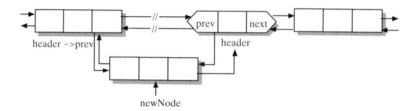

Figure 9-29
Insert node at the rear of a list

The upcoming table shows a summary of access and update operations for elements at the ends of a doubly linked list. For convenience, we list the operations under the familiar function names front(), push_front(), pop_back(), and so forth. The functions are not included in the dnode library.

Operation Name	Implementation
push_front(*item*)	insert(*header−>next, item*)
pop_front()	erase(*header−>next*)
front()	value: *header−>next−>nodeValue*
push_back(*item*)	insert(*header, item*)
pop_back()	erase(*header−>prev*)
back()	value: *header−>prev−>nodeValue*

Program 9-3   WORD JUMBLE

This application uses doubly linked list operations to insert letters from a word randomly at both the front and the back of a list. The resulting characters in the list create a word-jumble puzzle. The program prompts the user to enter the number of words that the program should jumble. In each iteration of a loop, a prompt asks the user to enter a word (string). For each successive character word[0] to word[word.length() − 1], a random integer with value 0 or 1 specifies whether to insert the character at the front or the rear of the linked list. If the random number is 0, insert the character at the front of the list; otherwise, insert the character at the back of the list. For output, the program displays both the original word and the jumbled characters in the following format:

Word/Jumbled Word: <original word>   <jumbled character list>

The program outputs the linked list by using the function writeDLinkedList() from "d_nodel.h". For instance, with input "tank," the random sequence 1 0 0 1 creates the jumbled list of characters n − a − t − k ("natk"). After processing a word, we call the function clear(), which erases the nodes of the linked list in preparation for the input of a new word.

```
// File: prg9_3.cpp
// the program prompts the user to enter the number of words
// the program should jumble. in a loop, the user enters the words.
// program inserts each letter of word into a doubly linked list of
// characters based generating a random integer with value
// 0 or 1. if the value is 0, insert the character at the front of
// the linked list; otherwise, insert it at the back. the function
// insert() from "d_nodel.h" implements list insertion operations.
```

```
// displaying the list using the function writeDLinkedList()
// gives a jumbled version of the word. calling clear()
// deletes the list so the next iteration will create a new list.

#include <iostream>
#include <string>

#include "d_node.h"    // node class
#include "d_nodel.h"   // for writeDLinkedList(), insert(), erase()
#include "d_random.h" // use random integers

using namespace std;

// clear the list
template <typename T>
void clear(dnode<T> *header);

int main()
{
    // header node for list holding jumbled characters
    dnode<char> *header = new dnode<char>;
    string word;
    int numWords, i, j;
    randomNumber rnd;
    // prompt for the number of words to enter
    cout << "How many words will you enter? ";
    cin >> numWords;
    cout << endl;
    for (i = 0; i < numWords; i++)
    {
        cout << "Word:       ";
        cin >> word;

        // use rnd.random(2) to determine if the char is inserted
        // at the front (value = 0) or back (value = 1) of the list
        for (j = 0; j < word.length(); j++)
            if (rnd.random(2) == 0)
                // insert at the front of the list
                insert(header->next, word[j]);
            else
                // insert at the back of the list
                insert(header, word[j]);

        // output the word and its jumbled variation
        cout << "Word/Jumbled Word: " << word << "   ";
        writeDLinkedList(header);
        cout << endl << endl;

        // clear the list in preparation for the next word
        clear(header);
    }
```

```
    return 0;
    }

template <typename T>
void clear(dnode<T> *header)
{
    // repeatedly remove the first node in the list
    // until the list is empty. this condition occurs
    // when the header points to itself
    while(header->next != header)
        erase(header->next);
}
```

```
Run:

How many words will you enter? 4

Word: C++
Word/Jumbled Word: C++    +   C   +

Word: before
Word/Jumbled Word: before   o   f   e   b   r   e

Word: jumbled
Word/Jumbled Word: jumbled   d   b   j   u   m   l   e

Word: link
Word/Jumbled Word: link   k   n   i   l
```

9-7   THE JOSEPHUS PROBLEM

In the world of puzzles, there is a challenge called the Josephus problem, which resembles the game of musical chairs. We introduce the problem in this chapter, because it has an elegant circular-list solution. The following is a version of the challenge:

> A travel agent selects n customers to compete in the finals of a contest for a free world cruise. The agent places the customers in a circle and then draws a number m ($1 <= m <= n$) from a hat. The game is played by having the agent walk clockwise around a circle, stopping at every mth contestant. The agent asks the selected person to leave the game and then continues the clockwise walk. Over time, the number of remaining contestants dwindles until only one survivor remains. This person is the winner of the world cruise. Figure 9-30 illustrates the Josephus Problem for $n = 6$ and $m = 3$.

The function josephus() assumes that n contestants compete for the cruise and that the deselection process removes every mth contestant. The values n and m are function arguments. A circular doubly linked list, called dList, stores the contestants with integer values 1, 2, . . ., n. In an iterative process, the algorithm sequences through the ring of remaining nodes and removes the mth node from the list. Be-

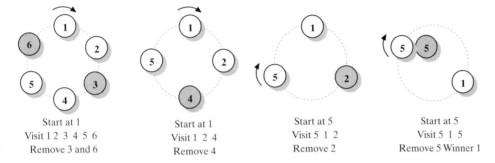

Start at 1
Visit 1 2 3 4 5 6
Remove 3 and 6

Start at 1
Visit 1 2 4
Remove 4

Start at 5
Visit 5 1 2
Remove 2

Start at 5
Visit 5 1 5
Remove 5 Winner 1

Figure 9-30
Removing contestants in the Josephus Problem with n = 6, m = 3

cause there are n contestants for the cruise, the function uses $n - 1$ iterations. The process starts by assigning a node pointer to reference the first node. Starting with this node, a series of $m - 1$ steps moves the pointer forward to the location of the first node (contestant) to remove. To avoid invalidating the pointer when we delete the node, we first move the pointer forward one position and then delete the predecessor node. The next iteration picks up at the current pointer position and repeats the process of moving the pointer forward $m - 1$ steps and deleting a node. Because the nodes are stored in a doubly linked list, each movement of the pointer must check for the header so that it is not counted or deleted. At the end of the $n - 1$ iterations, the pointer identifies the winner of the cruise. Each iteration outputs the deselected contestant. The function terminates by displaying the winner.

josephus():

```
void josephus(int n, int m)
{
    // declare the circular doubly linked list dList and scan pointer
    dnode<int> *dList = new dnode<int>, *curr;
    int i, j;

    // initialize the list of contestants 1 2 3 ... n
    for (i = 1; i <= n; i++)
        insert(dList, i);
    // curr moves around the list, starting at person 1
    curr = dList->next;

    // delete all but one person from the list
    for(i=1; i < n; i++)
    {
        // counting current person at curr, visit m persons.
        // we must advance m-1 times.
        for(j=1; j <= m-1; j++)
        {
            // advance the pointer
            curr = curr->next;

            // if curr at the header, move again
```

```
            if (curr == dList)
                curr = curr->next;
        }
        cout << "Delete contestant " << curr->nodeValue
            << endl;

        // advance curr and erase the node we just left
        curr = curr->next;
        erase(curr->prev);

        // might have deleted the rear of the list, so
        // curr is now at the header. move again
        if (curr == dList)
            curr = curr->next;
    }

    cout << endl << "Contestant " << curr->nodeValue
        << " wins the cruise" << endl;
    // delete the one remaining node and the list header
    delete curr;
    delete dList;
}
```

Program 9-4   THE JOSEPHUS PROBLEM

Let us see who wins the world-cruise contest. The upcoming program begins by prompting the user to enter the number of contestants, *n*. A random number in the range from 1 to *n* specifies the value *m*. A call to josephus() takes the arguments *n* and *m* and determines our winner.

```
// File: prg9_4.cpp
// the program prompts the user to enter the number of contestants
// n, in a world cruise contest and generates a random integer,m,
// between 1 and n. a call to the function josephus()
// outputs the winner of the contest. the function
// inserts the numbers 1, 2, 3, ..., n in a doubly
// linked list. a loop moves around the list in a circular fashion and
// erases every mth contestant until only 1 remains. this
// is the number of the winner

#include <iostream>

#include "d_dnode.h"
#include "d_nodel.h"
#include "d_random.h"

using namespace std;

// given an n item circular list, solve the Josephus problem
// by deleting every mth person until only one remains.
void josephus(int n, int m);
```

```
int main()
{
    // n is number of contestants
    // m is the rotation selector
    randomNumber rnd;
    int n, m;

    cout << "Enter the number of contestants:    ";
    cin >> n;

    // generate a random number between 1 and n
    m = 1 + rnd.random(n);
    cout << "Generated the random number " << m << endl;

    // solve the Josephus problem and output the cruise winner
    josephus(n, m);

    return 0;
}

/* implementation of josephus() given in the program discussion */
```

```
Run:

Enter the number of contestants: 10
Generated the random number 5
Delete contestant 5
Delete contestant 10
Delete contestant 6
Delete contestant 2
Delete contestant 9
Delete contestant 8
Delete contestant 1
Delete contestant 4
Delete contestant 7

Contestant 3 wins the cruise
```

THE MINILIST CLASS   9-8

With a knowledge of doubly linked lists, we are now in a position to implement the miniList class, which is a variation of the STL list class. Like the other "mini" classes, the implementation allows you to see how a programmer can declare an underlying structure to store the data and then code the operations. In the case of the miniList class, we choose a doubly linked list as the underlying structure. The miniList class also gives us the first opportunity to see an implementation of an iterator. In the miniList class, this is not a difficult task once you realize that we can represent an iterator object by using a dnode pointer. The problem involves implementing the iterator operations * (dereference operator), ++ and −− (increment and decrement), and the iterator comparisons == and !=. In the miniList class, we must also give meaning to the functions begin() and end(), which return iterators pointing to locations in the list. You can forsee that begin() will return an iterator whose underlying pointer value is *header−>next* and that end() will return a pointer to *header*.

miniList Class Private Members

The private data members in the miniList class include the header for the doubly linked list and an integer, called listSize, that contains a count of the number of elements in the list. The *header* is a dnode<*T*> pointer that each of the miniList constructors creates. Any of the insertion and deletion operations updates the value of listSize. The private members also include utility functions. Whenever an operation inserts a new node, we call getDNode() to allocate the node dynamically and return its address on the heap. The function throws a memoryAllocationError exception if the heap does not have enough space. A doubly linked list can use the insertion and deletion algorithms discussed in Section 9-5 to modify nodes at any position in the sequence. These are very powerful general-purpose operations that allow a programmer to copy a list, clear a list, and update the nodes at the ends of the list. The miniList class implements these algorithms in the private functions dinsert() and derase(). The upcoming code is the declaration of the miniList class private members. Figure 9-31 illustrates the value of the data members for a list with three integer elements.

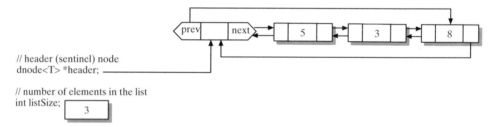

Figure 9-31
miniList object with three integer elements

Private Members of the miniList Class
```
dnode<T> *header;
    // header (sentinel) node

int listSize;
    // number of elements in the list

dnode<T> *getDNode(const T& item);
    // allocate a dnode object with the value item and
    // return a pointer to it. throw the memoryAllocationError
    // exception of the memory allocation fails
```

```
dnode<T> *dinsert(dnode<T> *curr, const T& item);
    // insert item before node curr of the linked list and
    // return the address of the new node

void derase(dnode<T> *curr);
    // erase node curr from the linked list.
    // Precondition:   the list is not empty. the functions that
    // call derase() check the precondition
```

miniList Class Constructors and Destructor

The underlying doubly linked list is a dynamic storage structure. As a result, the miniList class has the usual memory management operations, including constructors, a destructor, a copy constructor, and an overloaded assignment operator.

Constructors:
```
miniList();
    // constructor. create an empty list
miniList(int n, const T& item = T());
    // constructor. build a list with n elements, all having
    // the value item
miniList(T* first, T* last);
    // constructor. build a list whose data comes from the
    // pointer range [first, last)
```

Copy Constructor, Destructor, and Overloaded Assignment Operator
```
miniList(const miniList<T>& obj);
    // copy constructor
~miniList();
    // destructor
miniList<T>& operator= (const miniList<T>& rhs);
    // overloaded assignment operator
```

We include an implementation of the constructor that initializes a list with *n* elements and an implementation of the copy constructor. These functions illustrate the use of dinsert() to build the underlying doubly linked list. The constructor takes the size *n* and the initial value *item* as arguments. After initialization of listSize to have the value *n*, a loop uses dinsert() to add *n* nodes into the list with value *item*. Each node has the same value, so insert each value at the front of the list by using the pointer argument *header−>next*.

Constructor:
```
template <typename T>
miniList<T>::miniList(int n, const T& value): listSize(n)
{
    int i;
```

```
        // create an empty list
        header = new dnode<T>;
        if (header == NULL)
           throw memoryAllocationError
              ("miniList(): memory allocation failure");
        // insert n copies of value at the front of the list
        for (i=0;i < n;i++)
           dinsert(header->next, value);
     }
```

The copy constructor creates a miniList object that is a copy of the object *obj*. The implementation creates a doubly linked list for the new object having the same size and node values as the doubly linked list obj.header. A loop copies the values from obj.header onto the back of the current list by using dinsert().

Copy Constructor:

```
     template <typename T>
     miniList<T>::miniList(const miniList<T>& obj):
                 listSize(obj.listSize)
     {
        // curr moves through the nodes in obj, and end marks the finish
        // of a traversal through obj
        dnode<T> *curr = obj.header->next, *end = obj.header;

        // create an empty list
        header = new dnode<T>;
        if (header == NULL)
           throw memoryAllocationError
              ("miniList(): memory allocation failure");

        // insert the values in the linked list obj.header
        // at the back of the current list
        while (curr != end)
        {
           dinsert(header, curr->nodeValue);
           curr = curr->next;
        }
     }
```

Functions Dealing with the Ends of a List

We use the miniList functions dinsert() and derase() to add or remove elements in a miniList object. Operations at the front of a list require the pointer to the first element. This is exactly *header−>next*. Operations at the back of a list use the pointer value header for an insertion and the pointer *header−>prev* for a deletion.

Let us see these ideas in action for the implementation of the miniList operations push_front() and pop_back(). The function push_front() inserts a new element before the first item in the list. Use header−>next as the pointer argument for dinsert(). After inserting the new node, increment the list size.

push_back():

```
template <typename T>
void miniList<T>::push_front(const T& item)
{
    // insert at the front
    dinsert(header->next, item);

    // increment the list size
    listSize++;
}
```

The function pop_back() removes the element at the back of the list. The element is the node pointed to by *header−>prev*. The operation has a precondition that the list be nonempty. If the condition is violated, the function throws an underflowError exception. Call derase() to remove the back of the list, and decrement the list size.

pop_back():

```
template <typename T>
void miniList<T>::pop_back()
{
    if (listSize == 0)
        throw underflowError("miniList pop_back(): list is empty");

    // erase the back
    derase(header->prev);

    // decrement the list size
    listSize--;
}
```

miniList Iterators

The miniList class has fully functional iterators. The iterator classes, iterator and const_iterator, are *nested classes* declared within the miniList class. The upcoming code is the declaration of the nested iterator class within the miniList class. The miniList class also contains a similar declaration of the nested const_iterator class. Consult the file "d_liter.h" for a complete listing of both the iterator and const_iterator classes. We place the iterator nested classes in the separate file "d_liter.h" and introduce them into the miniList class using *include* statements. This is done to decrease the complexity of viewing the miniList class.

```
template <typename T>
class miniList
{
    public:

        // include the iterator nested classes
```

```
#include "d_liter.h"
    ...
};
```

CLASS miniList::iterator	Declaration	"d_liter.h"

```
// miniList class iterator
class iterator
{
  public:
    iterator();
      // constructor

    bool operator== (const iterator& rhs) const;
    bool operator!= (const iterator& rhs) const;
      // comparison operators for iterators

    T& operator* ();
      // pointer dereference operator

    iterator& operator++ ();
      // prefix increment operator        // ++int //increment then use
                                                       new value
    iterator operator++ (int);
      // postfix increment operator       // int ++ //use old value then
                                                         increment

    iterator& operator-- ();
      // prefix decrement operator        // --int
    iterator operator-- (int);
      // postfix decrement operator       // int --

  private:
    dnode<T> *nodePtr;
      // pointer to current list node
    iterator(dnode<T> *p);
      // private constructor. converts p to an iterator
      // by assigning p to nodePtr
};
```

An iterator object has a single data member, called nodePtr, which is a dnode<*T*> pointer. A miniList iterator is a generalized pointer to a list element. The underlying data member is an actual pointer to a node in the doubly linked list. Figure 9-32 illustrates four different iterator positions in the list mList. The iterator values iterA and iterB are the return values for the list functions begin() and end(), respectively, corresponding to the front of the list and the position just past the end of the list. Iterator iterC is the location of back, and iterD is the location of the predecessor of iterC. The figure also includes the doubly linked list, whose nodes store the values for the elements in the list. The value iter.nodePtr is the pointer value corresponding to *iter*. The figure includes labels for the nodePtr values that correspond to the four list iterators.

```
iterA = mList.begin();   // iterA.nodePtr = header->next (front of list)
iterB = mList.end();     // iterB.nodePtr = header (past end of list)
iterC                    // iterC.nodePtr = header->prev (back of list)
iterD                    // iterD.nodePtr points at element 9
```

List with 4 elements and different iterator values

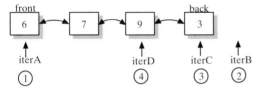

Corresponding doubly linked list with 4 nodes and different dnode <T> pointer values

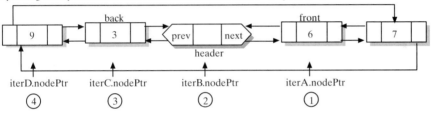

Figure 9-32
Comparison of iterator and associated dnode pointers

Defining the iterator as a nested class is purely an encapsulation technique. The nested class does not have special access to members of the miniList class; moreover, the miniList class has no special access rights to the members of the nested classes. When referring to a nested class outside the scope of the *parent class*, the class scope operator must be included. This is the reason for including the miniList scope operator in the declaration of an iterator or a const_iterator object.

☞ Note

```
miniList<T>::iterator iter;          // iterator for a miniList object
miniList<T>::const_iterator cIter;   // constant miniList iterator
```

Implementing Iterator Operations. We implement the iterator operations by using the nodePtr variable to reference a node in the doubly linked list. For instance, the dereference operator, *, accesses the nodeValue field in the node. Think of *iter as the value of the node pointed to by iter.nodePtr. The operator throws a referenceError exception if the list is empty.

Iterator dereference operator, *:
```
// pointer dereference operator
T& operator* ()
{
    // if the node's successor is itself, the list is empty
    if (nodePtr->next == nodePtr)
        throw
            referenceError("miniList iterator: reference error");

    return nodePtr->nodeValue;
}
```

If *obj* is a variable of a primitive type, the expression $++obj$ increments *obj* and returns the new value, whereas the expression *obj*++ also increments *obj*, but returns the original value. To overload the iterator increment and decrement operators and allow both the *prefix* ($++obj$, $--obj$) and *postfix* (*obj*++, *obj*−−) versions, each overloaded function must have a unique argument list that enables the compiler to determine which version the programmer intends. Overload the prefix version without an argument, as is customary when we implement a unary operator as a member function:

```
iterator operator++ ();
```

The postfix version of the increment operator uses a prototype that includes a formal argument of type *int*. When a compiler sees that a statement uses postfix increment, it provides 0 as the runtime argument. In the declaration of the operator function, it is necessary to specify that an *int* argument exists, but it is not necessary to specify a formal argument name:

```
iterator operator++ (int);
```

Implement the iterator postfix $++$ by making a copy of the current iterator in the object *tmp* (*tmp* = *this). Then advance nodePtr forward one node and return the object *tmp* as the value of the function:

operator++ (postfix form):
```
// postfix increment. move forward one node
iterator operator++ (int)
{
    // save the current value of the iterator
    iterator tmp = *this;

    // move to the successor of nodePtr
    nodePtr = nodePtr->next;

    return tmp; // return original iterator value
}
```

(handwritten note in left margin:)
//Prefix
nodePtr = nodePtr →next ;
return * this ;

The miniList Member Functions begin() and end()

The importance of header is most evident in the miniList functions begin() and end(). The function begin() returns an iterator that points to the first element in the list. This iterator has its nodePtr set to *header−>next*. The implementation of the operations makes use of the private iterator constructor. If you refer back to the iterator class declaration, you can note that the public section has a default constructor and the private section has a constructor with a dnode pointer argument. Programmers use the default constructor when declaring an iterator object. The private constructor takes a dnode<*T*> pointer and creates an iterator with the pointer value assigned to nodePtr:

```
iterator(dnode<T> *p);
    // private constructor. converts p to an iterator
    // by assigning p to nodePtr
```

The function begin() has a return statement that calls the private iterator constructor with *header−>next* as the argument:

begin():
```
template <typename T>
miniList<T>::iterator miniList<T>::begin()
{
    // private iterator constructor builds an iterator object
    // from the dnode pointer
    return iterator(header->next);
}
```

In the case of end(), we must position the iterator so it points just past the end of the list. In the doubly linked list, the header specifies this position. To implement the function, return an iterator object whose nodePtr value is header:

end():
```
template <typename T>
miniList<T>::iterator miniList<T>::end()
{
    // private constructor builds an iterator object
    // from the dnode pointer
    return iterator(header);
}
```

The General miniList Insert Function

The list insert() function takes an iterator position as an argument and adds a new element at the position. The return value from the function is an iterator pointing to the new element. The implementation is simple. Call dinsert() with the dnode pointer value corresponding to the iterator (pos.nodePtr), and then increment list-Size. The function dinsert() returns the pointer to the new node. Apply the private constructor to build an iterator object whose nodePtr variable is newNode, and return its value.

insert():

```
template <typename T>
miniList<T>::iterator miniList<T>::insert(iterator pos, const T& item)
{
    // record the current node's address in curr. newNode will be
    // the address of the node we insert
    dnode<T> *curr = pos.nodePtr, *newNode;
    // insert item before curr and capture the new node's address
    newNode = dinsert(curr, item);

    // increment the list size
    listSize++;

    // constructor converts newNode to an iterator
    return iterator(newNode);
}
```

9-9   SELECTING A SEQUENCE CONTAINER

The completion of this chapter marks the end of our study of sequence containers, including arrays, vectors, and lists. We have mentioned a fourth container class, called a deque, but have not provided an implementation. When designing an application that requires the storage of data by position, a programmer can choose among these four sequence containers. The decision can make a great difference in the performance of the program. We provide some guidelines:

- Use a C++ array only for problems for which you know the number of data items in advance. Because a vector also provides indexed access and has the ability to grow to meet the demands of the application, it is often advisable to use a vector instead of an array.

- Use a vector if the application needs index access and the program performs all insertions and deletions at the end of the sequence. The vector is the most efficient container for this type of access. This was our reasoning for using a vector to implement a stack. If the application requires infrequent modifications to the sequence at intermediate positions, a vector is still acceptable. However, applications requiring frequent insert and delete operations at intermediate locations should use a list container.

- Use a deque if the application needs index access and the application performs all insertions and deletions at both ends of the sequence. The deque is the fastest type of container for these operations; this is the reason that STL uses this container as the default for the implementation of the queue. A deque stores data in blocks that are linked together by a block map. When indexed access is used, the deque must access the block map to determine where the element resides in memory. This adds additional overhead to the operation. As a result, a deque does not execute index access as quickly as a vector or an array does.

- Use a list when the application requires frequent insertions and deletions at arbitrary locations in the list and direct (index) access is not required. For instance, a list is appropriate when creating an ordered list by repeated insertions of new elements into the sequence. The problem with a list is its access to the elements. Locating an element requires an $O(n)$ sequential search, starting at the front of the list. As a result, a list is not appropriate when an application must first search for the data before accessing or updating the value. These applications should use one of the associative containers, such as a set or map. These containers provide very fast running times for searches.

CHAPTER SUMMARY

- Efficient implementation of the list container requires a data structure that implements $O(1)$ insert and erase operations at any position in the sequence. It is not possible to meet these requirements when using a vector or an array to implement a list. Insertions and deletions inside a list will have running time $O(n)$. What we need is a structure that distributes data in separate units that are tied together like links in a chain. To insert or erase and element requires only that the links be reset. The linked list satisfies these requirements. There are two types of linked lists: singly linked lists and doubly linked lists. Our study began first with the singly linked list and then considered the much more flexible and efficient doubly linked list.

- A singly linked list contains nodes, where each node contains a value and a pointer (link) to the next node in the list. The list begins with a pointer to the first node of the list and terminates when a node has a NULL (0) pointer. We declare the pointer variable *front* to point to the first node of the list. For an empty list, *front* = NULL. As we insert items at the front of the list, *front* changes.

- Inserting at the front of a singly linked list requires that we set the pointer in the new node to the previous value of *front* and then update *front* to point at the new node. To erase the front, assign to *front* the pointer value of the first node, and then delete the node. These operations have running time $O(1)$.

- Inserting and erasing inside a singly linked list is more complicated than corresponding operations on the ends. The programmer must maintain a pointer to the current list node and a pointer to the previous node. Inserting or deleting involves changing the pointer value in the previous node.

- To efficiently insert at the back of a singly linked list, the programmer must maintain a pointer *back* to the last node in the list. The pointer has value NULL when the list is empty. Assign to *back* the address of the first node added to the list. To add other nodes at the back, allocate a new node, assign the pointer in node *back* to point to the new node, and assign to the pointer *back* the address of the new node. As an alternative to maintaining *back*, the programmer can perform an $O(n)$ scan to locate the back of the list and then perform an insertion. This approach is not acceptable unless the program requires this operation infrequently. Erasing the back of a singly linked list requires locating the node before the back, and this algorithm has running time $O(n)$. Programmers do not use a singly linked list when it is necessary to erase the back of the list frequently.

- A singly linked list is a very appropriate structure for implementing a stack or a queue, because all operations for these containers involve accessing and updating at one end of the list. Section 9-4 implements the queue ADT by using a singly linked list. The implementation provides an excellent application for the singly linked list and also provides an excellent opportunity to review the implementation of a destructor, copy constructor, and overloaded assignment operator.

- The doubly linked list provides the most flexible implementation for the sequential list. Its nodes have pointers to the next and the previous node, and so the program can traverse a list in either the forward or backward direction. To take full advantage of this structure, implement a circular doubly linked list with a header node. The header node contains the default value of type *T*, but the program never attempts to access this value. The header's *next* field points to the first node of the linked list, and its *prev* field points to the last node. Traverse a list by starting at the first node and follow the sequence of *next* nodes until you arrive back at the header. To traverse a list in reverse order, start at the last node and follow the sequence of *previous* nodes until arriving back at the header.

- Insertion before any node in a doubly linked list, including the header, requires four pointer assignments. When you have a pointer to a node, two assignment statements unlink the node from the list. Do not apply this operation to the header node. To insert a node at the front of the list, insert before the node following the header. To insert at the back of the list, insert before the header node. Remove the front of the list by removing the node following the header, and remove the back of the list by removing the node before the header. These operations are more involved in a singly linked list, because they involve handling the special case of an empty list. Removing the back of a singly linked list is an $O(n)$ operation and should be avoided unless the program will perform the operation infrequently. Section 9-7 states and solves the interesting Josephus problem, which illustrates doubly linked list operations.

- Section 9-8 discusses the implementation of the miniList class with a doubly linked list. The implementation of the push_front(), pop_front(), push_back(), and pop_back() operations is simple and follows directly from the discussion in Section 9-6. The miniList class provides our first opportunity to discuss the implementation of the nested iterator classes. Under the doubly linked list structure, an iterator object contains one data member, a node pointer. The miniList function begin() returns the address of the node following the header, and the function end() returns the address of the header.

- This chapter completes our discussion of the sequence containers. Section 9-9 presents some suggestions for deciding which container to use: array, vector, deque, or list. In general, the vector is superior to the array for most applications, because it expands at the back to meet the needs of the application and has index access. The deque also provides index access and expands automatically at either end. A deque is an excellent container to use for the implementation of a queue. Use a list for an application that does not require index access and that performs frequent insert or erase operations at intermediate locations in the sequence.

CLASSES AND LIBRARIES IN THE CHAPTER

Name	Implementation File
dnode	d_dnode.h
Linked list library	d_nodel.h
linkedQueue	d_lqueue.h
miniList	d_list.h
miniList iterators	d_liter.h
node	d_node.h
randomNumber	d_random.h

REVIEW EXERCISES

1. For what types of operations is a singly linked list more efficient than a vector?
2. **(a)** What is the running time for an insertion at the front of an n-element singly linked list?
   (b) What is the running time for an insertion at the back of an n-element singly linked list if the programmer maintains a pointer to the back of the list? What is the running time if the programmer maintains only a pointer to the front of the list?
3. Assume the following declarations:

   ```
   node<int> *front, *newNode, *curr, *nextNode;
   int i;
   ```

   (a) Display the resulting list after execution of the following statements:

   ```
   front = new node<int> (8);
   newNode = new node<int> (5);
   newNode->next = front->next;
   front->next = newNode;
   ```

   (b) Display the resulting list after execution of the following statements:

   ```
   front = new node<int> (7);
   front = new node<int> (15, front);

   curr = front->next;
   ```

```
for(i=4; i >= 1; i--)
{   newNode = new node<int> (i);
    curr->next = newNode;
    curr = newNode;
}
```

4. Call delFunc(front) for the lists in parts (a) and (b). Display the resulting list.

```
template <typename T>
void delFunc(node<T> * & front)
{
    node<T> *p = front, *q;

    while(p->next != NULL)
    {
      q = p;
      p = p->next;
      delete q;
    }
    front = p;
}
```

(a) Assume that T is the int type and the list is

    22   19   44   15   8   3

(b) Assume that T is the char type and the list is

    L I N K E D   L I S T

5. Implement the function find(), which searches for a value in a singly linked list:

```
// return a pointer to the first node with value item.
// if item is not in the list, return NULL
template <typename T>
node<T> *find(node<T> *front, const T& item);
```

6. Trace the code in the function f().

```
template <typename T>
void f(node<T> *front)
{
  node<T> *p = front;
  T value;

  if (front == NULL)
    return;

  while (p->next != NULL)
    p = p->next;

  value = p->nodeValue;
  p->nodeValue = front->nodeValue;
  front->nodeValue = value;
}
```

(a) Assume that the list is   `front -> 7  -> 2  -> 9  -> 5 -> NULL`

     The new list is   ____ ____ ____ ____ ____

(b) Assume that the list is   `front -> 'd' -> 't' -> 'a' -> 'g' -> 'z' -> NULL`

     The new list is   ____ ____ ____ ____ ____ ____

7. A program enters the integer values {1, 7, 2, 7, 9, 1, 9, 3} into a linked list front using the function f(). Give the resulting values in the list.

```
void f(node<int> * & front, int item)
{
   node<int> *p = front;
   while (p != NULL && p->nodeValue != item)
      p = p->next;
   if (p == NULL)
      front = new node<int>(item, front);
}
```

8. What is the output from execution of f(front), using the lists in parts (a) and (b)?

```
template <typename T>
void func(node<T> *front)
{
    stack<node<T> *> s;
    node<T> *curr = front;
    while (curr != NULL)
    {   s.push(curr);
        curr = curr->next;
    }
    while (!s.empty())
    {
        cout << (s.top())->nodeValue << "   ";
        s.pop();
    }
   cout <<endl;
}
```

(a) Assume the list is   `front -> 8 -> 7 -> 1 -> 5 -> 3 -> 2 -> NULL`

     The output of func() is   ____ ____ ____ ____ ____

(b) Assume that the list is   `front -> 8 -> 7 -> 3 -> 8 -> 3 -> 12 -> NULL`

     The output of func() is   ____ ____ ____ ____ ____

9. Implement the function replace(), which takes a linked list specified by the pointer front and two values, findItem and replItem, of type T. The function scans the list looking for all occurrences of findItem and replaces them with replItem.

```
template <typename T>
void replace(node<T> *front, const T& findItem, const T& replItem);
```

10. At each of the numbered comments, draw the doubly linked list.

```
dnode<int> *intList = new dnode<int>, *newNode, *curr;

newNode = new dnode<int> (5);
newNode->next = intList->next;
intList->next->prev = newNode;
newNode->prev = intList;
intList->next = newNode;       // #1

newNode = new dnode<int> (3);
newNode->prev = intList->prev;
intList->prev->next = newNode;
newNode->next = intList;
intList->prev = newNode;       // #2

curr = intList->next;
curr = curr->next;
curr->nodeValue = 15;          // #3

curr = curr->prev;
curr->prev->next = curr->next;
curr->next->prev = curr->prev;
delete curr;                   // #4
```

11. Why is inserting at the front or the rear of a doubly linked list an O(1) operation?

12. Implement the function size(), which returns the number of elements in a doubly linked list:

```
template <typename T>
int size(dnode<T> *header);
```

13. Describe the action of function f(), which takes a doubly linked list header as an argument:

```
template <typename T>
void f(dnode<T> *header)
{
    dnode<T> *p = header->next;
    if (header == header->next)
        return;
    do
    {
        insert(header->next, p->nodeValue);
        p = p->next;
        erase(p->prev);
    } while (p != header);
}
```

14. In the implementation of the miniList class, the code shown next is an alternative version of the function push_back() using the end() operation from the miniList class. Fill in the missing expression.

```
template <typename T>
void miniList<T>::push_back(const T& item)
{
    insert(_____);
}
```

Answers to Review Exercises

1. A linked list is more efficient when inserting or erasing an element at the front or in the interior of the sequence.

2. **(a)** O(1)
   (b) O(1) when maintaining *back*, O(n) otherwise.

3. **(a)**

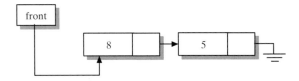

(b)

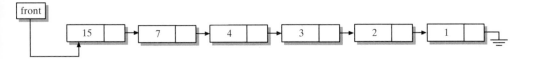

4. The function removes all but the rear node from the list.
   (a) Resulting list: 3
   (b) Resulting list: T

5.
```
// return a pointer to the first node with value item.
// if item is not in the list, return NULL
template <typename T>
node<T> *find(node<T> *front, const T& item)
{
    node<T> *curr = front;
    while (curr != NULL && curr->nodeValue != item)
        curr = curr->next;
    return curr;
}
```

6. **(a)** `front -> 5  -> 2  -> 9  -> 7 -> NULL`
   (b) `front -> 'z' -> 't' -> 'a' -> 'g' -> 'd' -> NULL`

7. Inserts the nonduplicate values in the list in reverse order:

```
front -> 3 -> 9 -> 2 -> 7 -> 1 -> NULL
```

8. The function uses a stack to display the elements of a linked list in reverse.
   (a) The output of func() is 2 3 5 1 7 8
   (b) The output of func() is 12 3 8 3 7 8

9.
```
template <typename T>
void replace(node<T> *front, const T& findItem, const T& replItem)
{
    node<T> *curr = front;

    while (curr != NULL)
    {
    if (curr->nodeValue == findItem)
    // replace findItem by replItem
    curr->nodeValue = replItem;
    curr = curr->next;
    }
}
```

10.

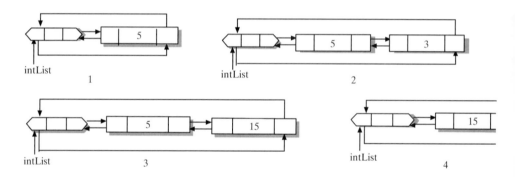

intList
        1

intList
        2

intList
        3

intList
        4

11. Each operation involves inserting a node after or before the header. Each insertion requires four pointer changes, regardless of the list size.

12.
```
template <typename T>
int size(dnode<T> *header)
{
    int count = 0;
    dnode<T> *curr = header->next;

    while(curr != header)
    {
        count++;
        curr = curr->next;
    }
    return count;
}
```

13. Reverses the order of the elements in the doubly linked list.

14. The implementation is

```
template <typename T>
void miniList<T>::push_back(const T& item)
{
    // insert before end()
    insert(end(), value);
}
```

WRITTEN EXERCISES

15. Assume that p, q, r, and nextNode are pointers to character nodes. Initially, the nodes for p and q are dynamically allocated with values X and A, respectively. The three upcoming statements build a portion of a linked list. After each statement, describe the resulting chain of nodes.

(a) `r = new node<char> ('M');`

(b) `q->next = r;`
`r->next = p;`

(c) `nextNode = q->next;`
`q->next = nextNode->next;`
`delete nextNode;`

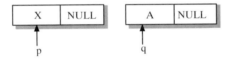

16. Use the following linked list of integer nodes for each part:

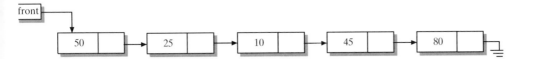

Assume the declaration

```
node<int> *front, *p, *newNode, *nextNode;
```

(a) Consider the following statement, which adds a new node to the list:

```
front = new node<int> (30,front);
```

The value of the first node in the list is _____
The value of the second node in the list is _____
The value of the third node in the list is _____

(b) Assume that *p* points at the node with value 10. Execute the following statements:

```
nextNode = p->next;
p->next = nextNode->next;
delete nextNode;
```

The integer value of node *p* after the statements is _____
The value of the node that is deleted from the list is _____

(c) The following loop scans the list:

```
p = front;
while (p != NULL)
    p = p->next;
cout << p->next;
```

Will the *cout* statement execute properly?

(d) Modify the code in part (c) so that it outputs the value 80.

(e) Trace the following loop:

```
int t;
node<int> *q;

p = front;
while (p->next != NULL)
{
    q = p->next;
    t = p->nodeValue + q->nodeValue;
    p->nodeValue = t;
    p = q;
}
```

What are the data values for each node in the resulting list?

17. Apply the following function to the lists in parts (a) and (b), and display the new list:

```
template <typename T>
void f(node<T> * & front)
{
    node<T> *curr, *prev;

    if (front == NULL)
        return;

    prev = NULL;
    curr = front;

    while (curr->next != NULL)
    {
        prev = curr;
        curr = curr->next;
    }
```

```
        if (prev == NULL)
            front = NULL;
        else
            prev->next = NULL;

        delete curr;
    }
```

(a) Assume that *front* points at the integer list

```
        front -> 2 -> 8 -> 5 -> 7 -> 2 -> 9 -> 25
```

(b) Assume that *front* points at the character list containing the elements "template."

18. Write a recursive version of the function outputReverse(), which outputs the nodes of a list in reverse order. The calling statement passes the front of the linked list to the argument *p*.

```
        template <typename T>
        void outputReverse(node<T> *p);
```

19. Extend the function eraseValue() to erase all occurrences of *target* in the linked list.

```
        template <typename T>
        void eraseAll(node<T> * & front, const T& target);
```

20. Write the following function

```
        template <typename T>
        node<T> *copy(node<T> *front);
```

which creates a duplicate of the list *front* and returns a pointer to the new list. The elements in the new list must be in the same order as those in the original list.

21. Assume that the doubly linked list *header* stores the elements of a priority queue. Implement the function pop(), which deletes the element with the largest value from the list (priority queue).

```
        template<typename T>
        void pop(dnode<T> *header);
```

22. Fill in the statements to build the following doubly linked list:

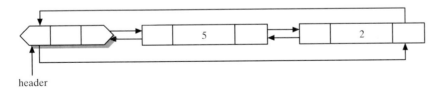

header

```
        dnode<int> *header = _____, *curr, *newNode;


        newNode = _____;
        newNode->next = _____;
        header->next->prev = _____;
        newNode->prev = _____;
        header->next = _____;
```

```
newNode = _____;
newNode->prev = _____;
header->prev->next = _____;
newNode->next = _____;
header->prev = _____;
```

23. Implement the function insertAfter(), which inserts *item* into a doubly linked list after the node pointed to by *curr*:

```
template <typename T>
void insertAfter(dnode<T> *curr, const T& item);
```

24. Implement the function unlinkAfter(), which unlinks the item after *curr* in a doubly linked list and returns its address:

```
template <typename T>
dnode<T> *unlinkAfter(dnode<T> *curr);
```

25. Implement the function

```
template <typename T>
void insertOrder(dnode<T> *header, const T& item);
```

which inserts *item* into a doubly linked list so that the data are in ascending order. Hint: See the function insertOrder() from Chapter 6.

26. Write a function eraseRange() that removes all nodes from a linked list in the pointer range [*first, last*):

```
template <typename T>
void eraseRange(dnode<T> *first, dnode<T> *last);
```

27. Implement the function reverseDList(), which reverses the order of a doubly linked list. Do not use a temporary list for the reversal. Hint: Use two pointers, *first* and *last*, that reference the ends of the list. Scan toward the center of the list, swapping elements until either *first* is equal to *last* or *last* is the predecessor of *first*.

```
template <typename T>
void reverseDList(dnode<T> *header);
```

PROGRAMMING EXERCISES

28. Implement a function countValue() that counts the number of times an item occurs in a linked list:

```
template <typename T>
int countValue(node<T> *front, const T& item);
```

Generate 20 random numbers in the range from 0 to 4, and insert each number at the front of a linked list. Output the list by using writeLinkedList(). In a loop, call the function countValue(), and display the number of occurrences of each value from 0 to 4 in the list.

29. Implement the function insertMax(), which takes the pointer *front* and an item of type *T* as arguments. The function inserts *item* at the front of the list only if it is greater than any current element in the list.

```
template <typename T>
void insertMax(node<T>* & front, const T& item);
```

Write a program that prompts the user for a value *n* and then inputs *n* values. For each value, use insertMax() to enter the value in a linked list. Output the resulting list by using writeLinkedList().

Run the program three times, using the following as input:

Run 1:	5	5	4	3	2	1	
Run 2:	4	1	2	3	4		
Run 3:	6	3	6	2	9	4	8

30. Create a linked list with the double values 5.5, 6.7, 15.3, 3.14, 2.718, 15.3, 3.5. Use the function copy() from Written Exercise 9-20 to make a copy of the list. Output both lists by using writeLinkedList().

31. Using the node class, write a program that enters five integers into a linked list by using the following algorithm:

For each input *N*, insert *N* at the front of the list. Scan the remainder of the list, deleting all nodes that are less than *N*.

Run the program three times, using the following as inputs

$$\{1, 2, 3, 4, 5\}$$
$$\{5, 4, 3, 2, 1\}$$
$$\{3, 5, 1, 2, 4\}$$

Output the resulting list.

32. Rewrite Program 9-1, using a doubly linked list to store the characters.

33. Write a program that prompts the user for an integer *n*. Input *n* integers, and store them at the back of a doubly linked list. Scan the list, and push the value of each node into a priority queue. Clear the priority queue with a series of top() and pop() operations that copy elements from the priority queue back into the linked list. Copy the elements to the linked list in such a way that the elements are in ascending order. Output the final list by using writeDLinkedList().

```
dnode<int> *intList = new dnode<int>;
priority_queue<int> pq;
```

34. Write a program that prompts the user for an integer *n* and uses a random-number generator to create *n* integers in the range from 0 to 99. Enter each random integer into a doubly linked list, using the function insertOrder() from Written Exercise 9-25. Output the list by using writeDLinkedList(). Use the function eraseRange() from Written Exercise 9-26 to remove all nodes with a value greater than 50. Output the modified list.

35. Modify Program 9-3 (the Josephus problem) so that it uses the miniList class.

PROGRAMMING PROJECT

36. The problem of merging ordered lists often occurs in list processing and is the basis for
the merge sort, which can be used to sort linked lists, vectors, and files. If list1 and list2 are
sorted doubly linked lists, remove elements from list2 and insert them into list1 so that
list1 is sorted. The list list2 should be empty at the conclusion of the algorithm.

```
// merge the ordered list, list2, into the
// ordered list, list1. list2 is empty at
// the conclusion of the merge
template <typename T>
void merge(dnode<T> *list1, dnode<T> *list2);
```

For the implementation, declare the pointers plist1 and plist2 to start at the beginning of each list:

```
// plist1 and plist2 move through list1 and list2, respectively
dnode<T> *plist1 = list1->next, *plist2 = list2->next, *p;
```

In a loop that advances each of plist1 and plist2 through its respective list, merge elements from list2 into list1 until you reach the end of one of the lists. Compare the values
at the current locations (plist1−>nodeValue and plist2−>nodeValue). If the value in list1
is smaller, advance plist1; otherwise, the value in list2 is less than or equal to the value in
list1. Save the value of plist2 in pointer object p, and advance plist2. Unlink *p* from list2,
and insert it into list1 before plist1.

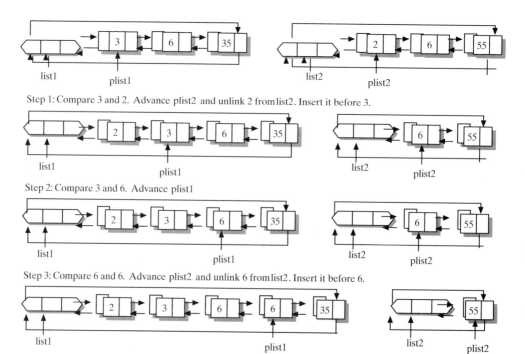

Step 1: Compare 3 and 2. Advance plist2 and unlink 2 from list2. Insert it before 3.

Step 2: Compare 3 and 6. Advance plist1

Step 3: Compare 6 and 6. Advance plist2 and unlink 6 from list2. Insert it before 6.

Step 4: Compare 6 and 55. Advance plist1.

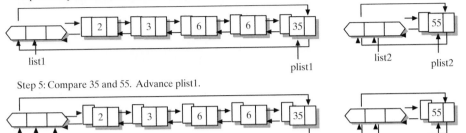

Step 5: Compare 35 and 55. Advance plist1.

Step 6: plist1 is at the end of list1. splice remaining element of list2 onto the end of list1.

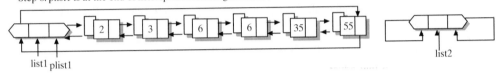

Figure 9-31
Merging two ordered linked lists

Any remaining values in list2 are larger than or equal to the values in list1. To conclude the implementation, remove any remaining nodes from list2, and insert them onto the end of list1. Figure 9-31 traces the algorithm for the two integer lists {3 6 35} and {2 6 55}.

Write a program that builds two integer doubly linked lists, listA and listB. Initialize them by inserting the values from array arrA onto the back of listA and the values from arrB onto the back of listB.

```
int arrA[12] = {1,3,6,9,12,23,33,45,55,68,88,95};
int arrB[8] = {2,8,12,25,33,48,55,75};
int arrASize = sizeof(arrA)/sizeof(int),
    arrBSize = sizeof(arrB)/sizeof(int);
dnode<int> *listA = new dnode<int>, *listB = new dnode<int>;
```

Using writeDLinkedList(), output the two linked lists. Call merge() to merge listB into listA, and output listA.

◆

CHAPTER 10

Binary Trees

OBJECTIVES

- To learn the definition of a general tree and become familiar with tree terminology.
- To understand that a tree is a nonlinear data structure.
- To understand that most tree applications involve binary trees, in which each parent has at most two children.
- To see that a complete binary tree with n nodes has a depth of $int(log_2 n)$ and that such trees locate data on short paths from the root.
- To understand that a tree can be degenerate and no more efficient as a storage structure than a linked list.
- To study the implementation of a binary tree, using a tnode object holding the data and pointers to the left and right subtrees of the node.
- To understand that there are six recursive tree-scanning algorithms and that the most frequently used ones are *inorder*, *postorder*, and *preorder*.
- To study the iterative algorithm that scans a tree level by level by using a queue.
- To become familiar with binary-tree algorithms by studying a series of applications.
- To understand the structure of a binary search tree that stores data by value, not position, and to become familiar with its ADT.
- To note that a binary search tree is an example of an associative container.
- To study applications of a binary search tree that include inventory maintenance for a video store.
- To study the implementation of selected member functions for a binary search tree container class.
- Optionally, to study the implementation of tree iterators.

OUTLINE

Arrays, vectors, and lists define sequence containers that access items by position. With arrays and vectors, programmers access the position by using an index; lists require the more general iterator concept to specify the location of an element. Many computer applications store data by value rather than position. For instance, a local telephone company uses the phone number to identify customer billing and service information. Appliance makers maintain a database of products using serial numbers. We call a value like a serial number a _key_, because it uniquely identifies the appliance.

A sequence container can store data by value. It is an inappropriate structure, however, because access to an element requires an O(n) scan of the sequence to locate the value. We need to design a new structure that stores data by their key in locations that allow for rapid access. With such a structure a program references the data through use of their key. For instance, the registrar of a college uses a social security number to search his or her collection of records and retrieves information on the units completed, GPA, major, and so forth for the student associated with the key. For this reason, the storage structure is called an _associative container_. The programmer interface for associative containers is similar to the interface for the sequence containers, except that objects are added, removed, or updated by value rather than by position.

In this chapter, you will study a data structure called a _tree_. Unlike the vector and list sequence containers, a tree is a _nonlinear_ structure in which each element can have multiple successors. In Section 10-1, we introduce tree terminology and define a special type of tree, called a _binary tree_, that allows an element to have at most two successors. Because general trees have restricted applications for things like file structures, we will focus on binary trees, which provide a variety of algorithms to store, access, and update the data. In Sections 10-2 to 10-4, we introduce the structure of a binary-tree node, which is the building block of the data structure, and design a series of scanning algorithms that allow us to evaluate attributes of the tree and modify its nodes. The main focus of the chapter is on the design of a tree container ADT called a _binary search tree_. The container class has a familiar interface that includes insert() and erase() operations, along with an iterator to scan and access the elements. Binary search trees are very powerful data structures, because they can store large collections of data while providing very efficient access and update operations. We illustrate applications for these trees and provide an implementation that will use many of the algorithms from the earlier sections of the chapter.

The interested reader can explore the implementation of the binary-search tree iterator in the optional Section 10-8.

This chapter presents the binary search tree as an ADT. In Chapter 11, we introduce the STL *set* and *map* containers, which are associative containers that use a binary search tree object as their underlying implementation structure. In Chapter 12, we introduce another container, called the *hash table*, that we also use to implement sets and maps. Our study of associative containers has been relatively long in coming. Our need to provide a systematic development of container classes and their implementation dictated our covering sequence containers first. The approach was never intended to give them priority. Associative containers are an integral part of data structures. You will soon discover that they lend themselves to a whole host of applications.

10-1   TREE STRUCTURES

A tree is a *hierarchical* structure that places elements in nodes along branches that originate from a *root*. For instance, an organization tree represents lines of authority in a corporation. The CEO is the root of the organization, while the divisional managers and supervisors are nodes at progressively lower levels in the organization (Figure 10-1). The term "hierarchical" has its origins in the religious distribution of authority from the bishop to the pastors, deacons, and so forth.

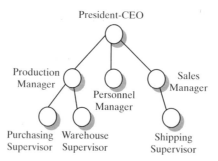

President-CEO

Production
Manager

Personnel
Manager

Sales
Manager

Purchasing   Warehouse
Supervisor   Supervisor

Shipping
Supervisor

Figure 10-1
Hierarchical-tree structure

Nodes in a tree are subdivided into levels in which the topmost level holds the root node. Any node in a tree can have multiple successors at the next level. Hence, a tree is a nonlinear structure. General trees, in which a node can have more than two successors, have limited application. Operating systems use a general tree to maintain file structures. The nodes of the tree are directories specified by a path from the root directory. Most applications involve a restricted category of trees, called *binary trees*, in which each node has at most two successors. For instance, a compiler builds binary trees while parsing a program's source code. The resulting trees provide information for an analyzer that must interpret the syntax. To illustrate this fact, consider the following infix expression:

```
a * b + (c-d)/e
```

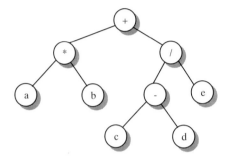

Figure 10-2
Binary expression tree for
a * b + (c−d)/e

The compiler parses the expression and creates an *expression tree*, in which the variables or constants (*a, b, c, d,* and *e*) occupy nodes at the end of a path (*leaf nodes*) and all nonleaf nodes hold operators (Figure 10-2). A binary-tree structure is appropriate, because only unary or binary operators are part of the expression..

Before we develop other examples of trees, let us step back and develop some terminology that will allow us to describe the features of trees. We will use the terminology to give a precise definition of a binary tree.

Tree Terminology

A tree structure is characterized as a collection of *nodes* that originate from a unique starting node, called the *root*. Each node consists of a value and a set of zero or more links to successor nodes. Using analogies from a family tree, we associate the terms *parent* and *children* to describe the relationship between a node and the successor nodes. We call the link from a parent to a child an *edge*. In Figure 10-3, node A is the root. As a parent, the root has nodes B, C, and D as children. The child node B is a parent for nodes E and F. From the perspective of a child, each nonroot node has a unique parent. We classify a node in a tree based on the number of its children. A *leaf node*, such as E, G, H, I, and J, is a node without any children. An *interior node* (nonleaf node) has at least one child.

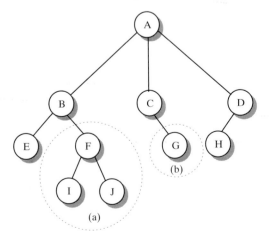

Figure 10-3
A general tree

Each node in a tree is the root of a *subtree*, which consists of the node and all of its descendants. In Figure 10-3(a), node F is the root of the subtree containing nodes F, I, and J, while G is a one-node subtree in Figure 10-3(b). Using the family-tree analogy, a subtree describes a node and all of its *descendants*. The definition of a subtree permits us to say that the root node A is a root of a subtree that happens to be the tree itself.

A path between a parent node P and any node N in its subtree is a sequence of nodes $P = X_0, X_1, \ldots, X_k = N$, where k is the length of the path. Each node X_i in the sequence is the parent of X_{i+1} for $0 \leq i \leq k - 1$. For instance, in Figure 10-4, the path from root A to node F is the sequence $A = X_0, X_1 = C, X_2 = F$, with length 2. The fact that each nonroot node has a single parent ensures that there is a unique path from any node to itself or one of its descendants. The length of a path between the root and any node of the tree defines a measure called the *level* of a node. The level of the root is zero. Each child of the root is a level-one node, the next generation consist of level-two nodes, and so forth. In Figure 10-4, F is a level-two node with a path length of 2.

The *depth* of a tree is the maximum level of any node in the tree. The concept of depth can also be described in terms of a path. The depth of a tree is the length of the longest path from the root to a node. In Figure 10-4, the depth of the tree is 3.

Binary Trees

Although general trees have some important applications, we focus on a restricted category of trees, called *binary trees*, in which each parent has no more than two children (Figure 10-5). A binary tree has a uniform structure that allows us to give a simple description of its node structure and to develop of variety of tree-handling algorithms. The limit on the number of possible children for a node is not a serious restriction, because most general trees have an equivalent binary-tree representation. We develop this fact in the exercises.

Each node in a binary tree has two links that can reference its children. We distinguish the links by the labels *left* and *right*. The left link connects the node to its *left*

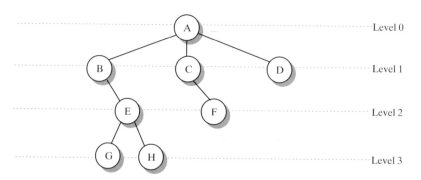

Figure 10-4
Tree node level and path length

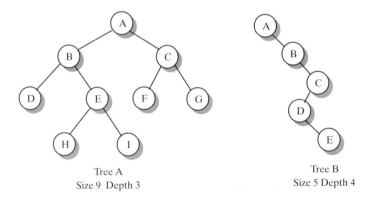

Tree A
Size 9 Depth 3

Tree B
Size 5 Depth 4

Figure 10-5
Depth of binary trees, including a degenerate tree

$child$, and the right link connects it to its $right$ $child$. Each child is the root of a subtree, so we can also view the left link of each node as a reference to its $left$ $subtree$
and the right link as a reference to its $right$ $subtree$. You will note that each subtree
of a node is itself a binary tree. This leads us to a recursive definition of a binary
tree. Such a tree defines the stopping condition, that views the tree as a set of nodes
consisting of a root and its two subtrees. By definition, a tree without any nodes is
a binary tree.

Definition: A binary tree T is a finite set of nodes with one of the following
properties:

(a) T is a tree if the set of nodes is empty. (An empty tree is a tree.)
(b) The set consists of a root R and exactly two distinct binary trees, the left
subtree T_L and the right subtree T_R. The nodes in T consist of node R and
all the nodes in T_L and T_R.

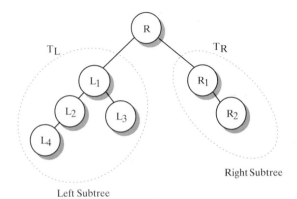

Left Subtree

Right Subtree

Example 10-1

Let us view the following binary tree with four nodes as a recursive structure. We represent an empty subtree by the graphic.

Binary Tree: root is A
   Left subtree of A: root is B
      Left subtree of B: an empty binary tree
      Right subtree of B: root is D
         Left subtree of D: an empty binary tree
         Right subtree of D: an empty binary tree
   Right subtree of A: root is C
      Left subtree of C: an empty binary tree
      Right subtree of C: an empty binary tree

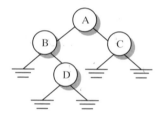

Density of a Binary Tree   At level zero in a binary tree, there is $1 = 2^0$ node, the root. Level one in the tree contains 1 or $2 = 2^1$ nodes, depending on the number of children the root has. The number of nodes at level two may range from 1 to $4 = 2^2$ nodes, with 4 occurring when the root has two children and each of the children has two children. In general, at any level n, a binary tree may contain from 1 to 2^n nodes. The number of nodes per level contributes to the density of the tree. Intuitively, density is a measure of the size of a tree (number of nodes) relative to the depth of the tree. In Figure 10-5, tree A contains nine nodes in a depth of 3, while tree B contains five nodes in a depth of 4. The latter case is a special form, called a *degenerate tree*, in which there is a single leaf node (E) and each interior node has only one child. An n-node degenerate tree has depth $n - 1$. A degenerate tree is equivalent to a linked list.

Trees with a higher density are important as data structures, because they can "pack" more nodes near the root. Access to the nodes is along relatively short paths from the root. Let us make this idea more precise. Degenerate trees are one extreme measure of density. At the other extreme, a *complete* binary tree of depth n is a tree in which each level from 0 to $n - 1$ has all possible nodes and all leaf nodes at level n occupy the leftmost positions in the tree. The largest possible complete binary tree with depth n is one that contains 2^n nodes at level n. In such a binary tree, every interior node has two children. Figure 10-6 distinguishes between complete and noncomplete binary trees.

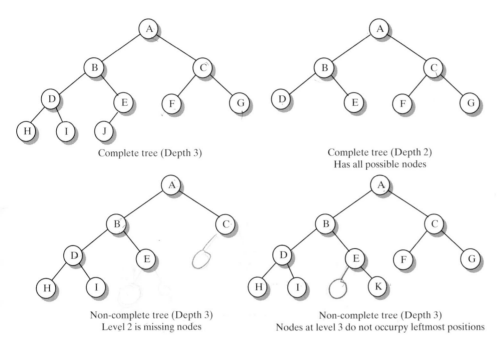

Figure 10-6
Complete and noncomplete binary trees

Evaluating Tree Density Complete binary trees are an ideal storage structure, because of their ability to pack a large number of nodes near the root. A little mathematical analysis highlights this fact. Assume we want to store n elements in a complete binary tree. We would like to know the depth of such a tree. We know the number of nodes that will occupy the first $d - 1$ levels in the tree. There is one (2^0) node (root) at level 0, two (2^1) nodes at level 1, four (2^2) nodes at level 2, and so forth. Through the first $d - 1$ levels, the total number of nodes is $2^d - 1$.

$$1 + 2 + 4 + \cdots + 2^{d-1} = 2^d - 1$$

At level d, the number of additional nodes ranges from a minimum of one to a maximum of 2^d. When the last level has one node, the number of nodes in the tree is

$$2^d - 1 + 1 = 2^d$$

When all interior nodes have two children, the number of nodes is

$$2^d - 1 + 2^d = 2^{d+1} - 1$$

If we put these two extreme cases together, the n nodes in the complete binary tree satisfy the inequality

$$2^d \leq n \leq 2^{d+1} - 1 < 2^{d+1}$$

After applying the logarithm base 2 to all terms in the inequality, we have

$$d \leq \log_2 n < d + 1$$

This shows that $\log_2$ n lies between the integer values d and $d + 1$, but cannot equal $d + 1$. The actual value of $\log_2 n$ as a real number is

$$\log_2 n = d.f_1 f_2 f_3 \ldots$$

The depth must be a whole number, so truncate $\log_2 n$ to an integer value k. This is the depth of a complete tree that holds the n elements.

$$k = \text{int}\,(\log_2 n)$$

Example 10-2

1. The maximum depth of a tree with five nodes is 4, which occurs when the tree is degenerate. The minimum depth of a tree with five nodes occurs when the tree is complete and is $\text{int}(\log_2 5) = 2$.

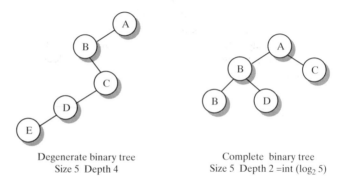

Degenerate binary tree
Size 5 Depth 4

Complete binary tree
Size 5 Depth 2 =int $(\log_2 5)$

2. For a complete binary tree with n nodes, the depth is $\text{int}(\log_2 n)$. Assuming that the tree has $n = 1,000,000$ elements, the depth of the tree is

$$\text{int}(\log_2 1000000) = \text{int}(19.931\ldots) = 19$$

10-2   BINARY-TREE NODES

In our implementation of binary trees, the elements are tnode objects. If we use a linked-list node as a model, a tree node contains a data value, called nodeValue, and two pointers, *left* and *right*. A value of NULL indicates an empty subtree. The root node defines an entry point into the binary tree; a pointer references a child node at the next level in the tree. A leaf node has a NULL *left* and *right* pointer. Figure 10-7 gives an abstract model of a binary tree, along with the corresponding representation with tnode objects. Nodes *F, G*, and *H* are leaf nodes.

The tnode class has two constructors that the programmer uses with the operator *new* to dynamically allocate tnode objects. The default constructor creates an uninitialized object. A second constructor has arguments that assign initial values to nodeValue and to the pointers *left* and *right*. The pointers have default value NULL.

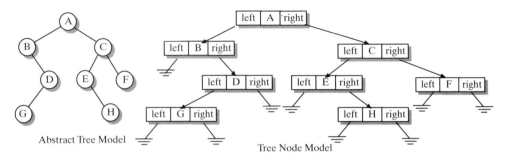

Figure 10-7
Binary-tree models

We declare the data in the tnode class as public members to simplify their use in implementing tree-based containers, such as the stree class, discussed in Sections 10-5 through 10-8. The tnode objects are the building blocks of the containers, but are not part of the public interface. Making the data in the tnode objects public does not violate the object-design principle of information hiding, because end users do not have access to these low-level objects. The following is a declaration of the tnode class with an implementation using inline code.

CLASS tnode	Declaration	"d_tnode.h"

```
// represents a node in a binary tree
template <typename T>
class tnode
{
   public:
         // tnode is a class implementation structure. making the
         // data public simplifies building class functions
         T nodeValue;
         tnode<T> *left, *right;

         // default constructor. data not initialized
         tnode()
         {}

         // initialize the data members
         tnode (const T& item, tnode<T> *lptr = NULL,
               tnode<T> *rptr = NULL):
                  nodeValue(item), left(lptr), right(rptr)
         {}
};
```

Building a Binary Tree

A binary tree consists of a collection of dynamically allocated tnode objects whose pointer values specify links to their children. If the call to new omits the pointer arguments to the constructor, the resulting node is a leaf node. If the call includes a

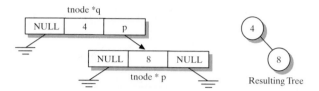

Figure 10-8
Leaf node and node with right child

tnode pointer as an argument, the newly allocated node uses the pointer to attach a child. The following statements declare two tnode<int> pointers, *p* and *q*, and dynamically allocate integer nodes. Node *p* is a leaf node with value 8; node *q* has value 4, with a link to *p* as its right child (Figure 10-8).

```
tnode<int> *p, *q;      // pointers to tnode objects with integer data

// p is a leaf node with value 8;
p = new tnode<int>(8);

// q is a node with value 4 and p as a right child
q = new tnode<int>(4, NULL, p);
```

Example 10-3

This example uses the tnode class to build a four-node tree. The first phase creates the two leaf nodes, 20 and 40, with NULL *left* and *right* pointers. Node 30 is next, with node 40 as its left child. The final statement creates the root node, 10, with nodes 20 and 30 as its children. Note that you build a tree from the "bottom up." Contrary to nature, you allocate the children first and then the parent.

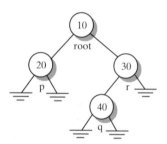

```
// pointers to integer tree nodes
tnode<int> *root, *p, *q, *r;

// allocate leaf nodes with values 20 and 40
p = new tnode<int>(20);
q = new tnode<int>(40);
```

```
// allocate node at level 1 with value 30
// and left child 40
r = new tnode<int>(30, q, NULL);

// allocate root node with value 10 and
// children 20 (left) and 30 (right)
root = new tnode<int>(10, p, r);
```

(handwritten annotations: "→ Right Node", "→ leftNode", "→ Value of node")

Function buildTree() Building trees by hand is a tedious process. Unfortunately, without algorithms to automate the process, we have no alternative. At the same time, we need some examples to illustrate the concepts in this chapter. To address this situation, we provide the function buildTree(), which builds three trees whose nodes contain character data.

```
// create one of three binary trees with character data. Argument n in
// the range from 0 to 2 selects from Tree 0, Tree 1, and Tree 2
tnode<char> *buildTree(int n);
```

The implementation, which is found in "d_tnodel.h", is not very glamorous. It builds the tree node by node, using the technique in Example 10-3. Figure 10-9 displays the sample trees.

Using buildTree() is very simple. First, declare a tnode<char> pointer as the root of the tree. Then, call buildTree() with an argument *n* in the range from 0 to 2, and assign the return value to the root pointer. For instance, the upcoming statements build Tree 0 and Tree 2 and assign them to the tnode<char> pointers root and bigRoot, respectively. The root of a tree is just a tnode<char> pointer and thus can have any name. In most applications, we suggest you call this pointer *root*, for obvious reasons.

```
tnode<char> *root, *bigRoot;    // declare the root pointers

root = buildTree(0);            // set up Tree 0 based at root
bigRoot = buildTree(2)          // set up Tree 2 based at bigRoot
```

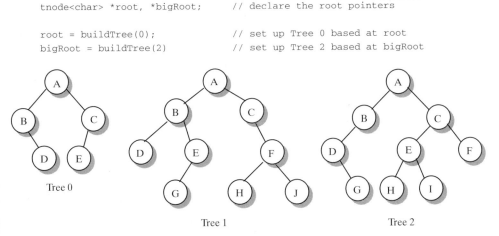

Figure 10-9
Trees created by buildTree()

10-3   BINARY TREE SCAN ALGORITHMS

A sequence container, such as a list or vector, allows us to scan the elements by using their positions in the sequence. Because a tree is a nonlinear structure, a linear scan is impossible, because there is no clear meaning for "next element." At each node, we can select between the left and right child. Based on the decision, we descend into the left or the right subtree of the node. If the decision is to go left, we arrive at the left child of the node and have another decision to select the left or the right child of this child node. As decisions begin to mount, you may wonder whether we will ever get back to the original node to select its right child. Without some organization, we face the possibility of skipping some of the elements or accessing elements multiple times. Fortunately, the recursive structure of a binary tree offers a variety of techniques that allow us to visit each node exactly once. The different tree-scan algorithms consider each node as the root of a tree (subtree) and identify tasks to perform at the node. These tasks include taking some action at the node and visiting both the left and right child of the node. The different scanning strategies depend on the order in which we perform the tasks.

In this section, we discuss the classical tree-scan algorithms and illustrate them by implementing functions that output tree nodes. The action at a node is simply to output the value of the node. In Section 10-4, we use the scanning algorithms to perform more meaningful tasks, such as copying or deleting the node, determining the level of the node, and so forth. For now, the emphasis is on the order in which we visit the nodes. Understanding the variety of ways to scan a tree is fundamental to your understanding of tree algorithms.

Recursive Tree Traversals

A binary tree is a recursive structure in which each node is specified by its value and its left and right subtrees. The power of recursion is manifest in a set of scanning algorithms that designate three separate actions at each node. The actions include visiting the node and performing some task (N), making a recursive descent to the left subtree (L), and making a recursive descent to the right subtree (R). A left or right descent into a subtree moves the scan to the left or right child, which is the root of the corresponding subtree. Once we arrive at the root of the subtree, the scan algorithm sets in place a repetition of the same three actions. The descent terminates when we reach an empty tree (*pointer* == NULL). The order in which we perform the N, L, and R actions determines the different recursive scan algorithms. Next, we develop the traversal algorithm in which the order of action is L N R. Once you understand the process, you will be able to scan a binary tree with different permutations on the order of activity.

Inorder Scan   The recursive tree traversals assume that the algorithm follows a specific order of action upon entry into each node. We refer to the action that performs a task, such as accessing the value of the node, as a *visit* and designate it with the letter N. A recursive descent into the left subtree (L) results from a decision to select the left child as the next node in the scan. A recursive descent into the right subtree (R) results from a selection of the right child as the next node. An inorder scan performs the visit (N) between the recursive descent into the left and the right subtree. The prefix "in" comes from the fact that the visit occurs between the descents into the two subtrees. In this example, we use the order LNR. A second in-order version of the algorithm could use the order RNL. The first action at a node is a recursive descent into the left subtree (L). The next action is a visit (N). The traversal completes its action at the node by performing a recursive descent into the right subtree (R). We summarize the order of action at each node as follows:

1. Traverse the left subtree ("go left").
2. Visit the node.
3. Traverse the right subtree ("go right").

After completing all of the operations at a node, return to the parent node and pick up with the unfinished actions at that node.

Let's trace the inorder scan of the nodes in Tree 0. The scan begins at node A, and a "visit" means to output the value of the node.

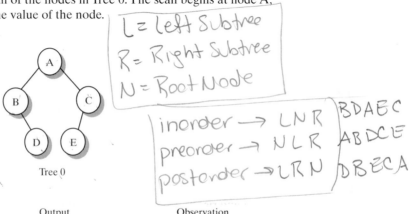

L = Left Subtree
R = Right Subtree
N = Root Node

inorder → LNR   BDAEC
preorder → NLR   ABDCE
postorder → LRN   DBECA

Tree 0

Node	Action	Output	Observation	
A:	Go left to B			
B:	Go left		Subtree is empty;	L_B is done
	Visit B	'B'		N_B is done
	Go right to D			
D:	Go left		Subtree is empty	L_D is done
	Visit D	'D'		N_D is done
	Go right		Subtree is empty	R_D is done;
	Return to B		Node D is done	
B:	Return to A		Node B is done	R_B is done
A:	Visit A	'A'		N_A is done
	Go right to C			
C:	Go left to E			L_C is done
E:	Go left		Subtree is empty	L_E is done
	Visit E	'E'		N_E is done
	Go right		Subtree is empty	R_E is done
	Return to C		Node E is done	
C:	Visit C	'C'		N_C is done
	Go right		Subtree is empty	R_B is done
	Return to A		Node C is done	
A:	Quit scan		Node A is done	

The traversal order for the nodes is B D A E C. The implementation of the inorder scan algorithm uses a recursive function. A stopping condition occurs when we descend to an empty subtree (tnode pointer t == NULL). The recursive step first descends the left tree (t−>*left*) of a node and then visits the node itself. The algorithm concludes by descending into the right tree (t−>*right*). The function inorderOutput() applies the algorithm to output the nodes of a binary tree, using an inorder scan. The file "d_tnodel.h" contains the implementation of inorderOutput(). Note that each recursive call includes the template type with the function name (See Section 6-2).

inorderOutput():
```
// inorder recursive output of the nodes in a binary tree.
// output separator after each node value. default value
// of separator is "  "
template <typename T>
void inorderOutput(tnode<T> *t, const string& separator = " ")
{
    // the recursive scan terminates on a empty subtree
    if (t != NULL)
    {
        inorderOutput<T>(t->left, separator);      // descend left
        cout << t->nodeValue << separator;         // output the node
        inorderOutput<T>(t->right, separator)      // descend right
    }
}
```

Example 10-4

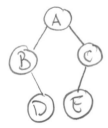

The postorder scan uses a different ordering of the actions at a node. The visit occurs after ("post") the scan completes recursive descents of both the left subtree and the right subtree. In this example, the order of actions is LRN (left, right, node):

1. Traverse the left subtree ("go left").
2. Traverse the right subtree ("go right").
3. Visit the node.

The table shown next is a brief trace of the postorder scan for Tree 0. Note that the order of visit to the nodes is D B E C A. We refer to this as a "bottom-up" scan, because we first visit the children before visiting the parent.

Action	Output	Observation
At node A, go left to node B		
At node B, go right to node D	D	D is a leaf node (L_D and R_D are NULL)
Back at B	B	L_B and R_B are complete
Back at A, go right to C		
At C, go left to E	E	E is a leaf node (L_E and R_E are NULL)
Back at C	C	L_C and R_C are complete
Back at A	A	L_A and R_A are complete
Quit scan		

The function postorderOutput () displays the nodes in a binary tree by first descending down the left subtree (t−>*left*) of a node and then the right subtree (t−>*right*). The output of the value of the node is the visit operation. The implementation of postorderOutput() is in the file "d_tnodel.h."

postorderOutput():
```
// postorder recursive output of the nodes in a binary tree.
// output separator after each node value. default value
// of separator is "  "
template <typename T>
void postorderOutput(tnode<T> *t, const string& separator = " ")
{
    // the recursive scan terminates on a empty subtree
    if (t != NULL)
    {
        postorderOutput(t->left, separator);     // descend left
        postorderOutput(t->right, separator);    // descend right
        cout << t->nodeValue << separator;       // output the node
    }
}
```

We have developed two tree-traversal algorithms. The others are simple permutations of the order of actions at a node. Define the *preorder* scan by first visiting the node ("pre") and then scanning the left and right subtrees (NLR). The other three algorithms descend to the right subtree before descending to the left subtree. The representations of the algorithms are given by NRL ("preright"), RNL ("inright"), and RLN ("postright").

Example 10-5

1. For the character tree Tree 2, the given lists describe the order of visit to the nodes for three scanning strategies. In each case, the descent into the left subtree occurs before the descent into the right subtree.

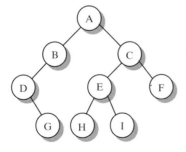

Tree 2

Preorder (NLR):   A B D G C E H I F
Inorder (LNR):   D G B A H E I C F
Postorder (LRN):   G D B H I E F C A

2. The RLN traversal of Tree 2 visits the nodes in the order F I H E C G D B A

Iterative Level-Order Scan

The recursive tree accesses elements by moving up and down through subtrees. Some applications, however, need to access elements by levels, with the root coming first (level 0), then the children of the root (level 1), followed by the next generation (level 2), and so forth. For obvious reasons, the algorithm is called a *level-order scan*.

A level-order scan is an iterative process that uses a queue as an intermediate storage container. Initially, the root enters the queue. An iterative step involves popping a node from the queue, performing some action with the node, and then pushing its children into the queue. Because siblings enter the queue during a visit to their parent, the siblings (on the same level) will exit the queue in successive iterations. The following figure illustrates the order of visits to the nodes:

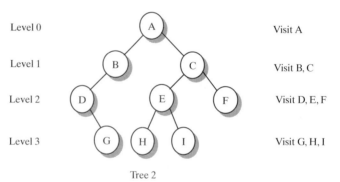

Tree 2

Level-Order Scan Algorithm The algorithm involves an initialization step and a *while* loop that pops the nodes, level by level, from a queue. The loop terminates when the queue is empty.

Initialization Step: Declare a queue of tnode pointers, and insert the root node pointer into the queue.

```
tnode<T> *root;
queue<tnode<T> *> q;

q.push(root);
```

Iterative Step: Delete a tnode pointer p from the queue, and visit the node. Conclude by pushing the non-NULL children of node p into the queue.

Example 10-6

The following steps illustrate the level-order scan algorithm for Tree 0:

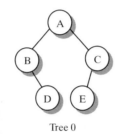

Tree 0

Initialization: Insert a pointer to node A into the queue. We use A in the figure to represent the pointer to the node with value A.

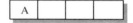

1. Delete node A from the queue.
   Visit A.
   Insert the children of A into the queue.
       Left child = B
       Right child = C

2. Delete node B from the queue.
   Visit B.
   Insert the children of B into the queue.
       Right child = D

3. Delete node C from the queue.

   Visit C.

Insert the children of C into the queue.

   Left child = E

4. Delete node D from the queue.

   Visit D.

D has no children.

5. Delete node E from the queue.

   Visit E

E has no children.

The algorithm terminates, because the queue is empty.

The function levelorderOutput() traverses the nodes of a binary tree in level order and outputs the value of each node. Locate the function in the file "d_tnodel.h".

levelorderOutput():

```
// traverse the binary tree level by level and output each node.
// output separator after each node value. default value
// of separator is "  "
template <typename T>
void levelorderOutput(tnode<T> *t, const string& separator = "  ")
{
    // store siblings of each node in a queue so that they are
    // visited in order at the next level of the tree
    queue<tnode<T> *> q;
    tnode<T> *p;

    // initialize the queue by inserting the root in the queue
    q.push(t);

    // continue the iterative process until the queue is empty
    while(!q.empty())
    {
        // delete front node from queue and output the node value
        p = q.front();
        q.pop();
        cout << p->nodeValue << separator;
```

```
            // if a left child exists, insert it in the queue
         if(p->left != NULL)
            q.push(p->left);

            // if a right child exists, insert next to its sibling
         if(p->right != NULL)
            q.push(p->right);
      }
   }
```

PROGRAM 10-1   SCANNING TREES

This program illustrates the inorder, the postorder, and the level-order scan algorithms. The
program begins by calling buildTree() to create Tree 1. The different scanning strategies use
the corresponding "output" functions from the tree node library "d_tnodel.h".

```
// File: prg10_1.cpp
// the program demonstrates the inorder and postorder
// recursive binary tree scanning algorithms and the
// iterative level-order scanning algorithm. using the
// function buildTree(), construct Tree 1 and call the
{// tree output algorithms from the library "d_tnodel.h".

#include <iostream>

#include "d_tnode.h"    // tnode class
#include "d_tnodel.h"   // tnode library

using namespace std;

int main()
{
   // root of the tree
   tnode<char> *root;

   // use the character Tree 1
   root = buildTree(1);

   // give inorder scan of nodes
   cout << "Inorder scan:        " ;
   inorderOutput(root);
   cout << endl;

   // give postorder scan of nodes
   cout << "Postorder scan:       " ;
   postorderOutput(root);
   cout << endl;

   // give level order scan of nodes
   cout << "Level-order scan:     " ;
```

```
      levelorderOutput(root);
      cout << endl;

      return 0;
}
```

```
Run:

Inorder scan:        D  B  G  E  A  C  H  F  I
Postorder scan:      D  G  E  B  H  I  F  C  A
Level-order scan:    A  B  C  D  E  F  G  H  I
```

10-4   USING TREE-SCAN ALGORITHMS

In this section, we employ scanning strategies to implement binary-tree algorithms.
For starters, we implement algorithms that count the number of leaf nodes and compute the depth of a tree. Anticipating the construction of the binary-search tree
class, we develop algorithms that copy and delete nodes in a tree. We implement all
of the algorithms as functions, which you will find in the tree library "d_tnodel.h."

Computing the Leaf Count

A node in a tree is a leaf node if it has no children. An algorithm for determining the
number of leaf nodes in a binary tree involves scanning each node and checking for
the presence of children. The order of the scan is irrelevant, so we can use any of the
tree traversal strategies. In the function countLeaf(), we include a reference argument, called count, and use a preorder scan, which first visits the node before descending into its left and right subtrees. The visit involves incrementing the variable
count if the node has no children. The calling statement must pass a runtime argument that is a variable with initial value 0.

countLeaf():
```
      // accumulate the number of leaf nodes in count.
      // assume that count initialized to 0
      template <typename T>
      void countLeaf (tnode<T> *t, int& count)
      {
          if (t != NULL)    // if the Root is Not NULL
          {
              // check if t is a leaf node (no children).
              // if so, increment count
              if (t->left == NULL && t->right == NULL)
                  count++;
              countLeaf(t->left, count);  // descend left
              countLeaf(t->right, count); // descend right
          }
      }
```

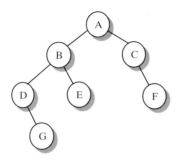

Figure 10-10
Binary tree of depth 3

Computing the Depth of a Tree

The depth of a tree is the "deepest" level in the tree. To see how we can design an algorithm to compute the depth, consider the character tree with root A (Figure 10-10). A look at the tree indicates that the depth is 3.

A little reflection will show that the order, in which of the nodes are scanned is critical. Let us use the analogy of a family tree. Suppose we select a preorder scan that visits node A first. During the visit, node A understands that it is a parent, because it has children B and C. Node A does not understand that it is a grandparent, because this information depends on node B's communicating back to node A that it is itself a parent. Ultimately, B will understand that it is a grandparent and can then communicate back to A that it is a great-grandparent. To find the depth of a tree, an early visit to a node is premature, because we must first have information passed back to the node from its children when they know the depth of their subtrees. We need to use a postorder scan that visits both subtrees before visiting the parent. In Figure 10-10, once node A recognizes that the depths of its left and right subtrees are 2 and 1, respectively, it can chose the greater depth, add one generation for itself, and conclude that it is the root of a tree of depth 3.

The function depth() takes a pointer to a tree node and returns the depth of the tree with root t. The function uses a postorder scan to first compute the depth of the left and right subtrees of node t. The resulting depth of the tree, which has t as the root, is 1 more than the maximum depth of the subtrees. In Figure 10-11, node B

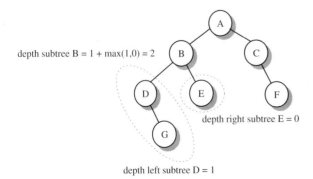

depth subtree B = 1 + max(1,0) = 2

depth right subtree E = 0

depth left subtree D = 1

Figure 10-11
Computing the depth of a
node from the depth of its
subtrees

has a left subtree D of depth 1 and a right subtree E of depth 0. The depth of the subtree with node B as the root is 2

For the stopping condition in the recursive scan, we define the depth of an empty tree to be -1. This is necessary so that a subtree with one node has depth 0.

$$depth(\text{leaf node}) = 1 + max(depth(\text{left subtree}), depth(\text{right subtree}))$$
$$= 1 + max(-1, -1) = 1 + -1 = 0$$

Figure 10-12 displays the order of visit (#i) to each node in the postorder scan. The subscript on each node label is the depth of its subtree. For instance, B is the fourth node visited, and its depth is 2.

depth():

```
// return the depth of the binary tree
template <typename T>
int depth (tnode<T> *t)
{
    int depthLeft, depthRight, depthval;

    if (t == NULL)
        // depth of an empty tree is -1
        depthval = -1;
    else
    {
        // find the depth of the left subtree of t
        depthLeft = depth(t->left);
        // find the depth of the right subtree of t
        depthRight = depth(t->right);
        // depth of the tree with root t is 1 + maximum
        // of the depths of the two subtrees
        depthval = 1 +
            (depthLeft > depthRight ? depthLeft : depthRight);
    }

    return depthval;
}
```

Handwritten annotations: "conditional expression", "T or F", "if T", "if F"

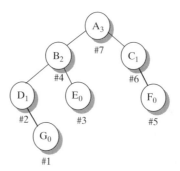

Figure 10-12
Tracing depth() for a postorder scan of a binary tree

PROGRAM 10-2   LEAF COUNT AND DEPTH

This program illustrates the use of the functions countLeaf() and depth() with the character tree Tree 1. Output includes the number of leaves and the depth of the tree.

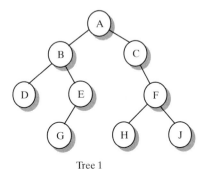

Tree 1

```
// File: prg10_2.cpp
// the program builds the sample Tree 1 and calls
// countLeaf() to determine the number of leaf nodes
// in the tree. it then calls depth() to compute
// the depth of the tree

#include <iostream>

#include "d_tnode.h"  // tnode class
#include "d_tnodel.h" // tnode library

using namespace std;

int main()
{
    // root of the tree
    tnode<char> *root;
    int leafCount;

    // use the character Tree 1
    root = buildTree(1);
    // we accumulate the number of leaf nodes in leafCount,
    // so it must have initial value 0
    leafCount = 0;
    // call countLeaf() and output leaf count
    countLeaf(root, leafCount);
    cout << "Number of leaf nodes is " << leafCount << endl;

    // make call to depth() and output the depth of the tree
    cout << "The depth of the tree is "
         << depth(root) << endl;
```

```
        return 0;
    }
```

```
    Run:

    Number of leaf nodes is 4
    The depth of the tree is 3
```

Copying a Binary Tree

A function that copies an entire tree introduces new concepts and prepares us for the construction of a binary search tree class that requires a copy constructor and assignment operator. The function copyTree() takes an initial tree and creates a duplicate (clone) tree. The function uses a postorder scan to visit the nodes of the tree. The traversal order ensures that we first create the nodes for both the left subtree and the right subtree. Only then is the parent node created with links to its subtrees. Thus, the function builds a new tree from the bottom up.

The character tree Tree 0 provides an example that illustrates the recursive copyTree() function. Assume that tnode<char> pointer root1 is the root of Tree 0. A call to copyTree() with root1 as the argument creates a second tree that is a clone of Tree 0 and returns its root pointer. The root of the new tree can be assigned to a second tnode<char> pointer root2 (Figure 10-13).

We trace the algorithm and illustrate the events that create the five nodes in the duplicate tree. At each node t in the postorder scan, we make separate recursive calls to copyTree() with *t−>left* and t−>*right* as arguments. The calls create the duplicate left and right subtrees for the node. The function returns pointers to the roots of these subtrees. Assume the pointer to the left subtree is newLeft and the pointer to the right subtree is newRight. Allocate a node whose value is the same as the corresponding node from the original tree and whose pointers are newLeft and newRight. To assist in the tracing of the algorithm, we include a subscript with the pointer variables newNode, newLeft, and newRight to indicate the association between the new node and the corresponding node of the original tree.

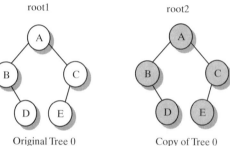

Original Tree 0
root1 =buildTree(0)

Copy of Tree 0
root2 =copyTree(root1)

Figure 10-13
Tree 0 and the copy of Tree 0
with roots root1 and root2,
respectively

Step 1: Starting at root A, create a copy of node D.

  At A. Go left to B (A−>*left*).

  At B. Go left (B−>*left* is NULL; newLeft$_B$ = NULL).

     Go right to D (B−>*right*).

  At D. Go left (D−>*left* is NULL; newLeft$_D$ = NULL).

     Go right (D−>*right* is NULL; newRight$_D$ = NULL).

     Allocate newNode$_D$ with value D

      and pointers newLeft$_D$ and newRight$_D$.

     Return newNode$_D$ to parent B.

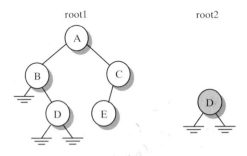

Step 2: Create a copy of node B.

  At B. newLeft$_B$ is NULL (Step 1).

     Assign newRight$_B$ = newNode$_D$ (Step 1)

      (root node for the right subtree).

     Allocate newNode$_B$ with value B

      and pointers newLeft$_B$ and newRight$_B$.

     Return newNode$_B$ as the root of the left subtree

      for parent A.

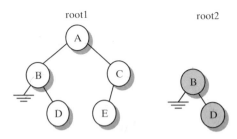

Step 3: Create a copy of node E.

  At A Go right to C (A−>*right*).

  At C Go left to E (C−>*left*).

  At E Go left (E−>*left* is NULL; newLeft$_E$ = NULL).

Go right (E−>*right* is NULL; newRight$_E$ = NULL).
Allocate newNode$_E$ with value E
and pointers newLeft$_E$ and newRight$_E$.
Return newNode$_E$ to parent C.

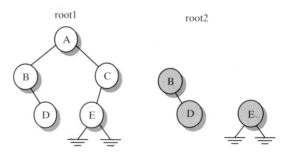

Step 4: Create a copy of node C.

At C   Assign newLeft$_C$ = newNode$_E$ (Step 3)
(root node for left subtree).
Go right (C−>*right* is NULL; newRight$_C$ = NULL).
Allocate newNode$_C$ with value C
and pointers newLeft$_C$ and newRight$_C$.
Return newNode$_C$ as the root of the right subtree
for parent A.

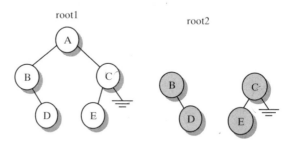

Step 5: Create a copy of node A.

At A   Assign newLeft$_A$ = newNode$_B$ (Step 2)
(root node for left subtree).
Assign newRight$_A$ = newNode$_C$ (Step 4)
(root node for right subtree).
Allocate newNode$_A$ with value A
and pointers newLeft$_A$ and newRight$_A$.
Return newNode$_A$ as the root of the tree
copy.

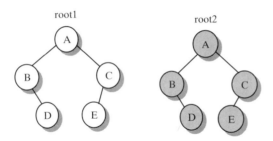

Each recursive call to copyTree() returns a pointer to the newly created tree. Because the function builds the root node as its last action, it returns the root pointer of the new tree to the calling statement.

copyTree():

```
// create copy of tree t and return a pointer to the new root
template <typename T>
tnode<T> *copyTree(tnode<T> *t)
{
    // newNode points at a new node that the algorithm
    // creates. newLptr. and newRptr point to the subtrees
    // of newNode
    tnode<T> *newLeft, *newRight, *newNode;

    // stop the recursive scan when we arrive at empty tree
    if (t == NULL)
        return NULL;
    // build the new tree from the bottom up by building the two
    // subtrees and then building the parent. at node t, make
    // a copy of the left subtree and assign its root node pointer
    // to newLeft. make a copy of the right subtree and assign its
    // root node pointer to newRight
    newLeft = copyTree(t->left);
    newRight = copyTree(t->right);

    // create a new node whose value is the same as the value in t
    // and whose children are the copied subtrees
    newNode = new tnode<T> (t->nodeValue, newLeft, newRight);

    // return a pointer to the root of the newly copied tree
    return newNode;
}
```

Deleting Tree Nodes

When an application uses a dynamic structure such as a tree, the program is responsible for deallocating unneeded memory. For a general binary tree, we design the deleteTree() function, which uses a postorder scan of the nodes. The ordering ensures that we delete the children of a node before deleting the node (parent).

deleteTree():
```
// traverse the nodes in the binary tree and delete each node
template <typename T>
void deleteTree(tnode<T> *t)
{
    // postorder scan. delete left and right
    // subtrees of t and then node t
    if (t != NULL)
    {
        deleteTree(t->left);
        deleteTree(t->right);
        delete t;
    }
}
```

The function clearTree() removes all of the nodes in a tree by calling deleteTree() and then assigns the root pointer to NULL. This function enables the root to be reused for a new tree.

clearTree():
```
template <typename T>
void clearTree(tnode<T> * & t)
{
    deleteTree(t);
    t = NULL;
}
```

Displaying a Binary Tree

For the programs and exercises in this chapter, we provide a function displayTree(), which outputs a picture of a binary tree. The output of the tree is vertical, with the nodes at each level on the same line.

displayTree():
```
// display a binary tree. output of a node value requires
// no more than maxCharacters
template <typename T>
void displayTree(tnode<T> *t, int maxCharacters);
```

Root of tree

You use the function by passing the root of the tree and the maximum number of characters required to output the value of a node. For instance, if the tree has integer values in the range from 0 to 99, pass 2 as the argument maxCharacters. If *string* is the template type of the tree, pass the length corresponding to the longest string as the value for maxCharacters.

The code fragment shown next uses buildTree() to create Tree 0 with single-character node values. A call to displayTree() shows the structure of the tree.

```
tnode<char> *root;

root = buildTree(0);
displayTree(root, 1);
```

```
Output:
     A
  B     C
    D   E
```

The interested reader will find a thorough explanation of the displayTree()
algorithm on the companion Web site. The algorithm introduces the concept of a   Note
shadow tree that has the same hierarchical structure as the source tree. Nodes
for elements in the *shadow tree*. contain a nodeValue and information that
specifies the position of the node. The algorithm makes use of an inorder scan to
build the shadow tree and a level-order scan to display the nodes.

PROGRAM 10-3   DISPLAYING, COPYING, AND DELETING TREES

This program demonstrates the algorithms for displaying, copying, and deleting trees. A call
to buildTree() with root pointer root1 constructs Tree 2. We wish to copy this tree and demonstrate that our copy algorithm works. For this purpose, we display the nodes of Tree 2 by using
displayTree(). Note that, because the data value in each node is a single character, the second
argument to displayTree() is 1. The program then makes a copy of Tree 2 using copyTree()
and displays the copied tree. It is good practice for any program to remove unneeded dynamic memory, so calls to clearTree() remove the nodes of the two trees and assign the two root
pointers to NULL.

```
// File: prg10_3.cpp
// the program builds the sample Tree 2 and displays the tree.
// by using copyTree(), the program makes a copy of Tree 2, and
// displays the copied tree. the program terminates after using
// clearTree() to delete the nodes in both trees

#include <iostream>

#include "d_tnode.h"    // tnode class
#include "d_tnodel.h"   // tnode library

using namespace std;

int main()
{
    // roots for two trees
    tnode<char> *root1, *root2;

    // build the character Tree 2 with root root2
    root1 = buildTree(2);
```

```
// display the tree
cout << "Original tree (Tree 2)" << endl;
displayTree(root1, 1);
cout << endl << endl;

// make a copy of root1 so its root is root2
root2 = copyTree(root1);

// display the tree copy
cout << "Copy of Tree 2" << endl;
displayTree(root2, 1);
cout << endl;

// delete the nodes in the two trees
clearTree(root1);
clearTree(root2);

return 0;
}
```

```
Run:

Original tree (Tree 2)
          A
      B           C
  D           E       F
    G       H   I

Copy of Tree 2
          A
      B           C
  D           E       F
    G       H   I
```

10-5   BINARY SEARCH TREES

Up to this point in the chapter, our discussion of binary trees has focused on the structure of the nodes and on algorithms to scan the elements. We have not associated with a binary tree any design structure that would dictate how a programmer should build and manage the tree. The examples assume the existence of the binary tree without any specifc ordering of the elements. In this section, we set out to design a binary tree as a storage structure that can hold a large collection of data with an ordering of elements that provide very efficient access and update operations. The resulting container structure is called a _binary search tree_ and includes operations that are the model for all associative containers.

This section introduces the structure of a binary search tree, including a description of operations to insert, delete, and access elements. We include these operations in the design of a binary search tree class ADT. With the declaration of the _stree_ class, you will see your first example of an associative container that stores elements by value. Like sequence containers, binary search trees have iterators that scan elements, and provide arguments and return values for search and update operations. In Section 10-6, we present two applications that feature the container operations and the use of tree iterators.

Introducing Binary Search Trees

A binary tree is a data structure that consists of nodes that reside on unique paths from the root. To design a binary tree as an efficient storage container, we must impose an ordering that associates the value of each element with its path from the root. The ordering enables us to take a value and execute a search on a path to locate the corresponding element. For this reason, the storage container is called a _binary search tree_.

A binary search tree orders the elements by using the relational operator $<$ for the specified template type T. The ordering compares each node with the value of elements in its subtree:

> _Ordering_: For each node, the data values in the left subtree are less than the value of the node, and the data values in the right subtree are greater than the value of the node.

Figure 10-14 illustrates binary search trees with a variety of shapes. Note that the order relation on the subtrees dictates that a binary search tree cannot have duplicate values. It is possible to allow duplicate values, but this complicates the design of a binary search tree container class. Programming Project 10-44 discusses the handling of duplicate values in a binary search tree.

A binary search tree has algorithms that maintain the ordering when elements are added or removed. The insert algorithm actually builds the tree. In the process, we discover a technique to access an existing tree element along its unique path from the root. Before we describe the binary search tree container as an ADT, let's explore the insert, find, and erase algorithms, using a set of examples.

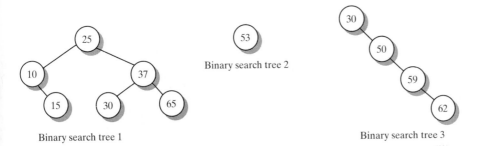

Binary search tree 1

Binary search tree 2

Binary search tree 3

Figure 10-14
Sample binary search trees

Building a Binary Search Tree

Elements enter a binary search tree via a specific ordering strategy. The first element becomes the root node. Subsequent elements enter the tree at the end of a specified path. Identifying the path is an iterative process that begins at the root. Each step involves comparing the value of the new element (*item*) with the value in the current node (*nodeValue*) on the path. The following is the algorithm based on the results of the comparison:

> If the value of the new element is less than the value of the current node (*item* < *nodeValue*), proceed to the left subtree (left child) of the node:
> - If the left subtree is not empty, repeat the process by comparing *item* with the root of the subtree.
> - If the left subtree is empty (left child == NULL), we have reached the end of a path of existing nodes and have the location for the new element. Allocate a new node with *item* as its value, and attach the node to the tree as the left child. This extends the path to the new element.

> If the value of the new element is greater than the value of the current node (*nodeValue* < *item*), proceed to the right subtree (right child) of the node:
> - If the right subtree is not empty, repeat the process by comparing *item* with the root of the subtree.
> - If the right subtree is empty (right child == NULL), allocate a new node with *item* as its value, and attach the node to the tree as the right child.

> If the value of the new element is equal to the value of the current node (*nodeValue* == *item*), perform no action, because the algorithm does not allow duplicate values.

Example 10-7

This example builds a binary search tree by adding the sequence of elements 35, 18, 25, 48, 72, 60.

> 35: Insert 35 as the root (Figure 10-15(a)).
> 18: Compare 18 with root 35. Go left, landing on an empty tree. Insert 18 as the left child of 35 (Figure 10-15(b)).

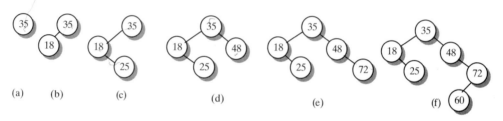

(a)   (b)   (c)   (d)   (e)   (f)

Figure 10-15
Inserting into a binary search tree

25: Compare 25 with the root 35. Go left, landing on node 18. Compare 25 with 18. Go right, landing on an empty tree. Insert 25 as the right child of 18 (Figure 10-15(c)).

48: Compare 48 with 35. Go right, landing on an empty tree. Insert 48 as the right child of 35 (Figure 10-15(d)).

72: Compare 72 with 35. Go right, landing on node 48. Compare 72 with 48 Go right, landing on an empty tree. Insert 72 as the right child of 48 (Figure 10-15(e)).

60: Compare 60 with 35. Go right, landing on node 48. Compare 60 with 48. Go right, landing on node 72. Compare with 72. Go left, landing on an empty tree. Insert 60 as the left child of 72 (Figure 10-15(f)).

Locating Data in a Binary Search Tree

Each node enters the tree along a specific path. That same path can be used to search for an item. The algorithm assumes that type T has the comparison operator $==$. A search for an item follows a path from the root, using the same steps required to add an element to the tree. Compare the value of each node on the path with the item. If a match occurs, we identify the location of the item. If the item is less than the node value, the path continues into the left subtree; otherwise, the path continues into the right subtree. If the path ends on an empty tree, the item is not in the tree. For instance, in the binary search tree in Figure 10-16, a search for 37 starts at the root and requires four comparisons.

Current Node		Action
Root = 50	Compare *item* = 37 and 50;	37 < 50, so move to the left subtree.
Node = 30	Compare *item* = 37 and 30;	37 > 30, so move to the right subtree.
Node = 35	Compare *item* = 37 and 35;	37 > 35, so move to the right subtree.
Node = 37	Compare *item* = 37 and 37.	Item found.

A search for 58 would require three comparisons with nodes along the path 50, 55, and 60. The search fails when the algorithm discovers that 60 does not have a left child (i.e., the left subtree is empty).

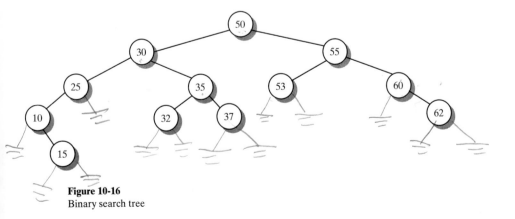

Figure 10-16
Binary search tree

Note that the ordering of a binary search tree ensures that an inorder scan of the tree visits the data in ascending order. For instance, an inorder scan of the tree in Figure 10-16 visits the data in the order

10   15   25   30   32   35   37   50   53   55   60   62

Removing a Binary Search Tree Node

In a linked list, the erase() operation unlinks a node and connects its predecessor to the next node. A binary search tree has a similar operation, although the reconnection of nodes is more complicated. Consider the problem of deleting the root, 25, from the search tree shown in the following figure. The first effect is to create two disjoint subtrees that require a new root:

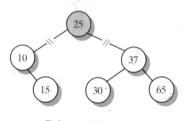

Delete node 25

At first glance, one might be tempted to choose a child of 25, say, 37, to replace its parent. This simple solution fails. We are left with nodes on the wrong side of the root (Figure 10-17(a)). The correct strategy looks for an element in the tree that is near 25 in value. Because the example is relatively small, we can identify that 15 or 30 would be a good choice. We choose node 30 and use it as a replacement for the deleted node, 25 (Figure 10-17(b)). We are not attempting to explain the algorithm, except to say that the process involves searching down the path from 25 to 37, and ultimately, 30, to locate an element near 25. The deletion involves disconnecting node 30 as the left child of 37, moving it to the root, and reconnecting the subtrees 10 and 37 as

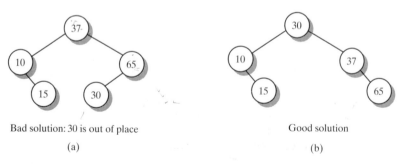

Bad solution: 30 is out of place   Good solution

(a)   (b)

Figure 10-17
Removing the root from a binary search tree

its left and right children. We point this out to illustrate that the erase algorithm, like the insert and find operations, involves an iterative scan of a path in a binary search tree. This ability to perform access and update operations by using paths is the fundamental reason for the efficiency of binary search trees as a storage container.

A Binary-Search Tree Class

A binary search tree is a structure that locates elements by value. With its operations, we can build a class that has an interface modeled on the STL container classes, including iterators. The resulting data structure is an associative container. In the design of the class, which we call *stree*, the operations size() and empty() identify the number of elements in the container. A default constructor creates an empty container; a second version uses an address range to initialize the tree with elements from a predefined array. Because a binary search tree container stores elements by value, and not by position, the stree class does not include operations such as push_back() or pop_front(), as these have meaning only for sequence containers. For illustration purposes, we include the function displayTree() in the class.

The binary search tree class supports both constant and nonconstant iterators. The iterators allow for an inorder traversal of the elements in the tree, starting at iterator location begin() and ending at iterator location end(). Using the dereference operator, *, a programmer can access the elements in a binary search tree container in ascending order. For this reason, we refer to the container as an *ordered associative container*. In its implementation, we will show you how the iterators produce an ordered scan of the elements.

Example 10-8
_____

1. A tree with integer data illustrates an stree constructor and the size() function:

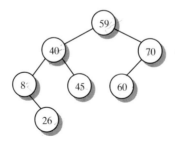

```
// declare an stree container with initial values
// from array arr
int arr[] = {59, 40, 70, 45, 8, 26, 60};
int arrSize = sizeof(arr)/sizeof(int);
stree<int> t(arr, arr+arrSize);

cout << t.size();        // Output: 7
```

2. The function writeSTree() uses a constant iterator to scan a tree container and output the values in ascending order. You can find the implementation in the library file "d_util.h."

```
template <typename T>
void writeSTree(const stree<T>& t, const string& separator = "  ")
{
  stree<T>::const_iterator iter = t.begin();

  while (iter != t.end())
  {
    cout << *iter << separator;
    iter++;
  }
}
```

```
Output from Example 10-8 (1):
8  26  40  45  59  60  70
```

Access and Update Operations

The access operation find() and the update operations insert() and erase() are the key functions in the stree class. The operations combine value and iterator arguments. To locate an element, call find() with the value as an argument. The return value is an iterator that references the location of the element in the tree. If the value is not found, the return iterator has value end().

find():
```
stree<T>::iterator find(const T& item);
```

The insert() operation requires some careful understanding. Before we look at the design of the function, let us explore an application that uses different features of an insert. An electronics store maintains a database of customer records, where the information includes the customer's name, address, phone number, and a list of products purchased. When a customer makes a new purchase, the retailer uses an insert to enter the customer's name and search the database. Depending on whether the customer is already in the database, the retailer either updates the existing list of purchases or fills in the missing fields for a new record. Assuming that the program maintains customer records in a search tree, the insert operation takes the customer's name as an argument and searches the existing records. The insert operation must return the location of the customer record along with a flag that indicates whether the insert added a new record or found an existing record. In the design of the insert() function, we could include reference arguments for the Boolean flag and the iterator location of the record. For instance,

```
void insert(const T& item, bool& success, iterator& iter);
```

Many search-tree applications require only a simple insert() that adds an element to the container. The applications do not need return information that specifies a flag indicating success (new element) or failure (duplicate element). For these cases, requiring reference arguments would be inconvenient, because a programmer would have to declare variables and pass them as runtime arguments with no intention of using their updated information. Another approach borrows a concept from STL. The insert() function returns a pair object that has separate iterator and Boolean data members called *first* and *second*. In the pair class, the data members are public. The syntax surrounding the declaration of a pair object is a little more complicated, because it must take into account two different template types. The concept is fairly simple, and you can think of the syntax as a mechanical technique to differentiate between the separate data members.

```
template <typename T1, typename T2>
class pair
{
    public:
        T1 first;
        T2 second;
    ...
};
```

Assume that an stree container stores integer elements. The declaration of an iterator–bool pair for the class includes two template arguments enclosed in angle brackets. To use the pair class in a program, include the header file <utility>:

```
                     T
pair<stree<int>::iterator, bool> pairObj;
```

An expression that includes the object's name and the value *first* accesses the iterator part of the object, and the data member *second* accesses the Boolean value:

```
pairObj.first    // iterator value in the pair
pairObj.second   // Boolean value in the pair
```

We use the concept of a pair object to describe the stree class insert() function. The operation takes a value of type T as an argument and returns an iterator–bool pair. If the insert adds a new element, the Boolean value of the pair is set to *true*. If the value already exists in the tree, the value is *false*. In either case, the iterator value is the location of the new or existing element in the tree.

insert():
```
template <typename T>
pair<stree<T>::iterator, bool> insert(const T& item);
```

To see how to use insert(), assume that a statement adds the element 17 to the search tree intTree, which contains integer values. The pair will contain an iterator that references a new or existing copy of the element 17 in the tree. The Boolean part distinguishes between the two situations.

```
pairObj = intTree.insert(17);

//  output value of element in the tree referenced by the iterator
cout << *(pairObj.first);

// test whether 17 is a new entry in the tree
if (pairObj.second)
   cout << "Insert added a new entry";
```

The stree class has versions of the erase() function that use value and iterator arguments. With a value argument, a search first identifies the location of the element in the tree and then removes it. If the value is not present, no action occurs. In either case, the function returns the number of elements removed (0 or 1). If the function uses a single iterator argument, the operation removes the element at the specified location. If two iterator arguments specify an iterator range [*first, last*), the operation removes all of the elements in the range. You could use the iterator range [begin(), end()) to clear the tree.

erase():
```
    int erase(const T& item);
    void erase(iterator pos);
    void erase(iterator first, iterator last);
```

To assist in your understanding of binary search tree operations, the container also includes the function displayTree(), which outputs a picture of a binary tree. The output of the tree is vertical, with the nodes at each level on the same line. Its argument is the maximum number of characters required to output the value in a node.

Example 10-9

Let us look at an example that builds a binary search tree container with characters from the string "patterns." The operations insert(), erase(), and find() access and update elements in the tree. Figure 10-18 displays the tree after repeated calls to insert() add the characters to the tree.

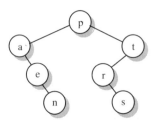

Figure 10-18
Using a Binary Search Tree to Remove Duplicates

```
   // declare an empty stree container for character data and an iterator
   stree<char> t;
   stree<char>::iterator tIter;

   // use pObj with insert()
   pair<stree<char>::iterator, bool> pObj;

   // use the string to initialize the elements in the container
   string str = "patterns";
   int i;
   // build the tree, noting duplicate letters
   for (i = 0; i < str.length(); i++)
   {
      pObj = t.insert(str[i]);
      if (pObj.second == false)
         cout << str[i] << " is a duplicate letter" << endl;
   }
   cout << "Initial tree" << endl;
   t.displayTree(1);

   // erase the character 'a' in the tree
   t.erase('a');
   cout << "Tree after deleting 'a'" << endl;
   t.displayTree(1);

   // look for 'p' and use the iterator to delete the letter if
   // the letter is found
   tIter = t.find('p');
   if (tIter != t.end())
     t.erase(tIter);
   cout << "Tree after deleting 'p'" << endl;
   t.displayTree(1);
```

```
Run:
t is a duplicate letter
Initial tree
```

```
Tree after deleting 'a'
     p
  e       t
    n   r
          s
Tree after deleting 'p'
     r
  e       t
    n   s
```

We summarize the interface for the stree class by listing the public section of the class, as follows.

| CLASS stree | Declaration | "d_stree.h" |

```
template <typename T>
class stree
{
   public:
      stree();
         // constructor. initialize root to NULL and size to 0
      stree(T *first, T *last);
         // constructor. insert the elements from the pointer
         // range [first, last) into the tree

      iterator find(const T& item);
         // search for item. if found, return an iterator pointing
         // at it in the tree; otherwise, return end()

      int empty() const;
         // indicate whether the tree is empty

      int size() const;
         // return the number of data items in the tree

      pair<iterator, bool> insert(const T& item);
         // if item is not in tree, insert it and
         // return a pair whose iterator component points
         // at the item, and whose bool component is true; if item
         // is not in the tree, return a pair whose iterator
         // component points at the existing item and whose
         // bool component is false
         // Postcondition:  the tree size increases by 1 if item
         // is not in the tree

      int erase(const T& item);
         // if item is in the tree, erase it, and return 1;
         // otherwise, return 0
         // Postcondition:   the tree size decreases by 1, if
         // item is in the tree

      void erase(iterator pos);
         // erase the item pointed to by pos.
         // Preconditions:   the tree is not empty and pos points
         // to an item in the tree. if the tree is empty, the
         // function throws the underflowError exception. if the
         // iterator is invalid, the function throws the
         // referenceError exception.
         // Postcondition:   the tree size decreases by 1
```

```
void erase(iterator first, iterator last);
        // erase all items in the range [first, last).
        // Precondition:   the tree is not empty. if the tree
        // is empty, the function throws the underflowError
        // exception.
        // Postcondition:   the size of the tree decreases by
        // the number of elements in the range [first, last)

    iterator begin();
        // return an iterator pointing to the first item inorder

    const_iterator begin() const;
        // constant version

    iterator end();
        // return iterator pointing just past end of the tree data

    const_iterator end() const;
        // constant version

    void displayTree(int maxCharacters);
        // tree display function. maxCharacters is the largest number
        // of characters required to output the value of a node
}
```

USING BINARY SEARCH TREES   10-6

An stree object is a powerful container for dynamic data storage. In this section, we provide two applications that exploit search tree properties. The first application acts on a vector containing duplicate values. By using a binary search tree as a filter, we copy the elements from the vector to the tree, which has the effect of sorting the collection and removing duplicates. A scan of the tree copies the elements back into the vector. A more practical application is that of a video store using stree objects to store the inventory of available films and to keep track of rented films. The application uses the find(), insert(), and erase() operations to process customer requests and move films from available inventory to the set of rented films.

Application: Removing Duplicates

An stree iterator traverses elements in sorted order. This enables us to generate a simple algorithm that removes the duplicates from a vector and, as a side effect, leaves the vector in sorted order. Use a search tree as a filter, with the elements copied from the vector to the tree, using the search tree insert() algorithm. The insert() ignores duplicate values. Using a tree iterator, copy the elements from the tree container back into the vector.

The function removeDuplicates() takes a vector v as a reference argument and implements the algorithm. A vector iterator scans the original sequence and copies the elements to the stree container. A tree iterator scans the tree container in order to copy the elements back into the vector. While we could scan the vector using an index, we choose an iterator that is a general scanning mechanism for containers. The code for removeDuplicates() can be modified for any container object to sort elements and remove duplicates.

removeDupliates():

```
// remove duplicate values from v and leave
// the remaining values in sorted order
template <<>typename T>
void removeDuplicates(vector<T>& v)
{
    // insert vector data into binary search tree t
    stree<T> t;
    // declare iterators for t and v
    stree<T>::iterator treeIter;
    vector<T>::iterator vectorIter;

    // insert each vector element into the search tree,
    // ignoring duplicate values
    vectorIter = v.begin();
    while (vectorIter != v.end())
    {
        t.insert(*vectorIter);
        vectorIter++;
    }

    // clear the vector
    v.resize(0);

    // traverse tree in ascending order, pushing each
    // element onto the back of v using push_back()
    treeIter = t.begin();

    while (treeIter != t.end())
    {
        v.push_back(*treeIter);
        treeIter+;
    }
}
```

PROGRAM 10-4 REMOVING DUPLICATES AND SORTING

Let us look at a program that illustrates the function removeDuplicates(). Use the integer array *arr* to initialize the vector *v*. There are duplicate values in *v*. After calling removeDuplicates(), we output the resulting vector by using the function writeVector() from the library "d_util.h."

```cpp
// File: prg10_4.cpp
// the program initializes the vector v with values from the
// integer array arr, which contains duplicates. a call to
// removeDuplicates() with argument v removes the duplicate values.
// the program concludes by displaying the unique values in v using
// writeVector()

#include <iostream>
#include <vector>

#include "d_stree.h"    // stree class
#include "d_util.h"      // for writeVector()

using namespace std;

// remove duplicate values from v and leave
// the remaining values in sorted order
template <typename T>
void removeDuplicates(vector<T>& v);

int main()
{
   int arr[] = {3, 6, 3, 33, 55, 5, 55, 15, 25, 3, 5, 2, 5, 3, 55};
   int arrSize = sizeof(arr)/sizeof(int);
   vector<int> v(arr, arr+arrSize);

   // remove duplicates and sort
   removeDuplicates(v);
   // output the modified vector
   writeVector(v);
   cout << endl;

   return 0;
}
/* the implementation of removeDuplicates() given in
   the program discussion */
```

```
Run:
2   3   5   6   15   25   33   55
```

Application: The Video Store

A video store maintains an inventory of movies that includes multiple titles. When a customer makes an inquiry, the clerk checks the inventory to see whether the title is available. If so, the rental transaction requires updating both the inventory and the database of rented films. The update decreases the number of copies of the title in inventory and increments a similar rented-film entry. When a customer returns a film, the clerk reverses the process by removing a copy from the collection of rented films and adding it to the inventory. The application presented here simulates inventory management at a video store by having a series of customers request and return film titles. The simulation uses two stree objects, *inventory* and *rentals*, to store the collection of available films and the set of rented films, respectively.

Each element in the binary search trees is a record consisting of the title of the film and the number of copies. We use the *video* class to describe each record. The class has the member function getCopies() to access the number of copies and the member function updateCopies() to update the number of copies. The class also defines three overloaded operators. The operators == and < compare film titles and enable the simulation to store video objects in a binary search tree. The overloaded stream output operator << displays a video object in the format

    film title (# copies)

The following is a declaration of the class, which is implemented with inline code in the file "d_video.h."

CLASS video	Declaration	"d_video.h"

```
class video
{
   public:
      video(const string& film = "", int copies = 1);
        // constructor. initialize film title and numCopies

      void updateCopies(int n);
        // add n to the number of copies. note that if n < 0
        // the function decreases the number of copies

      int getCopies();
        // return the number of copies of the film title

      friend bool operator== (const video& lhs, const video& rhs);
        // two video objects are "equal" if they have the same title

      friend bool operator< (const video& lhs, const video& rhs);
        // compare video objects by comparing film titles

      friend ostream& operator<< (ostream& ostr, const video& obj);
        // output a video object

   private:
      string filmTitle;
        // title of the film
      int numCopies;
        // number of copies (>= 0)
};
```

Designing the Video Simulation The function setupInventory() reads film titles from the file "films.dat" and inserts them into the inventory container (search
tree). Each line of the file is a string representing the title of a film. The function
reads each title using the string operation getline() and creates a video object with
specified title and default copy count of 1. The insert() function, with the *video* object as the argument, updates the inventory. If the film is not in the inventory, the
function places the corresponding *video* object in the tree and returns a pair whose
second data member is *true*; otherwise, it returns a pair whose second data member
is *false*. In this situation, setupInventory() uses the iterator member of the pair and
applies updateCopies() to increment the number of copies of the film.

setupInventory():

```
void setupInventory(stree<video>& inventory)
{
    ifstream filmFile;   // input stream
    string filmName;     // individual file names
    // use with stree insert()
    pair<stree<video>::iterator, bool> p;

    // open the file "films.dat"
    filmFile.open("films.dat");
    if (!filmFile)
    {
        cerr << "File 'films.dat' not found!" << endl;
        exit(1);
    }

    // read lines until EOF; insert names in inventory list
    while(true)
    {
        getline(filmFile, filmName, '\n');
        if (!filmFile)
            break;

        // try an insertion with default of 1 copy
        p = inventory.insert(video(filmName));
        // see if video already in the inventory
        if (p.second == false)
            // increment number of copies
            (*(p.first)).updateCopies(1);
    }
}
```

The simulation processes a series of customer rental and return transactions.
The two actions involve similar algorithms, which are implemented by the functions
rentalTransaction() and returnTransaction(), respectively. Let us look at the rental
algorithm. A rental transaction begins with a call to find() to search for a matching
title in the inventory tree. If the return iterator has the value inventory.end(), the

video store does not carry the title; otherwise, the iterator and the function get-Copies() can be used to determine if the film is available. A count of zero indicates that all of the copies are checked out. An actual rental occurs when the count is not zero. The function updateCopies() decreases the inventory count for the film. An insert() helps update the title in the rental tree. The operation returns the iterator–bool pair that indicates whether the insert found a duplicate or a new video entry enters the tree. In the case that a duplicate is found, a call to updateCopies()increases the rental count by one.

rentalTransaction():

```
void rentalTransaction(stree<video>& inventory, stree<video>& rentals,
                       const string& filmName)
{
   stree<video>::iterator filmIter;
   // use pObj with stree insert()
   pair<stree<video>::iterator, bool> pObj;

   // is film available?
   filmIter = inventory.find(video(filmName));
   if ( filmIter == inventory.end())
      // film is not in the store's inventory
      cout << "Film " << filmName << " is not in inventory" << endl;
   else if ((*filmIter).getCopies() == 0)
      // all copies are checked out
      cout << "All copies of " << filmName << " are checked out"
           << endl;
   else
   {
      // decrease the number of copies in the inventory
      // by 1
      (*filmIter).updateCopies(-1);

      // attempt to insert the film into rentalList. if it is
      // inserted, the number of copies will be 1
      pObj = rentals.insert(video(filmName));
      // if film not inserted, increase number of rented copies
      // by 1
      if (pObj.second == false)
         (*(pObj.first)).updateCopies(1);
   }
}
```

PROGRAM 10-5   RECORD KEEPING IN A VIDEO STORE

Let us run the video store simulation. After the inventory list has been set up, a loop prompts the store clerk to enter "Rent" or "Return," followed by the film name for the rental or check-in of a film. Entering "Done" followed by a blank terminates the program. The functions rentalTransaction() and returnTransaction() process the two activities.

```cpp
// File: prg10_5.cpp
// the program simulates inventory maintenance for a
// video store. the program stores the title of a film
// and the number of copies the store owns in a video
// object. the video class has functions that access
// and update the number of copies, compare objects
// by title, and output a title and the number of copies.
// the function setupInventory() inputs film titles
// from the file "films.dat" and creates the stree
// object inventory of video data. Output begins with a
// listing of the films in inventory;  an interactive loop reads
// transaction information indicating whether a customer wishes
// to rent a film or return a film, or whether the business day
// is over. for a rental, a call to rentalTransaction() updates the
// inventory by reducing the number of copies of the film by 1, and
// adds the film to the rentals tree that maintains a database
// of rented films. when a customer returns a film, a call to
// returnTransaction() removes 1 copy of the film from the rentals
// container and increases the number of copies in inventory container
// by 1. at the end of the business day, the program outputs
// the list of rented films and the films remaining in
// the inventory

#include <iostream>
#include <fstream>
#include string>
#include <utility>                // for pair class

#include "d_stree.h"              // stree class
#include "d_video.h"              // video class
#include "d_util.h"               // for writeSTree()

using namespace std;

// initialize inventoryList from file "films.dat"
void setupInventory(stree<video>& inventory);

// process the return of a film
void returnTransaction(stree<video>& inventory,
        stree<video>& rentals,const string& filmName);

// process the rental of a film
void rentalTransaction(stree<video>& inventory,
        stree<video>& rentals,const string& filmName);

int main()
{
   // the inventory and rental lists
   stree<video> inventory, rentals;
   // assign return value from find() to filmIter
   stree<video>::iterator filmIter;
```

```
                // input from store operator. transactionType = "Rent", "Return",
                // or "Done"
                string transactionType;

                // film requested by a customer
                string filmName;

                // read and output inventory file
                setupInventory(inventory);
                cout << "Initial inventory list:" << endl;
                writeSTree(inventory, "\n");
                cout << endl;

                // process customers by entering "Rental" or "Return"
                // followed by the film name or "Done" to end the program.
                // for "Rent", decrease number of copies in inventory by 1
                // and add the copy to the rental database. for "Return",
                // remove copy from rental database and increase number
                // of copies in inventory by 1
                cout << "Transactions:Enter type (Rent, Return, Done)" <<\ endl;
                cout << "followed by film name or space if done" <<\ endl << endl;
                while (true)
                {
                   // input the transaction type. the input must terminate with
                   // a blank
                   cout << "Transaction: ";
                   getline(cin, transactionType, ' ');
                   // if "Done", terminate the loop
                   if (transactionType == "Done")
                     break;

                   // get film name
                   getline(cin, filmName, '\n');

                   if (transactionType == "Return")
                      returnTransaction(inventory, rentals, filmName);
                   else
                      rentalTransaction(inventory, rentals, filmName);
                }
                cout << endl;

                // output the final rental and inventory lists.
                cout << "Rented Films: " << endl << endl;
                writeSTree(rentals, "\n");
                cout << endl;
                cout << "Films Remaining in Inventory: " << endl << endl;
                   writeSTree(inventory, "\n");

                   return 0;
             }
          /* implementation of setupInventory()and rentalTransaction()
          provided in the program discussion */
```

```
Run:

Initial inventory list:
Frequency (1)
Gladiator (2)
Lord of the Rings (4)
U-571 (2)

Transactions: Enter type (Rent, Return, Done)
followed by film name or space if done

Transaction: Rent Gladiator
Transaction: Rent Frequency
Transaction: Rent Shaft
Film Shaft is not in inventory
Transaction: Rent Frequency
All copies of Frequency are checked out
Transaction: Done

Rented Films:

Frequency (1)
Gladitor (1)

Films Remaining in Inventory:

Frequency (0)
Gladiator (2)
Lord of the Rings (4)
U-571 (2)
```

IMPLEMENTING THE STREE CLASS   10-7

In Section 10-2, we introduce the tnode class to describe the nodes in a binary tree. A tnode object has three data attributes, the value and pointers to the left and right child. For the stree class, we extend the structure of a tree node object to include a fourth data member, consisting of a pointer to the parent of the node. The stnode class describes the modified tree node object.

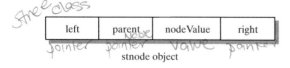

left	parent	nodeValue	right

stnode object

In the implementation of the member functions for the stree class, we maintain and update the parent field as we scan paths from the root. Retaining information on the parent of each node simplifies the implementation of both the iterator and const_iterator subclasses in stree (Section 10-8). The parent pointer value is critical for the iterator operations $++$ and $--$, which enable an iterator to scan the elements in an stree container in ascending or descending order. The parent of the root node is NULL. The upcoming code is a declaration of the stnode class. The constructor has four arguments that initialize the data members. All of the pointer arguments have a default value of NULL. Figure 10-19 displays a model of a binary search tree with its configuration, using stnode objects.

CLASS stnode	Declaration	"d_stree.h"

```
// declares a binary search tree node object
template <typename T>
class stnode
{
  public:
    // stnode is used to implement the binary search tree class
    // making the data public simplifies building the class functions

    T nodeValue;
        // node data
    stnode<T> *left, *right, *parent;
        // child pointers and pointer to the node's parent

    // constructor
    stnode (const T& item, stnode<T> *lptr = NULL,
          stnode<T> *rptr = NULL, stnode<T> *pptr = NULL);
};
```

The stree class declaration in Section 10-5 describes the interface for a binary search tree container. The container is a dynamic structure, so the class also includes the standard destructor, copy constructor, and overloaded assignment operator that allow us to initialize objects and perform assignment statements. The destructor is responsible for clearing the nodes when the program closes the scope of an object. The destructor calls the private function deleteTree(). In this section, we list the private

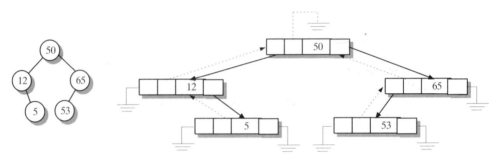

Figure 10-19
Binary search tree whose nodes have parent pointers

portion of the stree class. It includes the private function copyTree() for use by the copy constructor and overloaded assignment operator. The algorithms for delete-Tree() and copyTree() were developed in Section 10-4 as part of the general introduction to binary trees. The private function getSTNode() allocates an stnode object and throws a memoryAllocationError exception if the heap does not have sufficient memory. The function findNode() searches for the value *item* by starting at the root and applying the binary search tree rules (== success, < go left, > go right) until it locates item or encounters a NULL subtree. It returns a pointer to item, or NULL if item is not in the tree. The public-member functions find() and erase() use findNode().

```
CLASS stree            Declaration (private section)            "d_stree.h"

stnode<T> *root;
   // pointer to tree root
int treeSize;
   // number of elements in the tree

stnode<T> *getSTNode(const T& item,
          stnode<T> *lptr, stnode<T> *rptr, stnode<T> *pptr);
   // allocate a new tree node and return a pointer to it.
   // if memory allocation fails, the function throws the
   // memoryAllocationError exception

stnode<T> *copyTree(stnode<T> *t);
   // recursive function used by copy constructor and assignment
   // operator to assign the current tree as a copy of another tree

void deleteTree(stnode<T> *t);
   // recursive function used by destructor and assignment
   // operator to delete all the nodes in the tree

stnode<T> *findNode(const T& item) const;
   // search for item in the tree. if it is in the tree,
   // return a pointer to its node; otherwise, return NULL.
   // used by find() and erase()
```

The stree Class Data Members

The stree class contains a data member, called *root*, that is the starting point for the binary tree that stores the elements. Initially, root is NULL. The integer treeSize maintains the number of elements in the tree. The erase() and insert() functions are responsible for updating the size

```
// pointer to tree root
stnode<T> *root;
// number of elements in the tree
int treeSize;
```

Constructor, Destructor, and Assignment

The class contains two constructors that create both an empty binary search tree and one with initial values obtained from an array. A copy constructor and over-loaded assignment operator use the private copyTree() function to create a new bi-nary search tree for the current object. In this section, we give the implementation of the overloaded assignment operator.

The overloaded assignment operator copies the right-hand-side object to the current object. After checking that the object is not being assigned to itself, the func-tion clears the current tree by using the private function deleteTree() and then uses copyTree() to create a duplicate of the right-hand side (*rhs*). The function copies the tree size and returns a reference to the current object.

operator=:

```
template <typename T>
stree<T>& stree<T>::operator= (const stree<T>& rhs)
{
    // can't copy a tree to itself
    if (this == &rhs)
        return *this;

    // erase the existing tree nodes from memory
    clearTree();

    // copy tree rhs into current object
    root = copyTree(rhs.root);

    // set the tree size
    treeSize = rhs.treeSize;

    // return reference to current object
    return *this;
}
```

Update Operations

The insert() and erase() functions lie at the heart of the stree class. They are opera-tions that must maintain the binary search tree structure while modifying the tree. We provide a detailed implementation to highlight the importance of the algo-rithms. The algorithm for find() is very similar to the insert() algorithm. Consult the header file "d_stree.h" for details.

The insert() Operation The insert() function takes a new data item, search-es the tree, adds the item in the correct location, and returns an iterator–bool pair. If the item is already in the tree, the function returns a pair whose iterator compo-nent points to the existing node and whose Boolean component is false. If the item is a new entry, the iterator points at the new node and the Boolean value is true. The function iteratively traverses the path of the left and right subtrees until it locates the insertion point or finds a match with an existing value. For each step in the path, the algorithm maintains a record of the current node (*t*) and the parent of the current node (*parent*). The process terminates when an empty subtree (*t* = = NULL) is found. In this case, the new node replaces the NULL subtree as a child of the parent. For instance, the following steps insert 32 into the tree depicted by Figure 10-20:

1. The function begins at the root node and compares item 32 with the root value, 25 (Figure 10-20(a)). Because 32 > 25, we traverse the right subtree and look at node 35:

   t is node 35, and parent is node 25

2. Considering 35 as the root of its own subtree, we compare item 32 with the root value, 35, and traverse the left subtree of item 35 (Figure 10-20(b)):

   t is NULL, and *parent* is node 35

3. Create a leaf node with data value 32. Insert the new node as the left child of node 35 (Figure 10-20(c)):

```
newNode = getSTNode(item, NULL, NULL, parent);
parent->left = newNode;
```

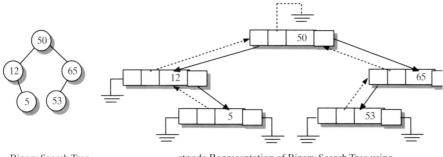

Binary Search Tree

stnode Representation of Binary Search Tree using
Parent Pointers

Figure 10-20
Inserting into a binary search tree

The pointers *parent* and *t* are local objects that change as we scan down the path to find the insertion point.

The optional Section 10-8 discusses the implementation of binary search tree iterators. In the implementation of insert(), an stree iterator is part of the iterator-bool return value. We create an iterator object pointing to node *t* with the expression

```
iterator(t, this)
```

The iterator implementation requires both the stnode address and the address of the stree object (this).

Note

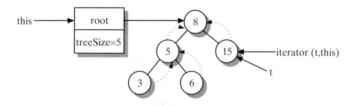

insert():

```
template <typename T>
pair<stree<T>::iterator, bool> stree<T>::insert(const T& item)
{
   {// t is current node in traversal, parent the previous node
   stnode<T> *t = root, *parent = NULL, *newNode;

   // terminate on on empty subtree
   while(t != NULL)
   {
      // update the parent pointer. then go left or right
      parent = t;
      // if a match occurs, return a pair whose iterator
      // component points at item in the tree and whose
      // bool component is false
      if (item == t->nodeValue)
         return pair<iterator, bool> (iterator(t, this), false);
      else if (item < t->nodeValue)
         t = t->left;
      else
         t = t->right;
   }

   // create the new leaf node
   newNode = getSTNode(item, NULL, NULL, parent);
   // if parent is NULL, insert as root node
   if (parent == NULL)
      root = newNode;
   else if (item < parent->nodeValue)
      // insert as left child
      parent->left = newNode;
   else
      // insert as right child
      parent->right = newNode;

   // increment size
   treeSize++;

   // return an pair whose iterator component points at
   // the new node and whose bool component is true
   return pair<iterator, bool> (iterator(newNode, this), true);
}
```

The erase() Operation Consider the erase() operation, which takes an stree iterator *pos* and removes the node from the tree to which it points. We will see in Section 10-8 that the data member *pos.nodePtr* is the address of the actual stnode in memory. We perform the deletion by finding a replacement node somewhere else in the tree and using it as a substitute for the deleted node. Issues surrounding this replacement node are critical to understanding the erase() algorithm. First, we must choose the node so that when it takes the place of the deleted node, its value maintains the structure of the tree. Second, subtrees for the deleted node and the replacement node become orphaned during the process and must be reconnected to the tree in such a way that the new tree has the proper ordering for the left and right subtrees of the nodes. Our discussion focuses on these issues.

Assign the address of the node we wish to remove, *pos.nodePtr*, to the pointer *dNodePtr*. In the discussion, we refer to the deleted node as D. A second pointer, *pNodePtr*, identifies the parent P of the deleted node:

```
pNodePtr = dNodePtr->parent;
```

Note that when pNodePtr is NULL, we are deleting the root. The erase() function sets out to find a replacement node R that will connect to the parent and thus take the place of the deleted node. The pointer rNodePtr identifies this replacement node R. The algorithm for finding a replacement considers four separate cases that depend on the number of children attached to node D. We draw our example of each case from the tree in Figure 10-21. In the annotated figures that illustrate each case, we show only selected parent pointers.

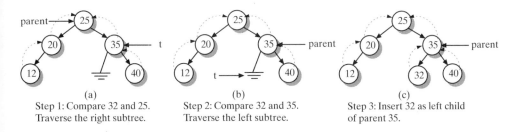

(a)	(b)	(c)
Step 1: Compare 32 and 25.	Step 2: Compare 32 and 35.	Step 3: Insert 32 as left child
Traverse the right subtree.	Traverse the left subtree.	of parent 35.

Figure 10-21
Sample tree for illustrating the erase() operation

Case A: Node D is a leaf node (i.e., it has no children). In this case, there is no need to find a replacement node. Simply update the parent node to have an empty subtree. In the figure, node D has value 10.

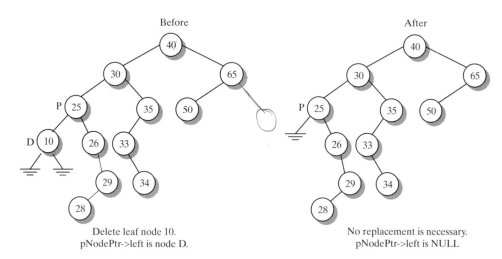

Before   After

Delete leaf node 10.   No replacement is necessary.
pNodePtr->left is node D.   pNodePtr->left is NULL

Accomplish the update by creating a NULL replacement node. When we attach the NULL replacement node, the parent points to NULL:

```
rNodePtr = NULL;
    . . .
pNodePtr->left = rNodePtr;  // complete the link to the parent node P
```

Case B: Node D has a left child, but no right child. In this case, the left child becomes the replacement node R. Attach the left subtree of D (the tree with root R) to the parent. In the figure, node D has value 35, and the node 33 becomes replacement node R.

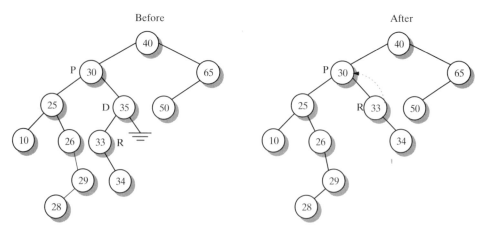

Before   After

Delete node 35 with only a left child: Attach node R to the parent.
Node R is the left child.

Perform the update by setting the replacement R to be the left child of D and then attaching node R to the parent:

```
rNodePtr = dNodePtr->left;
if (rNodePtr != NULL)
   // the parent of R is now the parent of D
   rNodePtr->parent = pNodePtr;
        . . .
pNodePtr->right = rNodePtr;   // complete the link to the parent node P
```

Case C: Node D has a right child, but no left child. This situation parallels
the one described in Case B. The right child becomes the replacement node R. Attach the right subtree of D (the tree with root R) to
the parent. In the figure, node D has the value 26, and node 29 becomes the replacement node R.

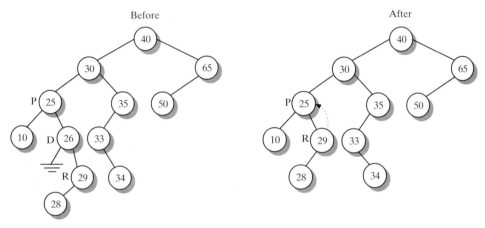

Delete node 26 with only a right child: Attach node R to the parent.
   Node R is the right child.

As in Case B, perform the update by setting the replacement node R to be the
right child of D and then attaching node R to the parent:

```
rNodePtr = dNodePtr->right;
if (rNodePtr != NULL)
   // the parent of R is now the parent of D
   rNodePtr->parent = pNodePtr;
        . . .
pNodePtr->right = rNodePtr;     // complete the link to parent node P
```

Case D: Node D has two children. This is the most interesting case, since removing D orphans both its left and right subtrees.

A node with two children has some elements in its subtrees that are less
than and some elements that are greater than its value. The algorithm must select a replacement node that maintains the correct ordering among the items.
Consider the tree in Figure 10-21. After deleting node 30, we create two orphaned subtrees that must be reattached to the tree (Figure 10-22). We need a

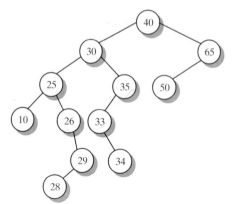

Figure 10-22
Deleting a node with two
children

strategy to select a replacement node from the subtrees of 30. The resulting tree must satisfy the binary search tree properties. Select as the replacement node R the leftmost node in the right subtree of D. This is the smallest node whose data value is greater than that of D. Note that node R has an empty left subtree, but might have a nonempty right subtree Unlink node R from the tree, connect its right subtree to its parent, and then use R in place of the deleted node. In the sample tree, node 33 is the replacement node. We connect its right child, node 34, to its parent node, 35. Finally, replace the deleted node, 30, with the replacement node 33.

Apply a simple algorithm to find node R:

Step 1: Because the replacement node *R* is greater than the deleted node *D*, move to the right child of *D*. In the example, move to node 35.

Step 2: Because R is the smallest of the nodes in the right subtree, locate its value by descending the path of left subtrees. During the descent, keep track of the predecessor node, which is called *pOfRNodePtr* (parent of the replacement node). In our example, descend to node 33, with pOfRNodePtr referencing node 35.

The descent of the path of left subtrees begins at the right child of the deleted node. The descent contains two cases. If the left subtree of the right child is empty, no descent actually occurs. The current location is the replacement node R, and pOfRNodePtr is the deleted node D. To update the tree, attach the left subtree of D as the left subtree of R, and attach the parent of the deleted node P to R. The deletion of node 25 in Figure 10-21 illustrates this case.

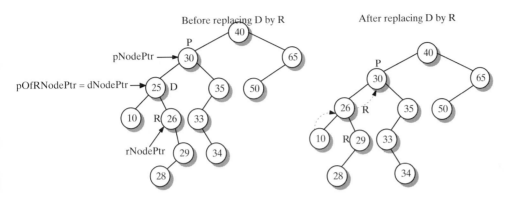

```
// right child of deleted node is the replacement.
// assign left subtree of D to left subtree of R
rNodePtr->left = dNodePtr->left;
// assign the parent of D as the parent of R
rNodePtr->parent = pNodePtr;
// assign the left child of D to have parent R
dNodePtr->left->parent = rNodePtr;
        . . .
// in the figure, D is a left child of P
pNodePtr->left = rNodePtr;
```

If the left subtree of the right child of D is not empty, the algorithm requires a series of descents of its left subtree. The scan ends with a leaf node or a node that has only a right subtree. Unlink node R from the tree, and relink the right subtree of R as the left subtree of the parent node pOfRNodePtr. We illustrate the required statements with the deletion of node 30 in Figure 10-21.

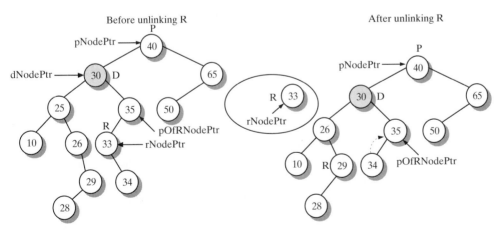

```
// we moved at least one node down a left branch
// of the right child of D. unlink R from tree by
```

```
// assigning its right subtree as the left child of
// the parent of R
pOfRNodePtr->left = rNodePtr->right;

// the parent of the right child of R is the
// parent of R
if (rNodePtr->right != NULL)
    rNodePtr->right->parent = pOfRNodePtr;
```

The algorithm for Case D finishes by substituting node R for the deleted node.
First, attach the children of D as the children of R. The parent of R must be the parent of D, and the children of D must now have parent R. As a result of these assignments, R replaces D as the root of the subtree formed by D.

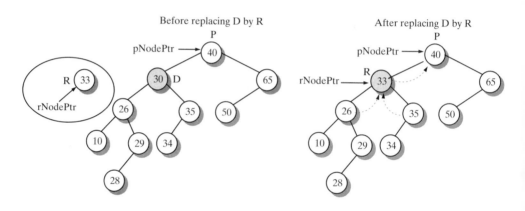

```
// put replacement node in place of dNodePtr
// assign children of R to be those of D
rNodePtr->left = dNodePtr->left;
rNodePtr->right = dNodePtr-> right;
// assign the parent of R to be the parent of D
rNodePtr->parent = pNodePtr;
// assign the parent pointer in the children
// of R to point at R
rNodePtr->left->parent = rNodePtr;
rNodePtr->right->parent = rNodePtr;
```

After handling the appropriate case A through D, erase() concludes by completing
the link to the parent node P, deleting node D, and decrementing the size of the tree:

```
// deleting the root node. assign new root
if (pNodePtr == NULL)
    root = rNodePtr;
// attach R to the correct branch of P
else if (dNodePtr->nodeValue < pNodePtr->nodeValue)
    pNodePtr->left = rNodePtr;
else
    pNodePtr->right = rNodePtr;
```

```
// delete the node from memory and decrement tree size
delete dNodePtr;
treeSize--;
```

An alternative to the approach of linking R into the tree in place of D is to leave node D in place, copy the data in R to D, and then unlink and destroy R. However, if the data consume a large amount of memory, this is a costly operation. Our approach involves only pointer changes.

Note

Complexity of Binary Search Tree Operations

The best-case complexity for the find(), insert(), and erase() operations occurs when the tree is complete. For a complete tree, the maximum number of comparisons needed to reach a leaf node is $O(\log_2 n)$. It follows that these operations have $O(\log_2 n)$ complexity in their best case. The worst case for these operations occurs when the tree is degenerate. In the case of a degenerate tree, the tree reduces to a linked list, and the functions have $O(n)$ complexity. An advanced mathematical analysis shows that the average case has complexity $O(\log_2 n)$. In general, the binary search tree algorithms work well; however, the worst case is linear. In Chapter 12, we eliminate the worst-case condition by extending the search tree concept to create balanced red–black trees.

THE STREE ITERATOR (Optional)   10-8

Iterators have basic operations that allow a program to scan the elements in a container and access their values. A nonconstant iterator also allows a program to update the container value. We have seen the implementation for the list iterator in Chapter 9. Its implementation mirrored the linear ordering of the container elements. Developing an iterator for a binary search tree is more difficult. For a binary search tree container, an iterator should move through tree's elements in order. However, successive elements in an inorder scan can be widely separated from each other. For instance, in the tree in Figure 10-23, the successor of element 23 is the root, 25, which is four levels up the tree. Section 10-3 discusses an algorithm to perform a recursive inorder scan of a binary tree. The problem with a recursive traversal is that there is no escape from the recursive process until it completes. A program cannot stop the scan, perform various operations on the data, and then continue the scan at another node in the tree. An iterator must allow the program to visit a node, perform an action, move to the next node in order, perhaps perform another action, and so forth. This requires an iterative algorithm. We must simulate a recursive scan without the "no escape" limitation.

The stree container provides nested classes that declare constant and nonconstant iterators. The public members of the classes provide the standard iterator interface. This includes the dereference operator, *; the increment and decrement operators, + + and − −; and the iterator comparison operators, == and !=. The upcoming code is the declaration of the iterator class. The const_iterator class has a

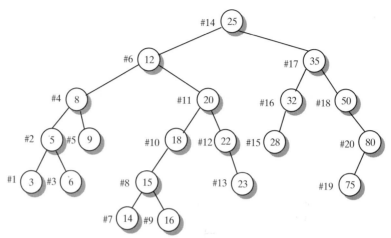

Binary Search Tree Iterator Traversal
#n labels the order of node visits

Figure 10-23
The inorder sequence

similar declaration, except that a const_iterator treats the tree nodes as having constant data.

CLASS stree<T>::iterator	Declaration	"d_stiter.h"

```
class iterator
{
    public:

        iterator();
            // constructor

        bool operator== (const iterator& rhs) const;
            // equality for iterators
        bool operator!= (const iterator& rhs) const;
            // inequality for iterators

        T& operator* () const;
            // pointer dereference operator

        iterator& operator++ ();
            // prefix increment. move to next node inorder

        iterator operator++ (int);
            // postfix increment

        iterator& operator-- ();
            // prefix decrement. move to previous node inorder
```

```
       iterator operator-- (int);
          // postfix decrement

   private:
       // nodePtr is the current location in the tree. we can move
       // freely about the tree using left, right, and parent.
       // tree is the address of the stree object associated
       // with this iterator. it is used only to access the
       // root pointer, which is needed for ++ and --
       // when the iterator value is end()
       stnode<T> *nodePtr;
       stree<T> *tree;

       // used to construct an iterator return value from
       // an stnode pointer
       iterator (stnode<T> *p, stree<T> *t):nodePtr(p), tree(t)
       {}
};
```

Note that, with the exception of the data member *tree*, the private portion of
the stree iterator is identical to the miniList iterator in Section 9-8. The iterator data
value, nodePtr, points to the current node in the inorder traversal of the tree. We discuss the necessity for the data member *tree* in the next section.

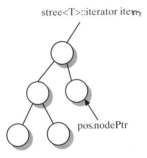

stree<T>::iterator item

pos.nodePtr

inorder

LNR

Implementing the stree Iterator

An iterative inorder traversal emulates the recursive scan. First, start at the root
node and traverse the chain of left subtrees. The process stops at a node with a
NULL left pointer. This becomes the first node the iterator visits in the inorder
scan. The stree member function begin() returns an iterator that references this
node. To build the return iterator, use the private constructor of the iterator class
that takes the stnode pointer and a pointer to the stree object as arguments:

stree begin():
```
    template <typename T>
    stree<T>::iterator stree<T>::begin()
```

```
    {
        stnode<T> *curr = root;

        // if the tree is not empty, the first node
        // inorder is the farthest node left from root
        if (curr != NULL)
            while (curr->left != NULL)
                curr = curr->left;

        // build return value using private constructor
        return iterator(curr, this);
    }
```

For instance, in Figure 10-23, iterator(*curr, this*) points to the node with value 3:

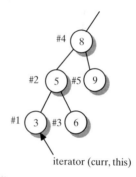

iterator (curr, this)

The implementation of end() must return an iterator that specifies the end of a tree traversal. We construct an iterator whose nodePtr value is NULL for this purpose. This is similar to a singly linked list, where a NULL pointer indicates the end of the list.

stree end():
```
    template <typename T>
    stree<T>::iterator stree<T>::end()
    {
        // end indicated by an iterator with NULL stnode pointer
        return iterator(NULL, this);
    }
```

The implementation for the iterator dereference operator, *, is simple. If nodePtr is NULL, the iterator is not pointing to a valid tree node; throw a referenceError exception. Otherwise, return a reference to the value of the node.

T& operator():*
```
    // dereference operator. return a reference to
    // the value pointed to by nodePtr
    T& operator* () const
    {
        if (nodePtr == NULL)
```

```
            throw referenceError
                ("stree iterator operator* (): NULL reference");

        return nodePtr->nodeValue;
    }
```

To implement the iterator operator $++$, we must execute a series of iterative steps that move us from the current node to the next node in order. We do not look at the left branch of the current tree node, because we have already visited the smaller values on the left subtree. We must either descend the right subtree or move up the tree. We summarize the possibilities with the following two rules:

- If the right subtree is not empty, obtain the next node in order by moving to the right child and then moving left until the node has a NULL pointer. For instance, in the tree in Figure 10-23, from the node with value 12, we must move to node 20 and then far left to node 14.
- If the right subtree is empty, obtain the next node in order by following a chain of parent pointers until we find a parent P for which our current node, nodePtr, is a left child. Node P is the next node in order. When this situation occurs, all the nodes on the left subtree of P have been visited, and it is time to visit P. For example, in Figure 10-23, if we are at the node with value 23, we move up the tree until we find that node 12 is the left child of node 25. The root node, 25, is the next node in order.

The implementation of the prefix operator $++$ follows these two rules. However, there are two special situations we must consider. When a traversal positions an iterator at the largest node in the tree, the next execution of $++$ must return the value end(). In Figure 10-23, the value of the node is 80. We know that the last node in the inorder scan of the tree is the final node on the path of right children from the root. When we invoke $++$ from this position, the second rule applies, because the right subtree is empty. As we move up the tree, we are always at a right child of the parent until we encounter the root node, whose parent is NULL. When this occurs, we conclude that we are currently at the last node and that the next iteration must stop with value end(). Another special case occurs when the iterator is, in fact, the value end(). This situation occurs when nodePtr $==$ NULL. In this case, the next node in order is the smallest value in the tree. To locate this smallest node, obtain the root pointer of the tree by using the data member, root, and move far left.

iterator& operator++():
```
    // preincrement. move forward to next larger value
    iterator& operator++ ()
    {
        stnode<T> *p;

        if (nodePtr == NULL)
        {
            // ++ from end(). get the root of the tree
            nodePtr = tree->root;
```

```
         // error! ++ requested for an empty tree
         if (nodePtr == NULL)
            throw underflowError
               ("stree iterator operator++ (): tree empty");

         // move to the smallest value in the tree,
         // which is the first node inorder
         while (nodePtr->left != NULL)
            nodePtr = nodePtr->left;
      }
      else
      if (nodePtr->right != NULL)
      {
         // successor is the furthest left node of
         // right subtree
         nodePtr = nodePtr->right;

         while (nodePtr->left != NULL)
            nodePtr = nodePtr->left;
      }
      else
      {
         // have already processed the left subtree, and
         // there is no right subtree. move up the tree,
         // looking for a parent for which nodePtr is a left child,
         // stopping if the parent becomes NULL. a non-NULL parent
         // is the successor. if parent is NULL, the original node
         // was the last node inorder, and its successor
         // is the end of the list
         p = nodePtr->parent;

         while (p != NULL && nodePtr == p->right)
         {
            nodePtr = p;
            p = p->parent;
         }

         // if we were previously at the right-most node in
         // the tree, nodePtr = NULL, and the iterator specifies
         // the end of the list
         nodePtr = p;
      }

      return *this;
}
```

We also implement the iterator operator $--$ by using an iterative algorithm.
The inorder predecessor is the node in the inorder scan that we visit just before the
current node. For instance, in Figure 10-23, the predecessor of node 25 is node 23,

and the predecessor of node 15 is node 12. Again, there are two rules upon which we base the algorithm:

- If the left subtree is not empty, determine the inorder predecessor of the node by moving to the left child and then moving right until the node has a NULL pointer. For instance, in the tree in Figure 10-23, from the node with value 25, we must move to node 12 and then far right to node 23. The predecessor is the last node visited on the left subtree of the current node.
- If the left subtree is empty, obtain the inorder predecessor of the node by following a chain of parent pointers until we find a parent P for which our current node, nodePtr, is a right child. Node P is the inorder predecessor. When this situation occurs, we got to the current node by moving right from P and then going far left. For example, in Figure 10-23, if we are at the node with value 14, we move up the tree until we find that node 20 is the right child of node 12. The node with value 12 is the predecessor of node 15.

The implementation of the prefix operator $--$ follows these two rules. As is the case with $++$, there are two special situations to consider. When the position of the iterator is the first node in order, the operator must return end(). The first node in order is the last node on the path of left children from root. In Figure 10-23, the node has the value 3. Another special case occurs when the iterator is, in fact, the value end(). This situation occurs when nodePtr $==$ NULL. In this case, the inorder successor is the largest value in the tree. You will note in "d_stiter.h" that the implementation of $--$ uses a parallel structure to that developed for the increment operator $++$.

CHAPTER SUMMARY

- A tree is a hierarchical structure that places elements in nodes along branches that originate from a root. Nodes in a tree are subdivided into levels; the topmost level holds only the root node. Any node in a tree can have multiple successors at the next level. Hence, a tree is a nonlinear structure. Most applications involve a restricted category of trees, called *binary trees*, in which each node has at most two successors. Trees have associated terminology with which you should be familiar. The terms include *parent*, *child*, *descendant*, *leaf node*, *interior node*, and *subtree*. We can mathematically measure a tree by computing its depth, which is the maximum level of any node in the tree. The root is at level 0.
- A binary tree is most effective as a storage structure if it has high density—that is, if data are located on relatively short paths from the root. A complete binary tree has the highest possible density, and an n-node complete binary tree has depth int($\log_2 n$). At the other extreme, a degenerate binary tree is equivalent to a linked list and exhibits $O(n)$ access times.
- A programmer implements a binary tree by using a class whose data include the value at the node and pointers to the left and right children of the node (left and right subtrees). This book implements the tnode class and supplies the function

buildTree() in "d_tnodel.h" to create one of three binary trees to use in algorithm development. The function builds the sample trees from the bottom up.

- A tree is a nonlinear structure, so a fundamental problem involves moving through trees in an organized fashion. There are six simple recursive algorithms for tree traversal. The most commonly used algorithms are inorder (LNR), postorder (LRN), and preorder (NLR). Many tree algorithms base their function on one of these traversal techniques. Another technique for tree traversal is to move left to right from level to level. This algorithm is iterative, and its implementation involves using a queue. The library "d_tnodel.h" contains algorithms that output the nodes of a tree via inorder, postorder, and level-order traversals.

- Section 10-4 uses tree-traversal algorithms to solve various problems for binary trees, such as counting the number of leaf nodes in a tree, computing the depth of a tree, copying a tree, and deleting all the nodes in a tree. The section introduces a function that provides a picture of a binary tree, using console output. The algorithm is relatively complex and is explained on the WWW site for the book.

- A binary search tree stores data by value instead of position and is an example of an associative container. The simple rules "== return," "< go left," and "> go right" until finding a NULL subtree make it easy to build a binary search tree that does not allow duplicate values. The insertion algorithm also defines the path to a data value in the tree. The removal of an item from a binary search tree is more difficult and involves finding a replacement node among the remaining values. Section 10-5 develops an ADT and associated API for the binary search tree container *stree*. Its use introduces the concept of a pair that allows the return of multiple values from a function.

- Section 10-6 provides two applications for binary search trees. Because the stree class does not allow duplicate values, we can use a search tree as a filter to remove duplicates from a vector. A more substantial application simulates the maintenance of inventory for a video store, using a database (tree) of available films and one of rented films. The application clearly demonstrates the majority of the features of the class.

- Section 10-7 discusses the implementation of selected member functions of the stree class. The class uses the algorithms for copying and deleting a tree presented in Section 10-4 for the implementation of the destructor, copy constructor, and overloaded assignment operator. The algorithm for insert() is relatively simple and follows directly from the rules for insertion into a binary search tree. The erase algorithm is somewhat difficult and involves a number of cases. In essence, it involves finding a replacement node, unlinking it from its position in the tree, and linking it in place of the deleted node.

- The optional Section 10-8 discusses the implementation of tree iterators. The implementation proceeds by developing an iterative process for moving forward to the inorder successor of a node or backward to the inorder predecessor. The implementation must pay special attention to the end of a traversal. In particular, if *iter* points to the largest node in the tree, iter++ must equal end(); if *iter* points to the smallest node of the tree, *iter*−− must equal end().

CLASSES AND LIBRARIES IN THE CHAPTER

Name	Header File
function writeVector()	d_util.h
pair	<utility>
Selected tree algorithms	d_tnodel.h
stree iterator nested classes	d_stiter.h
stree	d_stree.h
tnode	d_tnode.h
vector	<vector>
video	d_video.h

REVIEW EXERCISES

1. For each part of this question; use the following tree:

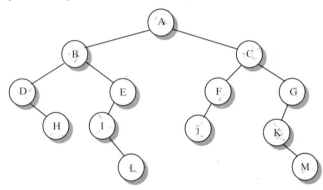

(a) What is the parent of node L?
(b) What is the depth of this tree?
(c) List the nodes in subtree B.
(d) List all of the leaf nodes.
(e) Give the order in which nodes are visited in an LRN (postorder) scan of the tree.
(f) Give the order in which nodes are visited in an RNL (in–right) scan of the tree.
(g) Assume the level-order scan algorithm uses a stack to hold the nodes instead of a queue. What is the resulting order of visit for the nodes?
(h) List all of the nodes at level 2 in the tree.

2. Draw a binary tree that contains seven nodes and has depth 3.
3. (a) A binary tree with all possible nodes has a depth of 8. How many nodes does it have?
   (b) A complete binary tree has 5125 nodes. What is its depth?
4. (a) What is the minimum number of leaf nodes in a binary tree with 63 nodes?
   (b) What is the maximum number of leaf nodes in a binary tree with 63 nodes?
5. (a) Display the tree created by the following statements:

```
tnode<char> *root, *a, *b, *c, *d, *e;

d = new tnode<char> ('D');
```

```
e = new tnode<char> ('E');
c = new tnode<char> ('C');
a = new tnode<char> ('A' , d, e);
b = new tnode<char> ('B', NULL, c);
root = new tnode<char> ('R', a, b);
```

(b) For the tree in part (a), list the order in which nodes are visited in an NLR (pre-order) scan.

6. Implement the function countNodes(), which returns the number of nodes in a binary tree as a reference argument:

```
template <typename T>
void countNodes(tnode<T> *t, int& count);
```

7. Trace the following tree-traversal function, and describe its action when it is applied to the binary tree Tree 2:

```
template <typename T>
int f(tnode<T> *t)
{ int n = 0, left, right;

  if (t != NULL)
  { if (t->left != NULL)
        n++;
    if (t->right != NULL)
        n++;
    left = f(t->left);
    right = f(t->right);
    return n + left + right;
  }
  else
      return 0;
}
```

8. Use the following tree, in its original form, for each part of this question:

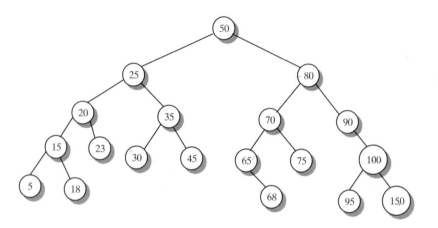

(a) If the value 33 is inserted into the tree, which node is its parent?

(b) If the value 64 is inserted into the tree, which node is its parent?

(c) When we delete node 30, the erase algorithm selects which node as the replacement node?

(d) When we delete node 90, the erase algorithm selects which node as the replacement node?

(e) If we delete the root node, 50, the erase algorithm selects which node as the replacement node?

(f) What sequence results from an RNL scan of the tree?

9. Which of the following lists represent a possible inorder scan of a binary search tree?

(a) 73 8 2 9 4 11   **(b)** 2 3 4 7 8 9 11

(c) 11 2 9 3 8 4 7   **(d)** All of the above

10. (a) Display the binary search tree formed by entering the following characters in the specified order:

P T, V, Z, S, F, C

(b) Using the tree from part (a), give the NLR scan of the nodes.

(c) Using the tree from part (a), give the LNR scan of the nodes.

(d) Using the tree from part (a), give the RNL scan of the nodes.

(e) Delete the node P, and draw the resulting tree.

11. Assume that we obtain the following integer sequence by traversing a binary search tree in preorder sequences:

20   15   10   17   16   18   25   22   21   24   35

Construct a tree that has such an ordering.

12. Assume that f() is a member function of the stree class. What is the action of the following function?

```
template <typename T>
T& stree<T>::f()
{
    stnode<T> *t = root;

    while (t->right != NULL)
        t = t->right;
    return t->nodeValue;
}
```

13. Use the function f() to insert values into a binary search tree:

```
template <typename T>
void f(stree<T>& t, const T& item)
{
    pair<stree<T>::iterator, bool> p;
    p = t.insert(item);
    if (p.second == false)
        t.erase(p.first);
}
```

(a) Display the tree that results from calling f() to load the values from array intArr:

```
int intArr[] = {5, 4, 7, 4, 8, 9, 1, 4, 8};
```

(b) Display the tree that results from calling f() to load the values from array *charArr*:

```
char charArr[] = {'t', 'j', 'v', 'a', 't', 'm', 'k', 'a'};
```

Answers to Review Exercises

1. (a) I **(b)** 4 **(c)** B D E H I L **(d)** H L J M
(e) H D L I E B J F M K G C A **(f)** G M K C F J A E L I B H D
(g) A C G K M F J B E I L D H **(h)** D E F G

2.

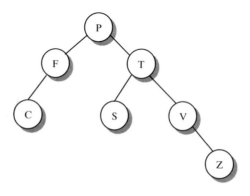

3. (a) $2^{8+1} - 1 = 2^9 - 1 = 511$ nodes
(b) depth $= \text{int}(\log_2 5125) = \text{int}(12.323...) = 12$
4. (a) 1 (degenerate tree)
(b) A tree of depth 5 with all possible nodes has $2^{5+1} - 1 = 2^6 - 1 = 63$ nodes. The last level has $2^5 = 32$ nodes.
5. (a)

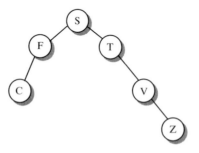

(b) R A D E B C
6. template <typename T>
```
void countNodes(tnode<T> *t, int& count)
{
    // use an inorder (LNR) traversal
    if (t != NULL)
```

```
    {
        // count nodes on left subtree
            countNodes(t->left, count);
            // count current node
            count++;
            // count nodes on right subtree
            countNodes(t->right, count);
        }
    }
```

7. Function f() returns the number of edges in a binary tree. For Tree 2, the function returns 8.

8. **(a)** 30   **(b)** 65   **(c)** NULL   **(d)** 100   **(e)** 65

   (f) 150 100 95 90 80 75 70 68 65 50 45 35 30 25 23 20 18 15 5

9. **(b)**

10. **(a)**

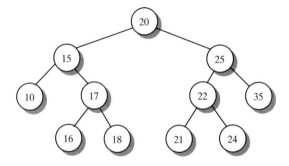

(b) P F C T S V Z
(c) C F P S T V Z
(d) Z V T S P F C
(e)

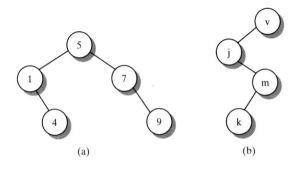

(a)   (b)

11.

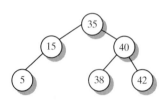

12. The function returns the largest node value in the search tree. The node is the farthest node to the right of the root.

13.

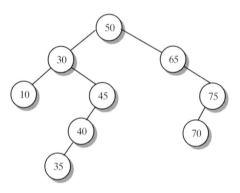

WRITTEN EXERCISES

14. Explain why a tree is a nonlinear data structure.

15. What is the minimum depth of a binary tree that contains
   (a) 15 nodes?　**(b)** 5 nodes?　**(c)** 91 nodes?

16. (a) Draw a binary tree that contains 10 nodes and has depth 5.
   (b) Draw a binary tree that contains 14 nodes and has depth 5.

17. A binary tree contains the data values 1 3 7 2 12.
   (a) Draw two trees of maximal depth containing the data.
   (b) Draw two complete binary trees in which the parent value is greater than either child value.

18. Draw all possible binary trees that contain three nodes.

19. Is it true that a binary tree with n nodes must have exactly $n - 1$ edges (non-NULL pointers)? Explain your answer.

20. (a) Draw the binary tree that the following allocations create.

```
tnode<int> *root, *a, *b, *c, *d, *e;

e = new tnode<int> (50);
d = new tnode<int> (20, NULL, e);
c = new tnode<int> (30);
b = new tnode<int> (45, c, NULL);
a = new tnode<int> (15, b, d);
root = new tnode<int> (10, NULL, a);
```

(b) List the nodes in the order of their visit for an NLR (preorder) scan.

(c) List the nodes in the order of their visit for an RLN (postorder) scan.

(d) List the nodes in the order of their visit for an LNR (inorder) scan.

21. Implement the function countNodes(), which returns the number of nodes in the subtree with root *t*:

```
template <typename T>
int countNodes(tnode<T> *t);
```

22. Trace the following tree-traversal function, f(), and describe its action:

```
template <typename T>
int f(tnode<T> *t)
{   int n = 0, leftValue, rightValue;

    if (t != NULL)
    {
        if (t->left != NULL || t->right != NULL)
            n++;
        leftValue = f(t->left);
        rightValue = f(t->right);
        return n + leftValue + rightValue;
    }
    else
        return 0;
}
```

23. Trace the following tree-traversal function, f(), and describe its action:

```
int f(tnode<int> *t)
{
    int sLeft, sRight;

    if (t != NULL)
    {
        sLeft = f(t->left);
        sRight = f(t->right);
        return   t->nodeValue + sLeft + sRight;
    }
    else
        return 0;
}
```

24. Using buildTree() as a model, implement a function buildIntTree() that builds the following binary tree:

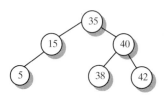

25. Implement the function

```
template <typename T>
void rlnOutput(tnode<T> *t, const string& separator = "   ");
```

that outputs a tree, using an RLN scan.

26. Use the following tree, in its original form, for each part of this question:

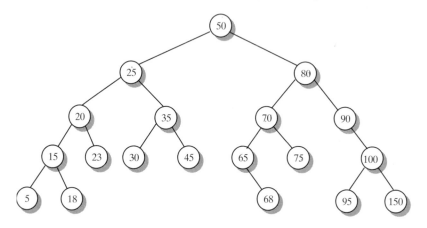

(a) If the value 33 is inserted into the tree, which node is its parent? 30
(b) If the value 72 is inserted into the tree, which node is its parent? 75
(c) If the root node 50 is deleted, the erase algorithm selects which node as the replacement node? 65
(d) If the node 30 is deleted, the erase algorithm selects which node as the replacement node?
(e) Traverse the tree, and list the nodes, via a preorder scan.
(f) Traverse the tree, and list the nodes, via an inorder scan.
(g) Traverse the tree, and list the nodes, via a postorder scan.
(h) Traverse the tree, and list the nodes, via a level-order scan.

27. For each sequence of characters, draw the binary search tree, and traverse the tree by using inorder, preorder, and postorder scans.
(a) M, T, V, F, U, N
(b) F, L, O, R, I, D, A
(c) R, O, T, A, R, Y, C, L, U, B

28. **(a)** Assume that we obtain the following integer sequence by traversing a binary search tree in preorder:

    50   45   35   15   40   46   65   75   70

    Construct a tree that has such an ordering.

    (b) Construct a binary search tree that would produce the following inorder traversal of its elements:

    40   45   46   50   65   70   75

29. Implement the stree member function

    ```
    template <typename T>
    T& stree<T>::min();
    ```

    which returns the minimum value in a binary search tree. Do this iteratively, and throw an underflowError exception if the tree is empty.

30. Use the integers from one to nine to build a nine-node binary search tree with no duplicate data values.

    (a) Give the possible root node values if the depth of the tree is 4.

    (b) Answer part (a) for depths of 5, 6, 7, and 8.

31. Assume the following iterative function is a member of the stree class and determines the depth of item in the tree.

    ```
    template <typename T>
    int stree<T>::nodeLevel(const T& item);
    ```

    Implement the Function. Return −1 if item is not in the tree, and throw the underflowError exception if the tree is empty.

32. To erase a node with two children, we have chosen the replacement node as the node with the smallest value on the right subtree. Propose an alternative node, and describe the algorithm for locating it.

33. **(a)** Why don't we implement tree iterators by using a recursive algorithm?

    (b) Explain why each node in our implementation of a binary search tree has a parent pointer.

34. Assume that the function stlevel() is a member of the stree class and that it takes a pointer to a search tree node and returns the level of the node in the search tree. Implement the function. Hint: Follow the parent pointer to the root.

    ```
    template <typename T>
    int stree<T>::stlevel(stnode<T> *t);
    ```

PROGRAMMING EXERCISES

35. Write a function

    ```
    template <typename T>
    int countOneChild(tnode<T> *t);
    ```

    that counts the number of interior nodes in a binary tree having one child. Test the function in a program that uses buildTree() from "d_tnodel.h" to allocate Tree 1 and Tree 2. Call countOneChild() for each tree, and output the results.

36. Use the function rlnOutput() in Written Exercise 10-25 and buildTree() to output Tree 1 in RLN order.

37. Implement the function max(), which returns the maximum value in the tree. Hint: Use a design similar to the depth() algorithm of Section 10-4.

```
// return a pointer to a node having the maximum value
// for the nodes in the tree
template <typename T>
tnode<T> *max(tnode<T> *t)
```

Write a program that calls max() to display the maximum value in the integer tree created by the function buildIntTree() from Written Exercise 10-24.

38. In a program, declare the stree object charTree with initial values from array arr. Display the tree by using the member function displayTree().

```
char arr[] = { 'S', 'J', 'K', 'L', 'X', 'F', 'E', 'Z' };
```

39. A program prompts the user to enter an integer *n* specifying the number of elements that will be added to a vector *v*. Use the random-number generator to create *n* integer values in the range from 0 to 99, adding each value to the vector. Output the elements by using writeVector(). Copy the elements from the vector into the binary search tree *vtree*, and output the ordered list by using writeSTree() from "d_util.h".

40. Write a program that declares the stree object intTree with initial values from array *intArr*:

```
int intArr[] = {14, 79, 18, 2, 91, 35, 28};
```

Using an iterator, output the smallest and the largest element in the tree.

41. (a) Implement a function count() that counts the number of stree values in the iterator range *first, last*):

```
template <typename T>
int count(stree<T>::iterator first,
          stree<T>::iterator last);
```

(b) In a program, create the binary search tree *t* with values determined by the array *intArr*:

```
int intArr[] = {22, 19, 87, 42, 9, 17, 1, 56, 48, 75};
```

Include an output statement that uses size() to determine the number of elements in the tree. With a second output statement, use count() to identify the number of elements in the tree. Use find() to locate the positions of nodes 9 and 42 in the tree. Using count(), determine the number of elements in the range [9, 42). Note: Call count() using the syntax

```
count<int> (...)
```

42. Implement the class integer in the header file "int.h."

```
class integer
{
   public:
      // constructor. initialize intValue and set count = 1
      integer(int n);

      // return intValue
```

```
      int getInt();
      // return count
      int getCount();

      // increment count
      void incCount();

      // compare integer objects by intValue
      friend bool operator< (const integer& lhs, const integer& rhs);
      friend bool operator== (const integer& lhs, const integer& rhs);

      / output object in format intValue (count)
      friend ostream& operator<< (ostream& ostr, const integer& obj);
   private:
      // the integer and its count
      int intValue;
      int count;
};
```

Declare a binary search tree *integerTree*. Write a main program that generates 10,000 random integers in the range from zero to six. For each value, construct an integer object, and search the tree. If the value is in the tree, increment its count; otherwise, insert the value, with a count of 1. Using a tree iterator, traverse the tree, and output its nodes in order. Picture the tree by calling displayTree().

PROGRAMMING PROJECTS

43. An arithmetic expression involving the binary operators addition ($+$), subtraction ($-$), multiplication (*), and division (/) can be represented by using a binary expression tree. In a binary expression tree, each operator has two children, which are either operands or subexpressions. Leaf nodes contain an operand; nonleaf nodes contain a binary operator. The left and right subtrees of an operator describe a subexpression that is evaluated and used as one of the operands for the operator. For instance, the expression a + b*c/d − e corresponds to the following binary expression tree:

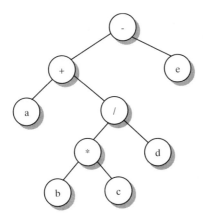

In a prefix expression, the operator appears before its operands. The following lists sample infix expressions and their prefix equivalents:

Infix expression	Prefix expression
a * b	* a b
a + b*c	+a*b c
(a + b)/c	/+a b c
a/(b*c/d + e/f*g)	/a + /*b c d*/e f g

(a) Perform preorder and postorder traversals of the binary expression tree. What relationship exists among these scans and the prefix (operator operand operand) and postfix (RPN) notation for the expression?

(b) For each arithmetic expression, build the corresponding expression tree. By scanning the tree, give the prefix and postfix form of the expression.

(1) a + b − c*d + e   **(2)** /a − b * cd
(3) a b c d/ − *   **(4)** * − / + a b c d eΔ

(c) Section 7-5 discusses the implementation of the class infix2Postfix, which converts an infix expression to postfix. The operands are integer values in the range from zero through nine. The class is in the header file "d_inftop.h". Modify the class so it deals with operands that are single-letter identifiers in the range from a through z, and place the modified class in the header file "inf2pstf.h".

(d) Implement an algorithm that takes a string containing a postfix expression and builds the expression tree. Hint: Model the algorithm after the postfix expression evaluation algorithm in Section 7-4. Instead of pushing values onto an integer stack, push the address of subtree roots onto a stack whose elements are of type tnode<char> *.

```
/// build an expression tree from a postfix expression.
// the operands are single letter identifiers in the range from
// 'a' .. 'z' and the operands are selected from the characters
// '+', '-', '*' and '/'
tnode<char> *buildExpTree (const string& pexp);
```

(e) Implement a scan of an expression tree that outputs the prefix form of the expression.

```
// output the prefix form of the expression represented
// by the tree
void prefixOutput(tnode<char> *exp);
```

(f) Write a program that inputs an infix expression and creates an expression tree Output the prefix form of the expression. Output the postfix form of the expression by traversing the tree using postorderOutput(), and display the tree by using displayTree(). These functions are located in "d_tnodel.h." Test the program with the expressions (a + b)/c and a + b*c/d + e/f *g.

44. We discuss the construction of sets and maps, using a binary search tree, in Chapter 11. A multiset is an extension of a set that allows duplicate values. Similarly, a multimap extends a map to allow duplicates. The implementation of multisets and multimaps requires that the underlying binary search tree allow duplicate values. This exercise extends the stree class to allow duplicate values.

Begin by copying the stree class to a new header file, "mstree.h," and rename the class as *mstree*. Remove the private-member function findNode() from the class. Copy "d_stiter.h" to "mtiter.h," and change stree references to mstree. Perform modifications to mstree in Steps 1–8.

Step 1.   Change the insert() member function so that it has the following prototype and operation:

```
iterator insert(const T& item);
   // insert item into the tree and return an iterator
   // positioned at the new element
   // Postcondition: the tree size increases by 1
```

To insert duplicate values, just move right if *item* >= *t−>nodeValue*.
In this way, we insert a duplicate value on the right subtree of an earlier occurrence of *item*.

Step 2.   Implement the following public-member functions:

```
iterator lower_bound(const T& item);
const_iterator lower_bound(const T& item) const;
```

These functions return an iterator pointing to the first element in order whose
value is >= *item*. If all elements in the tree are less than *item*, the functions return end(). As a consequence, if *item* is in the tree, the functions return an iterator pointing at the first occurrence, in order, of *item*.

Use the following implementation outline:

```
template <typename T>
mstree<T>::iterator mstree<T>::lower_bound(const T& item)

{
    stnode<T> *parent = NULL;
    stnode<T> *curr = root;

    // cycle until we find an empty subtree
    while (curr != NULL)
       if (!(curr->nodeValue < item))
       {
          < item <= curr->nodeValue. record curr
            as a possible lower bound and move
            to the left to look for an even
            smaller one >
       }
       else
          < keep the current parent and move right >
    return iterator(_____);
}
```

Step 3.   Implement the following public-member functions:

```
iterator upper_bound(const T& item);
const_iterator upper_bound(const T& item) const;
```

These functions return an iterator pointing to the first element in order whose
value is > item. If all elements in the tree are less than or equal to item, the functions return end(). As a consequence, if item is in the tree, the functions return
an iterator pointing just after the last occurrence, in order, of item.

```
template <typename T>
```

```
mstree<T >::iterator mstree<T>::upper_bound(const T& item)
{
    stnode<T> *parent = NULL;
    stnode<T> *curr = root;

    // cycle until we find an empty subtree
    while (curr != NULL)
       if (item < curr->nodeValue)
       {
          < record curr as a possible upper bound and
          move to the left to look for an even
          smaller one >
       }
       else
          < keep the current parent and move right >
    return iterator(_____);
}
```

Step 4.   Implement the following public-member functions:

```
pair<iterator, iterator>
equal_range(const T& item);
pair<const_iterator, const_iterator>
equal_range(const T& item) const;
```

These functions return a pair of iterators whose first element is equal to lower_bound() and whose second element is equal to upper_bound().

Step 5.   Change the find() member function so that it has the following prototype and operation:

```
iterator find(const T& item);
  // search for the first occurrence of item in the tree.
  // if found, return an iterator pointing at it in the tree;
  // otherwise, return end()
const_iterator find(const T& item) const;
  // constant version
```

Use lower_bound() to search for *item*, and decide whether the iterator it returns points at *item*.

Step 6.   Implement the following private-member functions:

```
int distance(iterator first, iterator last);
int distance(const_iterator first, const_iterator last) const;
```

These functions count the number of items in the range [*first, last*).

Step 7.   Implement the following public-member function:

```
int count(const T& item) const;
```

This function counts the number of occurrences of item in the tree. Use lower_bound() and upper_bound() to find an iterator range [first, last) that surrounds item, and call distance().

Step 8.   Implement the following public-member function:

```
int erase(const T& item);
   // erase all elements from the tree that match item and
   // return the number of elements that were erased
   // Postcondition: the tree size decreases by the number
   // of elements erased
```

Use equal_range() to find an iterator range [first, last) that surrounds item. Determine the number of items in the range using distance(), and call the version
of erase() that takes an iterator range to erase all occurrences of item.

Write a program that creates a tree containing the values from the integer array *arr*:

```
int arr[] = {5, 3, 4, 1, 5, 2, 3, 7, 2, 6, 2, 3, 10, 8, 1
             2, 15,9, 8, 2, 5, 3, 8, 1, 7, 0, 4, 9, 5};
int arrSize = sizeof(arr)/sizeof(int);
```

Perform the following actions with the tree:

1. Output the size of the tree.
2. Insert the value 8 into the tree.
3. Prompt for a value, and use find() to determine whether it exists in the tree.
4. Prompt for a value, and output the number of occurrences of the value in the tree.
   Using equal_range(), output each occurrence of the value.
5. Erase all occurrences of the value 2 from the tree.
6. Output the tree using displayTree().

◆

CHAPTER 11

Associative Containers

OBJECTIVES

- To understand that associative containers store elements by key and provide fast lookup operations.
- To understand that a set stores data of a single type, called a _key_.
- To understand that a map stores key–value pairs, where the key and the value may be of different types, so that you can look up a value by referencing its key.
- To understand that one technique of implementing a set or a map is to store the data in an underlying binary search tree and that balancing the tree guarantees $O(\log_2 n)$ search running time.
- To study the API for the STL set class and to apply a set in the construction of a simple spelling checker.
- To study the Sieve of Eratosthenes, which uses a set to find prime numbers.
- To study the implementation of set union, intersection, and difference for ordered sets.
- To study the API for the STL map class and to understand that its real power lies in effective use of the index operator.
- To see the development of a concordance by using the map container.
- To study an overview of the STL multiset class, where a key may occur two or more times in the set.
- To study the implementation of sets and maps by using a binary search tree to implement the miniSet and miniMap classes.

OUTLINE

In Chapter 10, we introduced the binary search tree and designed a programmer interface for the stree class operations. The interface included the find() function,
which accesses an element in the container; an insert() function, which adds a new
element or identifies a duplicate; and a series of erase() functions that use value and
iterator arguments. The discussion provided you with a first example of an associative container that stores elements by key. In this chapter, we introduce the set and
map classes, which are the associative containers for the Standard Template Library.
You will discover that the classes have an interface that is essentially the same as
that of the stree class. There is a good reason for this. STL does not provide a binary
search-tree as an application structure. It does, however, use a search-tree class as
the underlying implementation structure for its set and map classes. In this chapter,
we follow our customary pattern and develop a miniSet and a miniMap class. The
implementation of these associative containers follows the STL model by using the
stree class as the underlying storage structure. In Chapter 10, we designed the stree
class interface with an eye to the fact that we would use it to implement the miniSet
and miniMap classes.

OVERVIEW OF ASSOCIATIVE CONTAINERS   11-1

An associative container stores elements based on a key, which consists of one or
more attributes to uniquely identify each element. We will assume that a key consists of a single attribute. For instance, the Department of Motor Vehicles (DMV)
uses a license-plate number to identify a vehicle. The registrar of a school identifies
a student by a social security number. Each element enters the container with an associated key, and a program later uses the same key to retrieve the element.

Viewed as an ADT, an associative container is similar to the vector and list sequence containers we saw in earlier chapters. It is another storage structure with
operations to access and modify elements. The main difference is that associative-
container operations use the key rather than an index or a linear search algorithm
to retrieve an element. A programmer can use the key without concern for how elements are physically stored and how operations make the association between the
key and an element.

Associative-Container Categories

STL provides two types of associative containers, called *sets* and *maps*. The
structures of the elements distinguish between the containers. In a set, the data
value is the key, whereas a map stores an element as a key–value pair, where the key

and the value are treated as separate components. Let us explore this distinction further; it is critical to your understanding the difference between a set and a map.

A *set* is a template-based container with a single template type *T*. The type may be of int, double, string, or other simple type. The resulting container is a set of integers, a set of strings, or so forth (Figure 11-1).

```
set<int> intSet;
set<string> keyword;
set<time24> timeSet;    // set of time24 elements
```

An application might want to use a set to store a more complex data entry described by a record. Such an entry consists of two or more fields, including the key field. The key field uniquely identifies the entry. The other fields supply additional information. The task requires a bit more effort on the part of the programmer. A class describes the record by defining the fields as private data members.

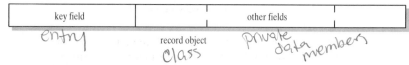

To support the set operations, the class overloads the operators == and < by comparing the key fields in the operands. For instance, the Department of Motor Vehicles declares the vehicle class with the license-plate number as a key of type *string*. Other fields might include the vehicle identification number, make of the vehicle, and so forth.

```
class vehicle
{
    public:
        . . .
        friend bool operator==(const vehicle& lhs, const vehicle& rhs);
        friend bool operator<(const vehicle& lhs, const vehicle& rhs);
    private:
        string license;
        . . .
};
```

18	45
12	67
54	89

intSet: Set of ints

"if"	"while"
"operator"	
"class"	"template"

keyword: Set of strings

| 9:15 | 4:45 |
| 17:00 | 23:59 |

timeSet: Set of time24 objects

Figure 11-1
Sets with integer, string, and time24 elements

The declaration of a set container for the DMV uses the class vehicle as the template type:

```
set<vehicle> vSet;
```

A lookup operation for vSet takes a vehicle object as an argument and uses the overloaded comparison operators to access the element by its key field. The operation returns the object from the set that matches the key in the argument. The program can then access or update the nonkey fields of the vehicle record.

Key–Value Data A map stores data as a *key–value pair*. In a pair, the first component is the key, and the second is the value. Each component may be of a different data type.

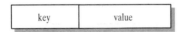

A map container has two template arguments, with the data types for the key and the value specifying the two template types. For instance, university administration might define a map with string–integer pairs to denote the number of majors in each of its degree programs. The name of the degree program is the key, and the number of majors is the value (Figure 11-2).

```
// declare the map degreeMajor with template types string and int.
map<string, int> degreeMajor;
```

A lookup operation with a map takes the key as an argument and returns an iterator pointing to a pair whose key component matches the argument. The program can then access or update the value component of the pair. For instance, the operation degreeMap.find("English") returns an iterator pointing to the pair ("English," 117).

The property of using the key to access the value component is analogous to an array that uses an integer index to access the value of an element. The map con-

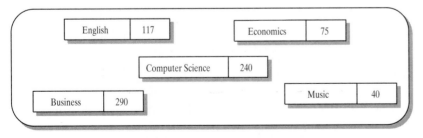

degreeMajor: Map of string-int pairs

Figure 11-2
Map of string–int Pairs with the degree major as the key and the number of majors as the value

tainer takes advantage of this feature by overloading the index operator, [] (The operator takes the key as an argument and returns a reference to the value) component in the pair. Like an array index, the operator can be used on both sides of an assignment statement.

```
degreeMajor["Mathematics"] = 54;           // insert pair in the map
cout << degreeMajor["Computer Science"];   // access value for the key
```

The first statement inserts the pair ("Mathematics," 54) into the map; the second statement searches for the pair corresponding to the key "Computer Science" and outputs the integer 240, which is the value component of the pair. The presence of an index operator leads us to refer to a map as an *associative array*. Note that the analogy with a standard array has two major differences. The index for a map is not limited to integer values, but can be of any type. Also, the map index corresponds to the key, which is a component of the pair. With a standard array, the index is an external value used to compute the location of the element in the sequence.

STL Associative Containers

The Standard Template Library defines both set and map containers. These containers do not allow duplicate keys, which is appropriate for most applications. For some problems, however, we might want to store data with duplicate keys. For these situations, STL provides the multiset and multimap containers. We discuss multisets in detail in Section 11-4. Most of the operations for sets and maps carry over to multisets and multimaps. Notable exceptions are the functions count() and equalRange(). These operations are specific to multisets and multimaps; they return the number of elements and the iterator range of elements with duplicate keys, respectively. Table 11-1 illustrates the four types of STL associative containers. The rows distinguish whether the container stores only the key or the key–value pair.

Implementing Associative Containers

In this chapter, our primary emphasis is on the development of sets and maps as application storage structures. To this end, we develop an API for each container and use them in a series of applications. We discuss the implementation of the containers in this chapter and use the simpler stree class from Chapter 10 to implement our miniSet and miniMap classes. In fact, programmers can use different design strategies to implement the set and map classes. STL uses a red–black search tree for this purpose. A red–black tree is a binary search tree that maintains balance between the left and right subtrees of a node. Let us briefly look a special case that illustrates the value of using a red–black tree rather than a simple stree object. Assume the stree object is degenerate of depth 4 and contains the integer values 1 to 5. By balancing

TABLE 11-1   ASSOCIATIVE CONTAINERS

	Unique Keys	Duplicate Keys
Key data only	set	multiset
Key–value pair	map	multimap

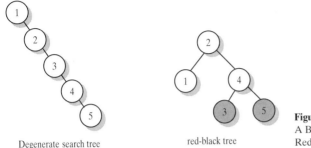

Figure 11-3
A Binary Search Tree and a
Red–Black Tree

Degenerate search tree   red-black tree

the subtrees, the corresponding red–black tree has depth 2 (Figure11-3). Searching a degenerate binary search tree has O(*n*) running time. The corresponding running time for the red–black tree is always O(log₂ *n*), or logarithmic. While maintaining balance in a red–black tree requires some overhead, there is no worst case, and hence the insert and find operations are logarithmic. Since the underlying storage structure is a search tree, sets and maps have iterators that scan the elements in ascending order of their keys. With this implementation, the STL classes implement *ordered associative containers*. We discuss red–black trees in Chapter 12.

In Chapter 12, we also develop hash tables, which store elements in clusters that depend on a hash function. Hash tables provide a different method of implementing associative structures, whose iterators do not access elements in order. Hash tables have O(*n*) worst-case running time for a search, but the average running time is O(1), or constant time.

SETS   11-2

A *set* is an associative container which stores keys that are objects of a specified data type. Duplicate keys are not allowed. The container uses the model of a mathematical set and serves applications for which the program simply wants to know whether an element is in the set. The set class has a constructor that creates an empty set, along with a constructor that that takes the address range for an array and creates the set with initial values from the array. A set is a dynamic structure, so its class has a destructor, copy constructor, and overloaded assignment operator that provide memory management operations. Like other containers, a set has operations size() and empty() to identity the number of elements in the collection. The basic set operations include the update functions insert() and erase(), along with the access function find(), which identifies whether an object is in the set. A set is an associative container, so it does not contain operations like push_back() or pop_front(), which are appropriate only in a sequence container.

All of our container classes have both constant and nonconstant iterators. These abstract locators provide a common interface that allows a programmer to scan the elements in a container. The function begin() returns an iterator pointing at the first element, and the function end() returns an iterator pointing just past the end of the list. Don't think that because a set has an iterator, the container stores elements by position. It doesn't. A set stores elements by key. Nevertheless, the set iterators define an access ordering, which scans the collection of elements. By default, the STL set class iterators scan the elements in ascending order of their keys. Hence, begin() points at the smallest element in the set, and end() points just past the largest element in the set.

Example 11-1

Let us use an example to illustrate some of the basic set and set iterator operations. Assume that setA and setB are sets of integer elements. The declaration of setA creates an empty set; the declaration of setB uses the pointer range for values in array arr to initialize the set. The object iter is an iterator for an integer set.

```
int arr[] = {8, 4, 2, 9};
int arrSize = sizeof(arr)/sizeof(int);
set<int> setA, setB(arr, arr+arrSize);
set<int>::iterator iter;     // set iterator

cout << setB.size();          // output:  4

// iterator points at smallest element with value 2
iter = setB.begin();

iter++;                       // position iter at next element
cout << *iter;                // output: 4

iter = setB.end();            // set iter at end of list
iter--;
cout << *iter;                // output: 9   (largest element)

setA = setB;                  // use assignment operator
```

Displaying a Container Using Iterators

For the array, vector, and list containers, we defined separate output functions to display the elements in the sequence. Now that we have more experience, we can use iterators to create a general output function writeContainer() that applies to any container having an iterator. The prototype for the function is as follows:

```
template <typename Iterator>
void writeContainer(Iterator first, Iterator last,
                    const string& separator = "  ");
```

The template header uses the identifier "Iterator" to emphasize that the arguments are iterators. The implementation of the function uses an iterator to scan the range [*first*, *last*) and the dereference operator, *, to access the value of the element. Each output inserts the separator string after the element.

> *writeContainer():*

```
// display the elements of a container in the iterator
// range [first, last). output separator between items.
// default value of separator = "  "
template <typename Iterator>
void writeContainer(Iterator first, Iterator last,
                    const string& separator = "  ")
{
    // declare iterator of type Iterator and initialize it
    // to have value first
    Iterator iter = first;

    while (iter != last)
    {
        cout << *iter << separator;
        iter++;
    }
}
```

We can use writeContainer() in place of writeArray(), writeVector(), and writeList(), which are specialized output functions—for instance,

```
int arr[] = {8, 4, 2, 9};
int arrSize = sizeof(arr)/sizeof(int);
vector<int> v(arr, arr+arrSize);
list<int> alist(arr, arr+arrSize);
set<int> aset(arr, arr+arrSize);

writeContainer(arr,arr+arrSize);                   // Array: 8 4 2 9
writeContainer(v.begin(),v.end());                 // Vector: 8 4 2 9
writeContainer(alist.begin(),alist.end());         // List: 8 4 2 9
// set output is in ascending order
writeContainer(aset.begin(),aset.end());           // Set: 2  4  8  9
```

For your convenience, writeContainer() is in the library file "d_util.h."

Set Access and Update Functions

The count() function takes a key data argument *item* of type *T* and searches the set looking for a match. An integer return value of 1 indicates that the item is in the set, while a return value of 0 means that the item is not in the set.

```
if(setObj.count(item) == 1)
   // item is in setObj
   ...
```

Like count(), the find() function takes a key data argument *item* of type *T* and searches the set, looking for a match. The return value is an iterator that locates *item* in the set. If the argument is not in the set, find() returns the iterator location end(). You can use find() to determine whether the set contains the element *item*. The iterator return value can be used to modify the nonkey fields of the item in the set or to erase the item from the set.

```
setIter = setObj.find(item);
if (setIter != setObj.end())
{
    // item is in setObj
    <modify non-key fields of *setIter>
}
```

The insert() operation takes the element item of type *T* as an argument and returns an iterator–bool pair. Recall that the data member first identifies the iterator component and data member second identifies the Boolean component. If *item* is a duplicate, the Boolean component is *false*. If *item* is not in the set, the insert operation adds the element to the set and assigns the Boolean component the value *true*. In either case, the iterator in the pair points to *item* in the set. Declare the return type as a pair object with template arguments set<*T*>::iterator and *bool*. For instance, assume that setA is an integer set with elements {8, 9, 1, 12, 5}. The upcoming statements declare an iterator–bool pair and attempt to insert the values 7 and 9 into the set. In the case of 9, an if statement determines that the value is a duplicate.

```
pair<set<int>::iterator, bool> p;

setA.insert(7);      // add 7 to the set
p = setA.insert(9);
if (p.second == false)
    cout << *p.first << " is a duplicate value";

// Output: 9 is a duplicate value
```

☞

Note

Note that the dot operator (.) has a higher priority than the dereference operator, *. As a result, the expression *p.first* is equivalent to *(p.first)*.

The set class uses the erase() operation to remove an element. The function has either a key or a set iterator as the argument to identify the element. If the element is not in the set, the operation simply returns. A special form of the erase() function takes an iterator range [*first, last*) and removes all elements within the range. The primary application for this function is clearing the set.

Example 11-2

Let us look at a set that stores the letters in the string "associative." The insert() operation build the set. The other operations update the elements.

```
string str = "associative";
set<char> charSet;        // creates an empty set
set<char>::iterator iter;

for (int i = 0; i < str.length(); i++)
    charSet.insert(str[i];

// length of string is 11; size of set is 8
// ('a','s','i' are duplicates)
cout << str.length() << "  " << charSet.size();

if (charSet.count('t') == 1)
{
    cout << "Erase 't' from the set" << endl;
    charSet.erase('t');       // remove 't' from the set
}
iter = charSet.find('s');  // locate 's' in the set
charSet.erase(iter);       // remove 's' from the set

// clear the set
charSet.erase(charSet.begin(), charSet.end());
```

We summarize the set operations in an API. Note that the functions find(), begin(), and end() have two versions that return either a constant or nonconstant iterator. We use the constant version when the set object is constant.

CLASS set	Constructors	\<set\>

set();
   Create an empty set. This is the default constructor.

EX| set <int> intSet;

set(*T *first, T *last*);
   Initialize the set by using the address range [*first, last*).

CLASS set	Operations	\<set\>

bool **empty**() *const*;
   Is the set empty?

int **size**() *const*;
   Return the number of elements in the set.

int **count**(*const T& key*) *const*;
   Search for *key* in the set, and return a value of 1 if it is in the set and a value of
   0 otherwise.

iterator **find**(*const T& key*);
   Search for key in the set and return an iterator pointing at it, or end() if it
   is not found.

const_iterator **find** (*const T& key*) *const*;
   Constant version.

pair<*iterator, bool*> **insert**(*const T& key*);
   If *key* is not in the set, insert it and then return a pair whose first element is an
   iterator pointing to the new element and whose second element is *true*.
   Otherwise, return a pair whose first element is an iterator pointing to the
   existing element and whose second element is *false*.
      Postcondition: The set size increases by 1 if *key* is not in the set.

int **erase**(*const T& key*);
   If key is in the set, erase it and return a value of 1; otherwise, return a value of 0.
      Postcondition: The set size decreases by 1 if *key* is in the set.

void **erase**(*iterator pos*);
   Erase the item pointed to by *pos*.
      Preconditions: The set is not empty, and *pos* points to a valid set element.
      Postcondition: The set size decreases by 1.

void **erase**(*iterator first, iterator last*);
   Erase the elements in the range [*first, last*).
      Precondition: The set is not empty.
      Postcondition: The set size decreases by the number of elements in the range.

iterator **begin**();
   Return an iterator pointing at the first member in the set.

const_iterator **begin**() *const*;
   Constant version of begin().

iterator **end**();
   Return an iterator pointing just past the last member in the set.

const_iterator **end**() *const*;
   Constant version of end().

A Simple Spelling Checker

Anyone who has used a word processor is familiar with a spelling checker. The software compares a word with a dictionary of correctly spelled words, accounting for
plurals, upper- and lowercase letters, and so forth. Typically, a spelling checker dis-

plays a word that appears to be misspelled and then does sophisticated pattern matching to identify words in the dictionary that are likely alternative spellings.

A set is an efficient container for storing the dictionary. We illustrate this fact with a very simple spelling checker. We create the dictionary as a set of strings containing approximately 25,000 words in lowercase. The operator $>>$ inputs the contents of a document as strings separated by whitespace. For each input, a call to find() determines whether the word is in the dictionary. If not, we assume it is misspelled and display the word, along with a prompt that allows the user to add the word to the dictionary, ignore it because it is actually spelled correctly, or confirm that the word is misspelled. For instance, the display format for the word "contians" is

```
contians
   'a' (add)   'i' (ignore)   'm'  (misspelled)
```

By adding the word to the dictionary, the user specifies that the word is actually correct and allows it to be used for subsequent dictionary lookups. When the choice is to ignore the word, the spelling checker continues with the next word. The "misspelled" response directs the spelling checker to add the word to a set of misspelled words. We conclude the process by displaying this set.

The function spellCheck() has filename as a string argument specifying the name of the document. In its initialization phase, the function opens the file "dict.dat" and uses its words to create the dictionary. After opening the document file, the spelling checker uses a loop to input each word from the document and check whether it is in the dictionary.

spellChecker();
```
void spellChecker(string& filename)
{
    // sets storing the dictionary and the misspelled words
    set<string> dictionary, misspelledWords;

    // dictionary and document streams
    ifstream dict, doc;
    string word;
    char response;

    // open "dict.dat"
    dict.open("dict.dat");
    if (!dict)
    {
        cerr << "Cannot open 'dict.dat'" << endl;
        exit(1);
    }

    // open the document file
    doc.open(filename.c_str());
    if (!doc)
    {
```

```
        cerr << "Cannot open " << filename << endl;
        exit(1);
    }

    // insert each word from the "dict.dat" into the dictionary set
    // while(true)
    {
        dict >> word;
        if (!dict)
            break;

        // insert into the dictionary
        dictionary.insert(word);
    }

    // read the document word by word and check spelling
    while(true)
    {
        doc >> word;
        if (!doc)
            break;
        // lookup word up in the dictionary. if not present
        // assume word is misspelled. prompt user to add
        // or ignore word
        if (dictionary.find(word) == dictionary.end())
        {
            cout << word << endl;
            cout << "'a' (add)  'i' (ignore)  'm'  (misspelled) ";
            cin >> response;
            // if response is 'a' add to dictionary; otherwise
            // add to the set of misspelled words
            if (response == 'a')
                dictionary.insert(word);
            else if (response == 'm')
                misspelledWords.insert(word);
        }
    }
    // display the set of misspelled words
    cout << endl << "Set of misspelled words" << endl;
    writeContainer(misspelledWords.begin(),
                    misspelledWords.end());
    cout << endl;
}
```

PROGRAM 11-1   A SIMPLE SPELLING CHECKER

Let us illustrate the use of the spelling checker. The program prompts the user for the name
of the document and then calls spellChecker(). To accommodate the fact that the dictionary
contains words in lowercase and the spelling checker uses only the >> operator to input a

word, the run uses a simple document with only lowercase alphabetic characters and no punctuation marks.

```cpp
// File: prg11_1.cpp
// input the name of a file containing lowercase letters
// and no punctuation marks. call spellChecker() to check
// its spelling. the function creates a dictionay by
// inserting the whitespace separated lowercase words in
// the file "dict.dat" into a set. the function then
// reads the words in the document, looking each up in
// the set. a word is considered misspelled if it is not
// in the set. in this situation, prompt the user
// to add the word to the dictionary (input 'a'), ignore the
// word because is it actually spelled correctly ('i') or
// confirm it as misspelled (input 'm')

#include <iostream>
#include <fstream>
#include <string>
#include <set>

#include "d_util.h"      // for writeContainer()

using namespace std;

// check filename for spelling errors
void spellChecker(string& filename);

int main()
{
   string fileName;

   cout << "Enter the document to spell check: ";
   cin >> fileName;

   // check the spelling
   spellChecker(fileName);

   return 0;
}
/* the function spellChecker implemented in the program discussion */
```

```
File "spell.tst"
teh message contians the url for the web-page
and a misspeled url for the email adress

Run:

Enter the document to spell check: spell.tst
```

```
teh
'a' (add)   'i' (ignore)   'm'  (misspelled) m
contians
'' (add)    'i' (ignore)   'm'  (misspelled) m
url
'a' (add)   'i' (ignore)   'm'  (misspelled) a
web-page
'a' (add)   'i' (ignore)   'm'  (misspelled) i
misspeled
'a' (add)   'i' (ignore)   'm'  (misspelled) m
email
'a' (add)   'i' (ignore)   'm'  (misspelled) i
adress
'a' (add)   'i' (ignore)   'm'  (misspelled) m
Set of misspelled words
adress   contians   misspeled   teh
```

Application: Sieve of Eratosthenes

The Greek mathematician and philosopher Eratosthenes lived in the third century B.C. He discovered an intriguing method of using sets to find all prime numbers less than or equal to an integer value n. A prime p is an integer greater than 1 that is divisible only by 1 and p (itself). The algorithm begins by initializing a set to contain all of the integers in the range 2 to n. A loop makes multiple passes over the elements in the set, using successive integer key values 2, 3, 4, ... Each pass "shakes free" nonprime numbers and lets them "filter through the sieve." At the end, only the prime numbers remain.

Begin with the integer $m = 2$, which is the smallest prime number. The pass scans the set and removes all multiples of 2, having the form $2 * k$, where $k \geq 2$. The multiples, $4 = 2*2, 6 = 3*2, 8 = 4 * 2, \ldots$. cannot be primes, because they are divisible by 2. At the end of the pass, we have removed all of the even numbers except 2, leaving the integers $2, 3, 5, 7, 9, \ldots$. Next, look at integer $m = 3$, which is a prime. As with value 2, remove all multiples of 3, starting at $6 = 2 * 3$. The multiples $6, 12 = 4 *3, 18 = 6*3$, and so forth, are even numbers, so they have already been removed from the set. The pass deletes the odd multiples of 3, including $9 = 3 * 3, 15 = 5*3$, $21= 7*3 \ldots$. The next key integer is $m = 4$, which is no longer in the set, because it was removed as a multiple of 2. The pass takes no action. Let us look at one more case, with $m = 5$. The value is still in the set and is a prime. The pass removes the multiples of 5 ($25, 35, 55, \ldots$) that remain in the set. The process continues until it removes all multiples of prime numbers. The numbers that remain in the sieve are the prime numbers in the range $2 \ldots n$.

Example 11-3

Figure11-4 illustrates the sieve of Eratosthenes finding all prime numbers in the range 2...25.

The function sieve() takes a set of integer elements as a reference argument, along with the integer n that specifies the upper bound of the list of primes. The function first initializes

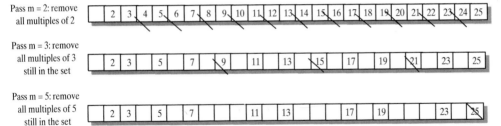

Pass m = 2: remove all multiples of 2

Pass m = 3: remove all multiples of 3 still in the set

Pass m = 5: remove all multiples of 5 still in the set

7, 11, 13, 17, 19, and 23 contain no multiples in the range 2 to 25
Primes {2, 3, 5, 7, 11, 13, 17, 19, 23}

Figure 11-4
Sieve of Eratosthenes: primes to 25

the set to contain all of the integers in the range 2 . . . n and then executes the algorithm for the Sieve of Eratosthenes. The algorithm uses an optimization feature by looking at key values in the range $2 \leq m \leq \sqrt{n}$. The limited number of key values still removes all nonprime numbers from the set. To verify this fact, assume that some nonprime (composite) number t = p*q remains in the set. If both factors p and q are greater than $\sqrt{n}$, then

$$t = p * q > \sqrt{n} * \sqrt{n} > n$$

Hence at least one factor, say p, must be $\leq \sqrt{n}$. This "small" factor is a key value (p = m) or a multiple of a key value (p = m * q) for pass m, where $2 \leq m \leq \sqrt{n}$. In either case, the pass removes t, because it is a multiple of m. Our assumption that a nonprime number remains in the set is not true.

In the implementation of sieve(), we test all numbers m such that m * m $\leq$ n , rather than computing the square root of n.

sieve():

```
void sieve(set<int>& s, int n)
{
    int m, i;

    // erase any previous values in s
    s.erase(s.begin(), s.end());

    // load the set with integers 2, 3, . . ., n
    for (m = 2; m < n; m++)
        s.insert(m);

    // find the primes using the Sieve of Eratosthenes.
    // look at all numbers from m = 2 to m * m > n ( n <= sqrt(n))
    for (m = 2; m * m <= n; m++)
        // check is m is still in the set; if so remove all higher
        // multiples of m starting with j = 2*m.
        if(s.find(m) != s.end())
        {
            i = 2 * m;      // i is successive multiples of m
            while (i <= n)
```

```
        {
            s.erase(i);
            i += m;      // update i to the next multiple of m
        }
    }
}
```

PROGRAM 11-2   SIEVE OF ERATOSTHENES

This following program uses the Sieve of Eratosthenes. A prompt asks the user to enter an integer *primeLimit*. A call to sieve() creates the set of primes in the range 2 to *primeLimit*. The program outputs all the primes, 10 per line.

```
// File: prg11_2.cpp
// the program prompts user for an integer upper limit and calls the
// sieve() to execute the Sieve of Eratosthenes. it creates a
// set containing the primes between 2 and the upper limit. using a
// set iterator, the program outputs all the primes, 10 per line

#include <iostream>
#include <iomanip>
#include <set>

using namespace std;

// apply the Sieve of Eratosthenes to remove all non-prime
// numbers from the integer set s = {2, 3, 4, ..., n}
void sieve(set<int>& s, int n);

int main()
{
    // set to hold the prime numbers
    set<int> primeSet;

    // used to output the final set of primes 10 numbers per line
    set<int>::iterator iter;
    int primeLimit, count = 0;

    cout << "Enter upper limit for the set of primes:    ";
    cin >> primeLimit;
    // use the sieve of Eratosthenes to remove the non-primes
    sieve(primeSet, primeLimit);

    // use iterator to scan the resulting set; output
    // 10 elements per line
    iter = primeSet.begin();
    while (iter != primeSet.end())
    {
```

```
        count++;
        cout << setw(5) << *iter;
        if (count % 10 == 0)
            cout << endl;
        iter++;
    }
    cout << endl;

    return 0;
}

/* Implementation of sieve() found in the program discussion */
```

```
Run:

Enter upper limit for the set of primes: 280
   2    3    5    7   11   13   17   19   23   29
  31   37   41   43   47   53   59   61   67   71
  73   79   83   89   97  101  103  107  109  113
 127  131  137  139  149  151  157  163  167  173
 179  181  191  193  197  199  211  223  227  229
 233  239  241  251  257  263  269  271  277
```

Set Operations

From your study of sets in mathematics, you are familiar with the binary operations union, intersection, and difference, which use sets as operands. To simplify notation, we introduce the arithmetic operators $+$, $*$, and $-$ for the set operations. Venn diagrams describe the results of the operations on two sets A and B. The upcoming statements are definitions for the operations, along with the corresponding Venn Diagram. Assume set $A = \{1, 3, 8, 9, 10\}$ and set $B = \{2, 3, 6, 9\}$.

Set-Union Operator + (A + B):
   The set of all elements x such that x is an element in set A *OR* x is an element in set B.
      Example: $A + B = \{1, 2, 3, 6, 8, 9, 10\}$

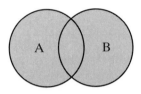

*Set-Intersection Operator * (A * B):*
   The set of all elements x such that x is an element in set A AND x is an element in set B.

Example: A * B = {3, 9}

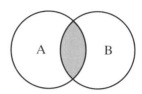

Set-Difference Operator − (A − B):
  The set of all elements *x* such that *x* is an element in set A, but *x* is not an element in set B.
    Example: A − B = {1, 8, 10}

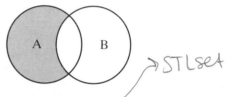

[handwritten left margin:]
#include <algorithum>
to use
Set_union(set1.begin(),
*   Set 1. end(),*
*   set 2. begin(),*
*   Set 2. end,*
*   insester(*
*   set 3,*
*   Set 3. begin()));*

[handwritten annotations:] → STLset   the class declaration [circled]

The set operations are not part of the class declaration. They have important appli-cations, however, so we provide them as free functions in the file "d_setops.h". STL uses a similar strategy by defining very general set operations that use iterator argu-ments and apply to any ordered container. Our implementation is specific to sets. The upcoming statements are the prototypes for the template-based functions that overload the binary operators +, *, and −. In each case, set<T> is the type for the arguments (operands) and the return value.

```
template <typename T>
set<T> operator+ (const set<T>& lhs, const set<T>& rhs);

template <typename T>
set<T> operator* (const set<T>& lhs, const set<T>& rhs);

template <typename T>
set<T> operator- (const set<T>& lhs, const set<T>& rhs);
```

Example 11-4

This example uses setA and setB with initial values provided by arrays arrA and arrB. The function writeContainer() outputs the elements in the resulting set.

```
int arrA[] = {1, 3, 4, 5, 7, 8, 11};
int arrB[] = {2, 4, 5, 8, 9};
set<int> setA(arrA, arrA+7), setB(arrB, arrB+5),setC;
```

Union: `setC = setA + setB;`
                `writeContainer(setC.begin(), setC.end());`
                   `Output: 1  2  3  4  5  7  8  9  11`

Intersection: `setC = setA * setB;`
                `writeContainer(setC.begin(), setC.end());`
                   `Output: 4  5  8`

Difference: `setC = setA - setB;`
                `writeContainer(setC.begin(), setC.end());`
                   `Output: 1  3  7  11`

Implementing Set Intersection   The implementation of the operator * (set intersection) uses iterators to scan each of the ordered sets. The algorithm makes a pairwise comparison of the elements, looking for a match that identifies an element as belonging to the intersection. Assume that *lhs* and *rhs* are the two set operands. Start by calling begin() to position the iterators *lhsIter* and *rhsIter* at the first element in the respective sets. Control the movement of the iterators by comparing the value of the elements pointed to by the iterators.

If **lhsIter* < **rhsIter*, then **lhsIter* is not an element in the intersection, and the iterator *lhsIter* moves forward to the next element in set *lhs* (Figure11-5(a)).

If **rhsIter* < **lhsIter*, then **rhsIter* is not an element in the intersection. The iterator *rhsIter* moves forward to the next element in set *rhs* (Figure 11-5(b)).

If **lhsIter* == **rhsIter*, then the iterators point to elements in the two sets with a common value. After inserting the value into the intersection, each iterator moves forward to the next element (Figure 11-5(c)).

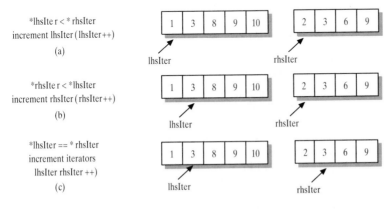

Figure 11-5
The Set Intersection operator *

The algorithm terminates when one of the iterators reaches the end of its list.

Set Intersection Operator *:

```
template <typename T>
set<T> operator* (const set<T>& lhs, const set<T>& rhs)
{
    // constuct intersection
    set<T> setIntersection;
    // iterators that traverse the sets
    set<T>::const_iterator lhsIter = lhs.begin(),
                           rhsIter = rhs.begin();

    // move forward as long as we have not reached the
    // end ofeither set
    while (lhsIter != lhs.end() && rhsIter != rhs.end())
        if (*lhsIter < *rhsIter)
            // *lhsIter is in lhs and not in rhs. move
            // iterator forward
            lhsIter++;
        else if (*rhsIter < *lhsIter)
            // *rhsIter is in rhs and not in lhs. move
            // iterator forward
            rhsIter++;
        else
        {
            // the same value is in both sets. insert one
            // value and move the iterators forward
            setIntersection.insert(*lhsIter);
            lhsIter++;
            rhsIter++;
        }
    return setIntersection;
}
```

Application: Updating Computer Accounts

Assume that the university computer center updates student accounts at the beginning of the fall semester. The administrator collects the names of students who desire an account for the current year and stores them in the set *currAcct*. A second set, called *oldAcct*, is the collection of accounts that were active during the previous academic year. The update process involves creating new accounts for first-time users of the system, deleting obsolete accounts that will no longer be active in the current year, and copying the carryover accounts for student wishing to maintain access to the system. The operations of set intersection and set difference identify the students for each of the update activities:

New Accounts: Accounts for the current year that were not active in the previous year.
    newAcct = currAcct − oldAcct

Obsolete Accounts: Accounts in the previous year that are not active in the current year.

$$obsoleteAcct = oldAcct - currAcct$$

Carryover Accounts: Accounts that were active in the previous year and continue to be active in the current year.

$$carryOverAcct = oldAcct * currAcct$$

PROGRAM 11-3   UPDATING COMPUTER ACCOUNTS

Let us look at a program that updates computer accounts. Assume that the login name iden-tifies each account. The administrator creates five sets containing the login names as string elements:

```
set<string> currAcct, oldAcct, newAcct, obsoleteAcct, carryoverAcct;
```

The program reads elements for the sets *oldAcct* and *currAcct* from the files "oldacct.dat" and "curracct.dat", respectively. The values of the other three sets are the results of set-inter-section and set-difference operations. After the displaying of a label for each set, a call to writeContainer() outputs the elements (login names) in the corresponding set.

```
// File: prg11_3.cpp
// the program reads file "curracct.dat" containing login names
// students who want a computer account for the current academic
// year. it reads the file "oldacct.dat" containing login names of
// students from the previous year. using set operations, program
// computes the set of new accounts, accounts carried over from the
// previous year, and accounts for students not requesting a
// current account. using writeContainer(), the program outputs
// the login names in the sets

#include <iostream>
#include <iomanip>
#include <fstream>
#include <string>
#include <set>

#include "d_setops.h"
#include "d_util.h"

using namespace std;

int main()
{
    // declare sets for current and new computer accounts
    set<string> oldAcct, currAcct, newAcct, carryOverAcct, obsoleteAcct;

    // objects used by the program
    string acct;
    ifstream finOldAcct, finCurrAcct;
```

```
// open file of old accounts and current accounts
finOldAcct.open("oldacct.dat");
finCurrAcct.open("curracct.dat");

// input the set of old accounts
while(true)
{
   finOldAcct >> acct;
   if (!finOldAcct)
      break;
   oldAcct.insert(acct);
}

// input the set of current accounts
while(true)
{
   finCurrAcct >> acct;
   if (!finCurrAcct)
      break;
   currAcct.insert(acct);
}

// use set intersection to determine the set of
// carryover accounts
carryOverAcct = currAcct * oldAcct;
// use set differnce to determine the set of new accounts
// and obsolete accounts
newAcct = currAcct - oldAcct;
obsoleteAcct = oldAcct - currAcct;
// output the set of old accounts
cout << "Old Accounts:  " << endl;
writeContainer(oldAcct.begin(), oldAcct.end());
cout << endl << endl;

// output the set of current accounts
cout << "Current Accounts:  " << endl;
writeContainer(currAcct.begin(), currAcct.end());
cout << endl << endl;

// output the set of new accounts
cout << "New Accounts:  " << endl;
writeContainer(newAcct.begin(), newAcct.end());
cout << endl << endl;

// output the set of carryover accounts
cout << "Carryover Accounts:  " << endl;
writeContainer(carryOverAcct.begin(), carryOverAcct.end());
cout << endl << endl;

// output the set of obsolete accounts
cout << "Obsolete Accounts:  " << endl;
```

```
        writeContainer(obsoleteAcct.begin(),obsoleteAcct.end();
        cout << endl;

        return 0;
    }
```

```
File "curracct.dat"

fbrue
ascott
wtubbs

File "oldacct.dat"

tmiller
lhung
fbrue
gharris

Run:

Old Accounts:
fbrue    gharris    lhung    tmiller

Current Accounts:
ascott    fbrue    wtubbs

New Accounts:
ascott    wtubbs

Carryover Accounts:
fbrue

Obsolete Accounts:
gharris    lhung    tmiller
```

Some versions of the set and multiset containers implement constant iterators only. For instance, if *iter* is a set iterator, an assignment such as

Note

```
    *iter = value;
```

is not allowed. Similarly, suppose we use the iterator to call a member function f() of an object, such as in the expression

```
    (*iter).f()
```

The function f() must be declared as a constant member function.

11-3   MAPS

A map is an associative container that stores data in a key–value pair. A pair consists of two components that have separate data types. As a storage structure, a map has an interface that closely resembles a set. In fact, you can think of a map as a "set of pairs" (Figure 11-6)

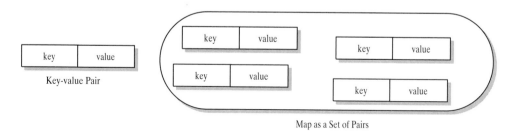

Map as a Set of Pairs

Figure 11-6
Map element is a key–value pair. the map structure is a set of pairs

The Map-Class Interface

The map-class interface has all of the operations found in the set class. Like any container, a map has both constant and nonconstant iterators. That is the easy part. You will not have to learn any new function names, and you can apply your knowledge of iterators to access elements in the map. The problems you will encounter, however, center on the fact that the elements in a map are pairs, not a single data item. The presence of key–value data affects the way you declare a map, add (insert) a new element into the map, and dereference an element pointed to by an iterator. Let us look at these issues one at a time.

A map has two template arguments, where the template types correspond to the key and the value components of a pair, respectively. The template arguments for a map include separate typename identifiers for the key and the value components of the key–value pair:

```
template <typename Key, typename T>
```

Often, the key type is a string. The value type can be any object type, including any of the container classes we have previously studied. For instance, the following statement declares *mapObj* as an empty map consisting of key–value pairs, where the key is a string and the value is an integer:

```
map<string, int> mapObj;
```

A program might use *mapObj* to store course information as key–value data, where the key component is the course name and the value component is the number of students registered (Figure11-7(a)).

ECON101	85
CS 173	27

ECON101	List of SSN's for students enrolled in ECON 101
CS 173	List of SSN's for students enrolled in CS 173

pair<string,int>
in mapObj

pair<string,list<string> >
in courseMap

(a)   (b)

Figure 11-7
Pair<string, int> data for the map mapObj and pair<string>, list<string> > data for
the map courseMap

If the program wants to maintain the list of the students in each course in the order they enrolled for the class, the map declaration can define the value component for each pair as a list of strings, where each string is a student's social security number (Figure 11-7(b))

```
map<string, list<string> > courseMap;
```

An element in a map container is a pair<*Key, T*> object. To simplify notation, the map class uses a typedef statement that equates the type pair<*Key, T*> with the identifier *value_type:*

```
typedef pair<Key,T> value_type;
```

Let us see how the typedef would apply to the declaration of an array of pair<*string, int*> objects that we use to initialize *mapObj*. Note that use of the identifier value_type requires the map class scope operator, because the class defines the identifier.

```
// declare an array of pair<string,int> objects corresponding to
// courses and their enrollment numbers
map<string,int>::value_type arr[] =
    {  map<string, int>::value_type ("ECON 101",85),
       map<string, int>::value_type ("CS 173",27),
       map<string, int>::value_type ("ENGL 25",30) };
```

You can see that the declaration of a pair object involves long type names. The syntax is correct, but clumsy and hard to read. A program can simplify the notation by defining its own typedef that equates map<*key,T*>::value_type with the identifier entry:

```
typedef map<string,int>::value_type entry;
```

Look at how this typedef simplifies the declaration of array *arr*, which we use to initialize *mapObj*:

```
entry arr[] = {entry("ECON 101",85),
               entry("CS 173",27),entry("ENGL 25",30) };
int arrSize = sizeof(arr)/sizeof(entry);
// declare mapObj using the address range for arr as arguments
map<string, int>mapObj(arr, arr+arrSize );
```

The iterator for a map specifies the location of an element in the container as a pair<*key,T*> object. The pair the iterator points to has data members first and second that reference the key and value components of the pair, respectively. To see how these data members apply, consider the following declaration of an iterator for a map<*key, T*> object:

```
map<Key,T>::iterator iter;
```

The dereference operator, *, combines with the data members to access the separate components of the element pointed to by *iter*. The dot operator has precedence, so the expression **iter* must be included in parentheses:

```
(*iter).first      // key component of the element
(*iter).second     // value component of the element
```

Example 11-5

1. The declaration creates an iterator for a map<*string, int*> object. A program can use the map operations begin() and end() to return iterator locations in the map container.

```
map<string, int>::iterator iter;
// set iter at the first element in mapObj; this is the element
// with the smallest key in lexographic order
iter = mapObj.begin();      // locates element ("CS 173", 27)

// output the separate components of the element
cout << (*iter).first;      // output: CS 173
cout << (*iter).second;     // output: 27
```

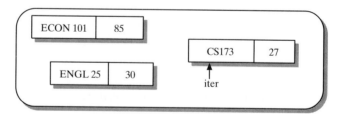

2. The function writeMap() uses a constant iterator to display the components for each element in a map. The function assumes that the << operator is defined for both the key and the value types. Because a map is the argument, the function requires two template arguments.

```
template <typename Key, typename T>
void writeMap(const map<Key,T>& m, const string& separator = "  ")
{
    map<Key, T>::const_iterator iter = m.begin();
```

```
      while(iter != m.end())
      {
          cout << (*iter).first << "  " << (*iter).second << separator;
          iter++;
      }
  }
```

Function call: `writeMap(mapObj, "\n");`

```
Output:  CS 173   27
         ECON 101   85
         ENGL 25   30
```

The function implementation is in the header file "d_util.h."

Map Operations

The map class has an insert function that takes an element of type pair<*key,T*> as the argument and returns an iterator–bool pair. You are familiar with the operation from the set class. If the insert finds a duplicate entry (i.e., same key), the operation returns a pair whose iterator component points at the duplicate and whose Boolean component is *false*. Otherwise, the operation adds the new entry and returns a pair whose iterator component points to the new location and whose Boolean component is *true*. The prototype for the insert() function uses value_type to reference the key–value pair argument.

```
pair<iterator,bool> insert(const value_type& kvpair);
```

We illustrate the use of insert() to add a course and its enrollment data to the map *mapObj*. In case the course is already in the map, we use the enrollment data from the argument to update the data in the map.

```
// typedef equates map value_type with the identifier entry
typedef map<string,int>::value_type entry;
string courseName;
int courseEnrollment;

// declare an iterator-bool pair for the return type
pair<map<string, int>::iterator, bool> p;

p = mapObj.insert(entry(courseName, courseEnrollment));

// test for a duplicate entry (p.second is false); if so, use the
// iterator p.first to update the enrollment data for the element
// *p.first
if (p.second == false)    // found a duplicate
   (*p.first).second = courseEnrollment;
```

You probably found the syntax in the previous example to be a bit daunting. In the next section, we discuss the overloaded index operator for maps, which greatly simplifies the addition and updating of entries in a map.

We identify an element in a map by its key, so the member functions find() and erase() use only the key as an argument. The find() function has two versions, which return either a constant or a nonconstant iterator. The return iterator points at a key–value pair if the search locates an entry with a matching key, but has the value end() if no match occurs. The erase() function removes the entry that matches the key. Two other versions of erase() take an iterator or an iterator range and delete the corresponding element(s).

Example 11-6

This example illustrates the find() and erase() functions for mapObj. At the same time, we also include the size() and empty() functions, which are common to all container classes.

```
cout << mapObj.size();          // Output: 3

// declare an iterator for the find() function
map<string, int>::iterator mapIter;

// iterator points at entry ("ECON 101", 85);
mapIter = mapObj.find("ECON 101");
cout << (*mapIter).second);     // Output: 85

mapObj.erase("ECON 101");       // delete entry ("ECON 101", 85);

mapIter = mapObj.begin();       // iterator points at ("CS 173", 27);
mapObj.erase(mapIter);          // delete the entry

// clear the map
mapObj.erase(mapObj.begin(), mapObj.end());

if (mapObj.empty())
   cout << "Map is empty"       // Output: Map is empty
```

Map Index Operator

The fact that a map stores elements as pairs with unique keys allows us to view the structure as an associative array indexed by the key. To implement this feature, the class overloads the index operator that takes a key as an argument and returns a reference to the value component of the entry.

```
// overloaded index operator returns value component of type T
T& operator[] (const Key& key)
```

The syntax has the familiar array-index format. The fact that the return type is a reference allows a program to use an index expression on either side of an assignment statement.

```
mapObj[key] = value;
cout << mapObj[key];    // outputs the value component
```

The presence of an index operator is one of the most powerful features of a map container. It simplifies notation and provides an alternative to the insert() operation. We will look at the features of the index operator in detail.

If an element with the specified key is in the map, the index operator can be used to retrieve or update the value corresponding to the key:

```
int courseEnrollment;

// the entry ("ENGL 25", 30) is already in the map. the index operator
// retrieves the value component
courseEnrollment = mapObj["ENGL 25"]; // assign value 30

// the entry ("CS 173", 27) is already in the map. the index operator
// updates the value component to have 29 students
mapObj["CS 173"] = 29;

// the entry ("ECON 101", 85) is already in the map. the statement
// adds 5 to the enrollment in the course
mapObj["ECON 101"] += 5;
```

When no pair with the specified key is in the map, the index operator acts like insert() and creates one for you. It adds a pair consisting of the key and the default value of type *T* to the map and returns a reference to the new entry. For instance, no entry with the key "MATH 51" is in the map. In the assignment statement shown next, the index operator creates the key–value pair (MATH 51, 0), adds it to the map, and returns a reference to the value field. The right-hand side of the assignment statement replaces the integer default value of 0 with 45.

```
// no entry has key "MATH 51"; the index operator adds the entry
// ("MATH 51", 0) to the map and assignment replaces 0 by 45 to
// create the map entry ("MATH 51", 45)
mapObj["MATH 51"] = 45;
```

As another example, if the program uses the index operator on the right-hand side of an assignment statement and no entry with the key is in the map, the operator creates a new map entry and returns the default value:

```
// no entry has key "BUS 31"; the index operator adds the entry
// ("BUS 31", 0) to the map and returns a reference to the value
courseEnrollment = mapObj["BUS 31"];    // assign value 0
```

PROGRAM 11-4   STUDENT WORK-TIME MAP

Map applications typically use the fact that the container is an associative array and employ the index operator to insert and update elements. Let us illustrate this fact with a program that maintains information on the total time a student works at a part-time job during a school week. We store the information in a map<*string, time*24> object called *studentWorker*, where the key component of an entry is the student's name and the value component is the accumulated time worked. The file "studwk.dat" consists of a series of separate data items that include the student's name and the time worked during a specific day. The file includes multiple entries for any student who works two or more days in the week. The program reads each line in the file, placing the name in the string *studName* and the hours worked into the time24 object *workTime*. A compound assignment statement updates the total weekly work time for the map entry that uses *studName* as the index:

```
// add a new student with workTime as time worked or update the
// accumulated work time if the student is already in the map
studentWorker[studName] += workTime;
```

When the name appears for the first time, the index operator creates a new entry with *studName* as the key and the default time 0:00 (midnight) as the value. The += operation adds *workTime* to 0:00, with the effect of initializing the value component of the entry to *workTime*. For input of a duplicate entry, the += operation simply updates the accumulated time by adding *workTime* to the current value. The program concludes by using the function writeMap() from "d_util.h" to display the student's name and the total work time in alphabetical order by name:

```
// File: prg11_4.cpp
// the program inputs file "studwk.dat", which contains student names
// and time worked during the week. the time is given in time24
// format. using the index operator, information is stored and
// updated in a map<string, time24> object called studentWorker.
// the program concludes by displaying the contents of the map,
// including the name and total time worked during the week

#include <iostream>
#include <fstream>
#include <iomanip>
#include <string>
#include <map>

#include "d_time24.h"  // time24 class
#include "d_util.h"     // for writeMap()

using namespace std;

int main()
{
   // a map<string, time24> object whose entries are student names
   // and total hours worked during a week
   map<string, time24> studentWorker;
   // map iterator
   map<string, time24>::iterator iter;
```

```
  // object used to input the data from file "studwk.dat"
  ifstream fin;
  string studName;
  time24 workTime;

  // open the file "studwk.dat"
  fin.open("studwk.dat");

  // input successive lines in the file consisting of the
  // student name and the scheduled work time
  while (true)
  {
    fin >> studName;
    if (!fin)
       break;
    fin >> workTime;

    // add a new student with workTime as time worked or update the
    // accumulated work time if the student is already in the map
    studentWorker[studName] += workTime;

  }

  // output the map, one key-value pair per line
  writeMap(studentWorker,"\n");
  return 0;
}
```

```
File: "studwk.dat"

Tolan   4:15
Dong    3:00
Tolan   3:15
Weber   5:30
Tolan   2:45
Brock   4:20
Dong    4:00
Dong    3:30
Tolan   3:15
Weber   2:30

Run:

Brock     4:20
Dong     10:30
Tolan    13:30
Weber     8:00
```

Case Study: Concordance

A *concordance* is a software tool that reads a text file and extracts all of the words in the file, along with the line numbers on which the words appear. Compilers often provide a concordance to evaluate the use of identifiers (including keywords) in a source-code file. This case study designs and implements such a concordance. It provides an excellent example of an application that combines the use of map and set containers.

Problem Analysis: The concordance takes a string specifying the source file. The software tool extracts all of the identifiers and displays them in an alphabetized list that includes the identifier, the number of lines in the file containing the identifier, and the line numbers on which the identifier appears. An identifier is a string that begins with a letter (A–Z, a–z) and is followed by zero or more other characters that are a letter or a digit (0–9). The concordance outputs the information for an identifier in the following format:

```
identifier      n:    l₁    l₂    l₃    l₄   . . .
```

Here, n is the number of lines containing the identifier and l_i ($i \geq 1$) is the list of line numbers on which it appears.

Program Design: The concordance uses a map to store each identifier as a pair<string, set<int> > entry. The identifier string is the key component, and the set of integer elements is the value component, which contains the collection of distinct line numbers corresponding to lines in the file that contain the identifier:

```
map<string, set<int> > concordance;
```

The concordance algorithm scans the source code one character at a time and extracts the identifiers. The design of the scan must recognize the start of an identifier and then store successive characters in a string until it reaches the end of the identifier. The resulting string, which is the identifier, is the key component for an entry in the map. An integer, *lineNumber*, maintains the current line number in the source file. Each scan of an end-of-line character increments *lineNumber*. Once the scan extracts an identifier, the algorithm must update the map. Recall that the value component of a map entry is a set containing the line numbers in which the identifier occurs. The update requires taking the entry with the identifier as a key and inserting the current value of *lineNumber* into the set component. Because a set does not allow duplicates, the insert() operation will ensure that the program stores a line number only once, in case the identifier appears two or more time on the same line. The design of the concordance algorithm boils down to two tasks: recognizing an identifier and updating the map. Let us look as these tasks separately.

Recognizing an Identifier: In order to extract an identifier, we declare a Boolean variable *beginIdentifer* that is initially set to *true* and a string *identifier* that is initially empty. If the scan reads a letter and *beginIdentifier* is *true*, we are at the start of an identifier. Setting *beginIdentifier* to *false* then allows the scan to add either letters or digits to the identifier string. The end of the identifier occurs when the scan reads a character that is neither a letter or a digit. After performing the map update, we set *beginIdentifier* back to *true* and *identifier* back to the empty string and repeat the process. Any time the scan reads an end-of-line character, we increment *lineNumber*. The following is an outline of the multiple-selection statement that processes the individual characters input during the scan of the source file:

```
if ch is a letter and beginIdentifier is true
{
   // begin building a new identifier
   add ch to identifier
   set beginIdentifier to false     // continue building identifier
}

else if ch is a letter or digit and beginIdentifier is false
   // continue appending ch to identifier
   add ch to identifier

else ch is not a letter or digit
{
   // we may have reached the end of the identifier
   if beginIdentifier is false and identifer != ""
      // we have an identifier
      update the map using identifier and lineNumber

   if ch is a newline
      increment lineNumber

   // reset the bool beginIdentifier and the string identifier
   set beginIdentifier to true
   set identifier to the empty string
}
```

Updating the Map: We use the identifier as an index to update the map. If the identifier is not yet in the map, the expression "concordance[*identifier*]" creates a new entry with an empty set as the value component. If the identifier is already in the map, then the expression simply accesses the set component of the corresponding entry. In either case, we insert the line number into the set by using the following statement:

```
concordance[identifier].insert(lineNumber);
```

Program Implementation: The function concordance() implements the software tool. Its argument is a string specifying the filename. After creating the map, the function calls writeConcordance() to create the output list.

concordance():
```
   // input filename and output a concordance
   void concordance(const string& filename)
   {
```

```cpp
// declare the concordance map
map<string, set<int> > concordanceMap;

// objects to create identifiers and maintain line numbers
char ch;
string identifier = "";
bool beginIdentifier = true;
int lineNumber = 1;

// file objects
ifstream fin;

// open the input file
fin.open(filename.c_str());

if (!fin)
{
   cerr << "Cannot open '" << filename << "'" << endl;
   exit(1);
}

// read the file character by character to determine each
// identifier and update line numbers
while(true)
{
   fin.get(ch);
   if (!fin)
      break;

   // check for a letter that begins an identifier
   if (isalpha(ch) && beginIdentifier)
   {
      // add char to identifier and continue scan
      identifier += ch;
      beginIdentifier = false;
   }

   // check if subsequent letter or digit in an identifier
   else if ((isalpha(ch) || isdigit(ch)) && !beginIdentifier)
      identifier += ch;

   // not part of an identifier
   else
   {
      // if we have just finished with an identifier,
      // use index operator to access a map entry with
      // identifier as the key. if not in the map, operator
      // adds an entry with an empty set as the value.
      // if in the map, operator accesses the set component.
      // in either case, insert the current line number
```

```
          if (!beginIdentifier && identifier != "")
              concordanceMap[identifier].insert(lineNumber);

          // increment lineNumber if ch == '\n'
          if (ch == '\n')
              lineNumber++;

          // reset objects preparing for next identifier
          beginIdentifier
          identifier = "";
       }
    }
    // output the concordanced
    writeConcordance (concordanceMap);
}

void writeConcordance(const map<string,set<int> >& concordance)
{  map<string, set<int> >::const_iterator iter =
                          concordance.begin();

   int i;

   while (iter != concordance.end())
   {  cout << (*iter).first;  // output key
      // pad output to 12 characters using blanks
      if ((*iter).first.length() < 12)
          for (i=0; i < 12 - (*iter).first.length(); i++
              cout << ' ';
      cout << setw(4) << (*iter).second.size() << ":  ";
      write Container((*iter).second.begin(), (*iter.second.end()));
      cout << endl;
      iter++;
   }
   cout << endl;
}
```

PROGRAM 11-5   SOURCE-FILE CONCORDANCE

This program outputs a concordance. Prompt the user to input the name of the file, and create the concordance listing by calling the function concordance().

```
// File: prg11_5.cpp
// prompt user for name of a text file containing identifiers,
// where an identifier begins with a letter ('A'..'Z', 'a'..'z')
// followed by 0 or more letters or digits ('0'..'9'). the function
// concordance() takes a file name as an argument and uses a map
// with key string and value set<int> to determine for each identifier
// the number of lines on which it occurs and the line numbers on
// which it appears. concordance() calls the writeConcordance() to
// display the results in the format
//          identifier       n:   line# line# line#  . . .
```

```cpp
#include <iostream>
#include <fstream>
#include <iomanip>
#include <cstdlib>
#include <string>
#include <set>
#include <map>
#include <ctype.h>   // for functions isalpha() and isdigit()

#include "d_util.h"

using namespace std;

// input filename and output a concordance
void concordance(const string& filename);

// output the identifier, the number of lines containing the
// identifier, and the list of lines having the identifier
void writeConcordance(const map<string,set<int> >& concordance);

int main()
{
   string filename;

   // get the file name
   cout << "Enter the file name: ";
   cin >> filename;
   cout << endl;

   // create the concordance
   concordance(filename);
   return 0;
}
/* function concordance() implemented in the program discussion */
```

```
File: "concord.txt"

int m, n;
double a = 3, b = 2, hypotenuse

cin << m;
if (n <= 5)
   n = 2*m;
else
   n = m * m;

cout << n << endl;

hypotenuse = sqrt(a*a + b*b);
cout << hypotenuse << endl;
```

```
Run:

Enter the file name: concord.txt

a                2:      2   12
b                2:      2   12
cin              1:      4
cout             2:      10   13
double           1:      2
else             1:      7
endl             2:      10   13
hypotenuse       3:      2   12   13
if               1:      5
int              1:      1
m                4:      1   4   6   8
n                5:      1   5   6   8   10
sqrt             1:      12
```

MULTISETS   11-4

The Standard Template Library defines multiset and multimap containers that extend the set and map classes by allowing duplicate entries. The containers have a slightly different interface that accounts for the possible presence of duplicate keys. Let us focus on multisets in some detail, because they illustrate the main differences without requiring the additional complexity of the map. The count() function takes the argument *item* of type *T* and returns the number of duplicate elements that match *item*. In a multiset, the value of count() may be greater than 1. An insert() operation will always add a new element to the multiset, because duplicate values are allowed. Rather than returning an iterator–bool pair, the function returns an iterator that points to the new element in the set. Like a set, multisets have several versions of the erase() operation that allow value or iterator arguments. When erase() uses a value argument, the operation removes all occurrences of elements from the multiset that match the value and returns the number of elements deleted. The operation with an iterator argument or an iterator range removes only the element(s) at the specified location(s).

Example 11-7

Assume that *msObj* is a multiset containing integer values from array *intArr*. The declaration of *msObj* uses the constructor that includes the address range of the array as its arguments. Like any container, the multiset class supports both constant and nonconstant iterators.

```
int intArr[] = {3, 5, 1, 5, 1, 9, 7, 5, 9};
int arrSize = sizeof(intArr)/sizeof(int);
multiset<int> msObj(intArr, intArr+arrSize);
multiset<int>::iterator iter;
```

1. Size operations that account for duplicates:

```
cout << msObj.size();          // output:  9
cout << msObj.count(5);        // output:  3
```

2. Adding an element to the multiset:

```
iter = msObj.insert(8);
cout << *iter;                 // output:  8
```

3. Removing elements from the multiset:

```
msObj.erase(9);                // remove two occurrences of 9

// set iterator to the smallest element in the multiset
iter = msObj.begin();          // *iter is 1
msObj.erase(iter);             // remove first occurrence of 1
```

Searching a multiset is bit more complicated, because we can encounter a range of elements that match the key. The function find() returns an iterator pointing to the first occurrence of the item in the multiset, or end() if the item is not found. To access all occurrences of an *item*, the multiset class provides a function called equal_range(), which takes item as an argument and returns a pair of iterators specifying the range of elements matching the key. As with other pair objects, we can use the identifiers *first* and *second* to reference each component. The concept is simple, but you have to be careful with notation. For instance, assume that *msObj* is a multiset of integer elements. The upcoming statements declare an iterator–iterator pair *p* for use by equal_range(). The iterator *p.first* points to the first occurrence of *item* in the multiset, and *p.second* points just past the last occurrence of *item* in the multiset.

```
pair<multiset<int>::iterator, multiset<int>::iterator> p;
p = equal_range(item);
```

We can use the iterator range along with erase() to delete all occurrences of *item* from the multiset. This is equivalent to calling erase(*item*). A more meaningful application uses the function writeContainer() to display the elements in the iterator range. Recall that elements in a multiset are often records consisting of a key field and other information. Elements are duplicates if they have the same key, even though the other information might differ.

```
// use the iterator-iterator pair p with components first and
// second to specify the iterator range
msObj.erase(p.first, p.second);
// remove duplicate occurrences of item

// output all occurrences of elements matching item
writeContainer(p.first, p.second);
```

We include an API listing of selected multiset functions:

CLASS multiset	Operations	{<}set{>}

int **count** (*const T& item*) *const*;
  Return the number of duplicate occurrences of *item* in the multiset.

pair<iterator, iterator> **equal_range**(*cons t T& item*);
  Return a pair of iterators such that all occurrences of *item* are in the
  iterator range [first member of *pair*, second member of pair).

iterator **insert**(*const T& item*);
  Insert *item* into the multiset, and return an iterator pointing at the new element.
    Postcondition: The element *item* is added to the multiset.

int **erase**(*const T& item*);
  Erase all occurrences of *item* from the multiset, and return the number of
  items erased.
    Postcondition: The size of the multiset is reduced by the number of oc-
                    curences of *item* in the multiset.

Application: Computer Software Products

Software applications often include both the name of the vendor and the name of
the product in their title. For instance, the C++ compiler used by the authors is Microsoft Visual C++. To illustrate the use of a multiset container, we develop a product class containing the strings *company* and *name* as private data members. The
class has access functions getCompany() and getName() to access the data members, as well as overloaded versions of the < and == operators. The operators compare product objects based on the company's attribute.

CLASS product	Declaration	"d_prod.h"

```
class product
{
   public:
      product(const string& cmpny = "", const string& nm = "" );

      string getCompany() const;
         // access the value of the product company

      string getName() const;
         // access the value of the product name

      friend bool operator< (const product& lhs, const product& rhs);
         // determine order of objects based on company

      friend bool operator== (const product& lhs, const product& rhs);
         // check for objects with the same company
```

```
    private:
        string company;
        string name;
};
```

This application declares a multiset<*product*> object *softwareSet* that contains elements from an array of products. Because the array includes objects with the same vendor, but different product names, it initializes the multiset with duplicate elements. The application illustrates the use of the count() and equal_range() functions.

PROGRAM 11-6 MULTISET OF COMPUTER SOFTWARE PRODUCTS

Let us look at a program that features a multiset. An array specifies a variety of software products from Microsoft, Adobe, Inprise, and Ramsoft. The array initializes the multiset container *softwareSet*. A prompt asks the user to input a vendor's name. The program uses the name with count() to determine the number of products in the set associated with the vendor. The most interesting part of the program is a loop that outputs the entire set of products in ascending order of vendor name. The format of the output is

```
Vendor: company
        Products: name₁   name₂   . . .
```

The loop uses an iterator to scan the multiset. For each vendor, a call to equal_range() defines the iterator range of products for the given vendor. An inner loop scans the range and outputs the product names. When the iterator reaches the end of the range, we have an element with a new vendor and a new sublist of products.

```
// File: prg11_6.cpp
// the program initializes the multiset softwareSet with software
// product entries. the multiset has duplicates, since some of the
// products have the same vendor. the program outputs the number of
// software products and prompts for a vendor. after outputting the
// number of products for the vendor, the program outputs the set
// of products in the format
//      Vendor: company
//            Products: name₁   name₂   . . .

#include <iostream>
#include <string>
#include <set>

#include "d_prod.h"

using namespace std;

int main()
{
    product prodArr[] =
        {product("Microsoft", "Word"), product("Inprise", "C++ Builder"),
         product("Microsoft", "Visual C++"), product("Ramsoft', "MAS"),
```

```
        product("Inprise", "J Builder"), product("Adobe", "Photoshop"),
        product("Microsoft", "Excel"), product("Adobe", "Illustrator")};
int prodArrSize = sizeof(prodArr)/sizeof(product);
// softwareSet is a multiset of product objects
multiset<product> softwareSet(prodArr, prodArr+prodArrSize);

// an iterator and iterator pair for the output
multiset<product>::iterator iter;
pair<multiset<product>::iterator, multiset<product>::iterator> p;

// vendor name used for input
string vendorName;

cout << "Number of software products = " << softwareSet.size()
     << endl << endl;

// prompt for the name of a vendor
cout << "Enter a vendor name:     ";
cin >> vendorName;
cout << endl;
cout << "There are " << softwareSet.count(product(vendorName, ""))
     << " " << vendorName << " products in the set" << endl;

// loop outputs the products in ascending order of vendor (company)
iter = softwareSet.begin();
while (iter != softwareSet.end())
{
    // determine the range of products with company
    p = softwareSet.equal_range(*iter);
    cout << "Vendor: " << (*iter).getCompany() << endl
         << "        Products: ";
    // output each product for the company
    while (iter != p.second)
    {
        cout << (*iter).getName() << "   ";
        iter++;
    }
    cout << endl;
}

    return 0;
}
```

```
Run:

Number of software products = 8

Enter a vendor name: Microsoft

There are 3 Microsoft products in the set
```

```
Vendor: Adobe
   Products: Photoshop  Illustrator
Vendor: Inprise
   Products: C++ Builder  J Builder
Vendor: Microsoft
   Products: Visual C++  Word  Excel
Vendor: Ramsoft
   Products: MAS
```

11-5   IMPLEMENTING SETS AND MAPS

Following our usual approach, we develop the miniSet and the miniMap classes modeled on the corresponding STL containers. The goal is to create classes that have most of the features of the STL class, with an accompanying implementation that is simpler to read and understand. For our classes, we use composition with an stree class as the underlying storage structure.

The design of the stree class interface anticipated the fact that it would be used to implement the miniSet class. This fact makes the implementation of the miniSet class almost trivial. Just declare an stree object *t* as a private data member and implement the miniSet functions by calling the corresponding stree functions for object *t*.

The problem of defining constant and nonconstant iterators for the miniSet class reduces to using the corresponding iterators in the stree class. Typedef statements provide the identification of the iterators in the two classes. The upcoming code is a partial listing of the miniSet class that illustrates our design approach. We provide implementations for the find() and insert() functions, along with one version of erase() that uses an iterator argument.

CLASS miniSet	Declaration	"d_set.h"

```
// implements a set which does not contain duplicate data values
template <typename T>
class miniSet
{
   public:

      // miniSet iterators are simply stree iterators
      typedef typename stree<T>::iterator iterator;
      typedef typename stree<T>::const_iterator const_iterator;

      . . .

   private:
      // set implemented using a binary search tree
      stree<T> t;
};
```

Implementing miniSet Operations

The find() function in the miniSet class takes an item of type T and returns the iterator pointing at the element *item* in the set, or end() if *item* is not in the set. The corresponding function in the stree class returns an stree iterator pointing at *item* in the binary search tree t, or the stree iterator end() if no match occurs. The typedef statement in the class declaration equates an stree iterator with a miniSet iterator.

find():

```
template <typename T>
miniSet<T>::iterator miniSet<T>::find (const T& item)
{
    // return stree iterator which is a miniSet iterator
    return t.find(item);
}
```

The insert() function takes an item of type T and returns an iterator-bool pair, where the iterator points to the element *item* in the miniSet and the Boolean value indicates whether insert() adds a new element to the set (*true*) or finds a duplicate (*false*). The insert() operation in a binary search tree has the desired return value. Implement the miniSet function by calling insert() with stree object t.

insert():

```
template <typename T>
pair<iterator, bool> miniSet<T>::insert(const T& item)
{
    // insert item into the binary search tree and return
    // the iterator-bool pair
    return t.insert(item);
}
```

One version of the erase() function in the miniSet class takes an iterator and removes the corresponding element. As with find() and insert(), the stree class has an identical operation. Unlike the STL classes, our "mini" classes use exception handling when a precondition fails. If the set is empty, the function throws the underflowError exception. When the iterator is invalid, it throws the referenceError exception. We could let the erase() function in the stree class throw the exception, but this would provide debugging information about the underlying search tree. We throw the exception, in the miniSet implementation with a message that explicitly references the error in the miniSet erase() operation.

erase():

```
template <typename T>
void miniSet<T>::erase(iterator pos)
{
    if (t.size() == 0)
        throw
            underflowError("miniSet erase(): set is empty");
```

```
        if (pos == end())
            throw
                referenceError("miniSet erase(): invalid iterator");

        // erase the item in the tree pointed to by pos
        t.erase(pos);
}
```

The miniMap Class

A map container is essentially a set of pairs consisting of key and value components. This fact is essential to your understanding of how we can use an stree object as an underlying storage structure in the implementation of the miniMap class. A map is a collection of key–value pairs with separate template types for the two components. The first task is to describe a pair object. This is done by using the miniPair class with two template arguments that include two public data members, *first* and *second*. STL calls this class pair, and it is the type we used for the STL map containers and the iterator–bool return type for the insert() functions in the set and map classes. The miniPair class has a default constructor that initializes the data members with the default values for the two template types. A second constructor assigns arguments to the data members. We will use miniPair objects for insert() and find() operations in the stree class, so the miniPair class must overload the < and == operators. The data member *first*, which is the key, is the basis for the comparison of two miniPair operands. We develop our own key–value pair class, because STL overloads < and == for pair operands. The comparisons use both the key and the value components, and we must compare only key attributes. The following is a declaration of the miniPair class.

CLASS miniPair	Declaration	"d_pair.h"

```
// substitute for the STL pair class. used by the miniMap class
template<typename T1, typename T2>
class miniPair
{
   public:
      T1 first;
      T2 second;
         // public data members

      miniPair();
         // default constructor

      miniPair(const T1& v1, const T2& v2);
         // constructor that initializes first and second

      friend bool operator< (const miniPair<T1,T2>& lhs,
                             const miniPair<T1,T2>& rhs);
         // overload < by comparing the first data members
```

```
friend bool operator== (const miniPair<T1,T2>& lhs,
                        const miniPair<T1,T2>& rhs);
   // overload == by comparing the first data members};

}
```

The implementation design for the miniMap class involves using composition, with a private stree object *t* serving as the underlying storage structure. Recall that the stree class has a single template argument. In order to have the object *t* store key–value pairs, we use miniPair as the template type for the stree object:

```
// declaration of the private stree object t
stree<miniPair<const Key,T> > t;
```

The object *t* is a search tree of pairs. The fact that the key type is constant ensures that no operation can update the key component of the key–value pair. Because the underlying storage structure is a search tree, no operation can destroy the tree structure. However, the value type *T* is not constant, so the programmer can modify the value component of a map entry.

Let us stop for a moment to appreciate the task at hand. Implementing a mini-Map class will involve calling the corresponding search tree operation for object *t*. When the miniMap operation includes only the key as an argument, we will need to create a miniPair argument for the search tree, because all that *t* knows is mini-Pair objects. For instance, the miniMap operation find() uses only the key as an argument. To create a miniPair object, use the default value for the data member *second*, and call the search tree find() with this object.

```
// pass a miniPair to stree find() that contains key as its
// first member and T() as its second
return t.find(miniPair<const Key,T>(key, T()));
```

Our miniSet implementation gives us a clue to the implementation of constant and nonconstant iterators in the miniMap class. We will use the iterators in the stree class. Like the miniSet class, a series of typedef statements equates the two iterator types:

```
typedef stree<miniPair<const Key,T> >::iterator iterator;

typedef stree<miniPair<const Key,T> >::const_iterator
        const_iterator;
```

By including the expression "const Key" in the typedef statement, we ensure that a miniMap iterator cannot update the key component and potentially destroy the underlying search tree *t*. Like STL, we simplify notation for the datatype in the miniMap class by equating the expression miniPair<*const Key*>,<*T*> with the term *value_type*.

```
typedef miniPair < const Key, T> value_type;
```

With this simplified notation, the function prototype for find() becomes

```
return t.find(value_type(key, T()));
```

The upcoming code is a partial declaration of the miniMap class. We include only the features that illustrate our implementation design. We demonstrate how these features apply by implementing the functions erase() and begin() in the mini-Map class. We have not discussed the overloaded index operator, which is so critical to the miniMap class. There is obviously no counterpart in the stree class, and so we treat the topic in its own section.

CLASS miniMap	Declaration	"d_map.h"

```
// implements a map containing key/value pairs.
// a map does not contain multiple copies of the same item.
// types T and Key must have a default constructor
template <typename Key, typename T>
class miniMap
{
   public:

        // miniMap iterators are simply stree iterators. an iterator cannot
        // change the key in a tree node, since the key attribute
        // of a miniPair object in the tree is const
        typedef typename stree<miniPair<const Key,T> >::iterator iterator;
        typedef typename stree<miniPair<const Key,T> >::const_iterator
                    const_iterator;

        // for convenience
        typedef miniPair<const Key, T> value_type;


        . . .

   private:
        // miniMap implemented using an stree of key-value pairs
        stree<miniPair<const Key,T> > t;
};
```

Implementing the miniMap Class

The implementation of the miniMap erase() function illustrates the conversion of a key argument to a miniPair object. Take the key argument, and create the corresponding miniPair object with the default value for the second component. The new miniPair object becomes the argument when the stree erase() function is called. The return value is 0 or 1, depending on whether the key corresponds to an entry in the map.

erase():
```
template <typename Key, typename T>
int miniMap<Key,T>::erase(const Key& key)
{
```

```
      // pass a miniPair to stree erase() that contains key as its
      // first member and T() as its second
      return t.erase(value_type(key, T()));
}
```

The miniMap function begin() returns an iterator pointing to the first element in the map. By equating the miniMap iterators with the stree iterators, we can use the search tree begin() to locate the first element in the tree list:

begin():
```
template <typename Key, typename T>
miniMap<Key,T>::iterator miniMap<Key,T>::begin()
{
    return t.begin();
}
```

The miniMap Index Operator

The map index operator takes a key as its argument and returns a reference to the value component of the corresponding key–value pair. What makes the operation so powerful is the fact that it adds a new entry in the map in case a pair matching the key does not yet exist. In other words, the index operator combines an insert operation with access to the value. These two features are actually combined in the stree insert() function. We use this fact to design implementation of the index operator.

The miniMap index operator appears in an expression of the form "*mapObj*[*key*]." The problem is to locate the entry value_type(*key, value*) in the map if it exists, or to create the entry value_type(*key, T()*) if there is no element matching the key. Start by creating the miniPair object *tmp* = value_type(*key, T()*). A call to the stree insert() function with argument *tmp* returns an iterator–bool pair whose iterator component *first* points at the newly added element or at an existing element that matches the key. To complete the implementation, use the iterator to return *second*, the value component of the pair.

Index Operator []:
```
template <typename Key, typename T>
T& miniMap<Key,T>::operator[] (const Key& key)
{
    // build a miniPair object consisting of key
    // and the default value T()
    value_type tmp(key, T());
    // will point to a pair in the map
    iterator iter;

    // try to insert tmp into the map. the iterator
    // component of the pair returned by t.insert()
    // points at either the newly created key/value
    // pair or a pair already in the map. return a
    // reference to the value in the pair
```

```
    iter = t.insert(tmp).first;

    return (*iter).second;
}
```

CHAPTER SUMMARY

- The set and map associative containers store and retrieve data by value rather than by position. A set is a collection of keys, where each key is unique. A map is a collection of key–value pairs that associate a key with a value. In a map, there is only one value associated with a key. The multiset and multimap containers allow multiple occurrences of a key. The associative containers implement fast insertion and retrieval of data by key.

- The STL set class uses one template argument to refer to the key type. The STL map class requires two template arguments, one for the key type and the other for the value. A binary search tree is an associative structure and is ideal for the implementation of sets and maps. Because a search-tree iterator traverses the tree in order, sets and maps implemented with a tree are said to be *ordered*. An ordinary binary search tree could be degenerate and have search running times that are linear $(O(n))$. By balancing the tree, one can guarantee that the worst-case time for a search is $O(\log_2 n)$.

- The API for the set is almost identical to that of the binary search tree class discussed in Chapter 10. Section 11-2 illustrates the set class by developing a simple spelling checker and by implenting the algorithm for finding prime numbers known as the Sieve of Eratosthenes. The section also discusses the set operations *union*, *intersection*, and *difference* and implements the algorithm for set intersection. The algorithm exploits the fact that set iterators traverse a set in order.

- Section 11-3 develops the map interface and operations and includes a detailed study of the map index operator. A map is often called an, *associative array*, because applying the index operator with the key as its argument returns the value associated with the key. The programmer rarely uses the insert() operation, because the index operator also serves the purpose of insert(). If no key–value pair with the specified key is in the map, it inserts one with the default value as the second component and returns a reference to this value. The programmer can build a map by using just the index operator. Section 11-3 concludes by developing a word concordance that uses a map.

- In a multiset, a key can occur more than once. In Section 11-4, we discuss the STL multiset class, which allows duplicate keys. Its interface is similar to that for a set, except for the functions count() and equal_range(), which deal with duplicates. Using equal_range() allows access to each duplicate in succession.

- Section 11-5 discusses the implementation of sets and maps. Implementing a set class is very simple. Include a binary search tree object by composition, and implement a set operation by calling the corresponding operation for the tree. The implementation of a map class is a little more involved. We implement a map by using a binary search tree of key–value pairs, where the key is constant. Having a constant key prohibits the alteration of a key that invalidates the structure of the tree. When implementing operations that have only a key argument, we construct a key–value pair with the default value and look this pair up in the map. The most interesting problem is implementing the map index operator. Create a pair with the index as the key and the default value as the second component. Call the insert() function of the underlying tree with the pair as an argument. This call returns an iterator–bool pair whose iterator component *first* points at the newly added element or at an existing element that matches the key. Use the iterator to return the value component of the pair, *second*.

CLASSES AND LIBRARIES IN THE CHAPTER

Name	Header File
map	<map>
miniMap	d_map.h
miniPair	d_pair.h
miniSet	d_set.h
multiset	<set>
product	d_prod.h
set operators	d_setops.h
set	<set>
time24	d_time24.h
writeContainer()	d_util.h

REVIEW EXERCISES

1. What additional operations must the rectangle class have if a programmer wishes to declare a set of rectangle elements?

2. The declaration shown next creates a set of characters with initial values created by the address range of an array. What is the output from the *cout* statement?

```
char charArr[] = "template";
int arrSize = sizeof(charArr)/sizeof(char) - 1;
set<char> charSet(charArr, charArr+arrSize);
cout << charSet.size();
```

3. Set A is a *subset* of set B if each element in A is an element in B. The subset relation can also be defined in terms of set intersection and set equality:

A is a subset of B if and only if A intersected with B is the set A.

Use this definition to implement the function that evaluates the subset relation $A <= B$.

```
// determine whether lhs is a subset of rhs
template <typename T>
bool subset(const set<T>& lhs, const set<T>& rhs);
```

4. Assume that insertItem() is a member function in the set class. The function has the same action as insert(), but returns only an iterator, rather than an iterator–bool pair. Hence, the programmer has no way to know whether the insert actually added a new element. Implement insertIterm().

```
template <typename T>
iterator set<T>::insertItem(const T& item);
```

5. Implement the function contains() as a member function in the set class. The function takes item of type *T* as an argument and returns *true* if the item is in the set and *false* otherwise.

```
template <typename T>
bool contains(const T& item);
```

6. What is the primary difference between a set container and a map container?

7. A program uses a map container to store pairs that consist of the name of a U.S. state and the name of the capital of the state.

(a) Declare the map *stateCapMap* for use in a program.

(b) Use a typedef to equate the type *entry* with the *value_type* of elements in the map.

(c) Use the result of part (b) to declare the array *stateCapArr* with four initial values:

(Texas, Austin), (Wisconsin, Madison), (Oregon, Salem), (New York, Albany)

Use the array to initialize the map *stateCapMap* in the declaration statement.

(d) Use the index operator to add the entry (Nevada, Carson City) to stateCapMap. Replicate the action of the index operator by using the map insert() operation.

(e) Assume that the state of Oregon decides to shift its capital from Salem to Portland. Use the index operator to carry out the update. Perform the update by using the find() function, which returns an iterator pointing to the (Oregon, Salem) pair.

8. Implement the function update() as a member function in the map class. The function takes a *value_type*(*key, newItem*) argument and updates the value component of the entry corresponding to the key only if the entry is already in the map.

```
template <typename Key, typename T>
void update(const map<Key,T>::value_type& kvpair);
```

9. The map<*string, list<string>* >object *mObj* contains an entry for which the key component is the name of a U.S. state and the value component is a list of cities in the state. Assume that program inputs the name of a state and the name of a city and wishes to add the information to *mObj*. Select the most appropriate instruction:

(a) *mObj.insert*(*state, city*);   **(b)** *mObj*[*state*] = city;

(c) *mObj.insert*(*state*)*.insert*(*city*);   **(d)** *mObj*[*state*]*.push_back*(*city*);

10. What is the action of function f()?

```
map<T, vector<T> > f(const multiset<T>& ms)
{
   map<T, vector<T> > m;
   pair(multiset<T>::iterator, multiset<T>::iterator> p;
   multiset<T>::iterator iter = ms.begin();

   while (iter != ms.end())
   {
     p = ms.equal_range(*iter);
     while (iter != p.second)
```

```
        {
            m[*iter].push_back(*iter);
            iter++;
        }
    }
    return m;
}
```

11. Distinguish between the index operation and the insert operation for a map:

```
    map<int, int> m;

    m[4] = 6;      // index operation
    m.insert(map<int, int>::value_type(4,6));
```

Answers to Review Exercises

1. A programmer must overload the < and == operators for rectangles, because set data is stored in a search tree.

2. The size is 6, because a set rejects duplicate values.

3.
```
template <typename T>
bool subset(const set<T>& lhs, const set<T>& rhs);
{  // use the set operation * for intersection
    return lhs * rhs == lhs;
}
```

4.
```
template <typename T>
iterator insertItem(const T& item)
{
    pair<set<T>::iterator, bool> p;
    p = insert(item);}  // call insert
    // return iterator (first) component of the pair
    return p.first;
}
```

5.
```
template <typename T>
bool contains(const T& item)
{
    // check the return iterator for find() to see if it
    // is the iterator value end() (not in the set)
    if (find(item) == end())
        return false;
    else
        return true;
}
```

6. A set stores elements that are treated as single value of type T. A map stores elements as key–value pairs. An element is partitioned into two separate components that may have different data types. The comparison operators < and == compare only the key component of an element.

7. **(a)** `map <string, string> stateCapMap;`
   (b) `typedef map <string, string> ::value_type  entry;`

(c)
```
entry stateCapArr[] = {
        entry("Texas", "Austin"), entry("Wisconsin", "Madison"),
        entry("Oregon", "Salem"), entry("New York", "Albany")};

   map<string, string> stateCapMap(stateCapArr, stateCapArr+4);
```

(d)
```
stateCapMap["Nevada"] =  "Carson City";
stateCapMap.insert(entry("Nevada", "Carson City"));
```

(e)
```
stateCapMap["Oregon"] = "Portland";

   map<string, string>::iterator mIter;
   mIter = find("Oregon");
   (*mItper).second =  "Portland";
```

8.
```
template <typename Key, typename T>
void update(const map<Key,T>::value_type& kvpair)
{
   map<Key, T>::iterator mIter;
   mIter = find(kvpair);
   if (mIter.first != end())
      (*mIter).second = kvpair.second;
}
```

9. If the state is not in the map, we need to create an entry with the state and city as the key–value pair. If the state is in the map, the city must merely be added onto the end of the list. This is statement (d):

```
mObj[state].push_back(city);
```

10. The function converts a multiset into a map by declaring a map element to have a key of type *T* and a vector of type *T* elements. Duplicate elements (i.e., the same key) in the multiset are written into a map element with the corresponding key, but with the duplicates stored in the vector.

11. The index operation will add the key–value pair (4, 6) to the map if no value with *key* = 4 exists. Otherwise, the operation updates the value component to 6. The insert operation executes only if no element with *key* = 4 exists. In this case, it adds the key–value pair (4, 6) to the map. Otherwise, the operation does not execute, and the value component for the element with *key* = 4 is unchanged.

WRITTEN EXERCISES

12. Declare a set *s* that that contains the characters from string *job*. Hint: Use the string member function c_str() to obtain the starting address of the characters in the string.

```
string job = "bowler";
```

13. Assume that *aList* is a list of type *T*. Implement the function removeDuplicates() by declaring a set of type T and copying the elements from *aList* into the set. Copy the elements from the set back to the list so that the nonduplicate elements appear in descending order.

```
template <typename T>
void removeDuplicates(list<T>& aList);
```

14. Set A is a subset of set B provided that each element of A is also an element of B. Implement the set relation as a function subset() that takes sets *lhs* and *rhs* as arguments and returns *true* if *lhs* is a subset of *rhs*.In the review exercises, the implementation uses set operations. Your implementation should use iterators *lhsIter* and *rhsIter* to scan the two ordered sets.

```
template <typename T>
bool subset(const set<T>& lhs, const set<T>& rhs);
```

15. The symmetric difference of set A and set B is defined as the set of all elements *x* that are contained in either A or B, but not in both.Using set operations, implement the function symDifference(), which takes *setA* and *setB* as arguments and returns the symmetric difference.

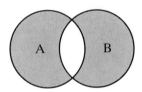

```
template <typename T>
set<T> symDifference(const set<T>& setA, const set<T>& setB);
```

16. The accompanying Venn diagrams illustrate the different set components that occur when three sets are combined. In each part (a)–(c), use the set operators +, *, and − to create an expression in terms of A, B, and C that describes the shaded region.

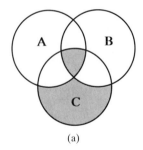

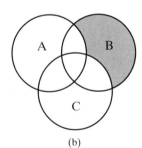

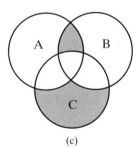

(a)   (b)   (c)

17. The following is part of a main program that includes the declaration of the integer array *intArr*:

```
int intArr[] = {15, 7, 32, 12};
map<int, vector<int> > m;
int i, j, value;
for(i = 0; i < 4; i++)
{
```

```
        value = intArr[i];
        j = 2;
        while(value > 1)
           if (value % j == 0)
           {
              m[intArr[i]].push_back(j);
              value /= j;
           }
           else
              j++;
   }
```

(a) Describe the action of each step in the *for* loop.

(b) List each entry in the map by giving first the key component and then the contents of the corresponding vector component.

18. Use the array *strList* of strings along with a `map<string,int>` object *mLength* to write code segments that perform designated tasks:

```
string strList[] = {"store", "map", "array", "set",
                                  "multimap", "string"};
int strListSize = sizeof(strList)/sizeof(string);
map<string,int> mLength;
int i;
```

(a) Write a loop that enters each string from the array into the map as the key–value pair (*string, string length*).

(b) Declare an iterator that locates elements in the map *mLength*. Use the iterator to output all strings that have a length of 5.

19. Assume that *setA* and *setB* are set<*char*> objects consisting of the distinct letters found in strings *strA* and *strB*, respectively. This exercise uses expressions that combine set operations. For instance, the expression

```
setC = setA - setA * setB
```

assigns to setC all of the letters that are in *strA*, but not in *strB*.

(a) Assign to *setC* all of the characters in the two strings that are not found in both strings.

(b) Declare a set called *setVowels* that contains the letters *a, e, i, o*, and *u*. Assign to *setD* all vowels that are not found in *strA*.

(c) Assign to setE all vowels that that are in either strA or strB.

(d) Assign to *setF* the consonants that are in the strings.

20. Implement the function randMap(), which takes an integer *n* as its argument and returns a map<*int, int*> container. After declaring a local map object, the function uses the random-number generator to produce *n* integers in the range 0–9. For each random integer *k*, create or update an entry in the map, where *k* is the key and the value maintains a frequency count on the number of times *k* is generated. The local map is the return value.

```
map<int,int> randMap(int n);
```

21. Assume that *v* is a vector of type *T*. Implement the function multisetSort() by declaring a multiset of type *T* and copying the elements from *v* into the multiset. To create a sorted sequence in the vector, copy the elements from the multiset back to the vector.

```
template <typename T>
void multisetSort(vector<T>& v);
```

22. (a) Let *ms* be a multiset of type *T*. Write a code segment that outputs the distinct elements of *ms* along with their count in the form

> element1 (<count1>) element2 (<count2>) element3 (<count3>) ...
> element4 (<count4>)

For example: if *ms* contains the elements from the array *arr* = { 2, 1, 3, 3, 1, 3, 5, 2, 3, 6}, the output is

> 1(2)   2(2)   3(4)   5(1| 6(1)

(b) Modify the output from part (a) so that the distinct elements are output one per line, with duplicates repeated on the line. Using array *arr* as the example.

> 1   1
> 2   2
> 3   3   3   3
> 5
> 6

23. Describe the action of function f().

```
template <typename T>
T f(const multiset<T>& ms, const T& item)
{
    multiset<T>::const_iterator iter;
    pair<multiset<T>::const_iterator, multiset<T>::const_iterator> p;
    T total = T();

    p = ms.equal_range(item);
    for (iter= p.first; iter!= p.second; iter++)
        total += *iter;

    return total;
}
```

PROGRAMMING EXERCISES

24. Write a program that declares three set objects *setA*, *setB*, and *setC* that store integer values. Using a loop, assign to *setA* the 25 integers from 0 to 24, and assign to *setB* 25 random integers in the range from 0 to 24. Output the size of *setB*. Using set operations, assign to *setC* the integers from 0 to 24 that were not randomly generated and assigned to *setB*. Output this set.

25. Write a program that declares an integer list *aList* with initial values copied from the array *arr*[] = {6, 7, 7, 2, 9, 7, 6, 6} Use the removeDuplicates() function in Written Exercise 11-13 to order the list. Output the elements of *aList* using writeList().

26. Use the strings *strA*, *strB*, and *strC* to initialize sets of characters *setA*, *setB*, and *setC* respectively.

> string *strA* = "hogtied," *strB* = "dog," *strC* = "horn";

(a) Write a program that uses the overloaded operator $<=$ in Review Exercise 11-3 to display messages that indicate whether *setB* is a subset of *setA* and whether *setC* is a subset of *setA*.

(b) Write a program that uses the function subset() from Written Exercise 11-14 to display messages that indicate whether *setB* is a subset of *setA* and whether *setC* is a subset of *setA*.

(c) Write a program that uses the function symDifference() in Written Exercise 11-15 to display the characters that are not common to *setA* and *setB* and the characters not common to *setA* and *setC*

Use the class shown next for Programming Exercise 11-27. The implementation for the class is in the "include" directory of the software distribution.

CLASS stateCity	**Declaration**	**"d_state.h"**

```
// object stores the state name and city in the state
class stateCity
{
   public:
      stateCity (const string& name = "", const string& city = "");

      friend ostream& operator<< (ostream& ostr, const stateCity& state);
         // output the state and city name in the format
         //    cityName, stateName

      friend bool operator< (const stateCity& a, const stateCity& b);
      friend bool operator== (const stateCity& a, const stateCity& b);
         // operators < and == must be defined to use with set object.
         // operators use only the stateName as the key

   private:
      string stateName, cityName;
};
```

27. **(a)** Write a program that declares a set object *s* having elements of type *stateCity* with the following as its initial values:

   ("Arizona", "Phoenix")   ("Illinois", "Chicago")   ("California", "Sacramento")

   Input the name of a state, and use the find() function to determine whether the state is in the set. If the object is present, use the operator to output the state and city; if it is not present, output a message to that effect.

(b) Using part (a) as a model, write a program that declares a multiset object *ms* with elements of type stateCity. Insert the following elements into the multiset:

   ("Arizona" ,"Phoenix"), ("Illinois" ,"Chicago"), ("Illinois", "Gary"),
   ("Nevada", "Reno") ("Illinois", "Evanston"), ("California", "Sacramento")

   Have the user enter a state name (string), and output all elements of *ms* that match the name.

28. Rather than using objects of type *stateCity*, implement Programming Exercise 11-27(a) by using a map with the state name (string) as the key and the city name (string) as the data value.

29. Write a program that uses the function randMap() in Written Exercise 11-20 to output the frequency of each integer in the range from 0 to 9 that is produced by calling the random-number generator *n* times. Prompt the user to input the value *n*.

30. Write a program that declares an integer vector *v* with initial values copied from the array arr[] = {6, 2, 8, 3, 8, 4, 3}. Use the multisetSort() function in Written Exercise 11-21 to order the vector. Output the elements of v by using writeContainer().

PROGRAMMING PROJECTS

31. (a) The class miniMultiSet uses the list class as the implementation structure for a multiset. Implement the class in the header file "mset_l.h". The list does not have to be ordered, but make sure that duplicate values occur in consecutive list elements.

```
template <typename T>
class miniMultiSet
{
    public:

        typedef typename list<T>::iterator iterator;
        typedef typename list<T>::const_iterator const_iterator;
            // miniMultiSet iterators are simply list iterators

        miniMultiSet();
            // default constructor

        miniMultiSet(T *first, T *last);
            // build a multiset whose data are determined by
            // the pointer range [first, last)

        bool empty() const;
            // is the multiset empty?

        int size() const;
            // return the number of elements in the multiset

        int count (const T& item) const;
            // return the number of duplicate occurrences of item
            // in the multiset

        iterator find(const T& item);
            // search for item in the multiset and return an iterator
            // pointing at the first occurrence matching item or end()
            // if it is not found
        const_iterator find(const T& item) const;
            // constant version

        pair<iterator, iterator> equal_range(const T& item);
            // return a pair of iterators such that all occurrences
```

```
            // of item are in the iterator range
            // [first member of pair, second member of pair)
    pair<const_iterator, const_iterator>
            equal_range(const T& item) const;
            // constant version
    iterator insert(const T& item);
            // insert item into the multiset and return an
            // iterator pointing at the new element.
            // Postcondition: the element item is added to the multiset

    int erase(const T& item);
            // erase all occurrences of item from the multiset
            // and return the number of items erased.
            // Postcondition: the size of the multiset is reduced
            // by the number of occurrences of item in the multiset

    void erase(iterator pos);
            // erase the item pointed to by pos.
            // Preconditions: the multiset is not empty and pos points
            // to an item in the multiset. if the multiset is empty,
            // the function throws the underflowError exception. if the
            // iterator is invalid, the function throws the
            // referenceError exception.
            // Postcondition: the multiset size decreases by 1

    void erase(iterator first, iterator last);
            // erase the elements in the range [first, last)
            // Precondition: the multiset is not empty. if the
            // multiset is empty, the function throws the
            // underflowError exception.
            // Postcondition: the multiset size decreases by the number
            // elements in the range

            //iterator begin();
            // return an iterator pointing at the first member
            // in the multiset
    const_iterator begin() const;
            // constant version of begin()

    iterator end();
            // return an iterator pointing just past the last
            // member in the multiset
    const_iterator end() const;
            // constant version of end()

private:
    list>T> multisetList;
            // multiset implemented using a list
    int distance(iterator first, iterator last);
            // return the number of items in the range [first, last)
```

```
        int distance(const_iterator first, const_iterator last) const;
           // constant version
   };
```

(b) Test the class by running Program 11-6.

32. The declaration for the miniMultiSet class is listed in Programming Project 11-31. Instead of implementing the class using a list, use the class *mstree* developed in Programming Project 10-44. Place the class in the header file "mset_t.h", and test it by running Program 11-6.

◆

CHAPTER 12

Advanced Associative Structures

OBJECTIVES

- To understand that hashing is an alternative to the use of binary search trees for locating data by value.
- To understand that the hash function converts a value of type T into an integer that, after division by the table size, produces a table index.
- To understand that hashing models its approach on direct access, using an index, but the table size is smaller and collisions can occur.
- To become familiar with the C++ concept of a function object.
- To study the design of hash functions for handling integer, real, and string data.
- To understand the two most commonly used algorithms for collision resolution, open probe addressing, and chaining with separate lists.
- To study the construction of a class that implements hashing using chaining.
- To compare and contrast the searching methods we have studied: sequential search, binary search, binary-tree search, and hashing.
- To see that the average-case running time for searching a hash table constructed with chaining is O(1).
- To see an implementation of unordered sets using a hash table.
- To study 2–3–4 trees as a model for a perfectly balanced tree with $O(\log_2 n)$ worst-case search running time.
- To understand that the balanced trees known as red–black trees come directly from the concept of a 2–3–4 tree.
- To study insertion into red–black trees by color changes and rotations and to understand that the motivation for these operations comes directly from insertion into 2–3–4 trees.
- To see that the worst-case running time for insertion, retrieval, and deletion in a red–black tree is $O(\log_2 n)$.
- To study the class rbtree, which implements a red–black tree container.

OUTLINE

The associative containers, sets, multisets, maps, and multimaps in Chapter 11 implement their operations by using a *binary* search tree. The container iterators access the binary search tree via an inorder implementation and thus access the data in sorted order. As a result, the structures are *ordered associative containers*. In this chapter, we develop a new type of associative container, called a *hash table*, that distributes the elements in clusters defined by their value. An associated function, called a *hash function*, maps a data item into a cluster, and the hash table inserts, updates, or erases the value in the cluster. Like a binary search tree, a hash table provides an implementation of sets and maps. Unlike a search tree, however, a hash-table iterator does not access the data in sorted order. As a result, the implementation of set and map containers by using a hash table creates *unordered associative containers*. Sections 12-1 through 12-4 discuss the hash table concept and include a declaration and implementation of the container class hash. We show how hash can be used to implement an unordered class. STL does not have a hash table class and does not provide unordered associative containers. Future releases of STL are likely to add the class to the containers in the library.

In this book, we develop a variety of search algorithms for sequence and tree containers. Section 12-5 compares and contrasts the runtime efficiency of the sequential and binary search algorithms and evaluates the binary search tree and hash table as search structures. The main topic in the section is a running time analysis of the hash table search algorithm called *chaining with separate lists*, which features constant running time $O(1)$ for its average case.

Binary search trees are designed for efficient access to data. In an application, the actual efficiency depends on the shape of the tree. A degenerate or "almost

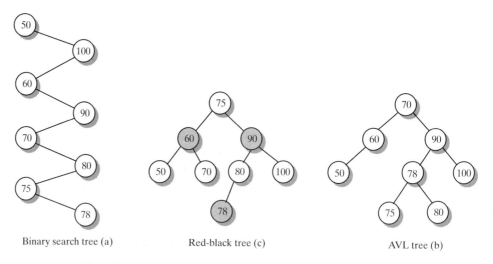

Binary search tree (a)   Red-black tree (c)   AVL tree (b)

Figure 12-1
Binary search tree, red–black tree, and AVL tree for insertion sequence 50, ~~100~~, 60, 90, 70, 80, 75, 78

degenerate" tree stores most of its n elements as a lone child of a parent. The shape resembles a linked list (Figure 12-1(a)) and has search efficiency O(n). A complete binary tree stores the n elements in a tree of minimum height by uniformly distributing the nodes in the left and right subtrees. Access to any element requires no more than int(log$_2$ n) + 1 comparisons, and the search efficiency is O(log$_2$ n). A complete tree represents an ideal shape for a search tree. The term "balanced" describes the distribution of nodes in the subtrees.

For many applications, we want assurance that our binary search tree does not result in a degenerate tree with worst-case access time. At the same time, we want the structure to have a measure of balance similar to that of a complete tree. Creating this type of search tree requires defining a special node structure and associated insert and delete algorithms. Section 12-6 introduces a balanced search tree called a *2–3–4 tree*. The description comes from the fact that each node has two, three, or four links (children). A 2–3–4 tree is perfectly balanced in the sense that no interior node has an empty link and all leaf nodes are at the same level in the tree. The concept of a red–black tree provides a representation of 2–3–4 trees. The trees feature nodes that have the color attribute BLACK or RED. We introduce red–black trees in Section 12-7 and describe their insert and delete operations. Figure 12-1(b) is a red–black tree of depth 3 that contains the same elements as does the degenerate search tree of depth 7. Modern data structures use red–black trees to implement ordered associative containers. In particular, STL provides a red–black tree class to support its implementation of sets and maps. The STL container class is a very sophisticated structure with multiple template arguments. In Section 12-8, we create a mini-rbtree class that implements a significant subset of the STL class. Our version gives you an opportunity to understand this important structure.

There are a number of tree-balancing algorithms that create binary search trees. One such structure is an *AVL tree*, named after the algorithm creators Adelson, Velskii, and Landis. For each node in an AVL tree, the difference in height between its two subtrees is at most 1 (Figure 12-1 (c)). Consult the WWW supplemental materials for a discussion of AVL trees.

Note

HASHING   12-1

In this book, we have developed array, vector, list, and binary search tree containers that allow retrieval of items. The efficiency of the search process depends on the container. For an unordered list stored in a sequence container, the sequential search has runtime efficiency $O(n)$. For an ordered list, the binary search provides $O(\log_2 n)$ search time. A binary search tree has an average search time of $O(\log_2 n)$. Ideally, we would like to design a container that can retrieve data in $O(1)$ time. In this way, access to an item is independent of the number of other items in the container. In Section 12-3, we will develop such a structure, called a *hash table*, that stores elements uniquely identified by their key. The main feature of this associative structure is a *hash function*, which takes a key as an argument and returns an entry point to the table. To gain some understanding of a hash function, you can view a hash table as an indexed sequence of items, such as an array or vector. A hash function is a locator function that takes a key and returns a table index. The memory access function for an array or vector is a model for the hash concept. In the following figure, the access function takes an index and computes the location of the item in the sequence.

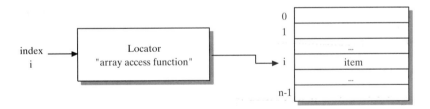

A hash function provides a different mode of access. Rather than starting with an index, a hash function begins with the key and evaluates an index that is used to locate the item in the table.

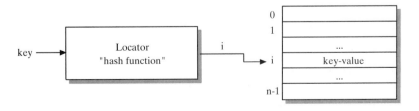

Using a Hash Function

The notion of a hash function and the table are related. Assume the table is an indexed list of n items in the range from 0 to $n - 1$. A hash function takes the key as an argument and returns an unsigned (positive) integer. In order that the integer can reference a table entry in the range from 0 to $n - 1$, we divide the hash value by n, using the remainder operator %. This creates the *hash table index.*

Hash Value: hf(key) = hashValue (unsigned integer)
HashTable index: hashValue % n

Let's begin with a simple hash function that assumes the key is an integer value. The function hf(intValue) = intValue is the identity function, which takes the key and returns intValue as hash value. The remainder after dividing intValue by n is the index into the table (hash table index).

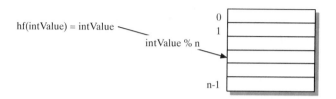

For instance, assume the table has $n = 7$ items, with indices 0, 1, ..., 6. The identity hash function hf() takes $key = 4$ and maps it to tableEntry[4]. For $key = 22$, the effect of the division step becomes apparent when we see how it maps the hash value into the available table indices.

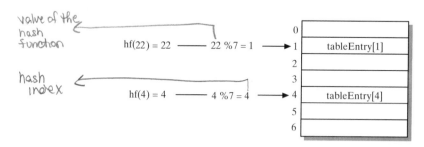

The need to divide the hash value by the table size can cause a problem. If two items have keys that differ by a multiple of seven, the hash process maps the items to the same table location. For instance, items with keys 22 and 36 map to index 1 in the table, and a *collision* occurs.

Your first response might be to treat a collision as an error in the hashing function. Putting such situations in context, however, you will see that avoiding collisions is often impossible or unrealistic. Consider a television manufacturer that uses a

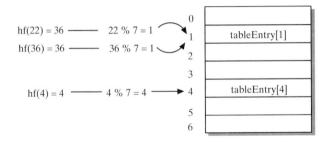

seven-digit serial number to distinguish between its different TV sets. If a data record uses the serial number as a key, the manufacturer's database would need to allocate 10 million records to handle all possible serial numbers. In most cases, a computer system does not have sufficient memory. Even if the resources are available, the strategy is inefficient, because the database needs to maintain only a few thousand records at any one time. A more realistic approach has the database use a table with $n = 10,000$ entries. The identity hash function creates a value that telescopes into the index range from 0 to 9999. For instance, the record corresponding to serial number 6482975 would be

$$hf(6482975) = 6482975 \rightarrow index\ i = 6482975\ \%\ 10000 = 2975$$

The effect of the hashing process is to map the serial number into the index specified by the low-order four digits of the number. If two records have serial numbers that end in the same four digits, hashing maps them into the same table location, and a collision results. Rather than viewing a collision as an error, treat it as a fact of life. The problem is to design the hashing process so it efficiently handles collisions. We will discuss this issue in the next two sections, when we design hash functions and the corresponding hash table.

DESIGNING HASH FUNCTIONS   12-2

The identity function for an integer key is an example of a hash function. We need other functions for different types of keys. Some general design principles guide the creation of all hash functions. Evaluation of a hash function should be efficient. The goal of the hashing process is efficient access to the corresponding table entry. A hash function's ability to compute the hash value efficiently is an important factor in attaining this goal. A hash function can produce collisions, particularly when the value is telescoped into the table range by using the % operator. Ideally, we would create a *perfect hash function* that produces no collisions. Short of this ideal situation, a hash function should produce uniformly distributed hash values. This spreads the hash table indices around the table, which helps minimize collisions.

Hash table applications involve data values that typically use strings or numeric values as the key. A design strategy must include hash functions that deal with integer, real, and string key types. The field of algorithms provides extensive research on this topic. We limit our discussion to a small set of hash functions that meet our design criteria.

We will use a hash function in the declaration of a hash container, so there must be a mechanism for associating the hash function with the container. C++ has syntax that allows a function to accept another function as an argument. This approach is clumsy, is not object oriented, and lacks efficiency. A better approach treats a function as an object defined by a class called a *function object type*. We define our hash functions as function object types and extend the template syntax to include the types as template arguments in the same way that we pass the data type as a template argument.

Function Objects

A function object is an object of a class that behaves like a function. Unlike ordinary functions, however, these objects can be created, stored, and destroyed like any other object and can have associated data members and operations. The definition of a function object begins with a template class that includes an overloaded version of the function call operator() as a member function. The argument list for operator() is the list of arguments required by the function.

Class declaration for a function object:

```
template<typename T>
class functionObject
{
   public:
      returnType operator() (arguments) const
      {
         // use arguments to create a returnValue
         . . .
         return returnValue;
      }
      . . .
};
```

For instance, consider the function object type *greaterThan*, which implements the > relational operator. The overloaded version of the "()" operator takes two arguments, x and y, of type T, compares their values, and returns a Boolean value indicating whether $x > y$:

```
template <typename T>
class greaterThan
{
   public:
      bool operator() (const T& x, const T& y) const
      {
         return x > y;
      }
};
```

The expression greaterThan<T> defines a type whose objects act like a function that compares two values of type T.

Example 12-1
_____

1. Like any template object declaration, we use the class name greaterThan and the template type to create a function object that evaluates the "greater than" condition. Function object *f* compares two integers:

```
greaterThan<int> f;
int a, b;

cin >> a >> b;

if (f(a,b))
    cout << a << " > " << b << endl;
else
    cout << a << " <= " << b << endl;
```

```
Input:   3   2
Output:  3 > 2
Input:   3   5
Output:  3 <= 5
```

The C++ compiler evaluates f(*a*, *b*) as f.operator()(a,b).

2. A programmer can use an anonymous object of type greaterThan<*T*> by adding the operator symbol () after the type, followed by the arguments enclosed within parentheses. The following is the meaning of terms in the declaration of an anonymous object that compares strings:

```
greaterThan<string> is the type.
greaterThan<int>() is an anonymous object of greaterThan<int> type.
greaterThan<int>()(x,y) evaluates x > y.
```

The anonymous object compares strings and indicates that "walk" is greater than "crawl":

```
string strA = "walk", strB = "crawl";

if (greaterThan<string>()(strA,strB))
    cout << strA << " > " << strB << endl;
```

```
Output: walk > crawl
```
_____

Illustrating Function Objects

Section 4-4 introduces the insertion sort for vectors. The implementation uses the < operator to sort the elements in ascending order. A separate implementation sorts the elements in descending order by replacing the < operator with the > operator. A more general approach uses a new version of insertionSort() with a function object to specify the type of ordering. The declaration of the function adds a function argument type, named *Compare*, to the template argument list and an object of type Compare to the function argument list:

```
template <typename T, typename Compare>
void insertionSort(vector<T>& v, Compare comp);
```

Like the template name *T*, there is no requirement to use the name "Compare" for the second argument. Following the lead of STL, we use *Compare*, because it is descriptive of the action of the function object.

The implementation of the insertionSort() simply applies the Compare object instead of using a specific C++ operator. This involves replacing the comparison expression "temp<$v[j-1]$" with the function object expression comp(temp, $v[j-1]$).

insertionSort():

```
template <typename T, typename Compare>
void insertionSort(vector<T>& v, Compare comp)
{
    int i, j, n = v.size();
    T temp;

    // place v[i] into the sublist
    //    v[0] ... v[i-1], 1 <= i <= n-1,
    // so it is in the correct position
    for (i = 1; i<n; i++)
    {
        // index j scans down list from v[i] looking for
        // correct position to locate target. assigns it to
        // v[j]
        j = i;
        temp = v[i];
        // locate insertion point by scanning downward as long
        // as comp(temp, v[j-1]) is true and we have not encountered
        // the beginning of the list
        while (j>0 && comp(temp, v[j-1]))
        {
            // shift elements up list to make room for insertion
            v[j] = v[j-1];
            j--;
        }
        // the location is found; insert temp
        v[j] = temp;
    }
}
```

PROGRAM 12-1 ILLUSTRATING FUNCTION OBJECTS

Let us look at a program that uses insertionSort() to order integers in both ascending and descending order. The function calls include the function object types *greaterThan* and *lessThan*. We include the implementation for lessThan that involves using the < operator to compare elements. Initially, a vector *v* has integer values from a predefined array *arr*. Calling insertionSort() with an lessThan<int> function object orders the elements in ascending order. The function writeVector() displays the ordered list. We repeat the process using the greaterThan<int> function object.

```cpp
// File: prg12_1.cpp
// the program demonstrates the use of function object types.
// it declares the function object types greaterThan and lessThan,
// whose objects evaluate the operators > and< respectively.
// a modified version of the insertion sort takes a second
// template argument that corresponds to a function object
// type. the function object is used to order elements. in
// this way, the function can sort a vector in either ascending
// or descending order. the program declares a vector and calls
// insertionSort() to order the values both ways. in each case,
// writeVector() outputs the sorted values

#include <iostream>
#include <vector>

#include "d_util.h"       // for writeVector()

using namespace std;

// objects of type greaterThan<T> evaluate x>y
// see Example 12-1 for its implementation

// objects of type lessThan<T> evaluate x<y
template<typename T>
class lessThan
{
   public:
      bool operator() (const T& x, const T& y) const
      {
         return x < y;
      }
};

// use insertion sort to order v using function object comp
template <typename T, typename Compare>
void insertionSort(vector<T>& v, Compare comp);

int main()
{
   int arr[] = {2, 1, 7, 8, 12, 15, 3, 5};
   int arrSize = sizeof(arr)/sizeof(int);
   vector<int> v(arr, arr+arrSize);

   // put the vector in ascending order
   insertionSort(v, lessThan<int>());
   // output it
```

```
        writeVector(v);
        cout <> endl;

        // put the vector in descending order
        insertionSort(v, greaterThan<int>());
        // output it
        writeVector(v);
        cout {} endl;

        return 0;
    }
    /* implementation for insertionSort() given in the program
       discussion */
```

```
Run:
1  2  3  5  7  8  12  15
15 12  8  7  5  3  2  1
```

☞

Note

STL implements the function object types *greater* and *less* in the header file <functional>. These types perform the same action as do our *greaterThan* and *lessThan* types. We will have occasion to use the STL function object types throughout the book, particularly when we develop heaps, in Chapter 14.

Integer Hash Functions

With an integer key, the identity function can serve as a good hash function provided that all or a portion of the number is random. Assume that the television manufacturer creates serial numbers, for which the low-order five digits are random. If we use a table with size $n = 10^k (k \le 5)$, the identify hash function maps the serial number to a random table index. For use with the hash class, we implement the identity function as the function object type hFintID. The operator () takes an integer as the argument and returns the corresponding unsigned integer value.

32 bit # w/
no
negative

```
class hFintID
{
    public:
        unsigned int operator()(int item) const
        { return (unsigned int) item; }
};
```

To call the identity hash function, declare an hFintID object and include the integer key as an argument:

```
hFintID hf;         // identity hash function object

hf(35) = 35         // call hf with argument 35
```

```
// index for a serial number in a 10000-element table
hf(0682401) % 10000 = 0682401 % 10000 = 2401
```

With other integer keys, the identify function might not be a good hash function, because the result after dividing by the table size might create too many collisions. For instance, assume our television manufacturer stamps each item with a serial number for which the last four digits record the year in which the item was made. If the manufacturer stores product information in a 10,000−element table, the identify hash function would map all of the products for a given year to the same index. Only products manufactured in different years would avoid a collision.

```
hf(9732001) = 9732001 -> index 9732001 % 10000 = 2001
hf(1362001) = 1362001 -> index 1362001 % 10000 = 2001
hf(8572001) = 8572001 -> index 8572001 % 10000 = 2001
```

In this case, we want a hash function that mixes up the digits in the serial number rather than using the low-order four digits. The *midsquare technique* provides a hash function algorithm that uses intermediate calculations to produce a random value. The technique takes an integer argument, converts it to an unsigned integer, squares its value, and returns a succession of bits that are extracted from the middle of the square. Assuming that the *int* type specifies a 32-bit number, the function object type hFint specifies a hash function that extracts the middle 16 bits from the square of the integer key:

```
class hFint
{
   public:
      unsigned int operator()(int item) const
      {
         unsigned int value = (unsigned int)item;

         value *= value;           // square the item
         value /= 256;             // discard the low order 8 bits
         return value % 65536;     // return item in range 0 to 65535
      }
};
```

Example 12-2

The general integer hash function maps three product serial numbers to an index in a 10,000-element table:

```
hFint hf;

hf(9732001) = 51491 -> index 51491 % 10000 = 1491
hf(1362001) = 26281 -> index 26281 % 10000 = 6281
hf(8572001) = 44732 -> index 44732 % 10000 = 4732
```

String Hash Functions

In the majority of hash table applications, the key is a string, such as a social security number (e.g., 467-29-1753), so it is important to implement an efficient hash function for strings. For instance, compilers often keep track of identifiers in a program by using a hash table. The sequence of characters in the string must be combined to form an unsigned integer. We describe such an algorithm that uses both multiplication and addition. Start with an integer value $n = 0$. For each succeeding string character, multiply n by 8 and add in the new character. As an example, consider the string key = "and." The computations proceed as follows:

```
n = (0 * 8) + 97 = 97            // ASCII value of 'a' is 97
n = (97 * 8) + 110 = 886         // ASCII value of 'n' is 110
n = (886 * 8) + 100 = 7188       // ASCII value of 'd' is 100
```

After this multiplication and addition have been executed for each character in the string, the integer value n could be negative on account of integer overflow. Taking the negative of n solves this problem. Return the remainder after dividing by a large prime number, which has the effect of further providing a random distribution of integer values. We use the prime number 2,049,982,463 for this purpose:

```
class hFstring
{
   public:
      unsigned int operator()(const string& item) const
      {
         unsigned int prime = 2049982463;

         int n = 0, i;

         for (i = 0; i < item.length(); i++)
            n = n*8 + item[i];

         return n > 0 ? (n % prime) : (-n % prime);
      }
};
```

Example 12-3

Declare a string hash function, and use it to evaluate the hash value for three words:

```
hFstring hfStr;

hfStr("and") = 7188
hfStr("multiplication") = 950233562
hfStr("algorithm") = 1885049517
```

A Custom Hash Function

For applications which involve keys that are not numbers or strings, a programmer must design a custom hash function object type for the key. The implementation of the operator() can use other hash functions. For instance, we now present a function object type called hFtime24 that enables the use of the hashing with time24 objects. The hash function takes a time24 object as an argument and applies the identity function to the time in minutes.

```
class hFtime24
{
   public:
      unsigned int operator() (const time24& t)
      {
         // apply hFintID() to t in minutes
         return hFintID() (t.getHour()*60 + t.getMinute());
      }
};
```

☞
Note

Most hash table applications use an integer or a string as the key. For the cases for which the key is a real number, we provide the class *hFreal*, which specifies a hash function that maps the real-number domain into a signed integer. Construction of the hash function for real numbers requires an understanding of the real-number storage format, which includes a sign, mantissa, and exponent. Consult the WWW supplemental materials for a discussion of this format and the algorithm to implement the operator ().

For convenience, we provide the declaration and implementation of the hash functions from this section in the header file "d_hashf.h".

DESIGNING HASH TABLES   12-3

In the previous section, we focused on the concept of a hash function. To understand its action, we described the link between a key and an indexed location in a hash table. In this section, we turn our attention to the design of a hash table. In the process, we define different storage models that work with a hash function to resolve collisions. The issue is clear. When two or more data items hash to the same table index, they cannot occupy the same position in the table. We are left with the option of locating one of the items at another position in the table or of redesigning the table to have separate containers at each index. In the latter case, a container holds all of the elements that hash to that location. These options represent two classical strategies for collision resolution, called *linear probe open addressing* and *chaining with separate lists*. The strategies result in two models for a hash-table container. We illustrate the linear probe open addressing model with an example, but we focus our attention on chaining with separate lists, because it represents the most commonly used design for a hash table.

Linear Probe Open Addressing

This technique assumes that the hash table is an indexed list (array or vector) of elements with an associated hash function. Initially, we tag each entry in the table as *empty*. To add an item to the table, apply the hash function to the key and find the remainder after division by the table size. The resulting index is a location in the table. If the location is empty, the algorithm inserts the item. Otherwise, it "probes" the table looking for the first open slot—hence the name of the algorithm. The probe starts at the next hash index and begins a sequential search at successive indices. The search wraps around to the start of the table after it probes the last table entry. An insertion occurs at the first open location. The search could cycle through all of the indices and return to the original hash location without finding an open slot. In this case, the table is full, and the algorithm throws an exception. Note that a hash table with open probe addressing is not a dynamic structure that increases its size to accommodate a new element.

If the hash table does not allow for values with duplicate keys, the algorithm must check whether the item is already in the list. A test for a match begins at the hash index and continues for each successive probe. The algorithm determines that the item is not a duplicate key when it finds an empty location in the table.

Example 12-4

A hash table of size 11 combines with the identity hash function to store eight distinct integer data items. The table lists the items and the corresponding hash index, whose value is *item* % 11.

Data Item	54	77	94	89	14	45	35	76
Hash Index	10	0	6	1	3	1	2	10

Insert 54, 77, 94, 89, 14:

The first five items hash to different indices. In each case, the table location is empty and the item is inserted at the hash index. Figure 12-2(a) displays the table with the annotation "1" next to the occupied cells, indicating that only one probe (test for empty) was necessary to insert the item.

Insert 45: The hash index for 45 is 1, which provides the first collision. The location is occupied by data value 89 from a previous insertion. The open probe picks up at index 2 and continues until the table has an open slot. This occurs immediately, because no item occupies the position at index 2. Inserting 45 requires only two probes (Figure 12-2(b)).

Insert 35: As the table begins to fill, the likelihood of collisions increases, along with the number of probes required to insert an item. With data value 35, which hashes to index 2, there is no collision with any previous value. However, we require additional probes, because the value 45 took slot 2 in response

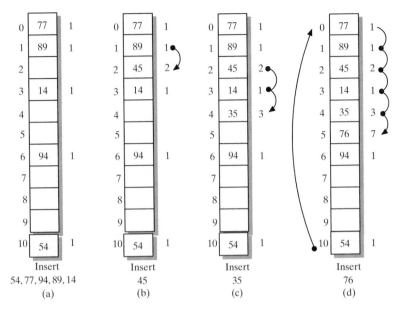

Figure 12-2
Hash table using linear probe addressing

to a collision with value 89. Value 35 requires three probes before landing at index 4 (Figure 12-2(c)).

Insert 76:   Adding 76 to the list dramatically illustrates a potential problem with linear probe addressing. The value hashes to index 10, but finds an open slot only after seven probes (Figure 12-2(d)).

The following code outline describes the linear probe insertion algorithm, assuming no duplicate values:

```
// compute the hash index for a table of size n
int index = hf(item) % n, origIndex;

// save the original hash index
origIndex = index;

// cycle through the table looking for an empty slot, a
// match or a table full condition (origindex == index).
do
{
    // test whether the table slot is empty or the key matches
    // the data field of the table entry
    if table[index] is empty
        insert item in table at table[index] and return
    else if table[index] matches item
        return
```

```
        // we are not yet successful. begin a probe starting at
        // the next table location
        index = (index+1) % n;
} while (index != origIndex);


// we have gone around the table without finding an open slot
// or a match. the table is full! throw the overflowError exception
throw overflowError;
```

Evaluating Linear Probe Addressing. If the size of the table is large relative to the number of items to store, linear probe addressing works well, because a good hash function generates indices that are evenly distributed over the table range, and collisions will be minimal. As the ratio of table size to the number of items approaches 1, inherent difficulties with the process becomes apparent. In the example, adding value 76 to the table requires 7 probes, which is more than 40% of the 17 probes required to store the entire table. Even though five of the eight data values hash to distinct indices, the linear probe algorithm requires an average of 2.1 probes per item. A phenomenon called *clustering* can occur when using linear probe addressing and will degrade performance. We discuss clustering in the exercises.

Chaining With Separate Lists

A second approach to hashing defines the hash table as an indexed sequence of containers, such as vectors or lists. Each container, called a *bucket*, holds a set of data items that hash to the same table location. This collision resolution strategy is referred to as *chaining with separate lists*.

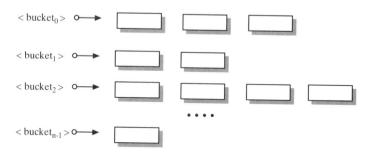

Assume that a bucket is a list. The hash table is a vector of list objects. To add an item, begin with the key, and use the hash function to identify the index for the appropriate bucket (list) in the vector. Insert the item at the rear of the list. In order to access an item in the table, the hash function locates the bucket and applies a sequential search of the list to find the item.

To illustrate a hash table that uses chaining with separate lists, consider the sequence of eight elements in Example 12-4. The table is a vector consisting of 11 list<int> containers. For reference, we repeat the list of elements and their hash index:

Data Item	54	77	94	89	14	45	35	76
Hash Index	10	0	6	1	3	1	2	10

Figure 12-3 displays the lists corresponding to the table indices. Each entry in a table includes the number of probes to add the element. We count an insertion at the back of the list as a probe.

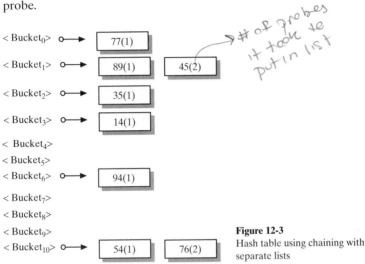

# of probes
it took to
put in list

Figure 12-3
Hash table using chaining with separate lists

Evaluating Chaining with Separate Lists   In the example, note that the total number of probes to insert the eight items is 10, an average of 1.25 probes per item. This compares favorably with the 2.1 probes required to insert an element when the table uses linear probe addressing. Chaining with separate lists is generally faster than linear probe addressing because the algorithm searches only keys that hash to the same table location. Furthermore, linear probe addressing assumes a fixed-length table, whereas the containers used in chaining grow as necessary, and hence the number of elements in the table is limited only by the amount of memory. In addition, deleting an element from the hash table is simple: Just erase it from the associated list. The primary disadvantage of chaining is the extra computing time and memory required to manage the containers.

THE HASH CLASS   12-4

This section develops the hash class that implements hashing by using chaining with separate lists. Recall that in Chapter 11, we used the stree class to implement ordered sets and maps. The hash class can be used to implement unordered sets and maps. Anticipating this application, the hash class has a public interface that is identical to that of the stree class, except for its two constructors. Let us look at a partial listing of the class declaration before we look at examples and an application. You will immediately see that most of the interface is identical to that of the stree class. The main difference lies in the presence of two template arguments in the hash class, in contrast to the single template argument for the stree class. Since the table size is an integral component of a hash object, the constructors require the table size (the number of buckets) as an argument. One version of the constructor creates an empty table, and the second version initializes the table with entries from a pointer range in an array or vector. Each constructor also has an argument that initializes the specific hash function the object uses. The default value for this argument is HashFunc(), the default function object. Like all of our containers, the hash class includes both iterator and const_iterator nested classes.

| **CLASS hash** | **Declaration (public section)** | **"d_hash.h"** |

```
template <typename T, typename HashFunc>
class hash
{
public:

    hash(int nbuckets, const HashFunc& hfunc = HashFunc());
        // constructor specifying the number of buckets
        // in the hash table and the hash function

    hash(T *first, T *last, int nbuckets,
                        const HashFunc& hfunc = HashFunc());
        // constructor with arguments including a pointer range
        // [first, last) of values to insert, the number of
        // buckets in the hash table, and the hash function

    // container size operations
    bool empty() const;
    int size() const;

    //access and update operations
    iterator find(const T& item);

    pair<iterator,bool> insert(const T& item);

    int erase(const T& item);
    void erase(iterator pos);
    void erase(iterator first, iterator last);

    //iterator access functions
    iterator begin();
    const_iterator begin() const;
    iterator end();
    const_iterator end() const;
    . . .
};
```

Example 12-5

Declaring a hash object requires template arguments for the element type and the hash function object type. You can use the hash functions in "d_hashf.h" for integer, real, and string types. If the table stores elements of other types, you must develop your own hash function object for the type.

1. Declare a hash table that stores integer values in 23 buckets, using the identity function. The template list includes the function object type hFintID.

```
#include "d_hash.h"        // hash class
#include "d_hashf.h"       // hash function object types
    . . .

// create an empty 23-bucket hash table of integers using the
// identity hash function
hash<int, hFintID> hInt(23);
```

2. A hash table consists of 101 buckets holding strings. The hash function object type is hFstring. The constructor initializes the table by using elements from the array strArr.

```
string strArr [] = {"a", "more", "bucket", "hash", "table", "class"};
int strArrSize = sizeof(strArr)/sizeof(string);
hash<string, hFstring> hString(strArr, strArr + strArrSize,101);
```

3. A hash table stores objects of type *employee*, where the social security number (ssn) specifies the key. The hash function object type hFemp takes an employee as an argument and uses the data member ssn to compute the hash value. We implement the class hFemp by using the hash function hFstring with the ssn field of the employee as an argument. By declaring hFemp as a friend in the employee class, the implementation of hFemp can access the private data of the class.

```
class employee
{
   public:
      employee(const string& snum, double sal):
         ssn(snum), salary(sal)
      {}
      . . .
      friend class hFemp;// hash function object type
   private:
      string ssn;
      double salary;
};

// hash function object type for employee
class hFemp
{
   public:
      unsigned int operator()(const employee& item) const
      {
         // apply hFstring() to the ssn component of item
         return hFstring() (item.ssn);
```

```
      }
  };
```

The following declaration creates a hash table with 157 buckets to store employee objects

```
hash<employee, hFemp> hEmp(157);
```

Application: Using A Hash Table

Hash tables, like binary search trees, are used to implement sets and maps. This is the most important application for the hash container. In some cases, however, you might want to use a hash container directly to implement an algorithm or another class. We provide a simple program that illustrates how you declare a hash object and call its member functions.

The hash table *ht* employs seven buckets to store an array of 10 integers that contains duplicate values. The function object hFintID implements the identity hash function. The declaration of a hash table requires two template arguments, so programmers often create an alias that simplifies notation for an iterator and an iterator–bool pair.

```
// typedef defines hashTable as an alias for an integer hash table
// that uses the identify function
typedef hash<int, hFintID> hashTable;

// using the alias hashTable, declare a hash table with 7 buckets
// and hash iterator
hashTable ht(7);
hashTable::iterator hIter;
// using the alias hashTable, declare a <iterator,bool> pair for the
// insert operation
pair<hashTable::iterator, bool> p;
```

The program uses the insert() function to add elements from the array into the table. The operation returns a pair where the second component is *true* when an insert occurs and *false* if a match is found. In either case, the iterator component of the pair is the location of the element in the table. The find() function takes an item and determines whether it is in the table. The return value is an iterator that locates the element in the table or has value end() if the element is not present.

We will discuss the hash table iterator in detail in the implementation of the class. With your knowledge of how a hash table stores elements, you can anticipate how an iterator operates. The value begin() is the location of the front of the list, corresponding to the first nonempty bucket. The increment operator, ++, moves the iterator to the next position in the current bucket or to the first position in the next nonempty bucket. To illustrate these ideas, assume that the array contains the elements {20, 16, 9, 14, 8, 17, 3, 9, 16, 12}. The following table lists the nonduplicate values and the corresponding hash index in the table (*value* % 7):

Data Item	20	16	9	14	8	17	3	12
Hash Index	6	2	2	0	1	3	3	5

Items that hash to the same index enter the table in sequential order. For instance, $bucket_2$ is the list 16 and 9, corresponding to the order of the elements in the array. The member function begin() returns an iterator pointing element 14, which is the first element in $bucket_0$. The iterator advances to locations for elements 8, 16, 9, and so forth. The order of access to the elements depends on their hash value, not their data value. This is in marked contrast to the binary search tree iterator, which scans elements in ascending order.

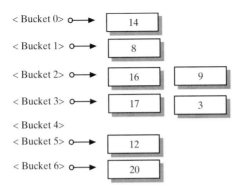

PROGRAM 12-2   USING A HASH TABLE CONTAINER

Let us create a program that implements the features of the application. The function insert() attempts to add elements from an array and returns an iterator–bool pair. We use the second component (of type bool) to note when the element is a duplicate. The user is twice prompted to enter a value and if present, delete the value from the table. The program concludes by listing the elements in the table, using an iterator. The order of output corresponds to our physical view of the table.

```
// File: prg12_2.cpp
// the program declares a hash table with integer data and
// the identity hash function object. it inserts the elements
// from the array intArr into the hash table, noting which
// values are duplicates that do not go into the table. after
// displaying the size of the hash table, a loop prompts the user
// for 2 values. if a value is in the table, the erase() operation
// deletes it. the program terminates by using an iterator to
// traverse and output the elements of the hash table

#include <iostream>

#include "d_hash.h"
```

```cpp
#include "d_hashf.h"

using namespace std;

int main()
{
   // array that holds 10 integers with some duplicates
   int intArr[] = {20, 16, 9, 14, 8, 17, 3, 9, 16, 12};
   int arrSize = sizeof(intArr)/sizeof(int);

   // alias describing integer hash table using identity function
   // object
   typedef hash<int, hFintID> hashTable;

   // hash table with 7 buckets and hash iterator
   hashTable ht(7);
   hashTable::iterator hIter;

   // <iterator,bool> pair for the insert operation
   pair<hashTable::iterator, bool> p;

   int item, i;

   // insert elements from intArr, noting duplicates
   for (i = 0; i < arrSize; i++)
   {
      p = ht.insert(intArr[i]);
      if (p.second == false)
         cout << "Duplicate value " << intArr[i] << endl;
   }

   // output the hash size which reflects duplicates
   cout << "Hash table size " << ht.size() << endl;

   // prompt for item to erase and indicate if not found
   for (i = 1; i <= 2; i++)
   {
      cout << "Enter a number to delete: ";
      cin >> item;

      if ((hIter = ht.find(item)) == ht.end())
         cout << "Item not found" << endl;
      else
         ht.erase(hIter);
   }

   // output the elements using an iterator to scan the table
   for (hIter = ht.begin(); hIter != ht.end(); hIter++)
      cout << *hIter << "   ";
```

```
    cout << endl;
    return 0;
}
```

```
Run:

Duplicate value 9
Duplicate value 16
Hash table size 8
Enter a number to delete:   10
Item not found
Enter a number to delete:   17
14   8   16   9   3   12   20
```

Hash Class Implementation

The hash class has four private data members that describe the hash table. The vector, called *bucket*, defines a sequence of list objects (buckets) that store the elements. The integer value *numBuckets* specifies the number of entries (buckets) in the vector, and *hashtableSize* records the number of entries in the hash table. The hash function *hf* is an object of the template type *HashFunc*, which is the hash function object for the element type *T*.

CLASS hash	Declaration (private section)	"d_hash.h"

```
private:
    int numBuckets;
        // number of buckets in the table
    vector<list<T> > bucket;
        // the hash table is a vector of lists
    HashFunc hf;
        // hash function
    int hashtableSize;
        // number of elements in the hash table
```

Constructors.   The class has two constructors that initialize the number of buckets (numBuckets) and allocate a vector of lists with that number of buckets. In addition, each constructor initializes the hash function and assigns 0 to the hash table size. The constructor that initializes the hash table with values from the pointer range [*first, last*) uses the insert() operation to place the values in the table. The function increments the hash table size. We list only the default constructor. Consult the file "d_hash.h" for a listing of the other constructor.

Constructor:
```
    // constructor. create an empty hash table
    template <typename T, typename HashFunc>
```

```
hash<T, HashFunc>::hash(int nbuckets, const HashFunc& hfunc):
            numBuckets(nbuckets), bucket(nbuckets), hf(hfunc),
            hashtableSize(0)
{}
```

Hash Table Insert Operation. The operation insert() uses the hash function *hf* to compute the hash value (bucket index) of argument *item* and sequentially searches the corresponding list object to verify whether *item* is in the list. If it finds a match, it returns a pair whose first component is a hash iterator that references *item* in the table and whose second component is *false*. Otherwise, it adds *item* at the back of the list and returns a pair whose first component is an iterator pointing to the new entry and whose second component is *true*.

```
template <typename T, typename HashFunc>
pair<hash>T, HashFunc>::iterator,bool>insert(const T& item);
```

To understand the code for insert(), we must anticipate our discussion of hash iterators. As you will see later in this section, a hash iterator has three components: a pointer to the hash table, the index of the current bucket, and the list iterator position of the element in the bucket.

hashTable — a pointer to the hash table object it traverses

currentBucket — the index of the current hash table bucket in the traversal

currentLoc — a list iterator pointing to the current value in the hash table

To create a hash iterator that references element *x* in the table, we use an iterator constructor with three arguments to initialize the components:

hash iterator object created by the constructor:
```
        iterator(hashTable, currentBucket, currentLoc)
```

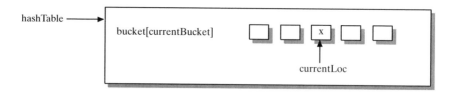

The algorithm for insert() computes the hash index for argument *item*. We call the index *hashIndex* and use it to identify the list *bucket[hashIndex]*. The list iterator *bucketIter* searchs the bucket for a match. The search terminates when the list iterator has value end() or identifies the location of a match. In the first case, the list insert() function adds *item* to the bucket and uses the return value from the list function insert() to update *bucketIter*. The Boolean variable *success* indicates whether the operation added a new element (*true*) or found a duplicate (*false*). In either case, the algorithm uses the values for *hashIndex*, *bucketIter*, and *success* to return an iterator–bool pair. The values hashIndex and bucketIter are arguments for a constructor that creates the iterator component of the pair.

insert():

```
template <typename T, typename HashFunc>
pair<hash<T, HashFunc>::iterator,bool>
hash<T, HashFunc>::insert(const T& item)
{
    // hashIndex is the bucket number
    int hashIndex = int(hf(item) % numBuckets);
    // for convenience, make myBucket an alias for bucket[hashIndex]
    list<T>& myBucket = bucket[hashIndex];
    // use iterator to traverse the list myBucket
    list<T>::iterator bucketIter;
    // specifies whether or not we do an insert
    bool success;

    // traverse list until we arrive at the end of
    // the bucket or find a match with item
    bucketIter = myBucket.begin();
    while (bucketIter != myBucket.end())
        if (*bucketIter == item)
            break;
        else
            bucketIter++;

    if (bucketIter == myBucket.end())
    {
        // at the end of the list, so item is not
        // in the hash table. call list class insert()
        // and assign its return value to bucketIter
        bucketIter = myBucket.insert(bucketIter, item);
        success = true;
        // increment the hash table size
        hashtableSize++;
    }
    else
        // item is in the hash table. duplicates not allowed.
        // no insertion
        success = false;

    // return a pair with iterator pointing at the new or
    // pre-existing item and success reflecting whether an
    // insert took place; pointer this references the hash table
    return pair<iterator,bool>
        (iterator(this, hashIndex, bucketIter), success);
}
```

Hash Table Erase Operations. The hash class has several versions of the erase() function. We describe the version that takes *item* as an argument and returns an integer value (0 or 1) to indicate whether the value is removed from the table. Implementation of this version of the function assumes use of the erase(*iter*) version that removes the element at location *iter*. The algorithm first calls find() to obtain an iterator pointing to *item* in the hash table. If the iterator is not end(), its value is an argument for the iterator version of erase(), and the return value is 1. If *item* is not in the table, the function returns 0.

erase():

```
template <typename T, typename HashFunc>
int hash<T, HashFunc>::erase(const T& item)
{
    iterator iter;
    int numberErased = 1;

    iter = find(item);
    if (iter != end())
        erase(iter);
    else
        numberErased = 0;

    return numberErased;
}
```

Implementing the Hash Iterators

The hash class gives us an excellent opportunity to study the design and implementation of iterators. Within the hash class, we declare *iterator* and *const_iterator* as nested classes. By making them friends, we give them access to all of the private data members of the hash class, including the vector object *bucket* and its size, *numBuckets*.

In designing an iterator class, we must develop a strategy for traversing the elements in the related container. For a hash table, the strategy begins with a search for the first nonempty bucket in the vector of lists. When we locate the bucket, we traverse all of the nodes in that list and then continue the process by looking for the next nonempty bucket. The iterator reaches the end of the table when it reaches the end of the list for the last nonempty bucket.

The design of an iterator class for any container follows a pattern. The private data members define the attributes of an iterator object. For instance, the private data member for a vector, list, or stree iterator is a pointer to the element or node in the corresponding container. The public member functions include the dereference operator, *; the increment operator, ++; and the comparison operators == and !=. If the container supports bidirectional iterators, the class also includes the decrement operator, −−. Implementing the == and != operators is simple; we merely compare iterator objects and return a value of true or false. The dereference operator accesses the element in the container pointed to by the iterator. The main task is the implementation of the increment operator, because this involves the traversal strategy.

Let us see how the design of an iterator class applies to hash tables. The private members include the pointer variable *hashTable*, which is the address of the corresponding hash table object. The pointer creates a link to the table, so that the iterator knows which collection of elements it is scanning. The other private members are the variable *currentBucket*, which is the index of the current bucket that the iterator

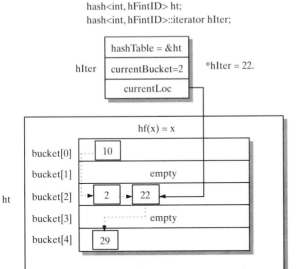

Figure 12-4
Hash iterator hIter
referencing element 22 in
table ht

is traversing, and the variable *currentLoc*, which is a list iterator pointing to the current hash table element. Put simply, the attributes for a hash iterator object identify its current location by specifying the table, the bucket, and the location in the bucket (list). Figure 12-4 illustrates the attributes for the hash table iterator *hIter*, which traverses a five-bucket table with four entries. The values for the attributes describe the iterator when it points at element 22 in table. The figure also includes a series of dotted lines that indicate the traversal order $(10, 2, 22, 29)$ for the elements.

The upcoming code is a declaration of the private section of the iterator class. The section includes the utility function findNext(), which is used by the increment operator, $++$, to move from the end of one bucket to the first element in the next nonempty bucket. The private constructor provides a function that creates an iterator object. The hash functions insert() and find() use this constructor to create a return iterator.

CLASS iterator	**Declaration (private section)**	**"d_hiter.h"**

```
hash<T,HashFunc> *hashTable;
   // points to the hash table container

int currentBucket;
   // index of current bucket being traversed
list<T>::iterator currentLoc;
   // points to the current element in the current bucket

iterator (hash<T,HashFunc> *ht, int b,
         list<T>::iterator loc);
   // used to construct an iterator return value
```

```
void findNext()
   // find next non-empty bucket and set currentLoc
   // to point at its first element
```

The function findNext() starts at bucket index *currentBucket* + 1 and searches for the first nonempty bucket within the range *currentBucket* + 1 ≤ *i* < *hashTable−>numBuckets*. Note that we need the pointer *hashTable* to identify the table. If the search is successful, the function sets *currentBucket* to *i* and *currentLoc* at the list iterator position for the first element of bucket *hashTable−>*bucket[*i*]. If all the buckets in the range are empty, findNext() assigns *currentBucket* the value −1, indicating that the iterator has arrived at the end of the hash table.

findNext():

```
   // find next nonempty bucket and set currentLoc
   // to point at its first element
   void findNext()
   {
      int i;

      // search from the next bucket to end of
      // table for a nonempty bucket
      for(i=currentBucket+1; i < hashTable->numBuckets; i++)
         if (!hashTable->bucket[i].empty())
         {
            // found a nonempty bucket. set
            // currentBucket index to i and
            // currentLoc to point at the first
            // element of the list
            currentBucket = i;
            currentLoc = hashTable->bucket[i].begin();
            return;
         }

      // we are at end()
      currentBucket = -1;
   }
```

Implementing the Increment Operator. The iterator preincrement operator, ++, advances the list iterator *currentLoc* forward (currentLoc++) and checks to see whether it has advanced to the end of the current list (currentLoc == hashTable−>bucket[currentBucket].end()). If so, a call to findNext() positions currentLoc at the first element of the next bucket or at the end of the table.

operator++:

```
   iterator& operator++ ()
   {
      // move to the next data value or the end of
```

```
        // the list
        currentLoc++;

        // if at end of list, call findNext() to
        // identify the next non-empty bucket in the table
        // and set currentLoc to its first element
        if (currentLoc == hashTable->bucket[currentBucket].end())
            findNext();

        return *this;
}
```

Implementing Hash Functions begin() and end() Each container provides member functions begin() and end(), which return iterator values pointing to the first element and immediately after the last element in the container. The functions are members of the container class, but must have knowledge of the traversal strategy used by an iterator. The hash class member function begin() creates an iterator object *tmp* that points at the first element in the table. The process involves assigning values to the three attributes of the iterator. The pointer, *hashTable*, is the address of the current table (*this*). Initially, *currentBucket* is −1. A call to *tmp*.findNext() positions the iterator at the first element of the hash table and updates the values for attributes *currentBucket* and *currentLoc*. The iterator *tmp* is the return value for begin().

begin():
```
    template <typename T, typename HashFunc>
    hash<T, HashFunc>::iterator hash<T, HashFunc>::begin()
    {
        hash<>T, HashFunc>::iterator tmp;

        tmp.hashTable = this;
        tmp.currentBucket = -1;
        // start at index -1 + 1 = 0 and search for a non-empty
        // list
        tmp.findNext();

        return tmp;
    }
```

The function end() simply builds and returns an iterator pointing to the current hash table, with its *currentBucket* variable set to −1.

end():
```
    template <typename T, typename HashFunc>
    hash<T, HashFunc>::iterator hash<T, HashFunc>::end()
    {
        hash<T, HashFunc>::iterator tmp;
```

```
        tmp.hashTable = this;
        // currentBucket of -1 means we are at end of the table
        tmp.currentBucket = -1;

        return tmp;
    }
```

Unordered Associative Containers

In Chapter 11, we developed the ordered set container and used the binary search tree class, stree, for its implementation. The interfaces for the two classes were almost identical; the implementation of the set container mainly involved defining a private stree object as the storage structure. Code for the set operations simply made calls to corresponding stree functions. At the implementation level, there is essentially no difference between an ordered set and a binary search tree. As abstract structures, however, they represent very different storage models. A programmer can use the mathematical concept of a set to view an ordered set object, while a binary search tree implies a hierarchical storage model.

With the hash class, we have a similar situation. We can design an unordered set container and use a hash object for the underlying storage in the implementation of the class. The requirement that the set be unordered flows from the traversal strategy used by the hash iterator. In many ways, an unordered set best describes a mathematical set.

The upcoming code is a declaration of the unordered set class, *uset*. We include only the data and constructors, because the remaining operations are identical to those for the set class. Because uset stores elements in a hash table, the class has two template arguments; the second argument is the hash function object type for the table. The constructors have a default argument for the *tableSize*, which gives an initial value of 1237. A programmer can modify the size if the application warrants. Just as we extended the binary search tree class to implement ordered maps, the hash class can be used to implement unordered maps (Programming Project 12-37).

CLASS uset	Declaration	"d_uset.h"

```
// implements an unordered set
template <typename T, typename HashFunc>
class uset
{
    public:
        uset(int tableSize = 1237, const HashFunc& hfunc = HashFunc());
            // default constructor
        uset(T *first, T *last, int tableSize = 1237,
            const HashFunc& hfunc = HashFunc());
            // build a set whose data are determined by pointer range
            // [first, last). . .
    private:
```

```
      hash<T,HashFunc> ht;
         // uset implemented using a hash table
};
```

Example 12-6

Let us compare the declaration and use of set and uset objects. Note the need to include a hash function object in the declaration.

   1. Two sets containing integers from the array intArr:

```
int intArr[] = {1300, 2474, 920};
set<int> oSet(intArr, intArr+3);            // ordered set
uset<int, hFintID> uSet(intArr, intArr+3);   // unordered set
```

   2. Declare iterators that are return values for the find() function:

```
set<int>::iterator oIter;
uset<int, hFintID>::iterator uIter;

oIter = oSet.find(200);     // oIter == oSet.end()
uIter = uSet.find(920);     // *uIter == 920
```

   3. Call writeContainer() to output the elements in the set. Output from *oSet* is ordered. The result for *uSet* depends on the hashing process.

```
hf(1300) = 1300 -> index 1300 % 1237 = 63
hf(2474) = 2474 -> index 2474 % 1237 = 0
hf(920) = 920 -> index 920 % 1237 = 920

writeContainer(oSet.begin(), oSet.end());
   Output:920  1300   2474

writeContainer(uSet.begin(), uSet.end());
   Output:2474   1300   920
```

Evaluating Ordered and Unordered Sets An unordered set class uses a hash table, so it provides constant-time performance for the insert(), erase(), and find() operations. Of course, this assumes that the programmer uses a good hash function that disperses the elements uniformly among the buckets. In the next section, we discuss hash table performance. The criteria provide a measure of efficiency for an unordered set iterator as it traverses the elements. An ordered set stores elements in a search tree. Access and update operations have runtime efficiency $O(\log_2 n)$. The application will dictate which set type is more appropriate. If the programmer needs very efficient access and updates without any concern for the ordering of the elements, the unordered set is appropriate, provided that the hashing process is efficient. When order is important, the ordered set container is more appropriate.

12-5   HASH TABLE PERFORMANCE

The hashing process includes both the hash function and the hash table. The design of the process has the goal of providing very efficient search operations. In this section, we develop methods that measure search performance for hash tables that use linear addressing and chaining with separate lists. Because we are interested primarily in tables that use chaining, they will be our focus. As with any performance analysis, we look at the search algorithm under both worst-case and average-case conditions.

The analysis of hashing performance depends upon the quality of the hashing function and the size of the hash table. A poor hash function maps all of the keys to a small set of indices; a good hash function provides a uniform distribution of hash values. A concept called *load factor* provides a measure of table density. If a hash table has m entries, and n is the number of elements currently in the table, the load factor λ for the table is

$$\lambda = n/m$$

In the case of linear addressing, m is the size of the vector (table range); for chaining with separate lists m is the number of buckets. When the table is empty, λ is 0. As we add more items to the table, λ increases. For linear probe addressing, λ attains the maximum value of 1 when the table is full ($m = n$). When the table uses chaining with separate lists, the individual buckets can grow as large as needed, and λ can increase without bound.

The worst case for hashing occurs when all data items hash to the same table location. If the table contains n elements, the search time is O(n), no better than that for the sequential search. To analyze the average case for a search, we assume that the hash function uniformly distributes indices around the hash table. That is, any data item is equally likely to hash into any of the m slots, independently of where any other element falls in the table. Making the table size a prime helps insure uniform distribution. Consider the case where the table uses chaining with separate lists. For the target called *item*, the running time to compute the hash value hf(*item*) is O(1), so the number of comparisons it takes to locate *item* depends on the length of the list at vector location bucket[hf(*item*)]. The assumption of a uniform hash distribution implies that we can expect $\lambda = n/m$ elements in each bucket. There are two cases. Either *item* is in the list and the search is successful, or *item* is not in the list and the search fails. On the average, an unsuccessful search makes λ comparisons before arriving at the end of a list and returning failure. Computing the average running time for a successful search is more difficult. Assume that *item* was originally the ith element to enter the table. At the time of its insertion, we would expect that the previous i − 1 elements are uniformly distributed among the m buckets in lists of size (i − 1)/m. The insert places *item* at the end of the list corresponding to its hash bucket. Hence, a search for *item* in bucket[hf(*item*)] requires 1 + (i − 1)/m comparisons, where the 1 is the comparison with the item itself. The expected number of comparisons for a successful search for an item is the average number of comparisons to locate each of the n elements in the table. The following calculation computes this average:

$$\frac{1}{n} \sum_{i=1}^{n} \left(1 + \frac{i-1}{m} \right) = \frac{n}{n} + \frac{1}{n} \sum_{i=1}^{n} \frac{i-1}{m} = 1 + \frac{1}{nm} \sum_{i=1}^{n} (i-1)$$

$$= 1 + \frac{1}{nm} (1 + 2 + 3 + \cdots + (n-1))$$

$$= 1 + \frac{1}{nm} \frac{n(n-1)}{2} = 1 + \frac{n-1}{2m}$$

$$= 1 + \frac{\lambda}{2} - \frac{1}{2m}$$

A mathematical analysis of linear probe addressing is beyond the scope of this book. We include the results in Table 12-1, which lists formulas for the average number of probes needed for successful and unsuccessful searches for each hashing method. The formulas assume a uniform hash distribution.

The table shows that linear probe addressing is reasonably good as long as the load factor λ remains small. In general, chaining is a better method. For instance, when the table is half full ($\lambda = 1/2$), chaining requires not more than 1.25 probes for a successful search, but linear probe requires 1.5. When the table is 2/3 full ($\lambda = 2/3$), chaining requires no more than 1.33 probes, but linear probe requires 2.

Fine-Tuning Hashing A closer look at Table 12-1 indicates that the performance of a hash table search using chaining is a function of the load factor λ. In theory, $\lambda = n/m$ can increase without bounds when the table stores elements in a fixed number of buckets. As λ grows, the search performance becomes linear, O(n). For this reason, a programmer does not use a hash table if there is no upper bound on the total number of elements. We can assume that the number of elements n in the hash table is bounded by some amount, say $R*m$. In this case, $\lambda = n/m \leq (R*m)/m = R$. The running time for a successful and an unsuccessful search satisfy the relationships

$$1 + \frac{\lambda}{2} - \frac{1}{2m} \leq 1 + \frac{R}{2} - \frac{1}{2m} \qquad \text{(successful search)}$$

$$\lambda \leq R \qquad \text{(unsuccessful search)}$$

TABLE 12-1   EFFICIENCY OF HASH METHODS

Hash table size = m, Number of elements in hash table = n, Load factor $\lambda = \frac{m}{n}$		
	Average Probes for Successful Search	Average Probes for Unsuccessful Search
Linear Probe	$\frac{1}{2} + \frac{1}{2(1-\lambda)}$	$\frac{1}{2} + \frac{1}{2(1-\lambda)^2}$
Chaining	$1 + \frac{\lambda}{2} - \frac{1}{2m}$	λ

The terms on the right-hand side of the inequalities are constants, so the average search has running time $O(1)$! That is, the running time is independent of the number of data items. The challenge is to make the constant time reasonably small, which is equivalent to saying that λ is reasonably small. The programmer can fine tune the hashing process by adjusting the number of buckets. The choice of m must take into account system resources and the need to have the hash function uniformly distribute its values in the index range from 0 to $m - 1$.

Comparing Search Algorithms

With the introduction of hash tables, we have now seen four classical search algorithms. Earlier in the book, we developed the sequential search, the binary search, and binary tree searching. For each algorithm, we determined the average running time of the search method by computing the average number of comparisons needed to locate an item. The running time of the sequential search is $O(n)$, whereas the running time of the binary search and binary search trees is $O(\log_2 n)$.

Clearly, hashing is a fast search method. However, each of the four search techniques has applications for which it is most useful or efficient. The sequential search (efficiency $O(n)$) is effective when the number of elements n is small and the data do not have to be sorted. The binary search (efficiency $O(\log_2 n)$) is very fast, but requires that the data be sorted in an array or vector. The binary search is not suited to situations for which the application repeatedly adds or removes data items, because of the overhead required to maintain order. For data that are dynamically changing, the binary search tree (efficiency $O(\log_2 n)$) and hashing (efficiency $O(1)$) are competitive, although the tree iterator has the nice side effect of scanning the data in order. Hashing is best used when quick access to unordered data is required.

Using Big-O measures, we can make theoretical comparisons between the four search methods. Let us run a program and make empirical comparisons. The program inputs 25,025 randomly ordered words into the vector *vrand*. A second input assigns the same collection of words in sorted order to the vector *vsort*. The elements in the randomized vector initialize the binary search tree container *bstree* and the hash table *ht*, which consists of 1373 buckets. The function object *hFstring* provides a hash function for the table. We use the following strategies to evaluate each search method:

- Use the words in vector *vsort* as keys for a sequential search of the random entries in the vector *vrand*.
- Use the words in vector *vrand* as keys for a binary search of the entries in the sorted vector *vsort*.
- Use the words in vector *vsort* as arguments to the function find(), which determines whether an item is in the search tree *bstree*.
- Use the words in vector *vsort* as arguments to the hash table function find(), which determines whether an item is in the hash table.

For each method, we use a timer object that starts when the searching begins and stops when it ends. A message displays the time required for each search technique.

PROGRAM 12-3   TIMING SEARCHES
_____

The program inputs 25,025 word lists from files "udict.dat" and "sdict.dat." The former file contains the words in random order, and the latter has the words in sorted order. Each word is on a separate line. A loop reads the words and inserts them into the vectors *vrand* and *vsort*, respectively. Declarations for the binary search tree *bstree* and the hash table *ht* use the address range for *vrand* to initialize the two containers.

```cpp
// File: prg12_3.cpp
// this program makes empirical comparisons of four searching methods.
// it inputs 25025 word from files "udict.dat" and "sdict.dat".
// the former file contains words in random order, and the latter
// in sorted order. the randomly ordered words are inserted into
// vector vrand as well as search tree bstree and hash table ht.
// the sorted words are inserted into vector vsort. for each
// search, a timer object determines the number of seconds
// required to search for all words in the container. the words
// in vsort are keys for the sequential search and the find()
// function in the search tree and hash table. the words in
// vrand are the keys for the binary search

#include <iostream>
#include <fstream>
#include <vector>

#include "d_stree.h"
#include "d_hash.h"
#include "d_hashf.h"
#include "d_timer.h"
#include "d_search.h"

using namespace std;

int main()
{
   // vectors that store strings in random and sorted order
   vector<string> vrand, vsort;
   // declare a binary search tree and hash table with elements
   // from vrand. the hash table has 1373 buckets.
   hash<string, hFstring> ht(1373);
   stree<string> bstree;

   // objects used in the search tests
   ifstream unsortedStrings, sortedStrings;
   string word;
   timer t;
   int len, method, i;
```

```
// open 25000+ word dictionaries
unsortedStrings.open("udict.dat");

sortedStrings.open("sdict.dat");

while(true)
{
   // input a word from the randomly ordered dictionary
   unsortedStrings >> word;
   if (!unsortedStrings)
      break;

   // insert word into the randomly ordered vector
   vrand.push_back(word);
   // insert word into the binary search tree
   bstree.insert(word);
   // insert word into the hash table
   ht.insert(word);

   // input a word from the sorted dictionary
   sortedStrings >> word;
   // insert word into the sorted vector
   vsort.push_back(word);
}
// output the number of words
len = vrand.size();
cout <> "Number of words is " << len << endl <<\ endl;

// test the four search methods
for (method = 0; method < 4; method++)
{
   // start the timer
   t.start();
   // implement the search
   switch(method)
   {
      // sequential search of random words with list of sorted words
      case   0:   for (i = 0; i<len; i++)
                      seqSearch(vrand, 0, len, vsort[i]);
                  t.stop();
                  cout << "Sequential search time is ";
                  break;
      // binary search of sorted words with list of random words
      case   1:   for (i = 0; i<len; i++)
                     binSearch(vsort, 0, len, vrand[i]);
                  t.stop();
                  cout << "Binary search time is ";
                  break;
      // binary tree search of random words with list of sorted words
      case   2:   for (i = 0; i<len; i++)
```

```
                        bstree.find(vsort[i]);
                    t.stop();
                    cout << "Binary tree search time is ";
                    break;
            // hash search of random words with list of sorted words
            case    3:   for (i = 0; i<len; i++)
                            ht.find(vsort[i]);
                    t.stop();  cout << "Hash search time is ";
                    break;
        }
        cout << t.time() << " seconds" << endl;
    }

    return 0;
}
```

```
Run:

Number of words is 25025

Sequential search time is 126.642 seconds
Binary search time is 0.21 seconds
Binary tree search time is 0.2 seconds
Hash search time is 0.121 seconds
```

In the run, the $O(n)$ sequential search requires 126.6 seconds, while the $O(\log_2 n)$ binary and binary search tree algorithms take 0.21 and 0.2 seconds, respectively. The hash table search is the most efficient, requiring 0.12 seconds. Increasing the table size and thus reducing the number of collisions could improve this efficiency.

2–3–4 TREES   12-6

In Chapter 11, we used the binary search tree class stree to implement the associative set and map containers. In most cases, applications build a set or map in such a way that the underlying storage structure (tree) is relatively balanced. By "balanced," we mean that, for most nodes, the depths of the left and right subtrees are approximately equal. When this happens, the set or map has very efficient $O(\log_2 n)$ insert(), erase(), and find() operations. In some cases, however, the storage of elements results in an unbalanced tree, because the location of nodes depends on the order of insertion. For instance, a set that uses the insertion sequence

5, 15, 20, 3, 9, 7, 12, 17, 6, 75, 100, 18, 25, 35, 40

produces the binary search tree in Figure 12-5(a), which does not have a nicely balanced shape. If we determine the number of comparisons required to locate each value and compute the average, we see that the tree requires 4.0 comparisons per

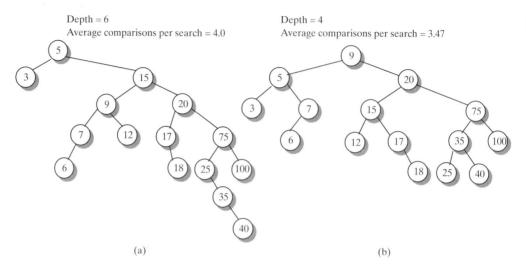

Depth = 6
Average comparisons per search = 4.0

Depth = 4
Average comparisons per search = 3.47

(a)   (b)

Figure 12-5
Two binary search trees

search. The tree in Figure 12-5(b) is also a binary search tree and contains the same data, but has a more balanced shape. It requires an average of 3.47 comparisons per search.

In the worst case, a set or map adds elements in order and thus creates a degenerate tree. The access and update operations become linear, O(n). We want to eliminate the worst case for binary search trees and build trees that have balance like the tree in Figure 12-5(b). This ensures that the set or map operations are always logarithmic.

To accomplish our task, we need to design new search-tree structures. We do this in two stages. We begin by extending the node structure for a binary search tree to a more general tree whose nodes can have more than one data value and more than two children. In particular, we design a 2–3–4 search tree, consisting of a collection of nodes that have two, three, or four children. The resulting structure is *perfectly balanced* in the sense that the depths of the left and right subtrees for each node are equal. While 2–3–4 trees satisfy our goal of balance, they are difficult and inefficient to implement. In the next section, we create representations of 2–3–4 trees, called red–black trees, that are binary trees with sufficient balance to ensure logarithmic search and update operations. We build the red–black trees by using a simple strategy that converts the nodes in a 2–3–4 tree into a binary search tree.

Let us look at a 2–3–4 tree. We begin by defining a *2-node* as a node containing a data value and pointers to two subtrees (hence, the name *2-node*). If A is the data value and the left subtree is not empty, the value of the root of the left subtree is less than A. Similarly, the value of the root of the right subtree is greater than A. A 2-node is simply a normal binary search tree node. A *3-node* is a node containing two ordered data values A and B such that A < B, as well as three pointers to subtrees. Value A cannot equal value B; we do not allow the 2–3–4 tree to have duplicate values. Assuming that the subtrees are not empty, the value of the root for the left subtree is less than A, the value of the root for the middle subtree lies between A and B, and the value of the root for the right subtree is greater than B. The final node structure in a 2–3–4 tree is the *4-node*. It contains three ordered data values A < B < C, along with four pointers to subtrees. The value of the root of the left subtree is less than A; the value of the root of the second subtree lies between A and B; the value of the root of the second subtree from the right lies between B and C; and the value of the root of the rightmost subtree is greater than C.

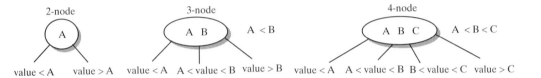

The tree in Figure 12-6 is a 2–3–4 tree containing integer data. A 2–3–4 tree is a search tree, and the process of locating a value in the tree is similar to the algorithm we use for finding data in a binary search tree. To locate an item, start at the root and compare the item with the values in the existing node. If no match occurs, move to the appropriate subtree. Repeat the process until you locate the data or encounter an empty subtree. For instance, to locate *item* = 7, begin at the root and compare the value 7 with the value 12. Because 7 is less than 12, move to the 4-node (4, 8, 10), which is the left child of the root. The value 7 is not in the node, but rather lies between values 4 and 8. Proceed to the second subtree from the left, landing in the 3-node (5, 7). The search concludes with a match at this node. When searching for *item* = 30, follow the branch from the root to the right subtree because 30 is greater than 12. In the 2-node, compare values 30 and 25, and proceed to the 3-node

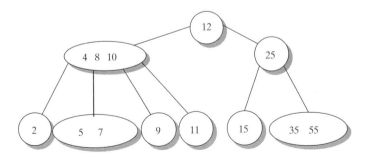

Figure 12-6
2–3–4 tree

(35, 55), because 30 is greater than 25. The next comparison finds that the value, 30 is less than value 35, and the search continues to the left subtree of the node, which is empty, telling us that the value 30 is not in the tree.

Inserting Into a 2–3–4 Tree

Building a 2–3–4 tree uses an insertion algorithm similar to that for a binary search tree. The process begins with a single node and adds elements until the node is full. The term *full* implies that the node is a 4-node with three elements. Before inserting the next element, split the 4-node into three 2-nodes, where the median value becomes the parent and the other two values become the left and right children:

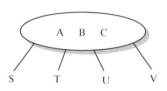
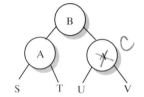

The next element then enters the tree under the insertion rule for a binary search tree. If the value is less than the parent, add the element in the left child node. If the value is greater than the parent, add the element in the right child node.

Let us apply the insertion strategy for 2–3–4 trees to the sequence 2, 15, 12, 4, 8, 10, 25, 35, 55, 11, 9, 5, 7. In the process, you will see how the strategy applies as the tree grows. In the end, the resulting tree is the 2–3–4 tree in Figure 12-6.

Insert 2, 15, 12: Create a 2-node with value 2 at the root. Combine 15 with 2 to form a 3-node at the root, and then conclude by adding 12. The root is a 4-node with values in the order 2 < 12 < 15.

Insert 2   Insert 15   Insert 12

Insert 4: There is no room in the 4-node for 4, and so we perform the first split. The middle value, 12, becomes the parent, and values 2 and 15 become the left and right child, respectively. The depth of the tree increases by 1, and it remains perfectly balanced. The element 4 then enters the tree. All insertions occur at a leaf node. Because 4 < 12, insert 4 into the left child of the root, creating the 3-node (2, 4).

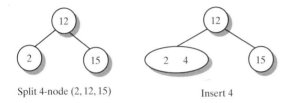

Split 4-node (2, 12, 15)   Insert 4

Insert 8:   The value 8 is less than the root value 12, and thus its inser-
                        tion is into the left child of the root. The resulting leaf node
                        becomes the 4-node $(2, 4, 8)$.

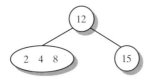

Insert 10:   The element should enter the left child of the root. Howev-
                        er, the node is full, and a split must occur. The middle value,
                        4, moves up to the parent (the root) and creates a 3-node
                        with $4 < 12$. The value 2 becomes the left child of the root,
                        and the value 8 becomes the middle child of the root. This
                        frees up room in the leaf nodes. The insertion rule com-
                        pares 10 with values in the root node and determines that
                        10 lies between 4 and 12. The new value enters the middle
                        child, creating the 3-node $(8, 10)$.

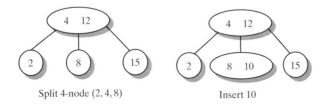

Split 4-node (2, 4, 8)   Insert 10

Insert 25, 35, 55:   Using the insertion rule, place 25 in the right child of the
                        root, because $25 > 12$. Similarly, place 35 in the same right
                        child, creating a 4-node$(15, 25, 35)$. The rule next indicates
                        that 55 should enter the right child of the root. However,
                        this node is now full and requires splitting. The middle
                        value, 25, moves to the root, creating the 4-node $(4, 12, 25)$.
                        The other two values, 15 and 35, then become children on
                        the right side of the tree. Complete the insertion by adding
                        55 to node 35.

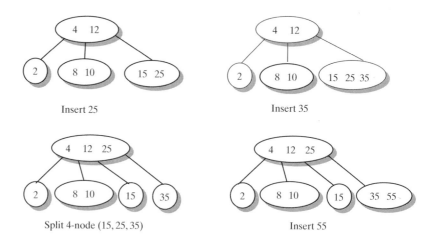

Insert 25

Insert 35

Split 4-node (15, 25, 35)

Insert 55

Before entering 11, let us observe the current status of the tree. The previous insertion of 55 caused a split of the 4-node (15, 25, 35) and a move of the middle value, 25, to the parent (root). In this case, the parent becomes a 4-node. Suppose the parent was already a 4-node. Then the split in the child would trigger a second split in the parent, with an element moving to the grandparent. As the tree gets bigger, an insertion at the bottom of the tree could begin a chain of splits back up the tree, perhaps all the way to the root. This bottom-up approach to splitting 4-nodes is inefficient, because the insertion must scan down the tree to find the insertion point and then retrace the path to split parent, grandparent, and so forth. A simpler technique splits all 4-nodes as they are encountered during the scan down the tree, looking for the insertion point. The top-down approach to splitting 4-nodes guarantees that whenever we come to the bottom of a tree, we are not inserting into a 4-node; we always insert into 2-node or a 3-node. The insertion transforms either a 2-node to a 3-node or a 3-node to a 4-node.

Insert 11: The top-down approach to splitting 4-nodes comes into play with the insertion of 11. The root is a 4-node, which splits into three 2-nodes having 12 as the new root. The split increases the depth of the tree by 1. The new element enters the 3-node (8, 10) in the right subtree of 4.

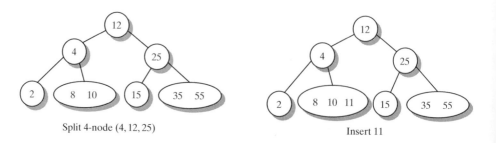

Split 4-node (4, 12, 25)

Insert 11

Insert 9:   In scanning the tree to find the insertion point for 9, we fol-
                    low the path from the root to node 4 and then to the 4-node
                    (8, 10, 11). With our top-down technique, we first split the 4-
                    node. In the new tree, the insertion point for 9 is the leaf
                    node 8 on the path 12, (4, 10), and 8.

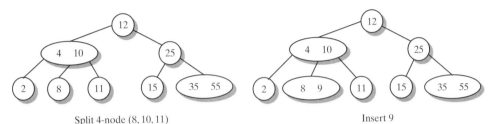

Split 4-node (8, 10, 11)   Insert 9

Insert 5, 7:   The path to insert 5 follows the left subtree of 12 and then
                    moves to the middle child of (4, 10), because 5 lies between
                    these two values. The element enters the 3-node (8, 9). A
                    similar path locates the insertion point for 7. However, the
                    leaf node is now the 4-node (5, 8, 9), which must be split.

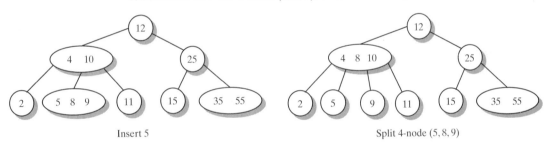

Insert 5   Split 4-node (5, 8, 9)

Inserting 7 into the 2-node with value 5 completes the
building of the 2–3–4 tree.

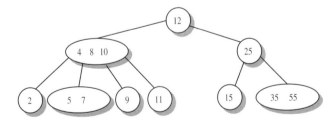

Running Time For 2–3–4 Tree Operations

Recall that in a complete binary tree with n nodes, the depth d is int($\log_2 n$), and a
path to locate a node in the tree has maximum length

$$\text{int}(\log_2 n) + 1$$

Assume that an n-element 2–3–4 tree has only 2-nodes. Because the tree is perfectly balanced, all of its interior nodes have two children, and the tree is complete. In searching for an element, the maximum number of nodes visited is int($\log_2 n$)+1. If the tree has 3- and 4-nodes, the length of the path will probably be lower. As a result, we can state the following property of 2–3–4 trees.

> **2–3–4 Trees Fact 1:**   In a 2–3–4 tree with n elements, the maximum number of nodes visited during the search for an element is int($\log_2 n$) + 1.

When performing an insertion, frequent node splits slow down an application that uses 2–3–4 trees. In the worst case, all nodes in the tree are 4-nodes. When traversing a path looking for an insertion point, the top-down technique for splitting 4-nodes requires at most int($\log_2 n$) + 1 splits. In fact, this case is unlikely to occur, and practice has shown that insertions require many fewer node splits on the average, because 2–3–4 trees do not tend to have many 4-nodes.

> **2–3–4 Trees Fact 2:**   Inserting an element into a 2–3–4 tree with n elements requires splitting no more than int($\log_2 n$) + 1 4-nodes and normally requires far fewer splits.

Implementing a 2–3–4 tree poses some problems. Because any node can have up to three values and four pointers, a node object would need to store seven data values, yet most nodes are not 4-nodes, so many of the data values are unused. A program might need to allocate a large amount of wasted space. Assume that the 2–3–4 tree contains n nodes. The corresponding objects must allocate $4 * n$ pointers. Because every node in the tree has a unique parent (except the root), the tree must have $n - 1$ edges (pointers in use). The number of unused pointers is

$$4n - (n - 1) = 3n + 1$$

which is approximately three fourths of the pointers. Besides the space consideration, handling the more complex structures is likely to make programs using 2–3–4 trees run more slowly than if the programs used standard binary search trees. The reason for creating a balanced tree is to eliminate the worst case of binary search trees and to make searches faster. Fortunately, there is a way to use the good balance and insertion features of a 2–3–4 tree by using an equivalent binary tree. In the next section, we develop a representation of a 2–3–4 tree as a red–black tree. The properties and operations for the new tree structure are derived from those we developed for 2–3–4 trees. A red–black tree has operations that require little more computation than those used by standard binary search trees.

12-7   RED–BLACK TREES

A red–black tree is a binary search tree in which each node has the color attribute BLACK or RED. It was designed as a representation of a 2–3–4 tree, using different color combinations to describe 3-nodes and 4-nodes. The link between these two types of trees is critical to your understanding the structure of a red–black tree and its operations.

We will motivate every red–black tree operation by looking at the corresponding 2–3–4 tree structure. Much of our presentation consists of pictures that illustrate how red–black tree algorithms must identify color patterns among the nodes and perform color changes and rotations to restructure the tree. In Section 12-9, we translate the pictures into algorithms that implement a red–black tree container class.

Figure 12-7 is an example of a red–black tree. We use a shaded node to represent a RED node. If you do not consider color, the tree is simply a binary search tree.

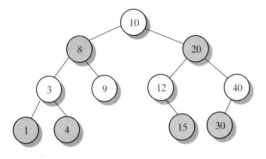

Figure 12-7
Red–Black Search Tree with
Integer Values

To indicate how a red–black tree is a representation of a 2–3–4 tree, we need a way to use binary nodes and colors to describe the 2–3–4 tree nodes. We use a simple scheme to represent a 2-node and a 4-node. A 3-node is more complex, because it has two possible red–black tree representations. A 2-node is an ordinary binary tree node. Assume that a 4-node has values A, B, and C. For the red–black tree, take the center node B as BLACK and values A and C as RED children.

A 3-node with values A and B has two possible representations using red–black tree nodes. Designate A as a BLACK node and B as its right RED child, or designate B as a BLACK node and A as its left RED child. With two choices for a 3-node, a red–black tree representation of a 2–3–4 tree is not unique (Figure 12-8). In the equivalent red–black tree structure, the subtree root has one pointer and the RED child has two.

In a red–black tree, look for the color grouping of nodes to indicate the configuration of 2-, 3-, and 4-nodes in the corresponding 2–3–4 tree. For instance, a grouping that includes a BLACK parent and two RED children corresponds to a 4-node; a collection that includes a BLACK parent and exactly one RED child corresponds to a 3-node.

4-node (A, B, C)
in a 2-3-4 Tree

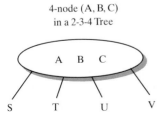

Representation with a black
parent and two red children

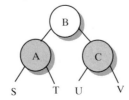

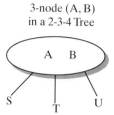

3-node (A, B)
in a 2-3-4 Tree

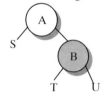

Representation with a black
parent and a red right child

Representation with a black
parent and a red left child

Figure 12-8
3-nodes in a red–black tree

Properties Of A Red–Black Tree

With the ability to represent each node in a 2–3–4 tree as a color-coordinated collection of nodes in a red–black tree, we can build the complete representation of a 2–3–4 tree as a red-black tree. The top-down technique starts at the root and then proceeds to the nodes at level 1, level 2, and so forth. For each node in the 2–3–4 tree, apply a red–black tree representation. Because 3-nodes have two possible representations, the conversion is not unique.

Let us go through an example in detail. The process will reveal important properties of red–black trees that we will use when we design algorithms to build the trees. Use the 2–3–4 tree in Figure 12-9, which consists of 11 values on two levels. The finished product will be the red–black tree in Figure 12-10.

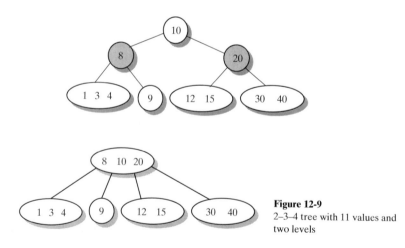

Figure 12-9
2–3–4 tree with 11 values and
two levels

Step 1   Converting the root node.

Convert the 4-node at the root into three red–black nodes, where the middle value is a BLACK node and the values 8 and 20 are RED children.

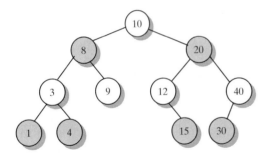

Figure 12-10
Red–black tree equivalent to
the 2–3–4 tree in Figure 12-9

Step 2 Converting the children of 8.

The left child node of 8 is a 4-node that converts to a BLACK parent
and two RED children. The right child, node 9, is a simple 2-node that
converts to a BLACK node.

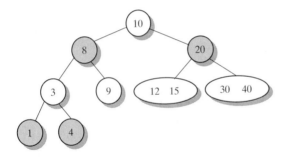

Step 3 Converting the children of 20.

Both children of node 20 are 3-nodes. They have two possible representations that depend on which value becomes the parent. For the 3-
node (12, 15), we let 12 be the BLACK parent and 15 be its RED right
child. For 3-node (30, 40), let 40 be the BLACK parent and 30 be its
RED left child (Figure 12-10).

The conversion process reveals important properties that apply to any
red–black tree. We list the properties and refer to steps in the conversion process to
provide the rationale:

Property 1. The root of a red–black tree is BLACK. If the root of the 2–3–4
tree is a 2-node, the root of the red–black tree is BLACK. Similarly, if the root of the 2–3–4 tree is a 3-node or a 4-node, the conversion to a red–black tree produces a BLACK parent at the root.

Property 2.   A RED parent never has a RED child; in other words, there are never two RED nodes in succession. In the conversion to a red–black tree, any RED node that is part of a 3- or a 4-node must be followed by a 2-, 3-, or 4-node, each of which has a BLACK node as the root of its subtree. In our sample tree, after step 1, the RED node 8 has one 4-node child and one 2-node child. The red node 20 has two 3-node children. In step 2, the 2-node 9 converts to a BLACK node. The 4-node (1, 3, 4) converts to a BLACK node 3 and two RED children. The BLACK parent follows the RED node 8. No matter which form of conversion is used for the 3-nodes (12, 15) and (30, 40), the parent is a BLACK node following the RED 20.

Property 3.   Every path from the root to an empty subtree (NULL pointer) has the same number of BLACK nodes. We call this number the *black height* of the tree; it defines the notion of balance for a red–black tree. In our sample tree, every path from the root to an empty subtree has two BLACK nodes. Every red–black tree has an equivalent 2–3–4 tree. Any path from the root of the 2–3–4 tree to an exterior (leaf) node falls on the same number of nodes, since the tree is perfectly balanced. As we move down a path in the red–black tree, each BLACK node we encounter corresponds to a level change in the 2–3–4 tree, so the number of BLACK nodes we encounter on any path to an empty subtree must be the same.

Inserting Nodes in a Red–Black Tree

Insertion into a red–black tree is more complicated than adding an element to an ordinary binary search tree. We must maintain the black height balance of the tree. The additional computation, however, is relatively small. The process follows a set of guidelines. Periodically, we must execute actions that restructure the tree. The guidelines are as follows:

Maintain the root as a BLACK node.

Enter a new node into the tree as a RED node, since each new node enters a 2-node or a 3-node.

Whenever the insertion results in two RED nodes in succession (RED parent and RED child), rotate nodes to create a BLACK parent while maintaining balance.

When scanning down a path to find the insertion location, split any 4-node (BLACK parent and two RED children). Recall that we perform this operation for a 2-3-4 tree.

The tree requires restructuring when we encounter two RED nodes in succession. This can occur when we insert a new node (RED node) at the bottom of the tree or at an intermediate node during the splitting of a 4-node. Let us look at these two situations separately. Examples illustrate the problem and motivate the solution.

Insertion at the Bottom of the Tree   Assume that a tree contains the nodes (5, 12), where node 5 is the root. Node 5 is BLACK (the root is BLACK), and node 12 is RED. Insertion of node 2 into the tree adds a RED left-child of the root, and we have a 4-node.

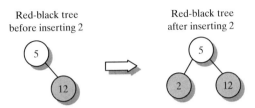

Rather than inserting 2, insertion of the value 14 into the tree places a RED node as the child of the existing RED node 12. Two RED nodes occur as successive right children, so a rotation is required. Move node 12 into position as the new root (BLACK), and set nodes 5 and 14 as the two RED children. The restructuring is called a *single (left) rotation*, since it creates a new parent by moving a node (node 12) up one level and to the left. In the figure, we illustrate the rotation. Note that the resulting tree is a 4-node (BLACK parent 12, RED children 5 and 14).

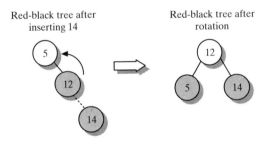

A different type of rotation results from the insertion of node 10. In the resulting tree, we have two successive RED nodes that are a right child and a left grand-child of node 5. A rotation moves node 10 up two levels to become the new BLACK root. The grandparent, node 5, becomes a RED left-child of node 10, and RED node 12 becomes the right child of node 10. Since the rotation creates a parent by moving a node up two levels and to the left, we refer to it as a *double (left) rotation*.

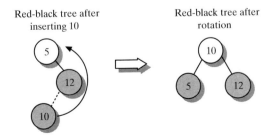

Splitting a 4-node During the scan down a path in a red–black tree, we encounter a 4-node when the subtree has a BLACK parent and two RED children. The algorithm requires an immediate splitting of the node. From our understanding of the 2–3–4 tree representation of a red–black tree, the split requires moving the BLACK parent up one level. We know that the node at the higher level could not be a 4-node, because it would have been split previously during the scan down the tree. Hence, moving the BLACK parent up one level will create a new 3-node or a new 4-node at the higher level. The fact that the BLACK parent must move up one level will be critical to our developing the algorithms that split the 4-node.

For discussion purposes, assume that X is the name of the BLACK parent in the 4-node. There are four situations that can occur when we discover a 4-node. The situations distinguish the color of the parent of X, called P, and, the orientation (left or right) of X as a child of P. Figure 12-11 illustrates the different possibilities.

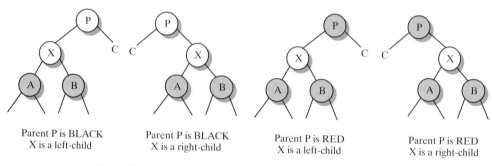

| Parent P is BLACK | Parent P is BLACK | Parent P is RED | Parent P is RED |
| X is a left-child | X is a right-child | X is a left-child | X is a right-child |

Figure 12-11
Four situations in the splitting of a 4-node

In each case, the splitting of a 4-node begins with a *color flip* that reverses the color of each of the nodes. The parent node X become RED, and its two children become BLACK. Making X RED has the effect of moving the node up one level. We are now in a position to look at the four different situations. When the parent node P is BLACK, the color flip is sufficient to split the 4-node, whether X is a left or right child of P. In Figure 12-12, the 4-node is a left child of P. The figure includes the 2–3–4 tree view of the red–black tree, before and after the color flip.

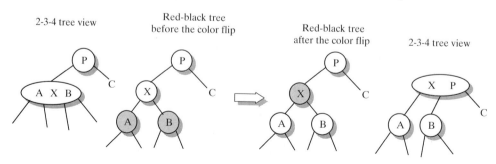

Figure 12-12
Splitting a 4-node that is the left child of a BLACK parent P

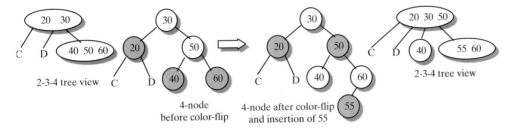

Figure 12-13
Splitting a 4-node prior to inserting node 55

Let us use an example to look at the situation where the parent P is BLACK and the 4-node is a right child of P. In Figure 12-13, the parent P is the root of the tree, and the 4-node includes values 40, 50, and 60. Assume that we discover the 4-node in the process of inserting node 55 into the tree. After the color flip, the new node enters the tree as the left child of node 60. Note that because the 3-node (20, 30) is represented with 20 as a RED node there is no color conflict.

Splitting a 4-node with Rotations   The previous examples illustrate that, when the parent of the 4-node is BLACK, a color flip is sufficient to the split the node. The red–black tree has proper structure. The situation is quite different when the parent is RED. The split will involve rotations that include the parent of P. We denote the node as G, to indicate that it is the grandparent of the BLACK node X. In Figure 12-14, consider the situation where P is a left child of G, and the 4-node is a left child of P. This left–left ordering of G, P, and X requires a single right rotation about P. The analogous situation is a right–right ordering of G, P, and X, which requires a single left rotation about P. In the figure, we begin with the usual color flip. The resulting nodes, P and X, create a color conflict, because they are both RED. A single right rotation about P makes node G a right child of P and copies the right subtree C of P across as the new left subtree of G. Node P changes color to BLACK, and the grandparent node G becomes RED. The changes in color maintain the black height of the tree. The term *single rotation* is derived from the fact that the subtree at P moves to the right and up one level in the tree. We include in Figure 12-14

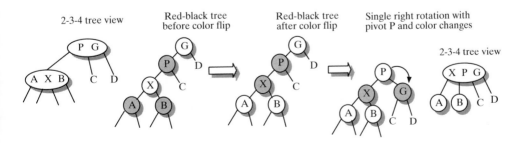

Figure 12-14
Splitting a 4-node oriented left–left from node G using a single right rotation

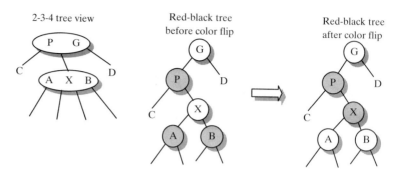

Figure 12-15
Splitting a 4-node oriented left–right from node G after the color flip

the 2–3–4 tree view of the red–black tree, before and after the color flip and rotation. The view was the motivation for the algorithm.

Rotations also occur in the splitting of a 4-node, when the parent P is a left child of G, and the 4-node is a right child of P. We illustrate this in Figure 12-15 and refer to the situation as a left–right order of nodes G, P, and X. An analogous right–left ordering has P as the right child of G, and the 4-node as the left child of P. The figure gives the order of nodes in the red–black tree before and after the color flip. The 2–3–4 tree view describes the ordering before the color flip.

To remove the color conflict, we use a double rotation, which consists of a single left rotation about X, followed by a single right rotation about X. In Figure 12-16, we illustrate each of these single rotations. You will note that these are just the rotations that we introduced in the previous section.

In Figure 12-16, we show the node configuration after each of the single rotations. The rotations and the coloring of the nodes are treated as separate operations. After the second rotation, color X as BLACK, make both the parent P and the grandparent G be RED. You will recognize that P X G is now a new 4-node, because the node is BLACK and its children are RED. The new 4-node will not be split until a subsequent insertion creates a new scan down the tree. In Figures 12-15 and 12-16, you can see the 2–3–4 tree

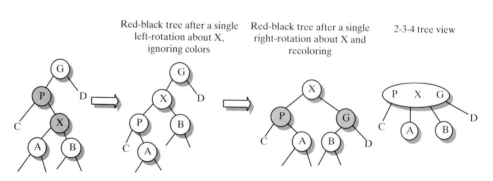

Figure 12-16
Splitting a 4-node with a double rotation

view of the red–black tree before and after the color flip and double rotation. You will also note that the reorientation involves two rotations – hence, the term *double rotation*.

Building A Red–Black Tree

In Section 12-7, we created a 2–3–4 tree with the insertion sequence 2, 15, 12, 4, 8, 10, 25, 35, 55, 11, 9, 5, 7. Let us use the first eight terms in the same sequence to illustrate red–black tree insertion algorithms. Each picture includes a view of the insertion into the red–black tree and the equivalent 2–3–4 tree. The interested reader can complete the sequence and produce the red–black tree in Figure 12-17.

Before beginning, note the general rules that apply at each step. Insert each node as a RED node. In this way, the insertion has no effect on the balance of the tree. If a color flip makes the root node RED, set the root to BLACK. This action just adds 1 to the BLACK height of the tree.

Insert node 2:   Insert node 2 into an empty tree as a RED node. Because node 2 is the root, change its color to BLACK.

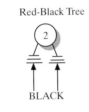

Insert nodes 15, 12:   We consider NULL to be a node with color BLACK. In this way, when we look at the root, we see two BLACK children and do not recolor the root:

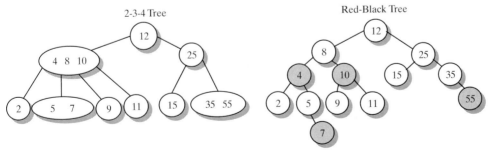

Figure 12-17
2–3–4 tree and red–black tree for the insertion sequence *2, 15, 12, 4, 8, 10, 25, 35, 55, 11, 9, 5, 7*

Element 15 enters the tree as a RED node and the right child of 2. The initial location for 12 is the left child of 15. Placing 12 in the tree as a RED node causes a color conflict and requires a rotation. The figure includes the NULL pointers, because they participate in rotations. Notice that 12 is an inside grandchild of 2, so we must perform a double left rotation. The two-step process creates a 4-node with 12 as the BLACK parent.

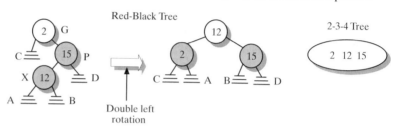

Insert node 4:   When we enter the tree at the root, we see a BLACK parent with two RED children, which make up a 4-node. Each 4-node on the insertion path must be split. A color flip implements the split. Insert 4 as the right RED child of 2, and color the root BLACK.

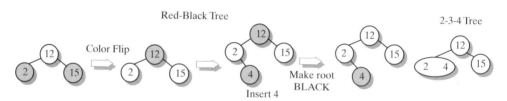

Insert node 8:   Insert 8 as the right RED child of 4; this action causes a color conflict. Because 8 is an outside grandchild of 2, perform a single left rotation. As in the insertion of 12, the NULL pointer participates in the rotation.

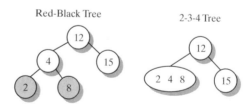

Insert node 10:   The 4-node (2, 4, 8) exists on the insertion path. The parent of the 4-node is a 2-node, so a color flip splits the node, and no rotation is necessary. Insert 10 as the RED right child of 8.

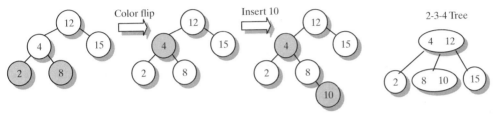

Insert nodes 25, 35:   Insert 25 as the RED right child of 15. No color conflict occurs. Insert 35 as the right RED child of 25, causing a color conflict that we correct with a single left rotation.

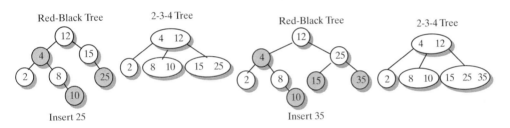

Search Running Time (Optional)

The purpose of building red–black trees is to ensure that the worst-case running time for a search is $O(\log_2 n)$. We should intuitively expect that this is true, because top-down 2–3–4 trees have a worst-case search time of $O(\log_2 n)$, and we build red–black trees by modeling our operations on top-down 2–3–4 trees. We apply some simple mathematics to develop the result in this section. The analysis relies on the following fact:

Let B be the BLACK height of the red–black tree and *blackNum* be the number of BLACK nodes. Then

$$2^B - 1 \le blackNum$$

The interested reader can prove this result by using mathematical induction. We use the inequality to show that the worst-case running time for searching a red–black tree with n elements is $O(\log_2 n)$. Since the number of BLACK nodes is no more than n.

$$2^B - 1 \le blackNum \le n$$

So, $\log_2(2^B) \le \log_2(n + 1)$, and $B \le \log_2(n + 1)$.

The greatest depth a red–black tree with BLACK height B can have is $2B - 1$. A tree attains this depth when it has a path to an empty subtree that alternates between BLACK and RED nodes. Such a path contains $2B$ nodes:

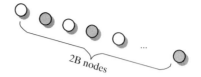

For instance, the tree in Figure 12-18 has a BLACK height of 2 and a path to an empty subtree with four nodes. Using the inequality that relates B and $\log_2(n + 1)$, the depth d of the tree satisfies the relation

$$d \le 2B - 1 < 2B \le 2 \log_2(n + 1)$$

Thus, the depth of the tree is $O(\log_2 n)$, and a search makes at most $O(\log_2 n)$ comparisons. An insertion also involves splitting 4-nodes. We must make at most $O(\log_2 n)$ comparisons on the way down the insertion path. From the discussion of 2–3–4 trees, we will split no more than $O(\log_2 n)$ 4-nodes, and each node split requires only color and pointer changes. Hence, the insertion has running time $O(\log_2 n)$.

Erasing a Node in a Red–Black Tree

Recall that erasing a node from an ordinary binary search tree is much more difficult than inserting a node. The same is true for a red–black tree. We will not develop the algorithm, but will just discuss some of the problems that it must handle. Recall that to erase a node, you find a replacement node and link it into the tree in place of the deleted node. If the replacement node is RED, the BLACK height of the tree is not changed, and no other action is necessary. In the the tree of Figure 12-19, when we delete the root, the replacement is the RED node 78.

When the replacement node is BLACK, we must make adjustments to the tree from the bottom up in order to maintain balance. In the original tree in Figure 12-19, if we search for and delete node 90, the replacement is the BLACK node 100. Node 100 assumes the position of node 90 in the tree and has color RED. As Figure 10-1 shows, the tree is out of balance. We regain balance by performing a right rotation and a recoloring of nodes. In general, the bottom-up algorithm that balances the tree when the replacement node is BLACK requires a series of color flips and at

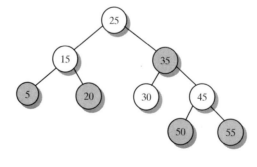

Figure 12-18
Red–black tree with maximal depth

Delete 75
Replacement node is RED

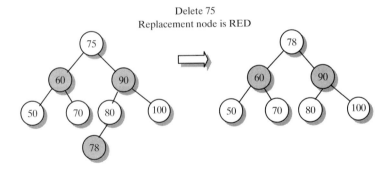

Figure 12-19
RED Replacement Node in a Deletion

most three rotations as it moves up the tree. Thus, the algorithm to delete a node from a red–black tree has running time $O(\log_2 n)$. The interested reader should consult Cormen, Leiserson, and Rivest, *Introduction to Algorithms* (McGraw-Hill, 2002) for a full discussion of the algorithm.

Delete 90
Replacement node is BLACK

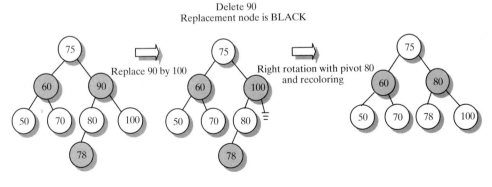

Figure 12-20
Replacement node is black during red–black tree node deletion

THE RBTREE CLASS   12-8

In Chapter 10, we implemented the binary search tree class stree with stnode objects including the node value, pointers to the left and right subtrees, and a parent pointer. To implement a red–black tree class, we extend the structure of a tree node object to include a fifth data member, consisting of the node color. The color of a node is the enumeration type *colorType*:

```
enum colorType {RED, BLACK}
```

The rbnode class describes the nodes in a red–black tree:

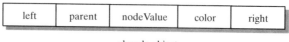

rbnode object

As with ordinary binary search trees, the implementations of the member functions for the rbtree class maintain and update the parent field of nodes. The parent of the root node is NULL. The parent pointer is critical for the iterator operations ++ and −−, whose implementation is identical to that of the iterators for the stree class. The upcoming code is a declaration of the rbnode class. The nondefault constructor has five arguments that initialize the data members. Figure 12-21 displays a model of a binary search tree with its configuration, using rbnode objects.

CLASS rbnode	Declaration	"d_rbtree.h"

```cpp
// each node of a red-black tree is of type rbnode
template <typename T>
class rbnode
{
   public:
      colorType color;     // node's color
      rbnode<T> *parent;   // node's parent
      rbnode<T> *left;     // node's left child
      rbnode<T> *right;    // node's right child
      T nodeValue;

      // constructors
      rbnode(const T& item, rbnode<T> *leftPtr, rbnode<T> *rightPtr,
         rbnode<T> *parentPtr, colorType c):
            nodeValue(item), left(leftPtr),
            right(rightPtr), parent(parentPtr), color(c)
      {}

      rbnode()
      {}
};
```

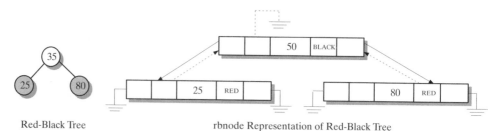

Red-Black Tree   rbnode Representation of Red-Black Tree

Figure 12-21
Black tree representation

The public interface of the rbtree class is identical to that of the stree class, whose API we presented in Section 10-5. The displayTree() operation indicates that a node is RED by following the data value with an asterisk (*).

PROGRAM 12-4   USING THE RBTREE CLASS

You have experience with binary search tree programs from our work with the stree class. Let us show how one of these programs would translate to red–black trees. An array contains initial values for the tree. The rbtree iterator scans elements in order, so a call to writeContainer() lists the elements in ascending order. We include calls to insert() and erase() to add elements 7 and 75 and then remove the root, 35. The function displayTree() illustrates the original tree and the trees produced by the update operations. Figure 12-22 provides a graphical view of the trees.

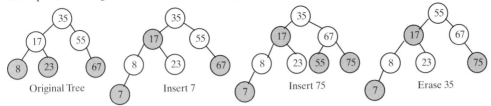

Figure 12-22
Trees in run of program 12-4

```
// File: prg12_4.cpp
// the program creates a red-black tree whose elements come from
// the integer array arr. a call to writeContainer() from
// "d_util.h" displays the tree data in ascending order. the
// program calls the displayTree() function from the rbtree
// class to output the tree and then inserts the values 7 and
// 75 into the tree. after each insertion, displayTree() is
// called to display the tree structure. the program concludes
// by deleting 35 (tree root) and displaying the final tree

#include <iostream>

#include "d_rbtree.h"
#include "d_util.h"

using namespace std;

int main()
{
    // initial red-black tree data
    int arr[] = {23, 35, 55, 17, 8, 67};
    int arrSize = sizeof(arr)/sizeof(int);
    rbtree<int> t(arr, arr+arrSize);

    // display the elements in order
    cout << "Listing of elements: ";
    writeContainer(t.begin(), t.end());
```

```
    cout << endl << endl;

    // display the initial tree
    t.displayTree(3);
    cout << endl;

    // insert operations add 7 and 75
    t.insert(7);
    cout << "Insert 7" << endl;
    t.displayTree(3);
    cout << endl << endl;

    t.insert(75);
    cout << "Insert 75" << endl;
    t.displayTree(3);
    cout << endl << endl;

    // erase the root 35
    t.erase(35);
    cout << "Erase 35" << endl;
    t.displayTree(3);
    cout << endl;

    return 0;
}
```

```
Run:

Listing of elements: 8   17   23   35   55   67


                  35
        17                55
8*          23*                67*

Insert 7

                        35
            17*                55
        8         23                67*
7*


Insert 75

                        35
            17*                      67
        8         23         55*          75*
7*


Erase 35

                        55
            17*                67
        8         23                75*
    7*
```

rbtree Class Private Section

The private functions in the rbtree class are similar to those found in the stree class. They include copyTree(), deleteTree(), findNode(), buildShadowTree(), and deleteShadowTree(). The function getRBNode() allocates an rbnode object and throws a memoryAllocationError exception if the heap does not have sufficient memory.

The private data members include the rbnode pointer NIL, which plays an important role in the tree operations. Rather than using the pointer value NULL (0) to indicate an empty subtree, we use NIL, which points to an actual rbnode object whose node value we do not initialize and whose child and parent pointers are NULL. Its color is BLACK, to ensure that a 3-node such as the following would not be taken as a 4-node:

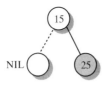

The use of NIL allows the node to participate in rotation operations like any other node. There is no point in having each rbtree object allocate its own rbnode node object pointed to by NIL. Declaring NIL static causes all rbtree objects to share one copy of NIL:

```
static rbnode<T> *NIL;
    // used instead of NULL to represent an empty subtree. NIL
    // is shared by all rbtree<T> objects. its pointers are NULL,
    // and its color is BLACK. it participates in rotations,
    // just like any other node
```

Splitting a 4-Node

In the implementation of the rbtree class, the function split4Node() and the rotate operations are fundamental. We discuss the splitting of a 4-node to give you an idea of how the class implements an algorithm. Code for the rotation operations is included in the header file "d_rbtree.h" and includes extensive documentation to assist your understanding of the algorithms.

The insert() function calls split4Node() to handle node splits and any required rotations. The argument to the function is a pointer x to a node whose children are RED (a 4-node). The function performs a color flip by changing the color of the children to BLACK and the color of x to RED. Once the color flip is complete, the operation must check the color of the parent of x. If the parent is RED, a color conflict occurs and requires a rotation. No matter what the rotation, the grandparent of x will be RED. A double rotation occurs if the orientation of the grandparent to the parent differs from the orientation of the parent to x. For instance, if p $==$ g $->$ right && x $==$ p $->$ left, we perform a double left rotation, as indicated in the following figure:

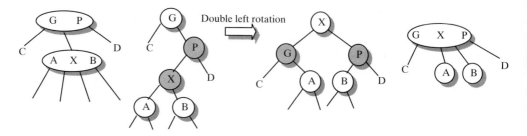

The double left rotation performs a single right rotation with pivot x. A double right rotation performs a single left rotation with pivot x. In either case, the color of x is BLACK. The double rotation concludes with a single rotation in the opposite direction with pivot x. For an ordinary single rotation, the pivot is p. Prepare for the single rotation by setting p to have value x.

We perform a single rotation with pivot p if the orientation of the grandparent to the parent is the same as the orientation of the parent to x. For instance, if p == g -> left && x == p -> left, we perform a single right rotation. In either case, the parent is BLACK.

split4Node():

```
template <typename T>
void rbtree<T>::split4Node(rbnode<T> *x)
{
  // perform the color flip
  x->color = RED;
  x->left->color = BLACK;
  x->right->color = BLACK;

  // if we split the root, we are done
  if (x == root)
     return;

  // to see if a rotation is required, we need the
  // parent of x. x is not root, so p != NIL
  rbnode<T> *p = x->parent;

  // a rotation is needed if the parent of x is RED
  if (p->color == RED)
  {
     // we need the grandparent of x. since the root
     // is BLACK, p cannot be root, so the grandparent
     // exists
     rbnode<T> *g = x->parent->parent;

     // the grandparent of x will be RED
     g->color = RED;
     // double rotation is required if x is an inside
     // grandchild. check this by seeing if the orientations
     // of p to g and x to p are different
```

```
            if ( p == g->left && x == p->right )
            {
                // perform a double right rotation
                // first move x up one level and p down
                rotateLeft(x);

                // node x will be BLACK
                x->color = BLACK;
                // prepare for a right single rotation
                p = x;
            }
            else if ( p == g->right && x == p->left )
            {
                // perform a double left rotation
                // first move x up one level and p down
                rotateRight(x);
                // node x will be BLACK
                x->color = BLACK;
                // prepare for a left single rotation
                p = x;
            }
            else
                // single rotation. parent will be BLACK
                p->color = BLACK;
            // perform a single rotation
            // move p up and g down
            if (p == g->left)
                rotateRight(p);
            else
                rotateLeft(p);
        }
    }
```

The Insert() Operation

The operation insert() is similar to the corresponding operation for an ordinary binary search tree. The only real difference is that we must perform restructuring operations on the way down the insertion path. The loop contains a statement that calls split4Node() when it encounters a node with two RED children. Upon completion of the loop, the function allocates a RED node and links it into the tree. If a color conflict occurs, call split4Node() to resolve it. Prior to returning, assign to the root the color BLACK.

insert():

```
        template <typename T>
        pair<rbtree>T>::iterator,bool> rbtree<T>::insert (const T& item)
        {
            rbnode<T> *curr = root, *parent = NIL, *newNode;
            // loop until we find the value in the tree or locate
            // the insertion point
```

```
    while (curr != NIL)
    {
        // if a match occurs, return an iterator-bool pair with the
        // iterator pointing at the match and Boolean value false
         ...
        // a node split is required if both children of curr are RED
        if (curr->left->color == RED && curr->right->color == RED)
                split4Node(curr);
        // move down the tree
        parent = curr;
        if (item<curr->nodeValue)
           curr = curr->left;
        else
           curr = curr->right;
    }
    // allocate and insert the element as a RED node
    ...
    // the insert may create a color conflict which is
    // dealt with by a call to spit4Node()
    if (parent->color == RED)
       split4Node(newNode);
    ...
    // the color of the root must be BLACK
    root->color = BLACK;
    // increment tree size and return an iterator-bool pair
    ...
}
```

CHAPTER SUMMARY

- The fastest searching technique is to know the index of the required value in a vector or array and apply the index to access the value. This is an O(1) algorithm. A hash table simulates this process by applying a hash function that converts the data value to an integer. After obtaining an index by dividing the value from the hash function by the table size and taking the remainder, access the table. Normally, the number of elements in the table is much smaller than the number of distinct data values, so collisions occur. To handle collisions, we must place a value that collides with an existing table element into the table in such a way that we can efficiently access it later. The two most commonly used algorithms for collision resolution are linear probe open addressing and chaining with separate lists.

- With linear probe addressing, the table is a vector or array of static size. After using the hash function to compute a table index, look up the entry in the table. If the values match, perform an update if necessary. If the table entry is empty, insert the value in the table. Otherwise, probe forward circularly, looking for a match or an empty table slot. If the probe returns to the original starting point, the table is full. For this algorithm, you can search table items that hashed to different table locations.

- For chaining with separate lists, the hash table is a vector of list objects. Each list is a sequence of colliding items. After applying the hash function to compute the table index, search the list for the data value. If it is found, update its value; otherwise, insert the value at the back of the list. With this algorithm, you search only items that collided at the same table location. In addition, there is no limitation on the number of values in the table, and deleting an item from the table involves only erasing it from its corresponding list. Deleting an item from a linear probe table is more difficult.

- It is critical to the performance of hashing that we compute the hash function efficiently. In addition, the hash function should uniformly distribute data over the table index range. In Section 12-2, we discuss efficient hash functions for integer and string data. We implement the functions as instances of function object types. The concept of a function object type is necessary; it is the means of communicating the hash function to the hash container class.

- Section 12-4 discusses the construction of the container class hash that implements chaining with separate lists. The iterators for the class do not traverse the data in sorted order. This class provides an alternative implementation structure for sets and maps.

- In Section 12-5, a relatively simple mathematical analysis shows that the average running time for a search of a hash table is $O(1)$. However, the worst case is $O(n)$. The section compares and contrasts the search algorithms we have discussed in the book. These include the sequential and binary searches, the binary tree search, and hashing.

- In a 2–3–4 tree, a node has either one value and two children, two values and three children, or three values and four children. Section 12-6 develops an algorithm for building a perfectly balanced 2–3–4 tree. The actual construction of 2–3–4 trees is complex, so we build an equivalent binary tree known as a red–black tree. We develop all operations on red–black trees by looking at the corresponding 2–3–4 tree.

- Section 12-7 discusses the construction and update of red–black trees. Using primarily pictures, we show how to insert into a red–black tree by modeling the operations with the corresponding 2–3–4 tree. Deleting a node from a red–black tree is rather difficult. We present only a basic idea of the problems involved.

- Section 12-8 implements the class rbtree, which builds a red–black tree. We discuss the implementation of the insertion algorithm in some detail. Although the class implements the erase() operation, the section does not discuss its implementation.

CLASSES AND LIBRARIES IN THE CHAPTER

Name	Header File
function writeContainer()	d_util.h
hash function object types	d_hashf.h
hash table iterators	d_hiter.h

hash   d_hash.h
rbtree   d_rbtree.h
seqSearch(), binSearch() functions   d_search.h
stree   d_stree.h
timer   d_timer.h

REVIEW EXERCISES

1. Consider the given hash function object type for strings. Give two strings whose length is ≥ 3 that collide after division by the table size. Is this a good hashing function? Why?

```
class stringHash
{
   public:
      unsigned int operator() (const string& s) const
      {
         int n = s.length();
         unsigned int hashval;

         if (n == 0)
            hashval = 0;
         else if (n == 1)
            hashval = s[0];
         else
            hashval = s[0] * 256 + s[1];

         return hashval;
      }
};
```

2. Assume that a hash function has the following characteristics:

Keys 77, 355, and 276 hash to 3.
Keys 945 and 579 hash to 5.
Key 517 hashes to 0.
Key 155 hashes to 2.
Perform insertions in order the 945, 77, 276, 355, 517, 155, 579.

(a) Using linear probe addressing, indicate the position of the data.

        0   1   2   3   4   5   6

(b) Which element requires the largest number of probes to be found in the table (if more than one element, give the element with the smallest index in the hash table)? _____

(c) Which element(s) can we access with a single probe?

_____ _____   _____ _____   _____ _____

(d) What is the load factor?

3. Use the hash function hf(x) = x, m = 11 to map an integer value to a hash table index.
   (a) Insert the data 15, 45, 36, 7, 77, 3, 6, 25, 29, 38, 11, 0, 95, 1 into the hash table, using chaining with separate lists.
   (b) What is the load factor? _____

Hash Table

0	
1	
2	
3	
4	
5	
6	
7	
8	
9	
10	

Handwritten notes:
14 = n = # of elements in table
11 = m = # of buckets
$^{14}/_{11}$ = λ

4. If a hash table with n elements uses chaining with separate lists, what are the average and worst-case complexities for a successful and an unsuccessful search?

Worst case for an unsuccessful search: O (___n___)
Worst case for a successful search: O (___n___)
Average case for an unsuccessful search: O (___1___)
Average case for a successful search: O (___1___)

Handwritten notes:
success chain: $1 + \frac{λ}{2} - \frac{1}{2m}$
fail chain: λ

5. (a) Declare a hash table *hint* with integer values having 101 buckets. Use the hash function object type hFint.
   (b) Declare a hash table *hstr* of strings having 1327 buckets.
   (c) Show how to create a hash function object type *hFsalaryAndYears*, for the given class. The double value is the key.

```
class salaryAndYears
{
    public:
        double salary;
        int yearsEmployed;
};
```

Handwritten notes:
success linear: $\frac{1}{2} + \frac{1}{2(1-λ)}$
fail linear: $\frac{1}{2} + \frac{1}{2(1-λ)^2}$

6. Is the given tree a valid 2–3–4 tree? If not, modify the tree so that it is.

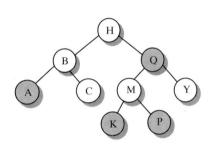

7. Draw a 2–3–4 tree that contains the characters in the string
SEARCHTWO

8. Consider the following insertion sequence:

15, 55, 28, 45, 32, 40, 35, 38, 36, 37

   (a) Draw the corresponding binary search tree.
   (b) Draw a red–black tree that corresponds to the data.

9. (a) If $v = \{3, 8, 12, 35, 2, 8, 12, 55\}$, what are the values in v after a call of the function f()?

```
template <typename T>
void f(vector<T>& v)
{
    rbtree<T> t;
    rbtree<T>::iterator i;
    vector<T>::iterator j;

    for(j=v.begin(); j != v.end(); j++)
        t.insert(*j);

    for(i=t.begin(), j=v.begin(); i!= t.end(); i++, j++)
        *j = *i;

    v.resize(t.size());
}
```

   (b) In general, what do you think is the running time for f() as a function of $n = $ v.size()?

10. (a) What is the worst-case complexity for insertion into a red–black tree?
O (_____).
   (b) The erase() algorithm used by rbtree moves up the tree, performing at most three rotations, until the tree is in balance. What is the worst-case complexity for the algorithm?   O (_____).

Answers To Review Exercises

1. The strings "cat," "catalog," and "car" all have the same first two characters; they collide. This is not a good hashing function. It does not mix up the characters of the string sufficiently to minimize the probability of collisions.

2. (a)

517	579	155	77	276	945	355
0	1	2	3	4	5	6

   (b) The value 579 requires four probes. The integer value 355 also requires four probes.
   (c) Access to the elements 517, 155, 77, and 945 require one probe.
   (d) The load factor is $\lambda = 7/7 = 1.0$.

3. (a)

Hash Table

0	77 11 0
1	45 1
2	
3	36 3 25
4	15
5	38
6	6
7	7 29 95
8	
9	
10	

(b) $\lambda = 14/11 \cong 1.2727$

4. Worst case for an unsuccessful search: $O(n)$
Worst case for a successful search: $O(n)$
Average case for an unsuccessful search: $O(1)$
Average case for a successful search: $O(1)$

5. (a) `hash<int, hFint> hint(101);`
(b) `hash<string, hFstring> hstr(1327);`
(c) `class hFsalaryAndYears`

```
    {
        public:
            unsigned int operator() (const salaryAndYears& obj)
            { return hFreal() (obj.salary); }
    };
```

6. The path {H, B, C} to an empty subtree has 3 BLACK nodes, and all the others have 2 BLACK nodes. The tree is not a red–black tree. The following tree is a red–black tree containing the same data:

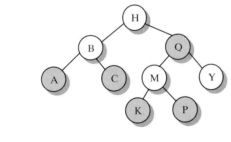

7.

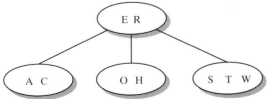

8. (a)

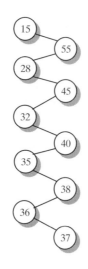

(b)

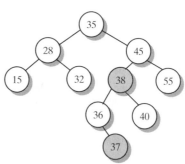

9. **(a)** The function f() removes duplicate values and sorts a vector in ascending order. The values in v after the call to f() are $v = \{2, 3, 8, 12, 35, 55\}$.

(b) The function inserts n values into the red–black tree. Each insertion requires $O(\log_2 n)$ running time, so building the tree has running time $O(n \log_2 n)$. Copying the data back into the vector is an $O(n)$ operation. The total running time is $O(n \log_2 n)$.

10. **(a)** $O(\log_2 n)$　　　**(b)** $O(\log_2 n)$

WRITTEN EXERCISES

11. Show that the identity hash function

$$hf(x) = x$$

is unacceptable if the table size m is even. Is the situation changed if m is odd?

12. This exercise investigates a hashing function for an integer value *item*. Generate a random real number x in the range $0 \le x < 1$. Let f be the fractional part of the product $x \, *item$ that is in the range $0 \le f < 1$. Multiply this number by m to obtain a hash value in the range

from 0 to $m - 1$. This algorithm is known as the *multiplicative method*. Implement a function object type *hFintM* that provides a hash function using this method:

```
class hFintM
{
   public:
     hFintM(int v = 1237);
         // constructor. initialize m. default value is a prime

     unsigned int operator()(int item) const;
         // hash function

     int getM();
     void setM(int v);
         // access and update m

   private:
      int m;
};
```

13. Assume that a hash function has the following characteristics:

> Keys 257 and 567 hash to 3.
> Keys 987 and 313 hash to 6.
> Keys 734, 189, and 575 hash to 5.
> Keys 122, 391 hash to 8.

Assume that we perform insertions in the order 257, 987, 122, 575, 189, 734, 567, 313, 391.

(a) Indicate the position of the data if we use linear probe addressing to resolve collisions.

ht

```
  0  1  2  3  4  5  6  7  8  9  10
+--+--+--+--+--+--+--+--+--+--+--+
|  |  |  |  |  |  |  |  |  |  |  |
+--+--+--+--+--+--+--+--+--+--+--+
```

(b) Indicate the position of the data if we use chaining with separate lists to resolve collisions.

Hash Table

```
0  +------------------------+
1  +------------------------+
2  +------------------------+
3  +------------------------+
4  +------------------------+
5  +------------------------+
6  +------------------------+
7  +------------------------+
8  +------------------------+
9  +------------------------+
10 +------------------------+
```

14. Repeat Written Exercise 12-13, but reverse the order of the insertions.

15. Use the hash function hf(x) = x, m = 11 to map an integer value to a hash table index. Insert the data 1, 13, 12, 53, 77, 29, 31, 22 into the hash table.

    (a) Construct the hash table by using linear probe addressing.

    (b) Construct the hash table by using chaining with separate lists.

    (c) For both techniques, determine the load factor, the average number of probes needed to locate a value in the table, and the average number of probes needed to determine that a value is not in the table. For linears probe addressing, when counting the number of probes needed to locate a value that is not in the table, count the discovery of an empty slot as a probe. For chaining with separate lists, record an encounter with the end of a list as a probe.

16. Consider the given hashing function object for strings. What can you say about strings "aefghk" and "gaefkh"? Is this a good hashing function? Why?

```
class hFstr
{
   public:
      unsigned int operator () (const string& s) const
      {
         int i;
         unsigned int hashval = 0;

         for(i=0;i < s.length();i++)
            hashval += s[i];

         return hashval;
      }
};
```

17. A programmer sometimes uses a technique called *folding* to develop hash functions. Partition the key into several parts, convert each part to an integer, and combine them to produce an integer value. Suppose a program must deal with a social security number as a key. Break the key into three groups of three digits, and add them. This produces an integer in the range 0 .. 2997. For instance, the social security number 523456795 produces the hash index 523 + 456 + 795 = 1774. Write the hash function object type *hFssn*, which takes a social security number and uses folding to return the hash value. You will need to extract the substrings and convert each to an integer. Perform the conversion by using the function atoi() in the library <cstdlib>.

```
// return the integer value of str
int atoi(const char *str);
```

For example,

```
string("523456795"), part;
int n;

part = s.substr(0,3);
n = atoi(part.c_str());
```

18. Consider the hash function object type

```
class hFint256
{
    public:
        unsigned int operator() (int item) const
        {
            return (item/16) % 256;
        }
};
```

(a) What is the size of the hash table?

(b) What are hFint256() (16) and hFint256() (257)?

(c) In general, what is the action of the hash function?

19. A problem with linear probe addressing is that it produces table *clustering*. Entries tend to "bunch together" in areas of the table as collisions occur.

Suppose there are m table entries. If the hashing function uniformly distributes indices, what is the probability of hashing to location p? Once data occupy table location p, location $p + 1$ can be occupied by data hashing to location p or location $p + 1$. What is the probability of filling location $p + 1$? What is the probability of filling slot $p + 2$? In general, explain why clustering occurs.

20. If the data are not located at the initial hashed index, the linear probe method presented executes the function

```
    index = (index+1) % m;    // look at next index
```

This is called a *rehash function*, and linear probe addressing is a method that resolves collisions by rehashing. As indicated in written exercise 19, this approach fosters clustering. A different rehash function can better distribute entries. We say that two integers p and q are *relatively prime* if they have no common divisors other than 1. For instance, 3 and 10 are relatively prime, as are 18 and 35. For linear probe addressing, use a rehash function of the form

```
    index = (index + d) % m;
```

where d and m are relatively prime. As we successively apply the relation, it can be shown that the sequence of indices covers the range $0 \ldots m - 1$. The traditional linear probe method uses $d = 1$.

(a) If d and m are not relatively prime, table entries are omitted. Show that if $d = 3$ and $m = 93$, the rehash function

```
index = (index + 3) % 93
```

covers only every third table entry.
(b) Show that if m is prime and $d < m$, then the entire table is covered by the rehash function.
(c) Do Written Exercise 12-15(a), using the rehash function

```
index = (index + 5) % 11
```

21. Hash tables are suited to applications where the primary operation is retrieval: Insert a data value, and then "look it up" many times. The linear probe hashing method is poorly suited to an application that requires that data elements be deleted from the hash table.

Consider the following hash table of 101 entries with hash function hf(*key*) = *key*

(a) Delete 304 by placing -1 (empty) in table location 1. What happens when we search for 707? Explain in general why just marking a slot as empty is not a correct solution to the problem of deletions.
(b) A solution to the problem involves placing a special value, *deletedData*, in the location of the deletion. When searching for a key, we skip table locations marked with *deletedData*. Use the key value -2 in the table to indicate that a deletion occurred at the particular table location. Show that this approach to deleting 304 allows a correct search for 707.

The insertion and retrieval operations in the linear probe algorithm must be modified to accommodate deletions.

(c) Describe an algorithm to delete a table element.
(d) Describe an algorithm to locate an element in the table.
(e) Describe an algorithm to insert an element in the table.
22. Recall that for hashing with chaining, in the average case,

$$U_n = \lambda,$$
$$S_n \cong 1 + \lambda/2$$

where U_n is the number of probes for an unsuccessful search of an n-element hash table and S_n is the number of probes for a successful search. Suppose $n = 1000$ and it is required that $U_n \le 1.75$ and $S_n \le 2.5$. Find the smallest acceptable value for m. Hint: Here are some prime numbers that could be helpful:

503 509 521 523 541 547 557 563 569 571 577 587 593 599

23. Another collision resolution method that is sometimes used is *chaining with coalescing lists.* This method is similar to linear probe addressing, except that we chain together colliding data values that must be circularly located further down the table in a linked list. Each chain might contain data whose keys hashed to different table locations. These lists have coalesced. For example, if $hf(x) = x$, $m = 7$, insert the integers 12, 3, 5, 20, and 7 into the table.

-1 designates an empty entry and a NULL pointer

0	20	1
1	7	-1
2	-1	-1
3	3	-1
4	-1	-1
5	12	6
6	5	0

Note that -1 designates an empty entry and a NULL pointer.

(a) Do Written Exercise 12-15(a), using chaining with coalescing lists.

(b) How do you think the runtime search efficiency of this method compares with that of linear probe addressing?

(c) Is the problem of performing deletions simpler than it is for linear probe addressing? Explain.

24. Given a set of keys $k_0, k_1, ... k_{n-1}$, a *perfect hashing function* hf() is a hash function that produces no collisions. It is not practical to find a perfect hashing function unless the set of keys is static. A situation for which a perfect hash function is desirable is a table of reserved words (such as "while", "template", and "class" in C++) that a compiler searches. When an identifier is read, only one probe is necessary to determine whether the identifier is a reserved word.

It is difficult to find a perfect hash function for a particular set of keys, and a general discussion of the subject is beyond the scope of this book. Furthermore, if a new set of keys is added to the set, the hash function normally is no longer perfect.

(a) Consider the set of integer keys 81, 129, 301, 38, 434, 216, 412, 487, 234 and the hashing function

$$hf(x) = (x + 18)/63$$

Is hf() a perfect hashing function?

(b) Consider the set of keys consisting of the strings

Bret, Jane, Shirley, Bryce, Michelle, Heather

Devise a perfect hash function for a table containing seven elements.

25. Consider the following hash function object:

```
class sHash
{
    public:
        unsigned int operator() (const string& s) const
        {   unsigned int hashval;
            if (s.length() == 0)
                hashval = 0;
            else
                hashval = s[0] + s[s.length()-1];
```

```
        return hashval;
    }
};
```

Declare a hash table of strings with 19 buckets that uses *sHash* as its hash function object type:

```
hash<string, sHash> ht(19);
```

Insert the strings "house", "dog", "printer", "animal", "tea", "key", "icon", and "course" into the hash table. The following table gives the hash function value for each string.

String	sHash() (String)
house	15
dog	13
printer	17
animal	15
tea	4
key	0
icon	6
course	10

Give the order in which an iterator visits the strings.

26. **(a)** Draw the binary search tree built when you insert the keys E A S Y Q U T I O N (in that order) into an initially empty tree.

   (b) Draw the 2–3–4 tree built when you insert the keys from part (a) into an initially empty tree.

   (b) Draw a red–black representation of the tree in part (b).

27. For the case of a double rotation with an inside left grandchild, draw the corresponding 2–3–4 tree configuration before and after the rotation and recoloration.

Double Rotation - X is inside left grandchild

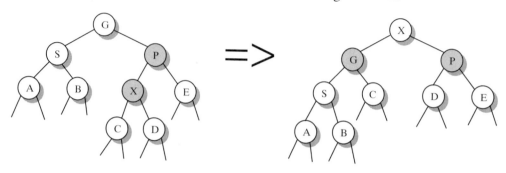

28. **(a)** Construct a 2–3–4 tree from the insertion sequence 20 30 5 45 25 36 42 33 55 3 2 4 67 28.

   (b) Draw a red–black representation of the tree in part (a).

29. (a) Draw the binary search tree that results when the letters A through G are inserted in order.

   (b) Draw the red–black tree that results when the letters A through G are inserted in order.

30. Build the red–black tree that results from inserting the values 2, 5, 3, 7, 9, 12, 1, 15, 18, 26, 4, 0, 19, 6, 25, in that order.

31. This exercise investigates what happens when we allow duplicates in a red–black tree. First, start with a 2–3–4 tree that allows duplicates. Using the rule "≥ move right," show that the following figure represents the 2–3–4 tree built by inserting the character data

   A A R D V A R K

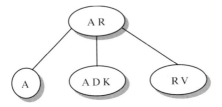

Convert the 2–3–4 tree to a red–black tree. Do nodes whose values equal that of a given node fall on both sides of that node? Will the algorithm "< go left, ≥ go right" find all duplicate values? If your answer to the question is no, can you propose an algorithm to locate all duplicate values?

PROGRAMMING EXERCISES

32. This exercise develops a simple spelling checker. The file "dict.dat" in the directory Ch12 of the program supplement contains 25,025 frequently used words, each on a separate line in lowercase. Read the file, and insert the words into a hash table with 1373 buckets. Prompt for the name of a document. Read the document, and separate it into a sequence of words converted to lowercase, where a word is defined by the function

```
// extract a word from fin
ifstream& getWord(ifstream& fin, string& w)
{
    char c;

    w = ""; // clear the string of characters

    while (fin.get(c) && !isalpha(c))
        ; // do nothing. just ignore c

    // return on end-of-file
    if (fin.eof())
        return fin;

    // record first letter of the word
    w += tolower(c);

    // collect letters and digits
```

```
        while (fin.get(c) && (isalpha(c) || isdigit(c)))
          w += tolower(c);

        return fin;
    }
```

Using the hash table, output a list of words that appear to be misspelled.

33. Implement the class integer and its associated function object type *hFinteger* in the header file "intv.h":

```
class integer
{
    public:
        // constructor. initialize intValue and set count = 1
        integer(int n = 0);

        // return intValue
        int getInt();
        // return count
        int getCount();

        // postfix ++. increment count
        integer operator++ (int);

        // compare integer objects by intValue
        friend bool operator< (const integer& lhs, const integer& rhs);
        friend bool operator== (const integer& lhs, const integer& rhs);

        // output object in format intValue(count)
        friend ostream& operator<< (ostream& ostr, const integer& obj);

        // allow hFinteger access to integer
        friend class hFinteger;

    private:
        // the integer and its count
        int intValue;
        int count;
};
class hFinteger
{
    public:
        unsigned int operator() (const integer& obj) const
        { <implementation> }
};
```

Implement a function toss() that uses a *randomNumber* object to simulate the tossing of *n* dice and returns the total:

```
// use rnd to simulate tossing n dice
int toss(int n, randomNumber& rnd);
```

Declare a hash table *diceHash* whose values are objects of type *integer* and whose table size is 17. The program should simulate the tossing of five dice a total of 1,000,000 times and compute the frequency for each total. For each toss, if the total is in the table, increment its count; otherwise, insert the total with a count of 1. Using a hash table iterator, traverse the table and insert the values into a vector. Use the insertionSort() from "d_sort.h" to order the vector and output the sorted dice totals and frequencies. For each total, also output the empirical probability, which is the ratio of the frequency and the total number of tosses.

34. This exercise compares different hashing functions.
    (a) Write a program that creates a hash table of strings whose values come from the ordered list of words in "sdict.dat." Use the hash function object type *hFstring* from "d_hashf.h," and set the hash table size to 1423. Start a timer object, and input strings from the file "udict.dat," which is a random ordering of "sdict.dat." Look up each string in the hash table. Upon reaching the end of file, output the time required for the search activity.
    (b) Repeat part (a), using the hash function object type *sHash* from Written Exercise 12-25.
    (c) Repeat part (a), using the hash function object type *hFstr* from Written Exercise 12-16. What conclusions can you draw from the programs?

35. (a) Using the class stree in "d_stree.h," write a program that constructs a binary search tree from the data values 20, 35, 5, 18, 7, 15, 22, 6, 37, 3, 19, 55, 38, 8, 2, 16, 12, 17, 13. Output the tree, using the member function displayTree(). Explain its shape.
    (b) Write a program that constructs a red–black tree from the same data values. Output the tree, using the member function displayTree (). Explain its shape.

36. (a) Repeat Programming Exercise 12-34(a), using a red–black tree to store the strings. However, create the tree from the strings in the file "udict.dat," and use the strings in "sdict.dat" to time the search operations.
    (b) Repeat part (a), but use an ordinary binary search tree instead. Discuss the results. What would happen if we build the tree from "sdict.dat" and search using the strings in "udict.dat"?

PROGRAMMING PROJECTS

37. (a) Implement the class *umapHashKey*, which creates a hash function for *miniPair* objects that uses only the key of the pair (*first*). The third template argument is a function object type that takes a *Key* argument. Place the class in the header file "umaphash.h".

```
// a hash function object type that applies KeyHashFunc
// to the key in a miniPair object
template <typename Key, typename T, typename KeyHashFunc>
class umapHashKey
{
   public:
      unsigned int
      operator()(const miniPair<const Key, T>& item) const;
};
```

   (b) Use the hash class to implement the unordered map class *umap*, and place it in the header file "umap.h". Use the miniMap class in "d_map.h" and the unordered set class uset in "d_uset.h" as a guide for your work. Run Program 11-4 using the unordered map class. Use umapHashKey to implement a hash function for miniPair<string, time24> objects that uses the only the string (key).

38. (a) Develop the class *openHash*, which maintains a hash table by using linear probe open addressing using the suggested class declaration. Place the class in the header file "openprob.h". Use Written Exercise 12-21 as a guide for implementing the erase() operation.

```
template <class T, class HashFunc>
  class openHash
  {
      public:
          class iterator;
          friend class iterator;
          class const_iterator;
          friend class const_iterator;
            // give the iterator classes access to private
            // section of openHash
          class iterator
          { ... };
          class const_iterator
          { ... };
          openHash(int nbuckets, const HashFunc& hfunc = HashFunc());
            // constructor specifying number of buckets in the
            // hash table and the hash function
          openHash(T *first, T *last,
                  int nbuckets, const HashFunc& hfunc = HashFunc());
            // constructor with arguments including a pointer range
            // [first, last) of values to insert, the number of
            // buckets in the hash table, and the hash function
              < remainder of public interface identical to that of hash >
      private:
          class tableRecord
          {
              public:
                  // entry available (true or false)
                  bool available;
                  T data;
                  tableRecord(): available(true)
                  {}
          };
          int numBuckets;
            // number of buckets in the table
          vector<tableRecord> bucket;
            // the hash table is a vector of tableRecord entries
          int hashtableSize;
            // number of elements in the hash table
          HashFunc hf;
            // the hash function
  };
```

(b) Use the openHash class to run Program 12-2.

(c) Do Programming Exercise 12-32 by using the openHash class. Use a hash table size 35353.

♦

Inheritance and Abstract Classes

OBJECTIVES

- To understand the concept of inheritance, in which a derived-class inherits data and operations from a base class.
- To understand the meaning of the protected section of a base class.
- To study the implementation of a derived class constructor and other member functions.
- To study the implementation of an employee hierarchy as an example of public inheritance.
- To study the design and implementation of a graphics hierarchy that allows the drawing of geometric figures and text.
- To see how the programmer can use inheritance to extend the vector class by adding index bounds checking.
- To study the use of inheritance for deriving an ordered list class from the STL list class.
- To understand the difference between static and dynamic binding of class member function calls.
- To understand the concept of polymorphism and its implementation in C++ by means of virtual member functions.
- To study examples of polymorphism, using the employee and graphics hierarchies.
- To understand the concept of pure virtual functions and their use in forming an abstract base class that serves as a template for implementing derived classes.

OUTLINE

Object composition defines one type of relationship among classes. A client class has one or more data members that are supplier class objects. As a result, we call object composition the "has a" relationship. Inheritance is another type of relationship. It involves sharing of attributes and operations among classes. A *base class* defines a set of common attributes and operations that it shares with derived classes. A *derived class* extends the resources provided by the base class by adding its own data members and member functions. For instance, a manufacturing company employs both salaried workers and others who work on an hourly basis. All of the employees share common attributes such as name, social security number, and date of hire. The attributes, along with access and update functions, describe the base class *employee*. The derived classes, *salaryEmployee* and *hourlyEmployee*, share the common attributes and operations of the employee class and define additional attributes and operations that the accounting office can use to produce payroll checks. In the case of a salaried employee, the office needs to know the annual salary, broken out in pay periods. Hourly employees receive paychecks based on the amount of time they worked and the hourly pay rate. Figure 13-1 illustrates the relationship between the base class and derived classes with arrows connecting the derived classes to the base class. The arrows highlight the fact that the derived class has access to the information stored in the base class.

Inheritance is often called the "is a" relationship; the reason is demonstrated by the fact that a salaried employee is also an employee and an hourly employee is also an employee.

Most of us associate the term *inheritance* with our parents, grandparents, and so forth. At conception, we inherit important attributes and characteristics from our parents. We become "like them" in very basic ways, but have our own uniqueness. The science of biology uses inheritance to describe the subdivision of the animal kingdom. For instance, the classification *animal* describes attributes shared by monkeys, cats, birds, and so forth. Although all share the attribute *animal*, there are dif-

Figure 13-1
Inheritance relationship between a base class and derived classes

ferent families of animals, each with its own special characteristics. Each of the animal types is further partitioned into *species*. The cat family includes lions, tigers, and cheetahs among its species. A hierarchy tree describes the entire animal organization, in which classifications at any level inherit the characteristics of all previous levels (Figure 13-2). For example, a cat is an animal, a tiger is a cat, and so forth. Relationships are valid over multiple levels, such as the fact that a tiger is an animal.

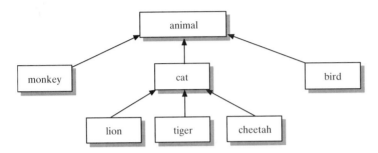

Figure 13-2
Hierarchy Tree Describing Inheritance Relations in the Animal Organization

In this chapter, we introduce the object-oriented concept of inheritance and its C++ syntax. Section 13-1 uses the employee hierarchy to illustrate the declaration and implementation of base and derived classes. Design of a graphics package is a classical application of inheritance. We develop a package that draws circle, rectangle, polygon, and line shapes in a window, as well as text. Section 13-2 discusses the use of inheritance in the design of the classes in the package, and Section 13-3 develops the supporting function library and provides a sample program.

The concept of inheritance has limited, but important, uses in data structures. In Section 13-4, we use inheritance to extend the functionality of the vector class by deriving a safe array class. The class has all the functions of the vector class and, in addition, provides an index operator that does bounds checking. As another example of inheritance in data structures, Section 13-5 derives an ordered list class from the list class by redefining the function insert().

Polymorphism adds an extra dimension to the use of inheritance. The term *polymorphism* is derived from ancient Greek and means "many forms." In programming, *polymorphism* means that a member function with the same name can be implemented in different classes. When an application needs the function, the particular version is dynamically determined at runtime. C++ implements polymorphism by using virtual member functions. Section 13-6 develops polymorphism and presents two application programs that illustrate the concepts.

The chapter concludes with a study of abstract base classes that are templates, or molds, for the construction of derived classes. A base class can specify the name, argument list, and return value that must be used for selected member functions in a derived class. Abstract base classes specify the design of a class that is likely to have different implementations. The section develops the stackInterface class as an example. It serves as a mold for the generation of different derived classes that implement the stack interface.

13-1   INHERITANCE IN C++

A C++ class *inheritance hierarchy* begins with a *base class* that defines a set of common attributes and operations that it shares with derived classes. A *derived class* inherits the resources of the base class and overrides or enhances their functionality with new capabilities. Let us look at the syntax that builds base and derived classes. The classes are separate, but related. The syntax must specify the access characteristics of the members so that each class can preserve an appropriate level of information hiding while fostering relationships among the members in the inheritance hierarchy. We begin by specifying the rules of access for general base and derived classes. You will see the rules in action when we apply them to the employee hierarchy.

The base class that starts an inheritance chain has no special designation. We must extend the derived-class declaration to include a reference to the base class:

Base Class

```
class baseCL
{
    public:
        <members>
    protected:
        <members>
    private:
        <members>
};
```

Derived Class

```
class derivedCL: public baseCL
{
    public:
        <members>
    private:
        <members>
};
```

In the declaration of a derived class, the keyword *public* in the class header specifies the use of *public inheritance*. Public inheritance determines the type of access that derived class objects and member functions have to the base class members. The private members in the base class remain private. Only the implementation of member functions in the base class can access these members. Any base or derived object, as well as any implementation of a member function in the derived class, can access the public members in the base class. In the base class, C++ allows for a new category of members called *protected members*. The scope of a protected member is the base class and all derived classes. This means that the base class and any derived class can access a protected member in the implementation of a member function.

Let's look at inheritance from the point of view of what a base or a derived class can access. A base class can access its private and protected members. Of course, it can also access its public members. A derived class can access the protected and public members of the base class, as well as all of the members in its own class. The importance of the "protected" label for members in the base class is the access it provides programmers when they implement derived-class member functions. Figure 13-3 illustrates a class hierarchy. The arrows on the left specify the access of member functions in the derived class to members of the base class. The functions can access only protected and public members of the base class. The right side of the diagram illustrates the access provided to a derived object. The object can access only the public members of the base and derived classes.

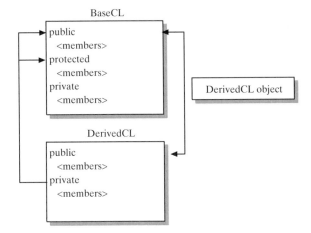

Figure 13-3
Access to class members, using public inheritance

In addition to public inheritance, C++ allows a programmer to declare a derived class with *private* and *protected inheritance*. These forms of inheritance modify the access of both derived class member functions and a derived object to the base-class members. The exercises discuss private inheritance. Protected inheritance has few applications, so we do not present it in the book.

Note

Declaring The Employee Hierarchy

Now that you understand how to declare base and derived classes with public inheritance and have the rules for access to base-class members, we can illustrate these ideas with the employee hierarchy that includes the employee base class, along with the derived salaryEmployee and hourlyEmployee classes. Let us start with the base class. The personnel office at a manufacturing plant sets up a record for each worker consisting of the worker's name and social security number. The record consists of two strings and represents data common to both salaried and hourly workers. The attributes are protected data members in the employee class. The constructor has arguments that initialize the data members. The arguments have the empty string as a default value. For operations, the employee class has public member functions setSSN() and setName() to update the data members and the output function displayEmployeeInfo(), which outputs labels, along with the name and social security number of the worker.

The upcoming code is a declaration of the employee class. We include in the listing a declaration of the member function payrollCheck(), which includes the attribute *virtual*. We will explain the meaning of the attribute *virtual* and the significance of payrollCheck() in Section 13-6 on polymorphism and virtual functions. The section will also explain why we include the attribute *virtual* for displayEmployeeInfo().

```
CLASS employee                    Declaration              "d_emp.h"

// base class for all employees
class employee
{
   public:
      employee(const string& name = "", const string& ssn = "");
         // constructor with default arguments for the attributes

      void setName (const string& name);
         // update the employee name

      void setSSN (const string& ssn);
         // update the Social Security Number

      virtual void displayEmployeeInfo() const;
         // output basic employee information

      virtual void payrollCheck() const;
         // function with this prototype will exist in each
         // derived class

   protected:
         // maintain an employee's name and Social Security Number
         string empName;
         string empSSN;
};
```

Employee Derived Classes   The accounting office at our manufacturing plant needs payroll information for each employee. Because the plant has workers both on fixed salary and on hourly pay, the office declares two classes that extend the attributes and operations of the base class. The new classes provide data and operations that focus on salary information. The salaryEmployee class has the data member *salary*, specifying the amount of payment on each payroll check. To update this amount, use the function setSalary(). The member function displayEmployee-Info() outputs the worker's name and social security number, along with the designation "salaried worker" and the weekly salary amount. The name and social security number, are information derived from the base class. The format for displayEmployeeInfo() is

```
Name: empName
Social Security Number: empSSN
Status:  salaried employee
Salary per week $salary
```

The accounting office uses the function payrollCheck() to cut a weekly payroll check. The function payrollCheck() produces a check in the form

```
Pay empName (empSSN) $salary
```

The upcoming code is the declaration of the salaryEmployee class. You will note that the constructor contains arguments to initialize the salary, along with the employee's name and social security number. We discuss the design and implementation of a derived-class constructor in the next section.

CLASS salaryEmployee **Declaration** **"d_emp.h"**

```
// salaried employee "is an" employee with fixed salary per pay period
class salaryEmployee : public employee
{
   public:
      salaryEmployee(const string& name, const string& ssn, double sal);
         // initialize employee attributes and monthly salary

      void setSalary(double sal);
         // update the monthly salary

      virtual void displayEmployeeInfo() const;
         // display employee info and status "salaried employee"

      virtual void payrollCheck();
         // output a payroll check
   private:
      double salary;            // salary per pay period
};
```

The hourlyEmployee class has a similar design. For salary information, the class declares private data members *hourlyPay* and *hoursWorked*. The update functions setHourlyPay() and setHoursWorked() enable the accounting office to adjust the hourly rate and the work schedule for the employee's check. The functions displayEmployeeInfo() and payrollCheck() play roles similar to those in the salaryEmployee class. The format for displayEmployeeInfo() is

```
Name: empName
Social Security Number:  empSSN
```

```
Status:     hourly employee
Payrate:    $hourlyPay per hour
Work schedule (hours per week) hoursWorked
```

The amount of payment to an hourly employee depends on the hourly rate and the schedule of hours. The function payrollCheck() produces a check in the form

```
Pay empName (empSSN) $(hourlyPay * hoursWorked)
```

CLASS hourlyEmployee	Declaration	"d_emp.h"

```
// hourly employee "is an" employee paid by the hour
class hourlyEmployee : public employee
{
   public:
      hourlyEmployee(const string& name, const string& ssn,
                     double hp, double hw)
         // initialize hourly pay rate and hours worked along
         // with attributes in the base class

      void setHourlyPay(double hp);
         // update the hourly pay rate

      void setHoursWorked(double hw);
         // update the hours worked during the pay period

      virtual void displayEmployeeInfo() const;
         // display employee info and status "hourly worker"

      virtual void payrollCheck();
         // output a payroll check
   private:
         // pay based on hourly pay and hours worked
         double hourlyPay;
         double hoursWorked;
};
```

The rules for access among members in an inheritance hierarchy apply to the implementation of the member functions in both the base and derived classes. Let us first look at special issues affecting the constructors in the derived classes. In the next section, we illustrate additional concepts, while implementing the member functions in the employee hierarchy.

Derived-Class Constructor

You can view a derived object as having two parts, the base portion and the derived portion. The base portion consists of the data members in the base class, and the derived portion consists of the data members in the derived class. For instance, a

salaryEmployee object has strings empName and empSSN from the base class and a
real number for the salary in the salaryEmployee class.

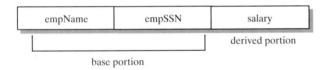

The constructor for a derived class must include arguments to initialize both the
base portion and the derived portion of an object. The implementation of a derived-
class constructor breaks into two tasks: Use the arguments associated with the base
portion of the object to initialize the data members in the base class, and then use
the other arguments to initialize the derived-class data members. In this way, a derived-class constructor first initializes the base portion of the object and then initializes the derived portion. Like any C++ class, the constructor in the derived class
can use an initialization list to assign the arguments to the data members. The list
initializes the base portion by including the base-class constructor and its arguments
as one of the terms. Assume that the constructor for baseCL includes a list of m arguments. The declaration of the derivedCL constructor must include m arguments
for the base portion of the object and an additional n arguments to initialize the derived portion:

```
// constructor for a deriveCL object with arguments for the base class
// and derived class data members
derivedCL (bArg1, bArg2, ..., bArgm, dArg1, dArg2, ..., dArgn);
```

The implementation of the constructor includes the term $baseCL(bArg_1, ..., bA_m)$ in
the initialization list:

Constructor derivedCL():
```
        derivedCL::derivedCL (bArg1, ..., bArgm, dArg1, ..., dArgn) :
           baseCL(bArg1, ..., bArgm), dData1(dArg1), . . ., dDatan(dArgn)
        { };
```

Example 13-1

---

1. The constructors for salaryEmployee and hourlyEmployee include the name and social security number as arguments for the base (employee) portion of the object. The
   additional arguments are specific to the payroll information in the derived portion of
   each object. In each class, the implementation of the constructor calls the employee
   base-class constructor with the name and social security number as arguments.

Constructor salaryEmployee():
```
salaryEmployee::salaryEmployee(const string& name,
   const string& ssn, double sal) : employee(name,ssn),salary(sal)
   {}
```

Constructor hourlyEmployee():
```
hourlyEmployee::hourlyEmployee(const string& name,
    const string& ssn, double hp, double hw) : employee(name,ssn),
        hourlyPay(hp), hoursWorked(hw)
{}
```

2. Let us use the constructors to declare salaryEmployee and hourlyEmployee objects:

```
// salaried employee Tom Baker (497-38-9178) earns $1750.00 per week
salaryEmployee sEmp("Tom Baker", "497-38-9178", 1750.00);

// Denise Rodgers (618-44-0193) is an hourly worker earning $12.00
// per hour with a schedule of 37.5 hours
hourlyEmployee sEmp("Denise Rodgers", "618-44-0193", 12.00, 37.5);
```

Note

The baseCL constructor in the initialization list executes before anything else. You must not omit the call to baseCL() and initialize base-class data members in the body of the constructor. If the base class has a default constructor and its default values are assumed, the derived class does not need to execute the default constructor explicitly. However, it is good practice to do so.

For objects in an inheritance chain, the runtime system calls destructors in the reverse order of the constructor calls. In the case of a derived object, the system calls the destructor for the derived class, followed by the destructor for the base class. Intuitively, a declaration creates the derived portion of an object after it creates the base portion of the object. When destroying the object, the runtime system destroys the derived portion first and then the base portion. If a derived class does not have a destructor, but the base class does, the compiler provides a *default destructor* for the derived class. This destructor destroys the derived-class members and executes the base-class destructor.

Implementing Member Functions

You are familiar with the procedures for implementing member functions in a class. In an inheritance hierarchy, the same procedures apply in both the base and derived classes when functions use only members of their class. We must be aware of the rules when a derived-class function needs to access members in the base class. You will quickly appreciate the importance of protected data in the base class. Another issue surfaces when base and derived classes have functions with the same prototype. We will need syntax to resolve name conflicts if the derived function wants to call the corresponding function in the base class. The employee hierarchy provides an excellent example to illustrate these concepts.

The member function setSalary() in the derived class updates the data member in the class. The implementation does not involve the base class.

setSalary():
```
void salaryEmployee::setSalary(double sal)
{ salary = sal; }
```

Resolving Name Conflicts The base and derived classes contain the public member function displayEmployeeInfo(). The functions have the same prototype, but perform different actions. The function in the employee base class outputs the name and social security number of the worker, using the format

```
Name: empName
Social Security Number:   empSSN
```

The derived-class versions of displayEmployeeInfo() call the base-class function and add additional output on the status of the employee (salaried or hourly worker) and salary or hourly pay information. For the implementation of a derived-class displayEmployeeInfo() function, we must understand that a member of a derived class is not in the same scope as the equivalent member (same name) in a base class. The declaration in the derived class hides the declaration in the base class, rather than overloading it. A programmer must use the class scope operator (::) to refer to a member of the same name in the base class. In the case of displayEmployeeInfo() in a derived class, a call to the equivalent function in the base class must include the expression "employee::".

hourlyEmployee displayEmployeeInfo():
```
// call displayEmployeeInfo from base class and output info
// on hourly rate and scheduled hours
void displayEmployeeInfo() const
{
    employee::displayEmployeeInfo();
    cout << "Status:   hourly employee" << endl;
    cout << "Payrate:  $" << setreal(1,2)
         << hourlyPay << " per hour" << endl;
    cout << "Work schedule (hours per week) " << hoursWorked
         << endl;
}
```

Accessing Protected Members. The base class declares some of its members as protected so that they can be accessed by member functions in a derived class. In the employee inheritance hierarchy, the data members in the base class are protected. The derived classes have the function payrollCheck(), which outputs the weekly payment for a worker. The functions display the employee's name, social security number in parentheses, and the amount of pay. The implementations of the functions have access to the data members empName and empSSN in the base class.

hourlyEmployee payrollCheck():
```
// cut a payroll check with the employee name, social security
// number in parentheses, and salary
virtual void payrollCheck() const
{
    cout << "Pay " << empName << " (" << empSSN
         << ")  $" << setreal(1,2) << salary  << endl;
}
```

Example 13-2

Let us look at different ways to handle data and operations in both the base and derived class. Object sEmp is a salaryEmployee object:

```
salaryEmployee sEmp("Tom Baker", "497-38-9178", 1750.00);
```

1. Display the salaryEmployee information about sEmp:

```
sEmp.displayEmployeeInfo();
    Output:
        Name: Tom Baker
        Social Security Number:  497-38-9178
        Status:   salaried employee
        Salary per week $1750.00
```

2. Display only the employee information about sEmp:

```
sEmp.employee::displayEmployeeInfo();
    Output:
        Name: Tom Baker
        Social Security Number:  497-38-9178
```

3. A program can declare an employee object and initialize it using a derived object. The operation copies the base portion of the derived object to the base object. For instance, in the following statements, the base portion (empName and empSSN) of sEmp initializes employee object *emp*:

```
employee emp = sEmp;
emp.displayEmployeeInfo();
    Output:
        Name: Tom Baker
        Social Security Number:  497-38-9178
```

You cannot use a base-class object to initialize a derived-class object, because the declaration does not include arguments for the derived portion of the object:

```
hourlyEmployee hemp = emp;      // error!
```

PROGRAM 13-1   ILLUSTRATING THE EMPLOYEE HIERARCHY

Let us illustrate the details from this section in a program. We start by declaring the hourlyEmployee object hEmp, and then we call displayEmployeeInfo() to describe the attributes of the object. We change the worker's hourly rate to $10.00 per hour through a call to setHourlyPay(). We conclude by calling payrollCheck() to pay the worker on the basis of the new hourly rate.

```
// File: prg13_1.cpp
// after declaring an hourly employee, Steve Howard, call
// displayEmployeeInfo() to output his data. change the employees
```

```cpp
// hourly pay to $10 using setHourlyPay() and call payrollCheck()
// to pay the worker using the new rate

#include <iostream>

#include "d_emp.h"

using namespace std;

int main()
{
   // declare an hourly employee
   hourlyEmployee hEmp("Steve Howard","896-54-3217",7.50,40);

   // output only the base class information on Steve Howard
   hEmp.employee::displayEmployeeInfo();
   cout << endl;

   // give Steve Howard a raise and output full set of information
   hEmp.setHourlyPay(10.00);
   hEmp.displayEmployeeInfo();
   cout << endl;

   // provide a weekly check
   hEmp.payrollCheck();
   cout << endl;

   return 0;
}
```

```
Run:

Name: Steve Howard
Social Security Number:   896-54-3217

Name: Steve Howard
Social Security Number:   896-54-3217
Status:    hourly employee
Payrate:  $10.00 per hour
Work schedule (hours per week) 40.00

Pay Steve Howard (896-54-3217)  $400.00
```

THE GRAPHICS HIERARCHY   13-2

This chapter develops a graphics package that enables a programmer to draw cir-
cles, rectangles, polygons, lines, and text on a drawing surface. Each of the graphical
elements in the package has a unique set of attributes that describe its objects. For

instance, a radius determines the shape of a circle; rectangles depend on their length and width. The graphics package consists of a collection of classes that describe the different figures. Each class defines the attributes of the figure as data members and includes operations to draw the figure and access and update its attributes. As an example, the circleShape class has a radius as the data member and operations to draw a circle and to access and update the radius. Similarly, the rectShape class has operations based on the dimensions length and width.

Despite the obvious differences among the figures in the package, we can identify a set of common attributes and operations. Assume the drawing surface is a coordinate system based at point (0,0). The x-axis is 10 units long the y-axis is 8 units long. Horizontal coordinates are positive moving to the right, and vertical coordinates are positive moving downward. Each figure has a *base point* that positions its location on the drawing surface, as well as a fill color chosen from a color palette. Figure 13-4 illustrates the drawing of a "lightgray" circle and a "darkgray" rectangle. The base point for the circle is its center. The base point for the rectangle is the upper left-hand corner. We specify the base point and dimensions of each figure relative to the 10-by-8 coordinate system.

The x- and-y-coordinates of the base point and the fill color are the data members for a base class called the *shape* class. The class has a constructor to initialize the data members and operations to access or update their values. Specifically, the shape class has functions getX() and getY(), which identify the current location of the base point in the coordinate system, and a function move(), which repositions the base point to another (x,y) coordinate. The shapeColor class defines a color palette containing 16 colors. By composition, the shape class includes a shapeColor object to specify the fill color of the figure. In the case of text, the color specifies the foreground color for the string. The following list of names identifies the colors in the palette:

white	blue	teal	green	turquoise	darkgray	brown	purple
lightblue	lightgray	gold	red	orange	pink	yellow	black

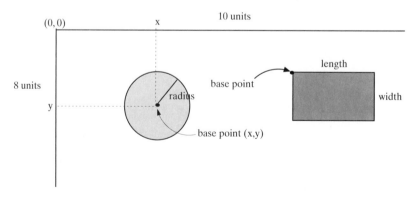

Figure 13-4
Circle and rectangle on the drawing surface with the base point, the color, and the dimensions of the figure

In order to access and update the color attribute, the base class has the member functions getColor() and setColor(). The shape class contains an erase() function that deletes the corresponding figure from the drawing surface. The class also specifies that draw() is a virtual function. This function cannot have an implementation in the base class, because it draws a specific shape that is known only in a derived class. The "=0" following the prototype specifies that the function must be implemented in a derived class. The declaration makes draw() a *pure virtual function* in the base class. Section 13-7 discusses pure virtual functions in detail. The following is a declaration for the shape class.

| **CLASS shape** | **Declaration** | **"d_shape.h"** |

```
// the graphics base class. maintains the base point and fill
// color. has functions to access and change these attributes.
// the graphics classes that draw specific figures inherit
// this class
class shape
{
   public:
       shape(double x, double y, shapeColor c);
           // the arguments initialize the base point (x,y) and
           // the fill color c

       double getX() const;
           // returns the x coordinate of the base point
       double getY() const;
           // returns the y coordinate of the base point

       void move(double x, double y);
           // sets base point to the new coordinates (x,y)

       shapeColor getColor() const;
           // returns the current fill color for the figure
       void setColor(shapeColor c);
           // set the fill color of the figure to the value c
           // from the color palette

       virtual void draw() = 0;
           // draw must be implemented in any derived class

       void erase();
           // removes the figure from the drawing surface
   protected:
       // location of the base point
       double baseX, baseY;

       // color of the shape
       shapeColor color;
};
```

Note

> You might question why the erase() function is in the base class; the operation
> would seem to be different for each figure. A graphics system such as Windows
> retains drawing information for each figure. An object, called a *handle*, provides
> the location of the bitmap image of the figure. We store the handle as a private
> member of the shape class. The erase() operation uses the handle to access the
> bitmap image and remove the figure.

The circleShape Class

Several derived classes describe the different figures in the graphics package. The
classes contain the unique attributes of a figure, along with a draw() function and
operations to access and update the attributes. Let us begin by describing the circle-
Shape class in detail. You are familiar with how the declaration of a derived class
uses public inheritance to extend the operands of the base class. In particular, you
understand why the constructor in a derived class must contain arguments to initialize both the base and derived portions of the object. The circleShape class illustrates
these concepts. The declarations of the other graphics classes are similar. In the next
section, we briefly describe these classes, focusing on the attributes of the different
figures, the meaning of "base point," and the declaration of the constructor.

The radius attribute determines the size of a circle. The radius is a private data
member of type *double* in the circleShape class. The member functions getRadius()
and setRadius() allow a programmer to access and update the radius. The class has
a draw() function to display the figure on the screen at the base-point location with
the specified fill color. The base point and color are attributes inherited from the
shape class. The constructor contains an argument list that specifies initial values for
the shape portion of the object, as well as the radius, which is the derived portion of
the object. The format for the list includes the *x*-coordinate and *y*-coordinate of the
base point, the radius, and finally the color. By default, the base point has coordinate
(0.0,0.0), the radius is 0.0, and the fill color is darkgray. The declaration of the circle-
Shape class uses public inheritance to specify access to the shape (base) class.

CLASS circleShape   **Declaration**   **"d_circsh.h"**

```
// declaration of circleShape class with base class shape
class circleShape : public shape
{
   public:
      circleShape(double x = 0.0, double y = 0.0,
                  double r = 0.0, shapeColor c = darkgray);
         // arguments for the base point, radius and color

      double getRadius() const;
         // return the current value of the radius

      void setRadius(double r);
         // update the value of radius
```

```
        void draw();
            // draw the circle on the window
    private:
        double radius;          // attribute describes a circle
};
```

Example 13-3

Let us illustrate how you declare a circleShape object and use member functions from the base class to reposition the object and change its color.

1. Declare a lightgray circle with radius 2.0 and base point at the center (5.0,4.0) of the drawing surface:

```
circleShape circ(5.0, 4.0, 2.0, lightgray);
```

2. Draw the figure, and then update the attributes. Shrink the radius to 1.0, reposition the center to the left at point (1.5, 4.0), and set the fill color to darkgray:

```
circ.draw();                    // figure (a)

// update the attributes
circ.setRadius(1.0);            // member function in circleShape class
circ.move(1.5,4.0);             // move() inherited from shape class
circ.setColor(darkgray);        // setColor() inherited from shape class

circ.draw();                    // figure (b)
```

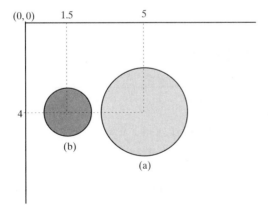

3. Declare a second circleShape object *newCirc*, using the default arguments. The "get" operations in the circleShape and shape classes extract the current attributes of the circ object and use them to update newCirc. Set newCirc to have a radius twice the size of that of circ, with a center that is three units to the right and one unit up from that of circ. Assume circ has its initial color of light gray. The example concludes by drawing both the circ and newCirc figures in the window.

```
// the initial base point is (0.0, 0.0), radius 0.0,color darkgray
circleShape newCirc;

// use attributes of circ to define those for newCirc
newX = circ.getX();              // newX = 1.5
newY = circ.getY();              // newY = 4.0;
newCirc.move(newX+3, newY-1);  // set the center at (4.5, 3.0)

// use the current radius of circ to compute radius for newCirc
newCirc.setRadius(2 * circ.getRadius());

// draw the two figures
circ.draw();
newCirc.draw();
```

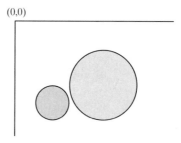

The Other Figure And Text Classes

Besides the circleShape class, the graphics package implements derived classes rect-
Shape, lineShape, polyShape, and textShape. The latter allows us to draw text on the
window. In each case, you must understand the attributes of an object and how we
use the base point to position it on the window. Appropriate "get" and "set" operations access and update the attributes.

The rectShape Class ("d_rectsh.h") The length and width determine the
shape of a rectangle. The dimensions are data members of type *double*. The functions getLength() and getWidth() return the current value of the length and width,
respectively. Using setSides() with length and width arguments updates the shape of

the rectangle. We noted before that the base point is the coordinate of the upper left-hand corner of the rectangle. The constructor includes five arguments; they initialize the *x*-coordinate and *y*-coordinate of the base point, the length, the width, and the fill color. The default values set the base point at the base point of the coordinate system, the length and width to 0.0, and the color to darkgray.

Constructor:
```
rectShape(double x = 0.0, double y = 0.0, double len = 0.0,
          double wid = 0.0, shapeColor c = darkgray);
```

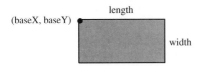

The lineShape Class ("d_linesh.") Two points determine a line. One of the points becomes the base point, and the other point, called the *end point*, has coordinates (endX,endY), which are data members in the derived class lineShape. The class inherits the operations getX(), getY(), and move() from the shape class to handle the base point. To access and update the end point, use the operations getEndX(), getEndY(), and setEndPoint(), which requires two arguments for the coordinates of the new end point. The constructor has five arguments, specifying coordinates for the base point, coordinates for the end point, and the color. The default values set all of the coordinates to 0.0 and the color to darkgray.

Constructor:
```
lineShape(double x = 0.0, double y = 0.0, double x2 = 0.0,
          double y2 = 0.0, shapeColor c = darkgray);
```

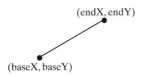

The polyShape Class ("d_polysh.h") The polyShape class describes regular polygons consisting of *n* lines of equal length. The base point of the polygon is its center point. The data members include the integer *numsides* and *length* of type *double*. Like the other graphics classes, the operations getLength(), setLength(), getN(), and setN() access and update the attributes. The constructor includes initial values for the number of sides and the length, along with arguments for the base point and fill color.

Constructor:
```
polyShape(double x = 0.0, double y = 0.0, int numsides = 4,
          double len = 0.0, shapeColor c = darkgray);
```

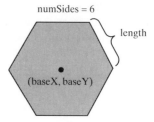

The textShape Class ("d_textsh.h")   Placing text on a window is a drawing operation. The textShape class stores a string in the data member *text* and includes the member functions getText() and setText(). The base point is the (*x,y*) coordinate of the first letter in the string, and the color attribute in the base class is the foreground color for the text. The constructor includes four arguments, specifying the base point, text, and color.

Constructor:
```
textShape(double x = 0.0, double y = 0.0, const string& s ="",
          shapeColor c = darkgray);
```

```
(baseX, baseY) ● The class textShape draws †
```

Example 13-4

Let us create an example that declares a variety of graphics objects. Figure 13-5 displays the figures on a single window.

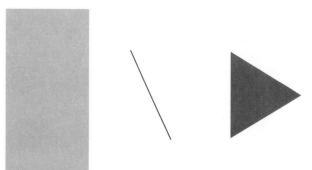

Figure 13-5
Drawing graphical figures
on a single window

```
// a 2 by 4 rectangle with base point (1.0, 1.0) and color lightgray
rectShape rect(1.0, 1.0, 2.0, 4.0, lightgray);

// a black line with base point (4.0, 2.0) and end point (5.0, 4.0)
lineShape line(4.0, 2.0, 5.0, 4.0, black);

// a darkgray triangle polygon (3-sides) of length 2.0; base point
(7.0,3.0)
polyShape triangle(7.0, 3.0, 3, 2.0, darkgray);

// the text "Graphical Figures" appears black below the figures
textShape label(3.0, 6.0, "Graphical Figures", black);
```

Figure 13-6 lists the inheritance hierarchy for the graphics package that includes the base class, derived classes, and all of their data members.

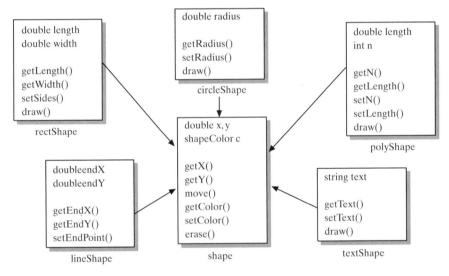

Figure 13-6
Inheritance hierarchy for the graphical package

Implementing The Polyshape Class

As an example of declaring and implementing the graphics package, we discuss the polyShape class. We chose this graphics class because it combines a data structure (array) and algorithm to allocate the key points of a polygon. The polyShape class creates regular polygons with the base point at the center of the figure. In order to draw a regular polygon with n sides, it is necessary to compute the n points (x_0, y_0), $(x_1, y_1), \ldots, (x_{n-1}, y_{n-1})$ that define the shape. We call these points the *vertices* of the

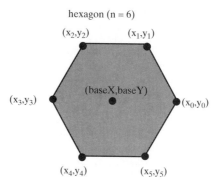

Figure 13-7
Points defining a regular
polygon

polygon. The private member function buildPoints() computes the vertices and
stores the *x*- and *y*-coordinates of the points in the vector<*double*> objects point_X
and point_Y. For instance, in Figure 13-7, the vectors point_X = $\{x_0, x_1, x_2, x_3, x_4, x_5\}$
and point_Y = $\{y_0, y_1, y_2, y_3, y_4, y_5\}$ store the points of the hexagon.
   The following is the declaration of the polyShape class.

CLASS polyShape   **Declaration**   **"d_polysh.h"**

```
class polyShape: public shape
{
   public:
      polyShape(double x = 0.0, double y = 0.0,
               int n = 4, double len = 0.0,
               shapeColor c = darkgray);
         // constructor. has arguments for the base point,
         // number of sides, the length of each side and the
         // color

      double getLength() const;
      void setLength(double len);
         // retrieve or set length of a side

      int getN() const;
      void setN(int numsides);
         // retrieve or set number of sides

      virtual void draw();
         // draw the polygon

   private:
      int numSides;
         // number of sides
      double length;
         // length of each side
```

```
    vector<double> point_X;
    vector<double> point_Y;
        // x and y-coordinates of the vertices
    void buildPoints();
        // construct the vertices
};
```

We now discuss the implementation of the constructor and the function build-Points(). The constructor calls the shape class constructor and passes it the coordinates (x,y) of the base point and the color. After assigning values for n (the number of sides) and *len*(the length of each side), the constructor initializes the two vector objects to have zero size. The function buildPoints() allocates the actual points for the coordinates that draw() uses to display the figure.

polyShape():
```
    // initialize base class, the number of sides
    // and the length of each side
    polyShape::polyShape(double x, double y, int n,
                    double len, shapeColor c):
            shape(x,y,c), numSides(n), length(len),
            point_X(0), point_Y(0)
    {}
```

The private member function buildPoints() computes the points that determine the polygon and by using trigonometry in its implementation. The distance from the center of the polygon to any vertex is $d = \dfrac{length}{2\sin(\pi/n)}$.

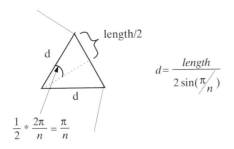

$$d = \frac{length}{2\sin(\pi/n)}$$

$$\frac{1}{2} * \frac{2\pi}{n} = \frac{\pi}{n}$$

If the counterclockwise angle at point (x_i, y_i) is θ, then

$$x_i = \text{baseX} + d * \cos(\theta) \quad \text{and} \quad y_i = \text{baseY} - d * \sin(\theta)$$

The loop in buildPoints() applies this formula at each point (x_i, y_i) when θ has angle $i*(2\pi/n)$ (Figure 13-8).

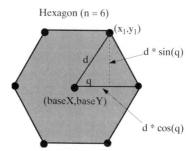

Hexagon (n = 6)

Figure 13-8
Calculations for buildPoints()

buildPoints():

```
void buildPoints()
{
    int side;
    double theta, d;
    const double PI = 3.141592653589793,
                 DELTA_THETA = (2.0*PI)/numSides;

    // allocate space for the numSides coordinates
    point_X.resize(numSides);
    point_Y.resize(numSides);

    d = length/(2.0*sin(PI/numSides));
    theta = 0.0;
    for(side = 0; side < numSides; side++)
    {
        point_X[side] = baseX + d*cos(theta);
        point_Y[side] = baseY - d*sin(theta);
        theta += DELTA_THETA;
    }
}
```

13-3   THE GRAPHICS SYSTEM

The graphics system allows a programmer to create a window and display figures from the graphics hierarchy. The drawing surface is a graphical window consisting of a grid of individual points, called *pixels*. On each computer, the resolution of the window depends on the size of the monitor and the quality of the video card. The graphics system recognizes the physical characteristics of each computer and scales the size of the window into a coordinate system 10 units wide by 8 units high (Figure 13-9). In order to create the window and control the flow of figures on the surface, we define a library of five free functions in the file "d_draw.h." The functions are implemented on Windows and Unix systems.

The two key operations in the library are the functions openWindow() and closeWindow(). Before drawing any figure, we must call openWindow() to create the drawing surface and initialize the coordinate system. A program terminates by

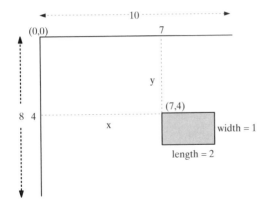

Figure 13-9
Drawing surface with a
lightgray 2-by-1 rectangle
located at position (7,4)

calling closeWindow(), which closes the drawing surface and shuts down the graphics system. During execution, we will need some way to pause in order to view the figures. The functions viewWindow() and delayWindow() provide this feature. A call to viewWindow() freezes the window until the user presses the ENTER key. The delayWindow() function takes an argument that specifies time in seconds. The window holds the current frame for the designated time before drawing the next figure. To clear the screen and create a white background, call eraseWindow(). The following is an API for the functions in "d_draw.h".

Graphics Library	Operations	"d_draw.h"

void **openWindow**();
    Initialize and open the drawing surface.

void **closeWindow** ();
    Shut down the drawing surface.

void **viewWindow** ();
    Halt the drawing of figures to allow the user to view the current status of the drawing surface. Continue execution by hitting the ENTER key.

void **delayWindow** (double *secs*);
    Wait *secs* seconds before executing the next instruction.

void **eraseWindow** ();
    Erase the entire drawing surface, and create a white background.

Example 13-5

The typical structure of a drawing program includes a call to openWindow(), the drawing of figures, a call to viewWindow() to freeze the current frame of the drawing, and a concluding call to closeWindow():

```
#include "d_draw.h"                  // access to the Graphics library

int main()
{
    <declaration of graphics objects>

    openWindow();                    // open the drawing surface
    <draw the figures>

    viewWindow();                    // pause for a keystroke
    closeWindow();                   // close the drawing surface

    return 0;
}
```

PROGRAM 13-2   BULL'S EYE

Let us combine many of the graphical components in a single program. We start with a black 4-by-4 square rectangle and a lightgray circle with radius 0.1. Position the figures about the center point,(5.0,4.0), of the window. This implies that the base point for the square is (3.0,2.0) and the base point for the circle is the center of the window. A loop provides animation. On each iteration, the radius of the circle increases by 0.125, and the figure is redrawn. A delay of one tenth of a second holds the current frame in the window. The loop terminates when the circle has radius 2.0; at this point, the circle is inscribed in the square. On the final frame, we draw the diagonals of the square and write the message "That's All Folks" below the square.

Note how the program uses the functions openWindow(), delayWindow(), viewWindow(), and closeWindow() to control the window and view the separate frames. The run captures four frames in the process, including the final frame with the diagonals and message.

```
// File: prg13_2.cpp
// draw a 4 x 4 black square centered at (5,4) in the drawing window.
// draw with a light gray circle with radius .125 centered at (5,4).
// after .1 seconds, draw the circle with the same center having a
// radius of .125 + .125. after pausing .1 seconds, continue this
// process with a circle whose radius increase by .125 until it
// reaches a radius of 2. at this point, the circle is inscribed in
// the square. draw the diagonals of the square and output the message
// "That's All Folks" below the square

#include "d_draw.h"      // graphics library
#include "d_rectsh.h"    // rectShape class
#include "d_circsh.h"    // circleShape class
#include "d_linesh.h"    // lineShape class
#include "d_textsh.h"    // textShape class
```

```
int main()
{
   // the black 4 x 4 square
   rectShape square(3.0,2.0,4.0,4.0,black);

   // circle that grows to size of the square
   circleShape circ(5.0,4.0,0,lightgray);
   // diagonal lines in the square
   lineShape diag1(3.0,2.0,7.0,6.0,black),
             diag2(3.0,6.0,7.0,2.0,black);

   // display message after the circle hits the bulls-eye
   textShape text(4.1,6.4,"That's All Folks", black);

   // initial radius of the circle
   double r = 0.125;

   // open the drawing window and draw the square
   openWindow();
   square.draw();

   do
   {
      // set the radius and draw the circle
      circ.setRadius(r);
      circ.draw();

      // increase radius by 0.125
      r += 0.125;

      // pause 1/10 second and then proceed
      delayWindow(.1);
   } while (r <= 2.0);

   // draw the diagonals for the square
   diag1.draw();
   diag2.draw();

   // draw the label "That's All Folks"
   text.draw();

   // pause to view the final figure
   viewWindow();

   // shutdown the drawing system
   closeWindow();

   return 0;
}
```

Run: (snapshot of 4 frames)

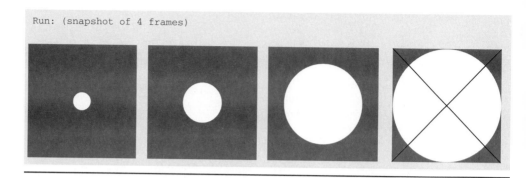

13-4   SAFE VECTORS

The design of the vector class extends the functionality of an array by adding dynamic memory allocation. A programmer might call push_back() and resize() to dynamically adjust storage while retaining access to the familiar array index notation. The design of the vector container has a serious limitation that we first noted with arrays: The container does not perform *index range checking* to ensure that the index operator references a valid element in the sequence. For a vector v and an index i, the expression $v[i]$ is proper only if $0 \leq i <$ v.size(). In this regard, a vector object has the same potential for error as an array. For instance, look at a simple *for* loop that shifts all elements on the tail of a vector one position to the left. The loop begins at index *pos* and scans to the end of the list:

```
for (i=pos; i < v.size(); i++)
    v[i] = v[i+1];
```

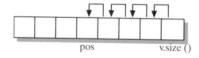

An error occurs, because the loop copies the element $v[$v.size()$]$, which is not in the range of valid entries, into the vector. A closer look shows that the loop test should be "$i <$ v.size() $- 1$."

The Standard Template Library provides the vector class without index range checking. A programmer should not attempt to rewrite the STL class to provide index range checking. More importantly, index checking requires additional overhead that is appropriate only during the implementation phase of a program. Once the program has been implemented and tested, its code executes more efficiently if index checking is not performed. Inheritance allows us to extend the vector class to a safeVector class that performs index checking. A programmer can use the derived class objects (safeVector) during implementation and testing of the program and then replace the objects with vectors for execution.

The design of the derived safeVector class includes constructors modeled after the corresponding vector operations. This enables a program to declare a safeVector object with the same arguments as the vector that is the base portion of the object. The derived class must create its own version of the overloaded index operator in order to implement index range checking. Inheritance gives a safeVector object access to all of the other vector functions.

CLASS safeVector	Declaration	"d_safev.h"

```
template <typename T>
class safeVector: public vector<T>
{
     public:
        safeVector();
           // default constructor creates an empty safeVector

        safeVector(int n, const T& value = T());
           // initialize the size of the safeVector and assign value to
           // to the elements

        safeVector(T *first, T *last);
           // initialize the safeVector with elements in the address
           // range of an array

        T& operator[] (int i);
           // overloaded index operator performs index range checking
};
```

Note that the safeVector class uses public inheritance to access members of the vector base class. Each of the three safeVector constructors builds the base-class portion of an object by passing its arguments to the base-class constructor in the initialization list. For instance, the constructor that creates a safeVector with a specified size and initial values uses the arguments to call the corresponding vector constructor:

Constructor safeVector():
```
         // call vector in the initialization list with arguments n and value
         safeVector::safeVector(int n, const T& value = T()) :
                  vector(n, value)
         {};
```

The index operator, [], in the safeVector class replaces the index operator for the vector class. Its implementation verifies that *i* is in the range $0 <= i < $ size() and throws the indexRangeError exception if not. This action normally terminates the program.

Index operator []:

```
T& operator[] (int i)
{
   if (i < 0 || i >= size())
      throw indexRangeError(
         "safeVector: index range error", i, size());

   // execute the index operator in the vector base class
   // and pass it the argument i
   return vector<T>::operator[] (i);
}
```

Example 13-6

An example illustrates how a programmer can use a safeVector constructor to create an object and then call the inherited vector operations:

```
// safeVector with 25 integers set to 100
safeVector<int> sv(25, 100);
int i, item;

// access the size() function in vector
cout << sv.size();          // Output: 25

// insert 10 additional elements 0, 1, ..., 9 in sv
for (int i = 0; i < 10; i++)
   sv.push_back(i);

// use [] operator to access an element. the previous insert operations
// placed the value 5 in sv[30]
item = sv[30] * 2;          // item = 10

try
{
   // index out of range
   sv[40] = 100;
}
catch (const indexRangeError& ire)
{
   cerr << ire.what() << endl;
}
Output:    safeVector: index range error   index 40   size = 35
```

13-5   ORDERED LISTS

The list class in Chapter 6 describes a general sequential list. For many applications, we need a list structure that stores elements in order. For these applications, we can use inheritance to build an orderedList class that modifies insert operations in the base list class to maintain an ordered sequence. The design of the orderedList class must focus on the operations that add or update an element in the list.

The derived class has a member function insert() that places items into the list in ascending order using the "<" operator. At the same time, the list base-class functions push_front(), push_back(), and insert() should not be available; they can destroy the list ordering. For instance, inserting 99 at the front of the list {2, 5, 7, 8, 12} creates a new list {99, 2, 5, 7, 8, 12} that is out of order. To prevent an orderedList object from calling these base-class operations, we hide them by declaring their prototypes in the private section of the derived class. Any attempt by an orderedList object to access one of the functions will produce a compiler error, because they are private members of the class. For instance, the sequence

```
orderedList<int> intList;
. . .
intList.push_front(99);
```

produces the error message "push_back: Cannot access private member declared in class orderedList."

An orderedList object can use the pop_back(), pop_front(), and erase() functions in the list class, because the operations remove an element and thus do not affect the order. The issue of iterators for an orderedList object requires some attention. The derived class should have access to the list version of erase(), which takes an iterator argument. Because the operation modifies the list, the argument must be a nonconstant iterator. To accommodate this flexibility, we allow the orderedList class to use the nonconstant iterator type from the base class. A programmer could unwisely use such an iterator and the deference operator, *, to modify the list and destroy the ordering. We assume a programmer would modify only nonkey attributes of the element and maintain the ordering by the key.

| CLASS orderedList | Declaration | "d_orderl.h" |

```
template <typename T>
 class orderedList: public list<T>
 {
    public:
       // constructor. implemented with inline code
       orderedList(): list<T>()
       {}

       orderedList(T *first, T *last);
          // constructor. build an ordered list whose data comes
          // from the pointer range [first, last)

       void insert(const T& item);
          // insert item into the ordered list
    private:
          // disallow access to insert functions in base class
```

```
        void push_front(const T& item);
        void push_back(const T& item);
        void insert(list<T>::iterator& pos, const T& item);
};
```

Example 13-7

This example includes an ordered list and both constant and nonconstant iterators. Note that each iterator declaration uses the container reference "orderedList<int>::". The actual iterator class is inherited from the list<*T*> class.

```
// create an empty list and two types of iterators
orderedList<int> intOrdList;

orderedList<int>::iterator ordIter;
orderedList<int>::const_iterator c_ordIter;
```

1. Create an ordered list, using insert():

```
intOrdList.insert(5);     // list: 5
intOrdList.insert(12);    // list: 5 12
intOrdList.insert(8);     // list: 5 8 12
```

2. Use a nonconstant iterator to delete an element from the list:

```
ordIter = intOrdList.begin();      // initialize iterator
ordIter++;                         // move to element with value 8
intOrdList.erase(ordIter);         // list: 5 12
cout << intOrdList.size();         // output: 2
```

3. Use a constant iterator to output the list:

```
c_ordIter = intOrdList.begin();
while (c_ordIter != intOrdList.end())
{
    cout << *c_ordIter << "  ";
    c_ordIter++;
}
```

Ordered List Class Implementation

Because orderedList inherits most of its operations from the base class, the implementation of the class reduces to finding an algorithm for the insert() operation. The operation uses a list iterator to sequentially search for the location at which to add the new element. After setting the iterator to the beginning of the list, the search looks for the first data value that is greater than or equal to the new item. The search terminates at an element in the list or at iterator location end() if the new value is larger than all existing values. In either case, use the insert() function from the base class to add the new value:

insert():

```
template <typename T>
void orderedList<T>::insert(const T& item)
{
    // curr starts at first element, stop marks end.
    // begin()/end() are base class fuctions
    list<T>::iterator curr = begin(), stop = end();

    // find insertion point, which may be at end of list
    while ((curr != stop) && (*curr < item))
        curr++;
    // do insertion using base class insert() function
    list<T>::insert(curr, item);
}
```

POLYMORPHISM AND VIRTUAL FUNCTIONS   13-6

Polymorphism is an important feature of inheritance and is fundamental to object-oriented programming. It allows two or more objects in an inheritance hierarchy to have identical member functions that perform distinct tasks. A program can use a single function call for the different objects and have the runtime system select a version of the function appropriate to the situation. C++ implements polymorphism by using *dynamic binding* of *virtual member functions*. This contrasts with *static binding*, which is the usual way of linking an object with a member function. We will now explore these concepts, using the displayEmployeeInfo() functions in the employee hierarchy.

Declare specific salaryEmployee and hourlyEmployee objects:

```
salaryEmployee sEmp("Louis Martin", "556-82-9011", 1500.00);
hourlyEmployee hEmp("Jill Vincent", "614-77-0827", 15.50, 30.0);

// display information about the salaried employee Louis Martin
hEmp.displayEmployeeInfo();
```

```
Output:
    Name: Louis Martin
    Social Security Number:  556-82-9011
    Status:  salaried employee
    Salary per week $1500.00
```

```
// display information about the hourly employee Jill Vincent
hEmp.displayEmployeeInfo();
```

```
Output:
    Name: Jill Vincent
    Social Security Number:  614-77-0827
```

```
Status:    hourly employee
Payrate:   $15.50 per hour
Work schedule (hours per week) 30.00
```

The statements call the appropriate version of the member function displayEmployeeInfo() by using the object name and the function name. The compiler realizes that the call is made to a specific version of the function. The process of referencing a specific object name and using the dot (.) member selection operator is known as *compile-time binding,* or *static binding.* All function calls up to this point in the book use static binding.

As another example of static binding, consider the function display(), which outputs the information in an employee object:

```
void display(employee emp)
{
    emp.displayEmployeeInfo();
}
```

The function passes the argument by value. The argument *emp* receives a copy of the runtime argument. Consider the following objects:

```
employee baseEmp("John Robinson", "569-54-1638");
salaryEmployee sEmp("Louis Martin", "556-82-9011", 1500.00);
hourlyEmployee hEmp("Joanna Smith", "296-52-6715", 15.50, 30);
```

The call

```
display(baseEmp);
```

outputs

```
Name: John Robinson
Social Security Number:  569-54-1638
```

Because salaryEmployee and hourlyEmployee are derived from employee (a salaried employee "is an" employee), sEmp or hEmp can be copied or assigned to a base-class object. Assignment copies the portion of the derived object's data that is in the employee class. If we pass hEmp to display(), the copy to the formal argument gives emp the base-class portion of hEmp.

```
// assign a salaryEmployee object to an employee object
baseEmp = sEmp;

// output employee information
baseEmp.displayEmployeeInfo();
cout << endl;

// copy hEmp to argument emp by copying base class portion
display(hEmp);
```

Output:

```
Name: Louis Martin
Social Security Number:  556-82-9011
```

```
Name: Joanna Smith
Social Security Number:  296-52-6715
```

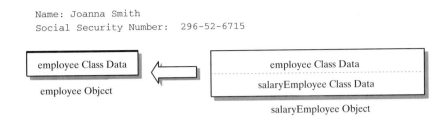

employee Object

salaryEmployee Object

At the same time, the assignment of an employee object to a salaryEmployee or hourlyEmployee object is not valid, because the derived-class data may be undefined. For instance, the following is an invalid assignment.

```
sEmp = baseEmp;  // salary in salaryEmployee class is not initialized
```

Dynamic Binding

We really want the function display() to recognize the type of the runtime object and call displayEmployeeInfo() for the specific argument. If a salaryEmployee object is the argument, we want display() to call displayEmployeeInfo() in the salaryEmployee class. Unfortunately, with static binding, the compiler makes the decision to call displayEmployeeInfo() for the base-class employee. What we need is a mechanism that will let display() make the decision about which version of displayEmployeeInfo() to call at runtime. C++ provides a mechanism, called *dynamic binding*, that solves our problem. Dynamic binding implements polymorphism. Invoke dynamic binding by declaring a *virtual member function* in a base class. The programmer places the keyword *virtual* in front of the declaration of the member function. To override the virtual function in the base class, derived classes declare a member function with precisely the same prototype, to imply that it has the same name, argument list, and return type. For instance, in the employee class, we declare the function displayEmployeeInfo() to be virtual. The corresponding functions in the derived salaryEmployee and hourlyEmployee classes have the same prototype, although they provide very different output, depending on the type of employee.

   In this section, we noted that you can assign a derived-class object to a base-class object, and the same rules apply to the assignment of pointer variables. The object assignment copies the base portion of the derived object to the base-class object and leaves the base-class object without any ability to reference the derived portion. The situation is quite different when the assignment involves pointer variables. This fact is critical to your understanding of how C++ implements dynamic binding. Assume that sEmp is a salaryEmployee object and empPtr is a pointer to an employee object. The assignment of the address of sEmp to empPtr initializes the pointer to reference the starting location of the base-class data members, which are only one portion of the salaryEmployee object Figure 13-10.

```
employee *empPtr;
salaryEmployee sEmp("Mike Morris", "569-34-0382", 1750.00);

empPtr = &sEmp;
```

sEmp

empPtr

Figure 13-10
Employee pointer references the starting address of the data members in a salaryEmployee object

Dynamic binding occurs when a statement uses the pointer empPtr to call the virtual function displayEmployeeInfo(). The runtime system recognizes the fact that the pointer references a salaryEmployee object and calls the function displayEmployeeInfo() in the salaryEmployee class, and not the one in the base class.

```
// execute function displayEmployeeInfo() using pointer empPtr
empPtr->displayEmployeeInfo();
    Output: Name: Mike Morris
            Social Security Number:  569-34-0382
            Status:    salaried employee
            Salary per week $1750.00
```

Note

In a derived class, member functions that override virtual functions in the base class can include the keyword *virtual* in their declaration. This is not a requirement; the function inherits the attribute *virtual* from the base class. We recommend that you add the keyword to the declaration, as a matter of good style; a programmer immediately realizes that a "virtual" form exists in the base class without having to check explicitly.

Example 13-8

In order to have the function display() use dynamic binding and output information for any employee, salaryEmployee, or hourlyEmployee object, modify the declaration to include a base-class pointer argument. Call the function by passing the address of the derived object, rather than the object itself.

```
void display(employee *empPtr)
{
    empPtr->displayEmployeeInfo();
}
```

The object *gRose* is a salaried employee, and *dBach* is an hourly worker. Output information on each employee by calling display() with the address of the object.

```
salaryEmployee gRose("Glenn Rose","345-83-8287", 1600.00);
hourlyEmployee dBach("Donald Bach","673-45-1835",12.50,40);

display(&gRose);
    Output:   Name: Glenn Rose
              Social Security Number:  345-83-8287
```

```
               Status:    salaried employee
               Salary per week $1600.00

  display(&dBach);
       Output:      Name: Donald Bach
                    Social Security Number:  673-45-1835
                    Status:   hourly employee
                    Payrate:  $12.50 per hour
                    Work schedule (hours per week) 40.00
```

Dynamic binding also applies when calling a virtual function using a class reference argument. Let the argument for display() be an employee reference:

☞
Note

```
void display(employee& empPtr)
{
    empPtr.displayEmployeeInfo();
}
```

Declare the object

```
salaryEmployee wGivens("William Givens","729-72-6284", 2000.00);
```

The statement

```
display(wGivens);
```

outputs

```
Name: William Givens
Social Security Number:  729-72-6284
Status:    salaried employee
Salary per week $2000.00
```

Application: Paying Employees With Polymorphism

We want to use polymorphism to create a weekly check for any employee. The employee base class declares the virtual function payrollCheck(). Each derived class overrides the virtual function by declaring its own payrollCheck() member function with the same prototype. Obviously, the implementation of the function differs depending on the class. The application can use polymorphism by declaring a base-class pointer variable and assigning to it the address of a derived object. When a statement uses the pointer variable to call payrollCheck(), the runtime system initiates dynamic binding. The system associates the base-class pointer with the corresponding derived object and calls the payrollCheck() function in the derived class.

The application in Program 13-3 uses polymorphism with the function pay(). The program passes the address of a derived object and lets the function pay() call the appropriate payrollCheck() operation to pay the specific type of employee:

pay():
```
void pay(employee *empPtr)
{
    empPtr->payrollCheck();
}
```

PROGRAM 13-3   PAYING EMPLOYEES USING MAP LOOKUP

Let us develop a program that uses the pay() function. To reinforce our understanding of data structures, assume that the accounting office stores the employees in a map where an element has the social security number as the key and a pointer to the employee as the value component:

```
map<string, employee *> empMap;
```

Using an employee pointer value allows the map to store pointers to both salaryEmployee and hourlyEmployee objects and use polymorphism when calling the pay() function.

The program declares two salaryEmployee and two hourlyEmployee objects. For each object, the map index operator takes the social security number as an index and assigns the address of the derived object as the value component:

```
empMap[empSSN] = &derivedEmployee;
```

A loop repeatedly prompts the user to input a social security number. A call to find() checks whether the number is valid. If so, pay() takes the pointer to the corresponding employee object (value component) as an argument and creates the payroll check. A message indicates when the social security number is not valid. The loop terminates when the user enters the social security number 000-00-0000.

```cpp
// File: prg13_3.cpp
// declare four employees and insert each employee into a map whose key
// is the SSN of a worker and whose value is a pointer to the employee
// object.in a loop, prompt for a Social Security Number and use find()
// to search the map for an entry with that SSN. if located, pass the
// pointer value to the function pay() that processes the paycheck for
// the employee. if the SSN is not valid, output a message. terminate
// the program when the user inputs the SSN "000-00-0000"

#include <iostream>
#include <fstream>
#include <map>

#include "d_emp.h"    // include the employee hierarchy

using namespace std;

// issue the pay check to the employee pointed to by emp
void pay(employee* emp);

int main()
{
    // declare four employees
    salaryEmployee sEmpA ("Bill Roberts","837-57-8293", 950.00);
    salaryEmployee sEmpB ("Dena Thomas","538-27-4981", 1300.00);
    hourlyEmployee hEmpA ("Sally Gere","583-73-5081", 15.00, 40.00);
    hourlyEmployee hEmpB ("Ty Le","654-20-2981", 30.00, 30.00);
```

```
    // database is a map with SSN as the key and a pointer
    // to the employee as the value
    map<string, employee*> empMap;
    string ssn;

    // insert the employees into the map
    empMap["837-57-8293"] = &sEmpA;
    empMap["538-27-4981"] = &sEmpB;
    empMap["583-73-5081"] = &hEmpA;
    empMap["654-20-2981"] = &hEmpB;

    while (true)
    {
        cout << "Enter Social Security Number: ";
        cin >> ssn;
        if (ssn == "000-00-0000")
            break;

        // search for ssn in the map and pay the
        // employee if found
        if (empMap.find(ssn) != empMap.end())
            pay(empMap[ssn]);
        else
            cout << "Not a recognized employee" << endl;
        cout << endl;
    }

    return 0;
}

void pay(employee* emp)
{
    // execute payrollCheck() for the type of employee
    // emp points at
    emp->payrollCheck();
}
```

```
Run:
Enter Social Security Number: 538-27-4981
Pay Dena Thomas (538-27-4981)  $1300.00

Enter Social Security Number: 691-45-7651
Not a recognized employee

Enter Social Security Number: 654-20-2981
Pay Ty Le (654-20-2981)  $900.00

Enter Social Security Number: 000-00-0000
```

Implementing Polymorphism In C++

C++ implements polymorphism by using a *virtual function table* that contains the locations of an object's virtual functions. Each object contains a pointer to the table. When a program calls a virtual function by using the address of an object, the run-time system follows the pointer to the table and executes the appropriate function.

Consider the following statements:

```
employee *p, *q;

p = new salaryEmployee(. . .);
q = new hourlyEmployee(. . .);

p->displayEmployeeInfo();  // Output: salaryEmployee information
q->displayEmployeeInfo();  // Output: hourlyEmployee information
```

Figure 13-11 shows class data members and a pointer to the virtual function table for the objects addressed by *p* and *q*.

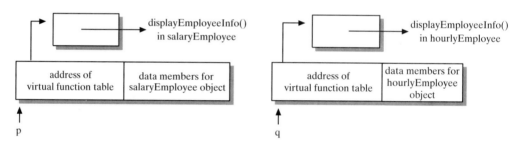

Figure 13-11
Virtual function table for dynamic binding (polymorphism)

PROGRAM 13-4   DRAWING GRAPHICS OBJECTS WITH POLYMORPHISM

The graphics hierarchy declares draw() as a virtual function. Let us use this fact to illustrate dynamic binding and polymorphism for circleShape and polyShape objects. The function collage() takes the address of a graphics figure as an argument and draws 15 copies of the figure in a 4-by-4 grid. The copies use the different nonwhite colors in the color palette.

The program shown next declares an array of three shape pointer variables and assigns to them dynamically allocated circle, hexagon, and triangle figures. In a loop, the program passes the shape pointers as arguments to the collage() function, which uses polymorphism to call the correct draw() operation. The resulting screen is a series of three 4-by-4 grids. After allowing the user to view the final display, the program clears the screen.

```
// File: prg13_4.cpp
// the function collage() forms a grid of identical
// shapes of the type pointed to by its argument.
// each row of the grid contains 4 figures. each
// of the 15 figures in the grid is draw in a
```

```
// different color from the palette. the program
// creates a circle, regular hexagon, and an
// equilateral triangle and calls collage()
// for each figure

#include "d_draw.h"      // for openWindow(), etc.
#include "d_circsh.h"    // use circleShape class
#include "d_polysh.h"    // use polyShape class

void collage(shape *sPtr);

int main()
{
   // pointers in the shape (base) class
   shape *fPtr[3];

   // create a blue circle with radius .75
   fPtr[0] = new circleShape(0, 0, 0.75, blue);
   // create a blue regular hexagon with sides of
   // length .75
   fPtr[1] = new polyShape(0, 0, 6, 0.75, blue);
   // create an equilateral triangle with sides of
   // length 1.5
   fPtr[2] = new polyShape(0, 0, 3, 1.5, blue);

   // open the drawing window
   openWindow();

   // create the collage of figures
   for (int i = 0; i < 3; i++)
      collage(fPtr[i]);

   // close the drawing window
   closeWindow();

   return 0;
}

void collage(shape *sPtr)
{
   // the initial color of the shape is blue
   shapeColor c = blue;
   int i;
   // draw 15 shapes, each in a different color
   // arranged in a grid of 4 figures across.
   // the figure base points for the 1st row
   // are (1,1), (3,1), (5,1), (7,1) and
   // for the second row are
   // (1,3), (3,3), (5,3), (7,3), etc.
   for (i = 0; i < 15; i++)
```

```
      {
         sPtr->move(2*(i%4) + 1.0, 2*(i/4) + 1.0);
         sPtr->draw();
         c++;
         sPtr->setColor(c);
      }

      viewWindow();
      eraseWindow();
   }
```

```
Run:
```

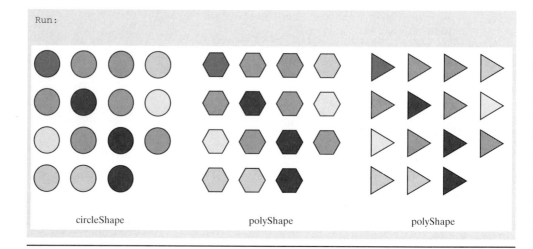

circleShape   polyShape   polyShape

Virtual Functions and the Destructor

Programmers must be aware of a design requirement for classes in an inheritance hierarchy when derived objects allocate dynamic memory. For memory management, the derived classes must have destructors. Using the standard approach to declaring a destructor will result in the compiler's creating code for static binding and cause memory leaks. We will illustrate this fact with an example and then provide a solution that involves declaring a virtual destructor in the base class.

The example includes a base class baseCL that deliberately does nothing. We want you to focus on problems that occur in the dynDerived class, which inherits baseCL and dynamically allocates a four-element integer array. For testing purposes, we declare a constructor and a destructor for the baseCL class. Each function outputs a message indicating that the runtime system is executing the operation.

baseCL class:
```
class baseCL
{
   public:
```

```
baseCL()
    { cout << "baseCL constructor - no action" << endl;}
~baseCL()         // not a virtual destructor
    { cout << "baseCL destructor - no action" << endl; }
};
```

The class dynDerived has an integer pointer as the data member. The constructor dynamically allocates a four-element array and outputs a message indicating the fact that the runtime system is calling the function. The destructor calls *delete* to deallocate the dynamic array and also outputs a message indicating that the operation is executing.

dynDerived class:
```
class dynDerived: public baseCL
{
   public:
      dynDerived() : baseCL()
      {
         cout << "dynDerived constructor - allocate 4-element array"
              << endl;
         dArr = new int [4];
      }

      ~dynDerived()
      {
         cout << "dynDerived destructor - deallocate";
              << 4-element array" << endl;
         delete [] dArr;
      }
   private:
      int *dArr;        // pointer to derived class dynamic array
};
```

PROGRAM 13-5   THE DESTRUCTOR AND STATIC BINDING

Let us look at a program which illustrates a problem that can occur when a derived object has dynamic memory. Declare basePtr as a baseCL pointer, and dynamically allocate a dynDerived object and assign its address to basePtr:

```
baseCL *basePtr = new dynDerived;    // construct a dynDerived object
```

The output statements in the constructors illustrate that the declaration of a dynDerived object first calls the constructor for the base portion and then calls the constructor for the derived portion. The derived constructor creates the dynamic four-element array. In an attempt to destroy the derived object, the program uses the *delete* operator with address basePtr:

```
delete basePtr:
```

On the surface, the operation looks fine; it seemingly reverses the action of the *new* statement that allocated the object. Unfortunately, the baseCL destructor is not virtual, and so the *delete* operation uses static binding. It calls only the base-class destructor and never calls the derived-class destructor. The statement does not destroy the dynamically allocated four-element array in the derived object.

```
// File: prg13_5a.cpp
// the program demonstrates the need for a virtual destructor
// in the base class. the base class, baseCL, does not declare
// a virtual destructor, and the derived class, dynDerived,
// allocates dynamic memory. after allocating a dynDerived object
// and storing the pointer in a baseCL pointer, the program calls
// delete which causes only the base class destructor to execute. the
// dynamic memory allocated by the derived object is not removed,
// causing a memory leak

#include <iostream>

using namespace std;

/* classes baseCL and dynDerived implemented in the
   program discussion */

int main()
{
    baseCL *basePtr = new dynDerived;

    delete basePtr;

    return 0;
}
```

```
Run: (baseCL destructor is not virtual):

In baseCL constructor - no action
In dynDerived constructor - allocate 4-element array
In baseCL destructor - no action
```

The solution requires declaring the baseCL destructor as virtual. When executing the *delete* operation, the system uses dynamic binding that identifies basePtr as the address of a dynDerived object. The runtime system first calls the derived-class destructor, which deallocates the four-element array, and then calls the base-class destructor. To fix the problem, simply declare the destructor ~baseCL() as virtual:

```
virtual ~baseCL()        // virtual destructor
{ cout << "In baseCL destructor - no action" << endl; }
```

A run of the program (source file "prg13_5b.cpp" in the software distribution) with the correct declaration of the baseCL destructor yields the following output:

```
Run: (baseCL destructor is virtual):

baseCL constructor - no action
```

```
dynDerived constructor - allocate 4-element array
dynDerived destructor - deallocate 4-element array
baseCL destructor - no action
```

From the example, we can develop a good design strategy for use in the declaration of a class. The strategy applies to classes that might be extended by a derived class that has dynamic memory.

> RULE: *Declare a virtual constructor, even if the destructor performs no action.*

Declare an empty destructor as follows:

```
virtual ~baseCL()
{}
```

This implements dynamic binding and ensures that the *delete* operator applied to a base-class pointer will cause execution of the destructor for the derived class.

ABSTRACT CLASSES   13-7

The use of polymorphism requires declaring a virtual function in the base class and overriding the function in the derived classes. At times, the base-class function performs meaningful action. For instance, the displayEmployeeInfo() function in the employee base class outputs the name and social security number of the worker. At other times, we declare a virtual base-class function merely for polymorphism, without any intention of using it. Dynamic binding will call only the derived versions of the function. The payrollCheck() function in the employee class is such an example. Its implementation would have an empty function body, because worker payment requires data found only in the derived classes.

Rather than forcing a programmer to declare essentially a "placeholder" function and create an empty implementation, C++ allows the use of pure virtual functions by appending " = 0" to the function prototype. A *pure virtual function* in a base class is a virtual function that has no implementation in the class. Besides enabling the function to be used with polymorphism, its presence in the base class ensures that each derived class must override the function as a member. A pure virtual function has the form

```
virtual returnType functionName(<argument list>)= 0;
```

In the shape class, we declare draw() as a pure virtual function. The operation is not meaningful for a shape object that specifies only the base point and the color for a geometric figure. By declaring draw() in the base class as a pure virtual function, we force each of the derived classes circleShape, rectShape, and so forth, to implement its own individual version of draw().

```
virtual void draw() = 0;
   // draw the shape. must be implemented in a derived class
```

We refer to a class that contains one or more pure virtual functions as an *abstract class*. A program must not declare an object of abstract class type.

Example 13-9

---

1. The shape class is an abstract class, because it contains the pure virtual function draw(). Attempting to declare a shape object results in a compiler error:

```
shape sh(4.0, 5.0, blue);
    // Error - cannot instantiate abstract class
```

2. The class circleShape is a derived class describing a circle with a base point, radius, and color. Because the base class is an abstract class, the declaration of circleShape must override draw() as a member.

An Abstract Class As An Interface

Object-oriented programming uses abstract classes to specify how a programmer must declare the public members of a class. The public members constitute the programmer interface for the class. To put the issue in context, recall how we dealt with the stack class. In Chapter 7, we introduced the STL stack container, whose interface consisted of the functions push(), pop(), top(), and so forth. In the same chapter, we created the miniStack class, whose implementation used a vector to store the elements in the stack. An exercise in Chapter 9 asked you to implement the linkedStack class by using a singly linked list. While the two classes used different implementation techniques, we assumed that each had the same interface as the STL stack class. By using an abstract class, we could force the assumptions to be true.

The idea is simple. Create an abstract class whose member functions have the prototype for the desired interface. Specify the functions to be pure virtual functions. As a result, the abstract class requires no implementation. To force a class to have the specified interface, declare it as a derived class with the abstract class as the base. The derived class must override the functions in the base class. Put another way, the derived class must inherit the interface specified by the abstract base class. You can think of the abstract base class as providing a mold for the derived classes.

The Stack Interface

Let us apply these concepts to the declaration of a listStack class that uses a list container to store the elements. We use the STL stack interface to create the abstract class stackInterface. The prototype for each member function is a pure virtual function.

```
// abstract base class that specifies the stack ADT
template <class T>
class stackInterface
{
   public:
       virtual void push(const T& item) = 0;
          // push item onto the stack
```

```
        virtual void pop() = 0;
            // remove item from top of the stack

        virtual T& top() = 0;
            // return reference to element on the top of the stack.

        virtual bool empty() const = 0;
            // determine whether the stack is empty

        virtual int size() const = 0;
            // determine the number of elements in the stack
};
```

Implement the listStack class as a derived class with stackInterface as the base class. The declaration of the public-member functions uses the prototypes from the base class. The compiler will note any variation in a function argument list or return type.

```
template <typename T>
class listStack : public stackInterface<T>
{
    public:
        . . .
        void pop();              // use prototypes from stackInterface
        . . .
    private:
        list<T> stackList;    // declare an empty list
};
```

The implementation of listStack uses the back of the list as the top of the stack. The push() and pop() operations simply call the list push_back() and pop_back() functions.

CHAPTER SUMMARY

- Section 13-1 introduces the concept of inheritance. Inheritance combines with object composition to create the primary techniques for reusing software. Inheritance involves a class hierarchy whose elements are base and derived classes. A base class provides member functions and data to a derived class. The derived class might choose to add its own member functions or redefine existing ones in the base class. Public inheritance expresses the "is a" relationship. A salaried employee "is an" employee, and a circleShape object "is a" shape. To illustrate public inheritance, the book introduces the employee, salaryEmployee, and hourlyEmployee hierarchy and uses them to develop the C++ syntax for inheritance. We develop the concepts further in Sections 13-2 and 13-3 with graphics classes such as circleShape and rectShape, which are derived from the common base class *shape*.

- The book discusses two applications of inheritance to data structures. In Section 13-4, we develop the class safeVector by deriving it from the vector class. The derived class overloads the index operator, "[]", to provide index bounds checking. A programmer can develop and debug an application using the safeVector class and then use the vector class for the final application. Section 13-5 develops an ordered list class by deriving it from the STL list class. The example shows how to mask off public members of the base class that should not be used by placing functions with the same prototypes in the private section of the derived class.

- Section 13-6 discusses the concept of polymorphism, which is fundamental to object-oriented programming. In fact, professionals often refer to object-oriented programming as "inheritance with runtime polymorphism." Polymorphism allows two or more objects in an inheritance hierarchy to have operations with the same prototype that perform distinct tasks. When an application calls such a function by using a pointer or reference to an object, the runtime system determines the required version. This is known as dynamic binding and contrasts with static binding, in which the compiler determines which function should be called. C++ implements polymorphism by declaring the functions with the keyword *virtual*. The section concludes by discussing use of the destructor in conjunction with polymorphism. To ensure that memory leaks do not occur, any class that may be used as a base class should define a virtual destructor.

- Section 13-7 discusses pure virtual functions and abstract classes. A pure virtual function declared in a base class forces the definition of the function in a derived class. The base class is known as an abstract class; it is a template or a mold for the construction of derived classes. A programmer uses an abstract base class to specify the design of a class that is likely to have different implementations.

CLASSES AND LIBRARIES IN THE CHAPTER

Name	Header File
circleShape	d_circsh.h
employee	d_emp.h
graphics library	d_draw.h
hourlyEmployee	d_emp.h
lineShape	d_linesh.h
map	<map>
orderedList	d_orderl.h
polyShape	d_polysh.h
rectShape	d_rectsh.h
safeVector	d_safev.h
salaryEmployee	d_emp.h
shape	d_shape.h
textShape	d_textsh.h

REVIEW EXERCISES

1. The base class *book* contains the protected data members *cover* and *pageLength*. The derived class *textbook* includes the string *subjectMatter* as a private data member. Each class has the member function describe(), along with a constructor.

```
enum coverType {HardCover, SoftCover};

class book
{
   public:
      book(coverType ct, int pglen): cover(ct), pageLength(pglen)
      {}

      virtual void describe()
      {
         cout << "A " << pageLength << " page";
         if (cover == HardCover)
            cout << " hard covered book" << endl;
         else
            cout << " soft covered book" << endl;
      }
   protected:
      coverType cover;
      int pageLength;
};

class textbook: public book
{
   public:
      // constructor
      _____            // (a)

      virtual void describe()
      {
         _____            // (b) describe book attributes
         cout << "Used for courses in " << subjectMatter << endl;
      }
   private:
      string subjectMatter;
};
```

(a) After declaring the constructor for the *textbook* class, give the constructor implementation, using inline code.
(b) Complete the implementation of describe() in the textbook class, where the missing statement calls describe() in the base class.
(c) Give a declaration for the book object *myDictionary*, which is a 625-page softcover book.
(d) Give a declaration for the textbook object *courseBook*, which is a hardcover computer science book with 850 pages.

   For parts (e) to (g), use the declarations from parts (c) and (d).

(e) What are the outputs from each of the following statements?

```
myDictionary.describe();
courseBook.describe();
```

(f) Write a statement that describes only the book attributes of the object courseBook.

(g) Are the following statements valid? Explain.

```
cout << courseBook.pageLength;
myDictionary.cover = HardCover;
```

2. In the given chart, a checkmark in any of the first two rows indicates that a statement in the implementation of a base- or derived-class function can access a private, protected, or public member of a class in an inheritance hierarchy. For example, the in the "Base" row indicates that a member function in the base class can access a private member in the base class. A checkmark in the third row would indicate that a derived object can access a private, protected, or public member of a class. Complete the chart, assuming that the base and derived classes are related with public inheritance.

Data ⟍ Statement	Private (Base)	Protected (Base)	Public (Base)	Private (Derived)	Public (Derived)
Base	✓				
Derived					
Client					

3. The class derivedCL inherits baseCL, using public inheritance. Both classes have a version of the function f(). For a series of objects, identify the output when f() is called.

```
class baseCL
{
   public:
      baseCL(int x = 1) : baseX(x), baseY(4)
      {}
      int f()
      { return baseX + baseY; }
   private:
      int baseX;
   protected:
      int baseY;
};

class derivedCL: public baseCL
{
   public:
```

```
      derivedCL() : x(10), y(11), baseCL(5)
      {};
      int f()
      {  y = baseCL::baseY * 2;
         x = 3;
         return x * y;
      }
   private:
      int x, y;
};
```

Assume the given declarations for objects base1Obj, base2Obj, and derivedObj in a main program. Give the output for each statement. If a statement is not valid, indicate that as the output.

```
baseCL base1Obj(2), base2Obj;
derivedCL derivedObj;
```

(a) cout << base1Obj.f();   // Output: _____
(b) cout << base2Obj.f();   // Output: _____
(c) cout << derivedObj.f();   // Output: _____
(d) cout << derivedObj.baseCL::f();   // Output: _____
(e) Assign a derived object to a base object:

```
      base2Obj = derivedObj;
      cout << base2Obj.f();     // Output: _____
```

(f) cout << base2Obj.derivedCL:f();   // Output: _____

4. A *for* loop enters data into the ordered list from an array. Trace the following code, and indicate the resulting list:

```
orderedList<int> alist;
int i, arr[] = {28, 45, 90, 17, 22, 87, 82, 38, 77, 50};

for (i = 0; i < 10; i++)
{
   if (!alist.empty() && arr[i] > alist.front())
      alist.eraseFront();
   alist.insert(arr[i]);
}
```

5. Are the following statements valid, given the fact that the safeVector class does not define its own iterator classes?

```
safeVector<int> sArr;
safeVector<int>::iterator iter;
iter = sArr.begin();
```

6. Why does the declaration of the derived orderedList class override push_back() as a private member function?

7. What is polymorphism? Give an example of its use.

8. This question uses the classes *book* and *textbook* discussed in Review Exercise 13-1. Assume the following function implementations:

```
void identify(book b)
{
    b.describe();
}

void identify(book *b)
{
    b->describe();
}
```

Declare the objects

```
book cookBook(HardCover, 150), *p;
textbook poetry(SoftCover, 500, "English"), *q;
```

What are the outputs of each of the follwoing sets of statements?

(a) ```p = &cookBook;```
```
identify(cookBook);
identify(p);
```

(b) ```q = &poetry;```
```
identify(q);
identify(poetry);
```

(c) ```p = &poetry;```
```
identify(p);
```

9. What is a pure virtual function? How does the concept relate to an abstract base class?

10. What is the format for an abstract base class when it is used as an interface in the declaration of derived class?

11. In the shape class, explain why
   (a) move() is not a virtual function.
   (b) draw() is a pure virtual function.

Answers To Review Exercises

1. (a) ```textbook(coverType ct, int pglen, const string& subject):```
```
        book(ct, pglen), subjectMatter(subject)
    {}
```

   (b) ```book::describe();```
   (c) ```book myDictionary(SoftCover, 625);```
   (d) ```textbook courseBook(HardCover, 850, "Computer Science");```
   (e) ```A 625 page soft covered book```
```
    A 850 page hard covered book
    Used for courses in Computer Science
```

   (f) `courseBook.book::describe();`

   (g) No. Each object is a protected data member of the *book* class. The objects can be accessed only by member functions of the *book* and *textbook* classes.

2.

Statement \\ Data	Private (Base)	Protected (Base)	Public (Base)	Private (Derived)	Public (Derived)
Base function	✓	✓	✓		
Derived function		✓	✓	✓	✓
Derived object			✓		✓

3. **(a)** 6   **(b)** 5   **(c)** 24   **(d)** 9   **(e)** 9   **(f)** Not a valid statement

4. The resulting list is 50 77 82 87 90.

5. The statements are valid. The safeVector class inherits the iterator and the member function begin() from the vector class.

6. Overriding push_back() as a private member function prevents an orderedList object from accessing the function and potentially destroying the list.

7. In a system of classes related by inheritance, a member function with the same name can be defined in different classes. The specific action of the member function will vary from class to class. When an application needs the function, the particular version is dynamically determined at runtime. In C++, polymorphism is implemented by using virtual member functions. The draw() operation in the graphics hierarchy is a virtual function. When it is called using a Shape pointer or reference to a derived object, the version draw() in the derived object is called.

8. **(a)** A 150 page hard covered book
      A 150 page hard covered book

   (b) A 500 page soft covered book
      Used for courses in English
      A 500 page soft covered book

   (c) A 500 page soft covered book
      Used for courses in English

9. A pure virtual function is a virtual function in a base class that has no implementation. Its declaration forces an implementation in a derived class. An abstract base class is a class with at least one pure virtual function.

10. The abstract base class declares a series of pure virtual functions that specify the interface (public member functions) for the derived class. The derived classes must override each of the functions in the base class.

11. **(a)** The function move() changes the base point for the figure. There is no need for it to be overridden in a derived class.

   (b) The *shape* class maintains the base point and color for the figure. There is no viable definition for draw() in the base class. However, declaring it as a pure virtual function ensures that each derived class will define draw() to sketch the figure on the drawing surface.

WRITTEN EXERCISES

12. Assume that the following strings represent names of C++ classes:

superBowl, television, series, comedy, academyAwards, drama, special

Develop an inheritance hierarchy of base and derived classes from this list. The hierarchy must maintain the "is a" relationship between base and derived classes.

13. Consider the following inheritance hierarchy:

```
class baseCL
{
   public:
      baseCL();
      void demoFunc();
   private:
      int m;
   protected:
      int n;
};
class derivedCL: public baseCL
{
   public:
      derivedCL();
      void demoFunc();
   private:
      int r;
};
```

(a) Which of the data members m, n, and r, can be accessed by a member function in the derived class?

(b) Which of the data members m, n, and r, can be accessed by a member function in the base class?

(c) Consider the declarations

```
baseCL bObj;
derivedCL dObj;
```

Which of the objects bObj and dObj can execute demoFunc() in the base class? If valid, give the C++ statement that provides the function call.

Which of the objects bObj and dObj can execute demoFunc() in the derived class? If valid, give the C++ statement that provides the function call.

14. Consider the following outline for a base and a derived class:

```
class baseCL
{
   public:
```

```
        // constructors
        baseCL(int v): bValue(v)
        {}

        baseCL(): bValue(0)
        {}
    protected:
        int bValue;
};

class derivedCL
{
    public:
        // constructors
        derivedCL(int v, int w);      // constructor ONE
        derivedCL(int w);             // constructor TWO
            ...
    private:
        int dValue;
};
```

(a) Use inline code to implement constructor ONE that assigns *v* to the base class and *w* to the derived class.

(b) Use inline code to implement constructor TWO that assigns *w* to the derived class and uses the default constructor for the base class.

15. When a class is derived from a base class by using *private inheritance*, the public members of the base class become private members of the derived class. The public and protected members of the base class are available only to the derived-class member functions, and not to a derived object. Thus, only the implementation of derived-class member functions may access base-class member functions. Private inheritance is referred to as *inheritance of the implementation.*

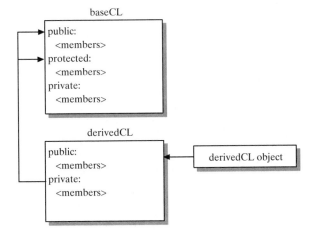

Look at Review Exercise 13-2. Fill in the chart, assuming that the base and derived classes are related by private inheritance.

Data / Statement	Private (Base)	Protected (Base)	Public (Base)	Private (Derived)	Public (Derived)
Base Class Functions	✓				
Derived Class Functions					
Derived Object					

16. The given program illustrates the order in which classes in an inheritance hierarchy make constructor and destructor calls. What is the output of the program?

```cpp
#include <iostream>

using namespace std;

class baseCL
{
    public:
        baseCL() { cout << "baseCL constructor" << endl; }
        ~baseCL() {cout << "baseCL destructor" << endl;}
};

class derivedCL : public baseCL
{
    public:
        derivedCL() { cout << " derivedCL constructor" << endl; }
        ~derivedCL(){ cout << " derivedCL destructor" << endl; }
};

int main()
{
    baseCL bObj;
    derivedCL dObj;

    return 0;
}
```

17. What is the output of the following program?

```cpp
#include <iostream>
#include <string>

using namespace std;

class baseCL
{
```

```
    public:
        baseCL(string s, int m = 0): msg(s), n(m)
        {}

        void output()
        {    cout << n << "   " << msg << endl; }

    private:
        string msg;
    protected:
        int n;
};

class derivedCL: public baseCL
{
    public:
        derivedCL(int m = 1): baseCL("Base",m-1),n(m)
        {}

        void output()
        {    cout << n << endl;
            baseCL::output();
        }
    private:
        int n;
};

int main()
{
    baseCL bObj("Base Class",1);
    derivedCL dObjA(4), dObjB;

    bObj.output();
    dObjA.output();
    dObjB.output();

    return 0;
}
```

18. Use the employee inheritance hierarchy that includes the derived classes salaryEmployee and hourlyEmployee in Section 13-1. For each statement, explain whether the assignment is valid.

```
employee genEmployee ("No Name", "000-00-0000");
hourlyEmployee rKarl("Ron Karl","867-49-3985", 8.00, 45);
```

(a) genEmployee = rKarl;
(b) rKarl = genEmployee;

19. The squareShape class is derived from the rectShape class by using public inheritance:

```
// declaration of squareShape class with base class rectShape
class squareShape: public rectShape
```

```
        {
           public:
                // constructor sets base point, length of side, and color
                squareShape(double xpos = 0.0, double ypos = 0.0,
                            double side = 0.0, shapeColor c = darkgray);
                // squareShape data access and update functions
                double getSide() const
                { _____ }
                void setSide(double s)
                { _____ }
        };
```

(a) Implement the constructor squareShape() as an inline function.
(b) Explain why the squareShape class does not need a draw() function.
(c) Implement getSide() as an inline function.
(d) Implement setSide() as an inline function.
(e) Declare a squareShape object with a length of 3, a base point at (4.0,4.0), and a fill color of red.

20. Use the employee hierarchy and the following statements for this problem:

```
employee boss("Mr. Boss", "555-33-5355"), *p;
salaryEmployee kRoss("Karen Ross", "156-23-8357", 3300.00),
          *q = &kRoss;
hourlyEmployee wJohns("William Johns".  "463-38-4772", 6.5, 40.00),
          *r = &wJohns;


p = &kRoss;
```

Indicate the version of displayEmploveeInfo() that is executed by each of the following function calls:

```
r->displayEmployeeInfo();
q->displayEmployeeInfo();
q->employee::displayEmployeeInfo();
p->displayEmployeelnfo();
```

21. Consider the following classes:

```
class baseCL
{

    public:
        baseCL(int a): one(a)
        {}

        virtual void identify()
        { cout << one << endl; }
    protected:
        int one;
};


class derivedCL: public baseCL
{
```

```
public:
   derivedCL(int a, int b): baseCL(a), two(b)
   {}

   virtual void identify()
   { cout << one << "  " << two << endl; }
protected:
   int two;
};
```

The following functions are used to identify the classes:

```
void announce1(baseCL x)
{
   x.identify();
}

void announce2(baseCL *x)
{
   x->identify();
}
```

(a) Give the output of the following code segment:

```
baseCL baseObj(7), *p;
derivedCL derivedObj(1,2);

announce1(baseObj);
announce2(&derivedObj);
p = &derivedObj;
p->identify();
```

(b) Give the output of the following code segment:

```
baseCL *arr[3];
derivedCL derivedObj(3,5);

announce1(derivedObj);
announce2(&derivedObj);
for(int i=0;i < 3;i++)
   if (i == 1)
      arr[i] = new baseCL(7);
   else
      arr[i] = new derivedCL(i,i + 1);
for(i=0;i < 3;i++)
   arr[i]->identify();
```

22. **(a)** Explain why the vector-class member functions size(), resize(), back(), push_back(), and pop_back() apply to objects of type safeVector.

    (b) What is the result of executing the following statements?

```
int arr[6] = {5, 7, 12, 15, 13, 17};
safeVector<int> v(arr, arr+6);
```

```
try
{
    cout << v.back() << endl;
    v.pop_back();
    v.pop_back();
    cout << v[0] << "   " << v[3] << endl;
    v.pop_back();
    v[2] = 25;
    v[3] = 9;
}
catch(const indexRangeError& re)
{
    cout << re.what() << endl;
}
```

23. Implement the function listSort() that orders the elements in vector *v*. The algorithm copies the elements of *v* into an orderedList object and then copies the sorted list back to the vector.

```
// sort vector v by inserting into an ordered list
template <typename T>
void listSort(vector<T>& v);
```

24. (a) Declare a template-based abstract base class *priorityQInterface* as an interface for a priority queue. The interface should use the design model for the STL priority_queue class.
    (b) Using inheritance, declare the class *listPriorityQ*, assuming that the orderedList object *pqList* stores the elements in the priority queue.
    (c) Using the declaration from part (b), implement the class *listPriorityQ*.

PROGRAMMING EXERCISES

25. A square is a rectangle whose length and width are the same. We can implement the square class from the rectangle base class by using public inheritance. Declare and implement the square class as a derived class, and place it in the header file "square_i.h". The constructor takes a side as the argument, with default value 0.0. The derived class has the member functions getSide() and setSide(), and the functions perimeter() and area() are available from the base class.
    In a program, prompt the user to enter the length of a side for the square object *sq*. Output the area and perimeter of the square. Double the length of the side, and output the measurements again.

26. Use the inheritance hierarchy for the classes *book* and *textbook* from Review Exercise 13-1. Place the two classes in the header file "textbook.h". Define the following *book* and *textbook* objects:

```
book bk1(HardCover, 250),
    *bk2 = new textbook(SoftCover, 360, "History");
textbook econ101(HardCover, 725, "Economics");
```

Write a program that outputs the book descriptions for bk1, *bk2, and econ101 and the textbook descriptions for *bk2 and econ101.

27. Place the squareShape class from Written Exercise 13-19 in the header file "sqshape.h". Use the class to draw a series of 5 nested squares in different colors about the point (5,4):

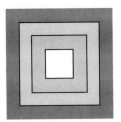

28. The *student* class defines the strings *studName* and *studSSN* as protected data members. A constructor has arguments that initialize the data. The class *studentAthlete* has a private data member *sport*, which describes the sport the student plays. Both classes have a member function identify(). The base class *student* outputs the student information in the form

```
student studName    Social Security Number studSSN
```

The function in the base class should support polymorphism, and the function in the derived *studentAthlete* class should add the information "Sport <sport>". In the file "student.h", declare and implement the two classes in an inheritance hierarchy.

In a program, initialize an array of five student pointers as follows:

```
student ja("John Anderson", "345-12-3547");
student bw("Bill Williams", "286-72-6194");
studentAthlete bj("Bob Johnson", "294-87-6285", "football");
studentAthlete dr("Dick Robinson", "669-289-9296", "baseball");

// list of student pointers
student* stud[] = {&ja, &bw, &bj, &dr};
```

In a loop, execute stud[i]−>identify(), for i from 0 to 3, and output the information about each student.

29. Assume that the *median* value in an *n*-element array or vector is the element at the middle index ($n/2$) if the list is sorted. For instance, consider the two integer arrays

```
int arrA[] = {5, 8, 1, 3, 6},
    arrB[] = {6, 12, 3, 9};
```

The median of arrA is 5, and the median of arrB is 9. Write a function

```
// return the median of v
template <class T>
T median (const vector<T>& v);
```

that returns the median of vector *v*. Use an orderedList object in the implementation to order the vector values. Then determine the median. Throw the underflowError exception if the vector is empty.

Write a program that inputs an integer *n* and allocates a vector of *n* integer values. Input *n* integers, and find their median value.

30. (a) Implement a function mode() that takes an iterator range for an increasing ordered sequence and returns an iterator pointing to the most frequently occurring value in the sequence. It also should compute the number of times the value occurs. If two or more elements occur with the same frequency, return the first element. Throw the underflowError exception if the sequence is empty.

```
// the range [first, last) is an increasing ordered sequence.
// mode() finds the most frequently occurring element and
// returns an iterator pointing to it. the reference argument
// numOccurrences is assigned the number of occurrences of the
// element
template <class Iterator>
Iterator mode(Iterator first, Iterator last,
              int& numOccurrences);
```

(b) Implement a function freq() that takes an orderedList object and outputs the number of times each element occurs in the list. The output order is from most frequent to least frequent.

```
// output each value in the list and its frequency of occurrence
// in the format "value(frequency)". the output order is from
// largest to smallest frequency
template <class T>
void freq(const orderedList<T>& aList);
```

For instance, freq() takes the list {2, 2, 6, 6, 6, 6, 9, 12, 12, 12} and produces the following output:

$$6(4) \quad 12(3) \quad 2(2) \quad 9(1)$$

Hint: Copy aList to another orderedList object. By repeatedly calling mode(), search the list for the most frequently occurring element, and execute a series of erase() operations until all occurrences of the element are removed from the list.

(c) Write a program that takes the integer array

```
int arr[] ={4, 5, 7, 3, 7, 2, 3, 8, 7, 12, 3, 7, 4, 5, 3, 12, 7};
int arrSize = sizeof(arr)/sizeof(int);
```

and outputs the frequency for each element in the array.

31. This exercise uses the function listSort() from Written Exercise 13-23. Declare the following vectors, sort them by using listSort(), and output the vectors by using the function writeContainer() from "d_util.h":

```
vector<int> with values {5, 8, 12, 25, 23, 1, 3, 3, 5, 15, 25, 5}
vector<string> with values {"Mississippi", "Alabama",
          "Massachusetts", "Arizona", "Maine"}
```

32. This exercise uses the abstract class *priorityQInterface* and the class *listPriorityQ* from Written Exercise 13-24. Place the interface and the implementation of *listPriorityQ* in the header file "pqi_lpq.h". Use *listPriorityQ* to run Program 8-4.

PROGRAMMING PROJECT

33. Implement a class *genVector* that generalizes the vector class to create a safe array with general starting and ending indices. For instance,

```
genVector <int> vA(1,10), vB(-1,8);
```

creates objects vA and vB with index ranges $1 <= i <= 10$ and $-1 < i < 8$, respectively. Objects of type *genVector* can be indexed within their defined range. For instance,

```
int i;
for(i=-1; i <= 8;i++)    // initialize all vector elements to 0
   vB[i] = 0;
```

Derive genVector from the vector class by using public inheritance. Override the index operator so it accepts indices in the correct range. Implement a derived member function resize() that resizes the vector and resets the beginning and ending indices. These actions prevent references to the vector index operator and resize() function unless the programmer uses the class scope operator "::".

```
template <typename T>
class genVector: public vector<T>
{
   public:
      genVector(int low, int high);
         // vector has high - low + 1 elements in range [low,high]

      T& operator[] (int i);
         // operator verifies that lower <= i <= upper.
         // if not, it throws the indexRangeError exception
      void resize(int lowIndex, int highIndex);
         // resize vector and set range to [lowIndex, highIndex]
   private:
      int lower;
      int upper;
};
```

Place genVector in the header file "genvec.h", and write a program that declares the following objects:

```
genVector<char> ucLetter(65,90);
genVector<double> tempVector(-10,25);
```

Initialize ucLetter so that ucLetter[65] = 'A', ..., ucLetter[90] = 'Z'. Initialize tempVector so that tempVector[*t*] is the Fahrenheit equivalent of Celsius temperature *t*. Recall that

```
F=9.0/5.0 * C+32
```

Output the contents of each vector.

◆

Heaps, Binary Files And Bit Sets

OBJECTIVES

- To understand that there is a representation of an array or vector as a complete binary tree.
- To learn how to compute the children and the parent of a node in an array-based tree.
- To understand that an array-based tree defines a path of children or a path of parents.
- To understand that heap order defines either a maximum or minimum heap within an array or vector.
- To study the heap as a container with operations that insert and erase an element from a heap and that order a vector as a heap.
- To study the running time of heap operations.
- To develop the fast heapsort algorithm for sorting a vector or array.
- To study the basics of binary file operations in C++, including direct access.
- To learn the bit operators in C++.
- To develop a bit vector class that creates an abstraction allowing the programmer to avoid working directly with low-level bit operators.
- To study the Huffman file compression and decompression algorithms that are implemented using heaps, binary files, and bit sets.

OUTLINE

In Chapter 10, we created trees as a collection of dynamically generated nodes. With some simple rules, we can view a direct-access container, such as an array or vector, as a binary tree. These trees are referred to as *array-based trees* and form the basis for a new container type, called a *heap*, whose insertion and deletion algorithms have $O(\log_2 n)$ running time. A heap stores elements with a heap-ordering principle that compares elements by using either the $<$ or the $>$ relational operator. The storage technique is designed to provide immediate access to the maximum element ($>$ order) or the minimum element ($<$ order) in the collection. In this way, a heap acts like a priority queue. In a maximum heap, a deletion (pop) removes the largest element from the container; a deletion from a minimum heap removes the smallest element. The operation then efficiently reorders the elements so that the next deletion can immediately access the appropriate element. An insertion locates an element in the heap so as to maintain the ordering principle.

In Section 14-2, we develop the *heap* insert, delete, and "heapification" operations. Because heap operations have logarithmic performance and deletions return the largest or the smallest value, the structure provides a famous and very efficient sorting algorithm, appropriately called the *heap sort*. The sort has no worst case and is an $O(\log_2)$ algorithm in all situations. We will use the class as the implementation for a priority queue. At this point, you will unerstand why we did not declare and implement a "mini" priority queue class in Chapter 8 when we presented the API for the priority_queue class. The reason is simple: we did not have the tools to provide an efficient implementation. With array-based trees and heaps, we can provide the implementation of the miniPQ class in Section 14-3.

Up to this point in the book, all applications have used text files, which contain character data. Most files used in practice, however, are binary files, which are not printable and contain arbitrary sequences of binary data. For instance, a word processor creates a binary file that specifies the document's content, along with formatting information. Only the word processor can open, display, and print a document, because it must extract format directives and prepare a screen or print-page image. While a thorough discussion of binary files is beyond the scope of this book, Section 14-4 provides very basic examples of creating, reading, and writing binary files.

C++ contains operators that manipulate groups of bits in characters and integers. Section 14-5 gives an overview of the C++ bit-handling operators and applies them in the construction of the bitVector class. This class allows the programmer to treat a stream of bits as if each bit is an element of an array, in effect eliminating much of the need to use the bit manipulation operators.

A compression algorithm reads data in a file, encodes the data, and writes the data to a new file whose size is appreciably smaller than the original. A decompression algorithm reads the compressed file and decodes it to restore the original file. One of the oldest and most easily understood compression schemes is the Huffman compression algorithm, named after its inventor, David Huffman. The algorithm finds many uses today. Section 14-6 implements Huffman compression and decompression. This case study uses all the concepts from the chapter, including minimum heaps, bitsets, and binary files.

14-1   ARRAY-BASED BINARY TREES

In Chapter 10, we built binary trees by using tree nodes. Each node has a data value and left and right pointer values that identify the left and right subtrees of the node, respectively. Insertions and deletions involve dynamically allocating/deallocating nodes and modifying pointer values. This representation handles trees ranging from degenerate to complete trees. In this section, we introduce a tree that uses an indexed container, such as an array or a vector, to store the data and indices to identify the nodes. For historical reasons, we use the term *array-based trees* to describe these trees, although most of our applications assume that a vector is the storage structure. We derive a very powerful relationship between the array or vector and a complete binary tree. The resulting structure enables us to define a heap and create functions that provide very efficient insertion and deletion operations. We discuss heaps in Section 14-2 and use them to implement the "mini" priority queue class miniPQ in section 14-3.

Recall from Chapter 10 that a complete binary tree of depth d contains all possible nodes through level d $-$ 1 and that nodes at level d occupy the leftmost positions in the tree. We can view a vector v, with its indexed structure, as a complete binary tree. The root is $v[0]$, the first-level children are $v[1]$ and $v[2]$, the second-level children are $v[3]$, $v[4]$, $v[5]$, $v[6]$, and so forth. Figure 14-1 illustrates a 10-element vector v viewed as a complete tree.

```
int arr[] = {5, 1, 3, 9, 6, 2, 4, 7, 0, 8};
int arrSize = sizeof(arr)/sizeof(int);
vector<int> v(arr, arr+arrSize);
```

The power of array-based trees becomes evident when an application requires access to node data. There are simple index calculations that identify the children

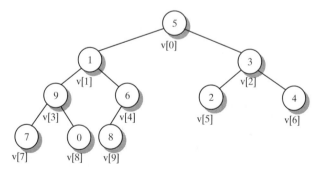

Figure 14-1
Complete Binary Tree for a Vector v with 10 Elements

and the parent of nodes. For each node $v[i]$ in an n-element vector, the following formulas compute the indices of the child nodes:

Item v[i]   Left child index is   2*i+1
             undefined if 2*i+1 ≥ n

Item v[i]   Right child index is   2*i+2.
             undefined if 2*i+2 ≥ n

A similar calculation allows us to identify the parent of any node $v[i]$. The index for the parent node is given by

Item v[i]   Parent index is   (i-1)/2
             undefined if i=0

Example 14-1

_____

Let us see how these index calculations apply to the array-based tree in Figure 14-1. Note especially how we can start at any node and move up the tree along the path of parents until we arrive at the root. With stree nodes in chapter 10, we had to maintain a parent pointer to carry out the same task in a binary search tree.

1. The root is $v[0]$, with a value of 5. Its left child has index $2 * 0 + 1 = 1$, and its right child has index $2 * 0 + 2 = 2$. The values for the children are $v[1] = 1$ and $v[2] = 3$.

2. Start at the root and select the path of left children:
   root index = 0
   left child of v[0] has index=2 * 0 + 1 = 1
   left child of v[1] has index = 2 * 1 + 1 = 3
   left child of v[3] has index = 2 * 3 + 1 = 7
   left child of v[7] is undefined (2 * 7 + 1 = 15 ≥ 10)
   Path: v[0] = 5, v[1] = 1, v[3] = 9, v[7] = 7

3. To identify the path of parents from any node $v[i]$, evaluate successive parent indices as $(i - 1)/2$. Assume that we start at $v[8] = 0$. Successive parent indices are $(8 - 1)/2 = 3, (3 - 1)/2 = 1$, and $(1 - 1)/2 = 0$, which is the root. The path of parents starting at $v[8]$ is $v[8] = 0, v[3] = 9, v[1] = 1, v[0] = 5$.

HEAPS   14-2

_____

An array-based tree has simple index calculations that access child and parent data. By imposing an ordering on the elements, we can create a structure that effectively utilizes these calculations to add and remove items within the tree structure. The structure, called a *heap*, has an order relationship between a parent and its children. For a *maximum heap*, the value of a parent is greater than or equal to the value of each of its children. For a *minimum heap*, the value of the parent is less than or equal to the value of each of its children. These situations are depicted in Figure 14-2, which illustrates these two types of heaps. In a maximum heap, the root contains

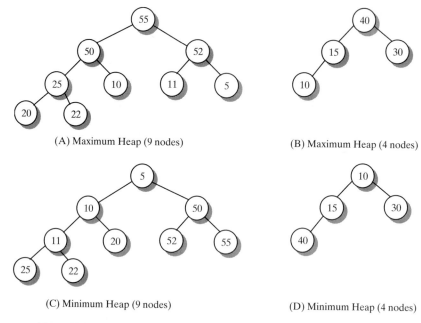

Figure 14-2
Maximum and Minimum Heaps

the largest element; in a minimum heap, the root contains the smallest element. Note that heap ordering defines a relationship between a parent and its child.

For the purposes of discussion, we assume that a heap is a maximum heap. When we declare heap functions, we include a comparison function object as an argument. This allows the programmer to specify the type of heap by passing either greater<T> or less<T> as the argument to distinguish between a maximum heap and a minimum heap.

Inserting Into A Heap

We discuss insertion in the context of understanding that a heap is an array-based tree with a vector as the underlying storage structure. What makes the tree a heap is the ordering of the elements. An insertion involves two separate operations. We must first add the element at the back of the vector by using push_back(). Depending on the value of the new element, this operation might destroy the heap order, because a parent might no longer be greater than its children. A second task involves restoring the heap order in the tree. We refer to this operation as *reheapifying* the tree. Let us look at an example to appreciate the problem. Figure 14-3(a) displays a heap with 10 integer values. After the execution of push_back() to insert value 50, the resulting array-based tree in Figure 14-3(b) is no longer a heap. Element $v[10]$ is out of place.

Reheapifying a tree after an insertion involves local repositioning of elements in the tree so that the heap order is reestablished. The example illustrates what we

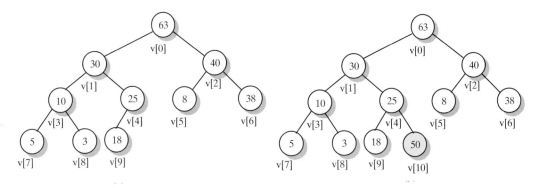

Figure 14-3
Heap before and after Insertion of Element 50 at the Back of the Vector

mean by "local." Element 50 is out of order relative to its parent, 25, and grandparent, 30. Only values along the path of parents are affected by the necessary readjustments. To reorder the tree, we provide the function pushHeap(), which has access to the vector, and the index *last*, which is the upper bound for the range [0, *last*) of elements to readjust. The algorithm assumes that the tree with elements $v[0]$ to $v[last - 2]$ is a heap and that only element $v[last - 1]$ could be out of order. The implementation of pushHeap() is an iterative process that looks at the path of parents. At each step, the value of the child is compared with the value of the parent, and, if the child is larger (out of order), the two elements exchange positions. Because the parent was already larger than the other child, replacing the parent node with a larger value will maintain the heap order. The effect of the exchange is to move (filter) the child up to the next higher level of the tree. The iterative process continues until we find a parent that is larger than the child and the heap order is ensured, or we arrive

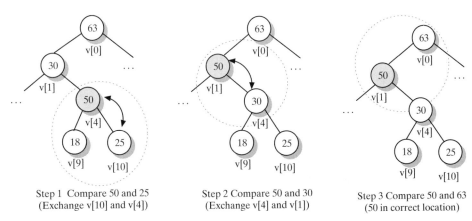

Step 1 Compare 50 and 25
(Exchange v[10] and v[4])

Step 2 Compare 50 and 30
(Exchange v[4] and v[1])

Step 3 Compare 50 and 63
(50 in correct location)

Figure 14-4
Reorder the Tree in pushHeap()

at the root. The later case occurs when the inserted element is a new maximum value, and its filtering up along the path of parents eventually locates it as the new root.

Let us look at the algorithm for the example in Figure 14-4. The first step compares element 50 with its parent, 25, and makes an exchange. We illustrate the operation by labeling only the affected nodes. The process continues by comparing element 50 (in $v[4]$) with its parent, 30, and performing a second exchange. The next iteration compares element 50 (in $v[1]$) with its parent (root), which has value 63. We have filtered element 50 up through the heap until it found a suitable position that restores heap ordering throughout the tree.

The declaration of pushHeap() includes the vector that stores the elements in the heap, the index *last*, and a comparison function object to specify the type of heap. Use the comparison function object greater<*T*>() for updating a maximum heap and less<*T*>() for updating a minimum heap. The function pushHeap() assumes that only the target value at $v[last - 1]$ can violate heap order and sets out along the path of parents to reposition *target*. The indices *currentPos* and *parentPos* move in tandem up the parent path, beginning with *currentPos* = *last* − 1. At each step, the index of the parent is (*currentPos* − 1)/2. The iterative process filters *target* up through the heap by exchanging its current position with that of its parent until we correctly position *target* or reach the root. In this last case, *target* becomes the new root value. We describe the algorithm as though it performs a series of exchanges between the child the parent nodes. Because an exchange requires three assignment statements, we implement the algorithm by copying the parent node to the child node as we move up the tree. This has the effect of moving successive nodes on the path down one level. The process terminates when the algorithm finds the location for *target*. The algorithm copies *target* into the location.

pushHeap():

```
// the vector elements in the range [0, last-1) are a heap.
// insert the element v[last-1] into the heap so that the
// range [0, last) is a heap. use the function object comp
// to perform comparisons
template <typename T, typename Compare>
void pushHeap(vector<T>& v, int last, Compare comp)
{
    // assume the new item is at location v[last-1] and that
    // the elements v[0] to v[i-2] are in heap order
    int currentPos, parentPos;
    T target;

    // currentPos is an index that traverses path of parents.
    // target is value hlist[i] and is repositioned in path
    currentPos = last-1;
    parentPos = (currentPos-1)/2;
    target = v[last-1];

    // traverse path of parents up to the root
    while (currentPos != 0)
```

```
      {
          // compare target and parent value
          if (comp(target,v[parentPos]))
          {
              // move data from parent position to current
              // position. update current position to parent
              // position. compute next parent
              v[currentPos] = v[parentPos];
              currentPos = parentPos;
              parentPos = (currentPos-1)/2;
          }
          else
              // if !comp(target, parentvalue), heap condition is ok.
              break;
      }
      // the correct location has been discovered. assign target
      v[currentPos] = target;
}
```

Deleting From A Heap

Deletion from a heap is restricted to the root only. Hence, the operation specifically removes the largest element. With a heap insertion, we assume the programmer has made a separate call to push_back() to first add the element at the back of the heap. Only then do we execute the function pushHeap() to reheapify the tree. In a similar way, we design the function popHeap() to exchange the root with the last element in the heap. The effect is to tuck the root away in a safe position. Unfortunately, the exchange can destroy the heap order: The new root might not be greater than its children. The algorithm then reheapifies the tree, minus its last value, by moving the new root down a path of children until it finds a location that restores heap order. Once popHeap() completes its task, the programmer can remove the maximum value from the vector by using pop_back().

Let us look at an example that illustrates the initial steps in the popHeap() algorithm. Figure 14-5 displays a heap before a deletion and then immediately after

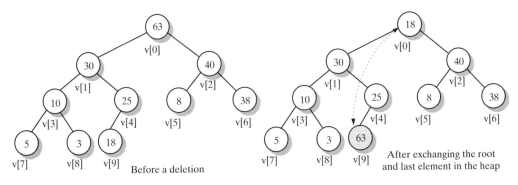

Figure 14-5
Exchanging Elements in popHeap()

we exchange the root with the last element in the tree. The exchange destroys the heap, because the new root is not greater than its children, 30 and 40. Note that we consider only the unshaded elements as part of the remaining heap.

To reheapify the tree after the exchange, the algorithm needs to move (filter) the root (target value 18) down the tree along a path of children until it locates a valid position that restores heap order. We need this filtering process later for the heap sort, so we create a separate function, called adjustHeap(), that performs the task. The function takes a vector; the integer *first*, which designates the index of the element that must filter down the tree; the index *last*, which designates the end of the heap; and the *Compare* function.

```
// filter the vector element v[first] down the heap with index
// range [first, last)
template <typename T, typename Compare>
void adjustHeap(vector<T>& v, int first, int last, Compare comp);
```

We will illustrate the iterative adjustHeap() algorithm when index *first* = 0 and we are dealing with a maximum heap. This is the situation for popHeap(), where the root must move down the tree until we reestablish heap order. Start by comparing the value of the root (*target*) with that of its two children. If the root is not larger than or equal to both children, we select the larger child and make a parent–child exchange. The child then becomes the root, and the parent moves to level 1 in the tree. The process continues until the target value is a parent larger than or equal to its children and heap order is restored, or the path lands on a leaf node, which becomes a valid position at which to store the target value. In the example, 18 exchanges positions with the larger child, 40. At level 1, 18 is greater than 8, but not 38, and so the parent and large child exchange, leaving 18 as a leaf node (Figure 14-6). Obviously, any leaf node satisfies heap order, because it has no children, so the algorithm terminates.

You can find a complete listing of adjustHeap() in "d_heap.h". We only highlight key code segments in the function. The function assigns the index first and the value at index first to variables *currentPos* and *target*, respectively. The loop takes the target and traverses down the path of children, using *currentPos* and *childPos* as the indices for the current node and its largest child, respectively. The value of *child-*

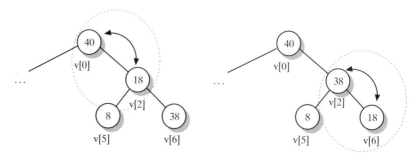

Step 1: Exchange 18 and 40   Step 2: Exchange 18 and 38

Figure 14-6
Adjusting the Heap for popHeap()

Pos is 2*currentPos* + 1 or 2*currentPos* + 2, depending on whether the left or right child is larger. An initial comparison establishes which child to consider:

```
// compute the left child index and begin a scan down
// path of children, stopping at end of list (last)
// or when we find a place for target
childPos = 2 * currentPos + 1;
while (childPos <= last-1)
{
   // index of right child is childPos+1. compare the
   // two children. change childPos if
   // comp (v[childPos+1], v[childPos]) is true
   if ((childPos+1 <= last-1) &&
         comp(v[childPos+1], v[childPos]))
      childPos = childPos + 1;
   ...
}
```

Inside this loop, a second comparison determines whether locating the target at *currentPos* violates the heap order. If so, the value of the largest child is copied up the tree to *currentPos*, and the process continues. If not, the loop terminates.

```
// compare selected child to target
if (comp(v[childPos],target))
{
   // comp(selected child, target) is true.
   // move selected child to the parent;
   // position of selected child is now vacated
   v[currentPos] = v[childPos];

   // update indices to continue the scan
   currentPos = childPos;
   childPos = 2 * currentPos + 1;
}
else
   // target belongs at currentPos.
   break;
```

After loop termination, the function assigns the target into the its final location at *currentPos*:

```
v[currentPos] = target;
```

The declaration of popHeap() includes the vector that stores the elements in the heap, the index *last*, and a comparison function object to specify the type of heap. Use the comparison function object greater<*T*>() for updating a maximum heap and less<*T*>() for updating a minimum heap. No matter whether the operation occurs in a maximum heap or a minimum heap, the root (*v*[0]) holds the optimal value. We use the term "optimal" to refer to the largest or the smallest element, depending on the type of heap. After exchanging this value with *v*[*last* − 1], the function calls adjustHeap() to position the new root and thus restore heap order. The reordering of the heap occurs only within the list from *v*[0] to *v*[*last* − 2], because this is the remaining heap.

popHeap():

```
// the vector elements in the range [0, last) are a heap.
// swap the first and last elements of the heap and then
// make the elements in the index range [0, last-1) a heap.
// use the function object comp to perform comparisons
template <typename T, typename Compare>
void popHeap(vector<T>& v, int last, Compare comp)
{
    T temp;

    // exchange the first and last element in the heap
    temp = v[0];
    v[0] = v[last-1];
    v[last-1] = temp;

    // filter down the root over range [0, last-1)
    adjustHeap(v, 0, last-1, comp);
}
```

PROGRAM 14-1   HEAP OPERATIONS

Let us look at a simple program that illustrates the heap functions. Array *arr* holds seven integer values in the range from 1 to 9. A loop inserts each array element at the back of vector *vA* and calls pushHeap() with the greater<*int*>() function object to reheapify the array-based tree as a maximum heap. A similar insert into *vB* with the less<*int*>() function object creates a minimum heap. A series of deletions repeatedly removes the optimal value from each heap. The operation involves calling popHeap() to place the optimal value at the back of the vector, outputting the value, and then removing it with the vector pop_back(). The maximum heap outputs the data in descending order; the minimum heap outputs the data in ascending order.

```
// File: prg14_1.cpp
// program illustrates pushHeap()/popHeap() for vectors vA and vB;
// vA is array-based tree for maximum heap and vB for minimum heap.
// loop copies 7 elements from arr to vA and vB using pushHeap()
// using objects greater<int>() and less<int>() respectively.
// calls to popHeap() remove elements from two heaps creating
// output in ascending and descending order

#include <iostream>
#include <vector>

#include "d_heap.h"
#include "d_util.h"

using namespace std;
int main()
{
    int arr[] = {5, 9, 2, 7, 1, 3, 8};
    int i, arrSize = sizeof(arr)/sizeof(int);
    vector<int> vA, vB;
```

```
// load arr element in vA as a maximum heap and
// in vB as a minumum heap
for (i = 0; i < arrSize; i++)
{
    vA.push_back(arr[i]);
    pushHeap(vA, vA.size(), greater<int>());
    vB.push_back(arr[i]);
    pushHeap(vB, vB.size(), less<int>());
}

// clear the heaps by popping elements. output the
// optimum value which is located at back of vector
cout << "Maximum heap: ";
while (!vA.empty())
{
    popHeap(vA, vA.size(), greater<int>());
    cout << vA.back() << "   ";
    vA.pop_back();
}
cout << endl;

cout << "Minimum heap: ";
while (!vB.empty())
{
    popHeap(vB, vB.size(), less<int>());
    cout << vB.back() << "   ";
    vB.pop_back();
}
cout << endl;
return 0;
}
```

```
Run:
Maximum heap: 9  8  7  5  3  2  1
Minimum heap: 1  2  3  5  7  8  9
```

Complexity of Heap Operations A heap stores elements in an array-based tree that is a complete tree. The pushHeap() and popHeap() operations reheapify the tree by moving up the path of parents for a push and down the path of largest children for a pop. Assuming that the heap has n elements, the maximum length for a path between a leaf node and the root is $\log_2 n$, so the runtime efficiencyof the algorithms is $O(\log_2 n)$.

The Heap Sort

The heap sort is a very efficient $O(n \log_2 n)$ in-place sorting algorithm. It uses the fact that a heap stores the optimal element in the root (index 0). To apply the heap sort to a vector v, we must first order the elements so that the vector, viewed as an array-based tree, is a heap. For the sake of discussion, assume we have performed this task. We will, in fact, develop the function makeHeap() in the next section. By seeing its application in the heap sort algorithm, you will better appreciate its value.

We execute the heap sort by repeatedly exchanging $v[0]$ with the value at the rear of the vector at locations $v[n - 1], v[n - 2], ..., v[1]$. After making the exchange, we must reheapify the tree. You no doubt recognize that each exchange and re-heapification is just the popHeap() operation, where the argument *last* is a value in the range from n down to 2. The first call to popHeap(), with last $= n$, copies the largest (smallest) element in the list to $v[n - 1]$. The next call copies the second largest (smallest) element to $v[n - 2]$, and so forth. If we call popHeap() with the greater<T> function object, the vector is sorted in ascending order. When popHeap() uses the less<T> function object, the sort is in descending order.

The following steps implement the heap sort for the five-element vector v, assuming a maximum heap:

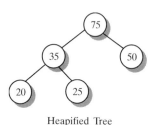

Heapified Tree

Call popHeap() with last = 5
deletes 75 and stores it in h[4]

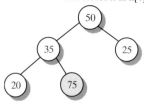

Call popHeap() with last = 4
deletes 50 and stores it in h[3]

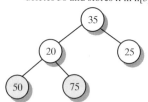

Calling popHeap() with last = 3
deletes 35 and stores it in h[2]

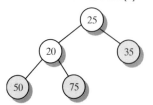

Calling popHeap() with last = 2
deletes 25 and stores it in h[1]

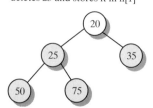

The only remaining element, 20, is at the root, so the vector is sorted: $v = 20, 25, 35, 50, 75$.

The upcoming code is an implementation of the heap sort algorithm. The first instruction calls makeHeap() to heapify the vector. You can find the function heapSort() in the header file "d_sort.h".

heapSort():

```
template <typename T, typename Compare>
void heapSort (vector<T>& v, Compare comp)
{
    //"heapify" the vector v
    makeHeap(v, comp);

    int i, n = v.size();

    // iteration that determines elements v[n-1] ... v[1]
    for(i = n; i>1;i--)
    {
        // call popHeap() to move next largest to v[n-1]
        popHeap(v, i, comp);
    }
}
```

PROGRAM 14-2   HEAP SORT IN ASCENDING AND DESCENDING ORDER

Let us illustrate the heap sort by ordering a random list of 15 integers in the range from 0 to 99. By calling the function with the greater<*int*>() function object, the vector is sorted in ascending order. A second call, with the function object less<*int*>(), sorts the list in descending order. Output displays the original list of elements and the lists after each sort.

```
// File: prg14_2.cpp
// program creates a 15-element vector of integers in range 0 to 99.
// a call to heapSort with greater<int>() object sorts the vector in
// ascending order; a second call to heapSort() with less<int>()
// sorts the list in descending order; output displays original
// list and the ordered lists

#include <iostream>
#include <vector>
#include <functional>

#include "d_sort.h"
#include "d_util.h"
#include "d_random.h"

using namespace std;
int main()
{
    // objects to store the elements and generate random numbers
    vector<int> v;
    randomNumber rnd;
    int i;
```

```
// create a vector with 15 random integers
for (i = 0; i<15; i++)
   v.push_back(rnd.random(100));

// display the original list
cout << "Original vector" << endl << "     ";
writeVector(v);
cout<<endl;

// call heapSort() with greater<int>() and display results
cout << "Sort in ascending order" << endl << "     ";
heapSort(v,greater<int>());
writeVector(v);
cout<<endl;

// call heapSort() with less<int>() and display results
cout << "Sort in descending order" << endl << "     ";
heapSort(v,less<int>());
writeVector(v);
cout<<endl;

return 0;

}
```

```
Run:

Original vector
   92   77   88   36   19   34   14   49   61   14   1   52   44   77   79

Sort in ascending order
    1   14   14   19   34   36   44   49   52   61   77   77   79   88   92

Sort in descending order
   92   88   79   77   77   61   52   49   44   36   34   19   14   14   1
```

Computational Efficiency of the Heap Sort An n-element vector corresponds to a complete binary tree of depth $k = \text{int}(\log_2 n)$. The initial phase to heapify the vector uses makeHeap(), which is an O(n) operation. During the second phase of the sort, popHeap() executes $n - 1$ times. Each operation has efficiency O($\log_2 n$). By combining the two phases, the worst-case complexity of the heap sort becomes is O(n) + O($n \log_2 n$) = O($n \log_2 n$).

The heap sort does not require any additional storage, so it is an in-place sort. Some O($n \log_2 n$) sorts have a worst-case behavior of O(n^2). For instance, the quicksort that we discuss in Chapter 15 is an example. In contrast, the heap sort has worst-case complexity O($n \log_2 n$), regardless of the initial distribution of the data.

Heapifying A Vector

Some applications, like the heap sort, start with a vector and need to reorder the elements so that the corresponding array-based tree is a heap. The reordering is called *heapifying* the vector. The algorithm makeHeap() successively applies the technique developed in adjustHeap() that moves an element down a path of children until it establishes heap ordering. All leaf nodes satisfy heap order (because they have no children), so the makeHeap() algorithm looks only at nonleaf nodes, beginning with the parent of the last node in the heap. The index of the last heap element is *heapSize* − 1, and thus its parent is at index

$$currentPos = \frac{(heapSize - 1) - 1}{2} = \frac{heapSize - 2}{2}$$

This index defines the last interior node in the heap. Starting at this parent node, we traverse the path of children until the parent can be located at a position that satisfies heap ordering. After handling this nonleaf node, we move to the next nonleaf node and repeat the process until finally we arrive at the root. As an example, consider the integer vector shown in the next figure. The unshaded nodes are leaf nodes with indices 5, 6, ..., 9. The first nonleaf node appears at index

$$currentPos = \frac{10 - 2}{2} = 4$$

Function makeHeap() will call adjust Heap() for the nonleaf nodes at indices 4, 3, ..., 0.

```
int arr[10] = {9, 12, 17, 30, 50, 20, 60, 65, 4, 19};
int arrSize = sizeof(arr)/sizeof(int);
vector<int> h(arr, arr+arrSize);
```

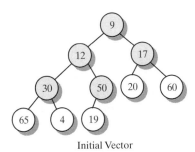

Initial Vector

The upcoming sequence of pictures illustrates the heapifying process for a maximum heap. We highlight the subtree that the algorithm is currently adjusting. Initially, the path is very short.

Locate element at index 4: The value $h[4] = 50$ is greater than its child $h[9] = 19$, and the heap condition for the subtree is satisfied. No exchanges occur (Figure A).

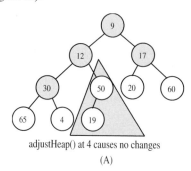

adjustHeap() at 4 causes no changes

(A)

Locate element at index 3: The value $h[3] = 30$ is less than its child $h[7] = 65$ and must exchange with its child (Figure B).

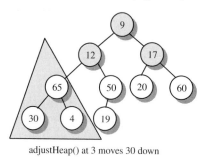

adjustHeap() at 3 moves 30 down

(B)

Locate element at index 2: The value $h[2] = 17$ is less than its child $h[6] = 60$ and must exchange with the child (Figure C).

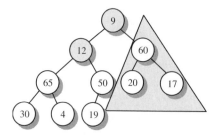

adjustHeap() at 2 moves 17 down

(C)

Locate element at index 1: The value $h[1] = 12$ is less than its child $h[3] = 65$ and must exchange with the child. The value 12 must subsequently exchange with 30 so that the heap condition is satisfied for the subtree (Figure D).

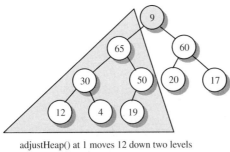

adjustHeap() at 1 moves 12 down two levels

(D)

Locate element at index 0: The process terminates at the root node. The value $h[0] = 9$ must exchange positions with its child $h[1] = 65$ and then continue down two more levels. The resulting tree is a heap (Figure E).

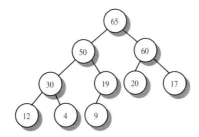

adjustHeap() at 0 moves 9 down three levels

(E)

The function makeHeap() takes a vector and a function object as arguments. The function object indicates whether the heapification creates a maximum or a minimum heap. Use the comparison function object greater<*T*>() to create a maximum heap and less<*T*>() to create a minimum heap. The code makes repeated calls to adjustHeap(), starting at the index (heapPos) of the first nonleaf node. Decrement the index down to 0 (root).

makeHeap():
```
// arrange the vector elements into a heap. use the function
// object comp to perform comparisons
template <typename T, typename Compare>
void makeHeap(vector<T>& v, Compare comp)
{
    int heapPos, lastPos;
```

```
            // start at 0 and restore heap ordering
            lastPos = v.size();
            heapPos = (lastPos - 2)/2;

            while (heapPos >= 0)
            {
                adjustHeap(v,heapPos, lastPos, comp);
                heapPos--;
            }
        }
```

14.3   IMPLEMENTING A PRIORITY QUEUE

The heap deletion operation removes the optimal element from the heap. If we take "optimal" to mean the element of highest priority, we observe that the deletion is just the pop() operation from a priority-queue. Heap insertion simply adds an element, much like the priority queue push() operation. Both the heap insertion and deletion operations update the underlying tree storage structure in such a way that it remains a heap; that is, they maintain the integrity of the storage structure. Putting these ideas together, we can use a heap to provide a very efficient implementation of a priority-queue class.

We illustrate this by developing the miniPQ class with the same interface used by the STL priority_queue class in Chapter 8. Recall that we never designed or implemented a "mini" priority queue class in that chapter, but rather referred you to the discussion on heaps. The upcoming code is a listing of the interface. Note that a second template argument specifies a function object type. The type defaults to greater<T>, which specifies that the largest element has highest priority. By including the function type less<T> in a declaration, the priority queue treats "smallest" as being of highest priority.

CLASS miniPQ	Declaration	"d_pqueue.h"

```
// maintain a priority queue containing elements of data type
// T using a comparison function object of type Compare
template <typename T, typename Compare = greater<T>>
class miniPQ
{
   public:
     miniPQ();
        // create empty priority queue
     int size() const;
        // return the number of elements in the priority queue
     bool empty() const;
        // is the priority queue empty?
     void push(const T& item);
        // insert item into the priority queue
        // Postcondition: the priority queue size increases by 1
     void pop();
```

```
        // remove the element of highest priority.
        // Precondition: the priority queue is not empty.
        // if condition fails, the function throws the
        // underflowError exception.
        // Postcondition: the priority queue size decreases by 1
     T& top();
        // return the element of highest priority
        // Precondition: the priority queue is not empty.
        // if the condition fails, the function throws the
        // underflowError exception
     const T& top() const;
        // constant version
  private:
     vector<T> pqList;
        // pqList holds the priority queue elements
     Compare comp;
        // function object used for comparisons
};
```

Example 14-2

You are familiar with STL priority queues from Chapter 8. Let us apply your understanding to the declaration and use of miniPQ objects.

1. Declaration a miniPQ container must include the template argument *T*. The comparator argument is optional, because it defaults to greater<*T*>:

```
// creates a maximum priority queue
miniPQ<int> pqMax;
```

A similar definition of a minimum priority queue must contain the function type less<T>:

```
miniPQ<int, less<int> > pqMin;
```

2. Assume that *pqMin* contains the elements 5, 9, 2, 7, 4. The top() and pop() operations access the smallest element in the list.

```
cout<<pqMin.top();              // output:   2
pqMin.pop();
cout<<pqMin.top();              // output:   4
```

Implementing The MiniPQ Class

The miniPQ class uses a heap as the underlying storage structure. Because a heap is just a vector viewed as an array-based tree, the vector private data member *pqList* is the storage container. A second data member, *comp*, is the function object that indicates whether *pqList* is a maximum or minimum heap.

Most of the miniPQ operations simply use features of the vector *pqList*. For instance, we implement size() by calling the vector size() function:

miniPQ size():XS
```
template <typename T, typename Compare>
int miniPQ<T,Compare>::size() const
{ return pqList.size(); }
```

The miniPQ top() operation returns the element of highest priority. This is just the element in the vector at index 0 (root). If the priority queue is empty, the function throws an underflow exception.

miniPQ top():
```
template <typename T, typename Compare>
T& miniPQ<T,Compare>::top()
{
    // check for an empty priority queue
    if (pqList.empty())
       throw underflowError("miniPQ top(): empty list");

    // return the root of the heap
    return pqList[0];
}
```

We designed the heap function popHeap() to support deletion of an element. The operation does not actually remove the optimal value from the heap, but rather copies it to the bottom of the tree (the back of the vector). The vector operation pop_back() deletes the element. This is the process used to implement the miniPQ pop() operation. After checking for an empty priority queue, call popHeap() with *pqList* as the heap argument. Then remove the optimal value from the back of *pqList*.

miniPQ pop():
```
    // remove the element of highest priority,
template <typename T, typename Compare>
void miniPQ<T,Compare>::pop()
{
// check for an empty priority queue
if (pqList.empty())
   throw underflowError("miniPQ pop(): empty list");

    // call popHeap() to put element at back of the vector
    popHeap(pqList, pqList.size(), comp);

    // delele element from back of pqList
    pqList.pop_back();
}
```

Many applications need to access data on disk files. In this section, we give an overview of binary file I/O, using the class *fstream* from the file <fstream>. The topics include functions to open and close a binary file, to access individual records in the file, and to execute block reads and writes of data in a file. A simple program illustrates the concepts. We use many of the concepts in this section in our study of file compression in Section 14-6. There, we develop the Huffman compression algorithm that creates a compressed image of either a text or a binary source file.

File Structure

A *text file* contains ASCII characters with a newline sequence separating lines. A *binary file* consists of data objects that vary from a single character (byte) to more complex structures that include integers, floating-point values, programmer-generated class objects, and arrays. In file terminology, we call each data object in a file a *record*. The logical view of a file pictures data as a sequence of records. The operating system allows a programmer to read and write individual data records. The operations use a system-maintained *file pointer*, which locates the current position in the file, meassured as a byte offset from the beginning of the file. If the pointer is at the beginning of the file, a read or write operation accesses the current data record and shifts the file pointer to the next record. This allows for sequential access to the file:

File as a sequential access structure

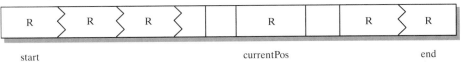

```
   R        R        R              R         R      R
```

start   currentPos   end

A programmer can also position the file pointer at a specific record. Combined with a read or write operation, this allows for direct access to the file, which can then be viewed as an external array of records:

File as a direct access structure

R_0	R_1	R_2	R_3	R_4			R_i			R_{n-2}	R_{n-1}
0	1	2	3	4			currentPos			n-2	n-1

The C++ file system is a hierarchical structure. The fstream class is a derived class that describes file objects that can be used for both input and output. We refer to the objects as streams, because they support the flow of data to and from a physical file that ordinarily resides on a hard disk. When creating an object, we use the open() function to associate the physical file name and access mode with a stream. The base class *ios* of the file system hierarchy defines the possible modes. Access the attributes of *ios* with the notation ios::attribute. You recognize "::" as the class scope operator that references the base class attribute.

Mode	Action
ios::in	open file for reading
ios::out	open file for writing
ios::trunc	truncate the file to have size 0 before reading or writing
ios::binary	open file in binary mode (not a text file)

Example 14-3

```
#include <iostream>
#include <fstream>
```

1. `fstream f;  // declare file stream object`

   ```
   // open text file "phone.txt" for input
   f.open("phone.txt", ios::in);
   ```

2. You can use the operator "|" to combine access modes. In Section 14-5, we introduce the operator as bitwise OR. By combining access modes, we make them all operative. In the following example, the stream *f* might read (input) data from a file and write (output) data to a file. The stream treats the data as binary data without any regard to end-of-line characters, that are in text files. If the file already exists, the open statement discards (truncates) any current data, leaving a file of length 0.

   ```
   fstream f;
   // truncate an existing file and open a binary file
   // for input and output
   f.open("studs.dat", ios::in | ios::out | ios::trunc | ios::binary);
   ```

Direct File Access

Each file object has a file pointer associated with it that identifies the current record for input or output. For an input file, the function tellg() returns in bytes the location of the current file pointer as an offset from the beginning of the file. For an output file, the function tellp() returns in bytes the location of the current file pointer. The functions seekg() and seekp() allow the application to reposition the current file pointers. The seek functions take an offset argument that measures the number of bytes from the beginning (ios::beg), ending (ios::end), or current position (ios::cur) in the file. If a file is used for both input and output, use the functions tellg() and seekg().

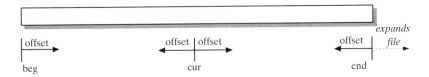

For instance, the statements shown next illustrate the action of the functions seekg() and tellg(). Define the stream *f* to handle integer data, where an integer occupies four bytes. The statements reference locations in the file "bin.dat", which we assume contains six integers, or 24 bytes of data.

```
// binary file of integer values
fstream f;

f.open("bin.dat", ios::in | ios::binary);
                ...
// reset current position to start of file.
// file pointer at byte 0
f.seekg(0, ios::beg);

// set current position at last data value.
// file pointer at byte 20
f.seekg(-sizeof(int), ios::end);
                ...
// assume current file pointer is at byte 12; move file.
// pointer forward 4 bytes to the next integer
f.seekg(sizeof(int), ios::cur);
                ...
// move to the end of the file
// file pointer at byte 24
f.seekg(0, ios::end);
// output number of bytes in the file
cout<<f.tellg();                              // Output: 24
// output the number of records in the file
cout<<f.tellg()/sizeof(int);                  // Output: 6
```

Input And Output For Binary Files

The fstream class has functions read() and write() that perform I/0 with a byte stream. Each function takes the address of a buffer and a count that indicates the number of bytes to transfer. The buffer is an array of characters that stores the data as they are sent or received from a device. I/0 operations with noncharacter data types require a type conversion, using the (char *) cast. This tells the compiler to consider the buffer to be an array of characters. Omission of the cast for a noncharacter array results in a compilation error. For instance, the following operations transfer a block of integer data to and from a file:

```
fstream f;
int intData;
// array of integers
int arr[20];

// read integer data as a "sizeof(int)" block of characters;
// reads the next 4 bytes into the variable intData
f.read((char *) &intData, sizeof(int));

// write 20 integers from array arr to stream f
// writes 20 * 4 = 80 bytes
f.write((char *)arr, sizeof(arr));
```

Application: Bank Account Records

Binary files often contain data that represent a record with multiple fields, where each record has the same size in bytes. We call these files *databases*. As an example of a database, consider a series of bank accounts. Associated with each account is an account number and a balance. Assume that the bank numbers the accounts 0, 1, 2, and so forth, and stores them in the database in that order. For example, record 5 of the database stores account number 5, and record 8 stores account number 8.

We create a bank-account database and access the records to illustrate many of the concepts and operations that apply to binary file streams. To store account information and provide update and output operations, we declare an account class. The function update() takes a transaction type 'D' (deposit) or 'W' (withdrawal) and modifies the account by a given amount.

CLASS account	Declaration	"d_acct.h"

```
// maintain bank account information
class account
{
   public:
      // constructor has initial account number and balance
      // with default values 0 and 0.0 respectively
      account (int n = 0, double bal = 0.0): acctNo(n), balance (bal)
      {}

      // update balance with deposit (D) or withdrawal (W)
      void update (char type, double amt)
      {
         if (type == 'D')
            balance += amt;
         else
            balance -= amt;
      }

      // output account fields
```

```
    friend ostream& operator<< (ostream& ostr, const account& acct)
    {
        ostr << acct.acctNo<<": " << acct.balance;
        return ostr;
    }

private:
    int acctNo;
    double balance;
};
```

A simple program uses an input/output stream acctFile to read and write account information to the file "acct.dat". We go through the design of the program step by step and display key code sequences. Initially, the program opens the file and truncates any existing data.

```
fstream acctFile;
// open the binary file for input and output. truncate a
// previous version of the file
acctFile.open("accounts.dat",ios::in | ios::out | ios::trunc |
              ios::binary);
```

Using the fstream function write(), we copy five "empty" accounts to the file, where the account numbers are 0, 1, ..., 4. Each write() copies sizeof(*account*) number of bytes from an account object to the file.

```
account acct;
// write 5 records with account number 0, 1, ..., 4
for (i=0; i<5; i++)
{
    // account(i) is anonymous object with number i
    acct = account(i);
    acctFile.write((char *)&acct, sizeof(account));
}
```

The main action in the program prompts the user to input an account number, a transaction type (D or W), and an amount. A call to seekg() locates the file pointer at the specified account record, and a call to read() inputs the record from the file. The account member function update() executes the transaction. Before writing the updated account back to the file, a call to seekg() must reposition the file pointer back to the original location. Remember, the read() call moved the file pointer forward sizeof(*account*) bytes.

```
// seek to record n
acctFile.seekg(n*sizeof(account), ios::beg);
// read the record and update the balance
acctFile.read((char *)&acct, sizeof(account));
acct.update(type, amt);
```

```
// seek back to the previous record
acctFile.seekg(-sizeof(account), ios::cur);
acctFile.write((char *) &acct, sizeof(account));
```

User input terminates when the account number is −1. To list the contents of the
file, the program calls outputAccounts(), which sequentially reads each data record,
starting at the first record. A seekg() call to the end of the file and a subsequent call
to tellg() reveals the total number of bytes in the file. Dividing this total by size-
of(*account*) gives the number of bank records in the file. A call to seekg() then positions the file pointer at the beginning of the file and allows the use of a loop to
sequentially scan the file.

PROGRAM 14-3 BANK ACCOUNT DATABASE

You have seen key components of the code for the application. Let us look at the complete
program and a run.

```
// File: prg14_3.cpp
// the program reads and writes account records to and from file
// accounts.dat"; an initial write creates 5 files with
// account numbers 0 to 4. The user enters a series of
// account numbers, transaction (deposit 'D' or withdrawal 'W',
// and amounts. The corresponding account is read from the file
// and updated based on the transaction . The data is written back
// to the file.  The program displays the current account
// information after the user enters account number -1

#include <iostream>
#include <fstream>
#include "d_acct.h"

using namespace std;

// output the records in a binary file of account objects
void outputAccounts(fstream& f);

int main()
{
   // binary file of part values
   fstream acctFile;
   account acct;

   int i, n;
   char type;
   double amt;

   // open the binary file for input and output. truncate a previous
   // version
   acctFile.open("accounts.dat",ios::in | ios::out |
            ios::trunc | ios::binary);
```

```
   if (!acctFile)
   {
      cerr << "Cannot create 'accounts.dat'" << endl;
      exit(1);
   }

   // write 5 records with account number 0, 1, ..., 4
   for (i=0;i<5;i++)
   {
      acct = account(i);
      acctFile.write((char *)&acct, sizeof(account));
   }

   // ask user to input account number and 'D' for deposit
   // and 'W' for withdrawal along with the ammount
   // update a record of the file; terminate with accout number -1
   while(true)
   {
      cout << "Enter acct#, type (D or W), and amount: ";
      cin>>n;
      if (n == -1)
         break;
      cin >> type >> amt;

      // seek to record n
      acctFile.seekg(n*sizeof(account), ios::beg);
      // read the record and update the balance
      acctFile.read((char *)&acct, sizeof(account));
      acct.update(type, amt);

      // seek back to the previous record
      acctFile.seekg(-int(sizeof(account)), ios::cur);
      acctFile.write((char *)& acct, sizeof(account));
   }

   // output final state of the account database
   cout << endl << "Final state of the accounts" << endl;
   outputAccounts(acctFile);

   return 0;
}

void outputAccounts(fstream& f)
{

   account acct;

   // go to the end of the file
   f.seekg(0, ios::end);
   // n = number of records in the file
```

```
    int n = f.tellg()/sizeof(account), i;

    // go back to the beginning of the file
    f.seekg(0, ios::beg);

    // read and output n records
    for (i=0; i<n; i++)
    {
        f.read((char *)& acct, sizeof(account));
        cout<<acct<<endl;
    }
}
```

```
Run:
Enter acct#, type (D or W), and amount: 3 D 200.00
Enter acct#, type (D or W), and amount: 1 D 500.00
Enter acct#, type (D or W), and amount: 4 W 150.00
Enter acct#, type (D or W), and amount: 2 D 800.00
Enter acct#, type (D or W), and amount: 4 D 225.00
Enter acct#, type (D or W), and amount: 2 W 475.00
Enter acct#, type (D or W), and amount: 1 W 100.00
Enter acct#, type (D or W), and amount: -1
Final state of the accounts
0: 0
1: 400
2: 325
3: 200
4: 75
```

14.5   BITSETS

Applications such as compiler code generation and compression algorithms create data that include specific sequences of bits. For instance, the machine code for an addition instruction is often a specific sequence of 16 bits. Certain bits have fixed values, but others belong to bit fields that indicate the source, destination and size of the data for the addition. For instance, assume the bit pattern for the add instruction could be where the x's are the source, y's are the size, and z's are the destination.

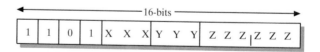

One add instruction might have the following bit sequence:

| 1 | 1 | 0 | 1 | 0 0 0 | 0 0 1 | 1 1 1 ¦ 0 0 1 |

Another might have the following bit sequence:

1	1	0	1	0 0 0	1 0 1	1 1 1 0 0 1

C++ allows manipulation of individual bits with the operators OR ($|$), AND ($\&$), NOT ($\sim$), and EOR ($\wedge$). The operators take integer or character operands. Table 14-1 defines the operators. The operator EOR may not be familiar. It produces a 1 only if the two bits differ. C++ applies the binary bit operators to n-bit integer values by executing the operation on each bit. Assume that

$$x = x_0 \, x_1 \, x_2 \, \ldots \, x_{n-2} \, x_{n-1}, \qquad y = y_0 \, y_1 \, y_2 \, \ldots \, y_{n-2} \, y_{n-1}$$

The result, $z = x \, op \, y$, is given by

$$z = z_0 \, z_1 \, z_2 \, \ldots \, z_{n-2} \, z_{n-1} = x_0 \, x_1 \, x_2 \, \ldots \, x_{n-2} \, x_{n-1} \, op \, y_0 \, y_1 \, y_2 \, \ldots \, y_{n-2} \, y_{n-1}$$

where

$$z_i = x_i \, op \, y_i, 0 \le i \le n - 1 \text{ and } op = |, \&, \wedge$$

The unary operator $\sim$ inverts the bits of its operand.

Example 14-4
_____

Declare the following unsigned eight-bit numbers:

```
unsigned char x = 182, y = 154;
```

In binary, $x = 10110110$ and $y = 10011010$. Apply the operators $|$, $\&$, and $\wedge$ to these operands:

(a)   x 10110110
$|$ y 10011010
10111110 (190)

(b)   x 10110110
$\&$ y 10011010
10010010 (146)

(c)   x 10110110
$\wedge$ y 10010010
00101100 (44)

(d) $\sim$x = 01001001 (73)

_____

TABLE 14-1   BIT OPERATIONS

x	y	$\sim x$	$x \mid y$	$x \& y$	$x \wedge y$
0	0	1	0	0	0
0	1	1	1	0	1
1	0	0	1	0	1
1	1	0	1	1	0

C++ also provides bit-shifting operators that shift the bits in an integer value left ($<<$) or right ($>>$). The expression $x<<n$ multiples x by 2^n, and $x>>n$ divides x by 2^n. An unsigned integer or character uses all of its bits to store a value ≥ 0. Shifting an unsigned number to the right fills the vacated bits on the left with 0:

$$x = 00101101 \qquad x<<1 = 01011010$$
$$x = 10110110 \qquad x>>2 = 00101101$$

For a signed number, the original leftmost bit fills the vacated bits. Generally, using a bit-shifting operator speeds up any computation that involves multiplying or dividing an integer value by a power of 2.

The bit operators are typically used with unsigned integer operands. We will apply them only in this situation.

The bitVector Class

Rather than requiring a programmer to use low-level bit operations, we develop the bitVector class as an alternative. A bitVector object treats on the left stream of n bits as an array, with bit 0 first bit on the left, bit 1 the second bit, and bit $n - 1$ the last bit on the right. For instance, if we use a bit vector to represent the five-bit stream 1 0 1 1 1, bit 0 is 1, bit 1 is 0, and bit 2 through bit 4 are 1. To be effective, a bit vector must supply operations that return the value of a particular bit in the bit stream and that set and clear individual bits. In addition, the class should provide overloaded versions of the bit-handling operators |, &, ^, $<<$, $>>$, and ~. For convenience, we also supply the class with file I/O operations.

CLASS bitVector	Declaration	"d_bitvec.h"

```
class bitVector
{

   public:
      // CONSTRUCTORS

      bitVector(int numBits = 16);
         // constructor. create a bit vector of 0 bits

      bitVector(int b[], int n);
         // constructor. create a bit vector whose
         // bits are initialized as follows:
         //    bit 0:   b[0]
         //    bit 1:   b[1]
         //             ...
         //    bit n-1: b[n-1]

      // ASSIGNMENT OPERATORS
      bitVector& operator= (int v);
         // assign the bit vector the bits of v
      bitVector& operator= (char c);
         // assign the bit vector the 8-bits of c
```

```
// ACCESS AND UPDATE FUNCTIONS
int size() const;
    // number of bits in the bit vector

// the functions bit(), set(), and clear() have
// the following precondition.
// Precondition: 0 <= i < numberOfBits. if the
// condition is violated, the function throws
// the indexRangeError exception

int bit(int i) const;
    // return value of bit i
void set(int i);
    // set bit i
void clear(int i);
    // clear bit i
void clear();
    // clear all bits in the bit vector


// BIT SET OPERATORS

// the operators ==, |, &, and ^ have
// the following precondition.
// Precondition:    the bit vectors must have the same size.
// if the condition is violated, the function throws
// the rangeError exception

friend bool operator== (const bitVector& x,
                        const bitVector& y);
    // bit vector equality
friend bitVector operator| (const bitVector& x,
                            const bitVector& y);
    // bitwise OR
friend bitVector operator& (const bitVector& x,
                            const bitVector& y);
    // bitwise AND
friend bitVector operator^ (const bitVector& x,
                            const bitVector& y);
    // bitwise EOR

friend bitVector operator<< (const bitVector& x, int n);
    // shift bit vector to the left n bits
friend bitVector operator>> (const bitVector& x, int n);
    // shift bit vector to the right n bits
bitVector operator~ ();
    // bitwise NOT


// BIT SET I/O
void write(fstream& ostr);
```

```
                       // output the bit vector to the binary file ostr
                void read(fstream& istr, int numBits);
                       // read the numBits bit vector from the binary file istr
                friend ostream& operator<< (ostream& ostr, const bitVector& x);
                       // output the bit vector in ASCII form

           private:
                int numberOfBits;
                       // number of bits in the vector

                int vectorSize;
                       // number of bytes in bit vector
                vector<unsigned char> member;
                       // the vector itself

                int vectorIndex(int i) const;
                       // determine the index of the vector element
                       // containing bit i

                unsigned char bitMask(int i) const;
                       // bit i is represented by a bit in member[vectorIndex(i)].
                       // return an unsigned char value with a 1 in the
                       // position that represents bit i
     };
```

The first constructor creates a bit vector, all of whose bits are 0. The second constructor simplifies the creation of short bit vectors by using a C++ integer array containing the values 0 and 1 to initialize the individual bits. The two assignment operators allow a convenient conversion between an integer or character and the corresponding bit vector. The stream operator << outputs the bits as a stream of ASCII characters '0' and '1'.

Example 14-5

Let use declare bitVector objects and use them in a sequence of operations.

1. Declaration

```
     int arr[] = {1, 0, 1, 1, 0, 1};
     int arrSize = sizeof(arr)/sizeof(int);

     // x is 1 0 1 1 0 1   and y is  0 0 0 0 0 0
     bitVector x(arr, arrSize), y(arrSize), z(arrSize);
```

2. Operations (assume result from previous operation)

```
     y.set(0);                    // y is 100000
     y.set(4);                    // y is 100010

     x.clear(2);                  // x is 100101
     cout <<x<< endl;
```

```
z = x | y;              // z is 100111
z = ~x;                 // z is 011010

x = x<<2;               // x is 010100
y = y>>3;               // y is 000100

z = x ^ y;              // z is 010000

// z has the 32-bits in the integer value 32
z = 31;                 // z is 00000000000000000000000000011111

// z has the 8-bits in the character 'a' ASCII 'a' = 97
z = 'a';                // z is 01100001
```

Implementing The Bitvector Class

The bitVector class uses the C++ bit operators on individual bits in a byte to efficiently implement a bitVector object. A vector of unsigned characters stores the range of individual bits with numbers 0 to *numberOfBits* − 1. The term *unsigned* means that the numerical value of a character is an unsigned number in the range from 0 to 255. The implementation views the vector, called *member*, as a stream of bits. The element *member*[0] provides eight bits, *member*[1] provides eight more bits, and so forth. There is a mapping from a bit in *member* to a bit number in the range 0 ... *numberOfBits*−1. The leftmost bit of *member*[0] represents bit 0, and the rightmost bit of *member*[0] represents bit 7. We continue with the leftmost bit of *member*[1] representing bit 8, and so forth. The following figure illustrates the storage scheme:

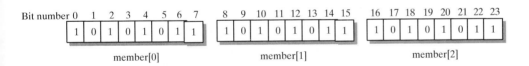

The private member functions vectorIndex() and bitMask() implement the storage scheme. The function vectorIndex() determines the vector element to which bit *i* belongs. Simply divide *i* by 8. In this way, $i = 0$ through $i = 7$ belongs to *member*[0], $i = 8$ through $i = 15$ belong to *member*[1], and so forth.

vectorIndex():
```
    // determine the index of the vector element
    // containing bit i
    int bitVector::vectorIndex(int i) const
    {
        // return i/8
        return i>>3;
    }
```

After locating the correct vector index, bitMask() returns an unsigned character value containing a 1 in the bit position representing *i*. This value, called a *mask*, can be used to set or clear the bit.

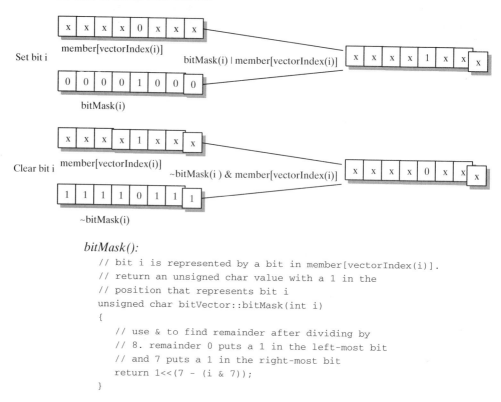

bitMask():

```
// bit i is represented by a bit in member[vectorIndex(i)].
// return an unsigned char value with a 1 in the
// position that represents bit i
unsigned char bitVector::bitMask(int i)
{
    // use & to find remainder after dividing by
    // 8. remainder 0 puts a 1 in the left-most bit
    // and 7 puts a 1 in the right-most bit
    return 1<<(7 - (i & 7));
}
```

The bitVector Constructors There are two constructors that create a bitVector object. One creates a bit vector initialized with a specified number of 0 bits; the second constructor initializes the bit vector by using a C++ integer array of 0 and 1 values. Build a bit vector of 0 bits by determining the number of unsigned-character vector elements needed to represent the range of bit numbers, and resize the vector member to have that number of elements. The resize() vector operator fills the vector with values of 0.

Constructor (creates empty bit vector):

```
bitVector::bitVector(int numBits) : numberOfBits(numBits)
{
    // number of unsigned characters needed to hold
    // numberOfBits elements
    vectorSize = (numberOfBits+7)>>3;
    // resize the vector with all bytes 0
    member.resize(vectorSize);
}
```

Set Operators The class implements the bitwise operations AND, OR, EOR, and NOT by overloading the C++ operators |, &, ^, and ~. For instance, to implement the bitwise OR operator (|), construct a bitVector object *tmp* of the same size as the arguments *x* and *y*. Assign its elements to be the bitwise OR of the vector elements representing the bit vector *x* and the bit vector *y*. Return this new bit vector as the value of the function. Note that the function throws the rangeError exception if *x* and *y* do not have the same size.

operator| ():
```
// bitwise OR
bitVector operator| (const bitVector& x, const bitVector& y)
{
   int i;

   // the bit vectors must have the same size
   if (x.numberOfBits != y.numberOfBits)
      throw
         rangeError("bitVector |: bit vectors not same size");

   // form the bitwise OR in tmp
   bitVector tmp(x.numberOfBits);

   // each vector element of tmp is the bitwise
   // OR of x and y
   for (i = 0; i<x.vectorSize; i++)
      tmp.member[i] = x.member[i] | y.member[i];

   // return the bitwise OR
   return tmp;
}
```

Bitwise NOT is a unary operator, so the class implements it as a member function. Create a bitVector object *tmp* of the same size as the current object. Create the new bitset by applying the bitwise NOT operator to the vector elements in *tmp*. Return the new bitvector as the value of the function.

operator~ ():
```
// bitwise NOT
bitVector bitVector::operator~ ()
{
   // form the bitwise NOT in tmp
   bitVector tmp(numberOfBits);

   // each vector element of tmp is the bitwise
   // NOT of the current object's member value.
   for (int i = 0; i<vectorSize; i++)
      tmp.member[i] = ~member[i];
```

```
   // return the bitwise NOT
   return tmp;
}
```

Bit Access and Modification Functions Functions like bit() and clear() access individual bits by applying the private functions vectorIndex() and bitMask(). The function bit() returns 1 if it finds a 1 in the bit corresponding to *i*, and 0 otherwise.

bit():
```
   // return value of bit i
   int bitVector::bit(int i) const
   {
      // is i in range 0 to numberOfBits-1 ?
      if (i<0 || i >= numberOfBits)
         throw indexRangeError(
            "bitVector bit(): bit out of range", i, numberOfBits);

      // return the bit corresponding to i
      if ((member[vectorIndex(i)] & bitMask(i)) != 0)
         return 1;
      else
         return 0;
   }
```

The function clear() turns off the bit corresponding to i. The process uses the AND operator and a mask that contains all 1's except for the specific *i* bit. Create the mask by using the bitwise NOT operator($\sim$).

clear():
```
   void bitVector::clear(int i)
   {
      // is i in range 0 to numberOfBits-1 ?
      if (i<0 || i >= numberOfBits)
         throw indexRangeError(
            "bitVector clear(): bit out of range", i, numberOfBits);

      // clear the bit corresponding to i. note
      // that ~bitMask(i) has a 0 in the bit
      // we are interested in an 1 in all others
      member[vectorIndex(i)] &= ~bitMask(i);
   }
```

14.6   CASE STUDY: HUFFMAN COMPRESSION

Data compression is a software technology that takes information and represents it in compact form. Compression algorithms create these compact representations by detecting patterns in the data and then representing them by using less information. The data can consist of a simple text file or a binary word processing file. More complex examples include sound and audio files. Most computer users have applied a compression program to save disk space.

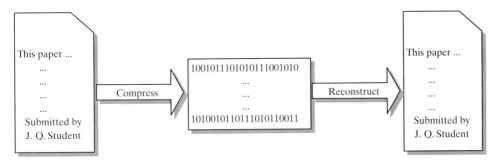

Figure 14-7
Lossless Compression

There are two basic types of data compression. With *lossless compression*, the data compression loses no information. The original data can be recovered exactly from the compressed data. We normally apply this type of compression to "discrete" data, such as text, word processing files, computer applications, and so forth (Figure 14-7). A *lossy compression* technique loses some information during compression, and the data cannot be recovered exactly (Figure 14-8). However, this type of compression tends to shrink the data further than do lossless compression techniques. Sound files often use this type of compression, because they can omit in the compressed image certain frequencies that cannot be detected by the human ear.

Evaluation of a compression algorithm can include a mathematical complexity analysis that determines its computing requirements. Other criteria assess how much compression the algorithm produces. When evaluating a lossy compression technique, another criterion to consider is how closely the decompressed image resembles the original. Often, a mathematical analysis is very difficult to perform, so we use the latter criterion. The *compression ratio* is the ratio of the number of bits in the original data to the number of bits in the compressed image. For instance, if a data file contains 500,000 bytes and the compressed data file contains 100,000 bytes, the compression ratio is 5:1.

In this section, we consider a compression technique, known as *Huffman compression*, that relies on counting the number of occurrences of each eight-bit charac-

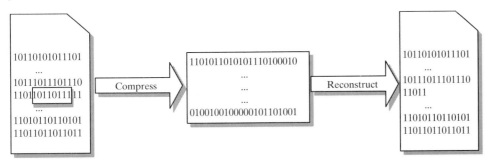

Figure 14-8
Lossy Compression

ter in the data and generating a sequence of optimal binary codes called *prefix codes*. Algorithms that perform optimization normally execute a series of steps requiring choices. At each step, a *greedy algorithm* always looks at the data on hand and makes the choice that looks best based on the local data. It hopes that the locally optimal choices will lead to an optimal solution to the whole problem. The Huffman algorithm is an example of a greedy algorithm.

Huffman compression is a popular and effective technique for data compression. The technique tends to be very effective for text files, where compression ratios of at least 1.8 (at least 45% reduction) are common. The technique is successful for binary files, but the savings are generally not as good. The algorithm generates a table that contains the frequency of occurrence of each character in the file. Using these frequencies, the algorithm assigns each character a string of bits known as its *bit code* and writes the bit code to the compressed image in place of the original character. It is hoped that the sum of the bit codes is smaller than the original file.

Suppose that a file contains only the characters "a" through "f" and that the characters have the frequencies specified in Table 14-2. For example, the character "e" occurs 20,000 times in the file. If we assign each character a fixed-length bit code, we will need three bits for each character ("a" = 000, "b" = 001, ..., "f" = 101), as shown in Table 14-2. If we replace each character by its bit code, the resulting compressed image uses a total of

$$(16(3) + 4(3) + 8(3) + 6(3) + 20(3) + 3(3)) \times 1000 = 171,000 \text{ bits}$$

Computers store data in eight-bit bytes, so the image will have a size of 21,375 bytes. The original file has a size of 57,000 bytes, so the compression ration is 2.67 (savings of 62.5%).

The goal of the Huffman algorithm is to create an "optimal" binary tree that represents the bit codes. We will explain the meaning of optimal when we develop the algorithm. For now, let us explore a tree that illustrates the issues. In the example, each leaf node contains a character and its frequency of occurrence. Each internal node contains the sum of the frequencies of its children. Starting at the root, a left child designates a bit of 0, and a right child designates a bit of 1. The tree grows until the branches create all bit codes as leaf nodes. The tree structure for the bit:

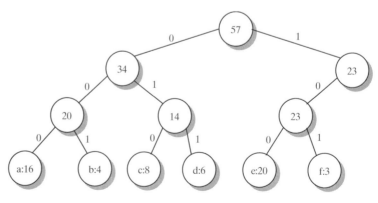

a = 000, b = 001, c = 010, d = 011, e = 100, f = 101

TABLE 14-2 BIT CODES

	a	b	c	d	e	f
Frequency (in thousands)	16	4	8	6	20	3
Fixed-length codeword	000	001	010	011	100	101

Note that, in the tree, no bit code is also a prefix for another bit code. This is guaranteed, because a character occurs only in a leaf node. Such codes are called *prefix codes*.

In the tree, each nonleaf node contains a frequency count. This becomes part of our strategy to create an optimal tree. Another issue of optimality involves the right subtree of the root. There are two codes beginning with 10, but no codes beginning with 11. The reason is that the tree is not a full binary tree. A *full binary tree* is one in which each interior node has two children. By converting the tree to a full tree, we can generate better bit codes for "a"–"f". If we replace the 23 on level 1 by its subtree, the following full tree results (Figure 14-9):

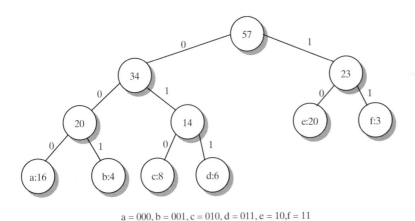

a = 000, b = 001, c = 010, d = 011, e = 10, f = 11

Figure 14-9
Prefix Codes for the Data in Table14-2

The bit codes for "e" and "f" are both one bit shorter, so the compressed file will now have

$$(16(3) + 4(3) + 8(3) + 6(3) + 20(2) + 3(2)) \times 1000 = 148,000 \text{ bits,}$$

which corresponds to a compression ratio of 3:1.

Now that we have seen a tree of bit codes, we can begin to understand the design of a file compression algorithm. Begin by reading the file and determining the frequencies of the characters in the file. Then, use the frequencies to build a tree of prefix codes that determines unique bit codes for each character. Write the tree to the compressed file, and then reread the source file. For each character in the second pass, write its corresponding bit code to the compressed file. For instance, using the tree in Figure 14-9, the bit codes for the characters in the string "ead" are 10 000 011.

To decompress a file, decode the stream of bits by using the prefix codes. To determine the first character of the original file, start at the root of the tree and read a bit from the compressed file. If the bit is 0, move to the left child; if the bit is 1, move to the right. Read the next bit, and move again. Continue until you encounter a leaf node, which is a character that corresponds to the bit code. No bit code is a prefix of any other bit code, so there is no ambiguity. Continue in this fashion until reaching the end of the compressed file. For instance, for our sample file and the tree in Figure 14-9, the bit sequence 1100001010 separates into the individual bit codes 11 000 010 10, which decodes to "face".

The overriding issue in using bit codes for compression is to choose an optimal tree. It can be shown that the optimal bit codes for a file are always represented by a full tree. It can be shown that any full tree with n leaf nodes has exactly $n-1$ internal nodes, and so it has a total of $n + (n-1) = 2n - 1$ nodes. Thus, if a file contains n unique characters and we compress it by replacing its characters by bit codes, the corresponding tree will have $2n-1$ nodes. There is a simple formula for the number of bits in the compressed image. For each character ch in the original file, let f(ch) be the frequency of the character and d(ch) be the depth of the leaf node containing ch. The depth of the node is also the number of bits in the bit code for ch. We refer to the number of bits necessary to compress the file as the *cost* of the tree, which we specify by the following relation:

$$\text{Cost} = \sum_{\substack{\text{all unique} \\ \text{ch in file}}} f(\text{ch})\, d(\text{ch})$$

It can be shown that a Huffman tree generates *optimal prefix codes*. That is, among all trees representing prefix codes, a Huffman tree gives the minimum cost. The Huffman algorithm constructs the tree so that the most frequently occurring characters correspond to leaf nodes near the top of the tree, and the least frequently occurring characters occur at the bottom. In this way, frequently occurring characters have short bit codes, and less frequently occurring characters have longer bit codes. As we describe the algorithm, we illustrate each step with the data in Table 14-2.

Building The Huffman Tree

For each of the n unique characters in a file, assign the character and its frequency to a tree node, and insert the node into a minimum priority queue ordered by frequency:

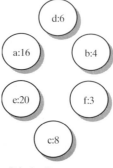

Priority Queue

In a loop remove two elements *x* and *y* from the priority queue, and attach them as children of a node whose frequency is the sum of the frequencies of its children. It does not matter which node is the left child and which node is the right child. The character value in an interior node is not used. Insert the resulting node into the priority queue:

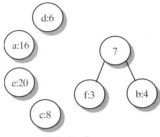

Priority Queue

The loop should, perform this action $n - 1$ times. Each loop iteration creates one of the $n-1$ interior nodes of the tree. Because each interior node has two children, the resulting tree is full. Figure 14-10 shows each step in the construction of a Huffman tree for the sample file.

$$(16(2) + 4(4) + 8(2) + 6(3) + 20(2) + 3(4)) \times 1000 = 134{,}000 \text{ bits,}$$

which corresponds to a compression ratio of 3.4.

Building the Huffman tree for file compression is simple to understand in principle. However, its implementation involves a great many details. The implementation uses a variety of tools we have developed, including the miniPQ class based on the heap, the bit vector, binary files, and inheritance.

Implementation Of Huffman Compression

An object of the class hCompress carries out the compression of a file. The class has a constructor that takes a source file name as an argument, along with the Boolean flag *verbose*. It opens the source file and creates a binary output file by adding the extension ".huf" to the name. When the *verbose* flag is true, the compression process includes accompanying progress messages. To use the same hCompress object for additional files, call setFile() with a new source file name. The public member function compress() executes the compression steps. To obtain some of the internal parameters of the compression process, we provide the functions compressionRatio() and size(), where the latter gives the number of nodes in the Huffman tree. For instructional purposes, we include the function displayTree(), which displays the resulting Huffman tree. The upcoming code is a declaration of hCompress, whose private member functions perform most of the tasks. The purpose of these functions will be clear in the next section.

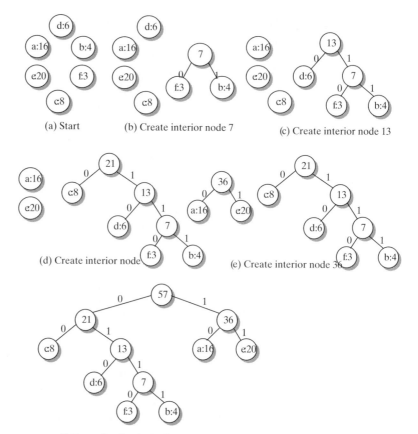

(a) Start   (b) Create interior node 7   (c) Create interior node 13

(d) Create interior node 21

(e) Create interior node 36

(f) Create interior node 57 to obtain the final tree

Figure 14-10
Construction of a Huffman Tree

CLASS hCompress	Declaration	"d_hcomp.h"

```
class hCompress
{
   public:
      hCompress(const string& fname, bool v = false);
         // constructor. call setFile() to open the
         // source file fname, and create a binary output file
         // by adding extension ".huf". any previous extension is
         // replaced. v determines if progress messages are
         // output

      void setFile(const string& fname);
         // open the source file fname and create a binary output
         // file with extension ".huf". throws the
```

```
        // fileOpenError exception if the input or output
        // file cannot be opened

    void compress();
        // compress the file

    double compressionRatio() const;
        // return the compression ratio

    int size() const;
        // return the number of nodes in the
        // Huffman tree

    void displayTree() const;
        // display the Huffman tree. recommended
        // only if tree size is <= 11

private:

    fstream source;
    fstream dest;
        // input and output streams
    vector<int> charFreq, charLoc;
        // charFreq used to count character frequencies. charLoc
        // maintains Huffman tree indices for characters present
        // in the file
    int numberLeaves;
        // numberLeaves is number of leaf nodes (character nodes)
        // in the tree
    short treeSize;
        // number of Huffman tree nodes in the compressed file
    vector<huffNode> tree;
        // stores the Huffman tree
    bool verbose;
        // are progress messages output?
    long fileSize;
        // size of the source file
    long totalBits;
        // total number of bits used in the compressed image
        // of the source file
    bool oneChar;
        // does the tree have only 1 unique character?
    bool filesOpen;
        // are source and dest open?

    void freqAnalysis();
        // determine the frequencies of the characters in the
        // source file and store them in charFreq. while doing
        // this, determine numberLeaves. also tabulate
```

```
            // fileSize so we can see how much savings the
            // compression algorithm gives us

        void buildTree();
            // build the Huffman tree

        void generateCodes();
            // for each leaf node, go up the tree and determine the Huffman
            // code for the character. compute the total number of bits of
            // compressed data

        void writeCompressedData();
            // reread the source file and write the Huffman codes specified
            // by the Huffman tree to the stream dest

        void treeData();
            // output Huffman tree data
};
```

The class is very simple to use. Just declare an hCompress object using the source file name, and call compress(). The function writes a compressed image to an output file whose name is the name of the source file with the extension ".huf". If the source file has an extension, ".huf" replaces the extension. If the second argument to the constructor is *true*, output messages trace the progress of the compression. The function displayTree() outputs the Huffman tree in vertical format. Use it only for small trees.

Example 14-6

This example shows the results of applying *verbose* Huffman compression to a file "demo.dat" that contains the characters "a" through "f" in precisely the frequencies specified in Table 14-2. After compressing the file, the statements output the compression ratio and call displayTree() to output the Huffman tree.

```
        hCompress hc("demo.dat", true);

        // compress the file
        hc.compress();

        // output the compression ratio
        cout << "The compression ratio = "
            << setreal(1,2)<< hc.compressionRatio()
            << endl << endl;

        hc.displayTree();
```

```
Output:
Frequency analysis ...
```

```
   File size: 57000 characters
   Number of unique characters: 6

Building the Huffman tree ...
   Number of nodes in Huffman tree: 11

Generating the Huffman codes ...

Tree has 11 entries.  Root index = 10

Index   Sym     Freq      Parent  Left    Right   NBits     Bits
  0      a      16000        9      -1      -1      2        10
  1      b       4000        6      -1      -1      4        0111
  2      c       8000        8      -1      -1      2        00
  3      d       6000        7      -1      -1      3        010
  4      e      20000        9      -1      -1      2        11
  5      f       3000        6      -1      -1      4        0110
  6     Int      7000        7       5       1
  7     Int     13000        8       3       6
  8     Int     21000       10       2       7
  9     Int     36000       10       0       4
 10     Int     57000        0       8       9

Generating the compressed file

The compression ratio = 3.39 (size of demo.huf = 16,822 bytes)

                                    57000
          21000                                   36000
  c:8000              13000                a:16000      e:20000
         d:6000                7000
                  f:3000         b:4000
```

Summary of compress(). The function compress() directs the file compression. We present an outline of its steps and then discuss the implementation of selected private functions. For the full implementation of compress() and the private functions, see the file "d_hcomp.h" in the software supplement. The charFreq vector contains 256 elements. Our example involves only six elements, for characters "a" through "f" that correspond to the index range from 97 to 102.

1. *Call freqAnalysis()*
   Read the file, and tabulate the number of occurrences of each character. The first time a character is input, increment a count of the number of leaf nodes. The algorithm uses the leaf-node count to allocate the Huffman tree. Also, compute the size of the file, to support the computation of the compression ratio.

		'a'	'b'	'c'	'd'	'e'	'f'		
0	1	97	98	99	100	101	102	254	255
		16000	4000	8000	6000	20000	3000		

vector<int>charFreq;

2. *Call buildTree()*
   Construct the Huffman tree for the file. Build it in a vector, because point-ers must be integer index values and not dynamically generated memory addresses that reference memory only during a specific run of the pro-gram.

3. *Call generateCodes()*
   For each leaf node, follow the path to the root, and determine the bit code for the character. In the process, determine the cost of the tree, which is the total number of code bits generated.

4. This completes all data gathering. The maximum number of nodes in the Huffman tree is $2 * 256 - 1 = 511$. Write the value to the compressed file as a 16-bit integer

5. Write the Huffman tree to the compressed file as a 32-bit integer.

6. Write the total number of bits in the bit codes to the compressed file.

7. *Call writeCompressedData()*
   Read the source file again. For each character, write its bit code to the com-pressed file.

From the actions of compress(), we see that the format of the compressed file is as follows:

Tree Size	Huffman Tree	Size of bit codes	Bit Codes

Building the Huffman Tree. The decompression algorithm requires tree nodes that contain child locations and, in the case of a leaf node, the character value. However, the compression algorithm requires that a node contain more data, such as the character frequency, the parent location, and the bit code for a character. A simple inheritance hierarchy implements these two different requirements. The base class diskHuffNode specifies the character data used by a leaf node and the lo-cations of the children.

CLASS diskHuffNode   Declaration   "d_hnode.h"

```
// NIL represents an empty subtree
const short NIL = -1;


// node object for the Huffman tree that goes in the
// compressed file
```

```
class diskHuffNode
{
   public:
      // character stored
      unsigned char ch;

      // pointers (indices) of children
      short left;
      short right;

      diskHuffNode (unsigned char c = 0, short lptr = NIL,
            short rptr = NIL): ch(c), left(lptr), right(rptr)
      {}
};
```

Use public inheritance (Chapter 13) to add the remaining attributes, by deriving the
class huffNode.

CLASS huffNode   **Declaration**   **"d_hnode.h"**

```
// maximum size of the bit code for a character
const int MAXBITSIZE = 255;

// node used to construct the Huffman tree. the compress application
// builds a node with these attributes plus those of the base class
// diskHuffNode. the attributes in this class are not needed in
// the uncompress application
class huffNode: public diskHuffNode
{
   public:
      int freq;              // frequency of the character ch
      int index;             // my index in the tree
      int parent;            // my parent in the tree
      int numberOfBits;      // number of bits in Huffman code for ch
      bitVector bits;        // bit vector holding the code

      huffNode (unsigned char c = 0, short lptr = NIL, short rptr = NIL,
                int f = 0, int indx = NIL, int p = 0,
                int numBits = 0, int maxSizeOfBits = MAXBITSIZE):
            diskHuffNode(c, lptr, rptr), freq(f), index(indx),
            parent(p), numberOfBits(numBits), bits(maxSizeOfBits)
      {}

      // necessary to build the priority queue
      friend bool operator< (const huffNode& lhs, const huffNode& rhs)
      {
         return lhs.freq < rhs.freq;
      }
};
```

The need for the data members will be explained as we continue our discussion of the implementation for the class hCompress. The priority queue uses the overloaded < operator as the algorithm builds the Huffman tree from the bottom up. It is theoretically possible for a bit code to have a size of 255 bits (Written Exercise 14-35). Only leaf nodes have a bits attribute with nonzero size.

The function buildTree() executes the priority-queue-based algorithm that constructs the tree in the vector data member tree. It requires some attention to detail, including the special case where the tree contains only one unique character. In this situation, in order to create a full tree with three nodes, the function creates an additional leaf node that is not used. The function creates leaf nodes in the index range from 0 to *numberLeaves*−1 that contain each character, its frequency, and the index of the node itself. It then executes a loop *numberLeaves*−1 times and builds the interior nodes. The fact that each node coming out of the queue contains a record of its own index allows the assignment of that index to the appropriate left or right location in the parent. It also allows the children's parent attribute to be set. The next figure shows the structure of the Huffman tree built for the demonstration file. The notation INT means that the node is internal. The ch, left, and right fields are data in the diskHuffNode base class. The freq, parent, and index fields are data in the derived huffNode class.

vector<huffNode> tree;

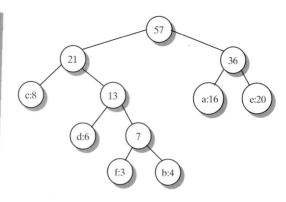

	ch	freq	parent	left	right	index
0	a	16	9	-1	-1	0
1	b	4	6	-1	-1	1
2	c	8	8	-1	-1	2
3	d	6	7	-1	-1	3
4	e	20	9	-1	-1	4
5	f	3	6	-1	-1	5
6	INT	7	7	5	1	6
7	INT	13	8	3	6	7
8	INT	21	10	2	7	8
9	INT	36	10	0	4	9
10	INT	57	0	8	9	10

Generating the Bit Codes   The function generateCodes() determines the bit codes by starting at each leaf node and following the path of parents until it finds the root node (parent = 0). As it makes each transition upward, it records a 0 bit if the node is a left child of its parent, and 1 otherwise. This process finds the bit codes in the reverse order, so the function reverses the bits when it assigns them to the bits data member of the leaf node.

Writing the Bit Codes   To output the bit codes, the function writeCompressed-Data() declares a bitVector object *compressedData* whose bit size is the cost of the

Huffman tree and all of whose bits are 0. It sets the file pointer to the beginning of
the file and inputs the characters again. The bit codes for each character were determined by generateCodes() and reside in the corresponding leaf node. For each 1-bit
in the bit codes for a character, set the next bit in compressedData; otherwise move
forward. For instance, if the first five characters of the sample file are "befae", initialize compressedData as follows:

Character	Bit Code	compressedData
b	0111	0111
e	11	011111
f	0110	0111110110
a	10	011111011010
e	11	01111101101011

Upon the conclusion of input, writeCompressedData() calls the write() member
function of the bitVector class to output the bits to the compressed file:

writeCompressedData():

```
// reread the source file and write the Huffman codes specified
// in the Huffman tree to the stream dest
void hCompress::writeCompressedData()
{
   // vector that will contain the Huffman codes for
   // the compressed file
   bitVector compressedData(totalBits);
   int bitPos, i, j;
   unsigned char ch;

   // clear end-of-file for the source file and set file
   // pointer to the beginning of the file
   source.clear(0);
   source.seekg(0, ios::beg);

   // bitPos is used to put bits into compressedData
   bitPos = 0;

   // re-read the source file and generate the Huffman codes in
   // compressedData
   while (true)
   {
      // get the next character
      ch = source.get();
      if (!source)
         break;

      // index of the tree node containing ch
      i = charLoc[ch];
```

```
      // put the bit code for tree[i].ch into the bit vector
      for (j=0;j<tree[i].numberOfBits; j++)
      {
         // only need to call set() if tree[i].bits.bit(j) is 1
         if (tree[i].bits.bit(j) == 1)
            compressedData.set(bitPos);
         // always advance bitPos
         bitPos++;
      }
   }

   // write the bit codes to the output file
   compressedData.write(dest);
}
```

The software supplement contains a textfile, "webster.dict", that has 234,946 words comprising 2,251,959 characters. Application of the Huffman algorithm gives a compression ratio of 1.8. The supplement also contains the file "mspaint.exe", which is a large binary file. In this case, all 255 characters occur, and the compression ratio is only 1.36.

Huffman Decompression

The class hDecompress performs Huffman decompression. The public member function decompress() decodes the file.

CLASS hDecompress   Declaration   "d_hdcomp.h"

```
class hDecompress
{
   public:
      hDecompress(const string& cname, const string& uname);
         // constructor. calls setFiles() to open Huffman
         // compressed file cname and assign the output
         // file name uname.

      void setFiles(const string& cname, const string& uname);
         // open Huffman compressed file cname
         // and assign the output file name uname.
         // throws the fileOpenError exception if a file
         // cannot be opened

      void decompress();
         // decompress the file
private:

      fstream source;
```

```
        fstream dest;
            // input and output streams

        bool filesOpen;
            // are source and dest open?
};
```

Example 14-7

The following statements prompt for the name of the compressed file and the name of the restored file, create an hDecompress object, and call decompress():

```
        string compFile, ucompFile;

        cout << "Compressed file name: ";
        cin >> compFile;
        cout << "Name for decompressed file: ";
        cin >> ucompFile;

        hDecompress ucomp(compFile, ucompFile);

        // decompress the file
        ucomp.decompress();
```

The function decompress() is straightforward. From the header data in the compressed file, input the size of the Huffman tree (treeSize), and then input the tree into the vector<diskHuffNode> object tree. Read the number of code bits (totalBits), and use the bitVector member function read() to place the bits in the bitVector object *bits*. Sequence through the object *bits*, tracing paths from the root to leaf nodes and writing each character to the destination file.

decompress():

```
        void hDecompress::decompress()
        {
            int i, bitPos;

            // treeSize and totalBits are read from the compressed file
            short treeSize;
            long totalBits;
            // treeSize diskHuffNode nodes are read from the compressed file
            // into tree
            vector<diskHuffNode> tree;
            // totalBits number of binary bits are read from the compressed
            // file into bits
            bitVector bits;
            // input the Huffman tree size
```

```
        source.read((char *)&treeSize, sizeof(short));

        // resize the vector holding the Huffman tree and
        // input the tree
        tree.resize(treeSize);
        source.read((char *)&tree[0], sizeof(diskHuffNode) * treeSize);

        // input the number of bits of Huffman code
        source.read((char *)&totalBits, sizeof(long));

        // input the Huffman codes for the characters
        bits.read(source, totalBits);

        // restore the original file by using the Huffman codes to
        // traverse the tree and write out the corresponding
        // characters
        bitPos = 0;
        while (bitPos<totalBits)
        {
            // root of the tree is at index treeSize-1
            i = treeSize-1;
            // follow the bits until we arrive at a leaf node
            while (tree[i].left != -1)
            {
                // if bit is 0, go left; otherwise, go right
                if (bits.bit(bitPos) == 0)
                    i = tree[i].left;
                else
                    i = tree[i].right;
                // we have used the current bit. move to the
                // next one
                bitPos++;
            }
            // we are at a leaf node. output the character
            // to the file
            dest.put(tree[i].ch);
        }

        // close the two streams
        source.close();
        dest.close();

        filesOpen = false;
    }
```

The software supplement for Chapter 14 contains the source files "hcompress.cpp" and "hdecompress.cpp", which use the Huffman compression and decompression classes. The accompanying data files "demo.dat", "webster.dict", and "mspaint.exe" allow the reader to experiment with the software.

CHAPTER SUMMARY

- There is a natural mapping from a vector or array v to a complete binary tree, called an *array-based* tree. The root is $v[0]$; the level-1 nodes from left to right are $v[1]$ and $v[2]$; the level-2 nodes are $v[3]$, $v[4]$, $v[5]$, and $v[6]$; and so forth. If i is the index of a node, its children are $v[2i+1]$ and $v[2i+2]$, and its parent is $v[(i-1)/2]$. By using these relations, it is possible to follow a path of children from the root to a leaf node and to follow the path of parents from a leaf node to the root.

- A heap is an array-based tree that has heap order. In a maximum heap, if $v[i]$ is a parent, then $v[i] \geq v[2i+1]$ and $v[i] \geq v[2i+2]$. In other words, a parent is $\geq$ its children. For a minimum heap, the parent is $\leq$ its children. It follows that in a maximum heap the root, $v[0]$, is the maximum value in the vector, and in a minimum heap, $v[0]$ is the minimum value. Insert into a heap by placing the new value at the back of the heap and filtering it up the tree. Delete the root of the heap by exchanging its value with the back of the heap and then filtering the new root down the tree, which now has one fewer element. Both of these operations have running time $O(\log_2 n)$. To convert a vector to a heap, apply the filter-down operation to the interior nodes, from the last interior node in the tree down to the root. This operation is termed *heapifying* the vector and has running time $O(n)$. The well-known $O(n\log_2 n)$ heapsort algorithm heapifies a vector and erases repeatedly from the heap, locating each deleted value in its final position.

- A binary file is a sequence of eight-bit characters without the requirement that a character be printable and with no concern for newline sequences, which terminate lines. A binary file is often organized as a sequence of records: record 0, record 1, record 2, ..., record $n-1$. The programmer often uses a binary file for both input and output, and the C++ file <fstream> contains the operations to support these types of files. During the opening of a binary file, the open() function must specify that the file is binary by using the attribute ios::binary. For direct access to a file record, use the function seekg(), which moves the file pointer to a file record. The function accepts an argument that specifies motion from the beginning of the file (ios::beg), from the current position of the file pointer (ios::cur), and from the end of the file (ios::end). Perform input from a binary file by using the stream function read(), which inputs a sequence of bytes from the file into a block of memory. Output from a block of memory to a binary file by using the stream function write().

- C++ supplies a series of bit manipulation operators: | (OR), & (AND), ^ (XOR), ~ (NOT),<<(shift left), and>>(shift right). A programmer can use these operators to perform operations on specific bits within a character or integer value. Rather than using these low-level operators, it is convenient to build a class that automates bit handling. The class bitVector supplies a high-level implementation for these operators through the use of operator overloading. It allows the programmer to treat a sequence of bits as an array, with bit 0 as the leftmost bit of the sequence. The operations bit(), set(), and clear() allow access to specific bits. In addition, the class has I/O operations for binary files and the stream operator <<, which outputs a bit vector as an ASCII sequence of 0 and 1 values.

- A file-compression algorithm encodes a file as sequence of characters that consumes less disk space than the original file. There are two types of compression algorithms: lossless compression and lossy compression. With lossless compression, the decompression algorithm restores the original file. A lossy compression algorithm loses some information during compression, and the data cannot be recovered exactly. Lossy compression algorithms are normally used with sound and video files. One approach to lossless compression is to count the frequency of occurrence of each character in the file and assign a prefix bit code to each character. With a prefix code, no bit code is the prefix of any other code. Generate the compressed image by replacing each character by its bit code. The size of the compressed file is the sum of the products of each bit-code length and the frequency of occurrence of the corresponding character. There is a natural tree representation for prefix codes. Each interior node contains the sum of the frequencies of its children. Begin at the root and move left for a 0 and right for a 1. Continue until reaching a leaf node that contains a character. The Huffman compression algorithm builds optimal prefix codes by constructing a full tree, with the most frequently occurring characters near the top of the tree. These characters have shorter bit codes. The less frequently occurring characters reside near the bottom of the tree and have longer bit codes. At each step of a loop, the algorithm uses a minimum heap to select the two nodes with smallest frequencies. It joins these two nodes to a parent and inserts the parent into the heap. If the file contains n distinct characters, the loop concludes after $n-1$ iterations, having built the Huffman tree. The bit sequences it defines are optimal prefix codes. Although the algorithm is easy to understand, it is not easy to implement. The implementation requires the use of a heap, bit operations, and binary files. The use of the bitVector class simplifies the construction of the classes hCompress and hDecompress, which perform Huffman compression and decompression. The technique works better with text files; they tend to have fewer unique characters than do binary files.

CLASSES AND LIBRARIES IN THE CHAPTER

Name	Header File
account	d_acct.h
bitVector	d_bitvec.h
diskHuffNode	d_hnode.h
hCompress	d_hcomp.h
hDecompress	d_hdcomp.h
heap	d_heap.h
heapSort()	d_sort.h
huffNode	d_hnode.h
miniPQ	d_pqueue.h
randomNumber	d_random.h
writeContainer()	d_util.h

REVIEW EXERCISES

1. Use the vector *v* for parts (a)–(d):

```
int arr[] = {3,5,6,7,1,3,9,12};
int arrSize = sizeof(arr)/sizeof(int);
vector<int> v(arr, arr+arrSize);
```

   (a) Draw the array-based tree that corresponds to the array.
   (b) What are indices of the children of node v[2]?
   (c) What is the index of the parent of node v[7]?
   (d) At which index do the leaf nodes begin?

2. Assume that *v* is an array-based tree with 80 members.
   (a) Is *v*[36] a leaf node?
   (b) What is the index of the first leaf node?
   (c) What is the depth of the tree?
   (d) How many leaf nodes does the tree have?

3. Start with the given minimum heap, and draw the tree after each operation. Execute the operations sequentially, each on the result of the previous operation.

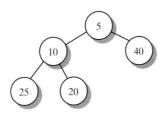

   (a) Insert the value 15.
   (b) Delete an element from the heap.

4. Start with the following tree, and heapify it to create a maximum heap:

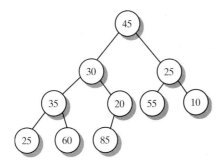

5. (a) What is the running time for deleting an item from an *n*-element priority queue that is implemented as a heap?
   (b) What is the running time for inserting an item into an *n*-element priority queue that is implemented as a heap?
   (c) What is the running time for heapifying an *n*-element array?

(d) What is the running time of the heap sort?

6. This exercise deals with a binary file of double values. For your reference, here are some constants that might be useful:

```
ios::in    ios::out    ios::trunc    ios::binary
ios::beg   ios::cur    ios::end
```

Declare an array of double elements, a single double object, and an fstream object, as follows:

```
double arr[] = { 3.14, 2.718, 3.8, 2.9, 5.5, 9.5, 6.7 };
double x;
fstream f;
```

Fill in code that does the following:

(a) Open a binary file "test.dat" for output. Do error checking.

```
f.open("test.dat", ios::out | ios::_____ | ios::_____);

if (___)
{
    cerr << "Cannot open 'test.dat'" << endl;
    exit(1);
}
```

(b) Write the records in *arr* to the file, and then close it.

```
f.write((_____)arr, sizeof(_____));
f._____;
```

(c) Reopen the file for reading and writing.

```
f.open("test.dat", ios::_____ | ios::_____ | ios::_____);
```

(d) Input the value at record 3, add 5 to the value, and write the new value to the file.

```
f.seekg(3*_____, ios::beg);
f.read((_____)&x, sizeof(_____));
x += 5.0;
f.seekg(-sizeof(_____),ios::___);
f.write(_____, _____);
```

(e) Append the value 8.9 to the file.

```
x = 8.9;
f.seekg(0, ios::_____);
f.write(_____, _____);
```

7. What is the output of the following statements?

```
int arr[] = {1, 0, 1, 1, 0, 1, 1, 0};
bitVector x, y(arr, 8), z, mask(8);
x = char(28); // 28 = 11100(base 2)
cout << (x | y) << endl;
cout << (x & y) << endl;
cout << (x ^ y) << endl;
x = y<<3;
```

```
    cout << x << endl;
    mask = ~mask;
    mask = mask>>1;
    mask = ~mask;
    x = y & mask;
    cout << x << endl;
```

8. Circle all statements that are true for a Huffman tree.
   (a) A Huffman tree is complete.
   (b) Every interior node has exactly two children.
   (c) Each character is in a leaf node.
   (d) The total number of bits generated by the tree is minimum.
   (e) Each interior node contains the product of its children's weights.
   (f) Each interior node contains the sum of its children's weights.
   (g) Nodes with a lower frequency are near the top of the tree.
   (h) Nodes with a lower frequency are near the bottom of the tree.

9. The file "data.txt" contains the following characters:
   ababbcabaac
   (a) Construct a Huffman tree for the file.
   (b) Write out the bits in the compressed file.

10. The Huffman algorithm is an example in a class of algorithms known as _____ algo-rithms.

Answers To Review Exercises

1. (a)

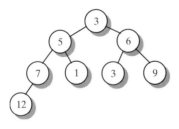

(b) 5, 6   **(c)**   3   **(d)**   4
2. (a) No   **(b)**   40   **(c)**   6   **(d)**   40
3. (a)

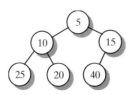

(b)

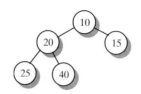

4.

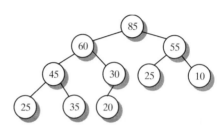

5. (a) $O(\log_2 n)$ **(b)** $O(\log_2 n)$ **(c)** $O(n)$ **(d)** $O(n \log_2 n)$

6. (a)
```
f.open("test.dat", ios::out | ios::trunc | ios::binary);
if (!f)
{
    cerr << "Cannot open 'test.dat'" << endl;
    exit(1);
}
```

(b)
```
f.write((char *)arr, sizeof(arr));
f.close();
```

(c)
```
f.open("test.dat", ios::in | ios::out | ios::binary);
```

(d)
```
f.seekg(3*sizeof(double), ios::beg);
f.read((char *)&x, sizeof(double));
x += 5.0;
f.seekg(-sizeof(double),ios::cur);
f.write((char *)&x, sizeof(double));
```

(e)
```
x = 8.9;
f.seekg(0, ios::end);
f.write((char *)&x, sizeof(double));
```

7. {10111110}
        {00010100}
        {10101010}
        {10110000}
        {10000000}

8. (b)   (c)   (d)   (f)   (h)

9. (a)

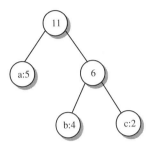

(b) 0 1 0 0 1 0 1 0 1 1 0 1 0 0 0 1 1

10. greedy

WRITTEN EXERCISES

11. Draw the complete tree corresponding to each of the following vectors:

    (a) `int a[8]= {15, 9, 3, 6, 2, 1, 4, 7};`
          `int aSize = sizeof(a)/sizeof(int);`
          `vector<int> v(a, a+aSize);`

    (b) `string b = "array-based tree";`
          `vector<char> w(b.c_str(), b.c_str()+b.length());`

12. For each of the following trees, give the corresponding vector:

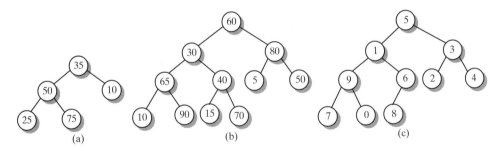

13. Assume that v is a an array-based tree with 70 members.

    (a) Is $v[45]$ a leaf node?
    (b) What is the index of the first leaf node?
    (c) What is the parent of $v[50]$?
    (d) What are the children of $v[10]$?
    (e) Does any item have exactly one child?
    (f) What is the depth of the tree?
    (g) How many leaf nodes does the tree have?

14. In a complete binary tree, show that the number of leaf nodes is greater than or equal to the number of nonleaf nodes. If the depth of the tree is d and there are 2^d nodes on level d, show that there are more leaf nodes than nonleaf nodes.

15. A complete binary tree B, containing 50 nodes, is stored in a vector.
  (a) What is the level of the tree?
  (b) How many nodes are leaf nodes? Nonleaf nodes?
  (c) What is the index of the parent of B[35]?
  (d) What are the indices of the children of node B[20]?
  (e) What is the index of the first node with no children? With one child?
  (f) What are the indices for all nodes at level 4 in the tree?

16. For each tree, indicate whether it is a heap (maximum or minimum).

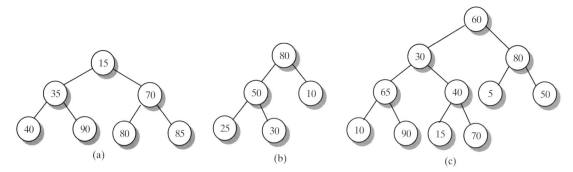

      (a)   (b)   (c)

17. Take each nonheap from Written Exercise 14-16 and create both a maximum heap and a minimum heap. For each minimum (maximum) heap, create the corresponding maximum (minimum) heap. Give your answer by drawing the tree.

18. Heapify the following tree to create a maximum heap:

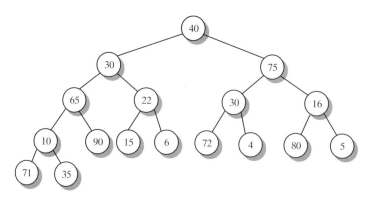

19. This exercise asks you to insert and erase elements in heaps (a) and (b). Corresponding to each heap, there is a sequence of operations that are to be executed sequentially. Use the result of the previous operation as you execute each part of the exercise. Draw the modified heaps at the conclusion of the operations. Treat an insert as an operation that adds the element at the end of the heap, using push_back(), and then calls pushHeap(). Treat an erase operation as one that calls popHeap() and then removes the element from the heap by using pop_back().

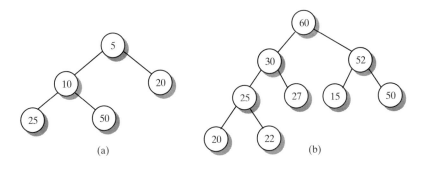

(a)   (b)

Heap (a)   Heap (b)

(a) insert 15   (a) erase
(b) insert 35   (b) insert 35
(c) erase   (c) insert 65
(d) insert 40   (d) erase
(e) insert 10   (e) erase
                  (f) insert 5

20. (a) What is the largest number of nodes that can exist in a tree that is both a minimum heap tree and a binary search tree? Do not allow for duplicate values.

(b) What is the largest number of nodes that can exist in a tree that is both a maximum heap tree and a binary search tree? Do not allow for duplicate values.

21. For the following heap, list the value of the nodes along the designated path:

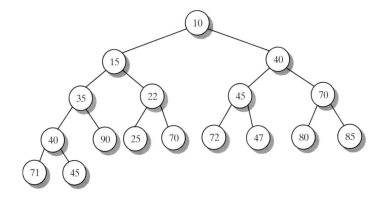

(a) the path of parents beginning with node 47;
(b) the path of parents beginning with node 71;
(c) the path of minimal children beginning with node 35;
(d) the path of minimal children beginning with node 10;
(e) the path of minimal children beginning with node 40 (level 1).

22. Begin with the vector, and build the corresponding maximum heap. List the new ordering for the vector.

(a)
```
int arr[] = {40, 20, 70, 30, 90, 10, 50, 100, 60, 80};
int arrSize = sizeof(arr)/sizeof(int);
vector<int> v(arr, arr + arrSize);
```

(b)
```
int arr[] = {3, 90, 45, 6, 16, 45, 33, 88};
int arrSize = sizeof(arr)/sizeof(int);
vector<int> v(arr, arrr + arrSize);
```

(c)
```
char str[]  = "heapify";
int strSize = sizeof(str)/sizeof(char) - 1;
vector<char> s(str, str + strSize);
```

(d)
```
char str[] = "minimal-heap";
int strSize = sizeof(str)/sizeof(char) - 1;
vector<char> s(str, str + strSize);
```

23. Implement the function erase() that removes the item at index *i* from the heap by first exchanging its value with the element at the end of the heap. After adjusting the heap, the function deletes the element by removing it from the underlying vector. The operation should run in O($\log_2 n$) time for an *n*-element heap.

```
// i is the index of an element in the heap with index
// range [0,last). erase v[i] and adjust the heap
template <typename T, typename Compare>
void erase(vector<T>& v, int i, int last, Compare comp);
```

Hint: The element moved into *v*[*i*] may have to move down or up the tree.

24. Implement the function isHeap() that determines whether the elements of a vector in the index range [0,*last*) form a heap:

```
// determine whether v[0] ... v[last-1] is a heap
template <typename T, typename Compare>
bool isHeap(const vector<T>& v, int last, Compare comp);
```

Hint: A one-element vector is a heap; otherwise, find the last parent in the heap. This parent will have either one or two children. Verify the heap condition for the parent. The remaining parents down to the root at index 0 have two children. Verify the heap condition for their children.

25. Trace the heapsort for a vector with elements {7, 12, 5, 2, 15, 25, 1}. Draw the initial heap, and show the status of the heap after every pop() operation. Also, show the contents of the vector at each step.

26. Consider the following declaration for an array of employee elements, a single employee object *r*, and an fstream object:

```
class employee
{
   public:
      int id;
      double salary;

      // constructor. initialize id and salary
      employee(int p, double sal): id(p), salary(sal)
      {}
      // default constructor. id and salary set to 0
```

```
        employee(): id(0), salary(0.0)
        {}
    };

    employee arr[] = { employee (1,35000.0), employee (2,65000.0),
                       employee (5,55000.0), employee (8,28500.0),
                       employee (15,75000.0), employee (25, 23000.0) };
    record r;
    fstream f;
```

(a) Open a binary file "employee.dat" for output only, truncating an existing version of the file. Do error checking.

(b) Write the records in *arr* to the file, and then close it. Use one call to the member function write(). Do not use a loop.

(c) Reopen the file for reading and writing.

(d) Input the value at record 4, add 500.0 to the salary field, and write the new value to the file.

(e) Append the values employee(45, 62500.0) and employee(77, 26500.0) to the file.

(f) Declare an integer variable *size* whose value is the number of records in the file. Use the tellg() member function.

(g) Using the value of the variable size from part (f), write a loop that outputs the records in the file.

27. Implement the following functions, which perform operations on a binary file that is open for input or output:

(a)
```
// set the file pointer to the first file record
void rewind(fstream& f);
```

(b)
```
// return the size of the file whose records
// have recSize bytes. the file pointer does not
// change after the function call
int fileSize(fstream& f, int recSize);
```

(c)
```
// write the obj into the record prior to the current
// value of the file pointer
template <typename T>
void update(fstream& f, const T& obj);
```

(d)
```
// add the contents of v at the end of the file
template <typename T
void append(fstream& f, const vector<T>& v);
```

28. Assume that the objects *x*, *y*, and *z* are defined as follows:

```
    unsigned short x = 14, y = 11, z;
```

What value is assigned to *z* as a result of each of the following statements?

(a) z = x | y;   (b) z = x & y;

(c) z = ~0 << 4;   (d) z = ~x & (y >> 1);

(e) z = (1 << 3) & x;

29. This exercise presents four functions that perform bit-handling operations. Match each function with one of the following descriptive phrases:

(a) Determine the number of bits in an *int* for a particular machine.

(b) Return the numerical value of the *n* bits of an unsigned integer, beginning at bit position *p*. Bit *p* = 0 is the least significant bit of the integer value.

(c) Return the result of inverting *n* bits of an unsigned integer, beginning at bit position *p*. Bit position 0 is the most significant bit of the integer value.

(d) Return the result of rotating the bits of an unsigned integer clockwise.

```
unsigned int one(unsigned int x, int b)
{
    int rightbit;
    int lshift = three() - 1;

    while (b--)
    {
        rightbit = x & 1;
        x = x>>1;
        rightbit = rightbit<<lshift;
        x = x | rightbit;
    }

    return x;
}

unsigned int two(unsigned int x, unsigned int p,
                 unsigned int n)
{
    unsigned mask = (unsigned int) (~(~0<<n));

    return (x>>(p-n+1)) & mask;
}

int three()
{
    int i = 0;
    unsigned int u = ~0;

    while (u != 0)
    {
        i++;

        u = u>>1;
    }

    return i;
}

unsigned int four(unsigned int x, int p, int n)
{
    unsigned int mask;
```

```
            mask = ~0;
            return x ^ (~(mask>>n)>>p);
    }
```

30. Consider the following bit vectors:

```
        int xarr[] = {1, 0, 1, 1, 0, 1, 0, 0},
            yarr[] = {0, 1, 1, 0, 1, 1, 0, 1};

        int xSize = sizeof(xarr)/sizeof(int),
            ySize = sizeof(yarr)/sizeof(int);
        bitVector x(xarr, xSize), y(yarr, ySize), mask(8);
```

Specify the output of the given statements. Each statement assumes the initial values for
x, *y*, and *mask*.

(a) cout << (x & y);

(b) cout << (x | y);

(c) cout << (x ^ y);

(d) cout << ~x;

(e) x=char(0);
     cout << ~x;

(f) cout << (x ^ y) << " " << (~x & y | x & ~y);

(g) mask = char(7);
     cout << (x & mask) << " ";
     mask = mask<<3;
     cout << (x & mask);

(h) mask.set(0);
     mask.set(1);
     mask = mask >> 4;
     cout << (mask & y) << " ";
     x = mask | x;
     x.clear(2);
     cout << x;

31. Consider the following set of frequencies:

   a:8   b:6   c:8   d:3   e:12   f:2   g:15

(a) Construct a binary tree for the fixed-length codes

   a->000, b->001, c->010, d->011, e->100, f->101, g->110

(b) Answer the following questions about the codes and tree in part (a):
   (i)   Are the codes prefix codes?
   (ii) Is the tree full?
   (iii) What is the cost of the tree?
   (iv) If your answer to part (ii) is no, modify the tree so it is full, and compute the cost
         of the modified tree.

(c) Construct a Huffman tree. What is the cost of the tree?

(d) What are the optimal prefix codes?

32. For a given file F, is the Huffman tree unique? If your answer is no, specify a file and show
   at least two Huffman trees that give the optimal prefix code.

33. Why is the Huffman algorithm classified as a greedy algorithm?

34. Is there a relationship between the cost of a Huffman tree and the sum of the frequencies in the internal nodes? If you find a relationship, supply an intuitive argument that shows you are correct.

35. Recall that the Fibonacci numbers are defined as follows:

$$f_0 = 0, \quad f_1 = 1,$$

$$f_n = f_{n-1} + f_{n-2}, \quad n \geq 2$$

They form the sequence $0, 1, 1, 2, 3, 5, 8, 13, 21, 34, 55, \ldots$. Suppose that the frequencies of the characters in a file F are based on Fibonacci numbers f_1 through f_8:

  a:1   b:1   c :2   d:3   e:5   f:8   g:13   h:21

(a) Determine a Huffman tree, and give the bit codes for the characters.

(b) If the frequencies of the characters correspond to Fibonacci numbers f_1 through f_n, what are the bit codes?

(c) What is the maximum depth of a full binary tree with n leaf nodes?

(d) Is it possible to construct a file whose longest optimal prefix code has 255 bits? If so, what would be the approximate size of the file in bytes? Is it practical to construct such a file?

PROGRAMMING EXERCISES

36. Implement adjustHeapRec() as a recursive version of adjustHeap(). Use the new function to implement makeHeapRec(), which is a modified version of makeHeap(), and popHeapRec(), which is a modified version of popHeap(). Test your work by creating a vector with 10 random integers in the range from 0 to 99, and output the resulting values. Call makeHeapRec() to heapify the vector, and output the vector. Use popHeap() to remove elements from the heap until it is empty. Output the final values in the vector.

37. A computer system runs programs (processes) by assigning a priority to each process. Priority 0 is the highest priority, and priority 39 is the lowest. Assume that when a user requests that a program be run, the operating system inserts a process request record into a priority queue. When the CPU is available, the operating system deletes the highest priority process request record and runs the corresponding process. The process request record has the following declaration:

```
class procReqRec
{
   public:
      procReqRec();
         // default constructor

      procReqRec(const string& nm, int p);
         // constructor

      int getPriority();
      string getName();
         // access functions
```

```
    void setPriority(int p);
    void setName(const string& nm);
        // update functions

    friend bool operator< (const procReqRec& left,
                                const procReqRec& right);
        // for maintenance of a minimum priority queue

    friend ostream operator<< (ostream& ostr,
                                const procReqRec& obj);
        // output a process request record in the format
        //    name: priority
private:
    string name;     // process name
    int priority;    // process priority
};
```

The name attribute identifies the process. Implement the processRequestRecord class in the header file "preqrec.h". Declare a miniPQ object *mpq*, and assign to it process request records, whose names are "Process A", "Process B", ..., "Process J" and whose priority values are random integers in the range from 0 to 39. Output and delete records from the priority queue until it is empty.

38. Consider a class that contains a data value and a priority level:

```
template <typename T>
class priorityData
{
    public:
        T data;
        int priority;

    friend bool operator< (const priorityData& lhs,
                           const priorityData& rhs)
    {
        return lhs.priority < rhs.priority;
    }

    friend bool operator> (const priorityData& lhs,
    const priorityData& rhs)
    {
        return lhs.priority > rhs.priority;
    }

};
```

Use the class and a miniPQ object to implement the class miniQueue in the header file "queue_p.h". (Hint: Declare a priority queue containing *priorityData* objects ordered by the priority level of each record. Define an integer *priorityLevel* that the class increments when inserting an item into the priority queue. Assign *priorityLevel* as the priority level of the record.)

Test your queue by reading five integers. Let push() store each item in the queue. Then, until the queue is empty, delete the items and output their values.

39. Use the model from Programming Exercise 14-38 to implement the class miniStack by using a priority queue. Place the class in the header file "stack_p.h". Test the new stack class by reading five integers. Let push() store the values in a stack. Until the stack is empty, delete the items by using pop(), and output their values.

40. Consider the following type:

```
class charRec
{
   public:
      char key;
      int count;

      friend bool operator< (const charRec& lhs, const charRec& rhs);
};
```

Create a binary file "letcount.dat" of 26 such records containing key values 'A', 'B', ..., 'Z' and a count of 0. Input the name of a text file. Read the file, character by character, and convert each alphabetic character to uppercase. Update the count field of the corresponding record in the binary file "letcount.dat". After updating the file, read through it, output the frequency count for each character, and insert each record into a vector. Use the heapsort to order "letcount.dat" in decreasing order of the count field, and output the results. Include a run that outputs a frequency count for the file "dict.dat" in the software distribution.

41. Use the bitVector class to develop a program that inputs an integer value and outputs it as a base-4 (quaternary) number. Obtain the quaternary representation for an integer by replacing each pair of bits in the binary representation by its value, from 0 to 3. For instance, the binary value

1 0 0 1 1 0 1 1 1 0 1 1 0 1 0 0

has the quaternary representation

2 1 2 3 2 3 1 0

(Hint: Make the declaration

```
int intSize = 8*sizeof(int);
bitVector b, lastTwoBits(intSize), mask(intSize);
```

and give mask the value 1 1 0 0 ... 0. Input the integer, and assign its value to b. In a loop, use the mask to isolate the two leftmost bits of b in *lastTwoBits*. Using the bit() function, convert the two bits into an integer value, and output it.)

42. Create a textfile "huf.dat" containing the following characters and frequencies:

a:17   b:8   c:16   d:18   e:36   f:8

Using pencil and paper, construct the Huffman tree and the corresponding bit codes. Use the hCompress class to compress the file. Output compression data and the Huffman tree, and compare these results with your hand calculations. Remove the original file, and use the class hDecompress to restore the original file from the compressed image. Verify that the decompression worked correctly.

PROGRAMMING PROJECT

43. The given declaration creates a text file class. Use the C++ fstream operations to implement the class in the header file "textfile.h".

```cpp
class textfile
{
    public:
        textfile();
            // constructor

        void assign(const string& fname);
            // sets file name

        void reset();
            // if file already open, seeks to beginning
            // of the file; otherwise, opens file fname
            // for input.
            // Preconditions: access type must be IN and it
            // must be possible to open the file. if the access
            // type is OUT, the function throws the fileError
            // exception, and if it is not possible to open
            // the file, it throws the fileOpenError exception

        void rewrite();
            // opens file for output and truncates any existing
            // version of the file.
            // Preconditions: the file must not be open and it
            // must be possible to open the file. if the file
            // is already open, the function throws the fileError
            // exception, and if it is not possible to open
            // the file, it throws the fileOpenError exception

        int endFile() const;
            // determine whether end-of-file has been reached.
            // Preconditions: the file must be open. if the file is
            // not open, the function throws the fileError exception

        void close();
            // close file

        int read(char arr[], int n);
            // read a maximum of n characters into array arr
            // and return the actual number of characters read.
            // Preconditions: access type must be IN, n must be >= 0,
            // and the file must be open. if any precondition is
            // violated, the function throws the fileError exception

        void write(char arr[],int n);
            // writes n characters from array arr to the file.
```

```
                          // Preconditions: access type must be OUT, n must be >= 0,
                          // and the file must be open. if any precondition is
                          // violated, the function throws the fileError exception
                 private:
                     enum access   {IN, OUT};
                          // defines the data flow of the file

                     fstream f;
                          // C++ file stream
                     string fileName;
                          // file name
                     access accesstype;
                          // data flow is IN or OUT
                     bool isOpen;
                          // true when a file is open
             };
```

To implement endFile(), use the fstream member function eof(). The fstream member function gcount() returns the number of bytes input from the stream and should be used in the implementation of read().

Write a program that uses the class to read the file "textfile.h", then to translate each lowercase letter to uppercase, and finally to write it to the file "textfile.uc". Use an operating-system utility to display the contents of "textfile.uc".

CHAPTER 15

Recursive Algorithms

OBJECTIVES

- To understand the algorithmic strategy of *divide and conquer*, which is simply illustrated by the problem of drawing a ruler.
- To study the O($n \log_2 n$) mergesort and quicksort algorithms, which apply the divide-and-conquer strategy.
- To see that the kth largest element in a vector can be computed with O(n) average running time by using the partitioning strategy of quicksort.
- To study recursive algorithms for enumerating all the subsets of a set and all the permutations of n numbers.
- To understand that a recursive function might not be efficient and that top-down dynamic programming might be helpful in improving its performance.
- To obtain an overview of bottom-up dynamic programming by using it to compute the combinations of n items taken k at a time and to solve the 0/1 knapsack problem.
- To obtain an overview of recursive backtracking strategy by studying the solution to the 8-Queens problem.

OUTLINE

Chapter 3 introduced the concept of recursion. The approach focused on the design of recursive algorithms in terms of stopping conditions and recursive steps. In a series of applications, we illustrated how a programmer uses recursive functions to solve problems. In this chapter, we take a more formal look at design principles for recursive algorithms.

A technique called *divide and conquer* is the basis for a rich variety of algorithms. In Section 15-1, we demonstrate the technique by discussing a function that draws a ruler. We then use *divide and conquer* to develop the recursive merge and quicksort algorithms, which have running time $O(n \log_2 n)$. A side effect of the strategy used by the quicksort algorithm is the development of a linear algorithm that finds the kth largest number in an unsorted vector.

Recursion finds many interesting applications in *combinatorics*, which is the branch of mathematics concerned with the enumeration of various sets of objects. Section 15-2 discusses two such problems. The first problem is to list all 2^n subsets of a set having n elements. For instance, if set $S = \{A, B\}$, the $2^2 = 4$ subsets are $\{\}$, $\{A\}$, $\{B\}$, and $\{A, B\}$. The second problem discusses the listing of all $n!$ permutations of the numbers $1...n$. As an example, if $n = 3$, the $3! = 6$ permutations are $123, 132, 213,$ $231, 312, 321.$

In Section 3-7, we discussed the Fibonacci numbers, which can be generated by a recursive function. In Section 15-3, we show that, although the recursive solution has the structure of a divide-and-conquer algorithm, it fails to partition the problem into independent subproblems and results in exponential running time. A technique called top-down dynamic programming can often improve the performance of a recursive function by eliminating redundant calculations. We illustrate the technique with the Fibonacci numbers and with the problem of generating the combination of n items taken k at a time. An alternative strategy, called *bottom-up dynamic programming*, evaluates a function by computing all the function values in order, starting at the lowest level and using previously computed values at each step to compute the current value. We illustrate this technique with the problem of computing combinations and by solving the famous 0/1 knapsack problem.

A number of advanced recursive algorithms can be solved by using a backtracking algorithm, in which we move step by step, creating a partial solution that appears to be consistent with the requirements of the final solution. If, at any step, we create a partial solution that is inconsistent with the final solution, we backtrack one or more steps to the last consistent partial solution. At times, backtracking can entail one step forward and n steps backward. The approach occurs frequently in operations research models, game theory, and the study of graphs. We illustrate backtracking by solving the famous 8-Queens problem.

15-1   DIVIDE-AND-CONQUER ALGORITHMS

Divide-and-conquer is a problem-solving technique that makes use of recursion. The strategy divides a problem into smaller subproblems that are solved as a stopping condition or in a recursive step. The solutions to the subproblems combine to build (conquer) the solution to the original problem. Divide-and-conquer algorithms typically contain two or more recursive calls. The algorithms are most efficient when the calls partition the data into disjoint collections and then work on the smaller data sets. The splitting of the data avoids costly recalculations of intermediate results. In the next section, we will develop a new strategy, called *dynamic programming*, that handles divide-and-conquer algorithms that involve overlapping data.

In this section, we begin with a simple divide-and-conquer algorithm that draws tick marks on a ruler. The algorithm allows us to understand the key elements of the strategy and view the recursive function calls as nodes in a tree. Two classical sorting algorithms are the main focus of the section. Earlier in the book, we developed the selection and insertion sort algorithms for arrays and vectors. The algorithms require $n - 1$ passes over the data. Each pass i must use an $O(n)$ scan of the sublist to correctly position the element $a[i]$. The need for $n - 1$ passes and the scanning of "long" sublists contribute to the relative inefficiency $(O(n^2))$ of the algorithms. An alternative sorting technique partitions the elements into smaller and smaller sublists, which are separately ordered and then combined to form the larger ordered list. This strategy produces $O(n \log_2 n)$ sorting algorithms. Combining the sublists by merging their elements is the basis for the mergesort algorithm. The mergesort has important applications in the external sorting of files. A more sophisticated algorithm partitions the list into two sublists by using a pivot value. The process places the pivot value in the correct location and produces a sublist of elements less than the pivot and a sublist of elements greater than the pivot. This recursive algorithm, called the *quicksort*, provides us with the fastest known sorting technique; one that works well in all but the most extreme cases. Quicksort is the algorithm of choice for data stored in an array or vector.

Building A Ruler

The task of creating a ruler with different-size tickmarks is a very simple example of the divide-and-conquer technique. A typical ruler is a sequence of inch-long blocks that have the longest mark at the end of each block. Each inch has a shorter mark at the $\frac{1}{2}$-inch point and progressively shorter marks at $\frac{1}{4}$-inch intervals, $\frac{1}{8}$-inch intervals, and so forth. The problem is to create a program that draws marks at regular intervals on a line. The sizes of the marks differ, depending on the specific interval. The recursive function drawRuler() provides the solution. Its algorithm assumes the existence of the function drawMark(), which takes a point x and an integer value h as arguments and draws a mark at point x with size proportional to h.

In drawRuler(), a series of recursive steps uses the variable h and the end points of an interval to draw a mark at the midpoint of the interval. The drawMark() function defines a constant baseHeight for the length of a mark and uses h to draw the mark with height $h *$ baseHeight. Given an initial value for h, the final recursive step will create tickmarks every $\frac{1}{2^h}$-inch interval. For instance, if h is initially set to 3, the ruler will have tickmarks every $\frac{1}{2^3} = \frac{1}{8}$ inch. The first recursive step draws a tickmark at $\frac{1}{2}$ inch (the midpoint) with height 3 * baseHeight. Let us trace the sequence of actions for the algorithm, assuming that h is initially 3 and the interval is 1 inch, with *low* = 0.0 and *high* = 1.0. Each step draws a tickmark at the midpoint of an interval. Using the midpoint to separate the interval into half-lines, the step makes two recursive calls to drawRuler() to draw smaller tickmarks at the midpoint of each half-line.

Recursive Step (h = 3)

Compute the midpoint of the interval $(0.0, 1.0)$:

```
midpt = (high + low)/2 = (1.0 + 0.0)/2 = 0.5 (1/2)
```

Draw a tickmark at midpoint $\frac{1}{2}$ with height 3 * baseHeight (Figure 15-1(a)):

```
drawMark(midpt, 3);
```

Partition the interval about the midpoint into half-lines. Make two recursive calls to drawRuler(), corresponding to the two intervals $(0.0, 0.5)$ and $(0.5, 1)$. A call uses the argument $h - 1$ to reduce the height of the tickmark in the half-line.

Recursive Step ($h = 2$):

For call drawRuler$(0.0, 0.5, 2)$,

```
midpt = (0.5 + 0.0)/2 = 0.25 (1/4)
```

Draw the tickmark at midpoint $\frac{1}{4}$ with height 2*baseHeight (Figure 15-1(b)).
For call drawRuler$(0.5, 1.0, 2)$,

```
midpt = (1.0 + 0.5)/2 = 0.75 (3/4)
```

Draw the tickmark at midpoint $\frac{3}{4}$ with height 2*baseHeight (Figure 15-1(b)).

Recursive Step ($h = 1$):

The algorithm executes four function calls with h = 1, since each of the two function calls in drawRuler() with h = 2 generates two function calls

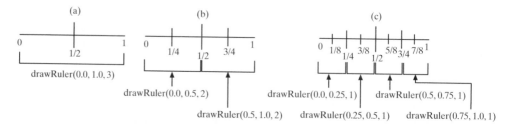

Figure 15-1
Tracing drawRuler$(0.0, 1.0, 3)$

with h = 1. The tickmarks occur at midpoints $\frac{1}{8}$ (0.125), $\frac{3}{8}$, $\frac{5}{8}$, and $\frac{7}{8}$, with height 1 * baseHeight (Figure 15-1(c)).

Stopping Condition (h = 0):

A function call terminates with the stopping condition $h = 0$.

We can view the tickmarks at successive recursive steps as nodes in a binary tree. The root level (the initial value of h) is a mark at the $\frac{1}{2}$-inch point. Each subsequent level creates two "child" marks for each "parent" mark. Using the analogy of a binary tree allows us to understand the design of a divide-and-conquer algorithm and to trace its implementation. We are traversing the binary tree by using one of the recursive scanning algorithms (Figure 15-2).

The drawRuler() function takes the end points of the segment and the value h as arguments. The first action is to draw a tickmark at the midpoint and then make two recursive calls to draw the marks in the two half-lines. The recursive calls correspond to a preorder scan of the corresponding binary tree.

drawRuler():

```
void drawRuler(double low, double high, int h)
{
    double midpt;

    if (h >= 1)
    {
        midpt = (high + low)/2;

        // draw the mark at midpt of [low, high)
        drawMark(midpt, h);

        // draw all marks on the left half-line, starting
        // with h-1
        drawRuler(low, midpt, h - 1);
        // draw all marks on the right half-line, starting
        // with h-1
        drawRuler(midpt, high, h - 1);
    }
}
```

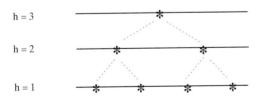

h = 3

h = 2

h = 1

Figure 15-2
Binary Tree of Tickmarks on a Line

In Chapter 15 of the software supplement, the program "prg15_ruler.cpp" illustrates the function drawRuler(). The implementation of drawMark() uses lineShape objects from the graphics package discussed in Chapter 13. The program draws the ruler with progressively smaller partitions that split the line at points $\frac{1}{2}$, $\frac{1}{4}$, ..., $\frac{1}{128}$.

Mergesort

As part of our study of arrays and vectors, we developed the selection sort and insertion sort algorithms, which arrange a sequence in ascending order. The algorithms use $n - 1$ passes to order the sequence. Each pass i requires an O(n) scan of a sublist to correctly position element $a[i]$. In the case of the selection sort, the pass selects an element from the unordered sublist with index range $[i, n)$, while the insertion sort scans the ordered sublist with index range $[0, i)$. The need for each pass to scan relatively long sublists contributes to the inefficiency of the algorithms and gives them running time O(n^2). In this section, we introduce a new sorting algorithm for arrays and vectors that uses recursion and the divide-and-conquer technique to order the sequence with running time O($n \log_2 n$) The mergesort recursively partitions a sequence into progressively smaller and smaller half-lists that are ultimately sorted. Recursive steps merge the sorted half-lists back into larger and larger ordered lists until the algorithm rebuilds the original sequence in ascending order. The partitioning and merge actions involve quite different algorithms, and so we discuss them separately. We begin with the merge algorithm, which assumes the presence of two distinct and sorted sublists. Its action combines the elements from the two sublists into a single sorted list.

The Merge Algorithm   The idea behind the merge algorithm is familiar to any teacher who has a large class and wants to return student exam papers in alphabetic order. The teacher splits the papers into two piles and sorts them separately. Assume that the piles contain the following ordered lists of names:

> **Pile 1:**   Alawab, Bender, Dolan, . . ., Martinez, and Re
> **Pile 2:**   Cardona, . . ., Nunez, Schwartz, Tong, and Walker

Sort the papers by merging the two piles. After choosing Alawab and Bender from pile 1, the teacher selects Cardona from pile 2. Eventually the teacher adds Re to the sorted set of papers, which exhausts the first pile. The merge process concludes by putting the remaining papers from the second pile (Schwartz, Tong, Walker) on the bottom.

    The merge algorithm takes a sequence of elements in a vector v having index range [*first*, *last*). The sequence consists of two ordered sublists separated by an intermediate index, called *mid*. Consider the following example, which describes a sequence of nine integer elements with index range [*first*, *last*). The sequence consists of the four-element sorted sublist sublistA and the five-element sublist sublistB, with index ranges [*first*, *mid*) and [*mid*, *last*), respectively.

		7	10	19	25	12	17	21	30	48		

sublist A   sublist B

first   mid   last

The merge algorithm uses indexA and indexB to scan the sublists separately. Initially, indexA has value *first* and indexB has value *mid*, corresponding to the beginning location in each index range. The scan compares the elements $v[indexA]$ and $v[indexB]$ and copies the smaller value to a temporary vector, tempVector. The corresponding index is incremented to the next location in the sublist. The process repeats until all of the elements in the vector are copied to tempVector. After completion of the pairwise scan of the two sublists, tempVector stores a copy of the elements from the two sublists in order. The algorithm concludes by copying the elements from tempVector back into the vector index range [*first*, *last*). Let us look at the steps for our example:

Step 1. Compare $v[indexA] = 7$ and $v[indexB] = 12$. Use push_back() to add the smaller element, 7, to tempVector. We chose element 7 from sublistA, so increment indexA to the next position in the sublist.

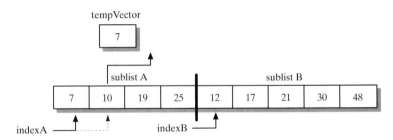

Step 2. Compare $v[indexA] = 10$ and $v[indexB] = 12$. Push a copy of the smaller element, 10, into tempVector. The smaller element, 10, is again an element in sublistA, and so indexA moves to the next position.

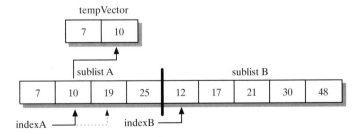

Step 3. The comparison of $v[indexA] = 19$ and $v[indexB] = 12$ provides the first opportunity to copy an element from sublistB to tempVector. Since an element has been chosen from sublistB, increment indexB.

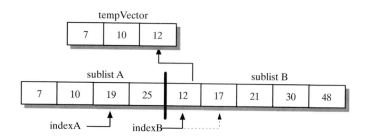

Steps 4–7:   The pairwise comparison of elements in the two sublists continues with the copy of values 17, 19, 21, and 25 to tempVector. At this point, indexA reaches the end of sublistA (indexA $==$ *mid*), and indexB references the value 30.

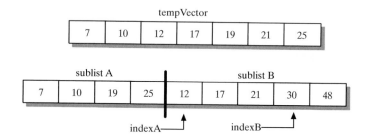

Step 8.   The merging process always exhausts one sublist first, leaving the tail of the second sublist. In this example, elements 30 and 48 in the tail of sublistB have not been copied to tempVector. The algorithm tests to identify the "uncompleted " sublist and copies the remaining elements from that sublist to tempVector. Step 8 copies the tail of sublistB to tempVector, terminating when indexB reaches the end of the sublist (indexB $==$ *last*).

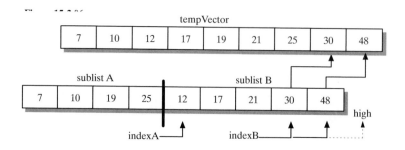

The merge algorithm concludes by copying the elements from tempVector back to the original list, starting at index *first*.

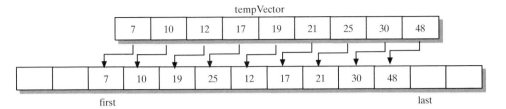

first   last

The Merge Function. The template-based merge() function takes a vector v as a reference argument, along with indices *first*, *mid*, and *last*. Index *mid* splits the elements in the sequence [*first*, *last*) into two ordered sublists with index ranges [*first*, *mid*) and [*mid*, *last*), respectively. A series of loops scans the sublists, using indices indexA and indexB. The first loop makes pairwise comparison of elements in the two sublists and copies elements to tempVector until one sublist is exhausted. A second loop copies the elements from the tail of the other sublist to the temporary vector. The process concludes by copying the elements from tempVector back to v, starting at index *first*.

merge():
```
// the elements in the ranges [first, mid) and [mid,last) are
// ordered. the function merges the ordered sequences into
// an ordered sequence in the range [first, last)
template <typename T>
void merge(vector<T>& v, int first, int mid, int last)
{
    // temporary vector to merge the sorted sublists
    vector<T> tempVector;
    int indexA, indexB, indexV;

    // set indexA to scan sublistA (index range [first, mid))
    // and indexB to scan sublistB (index range [mid, last))
    indexA = first;
    indexB = mid;

    // while both sublists are not exhausted, compare v[indexA] and
    // v[indexB]copy the smaller to tempVector using push_back()
    while (indexA < mid && indexB < last)
        if (v[indexA] < v[indexB])
        {
            tempVector.push_back(v[indexA]);    // copy to tempVector
            indexA++;                           // increment indexA
        }
        else
        {
            tempVector.push_back(v[indexB]);    // copy to tempVector
            indexB++;                           // increment indexB
        }
    // copy the tail of the sublist that is not exhausted
    while (indexA < mid)
```

```
        {
            tempVector.push_back(v[indexA]);
            indexA++;
        }

        while (indexB < last)
        {
            tempVector.push_back(v[indexB]);
            indexB++;
        }

        // copy vector tempVector using indexV to vector v using indexA
        // which is initially set to first
        indexA = first;

        // copy elements from temporary vector to original list
        for (indexV = 0; indexV < tempVector.size(); indexV++)
        {
            v[indexA] = tempVector [indexV];
            indexA++;
        }
    }
```

Let $n = last - first$ be the number of elements in the vector. The function merge() makes at most $n - 1$ comparisons, so it has linear $(O(n))$ worst-case running time.

Implementing the Merge Sort. The implementation of the mergesort algorithm reduces first to partitioning an initial list into ordered sublists and then using the merge() function to build an ordered list from the sublists. The recursive merge-Sort() function carries out this task. The function takes the vector v and the integers *first* and *last* to designate an index range of elements to be sorted. The function creates two half-lists by computing the index *midpt*, representing the midpoint of the index range:

```
int midpt = (last + first)/2;
```

The recursive step makes two calls to mergeSort(). The first call uses indices *first* and *midpt* to define the index range [*first*, *midpt*) for the lower half-list of the original sequence. A second call to mergeSort() uses indices *midpt* and *last* to define the index range [*midpt*, *last*) for the upper half-list. The process sets in motion a chain of recursive calls that partitions the original list into smaller and smaller sublists (half-lists) until their size is 1 (the stopping condition). Sublists of size 1 are obviously ordered. The function mergeSort() then calls merge(), which revisits the chain of recursive calls in reverse order, building successively larger ordered sublists. The final call to merge() creates the original vector in sorted order.

Figure 15-3 provides a binary tree whose nodes illustrate calls to mergeSort() for a vector v of size 11:

```
vector<int> v; // values: 25 10 7 19 3 48 12 17 56 30 21
```

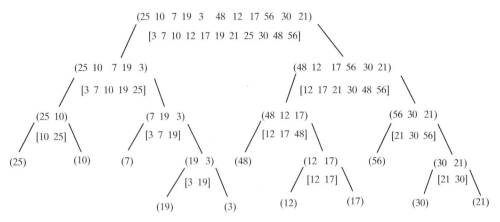

Figure 15-3
Binary Tree Illustrating the Partitioning and Merging of Sublists in mergeSort()

The root node corresponds to the original vector. Each left and right child node specifies the half-list used by the first (left) and the second (right) recursive call to mergeSort(). We enclose the half-lists in parentheses. The LRN (postorder) scan of a tree is the model for the algorithm. A call to merge() represents a visit and has the action of merging the sorted sublists from the child nodes. The tree describes the merged sublists by enclosing the elements in square brackets.

The partitioning process terminates when we reach a sublist of *size* = 1. The index range for a singleton sublist is [*first, first* + 1), where *first* + 1 = *last*. Thus, we continue the partitioning process only as long as *first* + 1 < *last*.

mergeSort()

```
// sorts v in the index range [first,last) by merging
// ordered sublists
template <typename T>
void mergeSort(vector<T>& v, int first, int last)
{
    // if the sublist has more than 1 element continue
    if (first + 1 < last)
    {
        // for sublists of size 2 or more, call mergeSort()
        // for the left and right sublists and then
        // merge the sorted sublists using merge()
        int midpt = (last + first) / 2;

        mergeSort(v, first, midpt);
        mergeSort(v, midpt, last);
        merge(v, first, midpt, last);
    }
}
```

You can find the implementation of mergeSort() with the other sorting algorithms in the header file "d_sort.h".

PROGRAM 15-1   ORDERING LISTS WITH MERGESORT

Let us create a test program that uses the mergesort algorithm for a vector of integers and a vector of strings. Each vector is initialized from an array. The integer example uses the list for Figure 15-3. After the sorting of the vectors, a call to writeContainer() outputs the resulting sequence.

```
// File: prg15_1.cpp
// the program initializes a vector of integers and a vector
// of strings. it then applies the function mergeSort() to
// each vector and outputs the result

#include <iostream>
#include <string>
#include <vector>

#include "d_sort.h"       // for mergeSort()
#include "d_util.h"       // for writeContainer()

using namespace std;

int main()
{
   // create an array of integers and of strings for the sort
   int intList[] = {25, 10, 7, 19, 3, 48, 12, 17, 56, 30, 21};

   string strList[] = {"Dallas","Akron","Wausau","Phoenix",
                       "Fairbanks","Miami"};

   vector<int> vIntList(intList, intList+11);
   vector<string> vStrList(strList,strList+6);

   // sort and then output each vector
   mergeSort(vIntList, 0, vIntList.size());
   cout << "Sorted integers: ";
   writeContainer(vIntList.begin(), vIntList.end());
   cout << endl;

   mergeSort(vStrList, 0, vStrList.size());
   cout << "Sorted strings:  ";
   writeContainer(vStrList.begin(), vStrList.end());
   cout << endl;

   return 0;
}
```

```
Run:
Sorted integers: 3  7  10  12  17  19  21  25  30  48  56
Sorted strings:  Akron  Dallas  Fairbanks  Miami  Phoenix  Wausau
```

Running Time of Mergesort: The partition and merge activities for the merge-sort are independent of the initial ordering of the list. Hence, it has the same runtime efficiency for the worst-case, best-case, and average-case conditions. An intuitive analysis of the process indicates that the running time for mergeSort() is $O(n \log_2 n)$.

To simplify the calculations, assume the list has $n = 2^k$ elements. Figure 15-4 is a binary tree illustrating the function calls in mergeSort(). At each level in the tree, we want to evaluate the amount of work that merge() performs. This is the operation that combines the half-lists into a single sorted list.

The first call to mergeSort() corresponds to level 0 of the tree. The two recursive calls produce half-lists of size $n/2$, and the merge() function combines the half-lists to create the ordered n-element list. At level 1, there are two calls to mergeSort(); each produces two additional recursive calls with lists of size $n/4$. Each merge joins two sublists of size $n/4$ to create an ordered list of size $n/2$. At level 2, there are $4 = 2^2$ recursive calls to merge(); each creates an ordered sublist of size $n/4$. In general, at level i, there are 2^i calls to merge(), and each call orders $n/2^i$ elements.

Level 0: $1 = 2^0$ call to merge(). The call orders n elements.

Level 1: $2 = 2^1$ calls to merge(). Each call orders $n/2$ elements.

Level 2: $4 = 2^2$ calls to merge(). Each call orders $n/4 =$ elements.

. . .

Level i: 2^i calls to merge(). Each call orders $n/2^i$ elements.

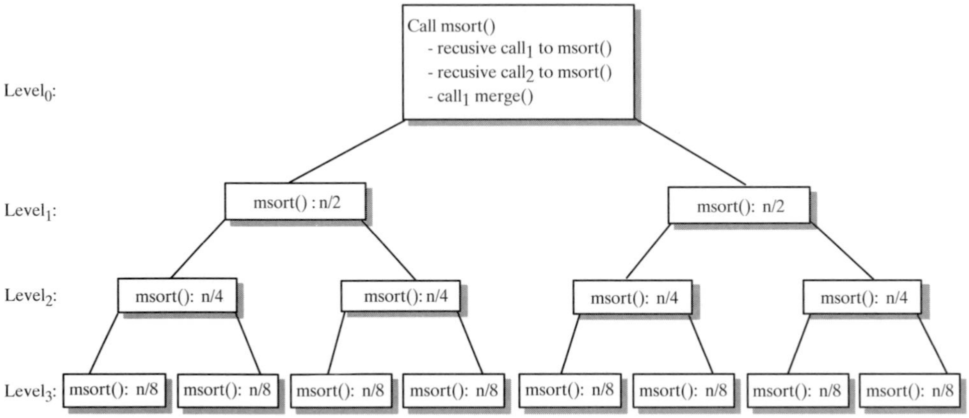

Figure 15-4
Function Calls in mergeSort()

At each level i in the tree, the combined 2^i calls to merge() order $2^i * (n/2^i) = n$ elements. The maximum number of comparisons for level i is $O(n)$, because merge() is a linear algorithm. Assuming that $n = 2^k$, the partition process terminates at level k with sublists of size $n/2^k = 1$. The total work done by all of the levels is

$$k*O(n) = \log_2 n * O(n) = O(n \log_2 n)$$

Quicksort

The famous quicksort algorithm uses another form of the divide-and-conquer strategy to order a list. The algorithm, designed by C. A. R. Hoare, uses a series of recursive calls to partition a list into smaller and smaller sublists about a value called the *pivot*. Each step chooses as its pivot the value at the midpoint of the list. The partitioning algorithm performs exchanges so that the pivot is in its final location, the lower sublist has only elements that are less than or equal to the pivot, and the upper sublist has only elements that are greater than or equal to the pivot. Unlike the merge sort, which copies elements to and from a temporary vector, quicksort is an "in-place" sorting algorithm, because it reorders the list by exchanging elements within the list. The best way to understand the overall design of the quicksort algorithm is by working through an example. Let v be a vector containing 10 integer values:

```
v = {800, 150, 300, 650, 550, 500, 400, 350, 450, 900}
```

Partition Level 0:   The list, which is all of v, has index range [*first, last*) = [0, 10). The value at the midpoint of the range becomes the pivot.

```
// pivot = v[mid] where mid = (last+first)/2
mid = (10 + 0)/5 = 5
pivot = v[5] = 500;
```

The algorithm separates the elements of v into two sublists, S_l and S_h. Sublist S_l is the lower sublist and contains the elements that are less than or equal to the pivot. The higher sublist, S_h, contains the elements that are greater than or equal to the pivot. The pivot (500) is a value that will ultimately lie between the two sublists. We begin by exchanging the pivot with the element at the low end of the index range. The exchange of $v[$ *first* $]$ and $v[mid]$ has the effect of moving the pivot to the front of the list and setting up a scan of the rest of the list, whose index range is [*first* $+$ 1, *last*). The scan uses two indices, scanUp and scanDown. The integer scanUp starts at position *first* $+$ 1 and moves up the list, locating the elements in sublist S_l. The integer scanDown starts at position *last* $-$ 1 and moves down the list, locating elements in sublist S_h.

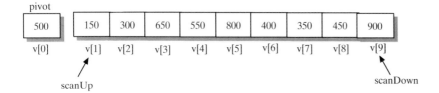

The scanning process begins with index scanUp and looks for an element that is greater than or equal to the pivot value. Such an element ultimately belongs in the upper sublist S_h. In an effort to find a location to store the element in S_h, the scan halts to allow scanDown to move down the list looking for an element that is less than or equal to the pivot. This scan halts when it locates an element that belongs in the lower sublist S_l. In the resulting situation, we have a pair of elements, pointed to by scanUp and scanDown, that are in the wrong sublists; $v[\text{scanUp}] \geq$ pivot and $v[\text{scanDown}] \leq$ pivot. A reordering of the list occurs by exchanging the elements at the two positions and then updating the two indices so that the scan with index scanUp can resume.

```
// exchange elements and thus place them in the proper sublists
exchange(v[scanUp],v[scanDown]);
scanUp++;              // set scanUp at next element up the list
scanDown--;            // set scanDown at next element down the list
```

In the example, scanUp stops at index 3 and scanDown stops at index 8. The elements 650 and 450 exchange positions, and the indices are moved to positions 4 and 7, respectively.

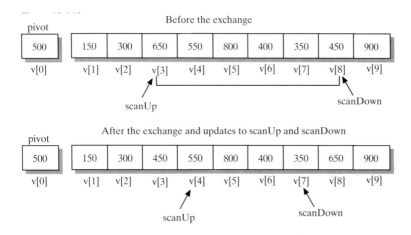

It is critical to understand that the two scans with indices scanUp and scan-Down work in tandem. They locate the next pair of elements that must be reordered to create the two sublists. In our example, we resume the scan up the list and have index scanUp halt at element $v[4] = 550 \geq 500$. Its partner, scanDown, moves down the list, halting at $v[7] = 350 \leq 500$. Elements $v[4]$ and $v[7]$ are the next pair that are in the wrong sublist. We exchange the elements and update the indices.

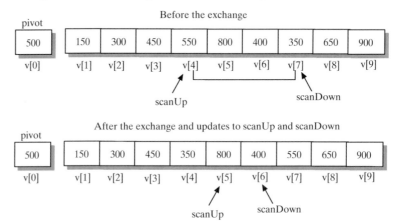

The scanning of the list resumes. Note that the two indices are closing in on each other and approaching the position in the list that separates the two sublists. Index scanUp halts at position 5 ($v[5] = 800$), and scanDown halts at position 6 ($v[6] = 400$). After exchanging the elements and updating the indices, the indices "pass or catch up with each other" and scanDown $\leq$ scanUp.

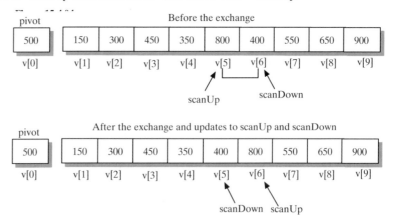

Once index scanDown becomes less than or equal to scanUp, the partitioning process terminates. The index scanDown marks the separation point between the two sublists and identifies the final location for the pivot value, which was temporarily stored in $v[0]$. Exchanging $v[0]$ and $v[\text{scanDown}]$ correctly positions the pivot value in the list.

Pivot in its final position

400	150	300	450	350	500	800	550	650	900
v[0]	v[1]	v[2]	v[3]	v[4]	v[5]	v[6]	v[7]	v[8]	v[9]

Note that the quicksort algorithm differs significantly from the mergesort, because the separation point between the two sublists depends on a value (pivot) and is not determined by splitting the list in half. When the process terminates, we are left with the element $v[5]$ in its correct position and the sublists S_1 ($v[0]$–$v[4]$) and S_h ($v[6]$–$v[9]$) in which all of the elements in S_1 are less than the elements in S_h.

400	150	300	450	350	500	800	550	650	900
v[0]	v[1]	v[2]	v[3]	v[4]	v[5]	v[6]	v[7]	v[8]	v[9]

└──────────v[0] - v[4] ──────────┘   └──────v[6] - v[9] ──────┘

Partition Level 1:   The algorithm recursively handles the two sublists S_1 and S_h separately.

Sublist S_1{400, 150, 300, 450, 350}: The index range of the sublist is [0, 5), with *first* = 0 and *last* = 5. The value of *mid* = (*last* + *first*)/2 = 2 and the pivot is $v[mid]$ = 300. Exchange *pivot* and $v[first]$, and assign initial values to the indices scanUp and scanDown:

```
scanUp = first + 1 = 1
scanDown = last - 1 = 4
```

The index scanUp moves up the list, stopping at index 2 ($v[2]$ = 400 > 300). The index scanDown then moves down the list, stopping at index 1 ($v[1]$ = 150 < 300).

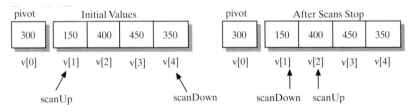

Because scanDown ≤ scanUp, the scan halts, and scanDown is the separation point between the two sublists. Complete the process by exchanging $v[$scanDown$]$ = 150 and $v[first]$ = 300. Note that, after locating the pivot, we are left with a one-element sublist $v[0]$ and a three-element sublist $v[2]$–$v[4]$. The recursive process terminates on an empty or one-element sublist, and so partition level 2 will order only the upper sublist, $v[2]$–$v[4]$.

150	300	400	450	350
v[0]	v[1]	v[2]	v[3]	v[4]

Sublist s_h   {800, 550, 650, 900}: The index range of the sublist is [6, 10); *first* = 6, *last* = 10. The midpoint is index 8, and the pivot is $v[mid]$ = 650. Exchange the pivot and $v[first]$, and assign initial values to the indices scanUp and scanDown:

```
scanUp = 7 = first + 1
scanDown = 9 = last - 1
```

Index scanUp moves up the list, stopping at position 8 ($v[8] = 800 > 650$). Index scanDown then moves down the list, stopping at position 7 ($v[7] = 550 < 650$).

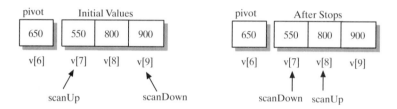

Exchanging v[scanDown] and v[first] = 650 locates 650 in the correct location at index 7. The partition leaves a one-element lower sublist and a two-element upper sublist.

550	650	800	900
v[6]	v[7]	v[8]	v[9]

Partition Level 2:   The ordering in partition level 1 produces two single-element sublists that are ordered and two sublists that contain two or more elements (*last − first* >= 2).

150	300	400	450	350	500	550	650	800	900
v[0]	v[1]	v[2]	v[3]	v[4]	v[5]	v[6]	v[7]	v[8]	v[9]

The recursive step continues only with these larger sublists. Ordering a two-element sublist is more efficient if we just compare the elements and make an exchange if necessary. This strategy applies to the sublist $v[8] \ldots v[9]$. The partitioning process continues only with sublist $v[2] \ldots v[4]$, which has a pivot value $v[3] = 450$. The following figure displays the sublist before and after the partitioning:

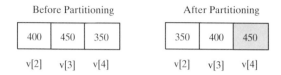

After the completion of partition level 2, the next level considers the two-element sublist $v[2] \ldots v[3]$ and makes no exchange. At this point, all of the elements in the original vector are in their correct locations, and the list is sorted in ascending order.

150	300	350	400	450	500	550	650	800	900
v[0]	v[1]	v[2]	v[3]	v[4]	v[5]	v[6]	v[7]	v[8]	v[9]

Quicksort Implementation. The recursive step in the quicksort algorithm reorders elements in the index range [*first, last*) about a pivot value. We provide the function pivotIndex() to perform this task. The function takes a vector v and two indices, *first* and *last*, specifying the index range. The function selects the value of the midpoint of the list as the pivot. The return value is the final location (index) of the pivot value after partitioning the list into two sublists consisting of elements that are less than or equal to the pivot and elements that are greater than or equal to the pivot.

```
template <typename T>
int pivotIndex(vector<T>& v, int first, int last);
```

The previous section illustrated the algorithm for pivotIndex(). After identifying the pivot value, the function exchanges the value with $v[first]$ and assigns index scanUp the value *first* + 1 and index scanDown the value *last* − 1. The two indices work in tandem to scan up and down the list. The upward scan halts at an element that belongs in the upper sublist (elements greater than or equal to the pivot) or when scanUp passes scanDown in the index range.

```
// move up lower sublist; stop when scanUp enters the
// upper sublist or identifies an element >= pivot
while (scanUp <= scanDown && v[scanUp] < pivot)
    scanUp++;
```

The index scanDown moves down the list, as long as it references elements that are greater than the pivot.

```
// scan down upper sublist; stop when scanDown locates
// an element <= pivot; we guarantee we stop at v[first]
while (pivot < v[scanDown])
    scanDown--;
```

If the two scans halt with scanUp < scanDown, then each index points at an element that is in the wrong sublist. The reordering of the list occurs by exchanging the two elements. This tandem scanning of the list terminates when scanDown is less than or equal to scanUp. At this point, the location of index scanDown separates the list into two sublists. The function concludes the partitioning process by exchanging the pivot in $v[first]$ with $v[\text{scanDown}]$ and then setting scanDown as the return value.

pivotIndex():
```
// use as pivot the value at the midpoint of [first,last)
// locate the pivot in its final location so all elements
// to its left are <= to its value and all elements to the
// right are >= to its value. return the index of the pivot
template <typename T>
int pivotIndex(vector<T>& v, int first, int last)
{
    // index for the midpoint of [first,last) and the
    // indices that scan the index range in tandem
    int mid, scanUp, scanDown;
    // pivot value and object used for exchanges
    T pivot, temp;

    if (first == last)
        return last;
    else if (first == last-1)
        return first;
    else
    {
        mid = (last + first)/2;
        pivot = v[mid];

        // exchange the pivot and the low end of the range
        // and initialize the indices scanUp and scanDown.
        v[mid] = v[first];
        v[first] = pivot;

        scanUp = first + 1;
        scanDown = last - 1;

        // manage the indices to locate elements that are in
        // the wrong sublist; stop when scanDown <= scanUp
        for(;;)
        {
            // move up lower sublist; stop when scanUp enters
            // upper sublist or identifies an element >= pivot
            while (scanUp <= scanDown && v[scanUp] < pivot)
```

```
            scanUp++;
    // scan down upper sublist; stop when scanDown locates
    // an element <= pivot; insure a stop at v[first]
    while (pivot < v[scanDown])
        scanDown--;

    // if indices are not in their sublists, partition complete
    if (scanUp >= scanDown)
        break;

    // indices are still in their sublists and identify
    // two elements in wrong sublists. exchange
    temp = v[scanUp];
    v[scanUp] = v[scanDown];
    v[scanDown] = temp;

    scanUp++;
    scanDown--;
    }

    // copy pivot to index (scanDown) that partitions sublists
    // and return scanDown
    v[first] = v[scanDown];
    v[scanDown] = pivot;
    return scanDown;
    }
}
```

The quicksort algorithm recursively partitions a list into smaller and smaller sublists. The process terminates when the size of the list is 0 or 1; such a list is obviously ordered. For efficiency, we handle a list of size 2 by simply comparing the elements and making an exchange if necessary. A recursive step handles all other lists by first calling pivotIndex() to reorder the list and determine the index for the pivot and then making two calls to quicksort(). Letting pivotLoc be the return value from pivotIndex(), the first call to quicksort() uses the arguments *first* and pivotLoc to specify the index range for the lower sublist. The second call uses the arguments pivotLoc + 1 and *last* to specify the index range for the upper sublist.

quicksort():
```
    // sort a vector using quicksort
    template <typename T>
    void quicksort(vector<T>& v, int first, int last)
    {
        // index of the pivot
        int pivotLoc;
        // temp used for an exchange when [first,last) has
        // two elements
        T temp;
```

```
// if the range is not at least two elements, return
if (last - first <= 1)
   return;
// if sublist has two elements, compare v[first] and
// v[last-1] and exchange if necessary
else if (last - first == 2)
{
   if (v[last-1] < v[first])
   {
      temp = v[last-1];
      v[last-1] = v[first];
      v[first] = temp;
   }
   return;
}
else
{
   pivotLoc = pivotIndex(v, first, last);

   // make the recursive call
   quicksort(v, first, pivotLoc);

   // make the recursive call
   quicksort(v, pivotLoc + 1, last);
}
}
```

We include the implementations for the functions pivotIndex() and quicksort() in the header file "d_sort.h".

Running Time of Quicksort To measure the efficiency of the quicksort() algorithm, assume that n is a power of 2; that is, $n = 2^k$ ($k = \log_2 n$). In addition, assume that the pivot lies in the middle of each list, so that quicksort partitions the list into two equal-sized sublists. Under these rather ideal circumstances, we can get a handle on the number of comparisons.

For partition level 0, there are approximately n comparisons ($n + 1$, to be exact). The result of the process creates two sublists of approximate size $n/2$. In partition level 1, there are two sublists. Partitioning each sublist requires approximately $n/2$ comparisons. The total number of comparisons for the two sublists is $2*(n/2) = n$. In partition level 2, there are four sublists, which require a total $4*(n/4) = n$ comparisons, and so forth. Eventually, the partition process terminates after k levels with sublists having size 1. The total number of comparisons is approximately

$$n + 2(n/2) + 4(n/4) + \cdots + n(n/n) = n + n + \cdots + n$$
$$= n*k$$
$$= n * \log_2 n$$

The ideal case we have discussed is actually realized when the vector is already sorted in ascending order. In this case, the pivot is precisely in the middle of the list.

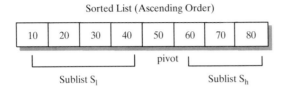

Sorted List (Ascending Order)

| 10 | 20 | 30 | 40 | 50 | 60 | 70 | 80 |

Sublist S_l pivot   Sublist S_h

If the vector is initially sorted in descending order, partition level 0 locates the pivot in the middle of the list and exchanges each element in both the lower and upper sublists. The resulting list is almost sorted, and the algorithm has the same running time, $O(n \log_2 n)$.

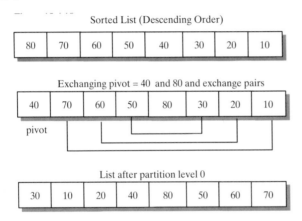

Sorted List (Descending Order)

| 80 | 70 | 60 | 50 | 40 | 30 | 20 | 10 |

Exchanging pivot = 40 and 80 and exchange pairs

| 40 | 70 | 60 | 50 | 80 | 30 | 20 | 10 |

pivot

List after partition level 0

| 30 | 10 | 20 | 40 | 80 | 50 | 60 | 70 |

For an arbitrary vector, a somewhat complex mathematical calculation verifies that the average running time, $T(n)$, for quicksort() satisfies the relation

$$T(n) = 1.39 \, n \log_2 n$$

This shows that the average running time for quicksort is $O(n \log_2 n)$.

Note

The worst-case scenario for quicksort() occurs when the pivot consistently splits off a one-element sublist and leaves the rest of the elements in the second sublist. This occurs, for example, when the pivot is always the smallest or the largest element in its sublist. For example, the data 5, 3, 1, 2, 9 exhibit this behavior. In partition level 0, there are $n + 1$ comparisons, and the large sublist contains $n - 1$ elements. In partition level 1, there are n comparisons, and the large sublist contains $n - 2$ elements, and so forth. The total number of comparisons is no more than

$$(n + 1) + n + n - 2 + \cdots + 2 + 1 = n(n + 1)/2$$

and the complexity is $O(n^2)$, which is no better than the selection or insertion sort. However, the worst case is very unlikely to occur in practice. In general, the overall performance of quicksort is superior to that of all the other sorts we have discussed.

Comparison Of Sorting Algorithms

This book's study of sorting algorithms is complete. We have seen quadratic $(O(n^2))$ algorithms: the selection sort in Chapter 3 and the insertion sort in Chapter 4. These algorithms all have one characteristic in common: They function by strictly comparing adjacent vector elements. It can be shown, by using a mathematical argument, that such sorting algorithms can never have a complexity better than $O(n^2)$. In other words, if you devise a new sorting method that always compares adjacent elements and you think its complexity is $O(n \log_2 n)$, you are wrong!

We discussed the heap sort in Chapter 14, and the mergesort and quicksort in this section. All of these sorts exhibit $O(n \log_2 n)$ performance and function by making comparisons of nonadjacent vector elements. In practice, the quicksort is the algorithm of choice for most sorting tasks. Its $O(n^2)$ worst-case running time has very little likelihood of occurring. Its partition strategy very efficiently moves elements to their final positions in the vector. The heap sort can be counted on for $O(n \log_2 n)$ performance under all conditions. The merge sort is encumbered by having to allocate additional memory, which also slows down its performance.

Can we do any better than the $O(n \log_2 n)$ performance of quicksort? An interesting mathematical result shows that any algorithm which performs sorting using comparisons cannot have a worst-case performance better than $O(n \log_2 n)$. A similar result also applies to the average-case performance. A sorting algorithm based on comparisons cannot be $O(n)$! To obtain linear performance, you have to use a sorting algorithm that does not use comparisons, such as the radix sort we discussed in Chapter 8.

PROGRAM 15-2   COMPARING SORTS

The following program compares the performance of the quicksort, heap, merge, and insertion sorts. Each sorting algorithm is given the same 100,000-element vector of random integers in the range from 0 to 999999. For each sort, the main program calls the function timeSort(), which uses the timer class to record the sorting time in seconds. After timing the sort, timeSort() calls the function outputFirst_Last(), which outputs the first and last five elements of the vector. The function timeSort() concludes by displaying the sorting time along with a string identifying the sort. The insertion sort, whose efficiency is $O(n^2)$, allows us to vividly contrast a slower sorting algorithm with the faster $O(n \log_2 n)$ sorts.

Consult the file "prg15_2.cpp" of the software supplement for the implementation of the functions timeSort() and outputFirst_Last().

```
// File: prg15_2.cpp
// the program compares the performance of heapsort, mergesort,
// quicksort, and the insertion sort. vectors v1, v2, v3, and v4
// are initialized with the same 100,000 random numbers in the
// range 0 to 999999. the program calls the function timeSort()
```

```
// with each vector as an argument and arguments that identify
// the sorting algorithm. the function times the sorting of the
// vector and calls outputFirst_Last() to display the first and
// last 5 values in the sorted vector. the function timeSort()
// then outputs the name of the sorting algorithm and the time
// it required to sort the vector. the program illustrates the
// general superiority of quicksort and the excellent speed
// of heapsort. mergesort has a slower time because it is not an
// in-place sorting algorithm. the results vividly contrast an
// O(n log n) algorithm with the quadratic insertion sort

#include <iostream>
#include <string>
#include <vector>
#include <functional>          // greater<T> for heapSort()

#include "d_random.h"          // randomNumber class
#include "d_sort.h"            // vector sorting algorithms
#include "d_timer.h"           // timer class

using namespace std;

// outputs the first 5 and last 5 items in the vector
void outputFirst_Last(const vector<int>& v);

// types of sorts we will test
enum sortType {HEAPSORT, MERGESORT, QUICKSORT, INSERTIONSORT};

// apply the specified sort to v and time it.
// output the result using sortName as a descriptive
// label
void timeSort(vector<int>& v ,sortType sort,
            const string& sortName);
int main()
{
   const int VECTORSIZE = 100000;
   vector<int> v1, v2, v3, v4;
   int rndNum, i;
   randomNumber rnd;

   // load the vectors with the same sequence of 100000
   // random numbers in the range 0 to 999999
   for(i=0;i < VECTORSIZE;i++)
   {
      rndNum = rnd.random(1000000);
      v1.push_back(rndNum);
      v2.push_back(rndNum);
      v3.push_back(rndNum);
      v4.push_back(rndNum);
   }
```

```
        // time heap sort
        timeSort(v1,HEAPSORT,"Heap sort");
        // repeat process for the merge sort
        timeSort(v2,MERGESORT,"Merge sort");

        // repeat process for the quick sort
        timeSort(v3,QUICKSORT,"Quick sort");

        // repeat process for the insertion sort
        timeSort(v4,INSERTIONSORT,"Insertion sort");

        return 0;
    }

/* implementation for outputFirst_Last() and timeSort() in
"prg15_2.cpp" of the software supplement */
```

```
Run:

8  11  45  55  61  . . .  999956  999961  999969  999972  999985
Heap sort time is 0.07

8  11  45  55  61  . . .  999956  999961  999969  999972  999985
Merge sort time is 0.39

8  11  45  55  61  . . .  999956  999961  999969  999972  999985
Quick sort time is 0.04

8  11  45  55  61  . . .  999956  999961  999969  999972  999985
Insertion sort time is 33.909
```

Application: Finding the Kth-Largest Element

An application could need to find the median value in a vector, which is a value M such that half the vector elements are $<= M$ and the remaining values are $>= M$. For instance, the Bureau of Labor Statistics reports the median family income as the middle value in a random sample of family incomes. In general, it can be necessary to locate the kth largest element of a vector. For instance, the SAT Testing Service identifies the quartile scores for students taking the college entrance exam. The quartile scores are the $n/4^{th}$, $n/2^{th}$ (median), and $3*n/4^{th}$(-largest) vector elements. We can solve the problem of finding the kth-largest element by first sorting the vector and then simply accessing the element at position k. This is an inefficient algorithm, however, because the sort requires additional work to order all of the elements. We simply need to locate the position of the kth-largest value (kLargest) in the list by partitioning the elements into two disjoint sublists. The lower sublist must contain k elements that are less than or equal to kLargest, and the upper sublist must contain elements that are greater than or equal to kLargest. Figure 15-5 illus-

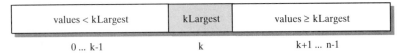

values < kLargest	kLargest	values ≥ kLargest
0 ... k-1	k	k+1 ... n-1

Figure 15-5
Partition of a List about the Position of the kth-Largest Element

trates the partition. The elements in the lower sublist do not need to be ordered, but only to have values that are less than or equal to kLargest. The opposite condition applies to the upper sublist.

We will apply the quicksort algorithm to create the partition. The function findK() takes a vector, the index range [*first, last*), and the position *k* as arguments. It modifies the vector so that the *k*th-largest element is at index *k*. A call to pivotIndex() reorders the current vector range about a pivot value, so that elements smaller than or equal to the pivot are in the lower sublist and elements greater than or equal to the pivot are in the upper sublist. The return value is the index of the pivot. If the index is *k*, then the pivot is the *k*th-largest element and the function returns. If the index is greater than *k*, then a recursive call to pivotIndex() with index range [*first, index*) continues the search for the *k*th-largest element in the lower sublist. Otherwise, a recursive call to pivotIndex() with index range [*index* + 1, *last*) continues the search in the upper sublist.

findK():
```
// locate the kth largest element of v at index k
template <typename T>
void findK(vector<T>& v, int first, int last, int k)
{

   int index;

   // partition range [first,last) in v about the
   // pivot v[index]
   index = pivotIndex(v, first, last);

   // if index == k, we are done. kth largest is v[k]
   if (index == k)
      return;
   else if(k < index)
      // search in lower sublist [first,index)
      findK(v, first, index, k);
   else
      // search in upper sublist [index+1,last)
      findK(v, index+1, last, k);
}
```

The function can be found in the library file "d_sort.h".

Example 15-1

Assume that the vector v contains n scores in the range from lowScore = 250 to highScore = 750. Let us use findK() to list the median score, the range of scores in the top 10%, and the range of scores in the bottom 25%:

```
int lowScore = 250, highScore = 750;
int arr[] = {250, 300, 350, 400, 400, 450, 500, 500, 550, 650,
             655, 700, 725, 735, 750};
int n = sizeof(arr)/sizeof(int);
vector<int> v(arr, arr+n);
```

1. Median:

```
k = n/2;
findK(v, 0, n, k);
cout << v[k] << endl;             // output: 500
```

2. Range for top 10%:

```
k = 9*n/10;
findK(v, 0, n, k);
cout << v[k] <<" - "
     << highScore << endl;        // output: 735 - 750
```

3. Range for bottom 25%:

```
k = n/4;
cout << lowScore << " - " << v[k]
     << endl;                     // output: 250 - 400
```

Running Time of findK(). This algorithm should have a faster running time than quicksort, because it rejects either the lower or the upper sublist at each stage. Let's investigate its running time for an n-element vector intuitively. Assume, as we did for quicksort, that the pivot always lies at the midpoint of the sublist. Under this assumption, locating the first pivot requires approximately n comparisons, finding the second pivot requires approximately $n/2$ comparisons, finding the third pivot requires approximately $n/4$ comparisons, and so forth. The whole process requires no more than

$$n + \frac{n}{2} + \frac{n}{4} + \frac{n}{8} + \cdots = n\left(1 + \frac{1}{2} + \frac{1}{4} + \frac{1}{8} + \cdots\right) = 2n$$

comparisons when we use the fact that the geometric series $1 + \frac{1}{2} + \frac{1}{4} + \frac{1}{8} + \cdots$ has the sum 2. This intuitive argument indicates that the average running time for findK() is $O(n)$, which is linear.

If the pivot is always the largest or smallest element in its sublist, findK() has the same worst-case running time as quicksort, which is $O(n^2)$.

A mathematical analysis similar to that for quicksort, but even more complex, shows that the average running time is approximately

$$2n + 2k \ln\left(\frac{n}{k}\right) + 2(n - k) \ln\left(\frac{n}{n - k}\right)$$

where ln is the natural logarithm function. For any $0 \le k < n$, this algorithm has linear running time. Note that locating the median requires approximately $2n(1 + \ln(2))$ comparisons.

☞

Note

COMBINATORICS   15-2

Recursion is a powerful programming strategy that often allows us to create natural and concise solutions to problems that would be very difficult to design and implement as an iterative process. Recursive algorithms require an understanding only of stopping conditions and recursive steps. A programmer can focus on the process design and leave the computer to manage intermediate calculations.

In this section, we develop several examples from combinatorics, which is the branch of mathematics concerned with the enumeration of various sets of objects.

Finding All Subsets

For a set S, we say that A is a subset of S if all of the elements of A are also elements of S. The empty set is a subset of S. The set of all subsets of a set S is called the *power set* of S. By mathematical induction, we can prove that if S has n elements, then the number of elements in its power set is 2^n. For instance, assume that $S = \{1, 2, 3\}$. Then the power set has $2^3 = 8$ subsets:

$$\{\} \quad \{1\} \quad \{2\} \quad \{3\} \quad \{1,2\} \quad \{1,3\} \quad \{2,3\} \quad \{1,2,3\}$$

(The notation $\{\}$ represents the empty set.) We can use a recursive algorithm to build all of the subsets in the power set. The function powerSet() takes a set S as an argument and returns the power set as a set<set<T> > object:

```
template <typename T>
set<set<T> > powerSet(set<T>& s).
```

Note that it is possible to form a set whose elements are set<T> objects, because the set container defines the operator $<$ for sets. The expression $s < t$ is true if s is lexicographically less than t. For instance,

$$\{1, 2, 3\} < \{2, 3\} \text{ is true}$$

but

$$\{2, 3\} < \{1, 5\} \text{ is false}$$

Start with set S of size n. Remove one of the elements, x, from the set to create a new set S' with $n - 1$ elements. The power set of S' contains 2^{n-1} subsets. Adding

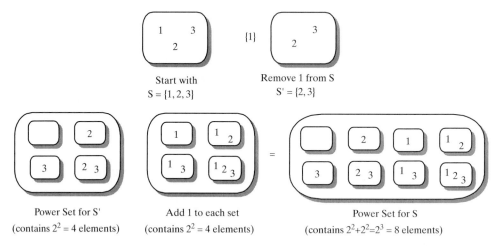

Figure 15-6
Algorithm powerSet() for Set S = {1, 2, 3}

the element x back into each of these subsets creates a second collection of 2^{n-1} subsets. The power set of S is the union of the power set of S' and the elements in the second collection. Figure 15-6 displays the situation for $S = \{1, 2, 3\}$. Assume that we remove element 1 from S to create set $S' = \{2, 3\}$.

This analysis leads us to a recursive definition for the power set of a set S. The stopping condition occurs when S has no elements. In this case, the power set has a single element, the empty set. If S is nonempty, select an element x in S and form the set $S' = S - \{x\}$. Then powerSet (S) is the union of powerSet (S') with sets formed by taking each set in powerSet (S') and adding the element x.

The function powerSet () takes a set S as a reference argument and uses an if/else statement to implement the recursive definition for power set. For the recursive step, the function uses iterator notation to remove temp = *(s.begin()), which corresponds to the first element in the set. Two set<set<T> > objects, sPrime and sPrimePlus, build the power set. Object sPrime is the power set of $s' = s - \{temp\}$, and object sPrimePlus is the collection of the subsets created from sPrime by adding temp to each subset of s'. The union of the two objects is the return value for the function.

powerSet():

```
// return the power set of s
template <typename T>
set<set<T> > powerSet(set<T>& s)
{
    // empty set
    set<T> empty;
```

```
// sPrime is power set not containing 1st element of s.
// sPrimePlus is the collection of the subsets created
// from sPrime by adding 1st element of s to each set
// in sPrime
set<set<T> > sPrime, sPrimePlus;
// will be the power set
set<set<T> > pset;

if (s.size() == 0)
   // s is empty, so sPrime contains the empty set
   pset.insert(empty);
else
{
   // record the 1st value in s
   T temp = *(s.begin());

   // erase the first value from s and compute the
   // the power set, sPrime, of the modified set
   s.erase(s.begin());
   sPrime = powerSet(s);

   // iterator that moves through sPrime
   set<set<T> >::iterator sIter;
   // tempSet is a set in sPrime
   set<T> tempSet;

   // move through sPrime
   sIter = sPrime.begin();
   while (sIter != sPrime.end())
   {
      // get current subset from sPrime
      tempSet = *sIter;
      // insert temp into it
      tempSet.insert(temp);
      // insert the subset into sPrimePlus
      sPrimePlus.insert(tempSet);
      // move the iterator forward
      sIter++;
   }

   // the power set for s is the union of sPrime
   // and sPrimePlus
   pset = sPrime + sPrimePlus;
}
// return the power set
return pset;
}
```

The implementation for powerSet() is in the file "d_pset.h".

PROGRAM 15-3   BUILDING A POWER SET

Let us look at a program that uses the function powerSet () to display a power set. A prompt asks the user to input an integer *n* in the range from 1 to 6. With the value for *n*, we build the set $\{1, 2, \ldots, n\}$ and then call the function to obtain the power set. After outputting the size of the power set, the program calls writePowerSet() to display each element, using "set bracket" notation. You can find the code for writePowerSet() in "d_pset.h".

```cpp
// File: prg15_3.cpp
// the program prompts for an integer value n and builds the set
// {1, 2, 3, ..., n}. it then calls the recursive function powerSet()
// that returns the power set of the set. the power set is the set
// of all subsets of the set and has 2^n elements. after displaying
// the size of the power set, the program calls the function
// writePowerSet() that outputs each subset using the notation
// {elt1, elt2, ..., eltm}

#include <iostream>
#include <iomanip>
#include <set>

#include "d_pset.h"

using namespace std;

int main()
{
   int n, i;
   // set of integers whose power set we construct
   set<int> s;
   // the power set
   set<set<int> > pSet;

   cout << "Enter a number 'n' between 1 and 6: ";
   cin >> n;

   // build the set {1,2,3,...,n}
   for (i=1;i <= n; i++)
      s.insert(i);

   // build the power set
   pSet = powerSet(s);

   // output the number of subsets and the the subsets
   cout << "Number of subsets is " << pSet.size()
        << endl << endl;
   writePowerSet(pSet);

   return 0;
}
```

```
Run:

Enter a number 'n' between 1 and 6: 4
Number of subsets is 16

{}  {1}  {1, 2}  {1, 2, 3}
{1, 2, 3, 4}  {1, 2, 4}  {1, 3}  {1, 3, 4}
{1, 4}  {2}  {2, 3}  {2, 3, 4}
{2, 4}  {3}  {3, 4}  {4}
```

Listing Permutations

A *permutation* of n items $(1, 2, \ldots, n)$ is an ordered arrangement of the items. For $n = 3$, the ordering $(1, 3, 2)$ is a permutation that is different from the orderings $(3, 2, 1), (1, 2, 3)$, and so forth. A classical combinatorics result determines that the number of permutations of n items is $n!$, a fact that is intuitively clear by looking at the individual positions in a permutation. For position 1, there are n choices from the list of n items. For position 2, there are $n - 1$ choices, because one item already occupies position 1. The number of choices decreases by one as we move down the position list. The total number of permutations is the product of the number of choices in each position:

$$\text{numPermuations}(n) = n * n - 1 * n - 2 * \ldots * 2 * 1 = n!$$

Number of choices by position

A more interesting recursive algorithm derives a listing of all the permutations of n items for $n >= 1$. For demonstration purposes, we derive by hand the 24 (4!) permutations of four items. A listing of the different permutations includes column labels corresponding to the first item. The rows are pairs of permutations with the same second item.

1	2	3	4
1234	2134	3124	4123
1243	2143	3142	4132
1324	2314	3214	4213
1342	2341	3241	4231
1423	2413	3412	4312
1432	2431	3421	4321

A hierarchy tree contains the paths that correspond to the permutations. We use the tree in the design of the algorithm. Level 1 contains the nodes for the four items 1, 2, 3, 4. Moving down the tree, we find that the subsequent levels split the nodes into 3 items, 2 items, and 1 item, respectively. The path of colored nodes corresponds to the permutation $(2, 3, 1, 4)$.

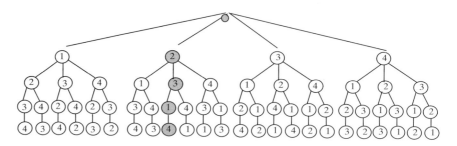

An algorithm for listing all of the permutations follows the paths of the tree. Each permutation is an n-element vector. A series of recursive steps build the $n!$ permutations by assigning values to successive positions in each vector. We start with the vector containing the elements $1, 2, \dots, n$. You can view the vector as the root of the hierarchy tree. Let us follow the process for $n = 4$.

Index 0:   Starting with the initial vector, an iterative process creates four vectors by exchanging each element in the index range $[0, 4)$ with the element at index 0. Level 1 defines the value of the first element of each vector in the hierarchy tree of permutations.

Figure 15-6.03

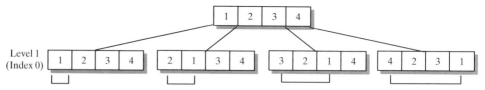

Index 1:   For each of the vectors from the first step (index 0), the algorithm makes a recursive call that creates three new vectors. A scan of the elements in the index range $[1, 4)$ creates a distinct ordering in the new vectors by exchanging each element with the element at index 1. Consider the vectors whose first element is 1 at level 1 of the tree. The three vectors have the value 2, 3, or 4 at index 1.

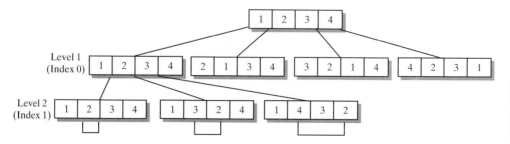

Index 2:   For each of the vectors from the second step (index 1), the algorithm makes a recursive call that creates two new vectors with an
ordering produced by exchanging the elements in the index range
[2,4]. The next figure shows the four new vectors that are derived at
level 3 from the vectors $\{1,3,2,4\}$ and $\{1,4,3,2\}$.

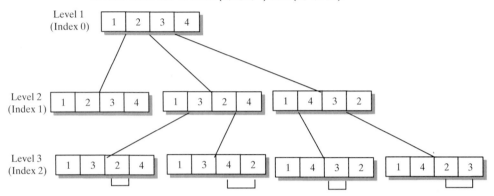

Each exchange at index $n - 2$ (level $n - 1$) creates a unique ordering and completes
the set of all permutations on the n items.

The permute() Function. The permute() function has two value arguments,
for the vector and the index. The recursive step uses a loop to exchange each element in the index range $[index, v.\text{size}())$ with $v[index]$. After each exchange, a recursive call passes the vector and $index + 1$ to permute(). The fact that the vector is a
value argument is critical. The recursive call creates a copy of the vector (permutation) for the next level in the tree. After ordering the first $v.\text{size}() - 1$ elements in
the vector, we reach a stopping condition, because the vector represents a unique
permutation. The function calls writeVector() to display the permutation.

permute():
```
// output the list of all permutations of the
// integer values in the range [index,permList.size())
void permute(vector<int> permList, int index)
{
    int temp, i, vSize = permList.size();

    if (index == vSize-1)
        // display the permutation
        writeVector(permList);
    else
    {
        // find all permutations over the range
        // [index, vSize)
        permute(permList, index+1);

        // exchange permList[index] with permList[i]
        // for i=index+1 to the end of the vector and
```

```
        // find all permutations
        for (i=index+1; i < vSize; i++)
        {
            temp = permList[i];
            permList[i] = permList[index];
            permList[index] = temp;

            permute(permList, index+1);
        }
    }
}
```

PROGRAM 15-4 LISTING PERMUTATIONS

Let us illustrate the permute() function with a program. A prompt asks the user to input the number of items, n. After the creation of the vector $\{1, 2, ..., n\}$, a call to permute() with index 0 begins the recursive process to create and list the permutations. You can locate the function permute() in the header file "d_perm.h"

```
// File: prg15_4.cpp
// the program prompts for an integer n and
// initializes a vector with the values {1,2,3,...,n}.
// it then calls the recursive function permute() that
// displays all n! permutations of the numbers 1 .. n

#include <iostream>
#include <vector>

#include "d_perm.h"  // for permute()

using namespace std;

int main()
{
    int n,i;
    vector<int> permList;

    cout << "Enter the size of the permutation list: ";
    cin >> n;

    for (i=0; i < n; i++)
        permList.push_back(i+1);  // initialize the vector
    cout << endl;

    // start creating permutation ordering at index 0
    permute(permList,0);

    return 0;
}
```

```
Run:
Enter the size of the permutation list: 3
1  2  3
1  3  2
2  1  3
2  3  1
3  1  2
3  2  1
```

DYNAMIC PROGRAMMING   15-3

In Chapter 3, we introduced the Fibonacci sequence. A simple recursive definition describes the sequence. The first two terms are 0 and 1. All subsequent terms are the sum of the two previous values.

$$\textit{Fibonacci Sequence: } 0, 1, 1, 2, 3, 5, 8, 13, 21, 34, 55, \ldots$$

Recursive Definition:

$$\text{fib}(n) = \begin{cases} 0, & n = 0 \\ 1, & n = 1 \\ \text{fib}(n-1) + \text{fib}(n-2), & n \geq 2 \end{cases}$$

The recursive implementation of fib() is a straightforward translation of the definition:

Recursive fib():
```
// recursive computation of the nth Finonacci number
int fib(int n)
{
    if (n <= 1)                     // stopping conditions
        return n;
    else
        return fib(n-1) + fib(n-2);  // recursive step
}
```

The execution of the function is far from straightforward. In Section 3-7, we showed that the number of function calls necessary to evaluate fib(n) increases exponentially. This means that the recursive computation of fib(n) is an exponential algorithm and is so inefficient as to be impractical for even small values of n. The problem stems from all of the redundant recursive calls. For instance, the hierarchy tree in Figure 15-7 illustrates the function calls required to compute fib(5) = 5. The redundancy is evident when you see that the execution makes multiple calls to fib(0) ... fib(3), including five calls to fib(1).

The format for fib() has the structure of a divide-and-conquer algorithm. It lacks, however, the efficiency ordinarily associated with this technique, because it fails to partition the problem into independent subproblems. Recall the design of the

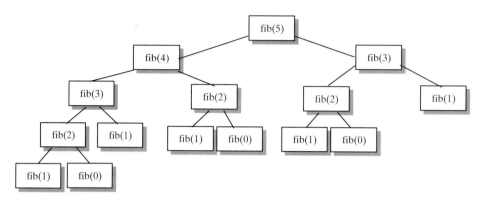

Figure 15-7
Tree of recursive calls for fib(5)

mergesort and quicksort algorithms that partition a list into separate (nonoverlapping) sublists. In general, when a divide-and-conquer strategy results in nonindependent subprograms, a straightforward recursive implementation often produces very poor running time, because the overlap can require a prohibitively large number of redundant calculations and function calls. In this section, we develop a new technique, called *dynamic programming*, that can often address the problem. The technique defines a *container* for storing intermediate results and then directly accesses values in the container rather than recomputing the result. We begin by developing a dynamic programming solution to the Fibonacci sequence problem. This will introduce you to the key concepts. Many important applications involve polynomials of the form $(1 + x)^n$. These mathematical expressions are the sum of terms consisting of binomial coefficients and powers of x. Computing binomial coefficients is an excellent example of dynamic programming and allows us to discover both a top-down and a bottom-up implementation of the technique. We conclude the section by looking at the famous knapsack problem from the field of operations research.

Top-Down Dynamic Programming

A slight change in the algorithm for fib() allows us to reduce redundancy and produce a function with running time $O(n)$. The approach includes, as an argument, a vector that stores the return values from intermediate function calls. The recursive step first checks the vector to see whether the result has already been computed and stored. If so, it directly accesses the value without requiring redundant calculations. If not, the recursive step executes and then adds the result to the vector for later access. The top-down strategy stores values as they are computed in the recursive descent to a stopping condition. Top-down dynamic programming is also referred to as *memorization*.

   Let us see how dynamic programming would affect the calculation of fib(5). In Figure 15-8, the unshaded nodes with numbers below the box have return values

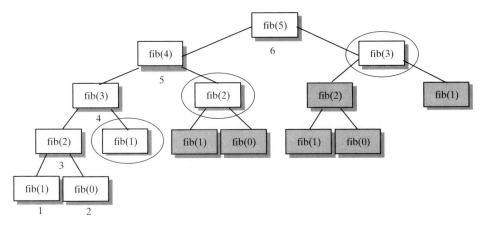

Figure 15-8
Improvement in fibonacci number computation by using dynamic programming

that are stored in the vector. The numbers below the nodes indicate the order of execution. The circled nodes have values that are already in the vector, because they involve calculations that were previously obtained. These values can be extracted from the vector and thus save the redundant calculations represented by the shaded nodes.

The function fibDyn() is the top-down dynamic-programming version for the fib() algorithm. The function fibDyn() includes an integer vector argument with at least $n + 1$ elements, whose initial values are -1. The vector stores intermediate Fibonacci numbers in the index range from 0 to n. The recursive step identifies a nonnegative value in the list as a previously computed result.

fibDyn():

```
// computation of the nth Fibonacci number using top down
// dynamic programming to avoid redundant recursive
// function calls
int fibDyn(int n, vector<int>& fibList)
{
    int fibValue;

    // check for a previously computed result and return
    if (fibList[n] >= 0)
        return fibList[n];

    // otherwise execute the recursive algorithm to obtain the result

    // stopping conditions
    if (n <= 1)
        fibValue = n;
    else
        // recursive step
```

```
         fibValue = fibDyn(n-1, fibList) + fibDyn(n-2, fibList);

    // store the result and return its value
    fibList[n] = fibValue;
    return fibValue;
}
```

☞

Note

The figure shows that $n + 1$ recursive calls reach the bottom of the tree. On the way back up, fibDyn(1), fibDyn(2), ..., fibDyn($n - 2$) return without performing more recursive calls. The number of function calls made to compute fibDyn(n) is $n + 1 + (n - 2) = 2n - 1$, so this algorithm for the computation of the Fibonacci numbers is linear.

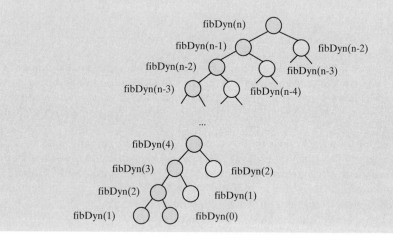

Example 15-2

---

1. We get a dramatic realization of how dynamic programming can improve efficiency by looking at the two Fibonacci functions fib() and fibDyn(), for large values of n. The example shows the number of function calls required to execute fib() and fibDyn() for $n = 20$ and $n = 40$.

```
n = 20:
    fib(20) is 6765
        Number of function calls is 21891
    fibDyn(20) is 6765
        Number of function calls is 39

n = 40:
    fib(40) is 102334155
        Number of function calls is 331160281
    fibDyn(40) is 102334155
        Number of function calls is 79
```

The functions fib() and fibDyn() are in the header file "d_fib.h".

2. If a program makes two or more calls to fibDyn(), the programmer must reset each vector element to -1 before making the next call to the function. The standard library free function fill(), from the file <algorithm>, is convenient for this purpose. The library function takes an iterator range and a value, and assigns the value to each element in the range. The following statements create a vector with 16 elements and use it to compute fibDyn(8) and fibDyn(15):

```
vector<int> fibList(16, -1);            // default value = -1

cout << fibDyn(8, fibList) << endl;     // output: 21
...
// fill each element of fibList with -1
fill(fibList.begin(), fibList.end(), -1);
cout << fibDyn(15, fibList) << endl;    // output: 610
```

Application: Combinations

Recursion finds a variety of applications in combinatorics. One such example is the definition of the function $C(n, k)$, which describes the number of different combinations of n items taken k at a time. The value of the function is defined in terms of factorials:

$$C(n, k) = \frac{n!}{(n - k)!k!} \quad n, k \geq 0 \quad \text{and} \quad n \geq k$$

Computing $C(n, k)$ directly from the equation can run into overflow problems, because factorials grow quickly as n gets large. With a 32-bit integer, $13! > 2^{32}$. We can use a recursive definition for $C(n, k)$ that allows for larger values of n. Let us first give the definition and then see why it makes sense.

$$C(n, k) = \begin{cases} 1, & k = 0 \quad \text{or} \quad k = n \\ n, & k = 1 \\ C(n - 1, k) + C(n - 1, k - 1), & \text{recursive step} \end{cases}$$

To understand the recursive step, consider a simple case with $n = 5$ and $k = 3$. The numbers are small, so we can anticipate the solution by using a little organization to produce an exhaustive list of the $C(5,3) = 10$ different combinations. Assume that the items are A, B, C, D, and E. The combinations are as follows:

{A,B,C}   {A,B,D}   {A,B,E}   {A,C,D}   {A,C,E}
{A,D,E}   {B,C,D}   {B,C,E}   {B,D,E}   {C,D,E}

We can get the same results by using a divide-and-conquer strategy that splits the problem into two simpler subproblems. We simplify the problem by removing item A from the collection, leaving the $n - 1 = 4$ items B, C, D, and E.

Subproblem 1:   Form all possible combinations from the four items taken three at a time. While these combinations do not include item *A*, they are, nevertheless, part of the *C*(5,3) combinations.

List 1:   (B,C,D)   (B,C,E)   (B,D,E)   (C,D,E)

Subproblem 2:   Form all possible combinations from the four items taken two at a time.

List 2:   (B,C)   (B,D)   (B,E)   (C,D)   (C,E)   (D,E)

Each of the six combinations is one item short of our desired three-element collection. We remedy this by adding item *A* to each group.

List 2 (with A):   (A,B,C)   (A,B,D)   (A,B,E)   (A,C,D)   (A,C,E)   (A,D,E)

The number of items in list 1 is $C(4,3) = 4$, and the number of items in list 2 is $C(4,2) = 6$. In general, we can evaluate $C(n,k)$ by adding the total number in list 1 $(C(n-1,k))$ and the total number in list 2 $(C(n-1, k-1))$:

```
C(n,k) = C(n-1, k) + C(n-1, k-1);   // recursive step
```

The stopping conditions consist of several extreme cases that can be directly evaluated. If $k = 0$ or $k = n$, there is only one combination: the empty collection, or the collection with all *n* items, respectively. If $k = 1$, then each of the *n* singleton collections consisting of one of the *n* items is a valid combination. By combining the stopping conditions and the recursive step, we can implement the function comm(n,k) = $C(n,k)$.

comm():
```
// recursive computation of C(n,k)
int comm(int n, int k)
{
    if (n == k || k == 0)                        // stopping condition
        return 1;
    else if (k == 1)
        return n;                                // stopping condition
    else
        return comm(n-1,k) + comm(n-1,k-1);   // recursive step
}
```

Like evaluating the recursive function fib(), evaluating comm() involves redundant calculations. For instance, computing comm(50,6) = 15890700 requires 3,813,767 function calls. A top-down dynamic programming implementation of comm() stores intermediate results in the matrix argument commMat, which has $n + 1$ rows and $k + 1$ columns, where commMat[i][j] is the solution for $C(i,j)$. The recursive function commDyn() checks on whether the value commMat[n][k] is nonzero. If so, it uses the matrix element as its return value.

commDyn():
```
// computation of C(n,k) using top down dynamic programming
// to avoid redundant recursive function calls
```

```
int commDyn(int n, int k, matrix<int>& commMat)
{
    int returnValue;

    // check if value is already computed
    if (commMat[n][k] != 0)
        return commMat[n][k];

    if (n == k || k == 0)
        returnValue = 1;
    else if (k == 1)
        returnValue = n;
    else
        // carry out the recursive step
        returnValue = commDyn(n-1,k,commMat) +
                      commDyn(n-1,k-1,commMat);

    // before returning, assign value to the matrix
    commMat[n][k] = returnValue;

    return returnValue;
}
```

Computing $C(50,6)$ by using commDyn() requires only 441 function calls, a little better than the almost four million calls required by comm().

Bottom-Up Dynamic Programming

Top-down dynamic programming moves through the recursive process and stores results as the algorithm computes them. This allows function calls to return without performing additional recursive calls. An alternative strategy, called *bottom-up dynamic programming*, evaluates a function by computing all the function values in order, starting at the lowest level and using previously computed values at each step to compute the current value. Let us apply this strategy to the function $C(n,k)$ by initializing a matrix with the solutions for $C(i,j)$, where $0 \leq i \leq n$ and $0 \leq j \leq n$. This involves computing a series of sequences:

$$
\begin{array}{lllll}
i = 0: & C(0,0) & & & \\
i = 1: & C(1,0) & C(1,1) & & \\
i = 2: & C(2,0) & C(2,1) & C(2,2) & \\
\cdots & & & & \\
i = n: & C(n,0) & C(n,1) & C(n,2) \cdots C(n,n-1) & C(n,n)
\end{array}
$$

The formula $C(n,k) = C(n-1,k) + C(n-1,k-1)$ indicates that we can compute intermediate values for entries in row i by using results from row $i - 1$. Table 15-1 displays the matrix for $n = 6$. We refer to the resulting grid as *Pascal's Triangle*.

In the table, note that the first entry ($C(i,0)$) and last entry ($C(i,i)$) in each row is a 1. The intermediate entries $C(i,j)$ for $1 \leq j \leq i - 1$ are the sum of entries from the previous row. We use this fact to give a bottom-up implementation for the function commDynB() that computes $C(n,k)$.

TABLE 15-1 PASCAL'S TRIANGLE FOR $N = 6$

i	$C(i,0)$	$C(i,1)$	$C(i,2)$	$C(i,)$	$C(i,4)$	$C(i,5)$	$C(i,6)$
0	1						
1	1	1					
2	1	2	1				
3	1	3	3	1			
4	1	4	6	4	1		
5	1	5	10	10	5	1	
6	1	6	15	20	15	6	1

commDynB():

```
// computation of C(n,k) using bottom up dynamic programming
int commDynB(int n, int k)
{
    // store all precomputed values. form Pascal's Triangle
    matrix<int> commMat(n+1,n+1);
    int i;

    // set row 0
    commMat[0][0] = 1;
    for (i = 1; i <= n; i++)
    {
        // set first and last entry to 1
        commMat[i][0] = 1;
        commMat[i][i] = 1;

        // use terms from row i-1
        for (int j = 1; j < i; j++)
            commMat[i][j] = commMat[i-1][j-1] + commMat[i-1][j];

    }
    // return value of the function
    return commMat[n][k];
}
```

The functions comm(), commDyn(), and commDynB() that compute $C(n,k)$ are in the header file "d_comm.h".

Knapsack Problem

Operations research is a branch of mathematics that solves, among other things, optimization problems. One such example is the knapsack problem, which can illustrate a dynamic programming solution. We are given a knapsack to hold a set of items that have specified sizes and values. The knapsack has a limited capacity, measured in volume. The problem is to find a subset of objects that will fit into the knapsack and provide the maximum value. The problem is a prototype for many important applications. Transport companies want to load a truck, freight car, or ship with cargo that returns a maximum profit. A contestant who wins a shopping spree wants to load the cart with items that represent the maximum value.

There are several versions of the knapsack problem. One version allows us to split items into fractional parts to fill up all of the space in the knapsack. For instance, a camper could cut a slab of bacon into small pieces or take only part of a bag of rice if necessary. The 0/1 version of the knapsack problem is more interesting. In this case, we are given a choice of selecting (1) or rejecting (0) an item from the collection. We explore this version.

A simple, but impractical, solution to the knapsack problem involves an exhaustive evaluation of every possible subset of items. Like finding all subsets in the power set, the algorithm has exponential running time $O(2^n)$. There is a dynamic programming solution that applies the *principle of optimality* to each item in the collection. The principle of optimality states that, no matter what the first decision, the remaining decisions must be optimal with respect to any state in the algorithm that results from the first decision.

Assume that we want to fill the knapsack from among a list of n items. Using bottom-up dynamic programming, we compute the values for an integer matrix maxValueMat. The row and column dimensions for the matrix are $n + 1$ and $capacity + 1$, respectively. The entry maxValueMat[i][cap] is the maximum value of a subset of items chosen from $\{item_1, item_2, \ldots, item_i\}$, where the total size of the elements in the subset is $\leq cap$. Assume that each item is a record with a value field and a size field. The mathematical definition of maxValueMat[i][cap] is

$$\max \sum_{j=1}^{i} a_j \, item_j.value \quad \text{subject to} \quad \sum_{j=1}^{i} a_j \, item_j.size \leq cap$$

where $a_j = 1$ if $item_j$ is in the subset and $a_j = 0$ if $item_j$ is not in the subset. After we build the matrix, matValueMat[n][$capacity$] is the solution to the problem.

Let us develop the algorithm to compute the matrix, using the following five items for a knapsack with capacity 12.

item	size	value
1	2	1
2	3	4
3	4	3
4	5	6
5	6	8

We will build the first three rows of the matrix. This is sufficient to develop the key elements of the algorithm. We start with $item_1$, having size 2 and value 1. The task is to assign values to maxValueMat[1][cap], where $0 \leq cap \leq capacity$. This is easy. Only when $cap >= 2$ do we have enough space for $item_1$. Placing it in the knapsack produces the value 1. The first row of the matrix becomes

0	1	2	3	4	5	6	7	8	9	10	11	12
row 1	0	0	1	1	1	1	1	1	1	1	1	1	1

$$\text{Contents of row 1}\quad \begin{cases} 0 & cap < 2 \\ item_1.value & cap \geq 2 \end{cases}$$

Row 2 in the matrix looks at the set $\{item_1, item_2\}$, where $item_2$ has size 3 and value 4. Again, $cap < 2$ is too small to hold any item. With $cap = 2$, there is room for only $item_1$ with value 1. We begin to understand the algorithm when $cap = 3$. Because $item_2.size = 3 \leq cap$, we can place $item_2$ in the knapsack. The effect is to create a value of 4 and leave no additional space in the knapsack ($cap - item_2.size = 0$). The new value 4 is an improvement over the value 1 from maxValueMat[1][3]. A similar analysis applies to $cap = 4$, except that placing $item_2$ in the knapsack leaves 1 unit of unused space. For $cap \geq 5$, the knapsack has room for both items, for a total value of 5.

	0	1	2	3	4	5	6	7	8	9	10	11	12
row 1	0	0	1	1	1	1	1	1	1	1	1	1	1
row 2	0	0	1	4	4	5	5	5	5	5	5	5	5

$$\text{Contents of row 2}\quad \begin{cases} 0 & cap < 2 \\ item_1.value & cap = 2 \\ item_2.value & 3 \leq cap \leq 4 \\ item\;.value + item_2.value & cap \geq 5 \end{cases}$$

For entries in row 3, we look at values created by filling the knapsack with any subset of the first three items. Row 2 contains the maximum value for each capacity when only the first two items are used. We need to determine whether adding the third item with size 4 and value 3 will improve the situation. When cap = 4, there is sufficient space to use the item. The effect is to produce a value of 3 and leave no additional space for any other item ($cap - item_3.size = 0$). From row 2, we already have a value of 4 by using only the first two items (maxValueMat[2][4] = 4). Adding $item_3$ does not improve the maximum value for the capacity, and so we retain the existing value:

```
maxValueMat[3][4] = maxValueMat[2][4] = 4
```

With $cap = 6$, adding $item_3$ contributes the value 3 and leaves two units of space, sufficient to add $item_1$. The total

$$item_3.value + maxValueMat[2][2] = 4$$

is not an improvement on the existing maximum value of 5 (maxValueMat[2][6]), which we derived in row 2 by using only the first two items, and so we again retain the value from row 2:

```
maxValueMat[3][6] = maxValueMat[2][6] = 5
```

When $cap = 7$, adding $item_3$ leaves 3 units of additional space. Using the maximum value for capacity 3 (maxValueMat[2][3] = 4) from row 2, we have a new value, 7, which is greater than the value, 5, from using only the first two items:

```
maxValueMat[3][7] = item₃.value + maxValueMat[2][7 - item₃.size]
                  = item₃.value + maxValueMat[2][3]
                  = 3 + 4
                  = 7
```

After completing all of the entries in row 3, we have

	0	1	2	3	4	5	6	7	8	9	10	11	12
row 1	0	0	1	1	1	1	1	1	1	1	1	1	1
row 2	0	0	1	4	4	5	5	5	5	5	5	5	5
row 3	0	0	1	4	4	5	5	7	7	8	8	8	8

Contents of row 3
$$\begin{cases} 0 & cap < 2 \\ item_1.value & cap = 2 \\ item_2.value & 3 \le cap \le 4 \\ item_1.value + item_2.value & 5 \le cap \le 6 \\ item_2.value + item_3.value & 7 \le cap \le 8 \\ item_1.value + item_2.value + item_3.value & cap \ge 9 \end{cases}$$

You have now seen all of the elements of the algorithm. In general, for row i, computing maxValueMat[i][cap] involves determining whether $item_i$ should be part of the subset of items from set $\{item_1, item_2, \ldots, item_i\}$, which produces the maximum value for the specified capacity. First, test whether the new item fits in the space:

```
if (cap - itemᵢ.space >= 0)
    <see if we can increase the value for the capacity cap>
```

Adding $item_i$ provides value, but reduces the space available to store items from the list $\{item_1, \ldots, item_{i-1}\}$. If we use $item_i$, the remaining capacity is ($cap - item_i.size$), and the maximum value for that capacity is the matrix entry maxValueMat[$i - 1$][$cap - item_i.size$]. The sum of this value and $item_i.value$ is the best we can do for this capacity by adding $item_i$. On the other hand, the entry maxValueMat[$i - 1$][cap] is the maximum value obtained from using only the elements $\{item_1, \ldots, item_{i-1}\}$. A test compares the effect of adding $item_i$ with the value that does not use $item_i$. The matrix entry is the larger value.

```
testMax = item_i.value + maxValueMat[i-1][cap - item_i.size];

// if new item increases value, use new value for matrix entry
if (testMax > maxValueMat[i-1][cap])
   maxValueMat[i][cap] = testMax;
else
   // retain maximum value provided by previous items
   maxValueMat[i][cap] = maxValueMat[i-1][cap];
```

In the next section, we declare the knapsack class and include the private member function buildMaxValueMat(), which builds the matrix by using the dynamic-programming algorithm. We include a complete listing of the function in the class implementation.

Designing the Knapsack Class We use object technology to design a solution for the knapsack problem. The class *item* describes the items in the knapsack. Two integer data members define the size and value of an object. To simplify access, we declare the members public. A constructor requires two arguments that have default value 0.

```
class item
{
   public:
      int size, value;
      item(int s = 0, int v = 0);
};
```

The knapsack class includes the vector itemList and the matrix maxValueMat as data members, along with integer variables for the capacity and number of items. The constructor takes the list and capacity as arguments and initializes the corresponding data members. The utility function buildMaxValueMat() implements the dynamic-programming version of the knapsack algorithm. For output, the function displayKnapsack() displays the maximum value and includes a list of the items that fit into the knapsack and produce the value. The listing also notes the amount of unused space. For diagnostic purposes, we include the function displayMaxValueMat(), which outputs the matrix.

| CLASS knapsack | Declaration | "d_ksack.h" |

```
class knapsack
{
   public:
      knapsack(vector<item>& v, int cap);
         // constructor. assigns v as the item list and calls
         // buildMaxValueMat() to implement the knapsack algorithm

      void displayKnapsack();
         // displays the capacity, the maximum value, the unused
         // space, and a list of the items with their size and value
```

```
    void displayMaxValueMat();
        // output the row/column values in the matrix
  private:
    int capacity;
    int numItems;
    vector<item> itemList;
    matrix<int> maxValueMat;


    void buildMaxValueMat();
        // implements the knapsack algorithm
};
```

Building the Value Matrix   We build the [row][column] entries in maxValue-Mat one element at a time. To simplify the calculations, all of the entries in row 0 have value 0. The outer loop uses the control variable *i* to scan the items in the row range, 1 ... numItems. An inner loop uses the control variable *cap* to compute the column values in the range 0 ... capacity. For each entry [*i*][*cap*], we use the value from the previous row to initialize the maximum value:

```
maxValueMat[i][cap] = maxValueMat[i−1][cap];
```

The effect is to assume that itemList[*i*] will not be added to knapsack. We override this assumption only after successfully completing a series of tests. The first test checks whether itemList[*i*] fits in the knapsack (*cap* − itemList[*i*].*size* >=0). A second test determines whether adding itemList[*i*] and sacrificing the space it occupies would produce a greater value. If so, the algorithm assigns the new value to the matrix entry.

buildMaxValueMat():

```
    void knapsack::buildMaxValueMat()
    {
        int i, cap, testMax;

        // compute entries in the matrix
        for (i = 1; i <= numItems; i++)
            for (cap = 1; cap <= capacity; cap++)
            {
                // keep the same max value by default
                maxValueMat[i][cap] = maxValueMat[i-1][cap];

                // test if itemList[i] fits into the knapsack
                if (cap-itemList[i].size >= 0)
                {
                    // test if maximum value increases
                    testMax = maxValueMat[i-1][cap-itemList[i].size] +
                            itemList[i].value;
                    // if yes, assign new max
                    if (testMax > maxValueMat[i-1][cap])
```

```
                                     maxValueMat[i][cap] = testMax;
                           }
                   }
           }
```

Identifying the Items: The matrix maxValueMat not only determines the maximum value for the specified capacity; it also provides information that will allow us to determine the items that fill the knapsack. The maximum value is max-ValueMat[numItems][*capacity*], which is an entry in the last row of the matrix. Starting with this entry, we can work back through the matrix to discover the other items in the knapsack. To understand the algorithm, recall how we built the matrix. In row i, maxValueMat[i][*cap*] is not equal to maxValueMat[$i-1$][*cap*] only if adding item-List[i] increases the value. This becomes the criterion for determining whether item-List[i] is in the knapsack.

Let us return to the our example and look at maxValueMat for capacity 12. Function displayMaxValueMat() provides the listing. The solution to the problem is maxValueMat[5][12] = 14.

```
Maximum value matrix for capacity 12
          1    2    3    4    5    6    7    8    9   10   11   12
1         0    1    1    1    1    1    1    1    1    1    1    1
2         0    1    4    4    5    5    5    5    5    5    5    5
3         0    1    4    4    5    5    7    7    8    8    8    8
4         0    1    4    4    6    6    7   10   10   11   11   13
5         0    1    4    4    6    8    8   10   12   12   14   14
```

Because maxValueMat[4][12] = 13, itemList[5] with size 6 and value 8 is in the knapsack. There are 6 units of unused space (*cap* − itemList[5].*size*) remaining, which can be filled from the sublist itemList[1] . . . itemList[4]. Working backwards, maxValueMat[4][6] indicates that the sublist produces the value 6. Now maxValue-Mat[3][6] = 5, so the test criterion indicates that itemList[4] with size 5 and value 6 is in the knapsack. Only one unit of additional space remains. Because the values maxValueMat [i][1] are identically 0 for rows 3, 2, and 1, we conclude that none of the corresponding items is in the knapsack. This fact is obvious; no item would fit into 1 unit of space. We conclude that the knapsack holds itemList[5] and item-List[4] and has one unit of unused space.

The function displayKnapsack() implements this algorithm. A loop scans the list of items in descending order and identifies an item in the knapsack when its presence adds value. The listing of the items in the knapsack includes their size and value.

displayKnapsack():
```
  void knapsack::displayKnapsack()
  {
     int i = numItems, cap = capacity;
     cout << endl << "Capacity:    " << capacity << "  Value:    "
          << maxValueMat[numItems][capacity] << endl << endl;
     cout << "Contents:    " << endl << endl;
     // scan list of items in reverse order
```

```
    while (i > 0)
    {
       // if values in successive rows are not equal,
       // itemList[i] is part of the solution
       if (maxValueMat[i][cap] != maxValueMat[i-1][cap])
       {
          cout << "   item" << i << '(' << itemList[i].size
               << ',' << itemList[i].value << ')' << endl;
          // look for maximum value remaining space
          cap -= itemList[i].size;
       }
       i--;
    }
    cout << "   Unused capacity:   " << cap << endl;
}
```

PROGRAM 15-5   FILLING THE KNAPSACK

We have provided the knapsack class, whose functions implement the knapsack algorithm. Let us put it all together in a program that defines a vector with the five items used in our examples. A prompt asks the user to enter a capacity. After using the value to create the knapsack object ks, the program calls displayKnapsack() to describe the solution.

```
// File: prg15_5.cpp
// the program demonstrates the dynamic-programming solution
// to the knapsack problem. the vector itemList contains
// five items, each with a specified size and value. after
// prompting for the capacity of the knapsack, the program
// declares a knapsack object for the items and the desired
// capacity. calling displayKnapsack() outputs the maximum
// value for the capacity, the contents of the knapsack, and
// the unused capacity

#include <iostream>
#include <vector>

#include "d_ksack.h"
int main()
{
   item itemArr[] = {item(2,1), item(3,4), item(4,3),
                     item(5,6), item(6,8)};
   int arrSize = sizeof(itemArr)/sizeof(item);
   vector<item> itemList(itemArr, itemArr+arrSize);
   int capacity;

   cout << "Enter the capacity: ";
   cin >> capacity;
   // create a knapsack object
   knapsack ks(itemList,capacity);
```

```
// ks.displayMaxValueMat();        // add for diagnostics
// display the solution
ks.displayKnapsack();
cout << endl << endl;

return 0;
}
```

```
Run 1:

Enter the capacity: 12

Capacity: 12   Value: 14

Contents:

    item5(6,8)
    item4(5,6)
    Unused capacity: 1

Run 2:

Enter the capacity: 19

Capacity: 19   Value: 21

Contents:

    item5(6,8)
    item4(5,6)
    item3(4,3)
    item2(3,4)
    Unused capacity: 1
```

Evaluating the Knapsack Problem Solution. The running time of our bottom-up dynamic-programming solution to the knapsack problem is $O(nC)$, where n is the number of items and C is the capacity. This follows directly from the fact that the algorithm builds a matrix of size $(n + 1) \times (C + 1)$ that has $O(nC)$ elements. The amount of computation depends critically on C. For instance, if $C = n$, the algorithm is $O(n^2)$, but if $C = 2^n$, the algorithm has running time $O(n2^n)$.

15-4   BACKTRACKING: THE EIGHT-QUEENS PROBLEM

Some recursive algorithms use the principle of *backtracking*. The principle applies when we are faced with a problem that requires a number of steps, with decisions at each step. In an effort to obtain a final solution, we move step by step, creating a partial solution that appears to be consistent with the requirements of the final solution. If, at any step, we create a partial solution that is inconsistent with a final solution, we backtrack one or more steps to the most recent consistent partial solution. At times, backtracking could entail one step forward and several steps backward. The eight-queens problem provides a classic example of backtracking.

On a chessboard, the queen is the most mobile piece. It can move horizontally in its row, vertically in its column, and along both diagonals. The problem attempts to position eight queens on a chessboard in such a way that no two can attack each other. To understand what "attack" means, think of a chessboard as an 8-by-8 grid with cells labeled as a (*row, col*) pair. One queen can attack another queen along a row (horizontally), along a column (vertically), or along the diagonals slope-up and slope-down. In Figure 15-9, the queen in cell (4,2) is vulnerable to a row attack by the queen in cell (4,6), to a column attack by the queen in cell (7,2), and to diagonal attacks by the queens in cells (2,0) and (1,5) respectively.

For a queen at cell (row_i, col_j), a second queen can launch a fatal attack from the following positions.

By row:	cells (row_i, col), where $0 \le col \le 7$
By column:	cells (row, col_j) where $0 \le row \le 7$
By slope-up:	all cells (*row, col*) that satisfy the equation
	$col + row = col_j + row_i, 0 \le row \le 7, 0 \le col \le 7$
By slope-down:	all cells (*row, col*) that satisfy the equation
	$col - row = col_j - row_i, 0 \le row \le 7, 0 \le col \le 7$

Example 15-3

Use Figure 15-9 with the queen in cell (4,2), with *row* = 4, *col* = 2. The locations for an attacking queen are as follows:

row: positions (4, *col*), where $0 \le col \le 7$ Cells: (4,0) (4,1) (4,3) (4,4)
                                                                                          (4,5) (4,6) (4,7)

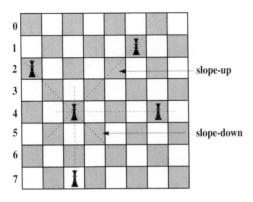

Figure 15-9
Attacking Queens for the Queen in Cell (4,2).

column:	positions $(row, 2)$, where $0 \leq row \leq 7$	Cells: (0,2) (1,2) (2,2) (3,2) (5,2) (6,2) (7,2)
slope-up:	positions (row, col) where $col + row = 6$	Cells: (6,0) (5,1) (3,3) (2,4) (1,5) (0,6)
slope-down:	positions (row, col) where $col - row = -2$	Cells: (2,0) (3,1) (5,3) (6,4) (7,5)

Problem Analysis

One could solve the eight-queens problem by a pure guess method, which looks at all possible arrangements of 8 queens on the 64-cell board. The total number of such arrangements is the combination of 64 cells taken 8 at a time:

$$C(64,8) = 4,426,165,368$$

A more structured approach uses a backtracking strategy that does not require our positioning all of the queens on the board at one time. We build a solution column by column, starting with column 0. In each succeeding column, *col*, we move from row 0 to row 1, and so forth, until we find a "safe" cell where the queen cannot be attacked by any of the other queens already positioned on the board in columns 0 ..col-1. Using this strategy, we observe the board after placing five queens in "safe" cells in columns 0 through 4 (Figure 15-10).

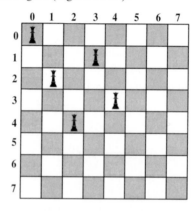

Figure 15-10
Location of Queens in Columns 0–4

The approach fails in column 5, because placing a queen in any of the eight rows leaves it vulnerable to attack by one of the five queens on the board. Table 15-2 identifies an attacking queen for each of the rows in column 5. In case two or more queens can attack, we select the queen from the smallest column.

TABLE 15-2   ATTACKING QUEENS FOR COLUMN 5

Row	Cell in Column 5	Attacking Queen	Row	Cell in Column 5	Attacking Queen
0	(0,5)	(0,0)	4	(4,5)	(4,2)
1	(1,5)	(4,2)	5	(5,5)	(0,0)
2	(2,5)	(2,1)	6	(6,5)	(2,1)
3	(3,5)	(1,3)	7	(7,5)	(4,2)

When the strategy hits a dead end, we backtrack one column and reposition the queen for that column. In our example, the backtracking algorithm undoes the successful step in column 4, which placed a queen in cell (3,4). At this point, we pick up the strategy for column 4 by looking at positions (4,4), (5,4), and so forth until we locate the next safe cell. Figure 15-11 illustrates that cells (4,4), (5,4), and (6,4) are open to attack and that a safe position first occurs at cell (7,4). After placing the a queen at that location, we move forward to column 5 and continue the algorithm.

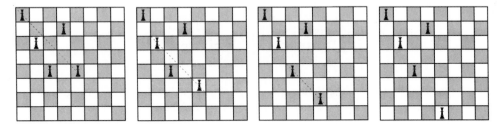

Figure 15-11
Backtracking to Column 4

Placing the queen in cell (7,4) is a short-lived success, because it does not permit any queen to be safely positioned in column 5. You can verify this from the figure. Faced with another dead end in column 5, we backtrack to column 4 and discover that this is also a dead end; there are no more rows in which to position a queen. The algorithm returns to column 3 and looks to reposition the queen that currently occupies cell (1,3). The strategy picks up by looking at row 2, then row 3, and so forth. You get the idea. Lest you think column 5 will always be a dead end, Figure 15-12 gives a partial solution that locates nonattacking queens in the first six columns.

With the previous discussion as background, let us leave the problem analysis phase of the eight-queens problem and move to program design.

Program Design

A solution to the problem involves finding a row for each of the columns from 0 to 7 so that a queen in cell (*row, col*) is safe from attack. An eight-element integer vector, queenList, stores the rows. A vector index corresponds to a column. Hence, queenList[*col*] = *row* indicates that a queen occupies cell (*row, col*) = (queenList[*col*], *col*).

```
// queen located in cell (queenList[col],col) for 0 <= col < 8
vector<int> queenList(8);
```

For the six queens in Figure 15-12, the values in the vector are as follows:

```
queenList[0] = 0        queenList[1] = 2
queenList[2] = 4        queenList[3] = 6
queenList[4] = 1        queenList[5] = 3
```

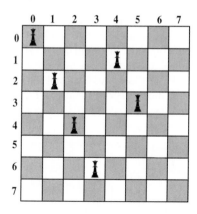

Figure 15-12
Eight-Queens Solution
through Column 5

The eight-queens algorithm begins at index *col* = 0 and assigns a value (*row*) to queenList[0]. For each successive index *col* > 0, the algorithm looks for a row so that a queen in cell (*row*, *col*) is not vulnerable to attack by any queen in cell (queenList[*i*], *i*), where 0 <= *i* < *col*. The row becomes the value queenList[*col*].

Recursive placeQueens() Function. The recursive function placeQueens() takes the vector queenList and an index *col* as arguments. The function assumes that the vector represents a partial solution to the eight-queens problem, with nonattacking queens in columns 0 to *col*−1. In column *col*, placeQueens() scans rows 0, 1, ..., 7 and searches for the first row that identifies cell (*row*, *col*) as a safe location for the next queen. If no row is found, the function returns *false*. On the other hand, if a row exists, the function assigns the value to queenList[*col*] and makes a recursive call with argument *col*+1 in an attempt to place a nonattacking queen in the next column. If the recursive call returns *false*, we know that the current partial solution (for columns from 1 through *col*) will not extend further, to the next column. The cell (*row*, *col*) might be a safe location, but it precludes finding a safe location in a subsequent column and so placeQueens() picks up the search for a safe location at index *row*+1. If *row*+1 == 8, the algorithm has exhausted all the rows, and the function returns *false*. This is the backtracking strategy for the algorithm. The stopping condition occurs when *col* =8, a column past the end of the board.

As part of its implementation, placeQueen() calls the Boolean function safeLocation(), which takes row and column indices and the vector queenList as arguments. The function determines whether a queen in the specified (*row*, *col*) cell is free from attack by the queens in the columns from 0 to *col*−1 identified by the vector. The function defines a cell (qRow, qCol) = (queenList[qCol], qCol) for each element in queenList and compares it with (*row*,*col*) to see whether the two cells lie on the same row, the same column, or diagonals (slope-up or slope-down).

safeLocation():
```
// non-attacking queens in columns 0 to col-1 ?
bool safeLocation(int row, int col, const vector<int>& queenList)
{
    int qRow, qCol;
```

```
    for (qCol = 0; qCol < col; qCol++)  // check previous columns only
    {
        qRow = queenList[qCol];
        if (qRow == row)                    // same row
            return false;
        else if (qCol == col)               // same col
            return false;
        // can they attack on a diagonal?
        else if(qCol-qRow == col-row || qCol+qRow == col+row)
            return false;
    }
    return true;
}
```

The function placeQueens() takes the current elements in queenList as a partial solution to the eight-queens problem and attempts to extend the partial solution to a complete solution. If this is possible, the function returns *true*; otherwise, it returns *false*.

placeQueens():
```
    // place a queen in columns col through 7
    bool placeQueens(vector<int>& queenList, int col)
    {
        int row;
        bool foundLocation;

        if (col == 8)  // stopping condition
            foundLocation = true;
        else
        {
            foundLocation = false;// start with row 0
            row = 0;
            while (row < 8 && !foundLocation)
            {
                // check whether cell (row, col) is safe; if so,
                // assign row to queenList and call placeQueens()
                // for next column; otherwise, go to the next row
                if (safeLocation(row,col,queenList) == true)
                {
                    // found good location
                    queenList[col] = row;

                    // recursive step. try to place queens in columns col+1
                    // through 7
                    foundLocation = placeQueens(queenList,col+1);
                    if (!foundLocation)
                        // use next row since current one does not lead
                        // to a solution
```

```
                           row++;
                   }
                   else
                       // current row fails. go to the next row
                       row++;

           } // end while
       }
       // pass success or failure back to previous col
       return foundLocation;
   }
```

The placeQueens() function attempts to find a solution to the eight-queens problem for the columns from *col* through 7, assuming that a partial solution exists in columns from 0 through *col*−1. We can choose any starting row in column 0 and attempt to extend it to a solution. We use the function queens() to launch the recursive process. The function takes the queenList array and a row as arguments and positions the first queen in (*row*,0). A call to the recursive function placeQueens() determines whether queens can be placed in the columns from 1 through 7. The main program calls this function with the starting row number for the queen in column 0.

queens():
```
       // try to find a solution to the 8-Queens problem starting
       // with a queen at (row,0)
       bool queens(vector<int>& queenList, int row)
       {
           // place first queen at (row,0)
           queenList[0] = row;
           // locate remaining queens in columns 1 through 7
           if (placeQueens(queenList, 1))
               return true;

               return false;
       }
```

The functions safeLocation(), placeQueens(), and queens() are located in the header file "d_queens.h" of the software supplement.

Displaying A Chessboard

In order to display a solution to the eight-queens problem, we create a class, called chessBoard, that draws an 8 × 8 grid of characters corresponding to the 64 cells on the board. A 'Q' designates the presence of a queen and a '-' designates an empty cell. The chessBoard class declares an 8-by-8 Boolean matrix, called *board*, as its private data member. Use the member function setQueens() and its vector argument queenList to place queens on the board. The function first "clears the board" by setting all of the values in the data member to *false*. The vector queenList identifies the location of each queen as a (*row*, *col*) pair. The function setQueens() sets the corresponding pair in the matrix to *true*. For instance, if queenList[*i*] = *k*, then the (*row*, *col*) pair (*k*, *i*) has a queen and board [*k*][*i*] is set to *true*. The member function draw-Board() displays the cells of the chessboard as a rectangular grid. Depending on the value of an entry in the matrix, the corresponding cell on the chessboard has the letter 'Q' or the symbol '-'. If board [*i*] [*j*] is *true*, drawBoard() places a 'Q' is cell (*i*, *j*); otherwise it places a '-'. To clear the board, call clearBoard(), which resets all of the Boolean values to *false*. Figure 15-13 illustrates the relationship between the matrix and the corresponding chessboard.

The following is a declaration of the chessBoard class. You can find the implementation in the header file "d_queens.h".

CLASS chessBoard	Declaration	"d_queens.h"

```
class chessBoard
{
   public:
      chessBoard();
         // default constructor

      void setQueens(const vector<int>& queenList);
         // set queens on board at cells (queenList[col], col)
         // 0 <= col < 8

      void clearBoard();
         // clear the board

      void drawBoard() const;
         // draw the board using symbols 'Q' or '-'
   private:
      // simulates chess board
      matrix<bool> board;
};
```

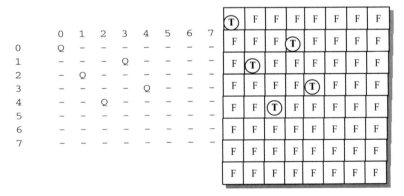

Figure 15-13
Chessboard and Boolean Matrix

Illustrating The Eight-Queens Problem

We are now in a position to illustrate the eight-queens problem. The recursive function placeQueens() carries out the backtracking algorithm by creating an eight-element array, queenList. Each index in the array corresponds to a column on the chessboard. The value queenList[*col*] is the row containing the nonattacking queen. The program declares a chessboard object, *board*, and passes the location of the queens on the board by using the function setQueens(). A call to drawBoard() displays the solution.

PROGRAM 15-6   ILLUSTRATING THE EIGHTQUEENS PROBLEM
_____

Let us find different solutions for the eight-queens problem. The following program asks the user to enter a row that positions the queen in column 0. With that input value, the program solves the eight-queens problem and outputs the solution.

```cpp
// File: prg15_6.cpp
// the program solves the eight-queens problem. it prompts the user for
// the starting row for the queen in column 0 and calls the recursive
// function queens() to determine whether there is a solution.
// if there is a solution, the position of the queens is passed to
// the chessboard object, board, and a call to its drawBoard() function
// shows the placement of the queens

#include <iostream>

#include "d_queens.h"

using namespace std;

int main ()
{
   int row;
   vector<int> queenList(8);
   chessBoard board;

  // enter a starting row for queen in column 0
   cout << "Enter row for queen in column 0: ";
   cin >> row;
   cout << endl;

   // see if there is a solution
   if (queens(queenList, row))
   {
      board.setQueens(queenList);
      // display the solution
      board.drawBoard();
   }
```

```
    else
        cout << "No solution" << endl;

    return 0;
}
```

```
RUN 1:

Enter row for queen in column 0: 2

    0 1 2 3 4 5 6 7
0   - Q - - - - - -
1   - - - - - Q - -
2   Q - - - - - - -
3   - - - - - - Q -
4   - - - Q - - - -
5   - - - - - - - Q
6   - - Q - - - - -
7   - - - - Q - - -


Run 2:

Enter row for queen in column 0: 5

    0 1 2 3 4 5 6 7
0   - Q - - - - - -
1   - - - Q - - - -
2   - - - - - Q - -
3   - - - - - - - Q
4   - - Q - - - - -
5   Q - - - - - - -
6   - - - - - - Q -
7   - - - - Q - - -
```

The file "d_gqueen.h" in the software supplement contains a version of the chessBoard class that implements a graphical version of drawBoard(). The program "prg15_6g.cpp" in Chapter 15 of the software supplement is a version of Program 15-6 that draws the eight-queens solution graphically.

CHAPTER SUMMARY

- A divide-and-conquer algorithm splits a problem into subproblems and works on each part separately. The algorithm collects the results of its work on the smaller pieces to form the solution of the whole problem. Section 15-1 illustrates this technique by discussing an algorithm that draws a ruler. A more substantial example of the divide-and-conquer strategy is the mergesort algorithm, according to which we split the range of elements to be sorted in half, sort each half, and then merge the sorted sublists together. The algorithm has running time $O(n \log_2 n)$, but requires the use of an auxiliary vector in order to perform the merge steps. The quicksort algorithm uses the divide-and-conquer strategy to perform in-place sorting. It uses a partitioning strategy that finds the final location of a pivot element within an interval [*first*,*last*). The pivot splits the interval into two parts, [*first*, pivotIndex), [pivotIndex, *last*). All elements in the lower interval have values $\geq$ *pivot*, and all elements in the upper interval have values $\leq$ pivot. The algorithm has average-case running time $O(n \log_2 n)$ and is the choice for most sorting applications. Quicksort does have a worst case of $O(n^2)$, but it is highly unlikely to occur in practice. The partitioning strategy of quicksort very easily provides a linear algorithm that finds the kth-largest element of a vector. A primary application of the algorithm is locating the median of n numbers.

- Recursion often applies to problems in combinatorics. Section 15-2 solves two such problems. A set of n elements has 2^n subsets, and the set of those subsets is called the power set. By using a divide-and-conquer strategy that finds the power set after removing an element from the set and then adds the element back into each subset, we implement a function that computes the power set. The section also uses recursion to list all the $n!$ permutations of the integers from 1 through n. The success of this algorithm depends on the passing of a vector *by value* to the recursive function.

- Section 15-3 provides an overview of dynamic programming. We illustrate top-down dynamic programming by using a vector to store Fibonacci numbers as a recursive function computes them. This avoids costly redundant recursive calls and leads to an $O(n)$ algorithm that computes the nth Fibonacci number. The recursive function that does not apply dynamic programming has exponential running time. The section also applies top-down dynamic programming to improve the recursive computation for $C(n,k)$, the combinations of n things taken k at a time. Another dynamic-programming strategy is bottom-up dynamic programming. It evaluates a function by computing all the function values in order, starting at the lowest level and using previously computed values at each step to compute the current value. We illustrate this technique by again visiting the problem of computing combinations. Dynamic programming often finds uses in optimization problems in operations research and other fields. Such problems are very well illustrated by the 0/1 knapsack problem. The section develops the knapsack class that solves the problem by using bottom-up dynamic programming.

- A backtracking algorithm finds a consistent partial solution to a problem and then tries to extend the partial solution to a complete solution by executing a recursive step. If the recursive step fails to find a solution, it returns to the previous state, and the algorithm tries again from a new, consistent partial solution. A backtracking algorithm takes "1 step forward and n steps backward."

Such algorithms have application for solving advanced problems in graph theory and operations research. The eight-queens problem provides a very interesting and relatively simple example of a backtracking algorithm. Section 15-4 solves this problem by developing a series of free functions and the class chessBoard.

CLASSES AND LIBRARIES IN THE CHAPTER

Name	Header File
eight-queens graphical solution	d_queens.h
eight-queens solution	d_queens.h
comm(), commDyn(), commDynB()	d_comm.h
fib(), fibDyn()	d_fib.h
knapsack	d_ksack.h
matrix	d_matrix.h
mergesort and quicksort algorithms	d_sort.h
permute()	d_perm.h
powerSet(), writePowerSet()	d_pset.h
randomNumber	d_random.h
timer	d_timer.h
writeContainer() function	d_util.h

REVIEW EXERCISES

1. Give the first six terms ($n = 0, 1, \ldots, 5$) in the numerical sequence generated by the recursive function f().

```
int f(int n)
{
   if (n == 0)
      return 1;
   else if(n == 1)
      return 2;
   else
      return 2*f(n-2) + f(n-1);
}
```

2. Use dynamic programming to rewrite f() in Review Exercise 15-1.

3. Plot on a graph the number of recursive calls used to compute fib(n) and fibDyn(n) for $n = 1, 3, 5, \ldots, 11$. Obtain your data by writing a program that adds an integer reference argument *count* to each function. Prior to calling fib() or fibDyn() in the main program, set *count* to 0. In each function, increment *count* as the first executable statement. After returning from the function, plot count as the y-value for x-value n.

4. Implement the template-based function max() by using a recursive divide-and-conquer strategy. The function takes a vector and two indices defining an index range. Partition the list about the midpoint, and then recursively call max() to obtain the maximum value in each sublist. The maximum value for the entire list is the larger of the two return values.

```
template <typename T>
int max(const vector<T>& v, int first, int last);
```

5. Using the binary tree of sublists for the mergesort in Section 15-1 as a model, create the tree for the max() function in Review Exercise 15-4. Assume that the list contains the elements {25, 7, 19, 48, 12, 56, 30, 21, 28}. Each of the child nodes is the half-list partitioned about the midpoint. Record the return value for the list below the parent node.

6. Develop a recursive function that counts the number of n-digit binary numbers that do not have two 1's in a row.

```
int no2Ones(int n);
```

For instance, if $n = 4$, the number of n-digit binary numbers that do not have two 1's in a row is 8. The numbers are 0000, 0001, 0010, 0100, 1000, 0101, 1001, and 1010.

7. Use top-down dynamic programming to improve the function no2Ones() in Review Exercise 15-6. Include a vector argument whose initial values are 0 that stores the intermediate results. The size of the vector should be at least $n + 1$.

```
int no2OnesDyn(int n, vector<int>& v);
```

8. Use bottom-up dynamic programming to modify the function no2Ones() in Review Exercise 15-6.

```
int no2OnesDynB(int n);
```

9. Vector v contains the integer values {55, 70, 40, 25, 50, 45, 30, 85, 20, 75}. List the elements after pass 0 of the quicksort algorithm.

10. Consider the problem of placing six nonattacking queens on a 6 × 6 chessboard. Use backtracking strategy with paper and pencil to place the queens, assuming that the queen in the first column begins in row 1 (the second row).

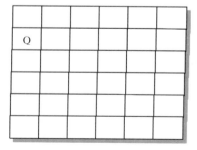

11. Trace the execution of the recursive function prefixEval(), which evaluates an arithmetic
expression defined with prefix notation. Assume that the string is

```
string strExp = "+ 2 * - 4 / 7 3 8"
```

prefixEval():
```
int prefixEval(const string& s, int& i)
{
   int value;

   if (i != s.length())
   {
      while (s[i] == ' ')
         i++;

      switch(s[i])
      {
         case '+':   i++; value = prefixEval(s, i) +
                                  prefixEval(s,i); break;
         case '-':   i++; value = prefixEval(s, i) -
                                  prefixEval(s,i); break;
         case '*':   i++; value = prefixEval(s, i) *
                                  prefixEval(s,i); break;
         case '/':   i++; value = prefixEval(s, i) /
                                  prefixEval(s,i); break;
         default:    value = int(s[i] - '0'); i++; break;
      }
   }
   else
      value = 0;

   return value;
}
```

Answers To Review Exercises

1. 1 2 4 8 16 32 64
2. Add a vector argument with initial values 0 that stores the intermediate results for f().
The vector must have size at least $n+1$. Check v to determine whether f() is already evaluated. If so, return the result from v. Otherwise, compute f(), and assign the result to v before returning the value.

```
int f(int n, vector<int>& v)
{
   int returnValue;
   if (v[n] != 0)
      return v[n];
```

```
        if (n == 0)
            returnValue = 1;
        else if(n == 1)
            returnValue = 2;
        else
            returnValue = 2*f(n-2,v) + f(n-1,v);

        v[n] = returnValue;

        return returnValue;
    }
```

3.

Effect of Dynamic Programming

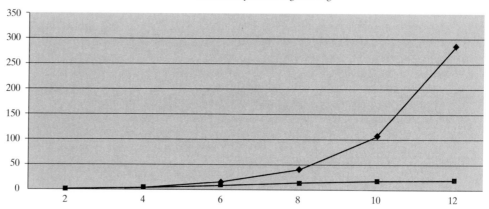

4. The stopping condition occurs when the index range contains one element ($last - first == 1$).

```
template <typename T>
int max(const vector<T>& v, int first, int last)
{
    int maxL, maxR, mid;

    if (last - first == 1)
        return v[first];
    else
    {
        mid = (first + last)/2;
        maxL = max(v, first, mid);
        maxR = max(v, mid, last);
        return (maxL >= maxR) ? maxL : maxR;
    }
}
```

5.

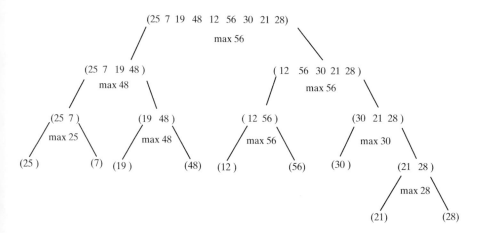

6. Assume that $n \geq 3$. If the binary representation of n begins with 0, the number of n-digit binary numbers that do not begin with 1 is no2Ones($n - 1$). If the binary representation of n begins with 1, the next digit must be 0, and the number returned by the function must be no2Ones($n - 2$). If $n = 2$, there are four possible binary representations: 00, 01, 10, 11; three of these do not have two successive 1's. Since no2Ones(1) = 2, we have the following recursive solution to the problem:

```
int no2Ones(int n)
{
    if (n == 1)
        return 2;
    else if (n == 2)
        return 3;
    else
        return no2Ones(n-1) + no2Ones(n-2);
}
```

7.
```
int no2OnesDyn(int n, vector<int>& v)
{
    int fval;

    if (v[n] != 0)
        return v[n];

    if (n == 1)
        fval = 2;
    else if (n == 2)
        fval = 3;
    else
        fval = no2Ones(n-1, v) + no2Ones(n-2, v);
```

```
        v[n] = fval;

        return fval;
    }
```

8.
```
int no2OnesDynB(int n)
   {
      // save two previous values using oneback
      // and twoback. fvalue will be the return
      // value
      int oneback, twoback, fvalue, i;

      if (n == 1)
         fvalue = 2;  // no2OnesDynB(1) = 2
      else if (n == 2)
         fvalue = 3;  // no2OnesDynB(2) = 3
      else
      {
         // initialize two previous values
         oneback = 3;
         twoback = 2;
         // form sums through i = n
         i = 3;
         while (i <= n)
         {
            // compute new value from 2 previous values
            fvalue = oneback + twoback;
            // change two previous values
            twoback = oneback;
            oneback = fvalue;
            i++;
         }
      }

      return fvalue;
   }
```

9. $\{30, 20, 40, 25, 45, 55, 50, 85, 70, 75\}$

10.

			Q		
Q					
				Q	
	Q				
					Q
		Q			

11. Value = 18

WRITTEN EXERCISES

12. Trace the function f() and indicate its action on the list object *alist*.

```
template <typename T>
void f(list<T>& alist, list<T>::iterator iter)
{
    if(iter != alist.end())
    {
        alist.push_front(*iter);
        alist.erase(iter++);
        f(alist,iter);
    }
}
```

13. In Section 3-2, we introduced an iterative version of the binary search that takes a vector, an index range, and a target and scans a list, looking for a match. The function returns the index of the match (index *last* if no match occurs). Implement a recursive version of the binary search algorithm.

```
template <typename T>
int binSearch(const vector<T> v, int first, int last, T target);
```

14. Trace the recursive function f().

```
int f(int n)
{
    if (n == 1 || n == 2)
        return 1;
    else
        return 2*f(n-1) + 3*f(n-2);
}
```

(a) Give the results for   **(i)** $f(4)$ **(ii)** $f(6)$ **(iii)** $f(1)$

(b) Using the model for the function fib() in Section 15-3, draw the "calling tree" (binary tree) that lists the recursive calls made during the execution of $f(7)$.

(c) Suppose that we use dynamic programming to store intermediate results and that in the recursive step the function call $f(n − 1)$ is made before the function call $f(n − 2)$. From part (b), circle all of the recursive calls (nodes) having values that are already in the vector. Shade nodes that represent redundant calculations that are saved by dynamic programming.

(d) Implement fDyn() as an alternative version for f(), using a vector and dynamic programming to store and access intermediate calculations.

```
int fDyn(int n, vector<int>& v);
```

15. Trace the following program and give the return value for each function call:

```
int h(int b, int n)
{
    if (n == 0)
        return 1;
    else
        return(b * h(b,n-1));
}
```

(a) What are values for h(), assuming function calls as follows:
   (i) h(5, 3)   (ii) h(3, 5)   (iii) h(2, 2)
(b) Describe the action of the function. What is the function in the <cmath> library that performs a similar calculation?

16. Use the quicksort algorithm to sort vector v. During each pass, list all exchanges of a pair of elements in the lower and upper sublist. List the ordering of the elements after each pass.

```
int arr[] = {790, 175, 284, 581, 374, 799, 852, 685, 486, 333};
int arrSize = sizeof(arr)/sizeof(int);
vector<int> v(arr, arr+arrSize);
```

17. In the quicksort algorithm, assume that the first element in the list, $v[first]$, is chosen as the pivot instead of the value at the midpoint of the list. What initial ordering of the elements would produce a worst-case running time?

18. We have considered the following sorting algorithms in this book:

   Heap, Insertion, Merge, Quicksort, Radix, Selection

For each sort, give the average and worst case running time and the space requirements, and make some additional comments about the efficiency of the algorithm. The additional comments may specify how probable the worst case is, the number of interchanges performed by the algorithm, and special situations that make the algorithm run faster.

19. A sorting algorithm is *stable* if two data items having the same value are not rearranged with respect to each other at any stage of the algorithm. For instance, in the five-element vector

   5_1 55   12 5_2 33

a stable sorting algorithm guarantees that the final ordering is

   5_1 5_2 12   33   55

Classify each of the algorithms in Written Exercise 15-18 as to their stability.

20. The following is a recursive definition for $f(a,b)$, where a and b are integer values with $a >= b$.

$$f(a,b) = \begin{cases} a - b & \text{if } a == 0 \text{ or } b == 0 \\ f(a - 1, b) + f(a, b - 1) \end{cases}$$

(a) Write a recursive function that implements f().
(b) Display the "calling tree" that lists the function calls required to execute $f(3,2)$.
(c) Implement a function fDyn() that uses dynamic programming and a matrix *mat* to store intermediate values. If $a \le b$, then $f(a,b) \ge 0$ Use the value $mat[a][b] = -1$ to indicate that $f(a,b)$ has not been computed. The dimension of *mat* must be at least $(a+1) \times (b+1)$.

21. The *generalized Fibonacci numbers* of order $k \ge 2$ are given by

$$F_n^k = \begin{cases} 0, & 0 \le n < k - 1 \\ 1, & n = k - 1 \\ \sum_{i=1}^{k} F_{n-i}^k, & n \ge k \end{cases}$$

For instance, the generalized Fibonacci numbers of order 2 are $\{0, 1, 1, 2, 3, 5, 8, 13, 21, 34, \ldots\}$, and those of order 3 are $\{0, 0, 1, 1, 2, 4, 7, 13, 24, 44, \ldots\}$.

(a) Implement a function, fibg(), that computes the generalized Fibonacci numbers of order k.

```
int fibg(int n, int k);
```

(b) Implement an iterative function, fibgDyn(), that finds the generalized Fibonacci numbers of order k by using bottom-up dynamic programming. Hint: Declare a vector of size $n+1$ to store intermediate values.

(c) What do you think is the running time for each algorithm? Hint: The running time for fibgDyn() depends on n and k.

22. For the knapsack problem, assume the following statements:

```
item itemArr[] = {item(3,1), item(2,1), item(5,8), item(3, 5)};
int arrSize = sizeof(itemArr)/sizeof(item);
vector<item> itemList(itemArr, itemArr+arrSize);

knapsack ks(itemList,12);
```

Build and display the matrix maxValueMat that determines the solution. What are the contents of the knapsack?

23. For two sequences of objects $\{s_0, s_1, s_2, \ldots, s_{n-1}\}$ and $\{t_0, t_1, t_2, \ldots, t_{m-1}\}$, with n and m elements, respectively, an *interleaving* is a permutation of $n + m$ objects such that within the permutation each original set retains the same relative ordering. That is, s_0 comes before s_1, s_1 before s_2, t_3 before t_4, etc. For instance, assume that $s = \{ab\}$ and $t = \{12\}$. The set of all interleavings of s and t contain six permutations:

　　ab12　a1b2　　a12b　　1ab2　　1a2b　　12ab

The permutations that appear in the set of interleavings have the relative-order restriction, so the set of all interleavings is a subset of the set of all permutations. There are $(m+n)!$ permutations of $m + n$ objects, and there are $(m+n)!/m!n!$ *interleavings*. For instance, the number of interleavings in the example is

　　$(2 + 2)!/2!2! = 4!/2*2 = 24/4 = 6$

A recursive function, interleavings(), outputs all the interleavings for the characters contained in two strings s and t. Assume that

　　$s = \text{“}s_0 s_1 s_2 \ldots s_{n-1}\text{”}$　　　and　　　$t = \text{“}t_0 t_1 t_2 \ldots t_{m-1}\text{”}$

The design of the function uses the next set of recursive steps and stopping conditions. During execution, i is the index of the current character we are looking at in s, and j is the index of the current character in t. As we apply the recursive step, the remaining characters that we must examine in the strings become smaller, so eventually we reach a stopping condition.

Recursive Steps:
　　Generate all interleavings of the remaining characters that begin with s_i:
　　...earlier characters ...'s_i' interleavings(“$s_{i+1}s_{i+2}\ldots s_{n-1}$”,“$t_j t_{j+1} t_{j+2} \ldots t_{m-1}$”)

　　Generate all interleavings of the remaining characters that begin with t_j:
　　...earlier characters ...'t_j' interleavings(“$s_i s_{i+1}s_{i+2}\ldots s_{n-1}$”, “$t_{j+1}t_{j+2}\ldots t_{m-1}$”)

Stopping Conditions:

> If string s is empty, add all remaining characters of t onto the end of the inter-leaving

> If string t is empty, add all remaining characters of s onto the end of the inter-leaving.

Implement the function interleavings().

```
// output all interleavings of the characters in s and t.
// i is the current position in s, and j is the current
// position in t. ci is the interleaving
void interleavings(const string& s, int i,
                   const string& t,  int j, string& ci);
```

PROGRAMMING EXERCISES

24. Use the binSearch() function from Written Exercise 15-13 in a program that initializes a vector with the elements from array arr.

```
int arr[] = {13, 18, 22, 30, 37, 42, 50, 57, 68, 81, 88};
int arrSize = sizeof(arr)/sizeof(int);
```

Prompt the user to input a target value and search the entire list, looking for a match. Use the return index in an output statement that determines whether a match occurs. Run the program with three different target values, exactly two of which are in the array.

25. In Written Exercise 15-14(d), you implemented the function fDyn(). Write a program that uses a loop to call the function for values $n = 1, 2, ..., 20$. Output the value for *n* and the return value on separate lines. Use the STL algorithm fill() to initialize the vector elements with value 0 before the second and subsequent calls to fDyn().

26. Implement a modified version of the quicksort algorithm, called quicksort15(), that repeatedly partitions a list into smaller sublists until the size of a sublist is less than or equal to 15. Handle the case of a one- or two-element sublist as before; however, if the sublist size is between 3 and 15, call insertionSort() to order the sublist. For this purpose, use the following version of insertionSort() from "d_sort.h":

```
// sort the elements of a vector of type T in the range
// [first, last) using insertion sort
template <typename T>
void insertionSort(vector<T>& v, int first, int last);
```

The prototype for quicksort15() is as follows:

```
template <typename T>
void quicksort15(vector<T>& v, int first, int last);
```

In a program, initialize a vector with 250 random integer values in the range from 0 to 999. Output the first 10 and the last 10 values in the vector after applying quicksort15() to order the vector.

27. In the quicksort algorithm, we chose the value at index *mid* = (*first*+*last*)/2 as the pivot. A modified version of the algorithm, called the Median-3 quicksort, takes the elements at indices *first*, *mid*, and *last*-1 and reorders (exchanges) them so that they are in order. The quicksort process begins by using $v[mid]$ as the pivot and exchanging the value with $v[first+1]$. The scan with index scanUp can then begin at index $first+2$, and scanDown begins at index $last - 2$. Implement the function quicksortMed_3(),which uses the median-3 algorithm. Include the following functions in your solution:

```
// exchange the values of x and y
template <typename T>
void exchange(T& x, T& y);


// define mid = (first + last)/2. put v[first], v[mid] and v[last-1]
// in order  v[first] <= v[mid] <= v[last-1], swap pivot v[mid]
// with v[first+1] and return pivot
template <typename T>
T& median3(vector<T>& v, int first, int last);


// using the value from median3() as the pivot,
// locate the pivot in its final location so all elements
// to its left are <= to its value and all elements to the
// right are >= to its value. return the index of the pivot

template <typename T>
int pivotIndexMed_3(vector<T>& v, int first, int last);


// median-3 quicksort of v over range [first, last)
template <typename T>
void quicksortMed_3(vector<T>& v, int first, int last);
```

In a program, initialize a vector with 250 random integer values in the range from 0 to 999. Output the first 10 and the last 10 values in the vector after applying quicksortMed_3() to order the vector.

28. This exercise uses the results of Written Exercise 15-21. Write a program that prompts for integer values n and k and outputs the generalized Fibonacci numbers of order k for $i = 0, 1, 2, ..., n$ by using the recursive function fibg(). Output the same sequence by using the iterative function fibgDyn().

29. This exercise uses the results of Written Exercise 15-23. Write a program that prompts for two strings, s and t, and outputs the set of all interleavings of the characters in s with those in t.

30. The function $(x + 1)^n$ has the expansion

$$(x+1)^n = C_{n,n}x^n + C_{n,n-1}x^{n-1} + C_{n,n-2}x^{n-2} + ... + C_{n,2}x^2 + C_{n,1}x^1 + C_{n,0}x^0$$

where $C_{n,k}$ is the combination of n items taken k at a time. Using the function commDynB() from Section 15-3, write a program that inputs n and outputs the terms of $(1+x)^n$. Represent x^k by using the notation $x\hat{\ }k$ In your output, omit the coefficient of the leading term (1), do not include $x\hat{\ }0$, and output x instead of $x\hat{\ }1$. For instance, your output for $n = 2$ should be

$$(1 \times x)\hat{\ }2 = x\hat{\ }2 + 2x + 1$$

31. The problem of finding the root of a real-valued function occurs frequently in mathematics, engineering, and the sciences. If $f(x)$ is a function, a root r of f() is a real number

such that $f(r) = 0$. In some few cases, roots can be computed by using an algebraic formula. For instance, all roots of the quadratic equation $f(x) = ax^2 + bx + c$ are given by the quadratic formula

$$r = \frac{-b \pm \sqrt{b^2 - 4ac}}{2a}$$

In general, however, there is no formula, and the roots must be found by using numerical methods.

If $f(a)$ and $f(b)$ are of opposite sign $(f(a) * f(b) < 0)$, and f is well behaved, then there is a root r of $f()$ between a and b.

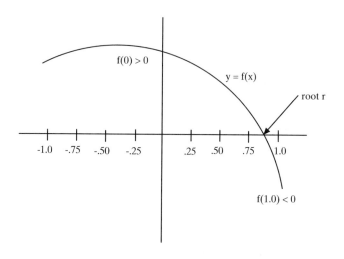

We define the bisection method as follows:

Let $m = (a + b)/2.0$ be the midpoint of the interval $a < x < b$. If $f(m)$ is 0.0, then $r = m$ is a root. If not, then either (1) $f(a)$ and $f(m)$ have opposite signs $(f(a)*f(m) < 0)$ or (2) $f(m)$ and $f(b)$ have opposite signs $(f(m)*f(b) < 0)$. If $f(m)*f(b) < 0$, then the root r lies in the interval $m < x < b$; otherwise, it lies in the interval $a < x < m$. In the figure, $m = (0.0 + 1.0)/2 = .5, f(.5) > 0$, and $f(1.0) < 0$, so there is a root in the interval $.5 < x < 1.0$. Perform the same process over with and the new interval, whose length is half the length of the original. Continue this process until the interval has become small enough or until we have found an exact root.

Write a recursive function

```
double bisect(double f(double x),
              double a, double b, double precision);
```

that finds the root of a function $f(x)$ passed as an argument. Terminate bisect() if $f(m)$ is 0.0 or if the length of the subinterval (a,b) is less than the precision. In either case, return m as the value of the function.

(a) Find the root of $f(x) = x^3 - 2x - 3$ that lies between 1 and 2. Use precision $= 10^{-15}$, and output the root using 10 decimal places.

(b) Let the function

```
double balance(double principal, double interest,
               int nmonths, double payment);
```

compute and return the balance after paying simple interest on the given principal with monthly interest for *nmonths* months. Use the bisection method to compute the payment on a $150,000 loan at 10% interest per year over 25 years.

32. Generalize the solution to the eight-queens problem to the *n*-queens problem, where the board is of size $n \times n$. Place the implementation for the software in the header file "nqueens.h". Position a queen in column 0, and attempt to place the other $n-1$ queens so that all *n* queens are nonattacking. Write a program that inputs n and a starting row in column 0 and determines whether there is a solution to the *n*-queens problem. If a solution exists, output the board that shows the placement of the queens.

33. Let S be a set of positive integers $\{x_0, x_1, x_2, \dots, x_{n-1}\}$ and *total* be a positive integer. The *subset-sum* problem asks whether there exists a subset of S that adds up exactly to the target value total. Here is an example:

$S=\{1, 4, 16, 64, 256, 1040, 1041, 1093, 1284, 1344\}$, total $= 3754$:
One solution: $\{1, 4, 16, 64, 1041, 1284, 1344\}$
Another solution: $\{1, 16, 64, 256, 1040, 1093, 1284\}$

The following is a description of a backtracking solution:

subsetsum():
```
// find a subset of the positive integers v[index], v[index+1], ...,
// v[v.size()-1[ that sums to total > 0. if subset[i] == true,
// v[i] is in the sum, 0 <= i < v.size()
bool subsetsum(const vector<int>& v, vector<bool>& subset,
               int total, int index);
```

Example:
> Input
> > $v = \{6, 26, 3, 15, 12, 8, 5, 18, 6, 25\}$
> > *total v* $= 28$, *index* $= 0$
> > *subset* $= \{false, false, false, false, false, false, false, false, false, false\}$
>
> Output
> > Return value *true*.
> > *subset* $= \{true, false, true, false, false, true, true, false, true, false\}$
> > $28 = 6 + 3 + 8 + 5 + 6$

Code outline:
```
bool subsetsum(const vector<int>& v, vector<bool>& subset,
               int total, int index)
{
   bool result;

   if (total == 0)
```

```
                result = true;      // success

          else if (index >= v.size() || total < 0)
              return false;         // failure

          else
          {
              subset[index] = true;

              < try using v[index] and moving forward. if this
                fails, do not use the current number and move
                forward>
          }

          return result;

      }
```

(a) When no solution exists that contains v[*index*], why can we move forward and try v[*index*+1] without considering the values v[0] to v[*index*−1]? Why is this a back-tracking algorithm?

(b) Implement subsetsum() in C++.

(c) Write a program that declares the following objects:

```
      int arr[] = {6,26,3,15,12,8,5,18,6,25};
      int arrSize = sizeof(arr)/sizeof(int);
      vector<int> v(arr,arr+arrSize);
      vector<bool> subset(arrSize);
```

Using subsetsum(), determine whether there is a subset of *v* that adds to *i* for all numbers $1 \le i \le 50$. For each success, output one such subset.

PROGRAMMING PROJECT

34. This problem is known as the *knight's tour*. You are given an $n \times n$ chessboard on which a knight (allowed to move according to the rules of chess only) is placed on the board with specified initial coordinates. The problem is to compute a tour of n^2-1 moves (if there is such a tour) in which the knight visits every square on the board once and once only. You are to write a program that solves the problem by using a backtracking approach.

NOTES:

1. Represent the board by a two-dimensional $n \times n$ matrix, all of whose initial values are 0.

```
      matrix<int> board(n,n,0);
```

Keep track of the order in which the knight reaches the squares by using the following convention:

board[i][j] = 0:   *square* (*i,j*) has not been visited
board[i][j] = k: *square* (*i,j*) is the kth square visited in the tour, where
                   $1<=k<=n^2$.

2. We must find a way to represent the list of possible moves from the current position. Given a particular position (i,j), there are eight potential candidates for the
knight's next move. Starting on the right and going counterclockwise, these moves
are as follows:

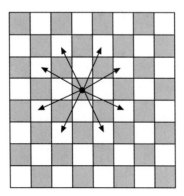

```
(i+2, j+1), (i+1, j+2), (i-1, j+2), (i-2, j+1),
(i-2, j-1), (i-1, j-2), (i+1, j-2), (i+2, j-1)
```

We can conveniently represent the preceding eight moves by using two arrays:

```
int dx[] = {2,1,-1,-2,-2,-1,1,2},
    dy[] = {1,2,2,1,-1,-2,-2,-1};
```

The knight at position (i,j) can move to position (u, v), where
$u=i+dx[m]$, $v=j+dy[m]$, for $0 \le m \le 7$.

Here is an outline of a function, knight(), that solves the problem:

```
// computes a tour of (n*n)-1 moves (if there is one) such
// that the knight visits every square on the board once
// and once only. the matrix object board is of size n x n.
// the values of (i,j) when the function is first called are
// the starting square for the knight, and k = 1. as the search
// for a solution progresses, the current position of the knight
// is (i,j). if (i,j) is in the tour, it will be the kth square
// visited by the knight. we record this information by
// assigning board[i][j] = k. if the square (i,j) is not on
// the tour, board[i][j] = 0. the search for a solution is
// successful if k reaches n*n, and knight() returns true;
// otherwise, knight() returns false to indicate that a tour
// does not exist
bool knight(matrix<int>& board, int k, int i, int j)
{
    bool result;
    int u, v, m;
    const int n = board.rows();
    static int dx[] = {2,1,-1,-2,-2,-1,1,2},
```

```
            dy[] = {1,2,2,1,-1,-2,-2,-1};

<assume this square will be move k>

if (k == n*n)
   // success! return true
   result = true;
else
{
   // assume result is false
   result = false;
   m = 0;

   // look at all 8 possible moves and see if one
   // leads to a solution
   while ( <no solution yet and there are moves to check>)
   {
       <use dx, dy to determine (u,v)>

       <if board[u][v] is on the board and has not been
       visited, try to find a solution by moving there>

       m++;
   }

   <if this position (i,j) did not work out, assign
   0 to board[i][j] and return false. we'll come


   return result;
}
```

Write a program that prompts for the board size and the starting position for the knight and determines whether there is a tour. If a tour exists, output the board, showing the sequence of moves.

Note: This algorithm performs an exhaustive search. For some positions, particularly near the edge of the board, the number of function calls the algorithm makes is very large. Here are some data concerning the amount of work the algorithm does:

n	Starting point	Number of function calls	Starting point	Number of function calls
5	(0,0)	8840	(0,3)	1,829,421 (no solution)
6	(0,0)	248,169	(0,3)	1,129,763,556

◆

Graphs

OBJECTIVES

- To understand the structure of both nonweighted and weighted graphs or digrafts.
- To master basic graph terminology.
- To become familiar with the graph API and to develop the ability to use it to build, update, and output a graph.
- To understand that the two means of implementing graphs are through the use either of adjacency lists or of an adjacency matrix.
- To master the overall design of the graph class, with particular emphasis on the vertex map and the vector of vertex information.
- To see the implementation of the breadth-first search, using a queue.
- To study the recursive depth-first visit from a starting vertex.
- To understand the depth-first search of a graph as a sequence of recursive depth-first visit operations.
- To understand the application of the depth-first search in determining whether a graph is acyclic.
- To understand the application of the depth-first search in performing a topological sort of a directed acyclic graph.
- To see how to use the depth-first search in computing the strong components of a graph.
- To study the use of the breadth-first search algorithm in computing the minimum distance from a starting to an ending vertex.
- To understand Dijkstra's algorithm for a weighted graph that computes a path from a starting to an ending vertex, the sum of whose edge weights is a minimum.
- To understand the structure of a spanning tree and to study Prim's algorithm for the computation of the minimum spanning tree for a connected, undirected graph.

OUTLINE

This chapter concludes our study of data structures by introducing graphs, which are nonlinear structures consisting of vertices and of edges that connect the vertices. Graphs are an important topic in finite mathematics, with applications in computer science and other areas of study. A graph is the most general container structure in the book, because the structure allows arbitrary relationships among the vertices. With structures like vectors and lists, there is a linear relationship among the objects, defined by their positions in the container. Trees are hierarchical structures in which the relationships flow from parent to child. In a graph, any vertex is potentially connected to any other vertex. Because of this generality, our study of graphs begins in Section 16-1 with terminology that describes the relationship among vertices and edges. As with other data structures, we provide a graph class, with iterators. Sections 16-2 and 16-3 discuss the class design and implementation.

The importance of graphs lies in their applications. Understanding these applications involves learning a variety of traversal algorithms. In Section 16-4, we introduce the depth-first and breadth-first search of vertices in a graph. Like tree-scanning algorithms, these traversals are the foundation for most of the graph algorithms. We use these traversal strategies to develop several classical graph algorithms. In Section 16-5, we use the traversal strategies to develop criteria for cycles in a graph and a method for identifying strong components. Many applications use directed acyclic graphs to determine precedence between data events. For instance, a graph might reflect course prerequisites, and we could want to list an order in which courses can be taken. We discuss the topological sort that provides this list in Section 16-5.

In Section 16-6, we introduce optimization algorithms. These include a shortest-path algorithm that determines the minimum number of edges that must be traversed in moving from a starting to an ending vertex. In contrast, when we associate a weight to the edges, Dijkstra's minimum-path algorithm determines a path from a starting to an ending vertex with minimum weight. The section concludes by presenting Prim's minimal-spanning-tree algorithm, which has applications to such problems as using the minimum amount of wire to make electrical connections in a building. There are many other graph algorithms, such as the maximum-flow problem for a network. An in-depth study of the many and far-reaching graph algorithms lies beyond the scope of this book.

GRAPH TERMINOLOGY   16-1

A graph consists of a set of *vertices* V, along with a set of *edges* E that connect pairs of vertices. An edge $e = (v_i, v_j)$ connects vertices v_i and v_j. A *self-loop* is an edge that connects a vertex to itself. We assume that none of our graphs have self-loops.

$$\text{Vertices} = \{v_1, v_2, v_3, \ldots, v_m\}$$
$$\text{Edges} = \{e_1, e_2, e_3, \ldots, e_n\}$$

For example, the buildings and the connecting walkways in the Civic Center form a graph. In Figure 16-1, the vertices consist of three government facilities, an opera, and library.

A *subgraph* is a subset of the vertices and edges. For instance, the government buildings along with their connecting walkways, form a subgraph. Two vertices in a graph are *adjacent* (*neighbors*) if there is an edge connecting the vertices. The term path describes a more general notion of connection. Two vertices v_s and v_e lie on a path, provided that there is a sequence of vertices beginning with v_s and ending with v_e such that each successive pair in the list is adjacent. The *length of the path* is the number of edges connecting the vertices.

$$P(v_s, v_e): v_s = v_0, v_1, v_2, \ldots, v_{(n-1)}v_n = v_e \qquad (v_i, v_{i+1}) \text{ are adjacent } 0 \le i \le n\text{-}1$$

$$\text{length } P(v_s, v_e) = n$$

For instance, in Figure 16-1, the Library and the Human Services building are adjacent vertices, whereas the Library and the Opera are not adjacent. These non-government building lie, however, on a path of length 3.

$$P(\text{Library, Opera}) = \text{Library - Human Services - City Hall - Opera.}$$

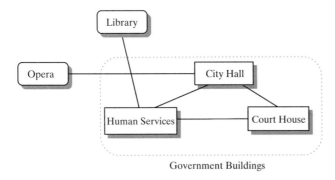

Government Buildings

Figure 16-1
Civic Center Graph

The path is a simple path provided each vertex occurs only once. If a path doubles back so that the same vertex appears twice in the list, the subpath that begins and ends at the duplicate vertex is a cycle. The Civic Center walkways allow a person to travel directly between Human Services and the Library along the edge (Human Services - Library) or to follow the path Human Services - City Hall - Court House - Human Services - Library. The subpath Human Services - City Hall - Court House - Human Services is a cycle.

The existence of a path indicates that two vertices are connected. In terms of access, we say one vertex is reachable from the other. The terminology can be extended to the entire graph. A graph is *connected* if each pair of vertices have a path between them. The Civic Center is an example. A *complete graph* is a connected graph in which each pair of vertices are linked by an edge. Figure 16-2 displays examples of connected, disconnected, and complete graphs.

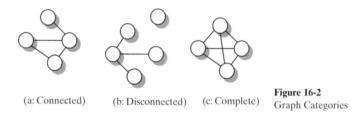

(a: Connected)   (b: Disconnected)   (c: Complete)

Figure 16-2
Graph Categories

Directed Graphs

Up to this point, we have described an edge as a pair that connects two vertices. Movement between vertices can occur in either direction. Edges of this type are called *undirected edges* or *arcs*, and the corresponding graphs are called *undirected graphs*. For many applications, such as a network system or a city map that includes one-way streets, we want the edges of the graph to have a direction representing flow. For these graphs, an edge is an ordered pair $E = (v_i, v_j)$ connecting vertex v_i to v_j. The graph provides a second edge, $E = (v_j, v_i)$, if the flow is in both directions. Graphs with ordered edges are called *directed graphs* or *digraphs*.Figure 16-3 is an example of a digraph with five vertices and seven edges. In this chapter, we develop the graph class and algorithms for digraphs. If we want an undirected graph, we provide a pair of directed edges to connect the vertices.

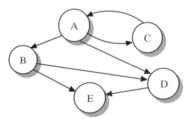

Vertices V = {A, B, C, D, E}
Edges E = {(A,B), (A,C), (A,D), (B,D), (B,E), (C,A), (D,E)}

Figure 16-3
Sample Digraph with 5
Vertices and 7 Edges

Much of the terminology for graphs carries over to digraphs. For instance, vertex v_j is adjacent to vertex v_i if there is a directed edge (v_i, v_j) between the vertices. A *directed path* (path) connecting vertices v_s and v_e is a sequence of directed edges that begin at v_s and end at v_e. Edges in a digraph allow flow in only one direction, so we must distinguish between the source and the destination vertices. The notation $E = (v_s, v_e)$ highlights the fact that the edge emanates from the source vertex v_s and terminates in the destination (ending) vertex v_e. The path $P(v_s, v_e)$ is a sequence of vertices that begins with v_s and ends with v_e. The number of the edges that emanate from a vertex v is called the *out-degree* of the vertex. The number of the edges that terminate in vertex v is the *in-degree* of the vertex. In Figure 16-3, vertex A has out-degree 3 and in-degree 1. The out-degree of vertex E is 0, while its in-degree is 2.

The concept of connectivity in a digraph distinguishes between a strongly connected and a weakly connected graph. A digraph is *strongly connected* if there is a path from any vertex to any other vertex. The digraph is *weakly connected* if, for each pair of vertices v_i and v_j, there is either a path $P(v_i, v_j)$ or a path $P(v_i, v_j)$. Figure 16-4 illustrates different types of connectedness for a digraph.

A *cycle* is a path of length 2 or more that connects a vertex to itself. In the directed graph of Figure 16-4(c), the vertices $\{A, B, C\}$ are in a cycle. A digraph that contains no cycles is called an *acyclic* digraph.

Weighted Graphs

Many graph applications require information not only about the presence of vertices and edges, but also associated values for the edges. In a transportation graph, the value of an edge might represent the distance between two locations or the amount of goods that can move between the locations. To handle these applications, we assign a value called the weight to each edge. A digraph that makes use of the weight of an edge is called a *weighted digraph*. Figure 16-5 illustrates a weighted job-scheduling digraph. The value of an edge defines the length of time to finish a task. In this section, we described a variety of graphs, including undirected graphs, directed graphs (digraphs), and weighted digraphs. In this chapter, we primarily discuss directed graphs in which an edge can store a weight. By assuming the weight to be 1

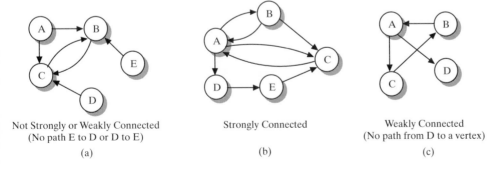

Not Strongly or Weakly Connected (No path E to D or D to E)	Strongly Connected	Weakly Connected (No path from D to a vertex)
(a)	(b)	(c)

Figure 16-4
Types of Connectedness for a Digraph

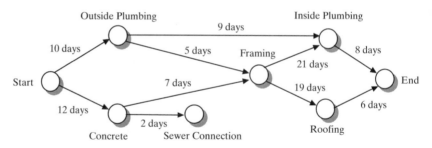

Figure 16-5
Home Construction Schedule

for each edge, the structure can include nonweighted digraphs. For convenience, we will use the term *graph* to refer to either a weighted or a nonweighted digraph.

16-2   THE GRAPH CLASS

In this section, we describe the graph class. You are familiar with graph terminology (from Section 16-1 and the general concept of an iterator, so we list the operations in the class as an API. The vertices are a set of elements of type *T*, and we specify an edge by giving the starting and ending vertex. In the next section, we discuss the design and implementation of the graph class.

Listing The Graph API

A graph consists of vertices and edges. The class has operations that access the properties of a graph, add or delete vertices and edges, update the weight of an edge, and identify the list of adjacent (neighbor) vertices for a specified vertex. The class also includes overloaded versions of the >> and << operators, to input a graph and display its key attributes. We discuss these operations in the next section.

| CLASS graph | Constructor | "d_graph.h" |

graph();
    Create an empty graph.

| CLASS graph | Operations | "d_graph.h" |

void **clear**();
    Remove all vertices and edges in the graph.
        Postcondition: The graph is empty.

bool **empty**() const;
    Return true if the graph has no vertices.

void **eraseEdge**(const *T&* v1, const *T&* v2);

Delete the edge ($v1$, $v2$) from the graph.
> Preconditions: Vertices $v1$ and $v2$ must be in the set of vertices.
> Postcondition: The number of edges is decreased by 1.

void **eraseVertex**(const *T*& *v*);
> Delete the vertex v from the graph.
>> Preconditions: Vertex v must be in the set of vertices.
>> Postconditions: The number of vertices is decreased by 1, and the operation removes all edges to or from v.

int **getWeight**(const *T*& *v1*, const *T*& *v2*) const;
> Return the weight of edge ($v1$, $v2$); if the edge does not exist, return -1.
>> Preconditions: Vertices $v1$ and $v2$ must be in the set of vertices.

set<*T*> **getNeighbors**(const *T*& *v*) const;
> Return the set of vertices adjacent to v.

int **inDegree**(const *T*& *v*) const;
> Return the number of edges that terminate in v.
>> Precondition: Vertex v must be in the set of vertices.

void **insertEdge**(const T& *v1*, const *T*& *v2*, int *w*);
> Add the edge ($v1$, $v2$), with the specified weight, to the set of edges.
>> Preconditions: Vertices $v1$ and $v2$ must be in the set of vertices and $v1 \neq v2$.
>> Postcondition: The number of edges is increased by 1.

void **insertVertex**((const *T*& *v*);
> Add vertex v to the set of vertices.
>> Postcondition: The number of vertices is increased by 1.

int **numberOfEdges**() const;
> Return the number of edges in the graph.

int **numberOfVertices**() const;
> Return the number of vertices in the graph.

int **outDegree**(const *T*& *v*) const;
> Return the number of the edges that originate at v.
>> Precondition: Vertex v must be in the set of vertices.

void **setWeight**(const *T*& *v1*, const *T*& *v2*, int *w*);
> Update the weight of the edge ($v1$, $v2$).
>> Preconditions: ($v1$, $v2$) must be an existing edge.
>> Postcondition: The weight of edge ($v1$, $v2$) is w.

istream& **operator>>** (istream& istr, graph<*T*>& *g*);
> Input from stream istr the number of vertices and their names, along with the number of edges and the edges. The input format for an edge consists of the starting and ending vertices and the weight. (See discussion.)

ostream& **operator**<< (ostream& ostr, const graph<*T*>& g);
  Output to stream ostr the list of vertices, with information on the edges that
  emanate from a vertex, the weight of an edge, and the in-degree and out-
  degree of a vertex. (See discussion.)

iterator **begin**();
  Return an iterator pointing at the first vertex in the graph.

const_iterator **begin**() const;
  Constant version of begin().

iterator **end**();
  Return an iterator pointing just past the last vertex in the graph.

const_iterator **end**() const;
  Constant version of end().

Example 16-1

Let us get some familiarity with the graph class. The two graphs in Figure 16-6 consists of vertices of type char.

1. Declaration of the graph.

```
graph<char> g;
```

Access the properties of the graph (Figure 16-6(a)):

```
cout << g.numberOfVertices():    // output: 4
cout << g.numberOfEdges():       // output: 5

// 'A' has in-degree 1; out-degree 2
cout << g.inDegree('A');         // output: 1
cout << g.outDegree('A');        // output: 2
cout << g.getWeight('B','D');    // output: 5
```

2. Update vertices, edges, and weights. The resulting graph is displayed in Figure 16-6(b).

```
g.eraseEdge('A', 'C');           // delete edge with weight 3

// delete vertex 'D' with edges ('B','D') and ('D','C')
g.eraseVertex('D');

g.setWeight('A','B',8);          // increase weight from 4 to 8
```

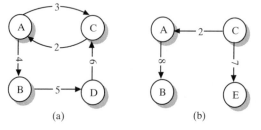

(a)   (b)

Figure 16-6
Graph Operations

```
g.insertVertex('E');        // add vertex 'E'
g.insertEdge('C','E',7);    // add edge ('C','E') with weight 7
```

Input and Output of Graphs. The graph class overloads the $>>$ operator to input the vertices, edges, and weights for a graph. The format treats the vertices and edges separately. Input begins with the number of vertices, followed by a list of the vertex names.

m (Number of Vertices m)

$\text{Vertex}_1 \ \text{Vertex}_2 \ldots \text{Vertex}_m$

For the edges, begin with their number, followed by a sequence of triples where the first two entries are the source and destination vertices of an edge and the third entry is the weight of that edge. For nonweighted graphs, assign the weight of an edge as 1.

n (Number of Edges)

$\text{Source}_1 \quad \text{Destination}_1 \quad \text{Weight}_1$

$\text{Source}_2 \quad \text{Destination}_2 \quad \text{Weight}_2$

...

$\text{Source}_n \quad \text{Destination}_n \quad \text{Weight}_n$

For instance, the following is the input data for the graph in Figure 16-7.

```
5                    // data for the vertices
A  B  C  D  E
6                    // data for the edges
A  B  1
A  C  1
B  C  1
C  B  1
C  D  1
E  B  1
```

The overloaded $<<$ operator displays a graph. For each vertex, the output lists the set of adjacent vertices, along with the weight for the corresponding edge. Output for each vertex also includes its in-degree and out-degree.

Output Format:
```
vertex name: in-degree (value) out-degree (value)
    Edges:  (list of adjacent vertices and edge weights)
```

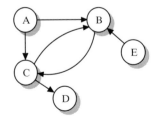

Figure 16-7
Graph Used to Illustrate Input
and Output

For the graph in Figure 16-7, the output is as follows:

   A: in-degree 0 out-degree 2
          Edges: *B* (1) *C* (1)
   B: in-degree 3 out-degree 1
          Edges: *C* (1)
   C: in-degree 2 out-degree 2
          Edges: *B* (1) *D* (1)
   D: in-degree 1 out-degree 0
          Edges:
   E: in-degree 0 out-degree 1
          Edges: *B* (1)

PROGRAM 16-1 GRAPH INPUT AND OUTPUT

Let us look at a simple program that uses the input and output operations along with the
member function getNeighbors(). The file "graphIO.dat" contains the input data. After the
reading of the graph, a call to getNeighbors() returns the set of adjacent vertices for vertex *A*.
The general container output function writeContainer() lists the vertices. The program concludes by using the output operator $<<$ to display the graph. We include a picture of the
graph in the listing of the input file.

```cpp
// File: prg16_1.cpp
// the program inputs the graph whose vertices are characters from
// file "graphIO.dat" and calls the function getNeighbors() to
// display the set of neighbors for 'A'. using writeContainer()
// from "d_util.h", a call to the overloaded stream operator
// displays the properties of the graph

#include <iostream>
#include <fstream>
#include <set>

#include "d_graph.h"    // the graph class
#include "d_util.h"     // function writeContainer()

using namespace std;

int main()
{
   // graph with vertices of type char
   graph<char> demoGraph;

   // edge set
   set<char> edgeSet;

   // input stream for graph data
   ifstream graphIn;

   // open stream and input the graph
   graphIn.open("graphIO.dat");
   graphIn >> demoGraph;
```

```
    // get set of neighbors of A and output with writeContainer
    edgeSet = demoGraph.getNeighbors('A');

    cout << "Neighbors of A are ";
    writeContainer(edgeSet.begin(), edgeSet.end());
    cout << endl << endl;

    // output the graph and its properties
    cout << demoGraph << endl;

    return 0;
}
```

```
Input file: graphIO.dat
5
A B C D E
8
A  B  4
A  C  7
A  D  6
B  A  2
C  B  3
C  E  2
D  E  4
E  C  1

Run:

Neighbors of A are B  C  D

A: in-degree 1  out-degree 3
    Edges: B (4)   C (7)   D (6)
B: in-degree 2  out-degree 1
    Edges: A (2)
C: in-degree 2  out-degree 2
    Edges: B (3)   E (2)
D: in-degree 1  out-degree 1
    Edges: E (4)
E: in-degree 2  out-degree 1
    Edges: C (1)
```

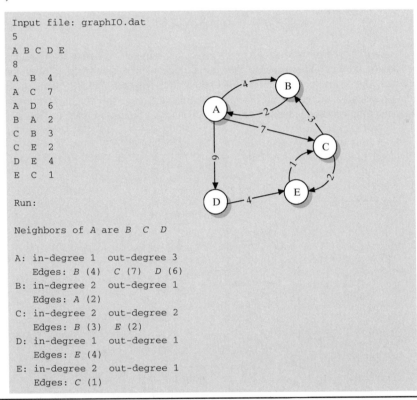

Representing Graphs

In the next section, we develop a design and implementation for the graph class. Before we do this, we need some way to represent the set of vertices and their edges. A simple technique stores the vertices as a list: $v_0, v_1, v_2, \ldots, v_{m-1}$. An *m*-by-*m* matrix, called an *adjacency matrix*, identifies the edges. An entry in row *i* and column *j* corresponds to the edge $e = (v_i, v_j)$. Its value is the weight of the edge, or -1 if the edge does not exist. For instance, Figure 16-8 shows a nonweighted and a weighted graph, with the corresponding adjacency matrices.

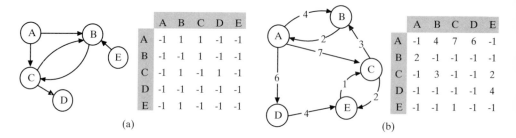

Figure 16-8
Graph Representation by Means of an Adjacency Matrix

Another representation of a graph associates with each vertex a set of its adjacent vertices (neighbors). This model is often more efficient, because it stores information for precisely the edges that actually belong to the graph. For each vertex, an element in the adjacency set is a pair consisting of the destination vertex and the weight of the edge. For the same graphs from Figure 16-8, we give the *adjacency set* representation (Figure 16-9).

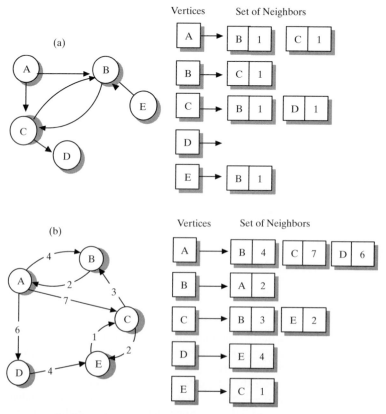

Figure 16-9
Graph Representation by Means of an Adjacency Set

The graph class uses the adjacency-set representation for a graph. A programming project develops the graph class via an adjacency matrix.

GRAPH CLASS DESIGN   16-3

The graph class is the most sophisticated container in the book. The complexity derives from the fact that we need separate data structures to store the vertices and the edges. In addition, we need to maintain information as we visit the vertices in a traversal of the graph. You will see that this information is critical in implementing many of the graph algorithms.

The graph class stores the vertices in a map container. Each vertex has an associated adjacency set that contains all of its adjacent vertices and the weight of each connecting edge. We define the neighbor class to provide a data type for each element in an adjacency set. The public data members in the class include the adjacent (destination) vertex dest and the weight of the edge. As we will see soon, dest is an integer index into the vector vInfo that contains vertex properties. The neighbor class contains a constructor that initializes the data members, plus overloaded operators < and == that compare two neighbors. The operators allow a set to contain neighbor objects.

CLASS neighbor	Declaration	"d_graph.h"

```
class neighbor
{
   public:
       int dest;
       // index of the destination vertex in the vector vInfo of vertex
       // properties
       int weight;
       // weight of traversing this edge

       neighbor(int d=0, int w=0);
       // constructor

       friend bool operator< (const neighbor& lhs, const neighbor& rhs);
       friend bool operator== (const neighbor& lhs, const neighbor& rhs);
       // operators for the neighbor class that compare the
       // destination vertices
};
```

Representing Vertex Information

The graph class stores the vertices in a map container. Each element in the map is a key–value pair, where the key is the vertex value. The value component is an index into a vector of vertexInfo objects where each object contains properties of the vector and information gained during visits to the vertex during execution of a graph algorithm. We introduce the vector in the next section. For now, let us focus on the structure of a vertexInfo object, which is associated with a vertex.

A vertexInfo object consists of seven data members. The first two members, called vtxMapLoc and edges, identify the vertex in the map and its adjacency set. A vertex is in the map as the key in a key–value pair. The data member, vtxMapLoc, is a map iterator that points to the pair. A vertex has an adjacency set that is a set<neighbor> object. The data member *edges* is the adjacency set of the vertex. A third data member, called *inDegree*, indicates the number of edges that terminate in the vertex. The other four members contain information that will be useful when we build a graph and design applications (Figure 16-10). We will discuss these members in context.

The vertexInfo class declares public data members and both a default constructor and a constructor that initializes the vtxMapLoc data member with the location of the vertex in the map. An enum, vertexColor defines three colors that we use in later scanning algorithms.

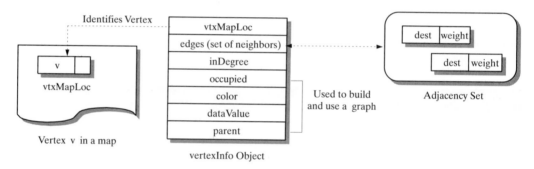

Figure 16-10
vertexInfo Object with Reference to the Map Location and the Adjacency Set

```
CLASS vertexInfo              Declaration              "d_graph.h"

// maintains vertex properties, including its set of
// neighbors
template <typename T>
class vertexInfo
{
   public:
      enum vertexColor { WHITE, GRAY, BLACK };
         // used by graph algorithms

      map<T,int>::iterator vtxMapLoc;
         // iterator pointing at a pair<T,int> object in vertex map

      set<neighbor> edges;
         // set of adjacent vertices for the current vertex
```

```
      int inDegree;
          // maintains the in-degree of the vertex

      bool occupied;
          // indicates whether object currently represents a vertex

      vertexColor color;
          // indicate if a vertex is marked in an algorithm
          // that traverses the vertices of a graph

      int dataValue;
          // available to algorithms for storing relevant data values

      int parent;
          // available to graph algorithms; holds parent which is a
          // vertex with an edge terminating in the current vertex

      vertexInfo();
          // default constructor

      vertexInfo(const map<T,int>::iterator& iter);
          // constructor with iterator pointing to a vertex in map
};
```

The Vertex Map And Vinfo List

To store the vertices in a graph, we provide a map<T,int> container, called vtxMap, where a vertex name is the key of type T. The int field of a map object is an index into a vector of vertexInfo objects, called vInfo. The size of the vector is initially the number of vertices in the graph, and there is a 1–1 correspondence between an entry in the map and a vertexInfo entry in the vector (Figure 16-11).

To understand the correspondence between the map, which contains the vertex names, and the vector, which contains information about the vertices, consider a vertex v in the graph. The key-value pair (v, index) is a vtxMap entry where index references the corresponding vertexInfo object in the vector vInfo.

```
      // index of entry in vInfo corresponding to vertex v in vtxMap
      vtxMap[v] = index;
```

The vertexInfo object vInfo[index] has fields that define the adjacency set for the vertex, its in-degree, and information we will use when visiting the vertex in a graph algorithm.

```
      // adjacency set containing the neighbors of v and the weight
      // of the edges emanating from v
```

```
vInfo[index].edges

// the in-degree of the vertex
vInfo[index].inDegree    // number of edges terminating at v
```

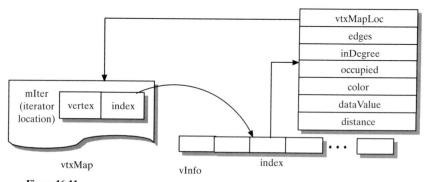

Figure 16-11
Vertex Map and Vector vInfo

If we start with an entry at index *i* in the vInfo vector, we can identify the corresponding vertex in vtxMap. The vtxMapLoc field holds an iterator pointing to a key–value pair in vtxMap.

```
vInfo[i].vtxMapLoc        // pointer to pair<T,int> object in vtxMap
```

The key portion of the pair is the vertex name for the vertex corresponding to vInfo[*i*]. Using the iterator dereference operator *, we can access each component of the key–value pair.

```
// member first accesses key component in the pair
(*vInfo[i].vtxMapLoc).first is the vertex name

// member second accesses value component which is an index
// into the vInfo vector; in this case the index is i
(*vInfo[i].vtxMapLoc).second is the vInfo index i
```

Example 16-2

This example describes the map vtxMap and the vector vInfo for vertices in the accompanying nonweighted digraph. Figure 16-12 includes the vertex map and a listing of the first three vertexInfo attributes for each vertex. The notation loc<*V*> denotes the iterator pointing to a map object, where <*V*> is one of the vertex names *A, B, C,* or *D*.

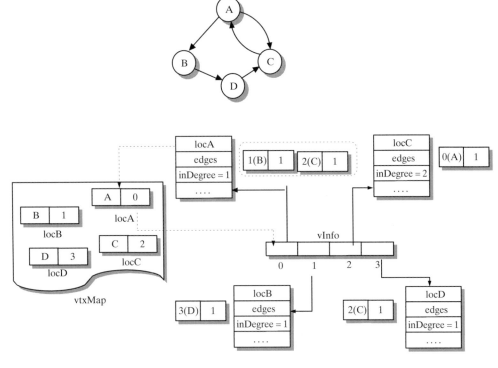

Figure 16-12
vtxmap and vinfo0 Example

Assume vertex A corresponds to index 0 in vInfo, vertex B corresponds to index 1, and so forth. In Figure 16-12, let us look at how to view vertex A. The dotted lines highlight the links between vtxMap['A'] = 0 and the element vInfo[0] in the vector. The vertexInfo data members include the following:

```
// iterator that references the map entry for vertex A
vInfo[0].vtxMapLoc = locA

vInfo[0].edges = adjacency set of vertex A

vInfo[0].inDegree = 1   // edge (C,A) terminates at A
```

The figure also includes a description of the first three fields in the vInfo entries for vertices B, C, and D.

Exploring the Adjacency Set of a Vertex. In the adjacency set, each element is a neighbor object containing an integer value for dest, the destination, and a weight. The integer value for dest is the index of the entry in vInfo that corresponds to the

956 Chapter 16 Graphs

adjacent vertex. For instance, in Example 16-2, vertex *B* is adjacent to *A*, because there is an edge $e = (A, B)$. The dest value for vertex *B* is 1. To identify that *B* is the adjacent vertex, use the vtxMapLoc field in vInfo[1] and the deference operator * to access the vector name in the map.

```
(*vInfo[1].vtxMapLoc).first is 'B'.
```

The edge attribute in a vertexInfo object defines the adjacency set for a vertex. To search the elements in the set, declare a set<neighbor> iterator and use the deference operator * to access the dest field. The value provides access to the vInfo entry and hence to all key attributes of the adjacent vertex.

The following code segment begins with vertex *A* and outputs all of its adjacent vertices. Comments describe the step-by-step process needed to access an adjacent vertex entry in vInfo and then return to the map container to extract the vertex name.

```
// locate vertexInfo object for A
int index = vtxMap['A'];

// to simplify notation, construct an alias for the adjacency set
set<neighbor>& edgeSet = vInfo[index].edges;

// use setIter to traverse the edge (adjacency) set
set<neighbor>::iterator setIter;

// index of vertexInfo object corresponding to an adjacent vertex
int aIndex;

// use a loop to search the edge set;
for (setIter=edgeSet.begin(); setIter != edgeSet.end(); setIter++)
{
    // " (*setIter).dest " is index into vInfo
    aIndex = (*setIter).dest;

    // use vtxMapLoc to access adjacent vertex in the map container.
    // data member first is the name of the vertex
    cout << (*vInfo[aIndex].vtxMapLoc).first << endl;
}
```

The 'Occupied' Field. The graph class maintains a 1–1 correspondence between entries in the vertex map and entries in the vertexInfo vector. Initially, the class builds the vector from the map by using push_back() to allocate each entry. The class must address the problem of removing a vertex. The operation removes an element from the map, but does not erase the corresponding entry in vInfo. To indicate whether an element in the vector corresponds to an existing vertex in the map, we use the "occupied" field. When building the graph, we assign the field the value true. Upon deleting a vertex in the map container, the field in the corresponding vertexInfo object is set to false.

Any code that searches the elements in the vInfo vector should first check the "occupied" field to determine whether the entry corresponds to an actual vertex.

```
for (i = 0; i < vInfo.size(); i++)
    if (vInfo[i].occupied)
        < entry corresponds to an actual vertex>
```

Graph Class Declaration

With the background from the previous section, the declaration of the graph class is straightforward. The private data members vtxMap, of type map<*T*,int>, and vInfo, of type vector<vertexInfo<*T*> >, store the vertices and the vertex information. The members numberOfVertices and numberOfEdges maintain size information for the graph. To handle the adding and removing of vertices, the class provides an *availability stack* to store indices for the vInfo vector. The operation of removing a vertex pushes the index for the corresponding vInfo element onto the stack. To add a vertex, first check the stack to see whether an index is available. If so, the vertex can use the corresponding vInfo element. Reusing elements in the vector assures more efficient memory management. The graph class includes the private function getvInfoIndex(), which takes a vertex argument and returns the corresponding index in vInfo or −1 if the vertex is not in the graph.

The following is a declaration that shows the private members in the graph class. The graph API from Section 16-2 describes public members of the class. Note that the class has a copy constructor and an overloaded assignment operator that we do not list in the API. These functions assure that the iterator values in vInfo point to the correct map entries. We will not discuss these functions further, and the interested reader should consult the source file "d_graph.h".

CLASS graph	Declaration	"d_graph.h"

```
template <typename T>
class graph
{
   public:

       <member functions listed in the graph class API>

   private:
       typedef map<T,int> vertexMap;

       vertexMap vtxMap;
          // store vertex in a map with its name as the key and
          // the index of the corresponding vertexInfo object
          // in the vInfo vector as the value

       vector<vertexInfo<T> > vInfo;
          //list of vertexInfo objects corresponding to the vertices
```

```
    int numVertices;
    int  numEdges;
        // current size (vertices and edges) of the graph

    stack<int> availStack;
        // stack for storing unused indices in vInfo

    int getvInfoIndex (const T& v) const;
        // uses vtxMap to obtain the index of v in vInfo
};
```

Graph Class Implementation

With a few examples, you can understand how we design algorithms to implement graph operations. Most of the details center on the interaction between the vertex map and the corresponding vector of vertexInfo objects. Let's look at the member functions getNeighbors(), inDegree(), outDegree(), insertEdge(), and deleteVertex(). We provide a full implementation of getNeighbors() to illustrate the interaction. For the other functions, we describe the steps in the algorithm and list small code blocks that perform the tasks. The deleteVertex() algorithm is the most interesting, because it draws on many of the design features of the graph class.

Identifying Neighbors. The function getNeighbors() takes a vertex *v* as an argument and returns the adjacency set of vertices. Begin by calling the private member function getvInfoIndex(), which returns the index of the corresponding element in vInfo. If the vertex is not in the set, throw a graphError exception. Otherwise, create an alias that references the set of neighbor objects from the edges field.

```
// position of vertexInfo object in vInfo
pos = getvInfoIndex(v);

// set of neighbor objects that reference the adjacent vertices
set<neighbor> & edgeSet = vInfo[pos].edges;
```

Using a set iterator, search each object in edgeSet, and use the dest field as the index for the vInfo entry that corresponds to the adjacent vertex. With this entry, use the vtxMapLoc field and the derefence operator * to identify the actual name of the adjacent vertex. Add the name to a set<*T*> container, which ultimately becomes the return value of the function.

getNeighbors()
```
// return a set containing the neighbors of v
template <typename T>
set<T> graph<T>::getNeighbors(const T& v) const
{
    // set returned
    set<T> adjVertices;
```

```
        // obtain the position of v from the map
        int pos = getvInfoIndex(v);

        // if v not in list of vertices, throw an exception
        if (pos == -1)
            throw
                graphError("graph getNeighbors():   vertex not in graph");

        // construct an alias for the set of edges in vertex pos
        const set<neighbor>& edgeSet = vInfo[pos].edges;
        // use setIter to traverse the edge set
        set<neighbor>::const_iterator setIter;

        // index of vertexInfo object corresponding to an adjacent vertex
        int aPos;

        for (setIter=edgeSet.begin(); setIter != edgeSet.end();
                setIter++)
        {   // "(*setIter).dest" is index into vInfo
            aPos = (*setIter).dest;
            // insert vertex data into a set. vInfo[aPos].vtxMapLoc
            // is a map iterator. dereference it to access the vertex
            adjVertices.insert ((*vInfo[aPos].vtxMapLoc).first);
        }

        return adjVertices;
    }
```

Evaluating In-Degree and Out-Degree. A vertexInfo element in the vector supplies information to evaluate the in-degree and out-degree of a vertex. Assume pos is the index for the entry in vInfo obtained by a call to getvInfoIndex(). The in-degree is a field in the entry.

```
    // in-degree of vertex v corresponding to vInfo[pos]
    vInfo[pos].inDegree
```

The out-degree of the vertex is the number of its adjacent vertices. This value is simply the size of the neighbor set called edges.

```
    // out-degree is the number of elements in the set of edges
    vInfo[pos].edges.size();
```

Adding an Edge. To insert an edge $e(v1, v2, w)$, we must add $v2$ as a neighbor of $v1$, increment the out-degree for $v1$ and the in-degree for $v2$, and update the private data member numEdges in the graph class. Start by finding the indices for the two vertex arguments in vInfo corresponding to $v1$ and $v2$.

```
    pos1 = getvInfoIndex(v1);
    pos2 = getvInfoIndex(v2);
```

If either $v1$ or $v2$ is not a valid vertex or $v1 == v2$ (self-loop), throw a graphError exception. Using pos2 and w as arguments, the operation adds a new neighbor object to the edge set for vertex $v1$, using the set insert() function. Increasing the size of the edge set automatically increases the out-degree for vertex $v1$. To increase the in-degree for vertex $v2$, the operation increments the inDegree field in vInfo[pos2]. If the edge is already in the set, no update is necessary.

```
// attempt to insert edge (pos2,w) into the edge set of vertex pos1
pair<set<neighbor>::iterator, bool> result =
    vInfo[pos1].edges.insert(neighbor(pos2,w));

// make sure edge was not already in the set
if (result.second)
{
    // increment the number of edges
    numEdges++;
    // the in-degree of v2 is one more
    vInfo[pos2].inDegree++;
}
```

Deleting a Vertex. Deleting a vertex is the most interesting function; it involves a series of disparate tasks. We describe the algorithm by outlining the order of operations and including implementation code.

The algorithm begins by finding the location of the vertex in the map and the index of the vextexInfo object in vInfo. Deleting the vertex will require calling the map erase() function, so we use the map find() function to locate the vertex. The function returns an iterator that combines with the dereference operator to access the index for the entry in vInfo. If the vertex is not in the graph, the function throws the graphError exception.

```
// search the map for the key v
mIter = vtxMap.find(v);
// if vertex is not present, terminate the erase
if (mIter == vtxMap.end())
    // if v not in list of vertices, throw an exception
    throw graphError("graph eraseVertex(): vertex not in the graph");
// obtain the index of v in vInfo
pos = (*mIter).second;
```

Task 1: Delete the vertex from the vertex map and decrement the number of vertices.

```
vtxMap.erase(mIter);

numVertices--;
```

Task 2: For the corresponding entry in vInfo, set the occupied field to false. Then push the index onto an availability stack for use by a vertex that might be added later.

```
vInfo[pos].occupied = false;
availStack.push(pos);
```

Task 3: Delete all edges that terminate in *v*. These edges have the form (v_i, v) and are found by searching the edge set for each vertex v_i and deleting those that indicate *v* as an adjacent vertex. The action of removing an edge from the set must also decrement the private data member numEdges.

```
// cycle through vInfo and remove all edges going to v
for (j=0; j < vInfo.size(); j++)
   // handle only occupied entries,
   if (vInfo.occupied)
   {
       // construct an alias for the set vInfo.edges
       set<neighbor>& edgeSet = vInfo.edges;

       sIter = edgeSet.begin();
       // cycle through the edge set
       while (sIter != edgeSet.end())
          if ((*sIter).dest == pos)
          {
              // found pos. remove it from the set and
              // decrement the edge count
              edgeSet.erase(sIter);
              numEdges--;
              break;
          }
          else
              // took no action. just move forward
              sIter++;
   }
```

Task 4: Delete all edges that emanate from *v*. These edges are simply the adjacency set for the vertex and have a representation as the set<neighbor> field called edges in the corresponding vertexInfo object. First, determine the number of edges and update the data member numEdges. Then, search the set of edges and decrement the in-degree for each adjacent vertex. Conclude by clearing the edge set.

```
// decrement numEdges by the number of edges for vertex v
numEdges -= vInfo[pos].edges.size();

// the in-degree for all of v's neighbors must be decreased by 1
set<neighbor>& edgesFromv = vInfo[pos].edges;
for (sIter=edgesFromv.begin(); sIter != edgesFromv.end();
   sIter++)
{
   j = (*sIter).dest;
```

```
            vInfo[j].inDegree--;
    }


    // clear the edge set. construct an alias for vInfo[pos].edges
    // and use erase to clear the set
    set<neighbor>& edgeSet = vInfo[pos].edges;
    edgeSet.erase(edgeSet.begin(), edgeSet.end());
```

Efficiency of Insert and Erase Operations. The insertEdge() function involves adding an element to the edge set for the source vertex. The current size of the edge set is less than or equal to E, where E is the number of edges in the graph. The set insert operation has logarithmic running time, so the efficiency of insert-Edge() is $O(\log_2 E)$. The big-O analysis for the eraseVertex() function is more complicated, because the operation involves a number of tasks. Locating and deleting the vertex from the map is $O(\log_2 V)$, where V is the number of vertices in the graph. The rest of the algorithm involves updating information in the edge set for the V entries of vInfo. To delete the edge set for the specified vertex and update the in-degree of each adjacent vertex, the elements in the set must be searched. This is an $O(E)$ operation. The most process-intensive task is removing all edges that terminate in the vertex and updating the edge count for the graph. This involves searching all of the entries in vInfo and then searching the edge set for each entry. There are V entries in the list and the total number of edges is E, so the task has efficiency $O(V + E)$. By combining the efficiencies of each task, we see that the total efficiency is $O(V + E)$.

16-4   GRAPH TRAVERSAL ALGORITHMS

In Chapter 10, we developed a series of scanning algorithms for binary trees. The algorithms described a preorder, inorder, and postorder scan of the tree by combining a visit to a node with a descent into its left and right subtrees. By beginning at the root, the algorithms visit each node of the tree exactly once: Each node lies on a unique path from the root. Traversing a graph is more involved. Graphs do not have a vertex, like a root, that defines a path to all of the other vertices. From any starting vertex, it might not be possible to visit all of the vertices in the graph. Scanning algorithms can determine only those vertices in the graph that are reachable from a starting vertex. In addition, a graph could have an edge between any two vertices, so traversing a path consisting of a sequence of adjacent vertices can result in a cycle. To avoid multiple visits to a vertex, the scanning algorithms need a strategy to mark a vertex once it has been visited.

Traditionally, graph traversal algorithms are termed search algorithms. In some cases, the scan has the traditional purpose of looking for a target value. In other cases, the search determines relationships between vertices and their edges. In this book, we will use the term graph search algorithms and graph traversal algorithms interchangeably. The algorithms reduce to two standard methods, the depth-first search and breadth-first search. The breadth-first search visits vertices in the order of their path length from a starting vertex. The depth-first search traverses vertices of a graph by making a series of recursive function calls that follow paths through the graph. Before we develop the algorithms, let us look at an example. Use the graph in Figure 16-13, with starting vertex A.

The breadth-first search generalizes the level-order scan in a binary tree. Starting with vertex A, we first visit its neighbors B, C, and G. There is no specific ordering among the neighbors, so visits to these three nodes depend on the arrangement of vertices in the adjacency set. Assume the order of visits for the first four vertices is

A, B, C, G // from A, vertex A has path length 0 ; B, C and G have path length 1

From vertex B, we visit its neighbor D with path length 2. The search concludes by visiting vertices E and F which are the neighbors of D with path length 3 from A. Depending on access to these neighbors, the breadth-first search could visit vertices in the order

A, B, C, G, D, E, F

Note that, in the breadth-first search of the graph, starting at vertex A allows us to visit all of the vertices in the graph. Had we started at vertex D, the breadth-first search would have included only vertices D, E, F, and G.

The concept of depth-first search begins with the notion of the depth-first visit from a starting vertex. In the example, the visit starts at A and begins a search down paths of neighbors until it reaches a vertex that has no neighbors or only neighbors that have already been visited. There is no ordering among vertices in an adjacency set, so the paths, (and hence the order of visit) to vertices can vary. Assume we start with the adjacent vertex B. The visit continues with vertex D, the only neighbor to B. At this point, the depth-first visit is looking at the path P(A, D) with vertices A, B, and D. Assume the search selects E as the neighbor of D. Because E does not have any adjacent vertices, we have gone as deeply as possible on this path and a formal visit of vertex E occurs. Backtracking to D, the depth-first visit pursues the other path, which goes from D to its neighbor F. At this point, the adjacency set for F con-

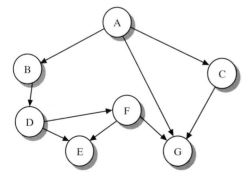

Figure 16-13
Demonstration Graph for
Depth-first and Breadth-first
Searches

tains vertices E and G. Since E is already visited, the depth-first visit proceeds to vertex G, which is as deep as the path can go. After visiting G, backtracking then visits vertices F, D, and B in that order. In the depth-first visit, we process a vertex only after we have performed the depth-first visit from all of its neighbors. The following list identifies the current order of visits to the vertices, in reverse order of processing.

B, D, F, G, E

We first processed E, then G, and so forth, and have currently finished with B. At this point, the depth-first visit backtracks to the starting vertex A and follows a path to C, which is the only unvisited neighbor of A. After visiting C, the depth-first visit concludes by visiting the starting vertex. The final list of visits in reverse order of processing is

A, C, B, D, F, G, E

We started the depth-first visit at A, so it is the last vertex to finish.

As we will see later in the section, the depth-first visit extends to all the vertices of the graph. This extension will define the concept of depth-first search. Unlike binary-tree scanning methods, there is no unique order of visits in either the breadth-first or depth-first search graph algorithms. The variations occur when the algorithms must select from among the set of neighbors for a particular vertex.

Breadth-First Search Algorithm

The breadth-first search of a graph emulates the level-order scan of a binary tree. The algorithm assumes a graph g and a starting vertex, called startVertex. The return value is the set of visited (reachable) vertices. The search first visits the startVertex (path length 0) and then its adjacent vertices (path length 1). The algorithm continues by visiting vertices with paths from startVertex of length 2, then of length 3, and so forth.

As in the level-order scan of a binary tree, we provide an iterative version of the breadth-first search that uses a queue to store the vertices awaiting a visit temporarily. At each iterative step, the algorithm deletes a vertex from the queue, marks it as visited, and then inserts it into visitSet, which is the set of visited vertices. The step concludes by placing all unvisited neighbors of the vertex in the queue. In order to maintain information on the "visit" status of each vertex, we associate a color (WHITE, GRAY, BLACK) with each vertex in the graph. Initially, all vertices have color WHITE. When a vertex enters the queue, its color is set to GRAY to indicate that it is in the process of being searched. Upon removal from the queue, the color is set to BLACK, indicating that the vertex has been visited. Using the color attribute assures that we do not visit a vertex more than once during the traversal.

The following are the iterative steps for the graph in Figure 16-14, assuming A is the starting vertex. The initial action pushes A into visitQueue, which is the queue that temporarily stores the vertices.

Step 1. Pop A from the queue, color it BLACK, and insert it into visitSet. The neighbors of A are vertices B, C, and G, which are still colored

WHITE (unprocessed). Push the vertices into the queue and color them GRAY. After the completion of the first iteration of the search, Figure (a) displays the elements in visitSet and visitQueue.

Step 2. Pop *B* from the queue and place it in visitSet with color BLACK. The only adjacent vertex for *B* is *D*, which is still colored WHITE. Color *D* GRAY and add it to the queue (Figure (b)).

Step 3. Remove *C* and place it in visitSet (Figure (c)). *C* has an adjacent vertex *G*, but the color of this neighbor is nonwhite indicating that it is either visited or in the queue awaiting a visit. In fact, *G* is in the queue with color GRAY. No new vertices enter the queue, and we are ready for the next step.

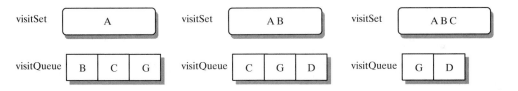

Steps 4–5: Continue the process by popping vertex *G* from the queue and placing it in visitSet (Figure (d)). *G* has no adjacent vertices, so continue to Step 5, which removes *D* from the queue. The neighbors, *E* and *F*, enter the queue (Figure (e)).

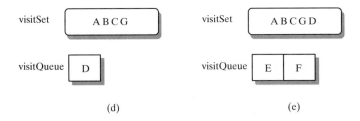

Steps 6–7: The previous steps identify the key issues in the algorithm. In Step 6, pop *E* from the queue and add it to visitSet (Figure (f)). *E* has no neighbors, so proceed to Step 7 and remove F from the queue. The adjacent vertices *E* and *G* are already visited (colored BLACK), so the algorithm can conclude with an empty queue (Figure (g)).

(f)

(g)

Implementing the Breadth-First Search. The algorithm for the breadth-first search is relatively easy to understand, and we implement it with the function bfs(). The function visits only the subset of vertices reachable from the starting vertex. The code for the function exploits the relationship between vtxMap, which is the map container storing the vertices, and the vector vInfo, which is the corresponding list of vertexInfo objects. We include a complete listing of the function, along with extensive comments to illustrate the design of the algorithm. The function takes a graph and a starting vertex of type *T* and returns a set<*T*> object containing the vertices reachable from the starting vertex. The function is included as a friend of the graph class in the file "d_graph.h". Note that the queue stores the index in vInfo corresponding to a vertex.

bfs():

```
// perform the breadth-first traversal from sVertex and
// return the set of reachable vertices
template <typename T>
set<T> bfs(graph<T>& g, const T& sVertex)
{
    // a queue to store indices of adjacent vertices from vInfo
    queue<int> visitQueue;

    // set of vertices in BFS
    set<T> visitSet;

    // use to store indices in vInfo
    int currVertex, neighborVertex;

    // use to search edge sets for unvisited vertices
    set<neighbor>::iterator adj;
    int i;

    // find the index of the starting vertex
    currVertex = g.getvInfoIndex(sVertex);

    // check for a nonexistent starting vertex
    if (currVertex == -1)
```

```
        throw graphError("graph bfs(): vertex not in the graph");

    // initialize all vertices in the graph to unvisited (WHITE)
    for (i=0;i < g.vInfo.size(); i++)
        if (g.vInfo[i].occupied)
            g.vInfo[i].color = vertexInfo<T>::WHITE;

    visitQueue.push(currVertex);     // initialize the queue

    while (!visitQueue.empty())
    {
        // remove a vertex from the queue
        currVertex = visitQueue.front();
        visitQueue.pop();
        // indicate that the vertex has been visited
        g.vInfo[currVertex].color = vertexInfo<T>::BLACK;

        // put the vertex in visitSet
        visitSet.insert((*(g.vInfo[currVertex].vtxMapLoc)).first);

        // create an alias for the edge set of currVertex
        set<neighbor>& edgeSet = g.vInfo[currVertex].edges;
        // sequence through the edge set and look for vertices
        // that have not been visited
        for (adj = edgeSet.begin(); adj != edgeSet.end(); adj++)
        {
            neighborVertex = (*adj).dest;
            // handle only unprocessed vertices
            if(g.vInfo[neighborVertex].color==vertexInfo<T>::WHITE)
            {
                g.vInfo[neighborVertex].color = vertexInfo<T>::GRAY;
                visitQueue.push(neighborVertex);
            }
        }
    }
    return visitSet;
}
```

Running Time for Breadth-First Search. In the breadth-first search algorithm, a loop colors each of the vertices WHITE. During execution of the algorithm, each vertex enters the queue at most once and hence is popped from the queue at most once. Each queue operation has efficiency $O(1)$, so the total running time for queue handling is $O(V)$, where V is the number of vertices. When a vertex enters the queue, the algorithm searches its adjacency set only once. The total number of elements in all of the adjacency sets is the number of edges in the graph (E); the running time to search the sets is at most $O(E)$. Combining the activities of initializing the graph, processing vertices on the queue, and searching the edges, the running time for the breadth-first search is $O(V + E)$.

Example 16-3

Let us create a code segment that calls bfs() with a specified starting vertex and outputs the set of reachable vertices. In general, you must provide declarations for the starting vertex and for the set, using the data type of the graph. The example uses the demonstration graph for the depth-first algorithm, which we repeat for your convenience.

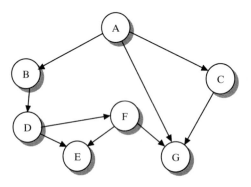

```
// declare the graph, startVertex and visitSet of type char
graph<char> g;
char startVertex;
set<char> visitSet;

// call bfs() with arguments g and startVertx
visitSet = bfs (g, startVertex);

// output the visitSet using writeContainer()
cout << "BFS visitSet from " << startVertex << ":    ";
writeContainer(visitSet.begin(),visitSet.end());
```

The following output represents three runs, assuming startVertex at *A, D,* and *E* respectively.

```
Run 1:
   BFS visitSet from A:    A   B   C   D   E   F   G

Run 2:
   BFS visitSet from D:    D   E   F   G

Run 3:
   BFS visitSet from E:    E
```

Depth-First Visit Algorithm

The depth-first visit of a graph emulates the postorder scan of a binary tree. The traversal follows paths of adjacent vertices, beginning with a WHITE (unvisited) starting vertex, until it reaches a vertex that has no neighbors or only neighbors that have already been visited. Visits to the vertices occur via backtracking. We provide a re-cursive form of the algorithm that collects the vertices in a list in the reverse order of their discovery. The ordering will allow us to use the algorithm in a variety of graph applications.

Each recursive step assumes we are at a current vertex on a path of adjacent vertices emanating from the starting vertex. The step takes the current vertex and colors it GRAY to denote that we make our first discovery of the vertex. The algo-rithm then proceeds to look at the set of neighboring vertices. For each undiscov-ered vertex (color WHITE) in the adjacency set, a recursive call continues the search deeper down a path. The scan will ultimately reach the end of a path where the vertex has no WHITE (undiscovered) neighbors. Only then do we actually start a recursively backtracking through the vertices and carry out formal visits. As part of each visit, the vertex is colored BLACK.

To understand the order of access to vertices, consider the graph in Figure 16-14, with a depth-first visit beginning at vertex A. We assume all the vertices of the graph are WHITE. After coloring vertex A GRAY, the visit selects between the neighbors B and C, which are both WHITE and thus undiscovered. If B is selected first, the visit proceeds recursively to vertices B, D, and G. G has no neighbors, so the algorithm makes G the first visit and colors it BLACK. Via backtracking, visits occur at vertices D and B in that order, with the color of each vertex changed from GRAY to BLACK. After backtracking to A, the algorithm selects C which is the other neighbor of A, colors it GRAY, and continues to vertices E and F, which form the adjacency set for C. Assuming that access in this set starts with E, the order of visits is E followed by F. Backtracking completes the algorithm with visits to vertex C and, finally, to the starting vertex A. In the figure, the notation d/f describes two integer values d and f that denote the order in which a vertex is discovered (colored GRAY) and visited (colored BLACK) during the scan. Graph applications some-times refer to these values as the "*discovery time*" and "*finishing time*" for a vertex.

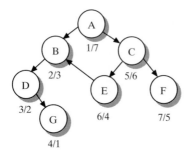

Figure 16-14
Graph Representing a Binary Tree

In the process of searching the graph, the depth-first visit algorithm maintains a list, called dfsList, that stores the vertices in descending order of their visit (finish-ing time). The vertex at the front of the list is the last vertex visited. This is, of course, the starting vertex. The vertex at the back of the list is the first vertex visited. The list, dfsList is the collection of vertices that are reachable from the starting vertex.

Recall that a vertex w is reachable from vertex v provided there is a path $P(v, w)$ connecting v to w. In the example, dfsList is

$$A, C, F, E, B, D, G$$

An intuitive interpretation of an element (vertex) in the list implies that a visit to the vertex during a depth-first visit occurs only after visits to vertices in the tail of the list. For instance, a visit to C occurs only after visits to vertices reachable from C, and these vertices are found in the tail of the list (vertices F, E, B, D, and G) and not vertex A. The list indicates that a visit to B results from searching activity involving only vertices D and G, which form the tail of the list.

The coloring of vertices in the recursive depth-first visit allows us to recognize the presence of a cycle within the set of reachable vertices. Recall that a cycle is a directed path of length 2 or more that connects a vertex to itself.

```
P(v, v):  v = v₁,  v₂,  ...,  vₘ₋₁,  vₘ = v        m > 1
```

At each recursive step in the traversal, the algorithm visits the adjacency set for the current vertex. If we are currently at vertex v and a neighbor vertex w has color GRAY, we say that (v, w) is a *back edge*. A back edge indicates the presence of a cycle. The reason is fairly simple. A GRAY vertex w must have been discovered in a prior recursive step. The vertex is not BLACK, so we have arrived at v along a path that emanates from w The length of the path depends on the number of recursive calls from the point when w was first discovered (colored GRAY) to the current vertex which identifies w as a neighbor. If we add the edge (v, w) to the path from w to v, the length of the new path is at least two and is a cycle. Conversely, if there is a cycle within its path, the depth-first visit algorithm will find a back edge. To see this, assume that w is the first vertex in a cycle discovered by the depth-first visit and that the cycle path is $w, ...,v, w..$ The visit will continue around the cycle and will eventually discover v. At this time, the vertex w is GRAY and so (v, w) is a back edge.

Implementing the Depth-First Visit. We have discussed the depth-first visit algorithm assuming a starting vertex. In this section, we create the function dfsVisit(), which implements the recursive depth-first visit from a starting vertex. This is a private utility function that we use in a variety of graph algorithms. In the process of executing dfsVisit(), we will identify a back edge in the case where the programmer explicitly tests for the presence of a cycle. The request is specified with a Boolean argument. We make the assumption that the starting vertex for dfsVisit() is WHITE. The function descends through the graph, discovering and processing all the WHITE vertices it finds.

The function dfsVist() includes a graph and a WHITE starting vertex sVertex as its first two arguments. The reference argument dfsList dynamically stores the list of visited vertices in reverse order of their finishing times. A fourth argument is the Boolean variable checkForCycle. We use this argument only for applications that require an acyclic graph. The function dfsVisit() routinely checks for a cycle. When the function detects one, its checks the Boolean flag and, if true, throws a graphError exception. A member function that uses dfsVisit() can test for a cycle by setting the argument to true and including the function call within a try/catch block.

dfsVisit():

```
// depth-first visit assuming a WHITE starting vertex. dfsList
// contains the visited vertices in reverse order of finishing time.
// when checkForCycle is true, the function throws an exception if
// it detects a cycle
template <typename T>
void dfsVisit(graph<T>& g, const T& sVertex, list<T>& dfsList,
              bool checkForCycle)
{
    // indices for vertex positions in vInfo
    int pos_sVertex, pos_neighbor;

    // iterator to scan the adjacency set of a vertex
    set<neighbor>::iterator adj;

    // alias to simplify access to the vector vInfo
    vector<vertexInfo<T> >& vlist = g.vInfo;

    // fetch the index for sVertex in vInfo; throw an exception
    // if the starting vertex is not in the graph
    pos_sVertex = g.getvInfoIndex(sVertex);

    if (pos_sVertex == -1)
       throw graphError("graph dfsVisit(): vertex not in the graph");

    // color vertex GRAY to note its discovery
    vlist[pos_sVertex].color = vertexInfo<T>::GRAY;

    // create an alias for the adjacency set of sVertex
    set<neighbor>& edgeSet = vlist[pos_sVertex].edges;

    // sequence through the adjacency set and look for vertices
    // that are not yet discovered (colored WHITE). recursively call
    // dfsVisit() for each such vertex. if a vertex in the adjacency
    // set is GRAY, the vertex was discovered during a previous
    // call and there is a cycle that begins and ends at the
    // vertex; if checkForCycle is true, throw an exception
    for (adj = edgeSet.begin(); adj != edgeSet.end(); adj++)
    {
        pos_neighbor = (*adj).dest;
        if (vlist[pos_neighbor].color == vertexInfo<T>::WHITE)
           dfsVisit(g,(*(g.vInfo[pos_neighbor].vtxMapLoc)).first,
                       dfsList, checkForCycle);
        else if (vlist[pos_neighbor].color == vertexInfo<T>::GRAY
```

```
            && checkForCycle)
         throw graphError("graph dfsVisit(): graph has a cycle");
   }

   // finished with vertex sVertex. make it BLACK and add it to
   // the front of dfsList
   vlist[pos_sVertex].color = vertexInfo<T>::BLACK;
   dfsList.push_front((*(g.vInfo[pos_sVertex].vtxMapLoc)).first);
}
```

Example 16-4

For the two parts of this example, we use the graph in Figure 16-15 and assume that all the
vertices of the graph are WHITE and that finishOrder is a list of characters.

1. Assume that the call to dfsVisit() has starting vertex *B*.

```
dfsVisit(g, 'B', finishOrder, false);
// finishOrder: B D E F C
```

2. Check for a cycle among the reachable vertices emanating from vertex *E*. The set of
    vertices includes *B*, *C*, *D*, *E*, and *F*. Catch an exception and include output that dis-
    plays the starting vertex. The dfsVisit() identifies cycle E-B-D-E.

```
try
{
   // set boolean flag checkForCycle true
   dfsVisit(g, 'E', finishOrder, true);
}
catch (graphError& ge)
{
   cout << "Searching graph from vertex " << 'E'
        << endl;
   cout << ge.what() << endl;
}

Output: Searching graph from vertex E
        graph dfsVisit(): graph has a cycle
```

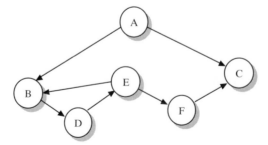

Figure 16-15
Graph for Example 16-4

Depth-First Search

The function dfsVisit() searches only vertices that are reachable from the starting vertex. Some algorithms, such as the topological sort and an algorithm that computes strong components, require a list of all graph vertices in order of decreasing finishing times. We provide a full depth-first search algorithm for all of the vertices in a graph in the function dfs(). We call this algorithm the *depth-first search*. The function dfs() takes the graph and a list, dfsList, as arguments and uses repeated calls to dfsVisit() to add vertices to the list. Initial activity clears the list and colors all of the vertices WHITE to indicate they are undiscovered. To identify starting vertices for calls to dfsVisit(), the algorithm sequentially searches the elements in vInfo and uses the next occupied and WHITE vertex as the starting vertex in a call to dfsVisit(). The call to dfsVisit() produces a list of vertices that are reachable from this starting vertex. The list is added to the front of dfsList. In the process, vertices in the list are colored BLACK. The sequential search of vInfo then finds the next WHITE vertex and repeats the call to dfsVisit(). The process terminates when we visit all vertices (every vertex is colored BLACK).

Each successive call to dfsVisit() accumulates vertices in dfsList in the reverse order of their visits (finishing times).

dfs():

```
// depth-first search. dfsList contains all the graph vertices in the
// reverse order of their finishing times
template <typename T>
void dfs(graph<T>& g, list<T>& dfsList)
{
    int i;

    // clear dfsList
    dfsList.erase(dfsList.begin(), dfsList.end());

    // initialize all vertices to WHITE
    for (i=0;i < g.vInfo.size(); i++)
        if (g.vInfo[i].occupied)
            g.vInfo[i].color = vertexInfo<T>::WHITE;

    // scan vInfo, calling dfsVisit() for each WHITE vertex.
```

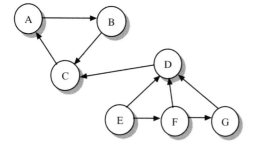

Figure 16-16
Graph for dfs() Example

```
        for (i=0;i < g.vInfo.size(); i++)
            if (g.vInfo[i].occupied && g.vInfo[i].color ==
                            vertexInfo<T>::WHITE)
                dfsVisit(g,(*(g.vInfo[i].vtxMapLoc)).first, dfsList, false);
    }
```

Example 16-5

To see how dfs() might execute, consider the graph in Figure 16-16. The first call to dfsVisit() uses the vertex corresponding to g.vInfo[0] as the starting vertex. We will trace two possible situations that correspond to starting with vertex A and vertex G respectively.

1. If *A* is the starting vertex, dfsVisit() accesses only the reachable vertices *A*, *B*, and *C*. The list of visits is

> dfsList: *A*   *B*   *C*

Assume that the next element in vInfo with a color field WHITE corresponds to the unvisited vertex *D*. The action of dfsVisit() adds only *D* to the list of visited vertices.

> dfsList: *D*   *A*   *B*   *C*

If *E* is the next vertex, dfsVisit() visits the vertices *G*, *F*, and *E* in that order, and the search is complete.

> dfsList: *E*   *F*   *G*   *D*   *A*   *B*   *C*

2. If *G* is the first vertex, dfsVisit() returns

> dfsList: *G*   *D*   *C*   *A*   *B*.

Only *E* and *F* are unvisited; let us assume that *E* is the next vertex for dfsVisit(). The final list is as follows:

> dfsList: *E*   *F*   *G*   *D*   *C*   *A*   *B*

An argument similar to that for the breadth-first search shows that that the running time for dfs() is O(V + E), where V is the number of vertices in the graph and E is the number of edges.

16-5   GRAPH TRAVERSAL APPLICATIONS

Section 16-4 develops algorithms that allow us to visit vertices in a graph systematically. We now want to do something during a visit and derive information about the graph. In this section, we look at three applications. We start by determining whether a graph is *acyclic*; that is, whether it contains a cycle. A digraph is an ideal structure for listing required courses and their prerequisites in a student's program. The topological sort creates a schedule (sequence of courses) that insures that a student will not take a course before completing all of its prerequisites. We conclude the section by developing an algorithm that identifies the strong components in a graph.

Acyclic Graphs

A graph is acyclic if it contains no cycles. This is a global property of the graph. The function dfsVisit() can identify a cycle, but only within the set of vertices that are reachable from a starting vertex. To check for a cycle anywhere in the graph, we traverse all of the vertices by using multiple calls to dfsVisit(). To see that this approach works, assume that the graph has a cycle that begins and ends at vertex v. The condition implies the existence of a path $P(v, v)$ of length at least two,

$$P(v, v): v = v_0, v_1, \ldots, v_{m-1}, v_m = v \; m \geq 2$$

where vertex v_{i+1} is a neighbor of v_i. Let v_s be the starting vertex for a call to dfsVisit() that reaches v. The depth-first traversal insures that there is a path $P(v_s, v)$ that connects v_s to v. By combining the paths $P(v_s, v)$ and $P(v, v)$, we note that all of the vertices in the cycle are reachable from v_s and thus are visited by dfsVisit(). By setting the checkForCycle flag to true, the function will find a back edge and identify the cycle.

The function acyclic() takes a graph as an argument and returns a Boolean value indicating whether a cycle is present. The implementation uses the strategy for dfs(). A loop searches the elements in vInfo and makes a call to dfsVisit() for each unvisited (WHITE) vertex with the argument checkForCycle set to true. By placing the function call within a try block, acyclic() can catch the exception thrown by dfsVisit() if it finds a cycle and return false. Otherwise, acyclic() returns true.

acyclic():

```
// determine if the graph is acyclic
template <typename T>
bool acyclic(graph<T>& g)
{
    int i;
    // use for calls to dfsVisit()
    list<T> dfsList;

    // initialize all vertices to WHITE
    for (i=0;i < g.vInfo.size(); i++)
        if (g.vInfo[i].occupied)
            g.vInfo[i].color = vertexInfo<T>::WHITE;

    // scan vInfo, calling dfsVisit() for each WHITE vertex.
    // catch a graphError exception in a call to dfsVisit()
    try
    {
        for (i=0;i < g.vInfo.size(); i++)
            if (g.vInfo[i].occupied && g.vInfo[i].color ==
                                    vertexInfo<T>::WHITE)
                dfsVisit(g, (*(g.vInfo[i].vtxMapLoc)).first,
                            dfsList, true);
    }

    catch (const graphError&)
    {
        return false;
    }
    return true;
}
```

PROGRAM 16-2 TESTING FOR CYCLES

Let us run acyclic() for the graph in Figure 16-17. Input for the graph comes from file "dag.dat".
Initially, the function determines that the graph is acyclic. By adding edge ('*E*', '*B*') we create a
cycle that a second call to the function identifies. The output simply displays these facts.

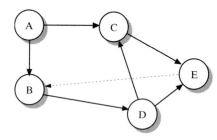

Figure 16-17
Test Graph for Calls to
Acyclic()

```
// File: prg16_2.cpp
// the program inputs a directed acyclic graph (DAG) from the file
// "dag.dat" and calls the graph algorithm acyclic() to verify that
// it has no cycles. adding an edge (E,B) creates a cycle in the
// graph. a call to acyclic() verifies the presence of the cycle

#include <iostream>
#include <fstream>
#include <string>

#include "d_graph.h"

using namespace std;

int main()
{
    graph<char> g;
    // the file that defines the graph
    ifstream graphIn;

    graphIn.open("dag.dat");

    // read the graph
    graphIn >> g;

    // determine if the graph is acyclic
    if (acyclic(g))
        cout << "Original graph is acyclic" << endl;
    else
        cout << "Original graph is not acyclic" << endl;

    // add edge (E,B) to create a cycle
    cout << "   Adding edge (E,B): ";
    g.insertEdge('E', 'B', 1);
```

```
   // retest the graph to see if it is acyclic
   if (acyclic(g))
      cout << "New graph is acyclic" << endl;
   else
      cout << "New graph is not acyclic" << endl;

   return 0;
}
```

```
Run:

Original graph is acyclic
   Adding edge (E,B): New graph is not acyclic
```

Topological Sort

In Section 16-4, we developed the depth-first function dfs(), which searches all of the vertices in a graph by using a series of calls to dfsVisit(). Function dfs() returns a list, called dfsList, that sequences the vertices in the reverse order of their finishing times. The order of vertices in dfsList depends on the selection of starting vertices for the calls to dfsVisit(). When the graph is acyclic, we will show that dfsList has a *topological order* that implies that, if $P(v, w)$ is a path from v to w, then v must occur before w in the list. We say that dfs() produces a *topological sort* of the vertices.

A topological sort has important applications for graphs that define a precedence order in the scheduling of activities. For instance, a department at a university stipulates a set of courses to define its major. Courses can have prerequisites, so the department uses a graph to direct a student's schedule. The courses are the vertices and the edges indicate prerequisites. For instance, Figure 16-18 is a graph of courses for a Religious Studies major. A student can elect courses R51 and R37 in any order, but R63 can be taken only after the student completes those two courses, because they are prerequisites. As another example, large construction projects can use a graph with precedence order to establish starting conditions for the subcontractors. Framers can begin to work only after the foundation is poured. Once the walls are raised, the roof, electrical, and heating subcontractors are free to start.

The previous examples are clearly acyclic graphs. A topological sort of the vertices (activities) provides the student a possible four-year schedule of courses or the contractor a schedule for the subcontractors.

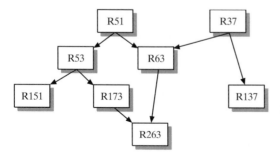

Figure 16-18
Major Program Graph Listing
Courses and Their
Prerequisites

From our knowledge of the dfs() algorithm, we can verify that dfsList produces a topological sort of the vertices, provided that the graph is acyclic. The analysis relies on the color status (WHITE, GRAY, or BLACK) of a vertex during a search. Assume $P(v, w)$ is a path from vertex v to vertex w. We must show that v comes before w in dfsList. This is equivalent to saying v has a later finishing time. Since dfs() searches all of the vertices in the graph, there is some starting vertex v_s used by dfsVisit() to visit v. Function dfsVisit() starts at vertex v_s and moves recursively along paths of neighbors. One of the recursive steps lands on v. At this point, vertex v is not yet visited. We check the current color of vertex w. There are three cases. Figure 16-19 provides a very simple example of each case.

BLACK: A vertex is BLACK only after it has been visited. Vertex w could be BLACK from a previous call to dfsVisit(), which used a starting vertex other than v_s. (Figure (a)). The other possibility is that w was visited by the current dfsVisit() when the recursive step chose a neighbor of v_s that led to w (figure (b)). In either case, vertex w has been visited and vertex v awaits its visit, so v has a later visit time.

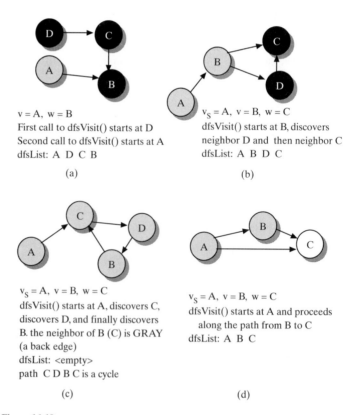

$v = A, \ w = B$
First call to dfsVisit() starts at D
Second call to dfsVisit() starts at A
dfsList: A D C B

(a)

$v_S = A, \ v = B, \ w = C$
dfsVisit() starts at B, discovers
neighbor D and then neighbor C
dfsList: A B D C

(b)

$v_S = A, \ v = B, \ w = C$
dfsVisit() starts at A, discovers C,
discovers D, and finally discovers
B. the neighbor of B (C) is GRAY
(a back edge)
dfsList: <empty>
path C D B C is a cycle

(c)

$v_S = A, \ v = B, \ w = C$
dfsVisit() starts at A and proceeds
along the path from B to C
dfsList: A B C

(d)

Figure 16-19
dfs() Options Assume $e = (v,w)$ is an Edge

GRAY: Vertex w is GRAY only if the recursive calls in dfsVisit() are fol-
            lowing a path from v_s to v that includes w. This implies there is a
            path $P(w, v)$ that connects w to v. The fact that there is a path from
            v to w means that v and w are involved in a cycle, contrary to the fact
            that the graph is acyclic (figure (c)).

WHITE: Because w is discovered after v, during backtracking w will be visit-
            ed before v (figure (d)).

The function topologicalSort() implements the sort algorithm. The result is
the dfsList from dfs(), so we use the code structure for the depth-first search function, with one modification: A topological sort requires an acyclic graph, so we modify dfs() by having the calls to dfsVisit() check for a cycle. This simply means setting
the argument checkForCycle to true and including the call in a try block. The catch
block in topologicalSort() catches an exception from dfsVisit() and throws a second
graphError exception.

topologicalSort():

```
// find a topological sort of an acyclic graph
template <typename T>
void topologicalSort(graph<T>& g, list<T>& tlist)
{
   int i;

   // clear the list that will contain the sort
   tlist.erase(tlist.begin(), tlist.end());

   for (i=0;i < g.vInfo.size(); i++)
      if (g.vInfo[i].occupied)
         g.vInfo[i].color = vertexInfo<T>::WHITE;

   // cycle through the vertices, calling dfsVisit() for each
   // WHITE vertex. check for a cycle
   try
   {
      for (i=0;i < g.vInfo.size(); i++)
         if (g.vInfo[i].occupied && g.vInfo[i].color ==
                                    vertexInfo<T>::WHITE)
            dfsVisit(g, (*(g.vInfo[i].vtxMapLoc)).first,
                     tlist, true);
   }

   catch(graphError&)
   {  throw
         graphError("graph topologicalSort(): graph has a cycle");
   }
}
```

PROGRAM 16-3   COURSE SCHEDULE

Let us create a schedule for a Religious Studies student. The graph of courses, with their prerequisites, is in Figure 16-18, and the graph input is from the file "courses.dat". After calling

topologicalSort() to create a precedence list, we output the list as a "possible schedule of courses".

```cpp
// File: prg16_3.cpp
// the program inputs a directed acyclic graph describing course
// prerequisites in a religious studies department. it performs
// a topological sort and outputs a possible schedule
// of courses

#include <iostream>
#include <string>
#include <list>

#include "d_graph.h"
#include "d_util.h"

using namespace std;

int main()
{
    // graph specifying the courses and prerequisite edges
    graph<string> g;

    // a list holding the topological order of courses
    list<string> tlist;

    // input file holding the vertex strings and edges
    ifstream graphIn;

    // open the file and input the graph
    graphIn.open("courses.dat");
    graphIn >> g;

    // execute a topological sort; store results in list
    topologicalSort(g,tlist);

    // output the list of possible courses
    cout << "Possible schedule of courses"
         << endl << "     ";
    writeContainer(tlist.begin(), tlist.end());
    cout << endl;

    return 0;
}
```

```
Run:
Possible schedule of courses
    R51   R53   R173   R151   R37   R137   R63   R263
```

The topological sort uses the algorithm for dfs(), so its running time is also $O(V+E)$, where V is the number of vertices in the graph and E is the number of edges.

Strong Components

A *strongly connected component* of a graph G is a maximal set of vertices SC in G that are mutually accessible. The set SC can contain a single vertex. If the component SC contains two or more vertices, for any two vertices v and w in SC, there is a path $P(v, w)$ and a path $P(w, v)$. In other words, the two vertices are reachable from each other. However, there is no way to get from a vertex in SC to a vertex in another component and back. Any graph can be partitioned into a unique set of strong components. For instance, the graph in Figure 16-20 has three strong components.

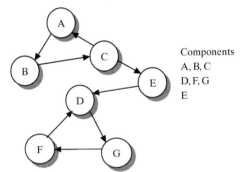

Components
A, B, C
D, F, G
E

Figure 16-20
Strong Components in a
Directed Graph

Graph theory provides an assortment of algorithms to identify strong components. We will discuss one such algorithm, which makes use the depth-first search dfs(). The algorithm introduces the transpose graph G^T for a graph G. The transpose has the same set of vertices V as graph G but a new edge set E^T consisting of the edges of G but with the opposite direction. More precisely, $e^T = (v,w)$ is in E^T if and only if $e = (w,v)$ is in E. Extending this fact to paths, it is clear that $P^T (v, w)$ is a path in G^T if and only if $P(w, v)$ is a path in G.

The algorithm first executes the depth-first search dfs() for the graph G and creates the list dfsList consisting of the vertices in G in the reverse order of their finishing times. After generating the transpose graph G^T, the algorithm concludes by making repeated calls to dfsVisit() for vertices in G^T. The starting vertices for the dfsVisit() calls use the order of vertices in dfsList. The list from each call to dfsVisit() is a strong component of G.

Let us trace the algorithm for the graph in Figure 16-20 and then show why it works. Figure 16-21 includes the original graph and its transpose. We assume that vInfo[0] refers to vertex A, vInfo[1] refers to vertex B, and so forth.

Step 1. Execute dfs() for graph G starting with vertex A. The function returns the list

$$\text{dfsList: } [A\ B\ C\ E\ D\ G\ F]$$

Step 2: Generate the transpose graph, G^T.

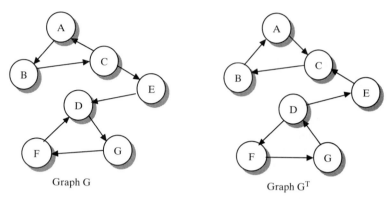

Figure 16-21
Graph *G* and Its Transpose G^T

Step 3. Execute a series of dfsVisit() calls for vertices in G^T. For the starting vertices, use the order of the elements in dfsList.

Start with vertex *A*: dfsVisit() visits vertices *A*, *B*, and *C* in G^T and produces the list [*A*, *C*, *B*]. The elements in the list form the set of vertices for a strong component SC_1.

$$SC_1 = \{A, B, C\}$$

The first call to dfsVisit() visits vertices *A*, *B*, and *C*, the next call to dfsVisit() takes the next unvisited vertex in dfsList, namely *E*. The function visits only vertex *E*, which is the second strong component SC_2.

$$SC_2 = \{E\}$$

Choose the next nonvisited vertex in dfsList, *D*, and make a call to dfsVisit() with starting vertex *D*. In G^T, the function visits vertices *D*, *F*, and *G*, which define the third strong component SC_3.

$$SC_3 = \{D, F, G\}$$

Now that you have seen an example of the strong-component algorithm, let us verify why it works. Assume SC is a set of vertices visited by a call to dfsVisit() in G^T, where the function uses v_s as the starting vertex. Vertex v_s is selected as the first remaining nonvisited vertex in dfsList. We show that, for any two vertices *v* and *w* in SC, there exist paths P(*v*, *w*) and P(*w*, *v*) in *G*. The vertices are in SC, so there are paths $P^T(v_s, v)$ and $P^T(v_s, w)$ *in* G^T and, hence, paths P(*v*, v_s) and, P(*w*, v_s) in *G*. We will establish the existence of paths P(v_s, *v*) and P(v_s, *w*). These show that there is a path P(*v*,*w*) through v_s and a path P(*w*,*v*) through v_s.

We first show that P(v_s, *v*) must exist. We proceed by assuming that no such path exists and derive a contradiction. In step 1 of the strong-component algorithm, dfs() searches all of the vertices in *G*. At some point, then, the search first dis-

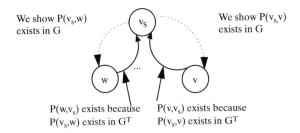

covers v having color WHITE. The contradiction stems from the fact that vertex v_s would have no valid color. Look at the different possible cases.

BLACK: Vertex v_s is BLACK only if it has already been visited—but then v_s would already be in dfsList and v would have a later finishing time. Step 3 would not select v_s before v as the starting vertex for dfsVisit(). Hence, the vertex v_s cannot be BLACK.

GRAY: Vertex v_s is GRAY only if the path of recursive calls to v includes v_s in the path. This implies a path $P(v_s, v)$, contrary to our assumption. Hence, the vertex v_s cannot be GRAY.

WHITE: Because v is WHITE (undiscovered) and there is a path $P(v, v_s)$, subsequent recursive calls to dfsVisit() will visit vertex v_s deeper in graph G, and thus v_s will have an earlier finish (visit) time and v_s will occur after v in dfsList. Hence, the vertex v_s cannot be WHITE.

Under the assumption that $P(v_s, v)$ does not exist, there is no possible valid color for v_s when we discover v. Thus, $P(v_s, v)$ must exist. The same argument shows that $P(v_s, w)$ must exist. This completes our argument that $P(v, w)$ and $P(w, v)$ exist, and so both v and w lie in the same strong component of G.

To complete our verification of the algorithm, we now show that, if x is any vertex in the strong component that includes v_s, it must be in SC. $P(x, v_s)$ exists, so $P^T(v_s, x)$ exists, and dfsVisit() in G^T with v_s as the starting vertex must reach x. If the color of x is WHITE, x will be a member of SC. The color of x cannot be GRAY, because v_s is the starting vertex of the dfsVisit() that produced SC. The color of x cannot be BLACK, because this implies x finishes in a dfsVisit() from another starting vertex, r. $P^T(x, v_s)$ exists, so the traversal from r would find v_s and it would not be the starting vertex for a scan in G^T. Thus, x must be in the set SC.

The function strongComponents() takes the graph and a vector of set<T> objects as arguments and implements the three steps of the algorithm. After calling dfs() to assign vertices in list dfsGList and then generating the transpose, the implementation uses elements in the dfsGList as starting vertices for calls to dfsVisit() in the transpose graph. Each function call creates a list dfsGTList, which the function copies to a set and then inserts into the vector. We include a listing of strongComponents() from "d_graph.h". Consult the file "d_graph.h" for the implementation of transpose().

strongComponents():

```
// find the strong components of the graph
template <typename T>
void strongComponents(graph<T>& g,
                      vector< set<T> >& component)

{
    // list of vertices visited by dfs() for graph g
    list<T> dfsGList;

    // list of vertices visited by dfsVisit() for
    // g transpose
    list<T> dfsGTList;

    // used to scan dfsGList and dfsGTList objects
    list<T>::iterator gIter, gtIter;

    // transpose of the graph
    graph<T> gt;

    // set for an individual strong component
    set<T> scSet;

    int i;

    // clear the return vector
    component.resize(0);

    // execute depth-first tranversal of g
    dfs(g, dfsGList);

    // compute gt
    gt = transpose(g);

    // initialize all vertices in gt to WHITE (unvisited)
    for (i=0;i < gt.vInfo.size(); i++)
        if (gt.vInfo[i].occupied)
            gt.vInfo[i].color = vertexInfo<T>::WHITE;

    // call dfsVisit() for gt from vertices in dfsGList
    gIter = dfsGList.begin();
    while(gIter != dfsGList.end())
    {
        // call dfsVisit() only if vertex is not visited
        if (gt.vInfo[gt.getvInfoIndex(*gIter)].color ==
                        vertexInfo<T>::WHITE)
        {
            // clear dfsGTList and scSet
            dfsGTList.erase(dfsGTList.begin(), dfsGTList.end());
            scSet.erase(scSet.begin(), scSet.end());

            // do dfsVisit() in gt with start vertex *gIter
```

```
            dfsVisit(gt, *gIter, dfsGTList, false);

            // copy vertices from the list to set scSet
            for (gtIter = dfsGTList.begin(); gtIter != dfsGTList.end();
                        gtIter++)
              scSet.insert(*gtIter);

            // add strong component set to the vector
            component.push_back(scSet);
        }
        gIter++;
    }
}
```

Example 16.6

Let us create a declaration to call the function strongComponents() and then display the
strong-component sets that are elements in a vector.

```
// declarations
graph<char> g;
vector<set<char> > vectSet;

// generate the strong components
strongComponents(g, vectSet);

// output the strong components
for (int i = 0; i < vectSet.size(); i++)
{
    cout << "Strong Component " << i+1 << ":    ";
    writeContainer(vectSet[i].begin(), vectSet[i].end());
    cout << endl;
}
Output for graph in Figure 16-20:
    Strong Component 1:    A  B  C
    Strong Component 2:    E
    Strong Component 3:    D  F  G
```

Recall that the depth-first search has running time $O(V+E)$, and that the computation for G^T is also $O(V+E)$. It follows that the running time for this algorithm
to compute the strong components is $O(V+E)$.

GRAPH-MINIMIZATION ALGORITHMS   16-6

Airlines use a graph to list the cities served and the set of available flights. Ideally, the
airline can provide a customer with a direct flight to the destination city. If this is not
possible, a scheduling algorithm should identify a flight with the fewest intermediate
stops, to prevent costly airport delay. We study this situation in the *shortest-path prob-*

lem, which seeks to find a path of shortest length connecting a source and a destination vertex. This algorithm assumes only nonweighted graphs, where an edge simply defines a link between two vertices. We next consider weighted graphs, which include a weight with each edge. The meaning of the weight varies with the application. In an airline graph, the weight could specify actual miles between connecting cities. A transportation system might associate weight with the cost of shipping cargo between terminals; network graphs might use weight to represent the volume of traffic between nodes. Weighted graphs introduce a variety of optimization algorithms. In this section, we look at two such examples. The Dijkstra algorithm identifies the minimum sum of the weights in moving from a starting to an ending vertex. The algorithm is similar to the shortest-path problem, which looks for a path of shortest length. The *minimum-spanning-tree algorithm* is a more general problem that applies to connected undirected graphs. The algorithm determines a set of edges that connect all of the vertices of the graph with a minimum total weight. Our examples illustrate design principles that apply to many graph-optimization problems.

Shortest-Path Algorithm

Airlines, transportation companies, and communication networks use graphs to describe links between hubs in their systems. To optimize customer service and the flow of cargo or data, these system often need to determine the shortest path between two points in the system. The general problem is to develop an algorithm that takes two vertices, sVertex and eVertex, and determines the path of minimum length connecting the vertices. The design of the algorithm must determine the length of the path and the vertices that define the path.

The bfs() algorithm traverses a graph from a starting vertex and identifies the reachable vertices in the order of their path length. The function visits the starting vertex first, followed by visits to its neighbors (path length 1) and then to vertices with successively larger path lengths. The design of the bfs() algorithm is ideal for the shortest-path problem. Starting with vertex sVertex, a search can fan out along paths of adjacent vertices until it locates the destination vertex, eVertex. In order to determine the path length from sVertex to eVertex and the vertices on the path, we need to modify bfs(). The key feature is our use of the parent and dataValue fields for the vertexInfo objects in the vector vInfo. An algorithm can associate its own meaning to the contents of dataValue. In our case, the variable stores the path length of the vertex from sVertex.

Like bfs(), the shortest-path algorithm includes a queue that indirectly stores the vertices, using the corresponding vInfo index. Each iterative step removes a vertex from the queue and searches its adjacency set to locate all of the unvisited neighbors and add them to the queue. The key difference between bfs() and the shortest-path algorithm involves the information that we maintain before pushing a neighbor on the queue. Assume that an iterative step is visiting vertex currPos and identifies neighborPos as an undiscovered neighbor. Recall that corrPos and neighborPos are the indices for elements in the vInfo vector corresponding to the current vertex and neighbor vertex respectively. The value currPos and the path length in the dataValue field permit updates to the parent and dataValue fields for neighborPos.

```
// currPos is the parent and the path length is one greater
vInfo[neighborPos].parent = currPos;
vInfo[neighborPos].dataValue = vInfo[currPos].dataValue + 1;
```

When the breadth-first search locates eVertex as a neighbor, the iterative process terminates and vInfo[eVertex].dataValue is the shortest path length. Furthermore, the process records the parent for each vertex, so the algorithm can retrace the path from eVertex to sVertex by using the parent variable.

Let us trace the algorithm for the graph in Figure 16-22, by finding the shortest path from F to C. A look at the graph reveals a series of possible paths.

$P(F, C): F, D, A, B, C$	(length 4)
$P(F, C): F, E, D, A, B, C$	(length 5)
$P(F, C): F, E, D, A, C$	(length 4)
$P(F, C): F, D, A, C$	(length 3)

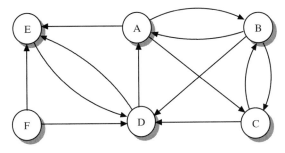

Figure 16-22
Shortest-Path Graph

Anticipating the result, the shortest path has length 3. Start the algorithm with sVertex = F. In the corresponding vertexInfo object, set dataValue (path length) to 0 and make sVertex its own parent. Initialize the queue by adding F as the first element.

Step 1:   Pop F from the queue. Identify the two neighbors, D and E, and update their vertexInfo records so that their colors are GRAY (discovered), path lengths are $1 = 0 + 1$, and F is the parent. Add the neighbors to the queue (Figure (a). Note that the queue stores a vertex by storing the index of the corresponding vInfo object. In the figure, we use a symbolic representation of a queue element like $D_{1,F}$ indicating that vertex D has path length 1 from F and F is its parent.

Step 2:   Pop D from the queue. Among its neighbors, vertex E is GRAY (discovered). The only undiscovered neighbor is vertex A, which goes into the queue with path length 2 and parent D (Figure (b).

Step 3:   Pop E from the queue. E has no undiscovered neighbors, so simply proceed to step 4 (Figure (c).

Step 4:   Pop *A* from the queue. The undiscovered neighbors include vertices *B* and *C*. *B* enters the queue with path length 3 and parent *A*, and *C* enters the queue with path length 3 and parent *A* (Figure (d).

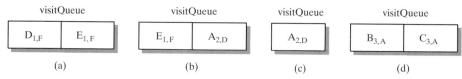

      (a)   (b)   (c)   (d)

Step 5 and 6:   Pop *B* from the queue. *B* has no undiscovered neighbors, so pop *C* from the queue. *C* is the destination vertex, so the algorithm concludes. All required return information is available.

Shortest path length = vInfo[eVertex].dataValue = 3

$P(F, C) = F\,D\,A\,C$
<discovery in reverse order> eVertex = C, parent(C) = A,
                                       parent(A) = D, parent(D) =
                                       F = sVertex

The function shortestPath() implements the algorithm. The arguments include the graph, the source and destination vertices, and a list for the path of vertices.

```
template <typename T>
int shortestPath(graph<T>& g, const T& sVertex,
            const T& eVertex, list<T>& path)
```

In the implementation, the Boolean variable foundShortestPath indicates whether the search discovers the ending vertex. Initially, the value is false. After the pushing of the starting vertex onto the queue, a loop continues until the algorithm finds the ending vertex or the queue becomes empty. When the loop identifies the ending vertex, the value of foundShortestPath is set to true and the loop exits. The function retraces the path, placing each vertex at the front of the list. The dataValue for eVertex is the return value. If the destination is never found (queue becomes empty), the function returns -1.

The code uses the structure of the breadth-first search. The algorithm performs additional computations in the loop that searches the adjacency set. Assume currPos is the current vertex that was popped from the queue. If currPos identifies the ending vertex, the loop terminates. Otherwise, for each vertex in the adjacency set of currPos, we update its color, dataValue (path length), and parent field in the vertexInfo object and push it into the queue.

```
while (!visitQueue.empty() && !foundShortestPath)
{
    // delete a queue entry, and color it BLACK
    currPos = visitQueue.front();
    visitQueue.pop();
```

```
        g.vInfo[currPos].color = vertexInfo<T>::BLACK;

        // if we are at eVertex, we have found the shortest
        // path from sVertex to eVertex
        if (currPos == pos_eVertex)
           foundShortestPath = true;
        else
        {
           // create an alias for the adjacency set of currPos
           set<neighbor>& edgeSet = g.vInfo[currPos].edges;
           // for all undiscovered neighbors, update the dataValue,
           // color, and parent fields in the vertexInfo object.
           for (eIter = edgeSet.begin(); eIter != edgeSet.end(); eIter++)
           {
              neighborPos = (*eIter).dest;

              if (g.vInfo[neighborPos].color == vertexInfo<T>::WHITE)
              {
                 g.vInfo[neighborPos].dataValue =
                                  g.vInfo[currPos].dataValue + 1;
                 g.vInfo[neighborPos].parent = currPos;
                 g.vInfo[neighborPos].color = vertexInfo<T>::GRAY;
                 // add neighbor vertex to the queue
                 visitQueue.push(neighborPos);
              }
           }
        }
     }
  }
```

If a path exists, the Boolean variable foundShortestPath is true. To find the path from sVertex to eVertex, begin at eVertex and follow the parent field back to sVertex. At each step, store the vertex at the front of the path list. Complete the algorithm by returning either the shortest path length in g.vInfo[pos_eVertex].dataValue or −1.

```
  // clear path and find the sequence of vertices
  // from sVertex to eVertex
  path.erase(path.begin(), path.end());
  if (foundShortestPath)
  {
     currPos = pos_eVertex;
     while (currPos != pos_sVertex)
     {
        path.push_front((*(g.vInfo[currPos].vtxMapLoc)).first);
        currPos = g.vInfo[currPos].parent;
     }
     path.push_front(sVertex);
     returnValue = g.vInfo[pos_eVertex].dataValue;
  }
  else
     returnValue = -1;
```

PROGRAM 16-4   FINDING SHORTEST PATHS

For the graph in Figure 16-22, the following program prompts the user to enter a source and a destination vertex. The function shortestPath() returns the length of the shortest path and a list of the path vertices. Output displays the length and then calls writeContainer() to list the path. File "shpath.dat" has the input data for the graph.

```cpp
// File: prg16_4.cpp
// the program inputs the graph specified by the file "shpath.dat"
// and prompts the user for a starting and an ending vertex. using
// the function shortestPath(), the program outputs the length
// of the shortest path from starting to ending vertex and the
// actual path

#include <iostream>
#include <fstream>
#include <list>
#include "d_graph.h"
#include "d_util.h"

using namespace std;

int main()
{
    // vertices are characters
    graph<char> g;

    char sVertex, eVertex;

    // minimum path to the destination vertex
    list<char> path;

    ifstream graphIn;
    graphIn.open("shpath.dat");

    // input the graph and then prompt for input of
    // source and destination vertices
    graphIn >> g;

    cout << "Enter starting and ending vertices: ";
    cin >> sVertex >> eVertex;

    cout   << "    Shortest path from " << sVertex << " to "
           << eVertex << " is "
           << shortestPath(g, sVertex, eVertex, path) << "    Path: ";
    writeContainer(path.begin(), path.end());
    cout << endl;

    return 0;
}
```

```
Run 1:

Enter start and end vertices: F C
   Shortest path from F to C is   3    Path: F  D  A  C

Run 2:

Enter start and end vertices: C F
   Shortest path from C to F is  -1    Path:

Run 3:

Enter start and end vertices: B B
   Shortest path from B to B is   0    Path: B
```

Dijkstra's Minimum-Path Algorithm

The shortest-path algorithm finds the path of shortest length connecting two vertices. The algorithm uses a breadth-first search of the vertices. We now introduce a similar algorithm for weighted graphs, known as *Dijkstra's algorithm*. The problem differs: We are interested in finding a path of minimum weight. As the graph in Figure 16-23 illustrates, the resulting paths might not be the same. Assume A is the starting vertex and E is the ending vertex. Three paths, $A–B–E$, $A–C–E$, and $A–D–E$, have path length 2, with weights 15, 14, and 13 respectively. The minimum Dijkstra path is $A–C–D–E$, with weight 11 but path length 3.

The Dijkstra algorithm uses a *greedy* strategy that solves the problem in stages. At each stage, we select the vertex x that defines a minimum path from the starting vertex. The term "greedy" indicates that the strategy attempts to maximize short term gains, even though the decision could need to be reversed as we discover new vertices. In the example, we first select vertex B among the neighbors of A, because it has the minimum weight, 3. Later, we will discover that the cost of adding the weight 12 for edge (B,E) would make C or D a better choice.

The minimum-path algorithm uses the iterative strategy that we employed for the shortest-path problem, with one major difference. The search uses a minimum priority queue, rather than a queue to store the vertices. To define objects in the priority

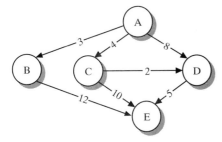

Figure 16-23
Weighted Graph Comparing
Shortest Path and Minimum
Path Connecting A to E

queue, we declare the minInfo class, which contains a vInfo index and the path weight as data members. The index represents the ending vertex for a path from the starting vertex and pathWeight is sum of the weights for the edges. The class overloads the < operator, using the pathWeight to compare objects.

```
class minInfo
{
   public:
      int endV;
      int pathWeight;
      friend bool operator< (minInfo lhs, minInfo rhs)
      { return lhs.pathWeight < rhs.pathWeight; }
};
```

Besides using a priority queue, the algorithm maintains data about each vertex in vInfo. The data include the color of the vertex and the current information about its minimum-path weight from the starting vertex. The variable dataValue maintains the minimum weight. Initially, each vertex is unvisited (WHITE) and its dataValue is set to INFINITY, which is a system-dependent value for the largest positive integer. Understanding the role of the dataValue variable is critical for the algorithm. The algorithm fans out from the starting vertex along paths of neighbors and reveals different routes that terminate at each vertex. At each step in the algorithm, the priority queue identifies a new vertex whose pathWeight value is the minimum path weight from the starting vertex . At no subsequent step would the search find a new path to the vertex with a smaller weight. Only at this point do we mark the vertex as visited. If this vertex is the ending vertex, the algorithm concludes. Otherwise, for each neighbor, we check the current value in the dataValue variable for the vertex and determine whether the new path to the neighbor has a smaller minimum weight. If so, we update dataValue to reflect our new understanding and insert the new path into the priority queue. We illustrate the algorithm by using the graph in Figure 16-24. Vertex A is the starting vertex and vertex D is the ending vertex. To simplify notation, let minInfo(v, w) designate a minInfo object with v as the ending vertex for path $P(A, v)$ and total path weight w.

The algorithm begins with vertex A. The initialization process assigns the pathWeight field for vertex A as 0 and creates the object minInfo(A, 0) that repre-

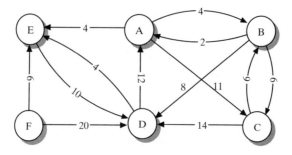

Figure 16-24
Sample Graph for the Dijkstra
Minimum-Path Algorithm
from A to D

sents a path from A to itself with initial weight 0. The object is the first entry in the priority queue.

priority queue

Each iterative step selects the minInfo object having the minimum weight. If the vertex is D, the pathWeight value is the solution to the minimum-path problem from A to D. Otherwise, the vertex is marked as visited, and the algorithm explores its unvisited neighbors.

Step 1:   Delete the only element in the priority queue. The minInfo object has vertex A and weight 0. After marking A as visited, look at the vertices B, C, and E, which are the unvisited neighbors of A. For each neighbor V, we do not have any current path $P(A, V)$ that has less path weight (dataValue = INFINITY), and so we create one by adding an edge. The weight of the path is the weight of the edge (A, V). Update the dataValue field for V and add the object minInfo(V, d) to the priority queue.

At the end of step 1, vertex A is marked as visited, and the minimum path from A to A has weight 0. Our current level of understanding has the minimum path weight from A to B as 4, from A to C as 11, and from A to E as 4. The three objects in the priority queue reflect this information.

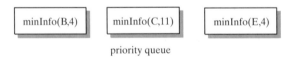

priority queue

Step 2:   The minInfo objects for vertex B and E have the same priority (path weight). Assume the pop() operation removes minInfo$(B, 4)$. We mark vertex B as visited, because its current path weight, 4, is the minimum path weight from A. Step 2 then considers the unmarked neighbors of B, which are C and D. We know there is a path of minimum weight 4 from A to B. The question is whether extending the path to C by adding the edge (B, C) would create a path to C of smaller weight than any other known path. From step 1, the current path weight (dataValue) for a known path to C is 11. The weight of the new path uses the weight to B and the weight of the edge (B, C).

$$\text{weight for path } A - B - C = \text{weight to } B + \text{weight } (B, C)$$
$$= 4 + 6 = 10$$

The new weight is less, so we update the current dataValue of C to 10 and insert the object minInfo(C, 10) in the priority queue. Creating a new path to D that uses the edge (B, D) is clearly better than the current weight, INFINITY, because we do not have an existing path for comparison. Update the current dataValue for D to 12 (4 + weight(B, D)), and insert minInfo(D, 12) into the priority queue.

Note that a vertex can occur in two or more minInfo objects. For instance, C is the ending vertex for paths of weight 10 and 11. When the time comes, the priority queue deletes the object with the smaller value.

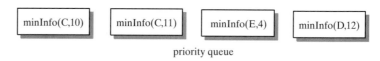

priority queue

Step 3:   Remove minInfo(E,4) from the priority queue and mark E as visited, with minimum path weight of 4. Vertex E has one unmarked neighbor, D. Extending the path from D to E by adding edge (D,E) has the following weight:

Path weight to E + weight(E,D) = 4 + 10 = 14.

The new path is no improvement over an existing path to D with weight 12. Go to the next step.

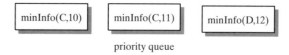

priority queue

Steps 4–5: Remove minInfo(C,10). After marking C, a check of its unmarked neighbors identifies D.

Extending the path from C to D by adding edge (C,D) creates a new path of weight 24, which is no improvement over a current path of length 12. Step 5 removes minInfo(C,11), but C is already marked, so we move to Step 6. The priority queue has one remaining element.

priority queue

Step 6:   Remove minInfo(D, 12). D is the ending vertex, so the algorithm terminates with a minimum path weight of 12 from A to D.

To see that the Dijkstra algorithm works, assume that the algorithm does not find the minimum path weight from the starting vertex v_s to the ending vertex v_e. Rather a second path connecting the vertices has smaller weight. Assume this second path and the Dijkstra path are the same up to vertex u and that the weight of the path found by Dijkstra's algorithm is W. The better path uses x as an unvisited intermediate vertex. The weight of $P(v_s, u)$ + weight(u, x) must be less than W, so $P(v_s, x)$ will come out of the priority queue before the path found by the algorithm. Continuing in this way, all the vertices on the better path will come out of the priority queue, and the algorithm will find the optimal path, contradicting our assumption that the algorithm does not find the minimum path.

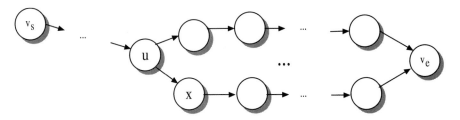

The function mininumPath() implements the Dijkstra algorithm. The function takes the graph and the starting and ending vertices as arguments, along with a list that stores the vertices on the path.

minimumPath():

```
template <typename T>
int minimumPath(graph<T>& g, const T& sVertex, const T& eVertex,
                list<T>& path);
```

The implementation in file "d_graph.h" follows the design of the shortest-path algorithm. We use the color and dataValue fields in vector vInfo to maintain the visit status and current path weight at a vertex. By updating the parent field, we can iterate back from the ending vertex to the starting vertex and place the vertices of the minimum path in list *path*. We use the miniPQ class from Chapter 14 to implement the priority queue, minPathPQ.

```
// heap (priority queue) that stores minInfo objects
miniPQ<minInfo, less<minInfo> > minPathPQ;
```

The Boolean variable foundMinPath indicates when the minimum path is found. The key element of the implementation is a loop that processes a vertex after deleting a corresponding minInfo object from the priority queue. Iteration continues until the ending vertex is deleted or the priority queue is empty. In the latter case, there is no minimum path, and the return value is -1.

```
// process vertices until we find a minimum path to
// eVertex or the priority queue is empty
while (!minPathPQ.empty())
{
    // delete a priority queue entry and record its
    // vertex and path weight from sVertex.
    vertexData = minPathPQ.top();
    minPathPQ.pop();
```

```
        currPos = vertexData.endV;

        // if we are at eVertex, we have found the minimum
        // path from sVertex to eVertex
        if (currPos == pos_eVertex)
        {
           foundMinPath = true;
           break;
        }

        if (g.vInfo[currPos].color != vertexInfo<T>::BLACK)
        {
           // mark the vertex so we don't look at it again
           g.vInfo[currPos].color = vertexInfo<T>::BLACK;

           // find all neighbors of the current vertex pos. for each
           // neighbor that has not been visited, generate a minInfo
           // object and insert it into the priority queue provided the
           // total weight to get to the neighbor is better than the
           // current dataValue in vInfo
           adj = g.vInfo[currPos].edges;
           for(adjIter = adj.begin();adjIter != adj.end();
                              adjIter++)
           {
              destPos = (*adjIter).dest;

              if (g.vInfo[destPos].color == vertexInfo<T>::WHITE)
              {
                 // compare total weight of adding edge to dataValue
                 if ((newMinWeight = (g.vInfo[currPos].dataValue +
                    (*adjIter).weight)) < g.vInfo[destPos].dataValue)
                 {
                    // add minVertexInfo object for new vertex and update
                    // dataValue in vInfo
                    vertexData.endV = destPos;
                    vertexData.pathWeight = newMinWeight;
                    g.vInfo[destPos].dataValue = newMinWeight;
                    g.vInfo[destPos].parent = currPos;
                    minPathPQ.push(vertexData);
                 }   // end "if" that checks weights
              }   // end "if" that checks if neighbor is not marked
           }   // end "for"
        }   // end "if" vertex not already marked
     }   // end "while"
```

If the algorithm identifies a minimum path weight, we can build the path by
starting at the ending vertex and using the parent variable to retrace the path back
to the starting vertex.

```
     // clear path and setup return
```

```
path.erase(path.begin(), path.end());
if (foundMinPath)
{
   currPos = pos_eVertex;
   while (currPos != pos_sVertex)
   {
      path.push_front((*(g.vInfo[currPos].vtxMapLoc)).first);
      currPos = g.vInfo[currPos].parent;
   }
   path.push_front(sVertex);
   returnValue = g.vInfo[pos_eVertex].dataValue;
}
else
   returnValue = -1;
```

PROGRAM 16-5   FINDING MINIMUM PATHS

Let us look at minimum paths for the sample graph in Figure 16-24. A prompt asks the user to enter the starting and ending vertices. Output gives the minimum path weight and the vertices on the path (or −1 if no path exists).

```
// File: prg16_5.cpp
// the program inputs the graph specified by the file "mpath.dat".
// in a loop that executes four times, a prompt directs the user
// to enter starting and ending vertices. by calling the algorithm
// minimumPath(), the program outputs the minimum path weight and
// the corresponding path from the starting to the ending vertex

#include <iostream>
#include <fstream>
#include <iomanip>
#include <list>

#include "d_graph.h"
#include "d_util.h"

using namespace std;

int main()
{
   // vertices are characters
   graph<char> g;
   char sVertex, eVertex;

   // minimum path to the destination vertex
   list<char> path;
   ifstream graphIn;
   graphIn.open("mpath.dat");

   // input the graph
```

```
    graphIn >> g;

    for (int i = 1; i <= 4; i++)
    {
       cout << "Enter start and end vertices: ";
       cin >> sVertex >> eVertex;

       cout   << "   Minimum path from " << sVertex << " to "
              << eVertex << " is " << setw(3)
              << minimumPath(g, sVertex, eVertex, path) << "   Path: ";
       writeContainer(path.begin(), path.end());
       cout << endl << endl;
    }

    return 0;
}
```

```
Run:

Enter start and end vertices: F C
   Minimum path from F to C is  38    Path: F  E  D  A  B  C

Enter start and end vertices: C F
   Minimum path from C to F is  -1    Path:

Enter start and end vertices: B B
   Minimum path from B to B is   0    Path: B

Enter start and end vertices: A C
   Minimum path from A to C is  10    Path: A  B  C
```

Running-Time Analysis. Coloring the vertices WHITE is an $O(V)$ operation. The actions in the loop "while (!minPathPQ.empty())" dominate the running time. In the worst case, the algorithm pushes all edges into the priority queue and pops all edges. Each push() and pop() operation is $O(\log_2 E)$, so the running time for all these priority-queue operations is $O(E \log_2 E)$. The running time for Dijkstra's algorithm is $O(V + E \log_2 E)$.

Minimum-Spanning Tree

The minimum-path algorithm finds an optimal path connecting a starting and ending vertex in a directed graph. A more general problem deals with a connected undirected graph and finds a set of edges that connect all of the vertices in a graph with the smallest total weight. The vertices and edges form a *minimum-spanning tree*. The concept has important applications. A network connects hubs in the system. The minimum-spanning tree links all of the nodes in the system with the least amount of cable (Figure 16-25). There is a variety of minimum-spanning-tree algorithms. One such algorithm, called Prim's algorithm, builds the tree in stages. At

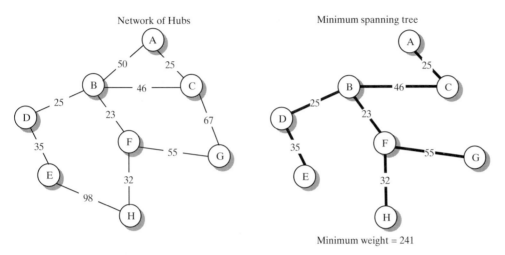

Figure 16-25
A Minimum-Spanning Tree

each stage, the algorithm adds a new vertex and an edge that connects the new vertex with the ones already in the tree. Its design is very similar to that of the Dijkstra minimum-path algorithm.

We can represent an undirected graph by assuring that if there is an edge (u,v) there is an edge (v,u) with the same weight. The iterative process begins with any initial vertex and maintains the two variables minSpanTreeSize and minSpanTreeWeight, which have initial values 0. Each step adds a new vertex to the spanning tree. Adding a vertex defines the meaning of "visit a vertex" in this algorithm. The process terminates when all of the vertices are added to the tree (minSpanTreeSize == g.size()). Adding a vertex also involves adding the edge of minimal weight that connects the vertex to those already in the tree. The weight of the edge updates the variable minSpanTreeWeight. Consider the graph in Figure 16-26(a), where A is selected as the first vertex in the spanning tree. There is no associated edge or weight for the initial vertex. Vertices $B, C,$ and D are neighbors of $A,$ so

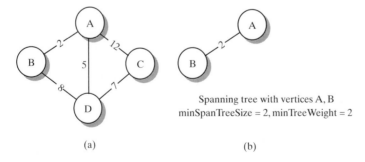

(a)   (b)

Spanning tree with vertices A, B
minSpanTreeSize = 2, minTreeWeight = 2

Figure 16-26
Minimum-Spanning Tree: Vertices A and B

they are candidates to become the next entry in the spanning tree. The edges connecting the vertices to A have weight 2, 12, and 5, respectively. Edge (A, B) has minimum weight, so B and that edge are added to the spanning tree. Figure 16-26(b) displays the spanning tree and the values for minSpanTreeSize and minSpanTreeWeight after the adding (visiting) of vertices A and B.

The key elements of the algorithm become clearer when we look at the next step. Search the edge set for each vertex that is already in the spanning tree (visited) and identify those edges that terminate at a nonvisited vertex. In the example, the edges are $e_1 = (A, C)$, $e_2 = (A, D)$, and $e_3 = (B, D)$. Note that edges e_1 and e_2 were part of step 1, which looked for neighbors of A. Only edge e_3, with weight 8, is new. Vertices C and D are candidates for the next entry in the spanning tree. Vertex D can enter with edge e_2 or e_3, and vertex C can enter with edge e_1. Among the three edges, e_2 has the minimum weight, 5, and so D becomes the next vertex in the spanning tree, with minSpanTreeWeight updated to 7 (Figure 16-27(a)). The last step adds vertex C to the tree. The available edges are e_1, with weight 12, and $e_4 = (D,C)$, with weight 7. The minimum choice is e_4, and the weight of the minimum spanning tree is 14 Figure 16-27(b).

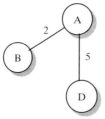

Spanning tree with vertices A, B, D
minSpanTreeSize = 3, minTreeWeight = 7

(a)

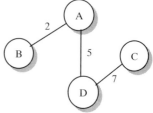

Spanning tree with vertices A, B, D, C
minSpanTreeSize = 4, minTreeWeight = 14

(b)

Figure 16-27
Completing the Minimum-Spanning-Tree Algorithm with Vertices D and C

Implementing Prim's Algorithm   We implement Prim's algorithm by using a priority queue of minInfo objects, much as we do in the Dijkstra minimum-path algorithm. An iterative step inserts an element into the priority queue when there is an edge $e = (v,w)$, where v is a vertex already in the minimum spanning tree, w is a vertex not in the tree, and adding the edge provides a smaller weight than the weight from any previously discovered edge that terminates in w. The endV field of a minInfo object is w, and the pathWeight field is the weight of the edge. Technically, endV is the index of the vertexInfo element in vector vInfo that corresponds to vertex w. We also use some of the fields in the vInfo entries.

color: Initially, all vertices are colored WHITE, to indicate that they are not in the spanning tree. When a vertex enters the tree, the color is set to BLACK. The colors BLACK and WHITE distinguish whether vertices are in the spanning tree.

dataValue: This is the weight of the minimum edge that would connect the vertex to an existing vertex that is already in the spanning tree. As the tree grows, dataValue is updated, because there are more and more available edges to connect the vertex to the tree. Initially, dataValue is INFINITY.

parent: This is the source vertex for the minimum edge associated with dataValue. The parent is a vertex in the spanning tree. Each update to dataValue has a corresponding update for the parent field.

Let us see how these implementation tools apply to the sample graph in Figure 16-26, where we select vertex A as the first vertex in the spanning tree.

Step 0: Create the object minInfo(A, 0) and push it onto the priority queue. The object creates an implied edge $e = (A, A)$ with weight 0. At the same time, set dataValue to 0 and parent to A in the vInfo element corresponding to A. For each step, we include a figure that lists the elements in the priority queue and the relevant fields for vertexInfo objects in vector vInfox.

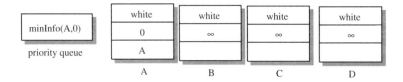

Step 1: Pop minInfo(A, 0) from the priority queue and color A BLACK. This has the effect of placing A in the spanning tree. With each deletion, we increment the variable minSpanTreeSize and add the dataValue to minSpanTreeWeight. The resulting variables have values 1 and 0. Search the adjacency list for A to locate the edges that could connect an adjacent vertex not in the spanning tree to the single vertex already in the tree. For each neighbor v, create the minInfo object with v as the ending vertex and the weight of the edge $e = (A, v)$ as the pathWeight. Also, update dataValue to the edge weight and set A as the parent.

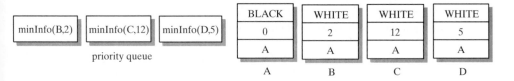

Step 2: Remove minInfo(B, 2) from the priority queue. If it is WHITE (not
visited), then color B BLACK. The importance of checking for
whether the vertex is already in the spanning tree will become clear in
the comment following step 4. Increment minSpanTreeSize to 2, and
update minSpanTreeWeight by adding the dataValue, 2. The spanning
tree now has two vertices, A and B. We have already taken care of vertex A, so we need only look for nonvisited (WHITE) neighbors of B
to find additional edges that would connect a vertex to the spanning
tree. In the example, D is such a neighbor, with edge (B, D) having
weight 8. This is a key point in the minimization algorithm. In the
vInfo object for D, the dataValue is 5. This implies that an edge already exists, which would connect D to the existing spanning tree. In
fact, it is edge (A, D), from step 1. This is a better (lower-weight) connection than the new edge (B, D), and so we take no action.

Step 3: Pop minInfo(D, 5) from the priority queue. D is WHITE; color it
BLACK. The number of vertices in the spanning tree (minSpanTree-
Size) is 3, and minSpanTreeWeight become 7 (5 + 2). The vertex has
only one WHITE neighbor, C. The edge (D, C) has weight 7, which is
less than the current "best" edge weight of 12 in the vertexInfo object
for C. The new edge is a better choice, and so we create minInfo(C, 7)
and update the vInfo entry variables so that dataValue is 7 and parent
is D. Push the minInfo object onto the priority queue.

Step 4: Remove minInfo(C, 7). The value for minSpanTreeWeight becomes
14 (7 + 7). Because minSpanTreeSize now equals the vertex size of
the graph, the process terminates. The weight for the minimum-spanning tree is 14.

Note that, in Step 3, vertex C appears twice in the priority queue. Initially it enters
the queue as a neighbor of A, where edge (A, C) has weight 12. Once D is in the
spanning tree, we look at its neighbors and find a better edge, (D, C), with weight 7.
In this step, we pop minInfo(C, 7) and put C into the spanning tree (color it

BLACK). In a larger example, a subsequent step may delete minInfo(C, 12) from the priority queue, but *C* would already be in the spanning tree (BLACK), so we would take no action, because we cannot connect *C* a second time with weight 12.

We want to use the information in the vInfo objects to build the minimum spanning tree. This involves creating a new graph, MST, that is the minimum spanning tree containing the vertices from the original graph and the minimal edges that were identified by the algorithm. We now make use of our effort to maintain the parent value. Search the vertices in the original graph and insert them into MST. For each vertex *v*, use the parent variable in the vInfo object to insert the edge *e* = (parent(*v*), *v*) into MST.

You can find the code for minSpanTree() in "d_graph.h". The function takes a graph *g* and a spanning tree MST as arguments, constructs MST, and returns the total weight for the minimal spanning tree.

```
template <typename T>
int minSpanTree(graph<T>& g, graph<T>& MST);
```

Let us look at a few of the code segments that implement the loop. After popping a minInfo object from the priority queue, we first check on whether the vertex (index currPos) is WHITE. If so, we proceed to update minSpanTreeWeight and minSpanTreeSize. The process terminates once all vertices are part of the spanning tree.

```
// delete a priority queue entry
vertexData = minTreePQ.top();
minTreePQ.pop();
currPos = vertexData.endV;

// if vertex is not part of the new graph (unvisited)
// add the weight of the edge to the total tree weight
// and increment the number of vertices in the tree
if (g.vInfo[currPos].color == vertexInfo<T>::WHITE)
{
    minSpanTreeWeight += vertexData.totalWeight;
    minSpanTreeSize++;

    // if we spanned all vertices, break
    if (minSpanTreeSize == g.numberOfVertices())
       break;

    // mark the vertex BLACK so we don't look at it again.
    g.vInfo[currPos].color = vertexInfo<T>::BLACK;
    . . .
}
```

With a new vertex in the spanning tree, we look at all of its WHITE neighbors and determine whether the edge connecting the vertex and the neighbor has less weight than any edge we may have discovered in a previous iteration. The weight (dataValue) for each neighbor is initially INFINITY, so the first edge weight will update dataValue. If the new edge is "better," create a minInfo object and update the dataValue and parent fields for the vInfo object corresponding to the neighbor (index destPos).

```
// find all unmarked neighbors of the vertex.
// adjIter is a set iterator pointing at the edge corresponding to
// vertices with index currPos and destPos
adj = g.vInfo[currPos].edges;
for(adjIter = adj.begin();adjIter != adj.end();   adjIter++)
{
   destPos = (*adjIter).dest;

   // if neighbor is unmarked, check whether adding the new
   // edge to the tree is better than using the current edge
   if (g.vInfo[destPos].color == vertexInfo<T>::WHITE)
   {
      if ((*adjIter).weight < g.vInfo[destPos].dataValue)
      {
         // if new edge is a better connection, create minInfo object
         // for new vertex. update dataValue and parent variables
         // in vertexInfo
         vertexData.endV = destPos;
         vertexData.pathWeight = (*adjIter).weight;
         g.vInfo[destPos].dataValue = (*adjIter).weight;
         g.vInfo[destPos].parent = currPos;
         minTreePQ.push(vertexData);
      }
   }
}
```

PROGRAM 16-6   MINIMUM SPANNING TREE
_____

After prompting the user for the name of the graph input file, the program constructs the graph and uses the algorithm minSpanTree() to compute the minimum spanning tree. The output displays the total weight for the resulting minimum spanning tree along with its vertices and edges.

We have used a single example to illustrate Prim's minimum-spanning-tree algorithm. The first run uses the graph in Figure 16-26 ("minspan.dat"), and the second run computes the tree for the graph in Figure 16-25 ("network.dat").

```
// File: prg16_6.cpp
// this program uses Prim's algorithm for a minimum spanning tree.
// it reads a graph input file with name entered by the user and
// calls minSpanTree() to build the minimum spanning tree for the
// graph. output includes the total weight for the tree as
// well as a listing of its vertices and edges

#include <iostream>
#include <fstream>
#include <cstdlib>
```

```
#include <string>

using namespace std;

#include "d_graph.h"

int main()
{
    // graph input file
    ifstream graphIn;
    // vertices are characters
    graph<char> g, minSpan;
    int weight;
    // graph file name
    string fileName;

    cout << "Graph input file: ";
    cin >> fileName;

    graphIn.open(fileName.c_str());
    if (!graphIn)
    {
        cerr << "Cannot open '" << fileName << "'" << endl;
        exit(1);
    }

    // input the graph
    graphIn >> g;

    // get minimum spanning tree and its weight
    weight = minSpanTree(g, minSpan);
    cout << "MST has weight " << weight << endl << endl;

    // display minumum spanning tree
    cout << " -- MST Graph --" << endl;
    cout << minSpan << endl;

    return 0;
}
```

```
Run 1:
Graph input file: minspan.dat
MST has weight 14

-- MST Graph --
A: in-degree 0   out-degree 2
   Edges: B (2)   D (5)
```

```
B: in-degree 1  out-degree 0
  Edges:
C: in-degree 1  out-degree 0
  Edges:
D: in-degree 1  out-degree 1
  Edges: C (7)


Run 2:


Graph input file: network.dat
MST has weight 241


-- MST Graph --
A: in-degree 0  out-degree 1
  Edges: C (25)
B: in-degree 1  out-degree 2
  Edges: D (25)  F (23)
C: in-degree 1  out-degree 1
  Edges: B (46)
D: in-degree 1  out-degree 1
  Edges: E (35)
E: in-degree 1  out-degree 0
  Edges:
F: in-degree 1  out-degree 2
  Edges: G (55)  H (32)
G: in-degree 1  out-degree 0
  Edges:
H: in-degree 1  out-degree 0
  Edges:
```

Running Time Analysis. Prim's algorithm is just a variation of Dijkstra's algorithm, so its running time is O($V + E \log_2 E$).

CHAPTER SUMMARY

- Section 16-1 develops the definition of an undirected and of a directed graph (digraph). Both types of graphs can be either weighted or nonweighted. The section discusses the types of applications that use graphs.

- Section 16-2 develops the API for the graph class. This is the most complex class in the book and describes a digraph. After showing how to use the primary class member functions, the representation of graphs is discussed. The two primary approaches are the use of adjacency lists or the use of an adjacency matrix.

- Section 16-3 develops the overall design of the graph class, paying particular attention to the vertex map and the vector, vInfo, of vertex properties. These properties include the set of adjacent vertices (edges). The class declaration is presented, along with the implementation of selected member functions.

- Section 16-4 develops the breadth-first and depth-first searches. The breadth-first search, bfs(), locates all vertices reachable from a starting vertex; the depth-first search, dfs(), produces a list of all graph vertices in the reverse order of their finishing times. The depth-first search is supported by a recursive depth-first visit function, dfsVisit(), that does most of the work.

- By application of the depth-first search strategy, an algorithm can check to see whether a graph is acyclic (has no cycles) and can perform a topological sort of a directed acyclic graph (DAG). The depth-first search also forms the basis for an efficient algorithm that finds the strong components of a graph. Section 16-5 discusses these algorithms.

- Many very important graph applications find minimum values in a graph. The breadth-first search can be used to find the minimum distance from a starting vertex to an ending vertex in a graph. If the graph has weights, Dijkstra's algorithm uses a priority queue to determine a path from a starting to an ending vertex, of minimum weight. This idea can be extended to Prim's algorithm, which computes the minimum-spanning tree in an undirected, connected graph. Section 16-6 discusses these algorithms.

CLASSES AND LIBRARIES IN THE CHAPTER

Name	Header File
graph	d_graph.h
miniPQ	d_pqueue.h
writeContainer()	d_util.h

REVIEW EXERCISES

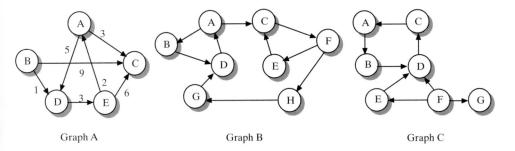

Graph A   Graph B   Graph C

1. Use graph A for parts (a) and (b).
   (a) Give the adjacency list representation for the graph.
   (b) Give the adjacency matrix representation for the graph.

2. Use graph B to answer the following questions on paths. If no path exists, respond "No path."
   (a) Find a directed path from E to B.
   (b) Find a directed path from B to E.
   (c) List all of the vertices that are adjacent to F.
   (d) List all of the vertices that have in-degree 2.
   (e) List all of the vertices that have out-degree 1.
   (f) List all of the vertices that have the same in-degree and out-degree.

3. (a) List the vertices in graph B in the reverse order of their visit (finish) time for a depth-first search (dfsVisit) that starts at vertex A. Repeat the process, but produce a different list by assuming that the scan accesses neighbors in a different order.
   (b) List the vertices in graph C in the reverse order of their visit (finish) time for a depth-first search that starts at vertex F and first accesses E as its neighbor. Repeat the process, but produce a different list by assuming that the search first accesses neighbor D.
   (c) Which starting indices would visit vertices $\{A, B, C, D\}$ by using the breadth-first scan (bfs)?

4. (a) Which of the graphs A, B, and C are strongly connected? weakly connected?
   (b) List the strong components of graph C.

5. Let v be a vertex in a graph. What is the meaning of the following output statement?

```
cout << vInfo[vtxMapv].edges.size();
```

6. Assume i is an index in the vInfo vector corresponding to vertex v.
   (a) What is the value of the following output:

```
cout << *(vInfo[i].vtxMapLoc).second;
```

   (b) Assume that a scan of the graph maintains the parent for each vertex in the scan. Write a statement that outputs the name of the parent for vertex v.

7. In the accompanying graph, identify minimum and shortest paths. For the minimum path, give the total weight. For the shortest path, give the total path length. In each case, list the path.
   (a) Shortest-path distance from A to G
   (b) Shortest-path distance from E to D
   (c) Shortest-path distance from H to F
   (d) Minimum path from A to H
   (d) Minimum path from B to G

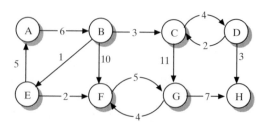

8. What is the prerequisite for a digraph to have a topological sort?

9. Determine the minimum spanning tree and its total weight for the following undirected graph.

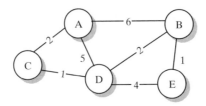

Answers to Review Exercises

1. (a) *A*: Edges: *C*(3) *D*(5)
      B: Edges: *C*(9) *D*(1)
      C: Edges:
      D: Edges: *E* (3)
      E: Edges: *A* (2) *C* (6)

  (b)

	A	*B*	*C*	*D*	*E*
A	0	0	3	5	0
B	0	0	9	1	0
C	0	0	0	0	0
D	0	0	0	0	3
E	2	0	6	0	0

2. (a) $P(E,B) = E - C - F - H - G - D - A - B$
  (b) $P(B,E) = B - D - A - C - F - E$
  (c) *E*, *H*
  (d) *C*, *D*
  (e) *B*, *C*, *D*, *E*, *G*, *H*
  (f) *B*, *E*, *G*, *H*

3. (a) *A*, *C*, *F*, *H*, *G*, *E*, *B*, *D*
      A, *B*, *D*, *C*, *F*, *E*, *H*, *G*
  (b) *F*, *G*, *E*, *D*, *C*, *A*, *B*
      F, *E*, *G*, *D*, *C*, *A*, *B*
  (c) *A*, *B*, *C*, *D*

4. (a) Strongly connected: *B*   Weakly connected: *A*   Neither: C
  (b) $\{A, B, C, D\}, \{E\}, \{F\}, \{G\}$

5. Size of the adjacency set for *v*

6. (a) *i*
  (b) cout << *(vInfo[vInfo[i].parent].vtxMapLoc).first;

7. (a) Shortest–path from *A* to *G* is 3. Path: *A* *B* *C* *G*
  (b) Shortest path from E to D is 4 Path: *E* *A* *B* *C* *D*
  (c) Shortest path from *H* to *F* is −1 Path:
  (d) Minimum path from *A* to *H* is 16 Path: *A* *B* *C* *D* *H*
  (e) Minimum path from *B* to *G* is 8 Path: *B* *E* *F* *G*.

8. Graph must be acyclic.

9. Total weight is 6.

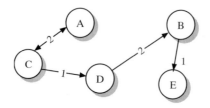

WRITTEN EXERCISES

For questions 16–10 through 16–14, use the following figure for the references to graph A and graph B.

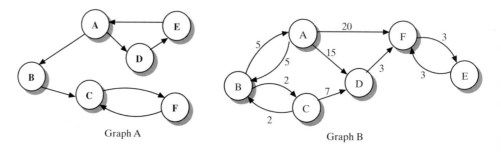

Graph A   Graph B

10. (a) Give the adjacency list and adjacency matrix representation for graph A.
   (b) Give the adjacency list and adjacency matrix representation for graph B.

11. Use graph B to answer the following questions on paths. If a path does not exists, respond "No path."
   (a) Find two distinct directed paths from vertex C to vertex E.
   (b) Find a directed path from vertex F to vertex B.
   (c) List all of the vertices that have out-degree 1.
   (d) List all of the vertices that have the same in-degree and out-degree.
   (e) Find a vertex that has maximum out-degree.

12. In graph A, find all distinct cycles.

13. (a) List the vertices in graph A in the reverse order of their visit (finish) time for a depth-first search that starts at vertex A. Repeat the process, and produce a different list by assuming that the scan accesses neighbors in a different order.
   (b) List the vertices in graph B in the reverse order of their visit (finish) time from a depth-first search starting at vertex C and first accessing neighbor D.
   (c) For both graph A and graph B, identify the starting vertices that would produce a breadth-first scan that visits all of the nodes in the graph.
   (d) In graph B, list a possible order of visits to vertices in a breadth-first scan that begins at vertex C.
   (e) List the elements in dfsList that result from a full depth-first scan (dfs()) of graph A. Assume that the first scan (dfsVisit()) begins at vertex B and that upon completing those recursive calls that dfsVisit() resumes at vertex A.

14. (a) Is graph A or graph B strongly connected? weakly connected?
   (b) List all of the strong components for each graph.

(c) If we add an edge in graph A from vertex C to vertex A, is the new graph strongly or weakly connected?

15. Use the accompanying graph to determine minimum and shortest paths. For the minimum path, give the total weight. For the shortest path, give the total path length. In each case, list a path providing the minimum value.
    (a) Shortest-path distance from C to D
    (b) Shortest-path distance from E to B
    (c) Shortest-path distance from C to F
    (d) Minimum path from C to D

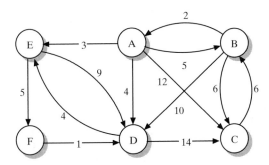

(e) Minimum path from E to B
(f) Minimum path from C to F

16. For the graph in Figure 16-28(a), replicate the trace of Dijkstra's algorithm from Section 16-6 to find the minimum path from vertex A to F. For each step, create the list of minInfo elements in the priority queue and indicate which element is removed from the queue.

17. For the graph in Figure 16-28(a), replicate the trace of Prim's algorithm from Section 16-6 to create a minimum-spanning tree. For each step, create the list of minInfo elements in the priority queue and indicate which vertices and edges are in the current spanning tree, along with the accumulated total weight.

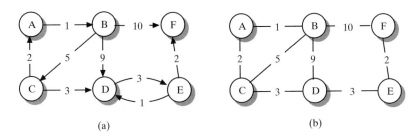

(a)   (b)

Figure 16-28
Graphs for Written Exercises 16–16 and 16–17

18. Give a topological sort for the following graph.

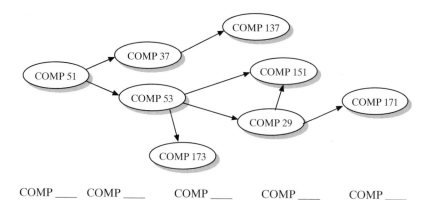

COMP ____   COMP ____   COMP ____   COMP ____   COMP ____
COMP ____   COMP ____   COMP ____

19. An Euler Tour of a strongly connected digraph is a cycle that visits each edge exactly once
(but a vertex may be visited more than once). A mathematical argument shows that a directed graph has an Euler Tour if and only if inDegree(v) = outDegree(v) for each vertex
v. Implement the function eulerTour() that takes a graph g as the argument and returns
true if the graph is strongly connected and has an Euler tour; otherwise, it returns false.

```
template <typename T>
bool eulerTour(graph<T>& g);
```

Hint: to determine whether a graph is strongly connected, compute the strong components of the graph and verify that there is only one.

Example: Graph A has an Euler Tour and graph B does not.

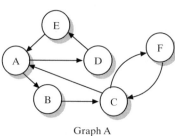

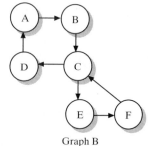

Graph A
Euler Tour: C A D E A B C F C

Graph B
No Euler Tour: indegree(C) != outdegre

20. (a) For each pair of vertices in a graph, we say that v_j is reachable from v_i if and only if
there is a directed path from v_i to v_j. This defines the reachability relation $R(v_i \text{ R } v_j)$.
For each vertex v_i, the breadth-first scan identifies the set of all vertices that are
reachable from v_i. If we use the scan for each vertex of the graph, we get a series of
reachablility sets that defines the relation R.

V_0:   <reachability set for v_0>
V_1:   <reachability set for v_1>

....

V_{n-1}:   <reachability set for v_{n-1}>

The same relation can also be described with an n-by-n reachability matrix that has a 1 in location (i,j) if and only if $v_i R v_j$. The following define the reachability sets and reachability matrix for the graph.

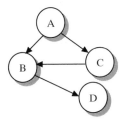

Reachability Sets   Reachability Matrix

A: $\{A, B, C, D\}$
B: $\{B, D\}$
C: $\{B, C, D\}$
D: $\{D\}$

	A	B	C	D
A	1	1	1	1
B	0	1	0	1
C	0	1	1	1
D	0	0	0	1

Implement the function reachMat() that takes a graph as its argument and returns the reachability matrix.

```
template <typename T>
matrix<int> reachMat(graph<T>& g);
```

Hint: Use an iterator to scan the vertices in the graph. For each vertex, call bfs() to obtain the reachability set. This set determines a row of the reachability matrix. With a second iterator, scan the vertices in the graph. This set determines the elements in the current row. Determine whether the vertex is in the set and, if yes, insert a 1 in the current column of the current row; otherwise, insert a 0. The rows and columns of the matrix have indices $0, 1, \ldots, n-1$. Index 0 corresponds to the first vertex scanned by a graph iterator, index 1 corresponds to the second vertex, and so forth.

(b) Determine the reachability matrix for graph A and graph B.

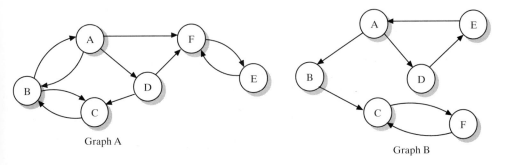

Graph A

Graph B

21. (a) Draw the graph that has the following adjacency list representation.

$$A: \text{ Edges: } B(2) \quad C(3)$$
$$B: \text{ Edges: } A(8) \quad D(3)$$
$$C: \text{ Edges: } A(2) \quad B(7)$$
$$D: \text{ Edges: } C(5) \quad B(8)$$
$$E: \text{ Edges: } A(2) \quad C(1)$$

(b) Draw the graph that has the following adjacency matrix representation.

	A	*B*	*C*	*D*	*E*
A	0	1	5	2	0
B	1	0	0	3	2
C	1	0	0	2	6
D	1	2	5	0	0
E	0	0	9	1	0

22. (a) Does the following graph have a cycle?

(b) Change the orientation for two edges so that the resulting graph is strongly connected.

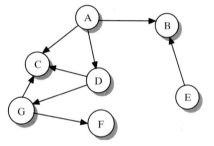

23. The following program builds the graph shown below and then executes graph class member functions. Give the output of the program, and draw the final graph.

```
#include <fstream>

#include "d_graph.h"

using namespace std;

int main()
{
    graph<char> g;
    ifstream fin;

    fin.open("wex16-23.dat");
    fin >> g;

    cout << g.numberOfVertices() << "  " << g.numberOfEdges() << endl;
    cout << g.inDegree('A') << "  " << g.outDegree('D') << endl;
    cout << g.getWeight('D','C') << endl;

    g.insertVertex('G');

    g.insertEdge('F','G',1);
```

```
        g.insertEdge('G','D',2);
        g.insertEdge('G','E',1);

        g.setWeight('E','D', 5);

        g.eraseEdge('D','E');

        g.eraseVertex('C');

        return 0;
}
```

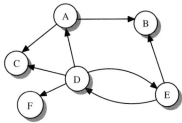

24. Assume the function pathConnected(g,s,e) returns true if there is a path from vertex *s* to vertex *e* in graph *g* and false otherwise.

```
template <typename T>
bool pathConnected(graph<T>& g, const T& s, const T& e);
```

Describe the action of the function f().

```
template <typename T>
vector<set<T> > f(graph<T>& g)
{
    graph<T>::iterator gIter;
    set<T> mks, pathSet;
    set<T>::iterator sIter;
    vector <set<T> > vectSet;

    for (gIter = g.begin(); gIter != g.end(); gIter++)
        if (mks.find(*gIter) == mks.end())
        {
            pathSet = bfs(g,*gIter);

            sIter = pathSet.begin();
            while (sIter != pathSet.end())
            {
                if(pathConnected(g,*sIter, *gIter))
                    mks.insert(*sIter++);
                else
                    pathSet.erase(*sIter++);
            }
            vectSet.push_back(pathSet);
        }
    return vectSet;
}
```

25. Assume that *g* is a graph and *v* is a vertex. For every vertex that is reachable from *v*, there is a path of minimum length. The function farReach() takes g and v as arguments and returns a vertex that has the longest minimum path from *v*. Note that there may be two or more vertices with the same longest minimum path from *v*. In this case, the function returns any one of the vertices.

```
template<typename T>
T farReach (graph<T>& g, const T& v);
```

   (a) Use the following (rather inefficient) algorithm to implement farReach(). Find the set of all vertices that are reachable from *v*. For each vertex *w* in the set, find the shortest path from *v* to *w*. Among these vertices, locate the vertex that is the farthest from *v*.

   (b) Develop a more efficient algorithm using the code for shortestPath() as a model. Assume that farReach() is a friend of the graph class.

26. A graph can represent a binary tree. The root is a vertex with in-degree 0, and each link from parent to child corresponds to an edge *e* = (parent,child). There cannot be a cycle in the graph. Assume gTree is a graph that corresponds to a binary tree. Implement the function leafNodes(), which returns the set of all vertices (nodes) that are leaf nodes. For instance, the adjacent graph represents a binary tree where *A* is the root.

```
template<typename T>
set<T> leafNodes(graph<T>& gTree);
```

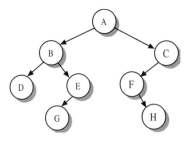

   HINT: Traverse the graph using a graph iterator and look at the out-degree of each vertex.

27. During a recursive depth-first search of a digraph, what is a back edge? What is the relation between a back edge and an acyclic graph?

28. If a graph algorithm is $O(V^2 + E)$, explain why we can equivalently write that the algorithm is $O(V^2)$.

29. A DAG (Directed Acyclic Graph) has n vertices. Give the minimum and the maximum number of strong components that exist in the graph.

30. Consider the following function f() that takes a graph as both an argument and a return value. Assume that f() is a friend of the graph class.

```
graph<T> f(graph<T>& g)
{
    int i, n = g.vInfo.size();
    set<neighbor>::iterator setIter;
    // initialize obj as a copy of g
    graph<T> obj = g;

    for (i=0;i < n;i++)
```

```
    {
        obj.vInfo[i].edges.erase(obj.vInfo[i].edges.begin(),
                                    obj.vInfo[i].edges.end());
        obj.vInfo[i].inDegree = 0;
    }
    for (i=0; i < n; i++)
        if (g.vInfo[i].occupied)
        {
            set<neighbor>& s = g.vInfo[i].edges;

            for (setIter = s.begin(); setIter != s.end(); setIter++)
            {
                obj.vInfo[(*setIter).dest].edges.insert
                            (neighbor(i,(*setIter).weight));
                obj.vInfo[i].inDegree++;
            }
        }
    return obj;
}
```

You are given the declaration

```
graph<char> g, newG;
```

For the following graph g, draw graph newG after the execution of the statement
`newG = f(g);`

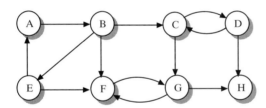

31. The function dfsVisit() uses a recursive algorithm for the depth-first scan. An iterative
    form, dfsIterVisit(), uses a stack to hold the vertices of the scan, similar to bfs(). The func-
    tion visits the vertices reachable from the starting vertex in preorder; that is, the function
    places the current vertex v at the back of the visit list, and then visits its neighbors. The
    function does not include a test for a cycle.

    ```
    template <typename T>
    void dfsIterVisit(graph<T>& g, const T& sVertex, list<T>& dfsList);
    ```

    Do not assume that dfsIterVisit() is a friend of the graph class. As a result, the function
    does not have access to the edges and the color variable of the vInfo entries for g. Obtain
    the neighbors of a vertex by using the member function getNeighbors(), and determine
    that a vertex has been visited by searching the visit list. Use the STL algorithm find()
    from <algorithm> for the search. The function takes an iterator range [first, last) and a
    value and returns an iterator pointing at the value or last if the value is not in the range.

    ```
    template <typename Iterator, typename T>
    Iterator find(Iterator first, Iterator last, const T& value);
    ```

32. Assume that a graph uses an adjacency matrix to represent the edges. Describe how you would update the matrix for the following algorithms.
   (a) Insert an edge.
   (b) Insert a new vertex.
   (c) Delete an edge.
   (d) Delete a vertex.

PROGRAMMING EXERCISES

In order to simplify your writing of programs, we use the following three graphs for most of the problems. In Programming Exercise 33, you will create the data file "graphA.dat" for graph A. The files for graph B and graph C are in the ch16 directory of the software supplement with file names "graphB.dat" and "graphC.dat", respectively.

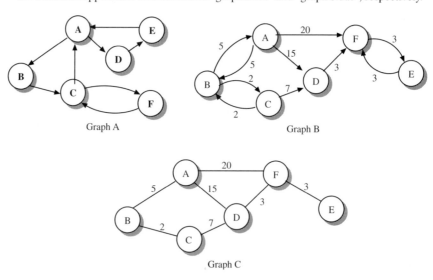

Graph A

Graph B

Graph C

33. Create the data file for graph A. In a program, input the file, and then include statements that carry out the following tasks.

   Insert an edge from F to D with weight 1.
   Delete vertex B.
   Erase the edge (A,D)
   Prompt the user to input a vertex, and list all of the neighbors of the vertex.
   Insert the new vertex G.
   Add the following edges with weight 1: $(G,C), (G,F), (D,G)$.
   Output the graph using the operator $<<$.

34. Using graph B, write a program that prompts the user to input a vertex. With the input value, carry out a breadth-first search, and use writeContainer() to display the set of reachable vertices. Perform a depth-first search of the entire graph, and call writeContainer() again to display the list of vertices in the reverse order of their finishing times.

35. Using graph B, create a program that determines the set of strong components. The components are returned as a vector of sets. Output the strong components. Remove from the graph all vertices that belong to a one-element strong component. After deleting the vertices, recompute and display the strong components for the updated graph.

36. Have the user input one of the vertices from graph B. For each of the other vertices v in the graph, determine the weight of the minimum path from the user supplied vertex to v. Output the vertex that has the largest minimum-path weight, the weight of the minimum path, and the path itself.

37. Written Exercise 16-19 contains the function eulerTour(). In a program, check your implementation of the function by using graph A and graph B. Output whether the graph has an Euler Tour.

38. The function reachMat() is found in Written Exercise 16-20. Write a program that inputs the name of a graph file, inputs the graph, and then calls reachMat() to create the reachability matrix. Output the result as a series of rows and columns. Optional: Enhance the output by including the names of the vertices as labels for the rows and columns. Run the program twice, and use graph B for one of the runs.

39. Written Exercise 16-22 asks you to determine whether the accompanying graph has a cycle and to change the orientation of two edges to make the graph strongly connected. Write a program that implements the exercise. Call acyclic() to determine whether the graph has a cyclic path; then select two edges to change orientation (delete and then re-insert the edge with the new orientation.), and use the function strongComponent() to verify that the new graph is strongly connected.

40. Write a program that checks your implementation of the function leafNodes() in Written Exercise 16-26. The program should input the graph that accompanies the exercise and output the set of leaf nodes.

41. Write a program that uses your implementation of dfsIterVisit() in Written Exercise 16-31. The program should input graph B and call dfsIterVisit() for each vertex in the graph. After each call, output the list.

PROGRAMMING PROJECT

42. Modify the graph class to use an adjacency matrix rather than an adjacency set to store the neighbors of a vertex. Implement only the class member functions, the stream operators, and the algorithm bfs(). Place the class in the header file "adjgraph.h".

Assume that the graph will contain no more than MAXGRAPHSIZE vertices. Use the map structure to store the vertices and their index into the vInfo vector. The vertex-Info object corresponding to a vertex does not store the adjacency set. Rather, the adjacency matrix is a data member in the graph class. The index from the map serves as a row or column index into the adjacency matrix as well as the index of the vertex in vInfo. When deleting a vertex, assign weight 0 to the entries in the corresponding row and column of the adjacency matrix, and use an availability stack to indicate that the index is available for reuse. Whenever an error occurs, such as a call to insertVertex() when the graph has MAXGRAPHSIZE vertices, throw the graphError exception.

Test the class by writing a program that inputs the graph in Figure 16-28(a) and outputs the result of a breadth-first search from vertex A. Delete vertex C and edge (B,E). Output the graph. Next, add vertex F and edges (F,A) with weight 3, (E,F) with weight 2, and (B,F) with weight 5. Output the final graph (Figure 16-29(b)).

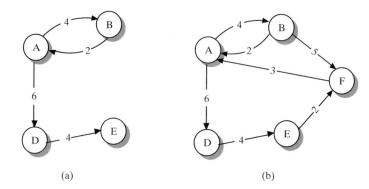

(a)   (b)

Figure 16-29
Graphs for Programming Project 16-42

For your convenience, the following is a listing of the private section for the class.

```
const int MAXGRAPHSIZE = 25;

template <class T>
class graph
{
   public:
      ...
   private:
      typedef map<T,int> vertexMap;

      vertexMap vtxMap;
         // store vertex in a map with its name as the key and the
         // index of the corresponding vertexInfo object
         // in the vInfo vector as the value

      matrix<int> edge;
         // adjacency matrix
      int numVertices;
      int numEdges;
         // current size (vertices and edges) of the graph

      vector<vertexInfo<T> > vInfo;
         // list of vertexInfo objects corresponding to the vertices

      stack<int> availStack;
         // availability stack for storing unused indices in vInfo

      int getVertexPos(const T& vertex) const;
         // member function to find vertex and identify its row
         // in the adjacency matrix and its index in vInfo
};
```

INDEX